CHRISTIANS AND JEWS
IN THE OTTOMAN EMPIRE

CHRISTIANS AND JEWS
IN THE
OTTOMAN EMPIRE

The Functioning of a Plural Society

EDITED BY
BENJAMIN BRAUDE
AND
BERNARD LEWIS

VOLUME I
THE CENTRAL LANDS

HM

HOLMES & MEIER PUBLISHERS, INC.
NEW YORK   LONDON

First published in the United States of America 1982 by
Holmes & Meier Publishers, Inc.
30 Irving Place
New York, N. Y. 10003

Great Britain:
Holmes & Meier Publishers, Ltd.
131 Trafalgar Road
Greenwich, London SE10 9TX

Library of Congress Cataloging in Publication Data
Main entry under title:

Christians and Jews in the Ottoman empire.

  Papers presented at an international symposium held
at Princeton University.
  Bibliography: Vol. II, p. 207.
  Includes index.
  CONTENTS: v. 1. The central lands. v. 2. The
Arabic-speaking lands.
    1. Christians in the Near East—Politics and
government—Congresses.   2. Jews in the Near East—
Politics and government—Congresses.   3. Christians
in Turkey—Politics and government—Congresses.
4. Jews in Turkey—Politics and government—Congresses.
5. Minorities—Near East—Congresses.   6. Minorities
—Turkey—Congresses.   I. Braude, Benjamin.
II. Lewis, Bernard.
DS58.C48 1980   956.1′01   80-11337

ISBN 0-8419-0519-3 (v. 1)

Manufactured in the United States of America

Contents

Abbreviations

ABCFM	American Board of Commissioners, Foreign Missions, Cambridge, Mass.
AE	Ministère des Affaires Etrangères, Paris
Arch. Prop.	Archives of the Sacred Congregation for the Propagation of the Faith, Rome
AUB	American University of Beirut
BBA	Başbakanlık Arşivi, Istanbul
BSOAS	*Bulletin of the School of Oriental and African Studies*
CC	Correspondance Consulaire, AE
DOP	*Dumbarton Oaks Papers*
DSA	*Dahiliye Sicill-i Ahval Defterleri, BBA*
EI²	*Encyclopedia of Islam,* second edition
FO	Foreign Office, Public Record Office Archive, London
IA	*İslâm Ansiklopedisi*
IFM	*İktisat Fakültesi Mecmuası,* Istanbul University
IJMES	*International Journal of Middle Eastern Studies*
JAOS	*Journal of the American Oriental Society*
JEEH	*Journal of European Economic History*
JEH	*Journal of Economic History*
JESHO	*Journal of the Economic and Social History of the Orient*
JQR	*Jewish Quarterly Review*
JRAS	*Journal of Royal Asiatic Society*
PRO	Public Record Office
REI	*Revue des Etudes Islamiques*
REJ	*Revue des Etudes Juives*
SA	*Sicill-i Ahval,* Hariciye Archives, Istanbul
SC	Scritture riferite nei Congressi, Arch. Prop.
SI	*Studia Islamica*
TOEM	Tarîh-i Osmânî Encümeni Mecmuası
USNA	United States National Archives

A Note on Transliteration

In view of the diversity of essays contained in these volumes, rigorous consistency has not always been possible or desirable. With certain exceptions Turkish has been transliterated according to official modern Turkish orthography and Arabic according to the system of the *Encyclopedia of Islam.* However, "ḳ" is rendered "q" and "dj" as "j". The ligatures below "ch", "dh", "gh", "kh", "sh", and "th" have been omitted.

Acknowledgments

These essays grew out of a research seminar and conference on "The *Millet* System: History and Legacy," that was conducted at Princeton University during the spring and summer of 1978. The scope of the book is somewhat narrower than that of the conference. Unfortunately considerations of space and unity of topic made it necessary to omit papers which dealt wholly or mainly with post-Ottoman or non-Ottoman topics. We gratefully acknowledge our debt to all those who participated in the seminar-conference.

A grant from the Ford Foundation to the Princeton University Program in Near Eastern Studies made possible the convening of the seminar-conference. Additional grants from both the Ford Foundation and Princeton University helped defray the costs of publication. Certain other costs were borne by the office of the Dean of the Graduate School of Arts and Sciences and the Department of History, both of Boston College.

The faculty, staff, and students of the Princeton Program and Department of Near Eastern Studies were especially helpful in the organization of the seminar-conference. Particular thanks are due Mrs. Mary Craparotta, Mrs. Grace Edelman, and Mrs. Judy Gross.

We benefited from able graduate assistance. Alan Iser, Near Eastern Languages and Civilizations at Harvard, reviewed the manuscript for consistency. Alan Makovsky, Near Eastern Studies at Princeton, reviewed the bibliography. Shayndel Feuerstein, Romance Languages and Literatures at Harvard, translated portions of the text from French to English. John Feeley and James Nealon of Boston College helped correct the galleys.

A special word of appreciation is due the late Morroe Berger who, as Chairman of the Program in Near Eastern Studies, first conceived this project and gained support for it. His death came before its publication. These volumes are dedicated to his memory.

Introduction

Benjamin Braude and Bernard Lewis

For nearly half a millennium the Ottomans ruled an empire as diverse as any in history. Remarkably, this polyethnic and multireligious society worked. Muslims, Christians, and Jews worshipped and studied side by side, enriching their distinct cultures. The legal traditions and practices of each community, particularly in matters of personal status—that is, death, marriage, and inheritance—were respected and enforced through the empire. Scores of languages and literatures employing a bewildering variety of scripts flourished. Opportunities for advancement and prosperity were open in varying degrees to all the empire's subjects. During their heyday the Ottomans created a society which allowed a great degree of communal autonomy while maintaining a fiscally sound and militarily strong central government.

The Ottoman Empire was a classic example of the plural society. An acute observer of similar societies in South Asia defined them with the following description which applies equally well to the Ottoman world:

> . . . probably the first thing that strikes the visitor is the medley of peoples. . . . It is in the strictest sense a medley, for they mix, but do not combine. Each group holds by its own religion, its own culture and language, its own ideas and ways. As individuals they meet, but only in the market-place, in buying and selling. There is a plural society, with different sections of the community, living side by side, but separately within the same political unit. Even in the economic sphere there is a division of labor along racial lines.[1]

For all their shortcomings, plural societies did allow diverse groups of people to live together with a minimum of bloodshed. In comparison with the nation-states which succeeded them, theirs is a remarkable record.

In recent years, spurred by an awareness of the ethnic strife that plagues so many nation-states, scholars have turned to the study of ethnicity and ethnically diverse states. Unfortunately, much of this work has been historically and geographically limited. The Islamic world has rarely been included in such studies despite the fact that one of the most enduring polyethnic states was the last great Islamic Empire, that of the Ottomans.

In recent studies on the Middle East, the dominant themes have been nationalism on the one hand and modernization on the other, to the neglect of religious and communal issues. The continuing importance of religion and community has become increasingly obvious and a serious and scholarly study of the background and implications of these factors is overdue.

The papers presented in these volumes attempt to answer both these needs. A subject as broad and complex as that presented here could easily fill many volumes. Considerations of space and sometimes of availability have forced us to omit many topics which could legitimately be included—as, for example, the smaller Christian sects of the Arabic-speaking lands, the Jewish community of Baghdad, the image of non-Muslims in Muslim fiction, drama, and folk literature. It is our hope that the topics discussed here will spur further research in the many important areas which have necessarily been omitted.

The policies of the Ottomans toward their Christian and Jewish subjects were part of a larger pattern of relations between Muslims and non-Muslims that emerged during centuries of Islamic rule. Before the House of Osman began its rise to power in the fourteenth century, Islam had conquered the Christian heartlands of the Middle East, all of North Africa, all of Iberia, and most of the Mediterranean islands. Clearly it is difficult to make generalizations about the status of non-Muslims in so vast an area for so long a time. Rendering the task even more difficult is the persistence of two opposing myths on the question of Muslim tolerance and intolerance. One depicts Islam and the Muslims as bigoted, intolerant, and oppressive; its best-known image is Gibbon's legendary figure of a fanatical warrior riding out of the desert, with the Quran in one hand and the sword in the other, offering his victims a choice between the two. The other myth is of an interfaith, interracial utopia in which Muslims, Christians, and Jews worked together in equality and harmony in a golden age of free intellectual endeavor.

Both myths are sadly distorted, relatively recent, and products of European, not Islamic, history. In the medieval past neither Christianity nor Islam greatly prized religious tolerance; neither condemned its absence in the other. The charge of Christendom against Islam was that its doctrines were false, not that they were imposed by force—a form of persuasion long seen as normal.

The charge of ruthless oppression began with the Renaissance. The self-identification of Christian Europe, threatened by the Turks, with the ancient Greeks who had resisted the Persians, led the West to see itself as engaged in a fight for freedom against Oriental despotism. This initiated a new line of thought about the Islamic Orient. It was reinforced during the Enlightenment of the eighteenth century, which had developed its own objections to religious intolerance. It was, of course, safer to criticize Islam than to criticize Christianity, in countries where the Church wielded considerable power, and Islam was sometimes used as a terrible example. Voltaire's *Mahomet* illustrates this point.

The other myth, that of the interfaith utopia, seems to have begun a little later, during the Reformation, when Islam was used as a stick with which some Protestant polemicists beat their opponents. Certain groups claimed an affinity with Islam as a strictly monotheistic religion; some even contrasted Turkish tolerance with Catholic repression. With the Enlightenment this myth too was reinforced. Sometimes Orientals, typically Turks or Persians, were used as a vehicle for social comment and criticism of the West. While Rousseau saw the Arabs and the Turks as perhaps no better and no worse than the Christians, Herder contrasted "the noble and valiant Saladin" with "the perfidious, depraved Christians."[2] Nineteenth-century Romanticism with its cult of Spain, as exemplified in the works of such writers as Theophile Gautier, Victor Hugo, and Washington Irving, extended the Spanish romantic myth from Christian to Muslim Spain. This tendency was also encouraged by European Jews. Told by their Christian compatriots that they were Semites and Orientals, they identified themselves with other Semites and Orientals, particularly with the Arabs of Spain. Such notable figures of Jewish origin as Benjamin Disraeli and Heinrich Heine turned to Muslim Spain where they found solace for themselves and a reproach and a model for their intolerant neighbors. In so doing they contributed greatly to the European glorification of medieval Islamic tolerance in the Andalusian golden age.

The truth, as usual, lies somewhere between these two extremes. The position of the non-Muslim in Islam in general and the Ottoman Empire in particular is more complex and more nuanced than either of these two oversimplified presentations would have us believe.

Before discussing the tolerance or intolerance of Islam, some definitions are necessary. First, what do we mean by "tolerance"—the absence of discrimination, or the absence of persecution? And what do we mean by "Islam"? The term may mean the original Islam—what Muslims conceive as the Islamic revelation vouchsafed by God to the Prophet Muhammad and embodied in the Holy Book of the Quran. Or it may mean the subsequent development of that revelation by the work of jurists and theologians leading to the whole imposing corpus of Islamic law, theology, tradition, and practice. Or in yet another definition, the word Islam may be used as the counterpart not of Christianity, but of Christendom, in other words, the whole civilization which has grown up under the aegis of Islam and which embraces much that would be non-Islamic or even anti-Islamic in the first and second meanings of the term. In this sense, Islam means not what Muslims were supposed or required to believe and do in accordance with the precepts of their religion, but what, for better or for worse, they actually thought and did—in other words, Islamic society and civilization as known to us from history and from present observation.

In this essay we shall be using "Islam" in both the second and third senses, that is, as the developed corpus of law and tradition and as the civilization which emerged under the influence of this corpus. As for "tolerance," the term is usually understood to indicate the willingness of a dominant religion to coexist with others. Muslims commonly subjected followers of other religions to discrimination but by and large without persecution. Thus Islam was intolerant by one definition of the term, tolerant by another. While persecution was rare and atypical, usually due to specific circumstances, discrimination was permanent and indeed necessary, inherent in the system and maintained by both Holy Law and common practice.

It is often said that Islam is an egalitarian religion. It certainly appears so if we compare the Islamic order at the time of its advent with the caste system of India to the east or the aristocratic privilege of Christian Europe to the west. By this standard, Islam is indeed an egalitarian religion, under the aegis of which was established an egalitarian society. Islam recognizes neither caste nor aristocracy. Though human nature caused both to obtrude from time to time, this happened despite Islam and not as part of it; when it did, it was seen and condemned by pious and conscientious Muslims as a non-Islamic innovation.

However, Islam does recognize certain basic inequalities, in its doctrines as well as in its practice. Most important among these are the three basic inequalities of master and slave, man and woman, believer and unbeliever. While a whole series of radical movements of social and religious protest arose among the Muslims, condemning and seeking to overthrow the barriers which arose from time to time between rich and poor, highborn and lowborn, Arab and non-Arab, white and black—all of which were seen as contrary to the true spirit of Islamic brotherhood—there were no movements of protest to question these three basic distinctions, sanctified by the Quran itself and regulated in detail by Holy Law, establishing the subordinate status of the slave, the woman, and the unbeliever.

All three inferior categories had their place and were seen as necessary for the conduct of the business of society. All had their functions, though occasional doubts were expressed about the unbeliever. There is, however, one very important difference among the three. Women could not become men; slaves could be freed, but only by legal process and by the will of the master and not of the slave. Unbelievers, on the other hand, were such entirely by their own choice. Their status of inferiority was voluntary—Muslims might say willful—and they themselves could easily end it at any time by an act of will. From the point of view of the Muslim, unbelievers were people to whom the truth had been offered in the final and perfect form of God's revelation, which they had willfully and foolishly refused.

Of the three groups of social inferiors, therefore, the unbeliever was the only one who remained so by his own choice. He was also the one whose disabilities were, on the whole, the least burdensome; these disparities may explain the need which was felt, for an unbeliever more than for a woman or a slave, to enforce or at least visibly to symbolize his inferiority.

The Quran says quite specifically that there is no constraint in religion, *lā ikrāha fī al-dīn* (2:256), and although this has recently been interpreted as being an expression of resignation rather than an encouragement of tolerance,[3] it was in the latter sense that it was generally interpreted. According to Muslim law and practice, men must not be compelled to change their religions, subject to one very important restriction—that their existing religion is a monotheistic one based on revelation. Islam recognizes Judaism, Christianity, and a rather mysterious third party, the Sabians, as earlier, incomplete, and superseded forms of Islam itself and therefore as containing genuine elements of divine revelation (see Volume 1, chapter 1 by C. E. Bosworth). Communities professing these religions are allowed the tolerance of the Islamic state. They are permitted to practice their religions subject to certain conditions, and to enjoy a considerable measure of communal autonomy. Those who are not so qualified, in other words those classified as polytheists and idolators, are not entitled to the toleration of the Islamic state and for them, according to the law, the choice is the Quran or the sword. The latter might in certain circumstances be commuted to slavery.

In this, as in many other things, Islamic practice on the whole turned out to be gentler than Islamic precept—the reverse of the situation in Christendom. The mysterious and not very precisely identified third group, the Sabians, made it possible by legal interpretation to extend the same kind of tolerance to Zoroastrians in Persia, Hindus in India, and other groups elsewhere.

In Muslim law and practice, the relationship between the Muslim state and the non-Muslim communities to which it extended its tolerance and protection was conceived as regulated by a pact called *dhimma;* those benefiting from it were known as *ahl al-dhimma,* people of the pact, or more briefly *dhimmi*s.

The medieval Muslim, like the medieval Christian, believed that he alone had the true faith and that those who believed otherwise would roast in everlasting hellfire. Unlike the medieval Christian, he saw no reason to anticipate the divine judgment in this world and was content to allow *dhimmi* non-Muslims to practice their own religions, maintain their own places of worship, and to a very large extent run their own affairs, provided that they recognized unequivocally the primacy of Islam and the supremacy of Muslims.

This recognition was expressed through a series of restrictions imposed by the Holy Law on the *dhimmi*s. The origins of these restrictions seem to go back to the very first period of the conquest and to be military in nature. When the Arab Muslims first conquered immense territories and were a tiny minority of conquerors amid a vast majority of the conquered, they needed certain security precautions for the protection of the governing and occupying groups. As so often in the early period, their actions, even though determined by practical considerations of expediency, were sanctified and incorporated in the Holy Law, so that what began as security restrictions became legal and social disabilities. The restrictions involved some limitation on the clothes the *dhimmi*s might wear, the beasts they might ride, the arms they might bear. There were limits on the building and use of places of worship. They were not to be higher than mosques. No new ones were to be built but only old ones restored. Christians and Jews were to wear distinguishing emblems on their clothes. This was the origin of the yellow badge, which was first introduced by a caliph in Baghdad in the ninth century and spread into Western lands—for Jews—in later medieval times. Even when attending the public baths, they were supposed to wear distinguishing signs suspended from cords around their necks so that they might not be mistaken for Muslims when disrobed in the public bathhouse. They were required to avoid noise and display in their ceremonies and at all times to show respect for Islam and deference to Muslims. Most of these disabilities have a social and symbolic rather than a tangible and practical character. The only real economic burden imposed on unbelievers was fiscal. They had to pay higher taxes, a system inherited from the previous empires of Iran and Byzantium. There are varying opinions among scholars as to how serious a burden the payment of these extra taxes imposed. Where we have documentary evidence, as from the eleventh-century records of the Jewish community of Cairo, it would seem that for the poorer classes at least the burden was heavy.

The fiscal differentiation between believer and unbeliever remained in force throughout the Islamic world until the nineteenth century and was never at any time or place allowed to lapse. The other disabilities seem to have varied considerably in their application. On the whole, one gets the impression that they were more often disregarded than strictly enforced. Partly, no doubt, such laxness may be attributed to the limited powers which a medieval state was able to exercise over the mass of its subjects, but partly also to a genuine disinclination on the part of rulers to impose these irksome restrictions.

These restrictions eventually became part of the Islamic way of life. Their symbolic purpose, as in many other societies and situations, was to demonstrate who belonged, however remotely, to the dominant group and who did not, and to maintain the distinction between them. The position of *dhimmi*s was in general tolerable but insecure. Humiliation was part of the pattern. The Arabic word *dhull,* meaning lowliness, abasement, abjectness, is often used by Muslim writers in this connection to denote the sense of humility which was felt to be appropriate to the non-Muslim and more especially the Jewish subjects. In spite of all this, their position was certainly very much better than that of non-Christians or of heretical Christians in medieval Europe.

Unlike the Jews in much of Europe, Jews and Christians under Muslim rule were rarely called upon to suffer exile or martyrdom for their faiths. They were not, as a matter of regular policy, confined to ghettoes either in the geographical or in the occupational sense. There were no restricted occupations and, with the exception of the holy cities in Arabia and some elsewhere, there were no restricted places. Though violence was rare, it did occur on occasion, and it may be useful to establish a typology of persecution or, rather, of the rationalizations offered by persecutors, which is not quite the same thing.

In pre-modern times by far the commonest rationalization was that the non-Muslim subjects were not keeping their place, were acting arrogantly, or getting above themselves. This expresses one of the fundamental political ideas of Islam—the idea or ideal of justice. In most Muslim political thought the central purpose of government, the main justification of authority, the cardinal virtue of the good ruler, is justice. The definition of justice has varied in different periods of Islamic history. In the earlier period, justice usually meant the enforcement of God's law, the maintenance and application of the Holy Law of Islam. Later, when the Holy Law of Islam was increasingly disregarded by Muslim rulers, it could no longer serve as touchstone of the just or unjust ruler, and the term justice came rather to have the sense of balance, of equilibrium—the maintenance of the social and political order, each group, each element in its proper place, giving what it must give and getting which it should get.

In either of these senses, the non-Muslim subjects had a certain place. If they seemed to be going beyond the place assigned to them, it was either, in the first sense of justice, a breach of the law, or, in the second sense, a disturbance of the social balance, and consequently a danger to the social and political order.

Trouble arose when Jews or Christians were seen to be getting too much wealth or too much power and enjoying them too visibly. The *locus classicus* of this is the massacre of Jews in Granada in 1066, usually ascribed to a reaction against a powerful and ostentatious Jewish vezir. Another striking example of such feelings occurred in Cairo in 1301 when the conspicuous consumption and haughty behavior of a Christian was said to have provoked the authorities to demand strict adherence to the sumptuary laws and other restrictions upon *dhimmi*s. Taking the law into their own hands, Muslim mobs in Cairo and other cities in Egypt and Syria destroyed a number of synagogues and churches, as well as some homes belonging to Christians and Jews.

A second rationalization is the accusation of what one might call traffic with the enemy, that is to say, with the enemies of Islam. This occurred at the time of the Crusades, when some Christian communities in the Muslim countries of the Middle East identified themselves with the Crusaders, and had to suffer the consequences after the Crusaders had gone. Jews were not directly affected by this. They had no love for the Crusaders, but they were sometimes caught in the backlash, the general feeling of resentment against non-Muslims seen—not without some basis—as disloyal subjects of the Muslim state.

A more striking example occurred in the time of the Mongol invasions. The Crusaders had only succeeded in establishing some small states along the Syrian and Palestinian littoral; the Mongols conquered the heartlands of Islam and destroyed the caliphate, thus establishing a non-Muslim ascendancy over the major centers of Islam for the first time since the days of the Prophet. The Mongol rulers found Christians and Jews—local people knowing the languages and the countries but not themselves Muslims—very useful instruments, and appointed some of them to high office. Afterward, when the Mongols themselves embraced Islam and adopted Muslim attitudes, there was a price to pay for past services to the pagan conquerors.

A similar role was played in more modern times by members of the non-Muslim minorities, who were in various ways useful and helpful to the European powers that came to dominate or influence much of the Islamic world. Some members of the minorities, and especially their upper classes, identified themselves with the European powers, adopting their languages, their culture, and at times even their citizenship—and after the end of empire and the withdrawal of Europe, there was again a reckoning to be paid by those who stayed behind.

A third type of persecution is that which arises in periods of strict and militant Islam. From time to time movements or rulers appear, who insist on the need to purify the faith, to remove the accretions and innovations which have corrupted it in the course of the centuries, and return to the authentic Islam of the Prophet and his companions. Such movements usually bring a wave of intolerance which affects not only Muslims but also the non-Muslim subjects of the Muslim state. The proper subordination of the unbeliever and the strict enforcement of the restrictions imposed on him are an obvious part of any such pious restoration.

Similar to these are the messianic and millenarian movements which sometimes arise in periods of upheaval and disorder. Such were the Almohades in medieval North Africa and Spain; such, too, were some messianically expressed nationalist and revivalist movements in more recent times, which claimed that the Kingdom of God—or the latest fashionable ideology—was about to be established on earth by the messianic or charismatic leader. In this process those who reject the new revelations and those who will not or cannot identify themselves with its bearers and exponents may no longer be accorded tolerance.

To these four types of persecution, originating from the populace, we may add two more of a rather more limited character, due to the rulers' initiative. One, of fairly common occurrence, is financial shortage. When a ruler is in financial straits, a simple way of raising money is to enforce some disagreeable and previously forgotten restriction, or to impose a new one, on the non-Muslims, who are then usually willing to pay the ruler to rescind his decrees. Another is when a ruler finds himself in a precarious situation, in conflict with powerful elements within his capital or ruling circle, and tries to mobilize support among the mob, usually at the expense of his non-Muslim subjects.

What in general were the attitudes of Muslims toward their *dhimmi* subjects? One important point should be made right away. There is little sign of any visceral hostility directed against Jews or any other group equivalent to the anti-Semitism of the Christian world. There were, however, unambiguously negative attitudes. In part, these were normal feelings of a dominant group toward subject groups, for which one can find parallels in virtually any society one cares to examine; in part, more specifically the contempt of the Muslim for those who had been given the opportunity to accept the truth and who willfully chose to persist in their disbelief; and in part, certain particular accusations against one group and not against the rest.

On the whole, in contrast to Christian anti-Semitism, the attitude is one not of envy or fear or hate but simply of contempt. This is expressed in various ways. There is no lack of polemic literature attacking the Christians and the Jews. The negative attributes ascribed to the subject religions and their followers are usually expressed in social and religious terms, very rarely in ethnic or racial terms, though this does occur occasionally. The language of abuse is often quite strong. The conventional epithets are apes for Jews and pigs for Christians (see Quran, 2: 61; 5: 65); modern political controversy offers parallels to this use of animal imagery for abuse. Greetings used when addressing Jews and Christians are different from those used when addressing Muslims, whether in conversation or in correspondence. Christians and Jews were forbidden to give their children distinctively Muslim names and, by Ottoman times, even these names which were shared by the religions, such as Joseph or David, were spelled differently for the three. There were a number of differences of this sort which the non-Muslims learned to accept and which, like the sartorial laws, were part of the symbolism of discrimination.

As well as the negative side, there is also a positive side. Relations between these communities and the Muslim state were regulated by law, by the *dhimma,* the contractual relationship deemed to exist between the Muslim state and the subject communities. The Holy Law conferred a certain status on the followers of these religions. They were therefore entitled to that status in accordance with God's law. If the law forbids them to rise above it, it also forbids Muslims to drag them down below it. We find at times some expression of respect for the *dhimmi*s, for their monotheism, for their learning, for their status as possessors of revealed books, even though these have been superseded by the Quran. Sometimes one finds that when a persecution begins the instigators are concerned to justify it in terms of the Holy Law. The usual argument is that the Jews or the Christians have violated the pact by exceeding their place. They have thus broken the conditions of the contract with Islam, and the Muslim state and people are no longer bound by it. On the other hand, on some occasions when an action against them was found contrary to law, it was stopped.

Also contributing to a positive attitude was the practical consideration that the *dhimmi*s were useful. They possessed skills which the Muslims needed and which Muslims either did not possess or did not care to acquire. In certain periods we find non-Muslims heavily engaged in trade and finance; in some periods, particularly in later centuries, we find them well represented in what one might call the dirty trades. As well as the more obviously disagreeable occupations, these sometimes included such trades as precious metals, banking, and diplomacy, i.e., dealing with foreigners, seen by strict Muslims as tainted and dangerous to the souls of those engaged in them.

Over the centuries the actual circumstances of *dhimmi* life varied considerably. One of the most important facts determining the treatment of Christians and Jews had little directly to do with the Holy Law, *dhimmi* uppishness, Islamic revivalism or millenarianism, fiscal hardship, or a ruler's unpopularity. It is easier to be tolerant when one feels strong than when one feels weak and endangered. The weakness or strength of the Muslim state, and, more generally, the relations between Islam and the outside world, affected the strict enforcement or lax disregard of the restrictions mandated by the Holy Law. Not surprisingly, as the Muslim world, compared with the Christian world, became weaker and poorer, the position of the non-Muslim subjects of the Muslim state deteriorated; they suffered from stricter enforcement of the restrictions and even, something which did not often happen previously, from a degree of social segregation. From the era of the Crusades, the twelfth and thirteenth centuries, and onward, there was a change in the balance of power between Islam and Christendom reflected in the deteriorating position of non-Muslims in the Muslim East.

It was against this background that the Ottoman Turks rose to power. The position of Christians and Jews had undergone a steady decline in the previous centuries, even as Islam itself was in disarray. The rise of this strong new dynasty promised to reverse both.

The expansion of the Ottomans from a small base on the fringes of the Muslim and Christian worlds recapitulated in some respects the early centuries of the Arab conquests. From the fourteenth century to the second half of the fifteenth century the Ottoman state consisted of a Muslim minority ruling a Christian majority. The success of the Ottoman thrust into Byzantium and the Balkans was facilitated by religious schism which had alienated the conquered peoples from their would-be Christian allies. However, unlike their Arab predecessors, the Ottomans had numerous examples in treating with the subject population. In addition to the norms which previous Mediterranean and Middle Eastern empires had developed—norms which were bequeathed through the legacy of Islamic civilization—the Ottomans had other precedents: the legal traditions of Islam, their own knowledge of the Byzantines, and the distinctive customs of the Turkish peoples. Each of these precedents, along with exigencies of the times, shaped Ottoman policy toward non-Muslims.

The first to come under Ottoman rule were the Greeks. The initial relation between these two people was not simply one of conqueror and conquered. Turk and Greek had developed a common culture of the frontier over the centuries of their conflict. Shifting alliances and borders had blurred some differences, but in the end the triumphant Ottoman state was clearly Muslim, however willing it might be to use the services of its Christian subjects (see Volume I, chapter 2, by İ. Metin Kunt). This was no *Byzance après Byzance*. But if the Ottoman state was not Byzantium, neither was it a Muslim theocracy, if by theocracy we mean a government whose ruler is divine and whose revealed laws are administered by a priestly order. The Ottoman sultan ruled as defender of the divine revelation vouchsafed to Muhammad, but he did not rule as a divinity nor was his empire administered by divines. Thus it was not out of a theocratic instinct that the Ottomans turned to the local remnants of the Orthodox Church to control their Orthodox populations. This was a practical policy. Similar considerations led the Ottomans to turn to the religious leaders of the other communities whom they conquered.

In addition to its obvious and practical advantages, the decision to allow a degree of autonomy to these communities was consistent with the traditions of Islamic law. However, not all the policies adopted by the Ottomans proceeded directly from this precedent. Two institutions which affected the lives of non-Muslims very greatly had little precedent in Islamic law and one may indeed have violated it.

The *sürgün* was a system of forced migration. It was used for two purposes—1) as punitive deportation directed against individuals and 2) as a socio-economic policy affecting entire communities. In the aftermath of the centuries-long war between Ottomans and Byzantines, the authorities used the *sürgün* as a means of forced colonization to repopulate devastated areas. Forced migration had been a policy of the Byzantines and earlier rulers, but as an economic tool it had not been commonly used by Islamic empires. Furthermore Islamic legal opinion had, on the whole, opposed deportations of non-Muslims for reasons other than security. The Ottoman *sürgün* brought Turks from Aksaray in Anatolia, Armenians from Ankara, and Jews from Salonica to repopulate Constantinople. After the conquest of Cyprus in the late sixteenth century, the same device was used to populate the island with landless Turcomans. The *sürgün* was not directed against Christians and Jews, as such, and its long-term effects were, for the most part, beneficial for both the empire and the peoples affected; but its initial impact was painful and since the majority of the Ottoman subjects were then non-Muslims it was they who bore more of its burdens. Those who were subject to the edict of forced migration regarded it as a disaster—it meant the destruction of long-established communities and the loss of lands and traditional places of business with no certainty that they would survive their migration or that the new settlements would be better. Because it meant such drastic disruption and because it often was the first Ottoman policy which directly affected their lives, the *sürgün* had a much greater impact upon the attitudes of Armenians and Jews toward the Ottomans than did the benign neglect of communal autonomy which structurally was a continuation of the *status quo ante*. (On the *sürgün* and the Jews, see Volume I, chapter 6 by Joseph Hacker). On the other hand, for the Greeks, and more generally the Orthodox Christians, who formed the overwhelming majority of the non-Muslim population, the loss of their political dominance and independence was the primary impact of the Ottoman triumph, and the *sürgün* along with the captivity and slavery were simply part and parcel of the general devastation.

However disruptive, the *sürgün* was not a continuous feature of Ottoman policy; once moved, the forced migrants were rarely moved again. The other Ottoman institution which affected non-Muslims was continuous. It was the *devşirme*, the periodic levy of unmarried male children from the Christian peasantry of the empire, imposed mainly on Slavs and Albanians, occasionally—in early times—on Armenians, rarely on Greeks and Jews. The *dev-*

şirme was in effect from the fourteenth century until late in the seventeenth century, but its heyday lasted only until the sixteenth century. Its perodicity and its precise toll varied, but its enforcement required that from time to time a certain number of Christians be trained as Ottoman soldiers or bureaucrats, converted to Islam, and made Turks. Although some Christians perceived this as a means to place a family member in a position of influence within the state, for most families and certainly for the Orthodox Church this levy was a heavy loss to bear.

More than the *sürgün* system, the *devşirme* was an unprecedented institution within the Middle East, for neither the Islamic nor the pre-Islamic empires ever adopted such a means of staffing the state. Furthermore, the provisions of the system were clearly at variance with the spirit of *dhimma*. While Islam did allow the taking of slaves from conquered populations during wartime, once the population was actually at peace under Islam such a levy was no longer permitted. In the absence of an Islamic precedent, the *devşirme* seems to have been an Ottoman invention.

Sürgün and *devşirme* were Ottoman policies which intruded into the lives of the *dhimmi* communities more violently than any other. However burdensome, the collection of poll tax and other taxes did not wreak havoc with the lives of Christians and Jews. As the proportion of non-Muslims to Muslims within the empire grew smaller—with the conquests of Syria and Egypt in 1517 Muslims became the overwhelming majority—and as the practices and needs of the empire became stronger, first *sürgün* and then *devşirme* came to affect the *dhimmi*s less and less. The local communal authorities grew increasingly able to mediate the policies of the government.

The framework within which the Christian and Jewish communal authorities functioned under Ottoman rule has been called the *millet* system. *Millet* was a term which originally meant a religious community and in the nineteenth century came to mean nation. Tradition has it that Sultan Mehmed II, in the period after the conquest of Constantinople, appointed as patriarch of Constantinople Gennadios Scholarios, a monk known for his opposition to rapprochement with the Latin West, and thereby made him the titular head of all the Orthodox faithful in the empire. Mehmed was reputed to have granted Patriarch Gennadios and the Orthodox Church a number of privileges which allowed fiscal and legal autonomy to the community. The Patriarch was responsible for his community's taxes and in return the state supported the authority of the patriarch. Comparable arrangements were said to have been made with the Armenians and the Jews.

Research presented in these volumes suggests that many of the accepted details regarding the *millet* system may be inaccurate and that its systemic nature may be greatly exaggerated (see Volume I, chapters 3, 4, 6 and Volume II, chapter 1 by Benjamin Braude, Kevork Bardakjian, Joseph Hacker, and Amnon Cohen respectively). Rather than a uniformly adopted system, it may be more accurately described as a series of *ad hoc* arrangements made over the years, which gave each of the major religious communities a degree of legal autonomy and authority with the acquiescence of the Ottoman state. Power could be held by either lay or religious figures—actual leadership varied with community, time and place. The degree to which communal authority was merely local or empirewide also varied.

Mehmed's recognition of the Greek Patriarchate in Constantinople, which had its own traditions of ecumenical authority, meant that for the Orthodox such empirewide authority existed, at least in theory. In practice, however, Constantinople had to contend with the autonomous traditions of Bulgarian Ohrid and Serbian Pec. On the other hand the Patriarchates of Antioch, Jerusalem, and Alexandria, richer in history but poorer in souls, proved less resistant to the dictates of their new capital after they came under Ottoman rule. Constantinople's claim to authority over all Orthodox Christians in the Empire, consistent with its ecumenical pretentions to universal authority, dovetailed with the Ottomans' own claims to universal empire, heir to the traditions of Byzantium and Rome.

As a result of Ottoman practice, millions of communicants of the Orthodox Church, speakers of Slavic, Romance, Semitic, and other languages, natives of Europe, Asia, and Africa, all came to be designated administratively as *Rum,* literally "Roman," meaning Greek Orthodox. It might seem strange that these peoples who in more recent times have variously asserted distinct Serbian, Greek, Bulgarian, Vlach, Montenegrin, Herzegovinian, Macedonian, Albanian, Yugoslavian, Rumanian, Arab, Syrian, Lebanese, Palestinian, or Jordanian national identity should have in the past accepted this all-embracing communal designation. Of course, to a degree that designation was not of their own choosing; the Islam-inspired understanding of the Ottomans recognized the primacy of religious affiliation and the expansionist imperative inherent in an Ecumenical Patriarchate ensured that Constantinople eagerly received the souls whom it regarded as rightfully its own.

The acceptance of *Rum,* however, was not merely submission to the edicts of the capital. It conformed to a perception which at least some *Rum* (notably the wealthier and more educated) had of themselves. Among the *Rum* people there appeared a disdain for Latin and Monophysite rivals and a certain pride in the imperial heritage of Byzantium and the Constantinople Patriarchate (see Volume I, chapter 10 by Richard Clogg). In the lands of the Middle East which spoke first Aramaic and later Arabic, those Christians who retained their loyalty to the Byzantine Church, resisting the appeal of Monophysitism and Islam, were originally called *Melkite* meaning kingsmen. Following the Vatican's success in gaining the conversion of some Arabic-speaking Orthodox to Rome, the term now also includes Arabic-speaking Catholics or Uniates of the Greek rite. Perhaps at first intended as an insult by local rivals, the term carried a certain nobility, a pretension to empire which its adherents could claim with pride. During the nineteenth century this was successfully exploited by the Romanov Empire, the third Rome, which stirred among the Arabic-speaking Orthodox a strong attachment to the tsar, the Russian motherland, and the Church of St. Petersburg. In southeastern Europe it was a Greek-speaking Vlach, Riga Velestiniul (as he was known in the Rumanian language, Rigas Velestinlis or Pheraios in Greek), whose revolutionary activities on behalf of a revived Byzantium earned him death at Ottoman hands. With more romance than truth, he is now claimed as an early martyr for modern Greek nationalism.

Although the ethnic composition of the other communities was simpler, administrative arrangements for Armenians and Jews proved more complex. They had different needs and traditions which made acceptance of the Greek Orthodox precedent of Constantinople-based leadership difficult. The traditions concerning Mehmed's grant of privilege to Armenians and Jews are even more uncertain. Even if such grants had in fact been made to the communal leaders in the capital it is not likely that they would have thereby gained power over all their coreligionists within the empire.

Unlike the Greeks, the Armenians had no patriarchate in Constantinople before the conquest (see Volume I, chapter 4 by Kevork Bardakjian). Their ecclesiastical centers were either the newly strengthened see of Ējmiacin (Etchmiadzin) or the see of Cilicia, both of which were then beyond the Ottoman borders. Since Mehmed had little desire for his subjects to be under an ultramontane authority, he fostered the development of an Armenian ecclesiastical center in Istanbul. But this Istanbul Patriarchate faced indifference and even opposition from the Armenians whom it was supposed to guide. Furthermore, Mehmed's successors were not as consistent in opposing ultramontane authority as he was.

For the Jews, the lack of a preexisting authority within the empire was less of a problem; there was no ultramontane authority either. The so-called Chief Rabbinate of the Ottoman Empire which arose after 1453 was an institution whose authority probably did not extend beyond the borders of Istanbul and whose existence did not survive the centrifugal pressures introduced by the large-scale immigration of Iberian Jewry during the early sixteenth century.

In the same century Selim's conquest of Syria and Egypt expanded the territory of the empire to include the heartlands of Islam, numerous Arabic-speaking Jewish communities and the ancient Christian churches of the East (see Volume II, chapter 1 by Amnon Cohen and chapter 2 by Muhammed Adnan Bakhit). Copts, Maronites, Jacobites, and other smaller sects now entered the Ottoman fold. Consistent with their *ad hoc* policies the conquerors were content, for the most part, to let local conditions determine the collection of taxes and relations with ecclesiastical authorities. When the Ottomans conquered large Catholic populations in Eastern Europe, local officials there too worked out the arrangements. There were of course significant differences between the *dhimmi*s of Syria and Egypt and those of Anatolia and Rumelia. For nearly a millennium the ancient communities of the East had lived under Islam, and the Ottoman conquest merely exchanged one Muslim master for another. The indigenous Christians and Jews of the Arabic-speaking lands had become linguistically assimilated to the Muslim population. Their distinctiveness was less obvious. Concomitantly, their numbers had dwindled and their influence upon society was small. Despite their centuries-old experience of Islam, the Arabic-speaking *dhimmi*s did not take an independent lead in dealing with Ottoman authorities. Rather from the sixteenth to the mid-nineteenth centuries they increasingly accepted the lead of their wealthier and more numerous coreligionists outside the Arab lands. The Patriarchates of Alexandria and Jerusalem, for instance, were henceforth held by ethnic Greeks. On the other hand, the Copts, who had no such external allies, remained the least ambitious Christians in the area (see Volume II, chapter 9 by Doris Behrens-Abouseif).

The institutional arrangements which prevailed during the early centuries of Ottoman rule provided the outer form of communal life, but rarely shaped its content. Western views of day-to-day life under Ottoman rule have been distorted by a number of misconceptions. For Christendom and its heirs the words Turk and Turkey have complex emotional associations over and above those suggested by Islam; for East Europeans in particular the traditional picture of the Turkish oppressor has become part of the national folklore. This image of the Turk has several sources. The first is fear, imprinted on the European mind during long periods when the Turks were thrusting into the heart of the continent and seemed to threaten the very existence of Christendom. Later Western travelers, failing to recognize in Turkish society the familiar virtues of their own countries, were blind to the real but different merits of the Ottoman order and found confirmation for their dislike in the tales of the Christian subjects of the sultans who were their main informants. Even more recent observers whose sympathies were with Islam tended to identify it with the Arabs and to blame the Ottomans for a decay which they did not cause and which they had, in fact, halted and for a while reversed.

A good example of the way in which travelers and other observers misunderstood and misinterpreted the conditions of non-Muslim life is provided by the word *raya*. According to most Western travelers, followed by most Western historians, the word *raya* means cattle and was applied to the Christian subjects of the Ottoman state, whose predatory attitude toward them was expressed in this term. However, Ottoman usage until the eighteenth century applied the term not to Christians as such but to the entire productive taxpaying population of the empire, irrespective of religion—in fact, to all who were not part of the civilian and military apparatus of government (see Volume I, chapter 8 by Kemal Karpat). Thus Muslim peasants were *raya,* but Christian cavalrymen were not. The word is derived from an Arabic root meaning to graze and might better be translated not as "cattle," but as "flock," expressing the well-known pastoral idea of government taken from the Psalms[4] and shared by Christendom and Islam. The extent of Western influence on Turkey may be seen in the fact that from the late eighteenth century onward, the Western misinterpretation of the term passed to the Turks themselves, who began to use it and sometimes apply it in this sense.

Western distortion was further elaborated and more widely disseminated during the nineteenth century, as the result of the struggle of the Balkan peoples against the Ottoman Empire to achieve independence. The liberal and nationalist movements against the Ottomans in the nineteenth century strongly reinforced the prevailing stereotype of the Muslim as oppressor—this time embodied in, and typified by, the Ottoman Turkish Empire.

Not all the nineteenth-century European mythmakers worked against the Turks. Among Jews in particular there developed a tinge of philo-Ottomanism which even colored the writings of a pioneer in modern Jewish historiography, Heinrich Graetz. Often this tinge was seen in a political sympathy for the Ottoman, and Jews in general came to be regarded and sometimes denounced in Europe as a pro-Turkish element.

In our own time yet another source of misinformation has been added. Since the spread of national movements in the Balkans and the Middle East many states have arisen from the ruins of the Ottoman Empire, each with its own national myth of liberation, and its own national brand of historiography. Like most liberated peoples, the Balkan and, later, Arab successor states of the Ottoman Empire tended to blame all the defeats and shortcomings of their societies upon the misrule of their fallen Imperial masters. Often more eloquent in Western languages than the Turks, and with better access to Western audiences, they succeeded in persuading many Western observers of the truth of their version of history.

Of all the liberated peoples the first to enthrall the West were the Greeks. The Hellenic past, however remote from the historical consciousness of the Greeks, was an essential element of European thought and it was in this perspective that Europeans saw the struggle of the Greeks against the Ottomans. The emerging Greek view thus gained ready acceptance. Depopulation, impoverishment, instability, insecurity, corruption, venality, intrigue, and deceit were all seen as faults of Ottoman origin. The more advanced observers might claim that those faults which could not be traced directly to the Turks should be ascribed to the Orthodox hierarchy, whose authority was, however, itself attributed to Ottoman "theocracy." In the course of their own struggles the other subject peoples—the Slavs, Wallachians, and Moldavians—accepted and adapted the Greek indictment. However, they added the Greeks themselves to the list of the accused, for they, as both laymen and ecclesiastics, often functioned as junior partners to the Turks in their dominion of the Balkans.

Clearly the Greek relationship to the Turks was the most complex. The sentimental view of history does not do justice to the very real achievements of the Greeks under Ottoman rule. The Ottomans allowed the Greek community to maintain its physical existence, language, sense of history, cultural traditions, and religious integrity over several centuries. In an exhortation delivered late in the eighteenth century, the Greek Patriarch of Jerusalem recognized the empire's role:

> See how clearly our Lord, boundless in mercy and all-wise, had undertaken to guard once more the unsullied Holy and Orthodox faith. . . . He raised out of

nothing this powerful empire of the Ottomans, in place of our Roman [Byzantine] Empire which had begun, in a certain way, to cause to deviate from the beliefs of the Orthodox faith, and he raised up the empire of the Ottomans higher than any other kingdom so as to show without doubt that it came about by divine will, and not by the power of man. . . .

The all-mighty Lord, then, has placed over us this high kingdom, "for there is no power but of God," so as to be to the people of the West a bridle, to us the people of the East a means of salvation. For this reason he puts into the heart of the Sultan of these Ottomans an inclination to keep free the religious beliefs of our Orthodox faith and, as a work of supererogation, to protect them, even to the point of occasionally chastising Christians who deviate from their faith, that they have always before their eyes the fear of God.[5]

For many the empire presented a wide field for personal advancement and success. In its service these Greeks were willing to work and make important contributions. Accordingly, some Greek writers of the late eighteenth century were more sympathetic to Ottoman rule than are their descendants today. The wealthy and lettered were oftentimes beneficiaries of Ottoman largesse and protection. As for the Church, its authority was often bolstered by the Ottomans who enforced its edicts. They had reason to be pro-Ottoman. To the extent that we know the feelings of the unlettered and the poor it would seem that, though their life was harder, they were not anti-Turk pure and simple, for their anger was as much directed against the Greek grandees.

It would thus be more accurate to discuss several Greek relationships to the Turks, not only because different elements of the population had their respective privileges and responsibilities, but also because different areas of population—mixed Muslim-Greek settlement as opposed to all-Greek settlement—had varying degrees of autonomy verging on effective independence. In addition, the day-to-day life of the Greeks depended upon both the general conditions of Ottoman power and administration and the status of other minority groups in the empire.

At the risk of overgeneralization in an area where there is all too little scholarly research, the following rough scheme of Greek-Ottoman history is presented. The earliest period from 1300 to 1450 was characterized by a degree of syncretism at the popular level in the absence of strong Greek leadership. The relationship between Greek and Turkish leaders showed a shifting pattern of alliance and hostility. After the conquest of Constantinople there emerged a structure of patriarchal leadership within a stable political setting, in which, however, the lot of the Church was by no means easy. Closely tied to the Constantinople patriarchate were wealthy Greek merchants—some with pretensions to Byzantine aristocracy. This period lasted from 1450 to 1600. From 1600 to 1800 the wealthy Greek families of the Phanar, an Istanbul district to which the patriarchate was moved in 1601, assumed increased wealth and political influence both within their own community and the empire at large. Among Greeks the Phanariotes manipulated the selection of the patriarch and his officials to suit the interests of their competing families. In the empire the Phanariotes controlled the revenue-producing principalities of Moldavia and Wallachia in addition to the influential chief dragomanate, which helped shape Ottoman foreign policy, and the post of dragoman to the fleet, who served the Ottoman high admiral and administered many of the Aegean islands.

During these centuries—1600–1800—there was a rise in European influence upon the Greeks—religious, economic, intellectual, and political. Protestant and Catholic missionaries and their protecting embassies vied for influence in Constantinople. Greek merchants who previously concentrated their foreign ventures in the Orthodox lands of Eastern Europe now traded in the West. The corrosive notions of the European Enlightenment, which started to penetrate Greek intellectual life, fostered new forms of political thinking in the Diaspora. The Greek ecclesiastical hierarchy viewed these developments with suspicion and distrust and combated them as best it could, but since the most disturbing of these trends flourished outside the empire, well beyond the confines of patriarchal authority, there was little the clergy could do.

During the last century and one quarter, from just before 1800 to 1923, the most drastic changes occurred, beginning with the French occupation of the formerly Venetian-held Ionian islands bordering Ottoman Greece, followed by the Greek War of Independence (1821–1832), and ending with the forced migration of Greeks, after the Treaty of Lausanne (1923), from Turkey and Bulgaria to Greece itself. Over this same period the Orthodox Church in Slavic and Arabic-speaking areas grew increasingly restive under Greek domination. A period which saw the first articulation of the Great Idea, the notion that Greece should control all the territories which had been under her sway in the past, a kind of neo-Byzantium, ended in ignominious withdrawal from all settlements back to her rocky outpost at the tip of the Balkan peninsula.

No less profound than the political and geographical transformation of the Greeks was the change in their historical consciousness and identity. In the eighteenth century Greeks claimed to be Romans, in the nineteenth century, Hellenes. The turning point in this transformation was the creation of an independent kingdom of Greece. Prior to its creation most Greeks of the Ottoman lands saw themselves as Romans, that is, as East Romans, heirs of Byzantium. The men of the Greek enlightenment propagated notions of Hellenism, a return to the glory of ancient and pagan Hellas. A key figure was Adamantios Koraes (1748–1833), a scientist, scholar, and man of letters who played a crucial role in the Greek intellectual revival.

But the intellectuals and merchants who formulated such notions in the distant European centers of the Greek diaspora—Koraes spent many years in Montpelier and Paris—were not the men who did battle. The Greek mountaineers and peasants, pirates and brigands who fought the Ottoman forces through years of protracted struggle would have found a return to Hellenism as alien if not as repulsive as conversion to Islam. The popular cry was for a return to the Romaic past, that is, Christian Constantinople and not pagan

Athens. The remains of classical Greece were as mysterious to the Greek peasant as were the monuments of Pharaonic Egypt to the *fellah;* both thought them the work of an ancient race of giants or genies. The claim to these legacies by latter-day Greece and Egypt developed from the eighteenth and nineteenth centuries as a consequence of European archaeological discoveries and European concepts of ethnic and territorial nationhood.

Another external element which had a great impact upon the Greeks and the empire as a whole was the French Revolution. The ideas of the Revolution—liberty and equality—were clearly disruptive of the traditional order. When coupled with French military success these ideas became the most dangerous force challenging the Ottoman Empire at the end of the eighteenth century. In 1797 the Treaty of Campo Formio partitioned the Republic of Venice and bestowed upon France many former Venetian possessions along the Ottoman Adriatic coast. From these islands the French launched a propaganda campaign directed at the empire's Greek subjects. They organized speeches and ceremonies which recalled the ancient glories and liberties of Hellas and promised their restoration. More significantly, French intelligence made contact with rebels and dissidents on the mainland and rumors abounded that the French planned an invasion to annex parts of Greece. It was finally Egypt, not Greece, which was France's target, but the mere presence of France along the borders of Ottoman Europe proved disturbing.

The immediate cause of the Greek rising, which eventually produced the independent Greek kingdom, may be seen in the centralizing policies of Sultan Mahmud II. During the late eighteenth and early nineteenth centuries, the Greek maritime and mercantile communities had prospered greatly. The Ottoman flag, neutral during some of the crucial years of the revolutionary and Napoleonic wars, had given them considerable commercial advantages; the loose and highly decentralized administration of the Ottoman Empire in that period allowed them the opportunity to develop their own administrative, political, and even military institutions. The local rulers and dynasts who governed much of Greece were for the most part Muslims. They presided, however, over largely Greek principalities, were served by Greek ministers and agents, and even employed Greek troops. The attempt by Mahmud II to restore the direct authority of the Ottoman central government thus represented in effect a severe curtailment of liberties which the Greeks already enjoyed, and it was the defense of these liberties, as much as the acquisition of new ones, that motivated the struggle of the Greeks against Ottoman rule.

The French occupation of some of the Greek lands had additional significance, for it presaged a process of occupation, agitation, and rebellion which was to afflict the empire in its last century. The French in Ionia, the Russians in Armenia, and the British in Egypt, each in different ways, used territory they had seized in or adjacent to the empire as a base from which to stir dissident elements to rebel. The Russians supported an Armenian revolutionary movement and the British armed and financed an Arab revolt.

In each instance of rebellion the external power aided and abetted in the recreation of a mythic past which bore little relation to the actual consciousness of the rebels but which took on a life of its own once the struggle was over. The contribution of the Hellenic revival to the popular struggle against the Ottomans was small. In the end, however, it was Hellenism which took over the cause. Unfortunately for the dreamers of a revived Byzantium, the notion of Hellas excluded the non-Greek-speaking Orthodox peoples as barbarians.

Thus the ties which had previously brought together the Serbs, Bulgars, Macedonians, Moldavians, Wallachians, Greeks and others now started to fray. The transformation of the Greek self-image and reality had an even more penetrating impact upon the position of millions of Greeks who remained within the empire. For many of these the politics, ideals, and even language of the new Greek kingdom were alien. Nonetheless, the creation of this new state rendered the position of the Ottoman Greek community increasingly difficult and eventually helped sound its death knell.

The central theme of Greek history through centuries of Ottoman rule was a sense of imperial loss. Greece's golden age was Byzantium; the classical past was rejected as barbarian paganism. Under the Ottomans the Patriarchate of Constantinople represented a kind of successor state to Justinians's empire. The boundaries—if there were boundaries to an ecumenical see—were the boundaries of his empire. Under the Ottoman aegis the Orthodox leadership could pretend to its greatest territorial extent. The emergence of Hellas redeemed shattered the pretense and ambiguity of the Greek position under the Ottomans. Dreams of empire could not compete with the realities of statehood. Eventually the Greeks were forced to choose the constricted reality and lose—if not forsake—the larger dream.

The gap between Armenian reality and Armenian dreams was even wider. The Armenians have been caught in the midst of nearly every struggle in Middle Eastern history and more often than not have chosen, or had chosen for them, the losing side. At one time or another the Greeks, the Persians, the Arabs, the Mongols, the Russians, and the Turks have been their enemies. Periods of Armenian independence have been brief and distant. Armenia's proudest memories have been the early adoption of Christianity and the determined adherence to Monophysite doctrines, a Christology it shares with the Copts of Egypt and the Jacobites of Syria.

Although Armenians, like Greeks, dreamed of a return to their own rule, the recollection of that rule has been much dimmer. The dispersal of the Armenian people following their repeated losses further complicated their dreams. While the Greeks could hold millenarian beliefs in the recapture of Constantinople, the Armenians had no single center to reclaim. The process of conquest, exile, and political revival on new soil—the moves from the Armenia of Van and Ararat and later Cappadocia to the Lesser Armenia of Cilicia during the eleventh century—although it preserved the territoriality of the Armenians, complicated their historical memory by creating new and conflicting national centers. Furthermore, their moves rarely gave them respite. They fled to Cilicia to escape the Seljuk Turks, but their new homeland became a base for the Crusades. Those who remained in historic Armenia suffered centuries of war as the Seljuks and Byzantines, marauding Turcomans, and then the Ottomans and Safavids fought over this land. The process of dispersal continued by *sürgün* and voluntary means, sending Armenians to the Black Sea region, the Balkans, and Eastern Europe, as well as to Iran and India.

During the heyday of Ottoman power, the fifteenth to early seventeenth centuries, the Armenians do not seem to have played a prominent role (see Volume I, chapter 7 by Robert Mantran). The privileges extended to Armenians by Shah ᶜAbbās, leader of Safavid Iran, who was building a great trading center in his capital, Isfahan, drew them eastward. The strength of Jewish merchant activities in the Ottoman Empire discouraged significant Armenian mercantile movement westward. In the eighteenth century, after the decline of the Safavids, the reduction of Iran to a chaos of warring factions, the Ottoman expansion into formerly Persian-held territory, and the weakening of the Jewish position in commerce, the Armenians began to rise to prominence in the life of the empire. Their position improved even more in the nineteenth century. They became the intendants of customshouses, the bankers to local pashas, the purveyors of luxury goods, the minters of coins, and the practitioners of long-distance trade.

Even during this period of increased activity in the entrepôts of Istanbul, Aleppo, and Izmir, the bulk of the Armenian population remained as they had been for centuries, peasants in Anatolia. In this region a figure who was to initiate a major movement for Armenian revival received his earliest schooling. Mekhitar of Sivas (1676–1749) founded an Armenian Catholic religious order which was to help lead the cultural resurgence and Westernization of his people. The Mekhitarist Fathers revived the Armenian language, cultivated Armenian literature, spread Western ideas through translations, established scholarly and popular journals, instituted a network of schools, and laid the foundation of modern Armenian historiography. All this was directed from monasteries outside the Ottoman Empire to which the Fathers had been exiled by the hostility of the established Armenian church.

In the course of the seventeenth and eighteenth centuries two challenges emerged to the traditional leadership of the Armenian community. The first came from the parvenus of wealth, the bankers, minters, and merchants, who came to be called the *amiras*. The second challenge came from the Catholic-tinged cultural revival inspired by the Mekhitarists. The *amiras* gained power and prestige within the Armenian community. Servants and advisers to Ottoman officials in both the capital and the provinces, they were in a better position to represent the Armenians than were the leaders of the Church (see Volume I, chapter 9 by Hagop Barsoumian). In the course of the eighteenth century the Armenian hierarchy parried the trust of the *amiras* by sharing power with them. In fact the Constantinople patriarchs used the influence of the capital's *amiras* to advance their own position over that of the other hierarchies.

The Catholic challenge was not as easily met. Eventually in 1830, supported by the French who regarded themselves protectors of Catholic interests in the empire, the Armenian Catholics received recognition from the Ottoman goverment as a community, *millet,* in their own right.

Though the Armenian Catholic problem seemed, at least on the surface, resolved, countless internal disputes remained to plague the Armenian community throughout the nineteenth century. For most of the period Armenian passions were directed more within the community than without, at the Ottoman government. Inspired by the ideas of the Enlightenment and the successive political revolutions of Europe, some Armenian thinkers of the mid-nineteenth century propagated new notions limiting the authority of the ruling *amira*-clergy coalition. The established leadership supported itself by appealing to the Divine Truth of the Bible which they claimed demanded obedience to both the Armenian and Ottoman authorities. The forces arguing for constitutional restraints also sought to bring their liberal notions to the population at large by educating the Armenian peasants in Anatolia whose welfare had been long neglected—or so they charged.

In the midst of these disputes the leaders of Armenian establishment, who had evolved an effective *modus vivendi* with the Ottoman authorities, found their position challenged from an unexpected quarter, the very Ottoman state to which they urged obedience. The reform decree of 1856 had a greater impact upon the Armenian community than it did on any other element of the empire. The issues of clerical versus lay control, participation by the community at large in selection of religious leaders, the nature of hierarchical authority, the notion of a constitution itself—issues which had provoked deep divisions among Armenians—were now addressed directly by the Ottomans. Among the Greeks and Jews such matters had not been the subject of prior controversy, so the Ottoman-sponsored reforms, which these communities eventually accepted, did not affect them in the same way. However, in the Armenian community the issue of reform was to be resolved with the Ottoman government, publicly at least, arrayed initially on the side of the new thinkers, the liberal constitutionalists, and the opponents of the traditional leadership. This emerging coalition of reform did not last long, but its existence for even a short time disturbed the traditional methods of political and social control which allowed Ottoman society to function. The political conflict within the community became ever more dangerous as it increasingly involved the Ottoman government. A constitution was drafted and eventually enforced which formed the basis for the organization and representation of the Armenian people for most of the remaining decades of Ottoman rule. This same document continues in our own day to govern the Armenians of Syria and Lebanon.

During the early constitutional period there was much reason to expect that the position of the Armenians in the empire would continue to improve.

Implementation of the Ottoman reform decrees opened up new possibilities for government service; the penetration of the economy by European firms opened up new jobs for people who had the skills, which many possessed; theater, music and the arts attracted Armenians of talent to the capital (see Volume I, chapter 15 by Roderic Davison). The so-called Armenian National Constitution seemed to inaugurate a new period of hope and opportunity for all the Armenians in the empire. Indeed it was a remarkable document: it recognized the right of all members of the community to have some voice in determining its affairs and it institutionalized a high degree of autonomy. By contrast the neighboring Armenian community in the Russian Empire seemed worse off. All their bishops were nominated by the tsar, who also had the right to choose the head of the Church from a final list submitted by an Armenian assembly. In addition, the Russian government appointed a pro-curator who supervised and even directed the Catholicos of Ejmiacin. Later the Russian goverment took even harsher steps; they compelled Armenian schools to use Russian as the language of instruction and they forcibly confiscated all the properties of the Armenian church.

Nonetheless Russia laid claim to be the protector of Ottoman Armenians. When Russia conquered the Caucasus early in the nineteenth century and created a province of Armenia with Armenian administrators and Armenian soldiers on the borders of the Ottoman Empire, hopes were stirred among Armenians who had imbibed the nationalist ideas of the West that together they might restore independence. The movement for national independence would in all likelihood have gained strength whatever policies the Ottomans pursued, but Ottoman support for policies which inadvertently undermined the authority of the traditional leadership in Istanbul contributed to the weakening of that element which cooperated with the government. Instead, in opposition to the Ottomans, the voices of the European-inspired Armenians and the voices of the Armenians of the eastern provinces, subject to the depredations of Kurdish and Turkish elements who took advantage of law-lessness and maladministration, now came increasingly to prevail in the Armenian community.

Tragically for the Armenians, their hopes for national independence repre-sented the severest threat to emerging Turkish nationalism. The Ottoman Turks could lose Greece, Serbia, Bulgaria, Albania, and even the Arab lands and still have a territorially viable national state. To a much greater degree than all the other Christian peoples, the Armenians were integrated with the Muslim population. Their misfortune was that in the past centuries they had got along well enough with Kurds, Turks, and other Muslims to inhabit the same towns and villages. No compact minority begging partition, they shared much of eastern and southern Anatolia with their Muslim neighbors. For the Turks to have lost the lands which the Armenians inhabited—territory stretching from the Caucasus to the Mediterranean—would have aborted Turkey. With the outbreak of World War I a terrible struggle between Turks and Armenians began. It ended with a disaster. In 1915, according to some observers, between one million and one and a half million Armenians perished. Once again the tragic themes of Armenian history were repeated.

The pattern of Jewish history under Ottoman rule ran contrary to that of the Greeks and Armenians. The heyday of Ottoman Jewry was during the sixteenth and seventeenth centuries; their centuries of decline were the eighteenth and nineteenth. The most significant date was 1492, the year of the expulsion of the Jews from Spain. Prior to the influx of Iberian Jews, Ottoman Jewry was small, poor, and spoke either Greek or Turkish. The Jews were divided into a Rabbinite community, that is followers of Talmudic Judaism, and a small Karaite community, a sect which traced its origins back to a break with Talmudic Judaism in the eighth century. Along with other Ottoman subjects, both were liable to forced migrations. Although there were individual exceptions, it would seem that the lot of most Jews in the early decades of Ottoman rule was not as prosperous as it was to be later, when for practical reasons the Ottomans opened their lands to the Iberian exiles. Of all the states in the Mediterranean region, the Ottoman Empire was the only one which had a need for skilled urban populations and possessed the administrative apparatus for handling thousands of immigrants. It was this combination of need and ability which made it possible for Jews to be received.

The numbers and cultural sophistication of these immigrants soon overwhelmed the indigenous Jewish communities, which subsequently, with few exceptions, became assimilated into Iberian Jewish culture. They abandoned Greek and Turkish for Ladino, i.e., Judaeo-Spanish. They also integrated the history of Iberian Jewry into their own. Of all the *dhimmi* communities, the Iberian Jews alone were Ottoman subjects by choice, not by conquest. This characteristic and the related lack of sympathy with Europe clearly marked them off from the Christian communities, and proved a source of suspicion in the eyes of their fellow subjects and of acceptance in the eyes of their masters. Jewish sources of the sixteenth century reflect a perception of the empire as a haven during times of trouble and persecution, and this image has held strong in the centuries that followed.

Through the early post-expulsion period the self-image of Ottoman Jewry was of a confident community, and its cultural and material achievements certainly justified this belief—the establishment of trade and industry, the growth and flowering of intellectual life, the participation of Jews in the mainstream of Ottoman commerce, and within limits, their perceptible role in science and in political and diplomatic affairs. Toward the end of the sixteenth century and the beginning of the seventeenth this picture of progress, wealth, and influence started to change. Jewish immigration to the Ottoman Empire, and thus contact with Europe, had diminished and emigration had begun.

The reason for this was twofold. Simply put, the major source of migrants, Iberian Jewry, was drying up. Those who wished to move eastward had done so and the rest who had chosen to settle in Europe and the New World were by now well established. Second, economic opportunities within the empire were diminishing. By the seventeenth century the woolen textile industry in Salonica, which was the largest single employer of Jewish labor in the entire country, was beginning to experience a series of crises from which it never recovered. The result of this decline was to reduce the economic base of the community and render it more subject to the vagaries of international commerce at a time when patterns of trade were shifting. The ties which Ottoman Jews established with their coreligionists in Italy became less profitable as this center declined. Ottoman Jews were not able to shift their network into central and eastern Europe. While there were large Jewish communities in those areas, they were Ashkenazi and therefore unlikely to provide the ties of family on which a Sefardi network must depend. The Greeks and Armenians had ethnic and family ties in eastern Europe which proved superior to the Jewish network.

This brings us to another cause of Jewish decline—the increasing competition of the Christians, particularly the Greeks and Armenians, but later also Arab Christians. The Christians had the advantage of numbers—there were far more of them than there were of Jews—and of education, in that they sent their children to Christian schools and often to Europe and European universities, while the Jews, having lost their commercial ties with the West, were for long confined to their own resources within the Ottoman Empire. The Christians had the advantage of patronage both from their church hierarchies (which the Jews lacked) and from Christian Europe, which naturally tended to favor Christians at the expense of Jews—and by now it was the favor of Europe, not of the Turks, that counted. Thus early in the seventeenth century, to quote one example among many, an Armenian replaced a Jew as customs intendant of Aleppo, aided in his appointment by the French consul.

Late in the seventeenth century a major crisis afflicted the Ottoman Jewish community. It came at the time of a shift in the economic base against a background of increased competition and loss of confidence. Nationalism never found as receptive an audience among Jews as it did among other communities of the empire, but the combination of mysticism and messianism which culminated in the Sabbatian movement of the late seventeenth century was at least as widespread and, in its own way, as inimical to Ottoman authority.

Mystical study and speculation had existed among Jews for many centuries. Originating in the Ottoman Empire was the study of Lurianic Kabbalah with its emphasis upon the messianic imperative. It was this doctrine—widely disseminated from Safed through the Jewries of the world—which allowed Sabbatai Sevi's messianic claims to gain a mass following. As news of "the messiah" spread, the Jews both within and outside the empire prepared themselves for his arrival—they performed acts of repentance, special fasts and prayers; the more practical-minded sold their goods, packed their bags, and prepared for the ingathering of the exiles to Palestine. The Ottoman authorities in Istanbul, preoccupied as they were with the campaign against Venetian Crete, did not immediately attempt to suppress the movement.

Eventually they quelled its more disturbing elements by arresting Sabbatai Sevi and ultimately "persuading" him to embrace Islam. The more overt agitation now subsided. Some of his followers adopted Islam outwardly. The majority remained Jews, though many still retained faith in him.

The social background and social impact of Sabbatianism have not been as thoroughly examined as has the spiritual. It has been claimed that in the aftermath of exhaustion and disappointment Ottoman Jewry reinforced the power and authority of rabbinic leadership and in the process lost the well-springs of its cultural and economic vitality. However, since the signs of decline had first appeared somewhat earlier it is more likely that the Sabbatian outburst hastened and exacerbated an already ongoing process.

Among the Ottoman Jews there was no intellectual revival comparable to those which renewed the cultural life of the Greeks and the Armenians. Neither in Hebrew nor in any of their vernaculars did they produce scholars or writers comparable to the Greek Koraes or the Armenian Mekhitar, either in quality or in influence. The nearest approach was of a Bosnian rabbi called Yehuda Alkalai (1798–1878) who from 1834 onward produced a series of books and pamphlets, proposing the establishment of Jewish colonies in Palestine as part of a program of Jewish self-redemption. This attempt to apply the lessons of Greek and Serb revival to Jewish life was entirely without impact among Ottoman Jews. It was not until much later that Alkalai acquired some retrospective historical importance as a precursor of Zionism.

In the nineteenth century the Jews, like the Christians and the Muslims, went through a phase of conflict—the struggle between reformers and conservatives. Among the Muslims, the Greeks, and the Armenians, the reformers won. Among the Jews, they lost. For this the Jews paid a price. Compared with their Christian neighbors they fell steadily behind.

The Jews had cast their lot, not surprisingly, with the reactionary forces among the Turks. The destruction in 1826 of the Janissary Corps, the old military order, with which the Jews had important links, was a heavy blow. The rise of Russia and the growth of Russian influence were also not very helpful to Jews in the Ottoman Empire. Later in the century there was a certain upswing in the entrepôt trade of Salonica with its ties to the West, but despite improved education, which was fostered most notably by the Alliance Israélite Universelle, the effort came too late (see Volume I, chapter 11 by Paul Dumont). They were caught in the circumstances which led to the end of the Ottoman Empire and the transformation of the entire region.

Language has barely been mentioned in this discussion of the major communities of the Ottoman Empire. In view of the role that language has played in determining national identity in the West, its relative lack of importance in the Ottoman context is significant. Greeks, Armenians, Jews, as well as Copts and non-Orthodox Christians in Arab lands each had a distinctive liturgical language. However, the language of ritual was not necessarily the language of the street or the home. While the hierarchy of the Greek Or-

thodox church was both ethnically and linguistically Greek, the parish clergy
and flock was a polyglot mass speaking almost as many languages as were
spoken in the empire itself. In the Balkans there were speakers of Slavic and,
in the case of Rumanian, a Romance language. To the south of Anatolia there
were Arabic-speakers. In Anatolia itself, according to observers during the
nineteenth century, the majority of the communicants of the church did not
know Greek at all, as their native language was Turkish or Armenian.[6] In
Anatolia the Greek Orthodox who were literate wrote in Greek script, but the
language many of them transcribed was Turkish or Armenian.

Early in the nineteenth century, under the influence of a Hellenizing trend
in the Greek community, an attempt was made to impose Greek upon the
many-tongued Orthodox flock. The words of the Hellenizing educator Daniel
of Moschopolis illustrate the sense of cultural superiority with which he
embarked upon this effort:

> Albanians, Wallachians, Bulgarians, speakers of other tongues, rejoice.
> And ready yourselves to become Greeks
> Abandoning your barbaric tongue, speech and customs.[7]

No other community was as linguistically diverse as the *Rum,* but members
of the Armenian churches, Gregorian, Catholic, and later Protestant, did not
necessarily speak Armenian. According to missionary reports, perhaps half
of the Armenian population of Anatolia spoke Turkish.

As the doctrines of nationalism spread among these communities, such
linguistic anomalies became a problem. Exacerbating the situation were the
cries for language reform which dominated the cultural life of Armenians and
Greeks during the nineteenth century. While the nationalist elites were judging the purity of the spoken dialect against a mythic classical model, the great
mass of the people they claimed as a nation continued speaking a different
language.

For the Jews and other Christians of the empire such linguistic anomalies
were less perplexing. Ottoman Jews spoke a variety of languages. In the
central lands Ladino dominated, but there were small pockets of Greek-
speakers in the Balkans. In the Kurdish areas of the empire there were communities of Jews who spoke Kurdish, others who spoke a dialect of ancient
Aramaic. Further to the south the Jews of Aleppo, Damascus, Baghdad,
Egypt, and Palestine for the most part spoke Arabic. Since nationalism barely
influenced these communities, linguistic diversity did not need to be explained away. For all, Hebrew remained the language of ritual and learning,
and, occasionally, literary expression; Hebrew script was commonly used by
Jews to write the languages they spoke.

In Ottoman Syria and Egypt, Christians spoke Arabic. Coptic and Syriac
were retained in liturgy alone. To a much greater degree than any other region
these lands were linguistically unified. The many centuries of Islamic rule had
brought about the triumph of Arabic over the preexisting languages.

Among these groups language was not imbued with that sacral character which makes of it the cultural determinant of nationhood. Whatever sacral quality there was to be ascribed to language was found in its script, not its sound. Thus the Greek Orthodox, the Jews, the Armenians, and many Syrian Christians wrote a large variety of different languages in their respective liturgical scripts. Spoken language was a means of communicating among peoples, not a means of distinguishing among them. In the nineteenth century language started to acquire the second role, but in the Ottoman Empire it never assumed the same importance it was to gain in Europe. Religion was more important than language in determining identity.

As we have seen, through the seventeenth, eighteenth, and nineteenth centuries the Ottoman empire faced an increasingly restive Christian population. In its external relations the empire confronted powers eager to exploit this restiveness. The disruptive notions of European thought, the Enlightenment, liberalism, and nationalism undermined the very different assumptions of Ottoman society. The powerful engines of Europe's capital and industry blasted the Ottoman economy. Each of these thrusts might have been resisted on its own; nothing could have withstood the combined thrusts. In the face of these challenges from within and without, the empire displayed a degree of patience, ingenuity, and flexibility which faltered in its twilight decades.

One of the earliest means by which Europe gained influence within the empire was through religious missions. A burst of such activity occurred early in the seventeenth century. For European Catholics and Protestants the Ottoman lands were something of a sideshow in the struggle for Reformation and Counter-Reformation. Constantinople, however, became one of the sites where the two sides fought over the neutral souls of Orthodoxy. Although the combatants at times had limited success in winning over a reigning patriarch to one doctrinal position or another, the Greek Orthodox did not join either side. Western Christendom had more success with Armenians and later with Christians in Syria and Egypt. The missionary effort created an intellectual beachhead in Ottoman territory. The schools and printing presses which the missionaries founded helped disseminate the ideas of the West.

Of all the challenges confronting the Ottomans, the most dangerous proved to be the notion of foreign protection. At its origin this protection was limited to Ottoman Christians and Jews, locally recruited for service to the foreigner as vice-consuls, interpreters, commercial agents, and more menial employees. The individual so employed was given a warrant, called *berat,* whose terms resembled diplomatic immunity, including in some instances exemption from Ottoman criminal jurisdiction, as well as reduced customs levies and other commercial privileges (see Volume I, chapter 13 by Charles Issawi).

From the point of view of Islamic law this warrant had the effect of removing its recipient from the status of a *dhimmi* to something approaching the status of a resident foreigner. *Dhimmi* status was subject only to the Holy Law of Islam and its governmental application, but resident foreigner status, as it evolved under Ottoman rule, was subject in addition to the terms of international agreements and understandings. Ultimately this status depended upon the balance of power between one state and another, and considerations of military security, diplomatic alliance, and economic advantage in practice determined its application.

As long as the Ottoman Empire was stronger than its rivals this elasticity did not pose a problem, but as the empire declined, some form of European protection became increasingly attractive. Christians and Jews with no claim whatsoever to a warrant of protection started obtaining them, and a brisk trade developed. Faced with such abuses the Ottoman government, which had previously allowed foreign diplomatic agencies to distribute them, now began to issue them directly to its subjects, non-Muslims and eventually even Muslim. The increased number of warrants diminished the competitive advantage afforded the holder and direct Ottoman sale removed the disruptive impact of distribution by foreign governments.

As the *berat* started to decline in importance, a new intrusion emerged. The Powers increasingly pressed claims to protection of entire communities. The Russians claimed the *Rum;* the French adopted the Catholics. Britain and Prussia competed for the protection of the small Protestant communities and occasionally extended it to the numerically more important Jews. Eventually the claims for protection led to the bestowal of citizenship on many Christians and some Jews (see Volume I, chapter 14 by A. Üner Turgay).

Early in the nineteenth century Russia added the Armenians to its list of protected communities. Fearing the growth of Russian influence, the Ottomans stopped the flow of offerings to Ejmiacin, the Armenian Catholicosate, which was in Russian hands. The chief dragoman of the Russian embassy suggested to a leading Ottoman official that they did not understand the significance of the Catholicosate; the more loyal a *millet* to its faith and church, the more loyal it would be to the state, and Armenian loyalty to the Ottoman state would thus be strengthened by their link with Ejmiacin. To which the Ottoman replied: "Yes, yes, now I understand the importance of the question. But it is up to you to set us a good example in this matter, which we would naturally follow." He went on to speak of the Muslim peoples in the Russian provinces of Kazan and Astrakhan whose religious life would benefit from a strengthening of their links with the Islamic caliphate, and the submission of their religious leaders to the jurisdiction of the chief Islamic jurisconsult in Istanbul. "When we see how this adds strength and cohesion to their religious affairs and thus increases their loyalty to the Russian state, we shall naturally take the necessary steps to strengthen the links of the Armenians with Ejmiacin."[8]

Now that Europeans proclaimed protection for entire communities, the Ottomans asserted the same claim for Muslim communities under Christian control. They developed the notion of political pan-Islam under the aegis of the Caliphate, an institution long defunct but now revived for this purpose. The Treaty of Küçük Kaynarca of 1774, skillfully misinterpreted by the Russians, provided the legal pretext for the tsarist right of intervention. The Caliphate was to provide a comparable pretext for Ottoman intervention on behalf of the Crimean Tatars whose political adhesion the sultan had been forced to renounce. It was a good stick with which to beat the Powers, for Russia in Central Asia, France in Algeria, and Britain in India all had substantial Muslim populations.

The threat, however, was not strong enough to stop European intervention, which now became more ingenious and more subtle. An effective method was the European sponsorship of internal reforms aimed at the equality of subjects of the empire. In order to forestall more drastic intervention the government issued a decree, the *Hatt-ı Hümayun* of 1856, as it became known in the West, which proclaimed the equality of all, Muslim and non-Muslim alike.

In the wake of this order, Cevdet Paşa, a high government official and acute observer of the Ottoman scene, noted the reactions of the Muslim and non-Muslim populations:

> In accordance with this ferman Muslim and non-Muslim subjects were to be made equal in all rights. This had a very adverse effect on the Muslims. Previously, one of the four points adopted as basis for peace agreements had been that certain privileges were accorded to Christians on condition that these did not infringe on the sovereign authority of the government. Now the question of (specific) privileges lost its significance; in the whole range of government, the non-Muslims were forthwith to be deemed the equals of the Muslims. Many Muslims began to grumble: "Today we have lost our sacred national rights, won by the blood of our fathers and forefathers. At a time when the Islamic *millet* was the ruling *millet,* it was deprived of this sacred right. This is a day of weeping and mourning for the people of Islam."
>
> As for the non-Muslims, this day, when they left the status of *raya* and gained equality with the ruling *millet,* was a day of rejoicing. But the patriarchs and other spiritual chiefs were displeased, because their appointments were incorporated in the ferman. Another point was that whereas in former times, in the Ottoman state, the communities were ranked, with the Muslims first, then the Greeks, then the Armenians, then the Jews, now all of them were put on the same level. Some Greeks objected to this, saying: "The government has put us together with the Jews. We were content with the supremacy of Islam."
>
> As a result of all this, just as the weather was overcast when the ferman was read in the audience chamber, so the faces of most of those present were grim. Only on the faces of a few of our Frenchified gentry dressed in the garb of Islam could expressions of joy be seen. Some notorious characters of this type were seen and heard to say: "If the non-Muslims are spread among the Muslims, neighborhoods will become mixed, the price of our properties will rise, and civilized amenities will expand." On this account they expressed satisfaction.[9]

Cevdet's skeptical view notwithstanding, a serious effort was made to implement reform (see Volume I, chapter 16 by Carter Findley). Advanced and official circles developed the notion of Ottomanism, the empire's attempt at creating patriotic loyalty to the sultan and the empire as a whole (see Volume I, chapter 18 by Enver Ziya Karal). Unfortunately, this secular and egalitarian (in religious, not social, terms) response to the centrifugal forces of religion and nation aroused little support. Working against it were the entrenched hierarchies of the religious communities, the eager spokesmen for the new national entities, and the defenders of Muslim privilege (on this last point see Volume II, chapter 4 by Moshe Maʿoz and chapter 5 by Samir Khalaf). Ottomanism had seemed a means of arousing the kind of patriotic loyalty which had earlier united diverse ethnic and cultural elements into France and Britain, but there was no comparable political tradition in the empire and in the nineteenth century the growing movements for unity were based on different assumptions and reflected different historical conditions. The kind of energies unleashed by the Risorgimento and the German Awakening were based on primordial instinct. These new notions of nationality once introduced into the empire would serve to disrupt rather than unify. In 1862 the then-Ottoman foreign minister, Ali Paşa, wrote a tragically prophetic note to his ambassador in Paris:

> Italy, which is inhabited only by a single race speaking the same language and professing the same religion, experiences so many difficulties in achieving its unification. . . . Judge what would happen in Turkey if free scope were given to all the different national aspirations which the revolutionaries and with them a certain government are trying to develop there. It would need a century and torrents of blood to establish a fairly stable state of affairs.[10]

Decades later, inspired by the unification of Italy and Germany, the Ottomans did try to arouse a movement based on what they considered to be comparable primordial instincts. They propagated the cause of pan-Islam, which heretofore had been largely used to score points in the chanceries of Europe; it was now transformed into a rallying cry carried to the entire world of Islam by the sultans' spokesmen. Unlikely a cause as it was, Ottomanism might have provided the basis for continued Ottoman unity, but pan-Islam only exacerbated tensions and divisions between Muslims and non-Muslims without achieving any political success.

As the cause of pan-Islam gained adherents and as the empire was increasingly threatened by its Christian adversaries, the situation of Ottoman Christians deteriorated. Problems arose not so much from grinding poverty and persecution as from the contradiction perceived between economic power and political powerlessness. In discussing the Greeks the English traveler Adolphus Slade made a series of observations which applied to other communities as well:

> The Turk committed an error, and generated the grievance, when he allowed the Greek the wealth and pursuits of a freeman, branding him at the same time as an inferior being. . . .
> In analysing the motive of this universal feeling amongst the *rayas* against the rule of the Ottoman, we find it to lie not in the direct oppression which affects a man's physical state, but in the broad sentiment which makes an insult be more resented than an injury—a taunt be more felt than a blow. . . . The Turkish clown

might insult the educated Greek; the Turkish urchin pelt the Greek priest; the Turkish "dancing girl" mock the Greek lady. The rarer the outrage, the more bitterly was it felt; even though never committed, the liability to it would be gall. At night, a surly pasha passing by, might order the lights in a Greek gentleman's house to be extinguished, and the music to cease; or the police might summon the master of the entertainment in the morning to answer for disturbing the peace of the neighbourhood with his frolics. These were the real stings of Turkish oppression, the true causes of Greek revolt, enhanced by intellect and education being on the side of the reviled; and the effect of white turbans and yellow slippers, noting the Turk, was as marked as that produced by the plumes and the red heels of the supercilious comparatively uneducated aristocracy of France.[11]

The picture Slade drew is a familiar one—the shabby aristocrat so convinced of his innate superiority that he remains oblivious to the fatal changes around him; the lower orders smarting from generations of abuse, about to seize control of the vast estate from its impoverished hereditary owner. For a long time the Ottomans ignored or pretended to ignore the insurgent social, economic, and ideological forces within their borders. Their historical instinct had been to view the major threat as military, coming from outside the empire. In accordance with the traditions of medieval Islam the *ahl al-dhimma* were dismissed as humble and lowly.

This image had begun to change just before Slade was writing. The shift of perception came at a cost which was ultimately paid by the Christians themselves. The posturings of humble subjects could be indulgently dismissed with imperial indifference—the proclamations of those claiming to be sovereign nations could be causes for war. During the eighteenth and nineteenth centuries the position of the Christians had been transformed in Muslim eyes. Initially they were *dhimmi*s, people protected by Islam, with their place and their obligations set by tradition. Were they to become too arrogant or too friendly with the enemy, they could be slapped down. But as the power of Europe increased, individual Christians and Jews moved into a status resembling that of resident aliens, their place, obligations, and privileges fixed not by tradition but by foreign powers. Eventually entire communities assumed a protected status. No longer the people protected by Islam, they became the peoples protected by Russia, France, and England. In terms of the Holy Law they were trying to leave the covenant of protection, *dhimma*, in order to become resident foreigners, that is, subjects of the *dar al-harb*, "the domain of war," rather than the *dar al-Islam*, "the domain of Islam." However, if they were subjects of "the domain of war," that is, the territory under non-Muslim control which the jurists regarded as appropriate for conquest, then they were no longer entitled to the protective status of even second-class citizenship. Reform and Ottomanism were the proposed remedy to this difficulty. But the effort failed. One could not be a citizen of a sovereign nation, the protégé of a foreign power, and the subject of a would-be egalitarian empire at one and the same time. Neither physics nor politics allows such things to occur, at least not for long.

There were further complications. In the nineteenth and twentieth centuries, the Muslim peasantry, weakened and impoverished by the heavy burdens of conscription and war, saw their Christian neighbors, exempt from these duties, grow in numbers and possessions. The same period witnessed the growth of a Muslim middle class whose economic aspirations brought it directly into conflict with Greeks, Armenians, and to a lesser degree Jews. There arose a vocal and articulate element eager to displace these minorities from their position of influence (see Volume I, chapter 19 by Feroz Ahmad and chapter 13 by Charles Issawi).

Pan-Islam had been the Ottoman response to the perception of ubiquitous pan-Christian threat: it represented the attempted transformation of a religio-political instinct into a politico-religious policy. Implicitly it raised the threat of holy war to gain its declared aim of Islamic unity under the leadership of the Ottoman sultan-caliph. In the event of such a war the position of the *dhimmi*s would be sensitive, but the position of those claiming protection from a warring nation would be grave indeed. This was the price that the Christians eventually paid for Ottoman recognition of their sovereign status. The Ottomans took a very long time to collect it. Even as late as the last decade of the nineteenth century, in the midst of the Greco-Turkish War, the authorities by and large left unmolested the Greek subjects of the empire who prayed for a Greek victory.

Muslim popular feeling toward non-Muslims became increasingly hostile. There were numerous riots and some massacres. The Young Turk Revolution of 1908, with its promised return to constitutionalism and Ottomanism, failed in its goals. The bitter hardship of the First World War and the events that followed sealed the fate of the Ottoman form of plural coexistence.

Notes

1. J. S. Furnivall, *Colonial Policy and Practice,* New York, 1956, pp. 304–305.

2. Jean-Jacques Rousseau, *The First and Second Discourses,* ed. Roger D. Masters, New York, 1964, p. 61 n and Johann Gottfried von Herder, *Reflections on the Philosophy of the History of Mankind,* ed. Frank E. Manuel, Chicago, 1968, p. 375.

3. Rudi Paret, "Sure 2,256: lā ikrāha fī d-dīni. Toleranz oder Resignation?" *Der Islam,* 45(1969), pp. 249–300.

4. Psalms, 79:13, 95:7, 100:3.

5.   Richard Clogg, ed. and tr., *The Movement for Greek Independence, 1770–1821*, London, 1976, p. 29.

6.   Roderic H. Davison, *Reform in the Ottoman Empire, 1856–1876*, Princeton, 1963, p. 62, n. 33.

7.   Clogg (cited n. 5), p. 91.

8.   Cevdet Paşa, *Tezakir,* ed. Cavid Baysun, Ankara, 1963, vol. 3, pp. 236–237.

9.   Ibid., vol. 1, pp. 67–68.

10.   Bernard Lewis, "Ali Pasha on Nationalism," *Middle Eastern Studies,* 10 (1977), p. 77.

11.   Adolphus Slade, *Turkey, Greece and Malta,* London, 1837, vol. 1, p. 216 and vol. 2, pp. 92–93.

I

THE ISLAMIC BACKGROUND

———————————— 1 ————————————

The Concept of *Dhimma* in Early Islam

C. E. BOSWORTH

I

The *millet* system, as it developed in the later centuries of classical Islam, owed its specifically Islamic legal bases to the very beginnings of Islam, to the events of Muhammad's Medinan years (622–632), when the Prophet and his followers had achieved majority power in one town at least of Arabia, and were therefore forced to consider the question of the Muslim community's relationship to minorities, in the case of Medina specifically, a Jewish minority.

However, systems for the regulation of minorities such as the Islamic *millet* system became were by no means alien to the older Near Eastern world, in which hardly any state or empire had ever achieved—or indeed sought—an ethnic or religious exclusiveness. Thus the two great empires of Muhammad's time, the Byzantine and the Sassanid ones, had to come to terms with the question of dissenting minorities. Where this dissent took the form of what seemed to be a schismatic and heretical deviation from the prevailing orthodoxy, or where some sort of challenge to the existing socio-religious order was involved, the claims to enforce uniformity of a powerful established church, under imperial patronage, in the case of Byzantium, or of a socially superior priestly caste, in the case of Zoroastrian Persia, could not be gainsaid. Hence Byzantium had to combat strenuously the Paulicians in eastern Anatolia and, later, the Bogomils in the Balkans, just as the Sassanid state and church successfully overcame the challenge in the eartly sixth century of Mazdakism and also managed to push Manichaeism out of the empire northwards and eastwards into Transoxania and Central Asia. But the existence of other great monotheistic faiths within the borders of the empires was— somewhat paradoxically in view of the external support which the devotees of such faiths could often call upon—felt as a lesser affront to the dominant religious susceptibilities than were the sectarian forms of that dominant faith. Something of respect for the founders of the other great faiths, for Moses and Christ as prophets and holy men, survived in Near Eastern minds, an attitude that was probably to influence Muhammad in his policy toward the *dhimmī*s. In the case of the Jews, there was an ethnic barrier which enabled the dominant castes to despise them for racial exclusiveness as well as for religious purblindness and to adopt something like an attitude of exasperated contempt, as if nothing better could be expected from such a people; and this in fact allowed the Jewish communities to survive. Moreover, the dissenting groups often fulfilled useful administrative, social or economic functions within the empires, thus permitting policies of discrimination against them but not policies of total extermination.

In the pre-Christian Roman Empire, Judaism had been a *religio licita,* but a hardening of attitudes took place after the conversion of Constantine. The Code of Theodosius II (438) restated a body of anti-Jewish legislation which had grown up in the previous decades. Thus chapters eight and nine of book XVI of the Code, *De Judaeis, Caelicolis et Samaritanis* and *Ne Christianum mancipium Judaeus habeat* forbade celebration of the feast of Purim, when it was believed that Jews burnt images of the cross, and Jews' holding Christian slaves (as the title of chapter nine implies), and also prohibited the construction of new synagogues and required the pulling down of old, structurally unsafe ones. The *Corpus iuris civilis* of Justinian I likewise subsumed a host of further discriminatory measures: *novella* 37 of 535 forbade the practice of Judaism altogether in the North African territories newly reconquered from the Vandals, and *novella* 146 of 553 actually interfered in Jewish doctrinal matters—something which was hardly ever to occur under Islam—by stipulating which *Targum* was to be used and forbidding use of the *Mishnah* for understanding the Torah. Already in 383 the council of Byzantine bishops had forbidden apostasy from Christianity, and Theodosius prescribed death for any Jews or Samaritans who persuaded Christians to abandon their faith.[1] Thus the general aim of Byzantine policy towards religious minorities, above all the Jews, was to keep them in a permanently inferior position; in several of the above measures, e.g., in regard to synagogue construction and proselytism, it foreshadowed later Islamic policy aimed at freezing the position of the *dhimmī* communities, presumably in the hope that over the course of time they would wither away naturally. The question of financial disabilities of the Jews in the Byzantine Empire is somewhat obscure, and specific documentation is lacking. Andreades thought it probable that the Jewish communities were liable to a special capitation tax.[2] In the pre-Christian period of the Roman Empire, the Jews had paid a fixed due to the imperial treasury, the *aurum coronarium* or *fiscus iudaicus,* and certain Arab geographical writers of the mid-ninth and early tenth centuries aver that the Byzantine state *(al-Rūm)* used to take one *dīnār per annum* from every Jew and Zoroastrian.[3]

In the Sassanid Empire, there were important Jewish communities in Mesopotamia and scattered across Persia proper as far as Khurasan and Soghdia. Since they were unsupported by any outside power, their presence posed no threat to the security of the state; hence they seem to have survived, as internally self-regulating communities, on their own enduring religious and intellectual resources. It was the Christians of the empire, much more numerous than the Jews (above all in Mesopotamia, but strongly represented in the towns of Persia, too) and at times looking outward to their coreligionists in countries like Byzantium and Armenia, who felt at times the persecuting hand of the Zoroastrian state church, though this seems most often to have fallen on the clergy rather than on the Christian laity. The church of the empire (after the schisms of the fifth century divided into Nestorian and Syrian Monophysite branches, with the former especially strong in the eastern parts) subsisted as a largely autonomous organization under its patriarchs or Catholicoi, as it was to do in Islam. But the church leaders do not seem to have had any fiscal responsibilities as under Islam, where the religious head, Patriarch or Exilarch, collected taxation from his community on behalf of the secular state; the mention that Shāpūr II (309–379) raised a double capitation tax from the Christians (i.e., double that normally levied on all his subjects, of whatever faith) and that he asked Simeon bar Sabbāᶜe to collect it, implies that this was not the norm. The building of new churches was prohibited as it was to be under Islam, but this regulation was often waived for diplomatic reasons; thus in the peace agreement between Justinian and Khusrau Anūshirvān (531–579) of 561, conversely, Zoroastrians in Byzantine territory were to be permitted to build fire temples). Juridically, the Christian communities were left to follow their own laws and customs, such as the Acts of the Synods of Ctesiphon of 410 and 420 for ecclesiastical matters and the Syro-Roman law code, the *Leges Constantini Theodosii Leonis,* for personal status, thus placing them on broadly the same footing as the Christian population within the Byzantine Empire. The question of apostasy from the dominant Zoroastrian faith is not entirely clear in the Zoroastrian legal literature. Certainly, high-born converts to Christianity, from the royal family, the nobility and the upper priesthood, courted death, which was often inflicted, as the Syriac Acts of the martyrs tells us, in a singularly barbarous fashion; and we hear of Christian martyrs as late as 615. Even so, such draconian punishment may not have been generally applied to those below the top social and religious ranks, since we know of several prominent ecclesiastics who were formerly Zoroastrians, such as Sābbā (d. 487), from a high Zoroastrian family, and the famous Nestorian Patriarch Mār Abhā (d. 552) was formerly a Zoroastrian official; and there are mentioned numerous Christians with Zoroastrian names, often containing theophoric elements, showing that they were not born Christians.[4] Persian imperial policy was more liberal than the later Islamic attitudes to conversion, since Al-Tabarī expressly records that Khusrau Parvīz (591–628) allowed conversions to Christianity from any faith except Zoroastrianism, whereas under Islam, conversions between the protected religions, e.g., of a Christian to Judaism and vice versa, were forbidden.[5]

In sum, the position of Christians and Jews in pre-Islamic Persia was precarious at certain times, such as those of warfare with Byzantium with respect to the Christians, but the Christians' numerousness, their high level of education and the ability of their faith to appeal even to the highest social classes of the Persians, all allowed them a generally not unfavorable position. Much in their social and legal status corresponds to the position of the Christian community under Islam (and one wonders whether the attitudes towards the *dhimmī*s elaborated later in Islam by such an Iraqi-centered *madhhab* as that of the *Hanafī* owed anything to the situation which the Arab conquerors found already prevailing in the early seventh century Persian Empire), but in certain respects it was superior. For one thing, the Persian emperors did not disdain to employ Christian soldiers in their army;[6] the Islamic *jizya* came to be regarded as in lieu of military service, but *dhimmī*s did not, after the first decades of Islam, have any option of either joining the Muslim forces and sharing in the privileges (primarily financial) of the Arab *muqātila* or of paying the *jizya*, till the *Tanzimat* period of the Ottoman Empire. Hence Sachau's conclusion was that "the struggle for existence by Christianity in Islam was much harder than in the time of the Zoroastrian Sassinid rule."[7]

II

The Quranic basis of the later doctrine of *dhimma* has as its background the numerous references to *jihād* against the unbelievers, arising out of Muhammad's gradual disillusionment with the Jews and Christians who failed, as he had originally hoped, to recognize the new faith of Islam as either the valid form of eternal revelation for the Arabs specifically, or as the latest, hence truest in its universal validity, form of God's message for all mankind. Also significant for the prehistory of the idea of *dhimma* is the document preserved in the *Sīra* of Ibn Isḥāq and known for convenience as the "Constitution of Medina." It has recently been recognized, e.g., by Watt and Serjeant, as in fact a highly composite document, parts of which antedate Badr (2/624) whilst others may postdate the massacre of the third great Jewish tribe of Quraiza (6/627). The main point for our present purpose is that it attempts to regulate *inter alia* the status of the Jews in Medina (though whether these Jews include the three major tribes or consist of smaller, splinter groups attached to the Arab tribes of the Ansār as confederates is unclear), either as a separate *umma* (if religion be the main test of an *umma*) or as part of the general *umma* of Yathrib-Medina (if territoriality be an important element in the definition of an *umma*); in any case, both the Muslims and the Jews are to retain their own *dīn* (here almost certainly meaning law as well as religion).[8]

It is here in the Constitution of Medina that we find the term *dhimma*, for section fifteen states that "the *dhimma* [here, it seems, "compact guaranteeing security"] of God is one," i.e., all within the *umma* are equally protected, and all are able to give protection to other members, so that complete solidarity, with everyone in the dual role of protector and protected, is assured for all.[9] The corollary would appear to be that no one outside the *umma* is to be protected, except under the temporary grants of *ḥilf* and *jiwār* which were traditional in ancient Arabian society. An increase in Muhammad's claims as religious leader and prophet is seen in his requirement of obedience "to God and His Messenger," paralleled by the fact that in his treaties with the out-lying tribes of Arabia who sent delegations to Medina we find mention both of "the *dhimma* of God" and "the *dhimma* of Muhammad," here clearly meaning "grant of protection." In some cases, there is mentioned the "*dhimma* of Muhammad" alone, possibly where tribes were still not yet Muslim in faith but nevertheless in political alliance with Muhammad, hence the Prophet's personal hesitancy about the propriety of extending God's *dhimma* to pagans. However, Muhammad seems later to have extended the *dhimma* of God to all tribes and individuals coming within his system of security and alliance; he never showed any compunction about employing non-Muslims in his fighting forces, as with the still pagan Quraish at Hunain, and the concept that only Muslims could share in the advantages of the Muslim *umma* develops only after the *Ridda* with the advent to power of the legalistic disciplinarian ᶜUmār b. al-Khaṭṭāb. The importance of the possibility of non-Muslim but political and military allies of the Prophet enjoying *dhimma* in these last years of Muhammad's life is that, in subsequent times, it was to be precisely the non-Muslim scriptuaries dwelling within Islamic society who were accorded this *dhimma* and became known as the *ahl al-dhimma* par excellence.

In the actual text of the Quran, we find the noun *dhimma* only twice, in *sūrat al-barā'a* (9:8, 10), coupled with a parallel word *ill* in the phrase "compact or agreement" (the lexicographers defining *ill* as "an agreement for mutual protection," "promise of protection," etc). But it is in this same *sūra,* so redolent of the atmosphere of *jihād,* that we find the Quranic crux for the subsequent legal basis of *dhimma* equals "protection of non-Muslims living with the *dār al-Islām*." In 9: 29, we have "Fight against those who disbelieve in God and the Last Day, who do not account forbidden what God and His Messenger have forbidden, and who do not follow the religion of truth, from amongst those who have been given the Book, until they pay the *jizya* in exchange for a benefaction granted to them, being in a humiliated position." The exact exegesis of the final phrases ᶜ*an yadin* and *wa-hum sāghirūna* has been much discussed,[10] but the general purport of the verse is clear: the People of the Book are exempted from the general sentence of being combatted till death, the inexorable fate of obdurate pagans, but the price of their preservation is to be reduction to a humiliating status in society as second-class citizens, liable to a poll tax—this last provision being presumably an echo of similar provisions which may have been imposed on minority faiths in the older Near Eastern empires (see above). What was thus envisaged in Islam was a sort of contract promising protection, *dhimma,* perpetually renewed with the Muslim state in return for acceptance of subordinate status and automatically revoked in the case of nonfulfillment by the *dhimmī*s (what happened when the Muslim authorities failed to implement the promised protection was left less clear).

Such a solution was based on sound pragmatic grounds. Even within the

Arabian peninsula, where the vestiges of ancient indigenous paganism soon crumbled and Islam became the majority faith, there were in the last years of Muhammad's life and during the caliphate of Abū Bakr, communities of Zoroastrians in Bahrain and Oman and of Christians in Najrān and other parts of southern Arabia who stood firm over their own faiths but were friendlily disposed toward the Prophet and his new creed, as is shown for example by the treaty which Muhammad made with the Christians of Najrān, by whose terms the people of that town were to aid the Prophet in time of war with weapons and beasts.[11] Outside the peninsula, some sort of *modus vivendi* with the vast populations soon to be subjugated by the generals of ᶜUmar and ᶜUthmān had to be hurriedly worked out. The Arab warriors were for long a dominant minority which had to concentrate itself in the *amsār* and in certain other urban centers; the broad consent, if only tacit, of the governed would have to be eventually secured. Moreover, one or two of the minorities formerly oppressed by the old regimes, like the Samaritans in central Palestine and perhaps some of the Jewish communities, had given positive assistance to the incoming Arabs. We do not have to picture the masses of Christian population across the Fertile Crescent as actually welcoming the conquerors—the age-old antipathy of sedentaries for Bedouins from the deep desert must have caused profound fear and disquiet at their approach—but the alienation of these Semitic populations, on social and religious grounds, from the Greek Melkite ecclesiastical hierarchy and the Byzantine Greek ruling elite of soldiers and officials was not conducive to wholehearted resistance against the invaders in most cases. Even where towns and regions did resist, and submitted eventually through force of arms rather than a peace treaty, mass enslavement or extermination (as had been possible in the limited confines of the Medinan oasis with the Banū Quraiẓa) was clearly not feasible.

Hence the *dhimma* system came into existence almost inevitably, but in a somewhat informal way; the elaboration of a tight legal system here was to be the work of later, systematizing jurists, above all in the Abbasid period. The first requirement was definition of the terms *ahl al-dhimma* and *ahl al-kitāb*. The Quran was somewhat vague. In three places (2:59/62; 5:70/69; 22:17) we have the Jews, Christians and Sābi'ūn linked together, but with the addition in the last verse, from *sūrat al-hajj*, of the Zoroastrians *(al-majūs)*, and traditional exegesis came to distinguish these from the polytheists *(alladhīn ashrakū* in this verse). The position of the Jews and Christians as scripturaries is clear enough. Whoever the original Sābi'ūn may have been—and they must have been some vestigial sectarian group on the fringes of Arabia—the designation later became an umbrella one under which various groups, like the so-called "Sabians" of Harrān, devotees of later classical paganism, were to claim *kitābī* status. The position of the Zoroastrians, somewhat uncertain because of their single mention only in the Quran, required very urgent clarification, for by 652 the last fugitive Sassanid emperor, Yazdagird III, was dead, and apart from remote regions like Dailam, the Caspian provinces and

Sīstān, all Persia lay under Muslim control. In any case, there had been Zoroastrian groups established in eastern and southern Arabia in pre-Islamic times, as we have noted above, conceivably including some native Arab converts. A *hadīth* attributed to the Prophet subsequently asserted that Muhammad expressly extended the terms of 9:29, to the Magians; some Persophile jurists were to maintain that the Zoroastrians had formerly been genuinely in possession of written scriptures, but these had been destroyed at a date before the advent of Islam.[12] In this fashion, a neat solution could be suggested for the difficulty that both the written Avestan originals of the Zoroastrian sacred texts and the Middle Persian translations, almost certainly made during the later Sassanid period (sixty century), seem to have been lost in the disruption of the Zoroastrian religious institution by the Arab invasions, and were only committed to writing again during the Zoroastrian literary renaissance of the ninth and early tenth centuries.[13]

When the Muslims first acquired a foothold in the Indian subcontinent through the conquest of Sind in the early eighth century, a situation arose similar to that of Persia; the teeming populations there could not be slaughtered *en bloc,* but how, in the absence of any Quranic *naṣṣ* (and the Majūs had at least been explicitly mentioned in the Holy Book in a context capable of bearing a favorable interpretation to the Zoroastrians), could the pagan Hindus be assimilated to *dhimmī* status? On the evidence of Balādhurī's account of the conquest of Sind, there were certainly massacres in the towns of Sind when the Arabs first arrived; but in some places, there was no resistance, especially, it seems, amongst the Buddhist minority, with their traditions of nonviolence (though it does not seem necessary to go as far as an Indian nationalist historian like R. C. Majumdar and claim that the Arab invasion was positively facilitated by the treachery of certain Buddhist priests and others who assisted the invaders, rather like the Samaritans are said to have done in Palestine). Peace treaties were made with the local communities according to Balādhurī again, on what had been standard conditions during the overrunning of the Fertile Crescent and Persia (see below), e.g., the requirement of giving hospitality to Muslims, and the commander Muhammad b. al-Qāsim al-Thaqafī is recorded as accepting the submission of the fortress and town of Rōr after several months' siege in return for tribute *(kharāj)* and as conceding that their idol temples should not be disturbed because, he proclaimed, "Idol temples are exactly like the churches and synagogues of the Christians and the fire temples of the Zoroastrians."[14]

Over the succeeding centuries, it became accordingly normal practice to concede to the Hindus and other non-Muslims the status of *ahl al-dhimma.* Here on the remote fringes of the Islamic world, it was obviously difficult to enforce the strict regulations of the *Sharīʿa* regarding *dhimmī*s. Territory not infrequently changed hands along the Hindu-Muslim frontier, and Muslims found themselves living under Hindu rulers (where in the case of the Rashṭrakūṭas of the Deccan, their Muslim subjects in the Bombay coastal region enjoyed much favor and religious and legal freedom[15]); and in this syncretistic environment, Islam came to adapt itself to the immemorial caste system of India, rather than attempt to change it. An interesting instance of what seems to be the adoption of an ancient Hindu discriminatory custom towards an inferior minority by the Muslim conquerors has been suggested by Y. Friedmann as the explanation of a puzzling passage in Balādhurī about the activities of an Abbasid governor in Sind during the caliphate of al-Muʻtasim (218–27/833–42). In this, the governor is dealing with the community of Jhats (Arabic, *Zuṭṭ*), considered an unclean group in the Hindu social system; he took the *jizya* from them, "sealed" their hands (i.e., the practice of giving a receipt for payment of poll tax in a particularly humiliating way, attested for Iraq and others of the central Islamic lands from the Umayyad period onwards), and ordered that every Jhat when he went out should be accompanied by a dog. The apparent explanation is that the dog is an unclean animal to both Hindus and Muslims, and the requirement that every member of the despised Jhat group should be distinguished by having him with a dog would thus be a peculiarly local form of *ghiyār*, distinguishing feature, analogous to the *zunnār* and the colored patches of the *dhimmī*s in the lands of the caliphate further west (see below).[16]

III

The treaties made by Muhammad and the commanders of the first Muslim armies as they overran the Arabian peninsula and then expanded over the whole Near East seem to have been *ad hoc* conventions, made by Muslim leaders on the spot with the chief or headman of the town or region in question. The historical sources providing details, such as Ibn ʻAbd al-Hakam for Egypt and Balādhurī for the conquered lands in general, date from up to two and a half centuries after the agreements were made, and as Fallal has remarked, the more detailed and circumstantial are the conditions of surrender, the more suspect are the documents.[17] The original agreements must in fact have been quite vague ones, often in the first place oral ones in an age when literacy, at least on the Arab side, was very rare, and when hardly any Coptic, Aramaic, or Persian native speakers could be expected to know Arabic anyway. It is certainly impossible to deduce a neat dichotomy, as later jurists were to do, between voluntary surrender according to a peace treaty (*ṣulḥan*) and conquest by force of arms (*ʻanwatan*). However, there are some broadly common features in these agreements. The subject peoples are above all required to pay the poll tax or *jizya* as the price of the *dhimma* extended to them. In addition, various services, express of *ṣughr* or humiliation, are demanded. They have to act as guides through unknown terrains for the Muslims, and give Muslim travellers shelter for between one and three nights and days: they have to keep up roads and bridges; they have to supply the Muslims with basic foodstuffs like corn, oil and honey and raw materials like pitch and timber for building purposes; and they must undertake not to provide aid or comfort for the Muslims' enemies. The *dhimma* received in exchange comprised freedom of person and freedom of legal status, i.e., continuance under personal law codes with access to personal courts; freedom to retain property (only houses abandoned by fugitive owners were to be taken over by the Muslims); and freedom of conscience and the exercise of monotheistic religion (only churches abandoned by their Christian congregations were to be turned into mosques). In the case of certain privileged groups who had rendered special services to the incomers (like the Samaritans who had acted as guides) or who lived in strategic areas on the borders of the Muslim empire and had to be specially conciliated (like the Mardaites or Jarājima of the Amanus region of northwestern Syria, bulwarks against a Byzantine revanche; the Arab tribes of Taghlib and Tanūkh in the upper Jazīra, adjoining the Byzantine frontier, who might have been tempted to go over to the Greeks; and the kingdom of Nubia, remote and protecting the Islamic province of Egypt from the unknown potential threats from inner Africa), exemptions from these general requirements were made often involving financial concessions or the privilege of fighting at the side of the Muslim warriors and thus sharing in the captured plunder.[18]

In all these agreements, the provisions are often summary in form and by no means rigorous. There is, for instance, no mention as yet of the *ghiyār* or *shiᶜār,* the requirement of distinctive dress for *dhimmi*s; the Muslim warriors, a small minority in the conquered lands in any case, were in these early years perfectly distinctive through their Bedouin dress and mounts and thus in no need further to distinguish themselves from what eventually became in most parts of the empire a non-Muslim minority only. The neat systematization of the social and legal rights and disabilities of the *dhimmī*s dates from a later time, as Islamic religion began to permeate for the first time the general fabric of Near Eastern society, whereas previously older attitudes of the Jāhiliyya had been still strongly held. Above all, this definition is a reflex of a general urge in all walks of life towards the erection of legal frameworks, in which each individual's rights and duties vis-à-vis the *sharīᶜa,* in the case of the Muslims, and vis-à-vis the Islamic state in the case of all peoples within the *dār al-islām,* Muslims and *kitābi*s alike.

The classic formulation of the general status of the *dhimmī*s was to be that of the so-called "Covenant of ᶜUmar." A forerunner of this is the document known as "the Prophet's edict to all the Christians" and then ". . . to all mankind," preserved by two oriental Christian sources, the anonymous Nestorian *Chronicle of Siᶜirt* and the Jacobite Barhebraeus's *Ecclesiastical Chronicle.* This edict is said to have been originally made by Muhammad with the Christians of Najrān. Various monasteries and other institutions of the Christian Orient later claimed to possess genuine copies of this document, confirmations of which were connected with various historical figures like the caliph Muᶜawiya and the Nestorian Catholicos Īshō'yahb II, and Fatal has noted that "une immense fortune était reservée à ce document"; "authentic" copies of it have continued to turn up till the present century, e.g., in 1909 at the Armenian Catholic Patriarchate in Istanbul. Nevertheless, it is a patent fabrication, probably the work of some Nestorian priest or monk.[19]

The "Covenant of ᶜUmar" itself exists *in extenso* only in authors of as late as the end of the eleventh century and the twelfth one, sc., in Abū Bakr al-Ṭurṭūshī's (d. 520/1126) *adab* work the *Sirāj al-mulūk* and in the *Ta'rīkh madīnat Dimashq* by Ibn 'Asākir (d. 571/1176), and then, with numerous variations, in subsequent authors, though certain of these authors do claim to be quoting much earlier authorities. It is true that the early Abbasid jurist Abū Yūsuf (d. 182/798) attributes in his *Kitāb al-kharāj* certain of the conditions of the "Covenant" as it was later constituted to 'Umar b. al-Khaṭṭāb's general Abū ᶜUbaida. Ṭurṭūshī's version claims to be an agreement made with the Christians of Syria at the time of their capitulation, without specifically mentioning any city like Damascus, Ḥims, Jerusalem, etc., although Ibn ᶜAsākir does state that the "Covenant" was in fact Abū ᶜUbaida's capitulation treaty with the people of Damascus and all Syria, elsewhere further citing Khālid b. al-Walīd's imposition of a capitulation treaty on the *dhimmi*s of Syria whose conditions resemble closely those of the "Covenant."

The essentials of the "Covenant," said to have been promulgated by ᶜUmar I in reply to a request for *amān* by the Christians of Syria and related on the authority of the Companion ᶜAbd al-Raḥmān b. Ghunm (d. 78/687), are as follows: the Christians undertake not to erect any new churches, monasteries or monks' hermitages, and not to repair those falling into ruin; to give hospitality to Muslim travellers for up to three days; not to shelter spies or harm the Muslims in any way; not to teach the Quran to their children; not to celebrate their religious services publicly; not to prevent any of their kinsfolk from freely embracing Islam; to show respect for the Muslims in various ways, such as rising in their presence; not to imitate the Muslims in matters of dress or hairstyle, to use their manner of language and their patronymics; not to use riding-beasts with saddles, or to bear any arms; not to have seals engraved in Arabic characters; not to sell alcoholic drinks; to shave the front of the hair and to wear the distinctive girdle or *zunnār;* not to parade the emblem of the cross publicly in Muslim quarters and markets, or to beat the *nāqūs* (wooden clappers used instead of bells to summon the faithful to worship) or to chant loudly; not to conduct public processions on Palm Sunday and at Easter; not to bury their dead in the same neighborhoods as Muslims are interred; not to keep slaves who have been the property of Muslims; and not to build houses which might overlook those of Muslims. The Christians agree to observe these conditions, in exchange for protection, and to regard contraventions as absolving the Muslim state from its obligation of *dhimma*.

Clearly, such provisions as the requirement of distinctive clothing, the prohibition of building houses overlooking the private quarters of Muslim houses and the forbidding of overt Christian ceremonial in public places where Muslims might be affronted, point to a society where Muslims and *dhimmi*s are inextricably mingled, and there is no indication of anything like the Jewish ghettos of mediaeval Europe or even of the specifically Jewish quarters of *mellāḥs* of later Islamic North Africa. The chronologically piecemeal character of the "Covenant" is apparent, and little of it seems to fit the conditions of the early conquest period in Syria; its attribution to the second caliph does however accord with the picture which grew up of ᶜUmar b. al-Khaṭṭāb as the great lawgiver and organizer of the military and administrative bases of the Islamic state. One may also suspect some confusion with the later Caliph ᶜUmar b. ᶜAbd al-ᶜAzīz (99–101/717–20), the "Hezekiah of the Umayyads" as Goldziher called him, who does seem to have endeavored to apply the letter of *sūra* 9:29, about humiliating the *dhimmīs*. The *Chronicle of Siᶜirt* states that ᶜUmar II was more hostile than previous rulers to the Christians, that he imposed hardships on them and on the celebration of their liturgy, and that he established the rule that the killing of a Christian by an Arab (i.e., a Muslim) did not necessitate the exaction of a life in retaliation but only a monetary payment. Michael the Syrian records similar policies, including a worsening of the financial means of support for Christian ecclesiastical institutions and increased incentives for Christians to become Muslims. It is indeed quite probable that ᶜUmar continued the policies of Arabization begun twenty years previously by his uncle ᶜAbd al-Malik, extending them from the administrative sphere to the personal religious one. The period of quiescence in Muslim-Christian relations during the decades immediately following the conquests was now coming to an end; to it there succeeded in the eighth century a sharpened consciousness of the intellectual and religious divisions of the three great monotheistic faiths and their communities, seen in the increasing appearance of Muslim-Christian polemical literature and the apologetic role of scholars like St. John of Damascus (d. 749?). The increasingly influential religious institution of *ᶜulamā'* and *fuqahā'* wished now to formalize what had earlier been a matter of varying local, somewhat informal, agreements, and inevitably, the dominating secular power worked in the direction of rigidity and of worsening the *dhimmīs*' legal status. Hence Tritton may well be right to some extent when he states that "it would seem that it (sc., the Covenant) was an exercise in the schools of law to draw up pattern treaties."[20]

IV

To recount the course of subsequent relations of the Muslims with the Jews and Christians would be a lengthy task, and is one which needs to be approached through monographs on specific communities at particular periods, as has in fact been done by Mann for the Jews in Fāṭimid Egypt, by Ashtor for the Jews in Mamlūk Egypt and in Muslim Spain, by Galante for the Jews of Istanbul, and by Simonet and de las Cagigas for the Mozarabs in Spain. Here, only a few of the general trends in these historical processes can be noted.

Further spasms of anti-*dhimmī* restrictions followed on ᶜUmar II's increasingly severe measures during the early Abbasid period, especially under

Hārūn al-Rashīd and under the strongly orthodox Sunnī and traditionalist al-Mutawakkil. Especially interesting is the requirement of distinctive dress, which Abū Yūsuf traces back to ᶜUmar II. The *zunnār* or girdle is always mentioned, but ᶜUmar II is said to have prohibited the *dhimmī*s from wearing the typically Muslim *qabā* or cloak, *ṭaylasān* or gown of the learned classes, and the *sirwāl* or trousers held round by bands of cloth. In the specially discriminatory senses of the two words, the *ghiyār* "mark of distinguishing" and *shiᶜar* "mark of recognition" make their appearance under the two Abbasid caliphs mentioned above. Al-Ṭabarī records under the year 191/807 that Hārūn al-Rashīd ordered one of his officials in Baghdad to see that the *dhimmī*s there were differentiated from the Muslims in matters of dress and mounts; this outburst of zeal was connected with an intensification of warfare with Byzantium, and the destruction of Christian churches along the frontier zone of the Taurus Mountains was also enjoined. Then in 239/853 al-Mutawakkil enjoined that the *dhimmī*s should wear two honey-colored (i.e., yellow) *durrāᶜas* and that they should ride only mules and donkeys, and not horses.[21] We now have the concept of a band or patch of a specific color being compulsorily placed over the shoulders of the *dhimmī*s garments. One Christian source says that al-Mutawakkil required the Christians to wear honey-colored *ṭaylasān*s together with the *zunnār,* and in subsequent times, patches of red and blue are also mentioned. The favored Muslim colors at this time were probably white (the official color of the Umayyads), black (that of the Abbasids) and green (that of the ᶜAlīds), but there does not really seem to have been any deep rationale behind these stipulations on color beyond that of pure differentiation. Only in Mamlūk times, when hostility towards the *dhimmī*s had intensified considerably, do we find for instance that according to Ibn Taghrībirdī, in 700/1301 the Jews in Egypt had to wear a yellow turban, Christians a blue one and Samaritans a red one, and in 755/1354 the requirement of similarly-colored garments was made (in the Fāṭimid period, however, the eccentric caliph al-Ḥākim had decreed black turbans for the *dhimmī*s, because black was the color of the detested Abbasids); another source states that the Jews and Christians of Egypt had to wear yellow leather boots with one red and one black garter. In Muslim Spain, where the numbers of the Mozarab Christians must have been not much less, and conceivably more, than those of the Muslims, regulations for the distinctive dress of Christians and Jews seem to have been imposed only with the advent of the Almoravids in the later eleventh century and then under the Almohads; the secretary of the Almoravides, Ibn ᶜAbdūn (d. 529/1134), demanded that such measures be imposed in Seville, but they do not appear actually to have been put into practice until Almohad times.[22]

The regulations concerning distinctive dress were only applied sporadically, as discussions in the Muslim sources of their frequent renewal show, and fell into desuetude toward modern times. Often it was on the fringes of the Islamic world, or in conservative and isolated regions of it, that discriminatory measures lasted longest. Thus until the establishment of the Protectorate in Morocco (1912), Jews there had to go on foot in their own quarters and had to take off their sandals or slippers when in the presence of Muslim dignitaries and when passing Muslim holy places.[23] Shiʿī areas of Islam were often more rigorous toward *dhimmī*s than the mainstream Sunnīs. Thus in the Zaydı highland zone of Yemen, the Jews' houses were limited in height and were further restricted in the use of external decoration. In the district of Yazd in central Persia, the Zoroastrian community, much oppressed within the Muslim environment, built low, fortress-like single-story houses, with covered-over courtyards for easier defense, until affairs began to improve for them in the later decades of the nineteenth century.[24]

Although protected by the contract of *dhimma,* the *dhimmī*s were never anything but second-class citizens in the Islamic social system, tolerated in large measure because they had special skills such as those of physicians, secretaries, financial experts, etc., or because they fulfilled functions which were necessary but obnoxious to Muslims, such as money-changing, tanning, wine-making, castrating slaves, etc. A Muslim might marry a *dhimmī* wife but not vice versa, for this would put a believing woman into the power of an unbeliever; for the same reason, a Muslim could own a *dhimmī* slave but not a *dhimmī* a Muslim one. The legal testimony of a *dhimmī* was not admissible in a judicial suit where a Muslim was one of the parties, because it was felt that infidelity, the obstinate failure to recognize the true light of Islam, was proof of defective morality and a consequent incapability of bearing legal witness. In the words of the Ḥanafī jurist Sarakhsī (d. 483/1090), "the word of a dishonest Muslim is more valuable than that of an honest *dhimmī.*" On the other hand, the deposition of a Muslim against a *dhimmī* was perfectly valid in law. It was further held by almost all schools of Islamic law (with the exception of the Ḥanafī one) that the *diya* or blood money payable on the killing of a *dhimmī* was only two-thirds or a half of that of a free Muslim.[25]

It is surprising that, in the face of legal and financial disabilities such as these outlined above, and of a relentless social and cultural Muslim pressure, if not of sustained persecution, that the *dhimmī* communities survived as well as they did in mediaeval Islam. Under the stigma of worldly subjugation to another faith, inevitably viewed by many as a manifestation of divine displeasure, and cut off from ready access to such centers of spiritual and cultural life as Rome and Constantinople, the standards of ecclesiastical discipline and clerical literacy amongst the Eastern Christian churches inexorably declined. Whenever a *dhimmī* was in difficulty under the laws of his own community, he could generally escape by a timely conversion to Islam, thereby putting himself outside the reach of his own legal system. In such a fashion, members of the highest clergy, such as bishops or Catholicoi of the Nestorian and Jacobite churches, not infrequently escaped the consequences of serious crimes like simony, unnatural vice and even murder.[26] Hence in several regions of the Islamic world, such as North Africa and Nubia in the west; Circassia, Daghistan and other parts of the northern Caucasus; and Persia and Central Asia in the east, Christianity disappeared completely by the fourteenth or fifteenth centuries. The mainly urban, though not exclusively urban, Jewish communities were more tenacious and Judaism survived even in a hostile environment like Yemen, where until the exodus of 1948 a high male literacy rate and a fervent attachment to the practices of rabbinical Judaism preserved the historic community there largely intact.[27]

Notes

1. *Encyclopaedia Judaica,* second edition, Jerusalem, 1972, s.v. "Byzantine Empire," vol. 4, cols. 1549–1555, and s.v. "Theodosius II," vol. 15, cols. 1101–1102.

2. A. Andreades, "Les Juifs et le fisc dans l'empire byzantine," *Mélanges Ch. Diehl,* Paris, 1930, vol. 1.

3. Ibn Khurradādhbih, *Al-Masālik wa-al-mamālik,* ed. M. J. de Goeje, Leiden, 1889, p. 111, repeated by Ibn al-Faqīh, *Mukhtasar kitāb al-buldān,* ed. de Geoje, Leiden, 1885, tr. H. Masse, *Abrégé du livre des pays,* Damascus, 1973, p. 176. Zoroastrians can only have been found in lands conquered by the Greeks from the Persians on the far eastern fringes of Asia Minor and in eastern Transcaucasia or Caucasian Albania.

4. For the general position of Christians in Sassanid Persia, see J. Labourt, *Le Christianisme dans l'empire perse sous la dynastie sassanide (224–632),* Paris, 1914; E. Sachau, "Von den rechtlichen Verhältnissen der Christen im Sassanidenreich," *Mitteilungen des Seminars für orientalische sprachen an der K. Friedrich-Wilhelms-Universität zu Berlin, Westasiatische Abteilung,* 10 (1907), pp. 69–95; and A. Christensen, *L'Iran sous les Sassanides,* second edition, Copenhagen, 1944, pp. 267–268, 298–299, and chapter 6, "Les Chrétiens de l'Iran," *passim.*

5. T. Nöldeke, *Geschichte der Perser und Araber zur Zeit der Sassaniden,* Leiden, 1879, pp. 287–288, cf. also pp. 74–76 n. and pp. 160–162 n.

6. Sachau (cited n. 4), pp. 79–80.

7. Ibid., p. 94.

8. Cf. W. M. Watt, *Muhammad at Medina,* Oxford, 1956, p. 221 ff.; R. B. Serjeant, "The 'Constitution of Medina'," *Islamic Quarterly,* 8 (1964), pp. 9–16 (who thinks that the Jews were to be a separate *umma* along with the Muslims); M. Rodinson, *Mohammed,* Harmondsworth, 1973, pp. 152–153 (who thinks that the Muslims and Jews were to form one *umma,* "the people of Medina as a whole, presenting a united front to the outside world"). Since this paper was written, the important article of R. B. Serjeant, "The *Sunnah Jāmi'ah,* Pacts with the Yathrib Jews, and the *Tahrīm* of Yathrib: Analysis and Translations of the Documents Comprised in the So-Called 'Constitution of Medina'," *BSOAS,* 41 (1978), pp. 1–42, has appeared. In it, Serjeant demonstrates clearly, by meticulous analysis of the Constitution into eight component documents, that his Document C affirms that each group of Jews in a *hilf*-relationship with one of the Arab tribes of Medina, was to form an *umma* with the Arab *mu'minūn; umma* he defines as a "(theocratic) confederation," and considers the document in question to have been composed early, perhaps only a few months after Muhammad's arrival at Medina.

9. The paragraph numbering here is that of Watt (cited n. 8), p. 222; the equivalent numbering by Serjeant, "Sunnah" (cited n. 8), p. 19 is sections 6–7 of his Document A.

10. The translation here follows essentially that of M. Bravmann in "A propos de Qur'an IX,

29," *Arabica,* 10 (1963), pp. 94–95: that the *jizya* is a benefaction granted in exchange for their lives (following Baidāwī on this verse), and that they have been left in a humiliating position because of their failure to fight till death in battle. This latter interpretation is assented to by C. Cahen, *ibid.,* p. 95, cf. also his earlier interpretation of the whole verse, "Quran IX, 29," *Arabica,* 9 (1962), pp. 76–79.

11. See Watt (cited n. 8), pp. 127–128.

12. A. J. Wensinck, *A Handbook of Early Muhammadan Tradition,* Leiden, 1927, p. 60, s.v. *djizya;* A. Fattal, *Le statut légal des non-musulmans en pays d'Islam,* Beirut, 1958, pp. 17–18.

13. See M. Boyce, "Middle Persian Literature," *Handbuch der Orientalistik, IV. Iranistik. 2. Literatur,* Part 1, Leiden-Cologne, 1968, p. 33 ff.

14. Al-Balādhurī, *Futūḥ al-buldān,* Cairo, 1959, pp. 425–427; Y. Friedman, "A Contribution to the Early History of Islam in India," *Studies in Memory of Gaston Wiet.* ed. M. Rosen-Ayalon, Jerusalem, 1977, pp. 325–329.

15. Cf. S. Maqbul Ahmad, s.v., "Balharā," *EI²*, vol. 1, p. 991 (an Arabized form of the title of the Rāshtrakūtas); amongst the Arabic sources stressing their benevolence towards the Muslims are al-Mas'udī *Murūj al-dhahab,* Paris ed., vol. 2, pp. 382–383, and the *Akhbār al-Sīn wa al-Hind,* ed. and tr. J. Sauvaget, Paris, 1948, p. 12, Section 25.

16. Al-Balādhurī (cited n. 14), p. 432; Friedmann (cited n. 14), pp. 331–332.

17. Fattal (cited n. 12), p. 58.

18. Ibid., pp. 58–60.

19. See for these two works, A. Baumstark, *Geschichte der syrischen Literatur,* Bonn, 1922, vol. 2, p. 312, and G. Graf, *Geschichte der christlichen arabischen Literatur,* Vatican City, 1944–1953, vol. 2, pp. 195–196, and for the "Edict" in general, Fattal (cited n. 12), pp. 27–33.

20. For detailed analyses of the "Covenant," see A. S. Tritton, *The Caliphs and Their Non-Muslim Subjects,* London, 1930, pp. 5–17, and Fattal (cited n. 12), pp. 60–69.

21. Al-Tabarī, *Ta'rīkh al-rusul wa-al-mulūk,* ed. de Goeje, Leiden, 1881, Series 3, vol. 2, pp. 712–713, 1419.

22. See on this question of distinctive clothing, Tritton (cited n. 20), pp. 115–126; I. Lichtenstadter, "The Distinctive Dress of Non-Muslims in Islamic Countries," *Historia Judaica,* 5 (1943), pp. 33–52; M. Perlmann, s.v. "Ghiyār," *EI²*, vol. 2, pp. 1075–1076.

23. E. Aubin, *La Maroc d'aujourd'hui,* Paris, 1904, p. 357; R. Le Tourneau, *Fès avant le Proctectorat, étude économique et social d'une ville de l'Occident musulman,* Casablanca, 1949, p. 185.

24. See M. Boyce, "The Zoroastrian Houses of Yazd," *Iran and Islam, In Memory of the Late Vladimir Minorsky,* ed. C. E. Bosworth, Edinburgh, 1974, pp. 125–147.

25. See Fattal (cited, n. 12), pp. 85 ff., and Cl. Cahen, s.v. "Dhimma," *EI²*, vol. 2, pp. 227–231.

26. See L. E. Browne, *The Eclipse of Christianity in Asia,* Cambridge, 1933, *passim.*

27. See S. D. Goitein, "The Jews of Yemen," in *Religion in the Middle East,* ed. Arthur J. Arberry, Cambridge, 1969, vol. 1, pp. 230–235.

II

THE EARLY HISTORY OF THE NON-MUSLIM COMMUNITIES UNDER OTTOMAN RULE

2

Transformation of *Zimmi* into *Askerî*

İ. METIN KUNT

I

My subject is the transformation of members of non-Muslim communities of the Ottoman realm into full-fledged members of the ruling group. The mechanisms of such transformation, principally the *devşirme* method of recruiting hand-picked non-Muslim youths to be trained as military administrative officers, have been fairly well-studied. Fresh evidence from archival sources, however, provides better understanding of how such mechanisms worked in reality. Documents have recently come to light suggesting an element of personal recommendation in *devşirme* recruitment and indicating the presence of non-Muslim subjects of the state in private households as slaves *(bende, gulâm)*. A review of these findings may culminate in a major change in our perception of the nature of the *devşirme* phenomenon.

*Zimmi*s also gained *askerî* status through a second channel, in this instance retaining their religious affiliation unlike *devşirme* recruits who converted to Islam. As Professor Inalcik has shown, the Ottomans directly incorporated into the ranks of their provincial cavalry (i.e., *timar*-holders) especially such members of the military groups or feudal forces as cooperated with them in the Balkan states they conquered.[1] Again new evidence, briefly noted earlier but now published in greater detail, shows that such direct entry by Christians into Ottoman provincial cavalry obtained also in Anatolia, and as late as the mid-sixteenth century.[2]

The two typically Ottoman socio-political mechanisms, allowing conquered military groups into their own *askerî* without first classifying them as *zimmi*, and levying *zimmi* youths through the *devşirme*, should be studied against the backdrop of Ottoman views of society as these views developed through the fourteenth and fifteenth centuries. Only against such a backdrop can these typical Ottoman mechanisms of inducting *zimmi*s into the military and administrative groups be properly appreciated. What seems anomalous in a traditional Islamic setting may be understandable and may even appear quite proper when viewed within the context of the specific conditions of the developing Ottoman state and society.

In Muslim states, so traditional wisdom goes, non-Muslims had a distinct and separate status. Individual non-Muslims could be important as influential citizens, typically as court physicians. At certain early points, when their talents and expertise were indispensible, some non-Muslims also occupied important positions in fairly large numbers in the bureaucracy and even in the army. But by Abbasid times a typically Islamic state and society had emerged. The *ulema* view of a universal Muslim society, *"dar al-Islam,"* wherein persons were defined according to religious beliefs and not by descent, became dominant. Also around the year 900 Abbasid caliphs ruled over a population in which the majority had by then been converted to Islam. *Dar al-Islam* was not only ruled by Muslims but came to be peopled by Muslims, too.[3] Non-Muslims, then, were by and large relegated to separate, secondary, and private roles, with few exceptional individuals remaining prominent in public affairs.

Ottoman society, however, at least to the end of the sixteenth century, differed from this early ideal of an Islamic state and society in two very important respects. First, the Ottoman state emerged out of a frontier group, the band of Osman. Even while in the course of the fourteenth century Ottoman *beys* were trying to develop a full-fledged state—complete with traditional state apparatus and educational institutions—frontier conditions, although ever further from the original nucleus both in time and space, nevertheless remained a significant strand in Ottoman consciousness. Secondly, by the fourteenth century, not solely in the frontier zones of the Muslim world but also in its heartlands, Abbasid Islamic ideals had become somewhat irrelevant, at least from the point of view of the state. The rise of Iranian dynasties, the establishment of the Seljuk Empire and other Turko-Iranian states, finally the conquest of major central Muslim areas by Mongols who were not even Muslims are the major steps in this development which culminated, by the mid-thirteenth century, in a different view of society. Irano-Islamic social and political philosophy, best exemplified by the *Ahlâk* of Nasīr al-Dīn Tūsī, philosopher, mathematician, and counsellor to the Mongols (d. 1274), and the Turco-Mongol idea of a military-based state organization became the two dominant features in the background of later political developments.[4]

II

Turning more closely to early Ottoman society it should be noted at the outset that the version of Islam practiced in the frontier zones of Anatolia around 1300 was one which freely allowed the retension of certain Turkish customs, some quite un-Islamic.[5] In addition, there are significant indications that religion was a secondary consideration if not a totally irrelevant one in the frontier zones of Anatolia around 1300. Included in Osman's band of frontiersmen, for example, were Byzantine renegades who kept their Christian beliefs, in some instances, to the end of their days. The most famous of such trusted and honored Christian associates of Osman was Köse Mihal, but there were other instances as well.[6] It appears their status as Christians was seen as their own affair; it certainly did not prevent them from being counted among the leaders of Osman's enterprise. These men were the more highly elevated forerunners of the Christian *timar*-holders that Inalcik has studied (see n. 1).

Even when religion was not viewed as a private affair, Muslims of the frontier society did not see much difference between the great monotheistic religions. "There will be a time when we shall all agree," said a Turk to Gregory Palamas, the archbishop of Salonica who was a captive of the Ottomans in 1355.[7] One may not agree with Arnakis's judgment that "the Ottoman court appears to have believed in the practicality of some kind of religious syncretism as a basis for the approach of the two peoples;"[8] the Turks clearly hoped the ultimate agreement would be within Islam. Still, they seem to have been fascinated with the proximity of Christianity and Islam and had difficulty in understanding why some Christians at least were so adamant in refusing to join Islam. During his few months in Ottoman lands, Palamas was engaged in at least three discussions on religious differences, the Turks trying to convince him that even if Christians did not convert they should at least honor Muhammad as a prophet of God as Muslims honored Jesus.

While these discussions seem on the whole to have been spontaneous, one was set up deliberately, in the presence of Orhan Bey and other Ottoman leaders. Orhan wanted Palamas to debate on religious matters, a particular group of people, called the *"chiones."* Arnakis believed the *chiones* were *ahi*s, members of artisans' brotherhoods with religious overtones, and insisted on his belief even after Wittek suggested *hoca*s, Muslim learned men, as a more probable reading for *chiones*.[9] Since then Meyendorff has convincingly shown that both Arnakis and Wittek were wrong; indeed that there was no need to presume *chiones* to be the corruption of any Turkish word.[10] It seems definite that *chiones* meant Christian apostates; the group Palamas encountered said specifically that they had "become Turk."[11] What better way to convince Palamas than to confront him with Christian apostates whom Orhan believed to be "wise and erudite men" as well.[12]

The attempt to minimize the differences and the hope that in the end all will come together, perhaps syncretic developments as well, may be seen in certain other features of early Ottoman society. Wittek, for example, has wondered, in the course of a discussion on religious toleration and ecumenical spirit, whether it was by chance that among the sons of Bayezid I, there were, besides Mehmed and Mustafa, a Süleyman (Solomon), Musa (Moses), and Isa (Jesus), or whether these names did not reflect a general current influential at the time. Wittek also saw in the Şeyh Bedreddin revolt of the fifteenth century "a kind if charitable communism, supported by a mystic love of God in which all differences of faith were overlooked."[13] And while Birge, in his study of the Bektaşi order, was hesitant to assert a dependent connection between the order and Christianity, nevertheless listed certain resemblances, "not with any claims as to origin, but only to show that in Bektashiism there was a system outwardly Moslem, but inwardly of so eclectic a nature as to make it possible for a primitive type of Christian in either Asia Minor or Albania to reconcile his old beliefs and priorities with an external situation where outward acceptance of Islam may have seemed necessary."[14] From the Ottoman *bey*'s court to folk beliefs and to a peasant uprising, one encounters symptoms of the same spirit of religious coming-together at the turn of the fifteenth century.

III

In the course of the fourteenth century, the Ottoman state had undergone a considerable evolution from the early days of Osman's band of frontiersmen. By the year 1400, the head of state was styled "sultan," no longer *"bey."* The change in the title reflected the elevation of the position from leader to ruler. Ottoman domains included a considerable portion of the Balkan peninsula as well as western and northern Anatolia. The frontier *bey*'s modest household grew to a palace organization, including bureaucrats and a central army, to rule over this state of considerable size. Although the invasion of Timur in 1402 was a major blow that scattered the Ottoman state into several pieces, the basic assumptions and institutions of the state which fully emerged around the middle of the fifteenth century were already to be noticed in the late fourteenth century; this fact indeed facilitated the recovery from invasion and defeat.[15]

In the emerging Ottoman state the position of the sultan was central. The institutions of the state, the bureaucracy and the standing army, were extensions of his household. He issued, in his name, laws based on local usage and general Ottoman practice for different regions of his realm, as well as regulations on state organization and procedure. Already in the fifteenth century Ottoman writers emphasized the sultan's position as the keystone in society who kept all other elements in their proper places and provided justice to all.[16] The laws of the sultan, *kanun,* made no reference to *şeriat* (Sharīᶜa); they were completely outside its sphere; in certain respects, as in parts of the criminal code, *kanun* unhesitatingly replaced specific *şer'i* injunctions.[17]

In this state the basic dividing line in society was that which separated the *askerî,* military, and other officials of the state, from the *raya* (or *reaya*), the subjects. This was a functional division between those who performed services for the state and therefore received remuneration as opposed to those who paid taxes; there was no reference to religion in this distinction. The *raya,* of course, included Muslim subjects as well as non-Muslim; all *raya* were liable to pay the same taxes, with the non-Muslims paying an additional *cizye.* Professor Inalcik has shown that among the *askerî* group, too, there were to be found non-Muslims (see n. 1). The Ottomans viewed the communities they conquered, like their own, to be composed of military men and subjects; the military of conquered societies could, if they were judged to be trustworthy, join the Ottoman *askerî* without converting to Islam. The simple and direct language of the fifteenth century chronicler Aşıkpaşazâde is quite expressive. When the town of Enez capitulated to Mehmed II's armies, he writes, the sultan "granted well-appointed 'fiefs' to its commander and military men."[18] Even in cases where a stronghold was captured by force, some, at least, of the Christian fighters wre allowed to join Ottoman forces. Upon the capture of Novobrdo, the Ottomans "placed Muslims in the fortress, and also those of the unbelievers whom they trusted, but those they did not trust they did not leave there."[19]

That there were non-Muslims in the armies of an outwardly Muslim state is not at all a paradox for, as Inalcik put it, the basic character of the Ottoman state was that of "a dynastic empire the only goal of which was to further its domination."[20] Christian *timar*-holders were subject to the same regulations as their Muslim counterparts, and there was no pressure or added incentive for them to convert to Islam.[21] Nor was this only a phenomenon of the Balkans in the fifteenth century, for we meet Christian *timar*-holders in eastern Anatolia and in Hungary in the mid-sixteenth century.[22]

Certain features of the incorporation of non-Muslim military men into the Ottoman *askerî* class may be further underlined here. To be sure, in time the Christian *timar*-holders tended to convert, although not particularly encouraged by the state to do so, as did the Byzantine collaborators in the early days of the Ottoman enterprise. The important consideration for our immediate purpose is not so much why but *how* such conversion happened. Clearly, conversion was a personal decision, not a group action, for we have examples of one of two brothers converting and the other remaining a Christian.[23] Even more important is the fact that, in some cases at least, conversion was achieved in two stages, first as becoming Turkish and only later as religious conversion. Inalcik has already drawn attention to a Christian *timar*-holder with a Turkish name, referred to in the register as "Kâfir Timurtaş" (Timurtaŝ the infidel).[24] That the term *"kâfir,"* "infidel," was not just a nickname which continued to be applied to Timurtaş even after he converted to Islam becomes obvious when he is referred to later in the entry as *"mezkûr kâfir,"* the aforementioned infidel.[25] It should be noted that the name this person took, Timurtaş, is a pre-Islamic Turkish name, underlining that he became Turkish and not Muslim. In another example we find that the brother of a Christian *timar*-holder bears the non-Islamic Turkish name Paşayiğit, although it is not specified that he still is a Christian.[26] It appears from such examples that when Christian *timar*-holders wished to become more like their Turkish counterparts, some of them perceived the primary characteristic of the conquering military as being Turkish and not necessarily as being Muslim. It was this primary characteristic that they adopted in their attempt to identify more closely with the Ottoman military class. They changed their names, taking care to choose Turkish names with non-Muslim connotations; they may also have become Turcophone. Turcification was a sufficient degree of conversion; they did not feel they also should become Muslims.

Another feature of the process of incorportion of conquered non-Muslim military men into the Ottoman military group is that such incorporation did not necessarily come about through state appointments. In a mid-fifteenth century register on Serbia, there were eight Christian *timar*-holders who were identified as *hizmetkâr,* servants, of the governor of the district.[27] It is significant that these men were not slaves *(gulâm)* but just "servants," i.e., members of the *bey*'s household as free men. Inalcik argues convincingly that they were military men who could not immediately be granted *timars*. They then placed themselves at the service of the governor, thereby gaining access to the *askerî* group as members of his household without lapsing into *raya* (subject) status. When they finally did achieve *timar* grants, this was not because of their preconquest status as military men but because they had been in service in a *bey*'s household—after all, slaves of *beys* too were awarded *timars*. In other words, their Ottomanization was complete when they started serving an Ottoman official and not necessarily directly the Ottoman state.

IV

Strictly speaking, the phenomenon under discussion to this point is not the transformation of *zimmi* into *askerî* for such men never experienced *zimmi* status. The Christian *timar*-holders should have become *zimmi* subjects in a more specifically Islamic state. In the Ottoman context they were directly incorporated into the military group. For those non-Muslims who were not military men and who were therefore recorded as *zimmi* subjects in cadastral registers after Ottoman conquest, the channel to Ottomanization was the *devşirme*. The practice of recruiting *zimmi* boys as the sultan's household slaves, an Ottoman innovation which served as an additional source of state slaves, has been well-studied.[28] My purpose here is not to describe the *devşirme* phenomenon but to draw attention to some of its lesser known features in the hope that such discussion will further our appreciation of the nature of the Ottoman state and its social mechanisms.

Before going on to discuss such specific features it might be underlined that it is difficult to find a *şer'i* basis for this phenomenon. Whatever dubious justification the Ottomans produced came around 1500, a century after the practice was initiated.[29] Recently the legality of the *devşirme* institution has received some further attention. Inalcik argues that the *devşirme* were not slaves and that, therefore, the institution was not against the *şeriat*.[30] He bases his argument on a passage, occurring in a fifteenth-century source recently translated into English, to the effect that while a *devşirme* "can leave his property to whomever he wants after his death," boys taken captive in enemy lands "after their deaths can leave nothing; rather, it goes to the emperor, except that if someone comports himself well and is so deserving that he be freed, he may leave it to whomever he wants."[31] According to the passage, obviously the *devşirme* were different than captives in terms of bequeathing property. But does this mean they were free, as Ménage asks, or could it also be taken to indicate that the *devşirme* were regularly manumitted?[32] In any case, the process of *devşirme,* gathering of boys, was an infringement of traditional rights accorded to *zimmi*s in Muslim societies. That this seems to have been irrelevant to the Ottomans, quite in keeping with the dynastic character of the state, is a further illustration that Islamic principles were secondary considerations in early Ottoman society.

Usually the *devşirme* is described as a state action, with officials of the *yeniçeri* corps conducting the periodic levy of children according to well-established rules and regulations. The admonitions contained in fermans authorizing each levy provide examples of the kinds of abuses commonly attempted and perpetuated. One irregularity, if not abuse, not cited in fermans and therefore not noted in modern scholarship, was that persons chosen for palace service tried to bring in, through the *devşirme,* their acquaintances. A late-sixteenth century critic of Ottoman society, the bureaucrat and historian Gelibolulu Âli, complains about persons brought into the palace because they are the "compatriot of this *vezir* and brother of that *ağa.*"[33]

A document which recently came to light in the Topkapi Palace Archives seems to furnish an example of how pages in the palace provided recommendations for friends and acquaintances back in their villages. The document (TPA, E. 9607) is undated and unsigned, nor is it addressed to any particular person; the catalogue assigns it to the sixteenth century. It is a list of twelve boys in certain villages of the districts *(kaza)* of Neretva and Sarayovası (in Bosnia). The Slavic place and personal names were obviously unfamiliar to the scribe and/or to the intended readers for the document is written in a very clear *nesih* script and all names are carefully vocalized. There is some annotation: "Raduya son of Narançik has three sons, the youngest is said to be a fine boy" *(Raduya veledi-i Narançik'in üç oğlu var imiş, amma kiçisi eyü oğlan imiş)*; and "Yorgo Licçuliyapik is said to have a capable boy" *(Yorgo Liçuliyapik'in bir yarar oğlu var imiş).* These expressions indicate that the writer of the list was reporting what he heard from others, but it is not clear whether the information was volunteered to him or whether the scribe systematically asked all the pages about boys they knew who should be chosen in the *devşirme.* In any case we have a direct link between the palace in Istanbul on the one hand and, on the other, *zimmi* boys in the villages of a faraway province of the empire.

Such intimate information on likely candidates for the *devşirme* is not the only personal element in the recruitment of *zimmi* youths into the Ottoman ruling group. There are indications that *zimmi* boys were taken not only into the sultan's household but were also present in lesser households as slaves. Examples are provided in sixteenth century lists, all in the Topkapi Palace Archives, of personal slaves belonging to certain *bâb üs-saâde ağas* (chief white eunuch of the imperial palace).[34] The terms used for slaves in such lists, sometimes interchangeably, are "kul," "gilmân," "bende," or simply "oğlan," but it seems by the mid-sixteenth century the distinction between "slave" and "servant" was obscure and perhaps totally irrelevant.

For our purposes these lists contain two points of direct relevance. A register (TPA, D. 10087) lists not only the names of 122 slaves but also how they came to be in the *ağa*'s household. Predictably, most were bought either at the slave market or from other Ottomans, some were presented to the *ağa* by palace or state officials. The curious thing is that several of the boys are stated to have become "slaves" of their own volition ("kendü iradesiyle bende olan")! Since it does not seem likely that they were non-Muslims from beyond the empire's boundaries come to volunteer their services, I propose that they must have been *zimmi* boys who were seeking employment in the household of an Ottoman official. This would be similar to Christian *hizmetkârs* (servants) attaching themselves to the household of a governor and eventually acquiring *timar* grants, a phenomenon we have noted above. However, in the case of the *zimmi* boys volunteering to become "slaves" they would not have to be from a military background. Perhaps some *zimmi* sought employment in Istanbul households because by the sixteenth century it had become increasingly difficult for *raya* volunteers, Muslim as well as non-Muslims, to receive *timar* grants in the provinces.

The second point provided by these lists with a bearing on our subject emerges when the ethnic-regional origins of such personal slaves are studied. Let us examine the provenance of the slaves Cafer Ağa left behind when he died in 1557.[35] There are 156 persons on the list; the ethnic origin of all but 13 is specified. Of the 143 persons whose ethnic origin is given, 31 were from the Caucasus (23 Circassians, 2 Georgians, 4 Abkhaz, 2 Mingrelians) and 112 from the northern and western reaches of the empire (52 Bosnians, 22 Hungarians, 16 Albanians, 7 Croatians, 7 *Frenk,* 3 Germans, 3 Greeks, 1 Wallachian, 1 Russian). These personal slaves presumably came from outside the empire, yet some of the "westerners" present a problem. Germans, Franks, and Russians were outside the realm; there were also Greeks (chiefly on Cyprus and Crete), some Hungarians, and some Croatians beyond Ottoman frontiers who could have been enslaved. However, it is difficult to explain the presence of Bosnians, Albanians, and Wallachians on the list, especially in such large numbers: the 52 Bosnians and the 16 Albanians constitute almost half of those persons whose provenance is noted. One possible explanation might be that such Bosnians, Albanians and Wallachians were captured in the event of uprisings in these areas against Ottoman rule. However, especially in the case of Bosnia, this explanation is not very likely. I would, therefore, suggest that there was a fairly regular and extensive system of *zimmi* boys joining private households, either by volunteering to become slaves, or through what might be termed "private *devşirme*" seems, at first sight, to be a contradiction in terms. I do not wish to convey the impression that Ottoman officials had their men roaming around the Balkan countryside to recruit boys against their or their families' will; any "private *devşirme*" must have been voluntary to a large extent. Was the master of this particular group, Cafer Ağa, a Bosnian himself who allowed into his household boys from his homeland as were recommended to him by relatives or friends still living there?

It is also relevant to our discussion what happened to these slaves Cafer Ağa left behind upon his death.[36] Fourteen of the *ağa*'s 156 slaves were already employed in the imperial palace while their master was still living. (We should note, by the way, that this fact indicates the palace was not homogeneously composed of the sultan's slaves but included the slaves of slaves as well.) Thirty-nine were young boys still involved in their studies *(okumakta idi)* who were ordered into the palace by the sultan immediately upon Cafer Ağa's death. Sixteen were outside Istanbul, presumably on various missions involving the *ağa*'s affairs in the provinces. The others, 101 persons (including the 14 already in the palace), petitioned the sultan to be allowed into the imperial household. They were then employed in various imperial corps (regiments of the household cavalry, the imperial workshops, etc.,) on the sultan's orders. Thus they truly became the sultan's slaves. Even if they had not been transferred into the imperial household they had attained *askerî* status as members of a private household, and, as such, were sometimes given state appointments outside the sultan's palace.

V

From the sixteenth to the seventeenth century Ottoman polity experienced a process of "Islamization" which, in the end, changed the main dividing line in society from that between *askerî* and *raya* to that between Muslim and non-Muslims precluding the possibility of non-Muslims among the *askerî*. The causes of this process are difficult to pinpoint. The empire may have become more actively *sunni* in outlook in a reaction to its confrontations on both its major frontiers. In the east, immediately after the establishment of the Safavi dynasty (1501), *Kizilbaş (ghulât)* religious views of the Türkmen tribes, the original supporters of Shah Ismail, and Twelver Shi'ism encompassing the sedentary population of Iran, were instituted in combination as state ideology. On the western frontier the main enemy the Ottomans faced from 1526 on, the Hapsburg Empire, was more powerful than earlier foes had been. The Hapsburg state, politically and militarily better organized and with a superior technology, succeeded in halting Ottoman advance into central Europe in the mid-sixteenth century. Thereafter the frontier became a rigid line, difficult to cross, on either side of which religious antagonism came to be felt more strongly.

At exactly the same time that the two main external foes of the empire were viewed as embodying rival religious ideologies, the Ottoman state gained control of the holiest cities of Islam. The Ottoman self-image became that of the leader and defender of Islam, not only against Christian Europe but also against the Safavi "heretics." By the seventeenth century the Ottoman sultan was styled *"Pâdişâh-i İslam"* and his armies *"asker-i Islam."* Perhaps the most significant feature of the "Islamization" of the state was the enhanced role of the *ulema* even as their own "bureaucratization" was completed with the development of the office of *şeyh ül-islam*.[37] Not only did the *ulema* come to play a significant role in state affairs, the relative importance of the two legal systems shifted away from *kanun* toward *şeriat*. While in the sixteenth century the *ulema* were busy demonstrating that Ottoman *kanun* did not contradict *şeriat* in the seventeenth century *şeriat* came to take precedence over *kanun*.[38]

Thus the fundamental orientation of the Ottoman state and the sources of its political ideas were quite different after 1600. Already in the sixteenth century, when the Muslim identity of the state became dominant, there were few Christian *askerî* left. Thereafter the remaining non-Muslim military were employed only in auxiliary services in the Balkans, typically charged with guarding specific passes, bridges, etc. Also around 1600 the other, and more significant, route for *zimmi*s to membership in the Ottoman military-administrative elite, the *devşirme* method of recruitment, was gradually abandoned. The *devşirme* recruitment was given up not because of the growing Islamic sensibility in society but because there were already too many candidates for offices by the second half of the sixteenth century; the one source of manpower which could be turned off most readily was the *devşirme*.[39] Although *devşirme* levies stopped because of institutional, not religious, reasons, the result was that the main avenue for *zimmi*s to Ottoman leadership was cut off, adding to the sense of alienation increasingly felt by Ottoman non-Muslims towards the state.

From then on until the nineteenth century very few *zimmi*s served the Ottoman government in any important office. These were the members of a handful of Istanbul Armenian *amira* families holding important financial positions, and Phanariot Greeks who monopolized the office of the dragoman and who, in the eighteenth century, supplied rulers for Wallachia and Moldavia. The following anecdote from the memoirs of Baron de Tott, a European observer of Ottoman society in the mid-eighteenth century, provides a sense of the pride such families had in their status:

> I have known an European very ill received by a considerable Grecian lady, whose husband had been hanged for some intrigue at Court, because he thought proper to lament her misfortune; and dwelt especially on the kind of death the deceased had suffered. "What kind of death would you wish him to have died?" cried she, in a rage. "Learn, Sir, that no person of my family ever died like a Baccal (grocer)."[40]

"To be punished for a crime against the state," Baron de Tott observes after telling this anecdote, "is to have been a person of importance in that State."

Such aristocratic *zimmi* families, however, were distinguished mainly in their own communities; they were not full-fledged members of the Muslim Ottoman established. In contrast to the extensive power they had in

Armenian and Greek communities, their political power in the general Ottoman system was very limited.[41] By the 1800s, ambitious non-Muslims were already seeking distinction in society as leaders of national movements.

Notes

1. Halil İnalcik, *Fatih Devri Üzerinde Tetkikler ve Vesīkalar*, Ankara, 1954, Chap. 4, "Stefan Duşan'dan Osmanlı İmperatorluğuna," pp. 137–184.

2. Ibid., p. 184, no. 190. For more recent publications see n. 22, below. Joseph Hacker has brought to my attention a Jewish *timar*-holder in the 1430s, *Suret-i Defter-i Sancak-ı Arvanid*, Halil İnalcik, ed. Ankara, 1954, p. 43, no. 98: *Timar-ı Hayo yahudi*.

3. On estimates of conversions to Islam, see the works of Richard W. Bulliet, "Conversion to Islam and the Emergence of Muslim Society in Iran," in *Conversion to Islam*, Nehemia Levzion, ed. New York, 1978, and *Conversion to Islam in the Middle Ages: An Essay in Quantitative History*, Cambridge, Ma., 1979.

4. Nasīr al-Din Tūsī, *The Nasirean Ethics*, G. M. Wickens, trans. London, 1964. For the type of state from the thirteenth century see Marshall G. S. Hodgson, *The Venture of Islam*, vol. 2: *The Expansion of Islam in the Middle Periods*, book 4, chapter 1: "After the Mongol Irruption: Politics and Society, 1259–1405," Chicago, 1974, pp. 386–436.

5. See the most recent studies of Speros Vryonis, Jr., "Nomadization and Islamization in Asia Minor," *Dumbarton Oaks Papers* 29 (1975), pp. 41–71, and especially his provocative article "Evidence on Human Sacrifice Among the Early Ottoman Turks," *Journal of Asian History*, 5 (1971), pp. 140–146.

6. G. Georgiades Arnakis, "Gregory Palamas Among the Turks and Documents of His Captivity as Historical Sources," *Speculum*, 26 (1951), pp. 104–118, especially pp. 115–16. In his comments on the original version of the present study, Andreas Tietze, too, emphasized the importance of the central Asian heritage in early Ottoman society, especially in terms of the flexibility to absorb outsiders and to give them positions of responsibility commensurate with their abilities. A new analysis of early Ottoman society as a "tribe" is in Rudi Paul Lindner, "Ottoman Government and Nomad Society," unpublished Ph.D. dissertation, University of California, Berkeley, 1976, especially Chap. 2, "Ottoman Success and Ottoman Settlements," pp. 15–61.

7. Arnakis, (cited n. 6), p. 110.

8. Ibid., p. 108.

9. Ibid., pp. 113–114; G. G. Arnakis, "Gregory Palamas, the *Xiones*, and the Fall of Gallipoli," *Byzantion*, 22 (1952), pp. 305–312; Paul Wittek, *"Xiones,"* *Byzantion*, 21 (1951), pp. 421–423.

10. J. Meyendorff, "Grecs, Turcs et Juifs en Asie Mineure au XIVe Siècle," *Byzantinische Forschungen*, 1 (1966), pp. 211–217.

11. Ibid., p. 213. In view of the usages Meyendorff notes to mean "converts to Judaism" (p. 215) and the fact that the specific *chiones* Palamas debated said that they became Turks when they realized the Turks respected the ten commendments of Moses; and because Palamas says that these people were obviously Jews and not Turks (pp. 212–213), Meyendorff and Lindner (cited n. 6), pp. 60–61, n. 132, believe them to have been Christian converts to Judaism in an effort to approach Turks. But the *chiones* say they have become Turks! Were they recent Turcophones but

Jewish, or converts to Islam for whom conversion was easier because the Turks respected the Old Testament?

12. Arnakis, (cited n. 6), p. 107.

13. Paul Wittek, "De le défaite d'Ankara a la prise de Constantinople," *Revue des Études islamiques,* 12 (1938), pp. 1–34, especially pp. 31–32.

14. John Kingsley Birge, *The Bektashi Order of Dervishes,* London, 1937 (reprint. 1965), pp. 215–218.

15. For the early development of the Ottoman state see Halil Inalcik, "Ottoman Methods of Conquest," *Studia Islamica,* 2 (1954), pp. 103–129, as well as Wittek (cited n. 13).

16. For Ottoman political views see H. Inalcik, "Süleyman the Lawgiver and Ottoman Law," *Archivum Ottomanicum,* 1 (1969), 105–138; H. Inalcik, *The Ottoman Empire: The Classical Age, 1300–1600,* London, 1973, 65–70; Bernard Lewis, *Istanbul and the Civilization of the Ottoman Empire,* Norman, Oklahoma, 1963, pp. 36–64. The fifteenth century historian Tursun Beg's *Tarih-i Ebu'l-feth* is now available in English, H. Inalcik and R. Murphey, trans. and eds., *History of the Conqueror,* Chicago, 1978.

17. On Ottoman *kanun* see, in addition to works cited in n. 16, Uriel Heyd (V. L. Ménage, ed.), *Studies in Old Ottoman Criminal Law,* Oxford, 1973, and Ömer Lütfi Barkan, "Türkiye'de Din ve Devlet İlişkilerinin Tarihsel Gelişimi," *Cumhuriyetin 50. Yılı Semineri,* Ankara, 1975, pp. 49–97.

18. *Aşıkpasazâde Tarihi,* Ali Bey, ed., İstanbul, 1332/1914, p. 145: "Pâdişâh dahi tekfurına ve sipahilerine eyü dirlikler itdi."

19. Ibid., p. 146: "Hisara müslümanlar koydılar; ve bu kafirlerden itimad itdiklerin kodılar, itimad itmediklerin komadılar."

20. İnalcik, (cited n. 1), p. 184.

21. Ibid., 166–167.

22. İsmet Miroğlu, *Bayburt Sancağı,* İstanbul, 1975, pp. 142–143; Table 18, p. 150, and *Kanunî Devri Budin Tahrir Defteri (1546–1562),* Gyula Kaldy-Nagy, ed. Ankara, 1971, pp. 7, 23, 30, 63–64, 66, 68, 86, 244, 253, 313, 337, 359, 361–364. (Some references are to scattered portions of the same person's *timar,* sometimes at different periods).

23. İnalcik, (cited n. 1), p. 145: "Timar-ı Mustafa ve Petros birader-i o . . ."

24. Ibid., p. 146, n. 46.

25. Ibid., p. 169, n. 124.

26. Ibid., p. 145: "Tîmar-ı Pavlo, Mikira'nīn oğluymuş, kardaşı Paşayiğit gözün, çıkarmiş, gözsüzdür, yılda bir eşkinci verirmiş."

27. Ibid., pp. 149–150, examples in n. 61.

28. For the *devşirme* phenomenon see Basilike Papoulia, *Ursprung und Wesen der Knaben-lese' im Osmanischen Reich,* Munich, 1963, and two extended reviews of this work by Speros Vryonis in *Balkan Studies,* 5 (1964), pp. 145–153 and by V. L. Ménage in *BSOAS,* 29 (1966), 64–78. Also see V. L. Ménage, "Dewshirme," *EI²,* vol. 2, pp. 210–213.

29. On the question of the legality of *devşirme* see, in addition to works cited in n. 27, P. Wittek, *"Devşirme and Shari'a", BSOAS,* 17 (1955), pp. 271–278 and V. L. Ménage, "Sidelights on the *Devşirme", BSOAS,* 18 (1956), pp. 181–183.

30. In comments at the panel on Islamic Military Institutions, Twelfth Annual Meeting of the Middle East Studies Association, 8–11 November 1978, Ann Arbor, Michigan.

31. Konstantin Mihailović, *Memoirs of a Janissary,* Benjamin Stolz, trans., historical commentary and notes by Svat Soucek, Ann Arbor 1975, p. 159.

32. V. L. Ménage, review of Mihailović's *Memoirs* in *BSOAS,* 40 (1977), pp. 155–160.

33. Gelibolulu Âli., *Mevâid ün-Nefâis fi Kavâid ül-Mecâlis,* İstanbul, 1956, pp. 20–21: "filân vezirin yurtdaşı imiş ve filân ağanın kardaşı imiş deyu . . ."

34.   One such list was published by Lajos Fekete, *Die Siyaqat-schrift in der Turkischen Finanz-verwaltung,* Budapest, 1955, document no. 7, vol. 1, pp. 170–175 and vol. 2, plate 9. I have studied two versions of another list and have published them, giving further references to similar lists, "Kullarīn Kullarī," *Boğaziçi University Journal-Humanities,* 3 (1975), pp. 27–42.

35.   Kunt (cited n. 34).

36.   Ibid., pp. 28–30.

37.   H. Inalcik, "The Nature of Traditional Society: Turkey," *Political Modernization in Japan and Turkey,* R. E. Ward and D. A. Rustow, eds., Princeton, 1964; R. W. Bulliet, "The Shaikh al-Islam and the Evolution of Islamic Society," *Studia Islamica,* 35 (1972), pp. 53–67; Marshall G. S. Hodgson, vol. 3 (cited n. 4), pp. 99–133, esp. pp. 107–111.

38.   See works cited in n. 17, above. Ottoman conservatism from about 1600 is also noted in the contributions of Epstein and Mantran to the present volume.

39.   İ. Metin Kunt, *Sancaktan Eyalete, Doçent* thesis, Istanbul 1978, pp. 110–124.

40.   Baron de Tott, *Memoirs,* London 1785, vol. 1, pp. 218–219.

41.   See the contribution by Barsoumian in this volume.

———————————— 3 ————————————

Foundation Myths of the *Millet* System

BENJAMIN BRAUDE

It is commonly supposed that the *millet* system was the framework within which the Ottoman state ruled its non-Muslim subjects. Basic to this view is the assumption that the Ottoman government usually dealt with *dhimmī*s of all denominations as members of a community, not as individuals. The *millet-başı,* be he patriarch or rabbi, was the administrative officer responsible to the state for his community, and to his community for the state. Through this office the fiscal and juridical autonomy of each recognized community, Greek, Armenian, or Jewish, was maintained.

Although this description is commonly accepted in the literature on the Ottoman Empire, it is unsatisfactory. The first to admit dissatisfaction were the authors of the most widely used account, Gibb and Bowen. They remarked that the primary sources for their book furnish little evidence on non-Muslims.[1] Indeed their authorities, mostly nineteenth century, are either outdated or the work of lawyers, not historians. These works by legal counselors or students of international diplomacy suffer from a tendency to telescope time present into time past. The result is that Gibb and Bowen's chapter on the *dhimmī*s projects back into the fifteenth and sixteenth centuries, forms and practices which arise only later.

Despite these evident weaknesses, few attempts have been made to reexamine Gibb and Bowen's description of the origins of the *millet* system in the light of subsequently available sources. This essay is the beginning of such an attempt. From this reexamination it emerges that the concept of the *millet* system originated through a combination of myths—myth in the sense of "fiction" or "illusion," and myth in the sense of "sacred tradition," "primordial revelation," or "exemplary model."

The Meaning of *Millet*

One source of illusion is the term itself. Broadly speaking, *millet* means a religiously-defined people. Although in the Quran (9:16) it refers to a pre-

Islamic community, *millat Ibrahim,* "the people of Abraham," and although in medieval usage it may mean Jews, Christians, or Muslims, its most common Ottoman Turkish usage, before the period of reform, denotes the community of Muslims in contradistinction to *dhimmī*s. It was in that sense that it appears in a legal opinion ascribed to the *Şeyhülislam,* Ebu Suud Efendi (1490–1574), the highest religious authority under Suleyman the Magnificent[2] and in the common phrase for the Ottoman Islamic community, *din ve devlet, mülk ve millet,* "religion and state, realm and people."

Accordingly *millet* does not commonly refer to non-Muslims. For instance, Pakalin does not so define it.[3] Nor is the term used with reference to *dhimmī*s in any of the following types of pre-Tanzimat sources which I have examined: capitation tax records,[4] cadastral records,[5] legal opinions on the standing of non-Muslims,[6] court records,[7] chancery decrees,[8] inquisitions postmortem,[9] and a variety of other materials.[10] From these it seems clear that *millet* in the empire's heyday did not denote an autonomous protected community of non-Muslim Ottoman subjects.

However the term does occasionally refer to Christians and Jews and it is worth examining these exceptional usages. It occurs in the well known *hadith,* quoted in Ottoman documents, that all Christians or all non-Muslims or all unbelievers constitute one *millet,* but as a tradition ascribed to the Prophet Muhammad, it can hardly be considered an example of Ottoman Turkish usage or administrative practice.[11] It also occurs in the work of the eighteenth-century historian, Raşid, where it signifies foreign Christian peoples *(milal)* in contradistinction to Ottoman Jews.[12] Raşid's usage suggests the one case in which the term had consistently been applied to non-Muslims, in sultanic letters to Christian heads-of-state, for this usage constituted a token of recognition extended to illustrious foreign Christians. Thus in correspondence with the doge of Venice, the king of France, and the queen of England, sultans Suleyman and Murat III, for example, would address them respectively as "the illustrious among the Christian *millet,*" "the pride of the Christian *millet,*" "exemplar of the women of the Christian *millet,*" and "the elect of the honored among the Christian *millet*".[13] The foregoing suggests that when *millet* does occasionally refer to non-Muslims in Ottoman usage it means foreign Christians as opposed to non-Muslim subjects.

Nonetheless there is a context in which the expression seems to refer to the Christians and Jews of the empire: in exceptional royal letters for highly influential Christians or Jews whose favor the Ottomans wish to gain or maintain. The earliest I have seen dates from 1412, a letter of Orhan son of Prince Suleyman to the Monastery of Saint Paul on Mount Athos in which he discusses a *timar* granted them by his father and in which he addresses "the pride of the Christian *millet.*"[14] Although the document discusses an internal administrative matter, the Christians to whom it was sent were not in any normal sense subjects of a Muslim Empire. Indeed there hardly was an empire after the fall of Bayezid. The subsequent interregnum of 1402 to 1413 created complicated political alliances between competing Ottoman factions and the Byzantines. Both Orhan and his father were so closely tied to Manuel II Palaeologus that at times they were more subjects than masters.[15] Thus the circumstance of this usage is closer to that of the correspondence with illustrious foreign Christians than to the internal administration of Christian affairs.

Later sources do use *millet,* but here again the examples are rare and arise in unusual circumstances. Two highly influential and wealthy Jews were described as leaders of respectively the Jewish or Mosaic *millet.* The term appears in an undated manuscript fragment which has been identified by Haim Gerber as a *mühimme defteri* of the period 1520–1530 (c.) concerning Abraham Castro, the head of the Mint in Ottoman Egypt. So great was his reputation that a later Hebrew source claimed he helped suppress a revolt against Ottoman rule in his province and helped rebuild the walls of Jerusalem. Whatever the truth Castro was important enough to merit an exceptional Ottoman title.[16] Another leading Jewish figure who gained even greater recognition was Joseph Nasi. As a confidante of Selim II and financier for the empire, Nasi rose to a position of greater influence than any other Jew and perhaps Christian in the history of the empire. Unique titles and honors (Duke of Naxos) were extended him. As another example the words *Musevi milletinin* ("of the Mosaic *millet*") were used in a sultanic letter of introduction to the king of Poland on behalf of Nasi's commercial agents.[17] The phrase is of two-fold significance, for its use of the term *millet* and for *Musevi* which is a more refined and polite term than the common *Yahudi* that appears elsewhere in the document to describe the agents themselves. The phrase then is clearly another instance of exceptional Ottoman usage in unusual circumstances: a sultanic letter to a Christian king on behalf of a Jewish favorite.

Why did Ottoman officials use *millet* for themselves, for Christian sovereigns, for rare Jewish favorites, but not for the mass of their non-Muslim subjects? The rarity of the usage may lie in the fact that the term was part of the formulaic vocabulary of the Ottoman foreign correspondence clerks but not of other government offices. That however begs the question, for why was the usage current in one department and not another? Perhaps the answer lies in the sense of sovereignty which the term seems to have connoted.[18] Sovereignty was possessed by Islamic Ottoman sultans and by powerful Christian rulers. It could be granted, albeit rarely, as part of an honorary title to individual Ottoman subjects, usually Jews, but it would not be extended to Ottoman Christians and Jews as a group. In addition, to extend the same term to both Christians outside the empire and those within might have suggested Ottoman recognition and acceptance of a unity between the two, a dangerous notion. Since the Jews did not constitute a sovereign group anywhere, the rare use of the term for individuals such as Castro and Nasi was merely honorific, entailing no political risk. This use of a different vocabulary for those within and those outside the empire extends to the terms for Christians themselves: *İseviye, Nasraniye,* and *Mesihiye,* literally, "Jesusist," "Nazarene," and "Messianist." These are consistently seen in correspondence abroad but somewhat less frequently in internal documents. Instead within the empire, Christian subjects would be called by less exalted, less religiously significant, and more restrictedly ethnic terms, *Rumi* (Greek), *Ermeni* (Armenian), and *Latin* (Roman Catholic). Of the three "external" terms, *Nasraniye* or *Nasara,* appear in internal documents, particularly in the Arabic-speaking lands. Jews, as indicated above, were *Yahudi* and rarely *Musevi.* More inclusive terms were *gebran* (Christian infidel), and *zimmi* (Turkish pronounciation of the Arabic *dhimmī*). The commonest term for a group of *dhimmī*s was *taife* (group, people, class, body of men, tribe) and less commonly *cemaat* (congregation, religious community).

A question remains—if the term *millet* was not typically used for the *ahl al-dhimma* prior to the nineteenth century, why is it today so used for all periods? One cause is the anachronizing influence of nineteenth-century practice on subsequent scholarship, an influence apparent in the misunderstanding of not only the term, but also the entire "system." Another cause for misuse today lies in the bivalence of Ottoman usage in the past: for purposes of external consumption Christians too were *"millet,"* but for internal administrative purposes, Christians and Jews, that is *ahl al-dhimma,* were simply a *"taife,"* or *"cemaat."* Working from the diplomatic correspondence alone, European orientalists concluded that the Ottomans customarily considered Christians and by extension, Jews, whether within or without Muslim rule, a *millet.* Thus Bernard de Paris in his *Vocabolario Italiano-Turchesco* (Rome, 1665) defined *"religione"* as *"millet,"* with the example, *"religione di Christo,"* i.e., *"millet-il-mesihiyye,"* the phrase he would have seen in countless letters of sultans preserved in Venice and Paris.[19] Meninski in his dictionary (Vienna, 1680; second edition, 1780) repeated Bernard's definition and his example.[20] The dictionaries based on Meninski (Richardson [1806] and Ciadyrgy [1832])[21] simply copied their source—again repeating the misleading example, *"millet-i mesihiyye,"* as did Bianchi and Kieffer (Paris, 1850).[22] Zenker (Lepzig, 1866–7) is the only lexicographer to note that the phrase customarily appears in diplomatic correspondence with European states, suggesting correctly the typical limits of Ottoman usage.[23]

In the nineteenth and early twentieth centuries the European lexicographic understanding (i.e., the specifically diplomatic usage of the term to include Christians) started to creep into normal Ottoman usage as well—though the earlier Muslim sense remained. The broadening of the term to include non-Muslims is documented in the various dictionaries of the period. It occurred gradually. Maliakas's Turkish-Greek dictionary (Istanbul, 1876) gives as its first example, *"millet-i islamiyye"* ("Muslim *millet*") and its second, "Christian *millet*."[24] Barbier de Meynard (Paris, 1886) clearly indicates the historic significance of the term with his example *"ehl-i millet,"* ("People of the *millet*") that is, the "Muslims of the Ottoman Empire," as opposed to the subject Christians and Jews, but he also recognizes the new inclusiveness of the term with another example, *"Millet-i osmaniyyeyi kabul edenler,"* "Those who accept Ottoman nationality."[25] Significantly, the "classic" usage of the term, the usage which is supposed to start with Mehmed the Conqueror in 1454, that is, the phrase *"rum milleti"* ("the Greek *millet"*), does not occur in these dictionaries prior to 1899.[26] Moreover in both Şemseddin Sami Fraseri's (Istanbul, 1901) and Ali Said's (Istanbul, 1912) dictionaries the normal sense of *millet* is still Muslim.[27]

At what precise point and how exactly did the external usage of the term start to influence the Ottoman vocabulary? The change may have occurred after the Treaty of Küçük Kaynarca (1774), for that document does not use the term. Although "Article Seven" discusses what one might expect to be called the Greek *millet,* the term used is not *"millet,"* but *"diyanet"* ("ritual and worship"). The terms *"millet"* and *"milel"* do occur in the treaty, but, in conformity with traditional usage, they refer to Christians outside the empire, in this case, the English and French nations *("milel")* who possessed trading rights now extended to Russia.[28]

It is with the reforming decrees of Mahmud II and Abdülmecid, in the nineteenth century, that the European understanding of *"millet"* clearly begins to enter the Ottoman institutional vocabulary. The external usage of the term suggests the external influence behind these decrees. One early usage of *"millet"* as *"ahl al-dhimma"* occurs in an order published in the *Takvim-i Vakayi,* February, 1835.[29] The order regularized the position of the Jewish community *("yahudi milleti")* and extended, for the first time, official recognition to a *Haham Başi.* Another source is the *Hatt-ı Şerif* of Gülhane (November 1839) which contains the phrase *"Tebaayi saltanati seniyyemizden olan ehli Islam ve mileli saire"* ("the people of Islam and other nations who are from among the subjects of our exalted sultanate"). Elsewhere in the decree these "other nations" are referred to by their normal title, *"zimmı."*[30] In the next decree of reform, the *Hatt-ı Hümayun* of 1856 *(İslahat Fırmanı)* the new usage of the term occurs alongside traditional Ottoman terminology. Thus the non-Muslim groups within the empire were most commonly called not *milletler* or *milel* but *cemaatlar,* their religious chiefs were called *patrikler ve cemaatbaşlar.* On the other hand, the administration of "national" affairs *(milletce olan maslahatlarinin idaresi)* is to be entrusted to a mixed lay-religious council for each "community" *(cemaat).* "Approval of the heads of the *millet" (rüesayi milletin tasvibi)* must be sought for building plans. Whatever the *"millet"* of the applicant *(herkangi milletin olursa olsun),* he is to be considered for a post in the state bureaucracy. Every "community" *("cemaat")* is authorized to establish *"millet"* schools *("milletçe mektepler").*[31]

The traditional meaning of *millet* as Muslim did not cease. In fact an issue of *Takvim-i Vakayi* which appeared just two numbers before the recognition of the Jewish *millet* described the sultan as "the shadow of God who is the protector of the state and the *millet."*[32] With the orders of the 1820s onward the term *"millet"* came to acquire the usage it now has in modern Western scholarship, a non-Muslim protected community, but prior to and even during these reforming decades *millet* could mean the exact opposite—the community of Islam in contradistinction to the non-Muslims under Islam's protection.

This discussion might seem like the pedantic arguments so beloved of nineteenth-century German classicists, arguments sometimes belittled by the line: "Homer never existed; his works were written by another poet of the same name." So what if the term *millet* was a late invention? What matters is not the term but the institution, or institutions—that is the reality it supposedly describes. Unfortunately over the past one hundred years the term, *"millet,"* has become a historiographical fetish with a life and meaning of its own. Because it is a Turkish-Arabic word, in the secondary literature it has assumed *ipso facto* an unjustified hoary, technical, administrative concreteness. The term has distorted the reality. Had the terms "communal" or "corporate" been substituted for *millet* this confusion would not have occurred, for these terms are clearly heuristic devices to shape a complex mass of unruly historical detail.

As a historiographical lesson this philological exercise may have been useful, but what does it tell us about the Ottoman government's policy toward non-Muslims? No philological exercise can answer that question completely, but it can help form the outline in which such questions can be posed. The lack of a general administrative term strongly suggests that there was no overall administrative system, structure, or set of institutions for dealing with non-Muslims. One might claim that the lack of an administrative term proves nothing in a premodern, prerational society where legally defined institutions barely existed. But the Ottoman Empire, at least in its heyday, was remarkably rational; it had many defined and functioning institutions. Thus an important distinction can be drawn between an institution with a title and a specific, explicit purpose (e.g., *devşirme, sürgün, iltizam*) and an undefined system with no title whatsoever. For these reasons the absence of an explicit technical term is highly significant in such a term-conscious bureaucracy. The absence of a term suggests the absence of an institutionalized policy toward non-Muslims. As for the so-called *millet* system, or, perhaps better, "the communal system," it was not an institution or even a group of institutions, but rather it was a set of arrangements, largely local, with considerable variation over time and place.

Foundation Myths

What are the foundation myths of the Greek, Armenian, and Jewish communities within the Ottoman Empire? To what degree are they accurate? A clear answer to these questions is difficult because the origins of non-Muslim autonomy are shrouded in legend and partisan historiography. The accounts of the Greek, Armenian, and Jewish "institutions" are strikingly similar—all are at variance with their prior communal practices and all bear the same patina of self-serving tradition.

Similarity is not proof of accuracy; quite the contrary, it is cause for suspicion. The Greeks, the Jews, and the Armenians all believed that Mehmed the Conqueror had a close personal relationship with their respective leaders. The Greeks claim that Mehmed himself knew Greek.[33] Mehmed in turn honored Gennadios with many gifts and tokens of esteem.[34] The Jews claim that Mehmed studied Hebrew to read the prophecies of the Book of Daniel which had foretold his imperial success. Mehmed enjoyed the company not only of Moses Capsali, the so-called chief rabbi, but also sought out other Jews who provided him with regular shipments of *kosher* food. The sultan particularly enjoyed the Passover *seder*.[35] The Armenians claim that Mehmed bestowed a personal promise of protection upon their leader, Yovakim, who responded by blessing the sultan's sword.[36]

What is also striking is that each foundation myth contradicts the practices and norms of its group. For the Greek Orthodox Church to have at its head a layman elevated through the ranks of the ecclesiastical hierarchy in one short day at the behest of a hostile infidel who treats the Patriarch-elect with the same ceremonial respect accorded by Byzantine emperors is a story that is surprising.[37] For the Jews the account is also suspect. The Jewish community has rarely been hierarchical; the norm has been congregational organizations jealously opposed to any superstructure of authority. Such antihierarchical tendencies were exacerbated during the all too frequent years when expulsions and persecutions threw together different Jewish communities into one city. Sultan Mehmed's policies of forced expulsion and resettlement in Constantinople created just such a factious lot.[38] As for the Armenians the account of their organization is the most unbelievable of all. With benefit of neither Sis nor Ējmiacin, Mehmed is supposed to have created an entirely new patriarchate—appointing to this see his favorite.[39]

These accounts may yield some information about the events surrounding Mehmed's consolidation of power in Constantinople, but they reveal even more about the mentalities of the subject peoples. The myths fulfilled a purpose—a polemical purpose—special pleading directed at the Ottoman court. In later centuries any claim based on the practice of the esteemed ancestor, the Conqueror, Mehmet II, was a claim surely to be honored. Just as devout Muslims ascribed all sorts of traditions to the Prophet and his Companions, so eager *dhimmī*s sought all sorts of tolerant acts in the behavior of Mehmed. Thus there grew a self-serving patina of tradition which colored the foundation accounts of each religious community.

In addition to the tendentious content of the chronicles there are other causes for doubt. One is that there is no external confirmation of the details or outline of any of these accounts. For each story the only sources are those of the community itself. The major Turkish chronicler, Aşıkpaşazâde (c. 1400–1480) ignores all patriarchs, rabbis, and *millet*s.[40]

Armenian sources present the fewest problems. There are no extant contemporary Armenian chronicles. As far as I can tell, the earliest Armenian history to discuss the founding of the Patriarchate dates from the eighteenth century.[41]

As for the Hebrew sources, the principal chronicle was composed around 1523 under circumstances which often undermine its reliability. Four problems beset the *Seder Eliyahu zuta* of Elijah Capsali (c. 1485–1555):[42] one, the Messianic message, which sacrifices concern with historical accuracy in order to herald the eminent arrival of the Redeemer; two, the biblically laden prose which shapes the facts to fit the verses; three, the family pride in a great-uncle (Moses the rabbi was related to Elijah the author), which exaggerates the former's position; and four, the confusion of tradition and practice in Crete, with which Elijah Capsali was familiar, with that in Constantinople, with which he was not. This last point requires a note of explanation. Elijah Capsali, as far as we know, never ventured into Muslim territory—his Crete was Venetian not Ottoman; apparently he knew no Turkish—his sources were Hebrew, Italian, perhaps Greek and oral traditions. It is understandable that the tasks, responsibilities, and prestige that Elijah knew from his own and his ancestors' positions as communal leaders in Crete might contaminate his account of the position of his great-uncle, Moses.[43] The other Hebrew source, *Divrey Yoseph* of Joseph Sambari (c. 1640–1703), suffers from different problems; both in time and place it is distant from the events of Mehmed's reign, for it was composed in Egypt during the second half of the seventeenth century.[44] To further complicate the story the secondary works have confused the two chronicles and accepted both uncritically.[45]

In contrast to the few Hebrew and Armenian chronicles the Greek sources are extensive, but they are also the most problematic. The Greek accounts are the most important because they have furnished the model for the structure of all the non-Muslim communities.[46] The source for this model is a chronicle which is now regarded as a forgery. Although suspicion about the provenance of the *Chronicon Maius* ascribed to Sphrantzes first arose in the 1930s, subsequent works on Ottoman history have not taken into account the Byzantinists' consensus against its authenticity.[47]

The general agreement is that the work, which had been ascribed to a Byzantine court official, Georgios Phrantzes, or rather Sphrantzes (c. 1401–1477) is in fact the product of Makarios Melissenos, Metropolitan of Monembasia, who flourished in the second half of the sixteenth century.[48] As such it belongs to the other late sixteenth-century chronicles, *The Political History of Constantinople* and *The Patriarchal History of Constantinople,* all three products of a highly interested party, the Greek Orthodox ecclesiastical establishment within the Ottoman Empire.[49]

Curiously, the Greek chronicles contemporary to the events of the Conquest are mostly silent about Mehmed and the Greek church. Only one describes the appointment of Gennadios to the Patriarchate. The authentic Sphrantzes says nothing;[50] Laonikos Chalkokandyles says nothing;[51] and Doukas says nothing.[52] Each does discuss Constantinople after the Capture so the silence on Mehmed and the Patriarchate is bizarre. Of course, an argument from silence is not convincing and there does remain a lone voice in the wilderness—Kritovoulos, *History of Mehmed the Conqueror.*[53] That

Kritovoulos's evidence should be the cornerstone of the privileged autonomous Greek Orthodox Patriarchate is full of irony. Nationalist Greek historians, notably Paparrhegopulos, have rejected him for alleged pro-Turkish tendencies.[54]

We should conclude that the primary and secondary accounts of the founding of the "*millet* system" are suspect. The primary accounts may contain forgeries or tendentious fables. The secondary accounts are faulty on two grounds: they accept uncritically the substance of the Greek, Hebrew and late Armenian chronicles, and they force this unverified substance into the mold of a problematic "*millet* system." The current view of relations between the Ottoman state and its non-Muslim subjects is a distortion of both fact and framework. None of the foregoing, however, is grounds for a total rejection of existing sources. Rather it is an appeal for a reexamination free of the misunderstandings of the past. The next three sections begin this reexamination.

The Greeks

Mehmed's initial policy was not to rely upon the Patriarchate to control the Greeks of the capital, but rather to turn to the leading Byzantine civil official still in the city, the Grand Duke Loukas Notaras. The contemporary sources assign Notaras a prominent and controversial role in the events during and after the Conquest. A few days later, Mehmed found the grand duke unreliable and had him executed.[55] Mehmed's choice of a civil official suggests that the Ottomans had no predisposition to use ecclesiastical authority to control non-Muslim groups. The Ottomans eventually did turn to the Church, but the patriarchal seat was not filled until January 1454, some six months after the Conquest.[56] The later Greek sources, notably Pseudo-Phrantzes and the *Patriarchal* and *Political Histories,* significantly ignore this period of lay power by dating the installation of Gennadios a few days after the Conquest, by claiming that Sultan Mehmet himself installed the patriarch with a resplendent ceremony similar to the ritual of the Byzantine Empire, and by insisting that the sultan give the patriarch a detailed declaration of rights and privileges.[57] Although these statements have no basis in the sources of the fifteenth century, they permeate the current secondary literature.[58] Another element of the Church's sixteenth-century attempt to rewrite history is the portrayal of Loukas Notaras. Pseudo-Phrantzes is decidedly hostile to him, while the *Patriarchal* and *Political Histories* ignore him.[59] As the alternative to the Church during Ottoman rule, Notaras must have been an object of concern among ecclesiastical officials. His execution shortly after the Conquest removed him as an active rival, but, as a martyr to the cause of Byzantine lay authority, he could have been a rallying point against both the Church and the sultan in the sixteenth century. Clearly it was in the interests of both to have him denigrated or ignored. Notaras was the most visible civil leader during this period of transition, but there were others who survived. Given the traditional conflict between laymen and clerics in Byzantium, it is likely that the passage of authority from civil to religious hands provoked a struggle within the Greek community.

Ultimately Mehmed did grant some form of recognition to Gennadios, however buffeted the patriarch's authority. Kritovoulos furnishes the only contemporary account of the sultan's actions. Though unsatisfactory in many respects, it is probably closer to the truth than the later accounts:

> During that period [the Sultan] . . . called back Gennadius, a very wise and remarkable man. He had already heard much through common report about the wisdom and prudence and virtue of this man. Therefore, immediately after the capture he sought for him, being anxious to see him and to hear some of this wisdom. And after a painstaking search he found him at Adrianople in a village, kept under guard in the home of one of the notables, but enjoying great honors. For his captor knew of his virtue, even though he himself was a military man.
>
> When the Sultan saw him, and had in a short time had proofs of his wisdom and prudence and virtue and also of his power as a speaker and of his religious character, he was greatly impressed with him, and held him in great honor and respect, and gave him the right to come to him at any time, and honored him with liberty and conversation. He enjoyed his various talks with him and his replies, and he loaded him with noble and costly gifts.
>
> In the end, he made him Patriarch and High Priest of the Christians, and gave him among many other rights and privileges the rule of the church and all its power and authority, no less than that enjoyed previously under the emperors. He also granted him the privilege of delivering before him fearlessly and freely many good disquisitions concerning the Christian faith and doctrine. And he himself went to his residence, taking with him the dignitaries and wise men of his court, and thus paid him great honor. And in many other ways he delighted the man.
>
> Thus the Sultan showed that he knew how to respect the true worth of any man, not only of military men but of every class, kings, and tyrants, and emperors. Furthermore the Sultan gave back the church to the Christians, by the will of God, together with a large portion of its properties.[60]

One difficulty with this story is that the nature of Kritovoulos's narrative dictates the very statements which are in question. The hero, consciously and explicitly, of the *History of Mehmed the Conqueror* is the sultan—all action stems from him. Whatever his actual involvement may have been, Kritovoulos makes him the center of the piece. Thus it is very difficult to be certain that Mehmed actually undertook all the deeds that the author ascribes to him.

Gennadios's own words, however, do seem to confirm many of the details of this account. The future patriarch was in fact taken prisoner to Edirne and he was kept in honorable captivity at the home of a powerful Muslim. The Ottomans did give "us"—"freedom in writing." The sultan did make many "gifts" to the Church.[61] Gennadios did write a tract on the Christian faith which was translated into Turkish.[62] Although it seems that Gennadios wrote nothing on the circumstances of his appointment, he does suggest that sometime later Mehmed tried to dissuade him from resigning his post. The difficulty with Gennadios's words is that he has a tendency to promote himself as "an indispensable advisor to powerful men."[63] One wonders what is truth and what is immodest exaggeration.

One more difficulty is that terms like "freedom" and "gifts" (*"eleutheria"* and *"dōra"*) have little concrete significance. If "freedom in writing" means a *berat,* was it personal or institutional? Is the "us,' the Greek Orthodox Church, the patriarchate, or the patriarch? If the sultan made "gifts" to the Church were they privileges, as one writer has argued, or, more likely, the annual presentation of one thousand florins given to the patriarch until 1469?[64] There is evidence to suggest that at least as far as the Ottoman government was concerned the authority granted was personal. How else to explain the issuance of a new *berat* upon the appointment of each new patriarch over the centuries? The Church was to claim that its power was institutionally recognized by Mehmed's *ferman* but around 1519 when Sultan Selim challenged this claim the then-reigning patriarch, Theoleptos, was unable to produce such a document despite a thorough search of the Church's archives.[65]

This discussion of the status of the Greek community after the Conquest has, perhaps, raised more questions than it has answered, but it has clarified a number of points. Whatever Mehmed's involvement in the selection of Gennadios as patriarch and the establishment of the "privileges" of the Ecumenical Patriarchate, it was more hesitant and less substantive than is normally claimed. The chronicles upon which such claims are made must be treated with caution.

The Jews

An examination of the Jewish foundation myths must begin at a more elementary level. Much of what has been claimed about the Jewish *millet* is not even based on the text of Elijah Capsali's *Seder Eliyahu zuta,* but rather on a confused mélange of it and the later and less reliable *Divrey Yoseph.* Further complicating the discussion is that unlike "patriarch," the terms, "chief rabbi," and *"haham başı,"* have little administrative significance in Jewish history and do not appear in the text of Elijah Capsali's chronicle. In order to discover what Mehmed did or did not give Moses Capsali and the Jews, we must first examine this chronicle:

> Among the Jews [whom the Sultan loved] there was the humble and saintly Rabbi Moses Capsali, of blessed memory, who lived in Constantinople from the days of the emperors of Greece. One day the king passed through the neighborhood of the Jews, and seeing there a vast number of people, he exclaimed in wonder: "Who will judge these people of mine, a nation so numerous!" Subsequently, when the king sat upon his throne with his ministers in attendance before him he again spoke up, saying, "Who is the judge and Rabbi of the Jews?" The ministers replied, "He is an old man, an ascetic, who fasts all the days of the year from the year's beginning to its end, who sleeps on the ground, and lives a life of distress whilst he labors in Torah. Thereupon the king had them bring the

Rabbi before him. When he came and stood before the king, the king addressed him: *"Hoca,"* ("my teacher," in the language of Togarmah) and spoke graciously to him. Even though the Rabbi did not know the language of Togarmah and the king had not met him previously, nevertheless the king relied upon reports he heard from all that the Rabbi's name was like pure oil, for, in friendship and in esteem, he turned not to bribes. And so the king ordered that he be mounted upon a horse and he sent a few of the servants and attendants on duty at the royal gate to accompany him to his home.[66]

We can learn much from this passage. The only Turkish title used for R. Moses Capsali was *hoca* and its significance was more honorific than substantive. His initial function was as judge and this role antedated Mehmet's contact with him. At most it would seem that Mehmet merely sanctioned an existing position which had arisen from the internal needs of the Jewish community, a position, moreover, which was consonant with the norms of Jewish practice. There is also much that we cannot learn. There is no evidence that the sultan appointed Capsali to the position of chief rabbi or *haham bası,* no evidence that such a post existed, no evidence that Capsali participated in Ottoman tax collection, no evidence that he had precedence over the patriarchs, and no evidence that he was the sole vehicle for Ottoman dealings with Jews or *vice versa.* As Joseph Hacker has demonstrated, contemporary sources suggest a limited role for Capsali. His authority did not apparently go beyond Constantinople and his successor as chief judge of this community, Elijah Mizrahi, seems to have had even less power.[67]

Barely a generation after the death of R. Elijah Mizrahi, in 1571 or thereabouts, the question of communal leadership surfaced *obiter dicta,* in a legal dispute regarding tax exemption:

The second tax is called in the language of the Ishmaelites, *rav akçesi,* for through it the Jews were allowed to have a Rabbi who leads [all the congregations of Constantinople] with "warrant of the kingdom" *(hormana demalkuta).* It is not known whether the king imposed it then upon the Jews as one of the royal statutes or whether the Jews asked the king to let them have the said Rabbi and in return for this undertook to give this second tax. In any event the matter of the Rabbi only lasted, because of our many sins, a very short time while the matter of this second tax still drags upon us, "until the Lord look down, and behold."[68]

What emerges from this passage is how little was actually known about the origins of Capsali's and Mizrahi's positions and this less than fifty years after the death of the second incumbent and in the very city where both flourished. Most uncertain was the involvement of the Ottoman authorities in the foundation of Capsali's position. What is clear is that the government was more eager to collect the tax than it was to fill or have filled whatever position of leadership Mizrahi left at his death. The Ottomans felt little institutional need for a Jewish "community-head" or at least not enough of a need to override the evident communal objections. In the absence of regular formal representation to the authorities, the Jewish communities of the empire employed a system of special envoys and court favorites to plead their causes—a custom prevalent among Iberian Jews before the expulsion. During the period under discussion the Jews never had what Gibb and Bowen have called, a *"Haham Başı,"* or "Chief Rabbi," with powers, similar to those enjoyed by the patriarch, over all his coreligionists in the empire.[69]

The Armenians

During the time of Mehmed the Conqueror, the Greeks in Istanbul had a communal leader, an institution, but uncertain Ottoman involvement. The Jews had a local communal leader but no institution, and little Ottoman involvement. What did the Armenians have? The consensus has been that the Armenians had a leader, Yovakim of Bursa, an institution, the patriarchate, and Ottoman involvement, a grant of powers from Mehmed II in 1461.[70] The source for this consensus is a late eighteenth-century history whose English version relates:

> Gregory the tenth, of Macu, having succeeded Kirakus in the pontificate of Etchmiatchin, proceeded with the repairs and improvements commenced by his predecessor. In the eleventh year of his spiritual sway Constantinople was taken from the Greeks by Sultan Mahomed Fathih, who a few years after brought thither from Prussia, Bishop Joakim the prelate of the city, with a few distinguished Armenian families, six in number, according to some. He also brought four Armenian families from Galatia, and some from the regions of Garaman, which he established in Samathia. Many more Armenians were brought by this monarch from various parts, and settled by him in Constantinople. Mahomed Fathih gave bishop Joakim letters patent, authorising him to assume the spiritual jurisdiction of all the Armenians situated in Greece and Asia Minor, and styling him "Batrig" or Patriarch: Hence sprung that patriarchate of Constantinople, which continues to this day.[71]

This excerpt comes from the pioneering work of Mik'ayēl Č'amč'ean (1738–1823), published first in Armenian and later in English. Similar accounts appeared in Italian and in the authoritative Armenian history of Maghak'ia Ormanian, Patriarch of Constantinople early in the twentieth century.[72] However Kevork Bardakjian, who has examined contemporary sources not previously available, has demonstrated the inaccuracy of this story.[73] Indeed there is no evidence for empirewide patriarchal authority established through Ottoman fiat. Rather, the authority and jurisdiction of the Constantinople Patriarchate evolved gradually over the centuries in fits and starts.

Bardakjian's argument is convincingly presented, but there is one exceptional instance which, while not contradictory, does illustrate the unique problems faced by the Ottoman Armenians. In 1479, Mehmed did attempt to create an Armenian patriarchal office and he did offer the post to two clerics.[74] This decision of Mehmed's was in contrast to his laissez-faire practice of sanctioning existing positions and leaders but not of creating new ones, a practice followed with Jews and Greeks. What might explain this apparent shift? An answer may be found in the political and military situation in eastern Anatolia. Unlike the Jews and the Greeks, the Armenians had a spiritual capital and demographic center which was outside the borders of the Ottoman Empire in adjacent hostile territory. Ējmiacin, Aghtamar and much of historic Armenia were under the control of two warring Turkmen factions, the Ak-Koyunlar and the Kara-Koyunlar. Their respective leaders, Uzun Hasan and Jihanshah, knew the value of the Armenian Catholicosates and populace in their midst. Erratically they pursued a policy of toleration towards these Christians, for they might reap two benefits, a strengthened basis for an alliance with Venice against the Ottomans, and support from among the Armenian subjects of the Ottomans.[75] The Ottoman fear of such a strategy gave impetus to the use of the *sürgün* system, causing the forced deportation of Armenians from sensitive areas to the relative security of Istanbul and the Balkans, and was reason enough to try to encourage an autonomous see, the so-called Patriarchate of Istanbul, as a focus of loyalty for Armenians within the empire.[76]

Over the centuries this post became a sort of *de facto* patriarchate, but its ecclesiastical legitimacy was grudgingly recognized, if at all. As late as 1678, Paul Rycaut dismissed the patriarchates set up under Ottoman auspices:

> It is true, that at Constantinople, and at Jerusalem, there are those who are called Armenian Patriarchs, but they are titular only made to please and content the Turks: who have judged it necessary and agreeable to the Armenian Faith, or rather to their own, that Patriarchs would remain in those places; and therefore have enjoined them to constitute such under that notion; by which means, the Armenian Church maintaining their Representatives at that place, they may always know from whom they may exact the money and Presents at a new Investiture, and may charge on him all those Avanias, or false pretences, which they may find most agreeable to their own advantage: Otherwise, I say, these Patriarchs are but titular, and are in reality no other than Deputies and Suffragans of the Patriarch, as are those at Smyrna or Angora, which Trade hath convocated great numbers of the Armenian Nation; or rather, they may be more properly called Bishops under those Patriarchs, having the name of Martabet, which in their language signifies a Superintendent, or Overseer of the Church.[77]

The chief patriarch resided in Ējmiacin and the so-called Patriarch of Constantinople was little more than a local bishop.[78]

One hundred years later when Č'amč'ean's *History* appeared, the complexities of the origins of the Patriarchate had been forgotten. The story of Yovakim and Mehmed may have been consistent with the purposes of Catholic Armenians, whom Č'amč'ean and Ormanian joined, for it bolstered the authority of sometimes Rome-leaning Constantinople over devotedly Monophysite Ējmiacin, but it was neither the whole story nor, in all likelihood, the true story of the Patriarchate.

What conclusions emerge from this discussion? First, the Ottomans had no consistent policy toward non-Muslims in the fifteenth and sixteenth centuries and perhaps later as well. Second, as administrative policy slowly began to emerge over the centuries it was accompanied by mythmaking which created justifications for new policies by attributing them to the past. For non-Muslims this invention meant distortion and pious forgery. For the Ottoman government this invention meant accepting as true non-Muslim claims which it previously had ignored. The adoption of the term *millet* was one stage of this acceptance, but the reforms of the *Tanzimat* opened many others. The story we have told is an old one, well-established in Near Eastern practice. The pact of ʿUmar and the Edict of the Prophet to the Christians are the best known of these legends; the founding of the *millet* system should be added to that list.[79]

Notes

1. Hamilton A. R. Gibb and Harold Bowen, *Islamic Society and the West*, London, 1966, vol. 1, part 2, p. 206, n. 1.

2. M. Ertuğrul Düzdağ, *Şeyhülislam Ebussuud Efendi Fetfaları Işığında 16 asır Türk Hayatı*, Istanbul, 1972, p. 176.

3. It does not appear alone; see Mehmet Zeki Pakalın, *Osmanlı Tarih Deyimleri ve Terimleri Sözlüğü*, Istanbul, 1953, vol. 2, p. 585. The term *millet başı* does appear, but its usage is restricted to local administration, a quarter or a village, rather than empirewide communal organization; furthermore the term does not appear until 1842.

Steen de Jehay, *De la situation legale des sujets ottomans non-Musulmans*, Brussels, 1906, p. 83, remarked that Turkish officials did not use the term *millet* after the beginning of the eighteenth century but he assumed that they did use the term earlier.

4. Ömer Lûtfi Barkan, "894 (1488/1489) yili Cizyesinin Tahsilatini ait Muhasebe Bilancolari," *Belgeler*, 1 (1964), 1–117.

5. In quoting the following documents Jennings never once uses the term *millet*: Başbakanlık Arşivi, Istanbul, Tapu Defier series—no. 33, Kayseri, 1500; no. 387, Karaman, Rum, Erzurum (circa 1523); no. 455, Konya (circa 1523); no. 205, Erzurum, 1540; no. 976, Kayseri (circa 1550); no. 288, Trabzon, 1554; no. 776, Amasya, 1642. Tapu ve Kadastro Arşivi, Ankara, Tapu defter series—no. 26, Amasya, 1576; no. 136, Kayseri, 1583; no. 29 Trabzon, 1583; no. 104, Karaman, 1587; no. 41, Erzurum, 1591. The terms which are used are *mahalle, cemaat,* and *taife*. See Ronald C. Jennings, "Urban Population in Anatolia in the Sixteenth Century," *IJMES*, 7 (1976), pp. 21–57.

6. The term does not appear in a collection of *fetveler* from the following legal scholars: Ebu-Suud Efendi, Pir Mehmed Üskübi, Kadi of Skopje (died 1611/12), Yahya Dhakayzade, Şeyhülislam (died 1649), Ali Çatacavi, Şeyhülislam (died 1691/2), Abdurahim Efendi Menteşizade, Şeyhülislam (died 1715); see Mario Grignaschi, "Le valeur du témoignage des sujets non-musulmans (dhimmī)," *Recueils de la Société Jean Bodin*, 18 (1963), pp. 211–323.

7. Halit Ongan, *Ankara'nın 1 Numaralı Şer'iye Siclii*, Ankara, 1958, *İki Numaralı Şeriye Sicili*, Ankara, 1974; nor, as far as I can tell in the records from Ankara, Kayseri, Konya, Karaman, Isparta, Tokat, Amasya, and Trabzon used in Ronald C. Jennings, "Loans and Credit in Early Seventeenth-Century Ottoman Judicial Records," *JESHO*, 16 (1973), pp. 168–216; nor as far as I can tell in the records from Sofia translated in Galab D. Galbov and Herbert W. Duda, *Die Protokollbücher des Kadiamtes Sofia*, Munich, 1960.

8. Eg., Ahmet Refik, *Hicri Onbirinci Asırda İstanbul Hayatı*, Istanbul, 1931; Dushanka Shopova, *Makedonia vo XVI–XVII Vek, Dokumenti od Carigradskite Arhivi*, Skopje, 1955, Bernard Lewis, *Notes and Documents from The Turkish Archives*, Jerusalem 1952.

9. Ömer Lûtfi Barkan, "Edirne Askeri Kassamina Ait Tereke Defterleri, 1549–1659," *Belgeler*, 3 (1966), pp. 1–477.

10. Josef Kabrda, *Le system fiscal de l'Eglise orthodoxe dans l'Empire ottoman (d'apres les documents Turcs)*, Brno, 1969; Dr. Sinasi Tekin of Harvard University has informed me that in the volume of Evliya Celebi which he is editing for publication the term, *millet*, is used occasionally for Muslims, but never for *dhimmīs*.

11. Grignaschi (cited n. 6), pp. 234–5; Haydar Aḥmad al-Shīhabī, *Lubnān fī ahd al-umarā'i alshihābīyīn*, ed. Asad Rustum and Fuad A. Bustaini, Beirut, 1933, vol. 1, p. 58.

12. Raşid, *Tarih Raşid*, Istanbul, 1865, vol. 2, pp. 587–88.

13. Mehmed Tayyib Gökbilgin, "Venedik Devlet Arşivindeki Türkçe Belgeler Kolleksiyonu," *Belgeler*, 5–8 (1968–71), pp. 128, 132, 116, 129; Akdes Nimet Kurat, *Türk İngiliz Münasebetlerinin Başlangıçı ve Gelişmesi*, Ankara, 1953, pp. 182, 187; A. N. Kurat, "İngiliz Devlet Arşivinde ve Kütüphanelerinde Türkiye Tarihine Ait Bazı Malzemeye Dair," *Ankara Universitesi Dil ve Tarih-Coğrafya Fakültesi Dergisi*, 7 (1949), p. 19.

14. Vančo Boškov, "Ein Nišān des Prinzen Orhan, Sohn Süleymān Çelebis, aus dem Jahre 1412 im Athoskloster Sankt Paulus," *Weiner Zeitschrift für die Kunde des Morgenlandes*, 71 (1979), pp. 130–131. I thank Prof. Andreas Tietze for bringing this article to my attention.

15. See John W. Barker, *Manuel II Palaeologus (1391–1425)*, New Brunswick, N.J., 1969, pp. 252–254; 281–284.

16. Haim Gerber, "An Unknown Turkish Document on Abraham di Castro," (in Hebrew) *Zion*, 45 (1980), pp. 158–163, English summary, p. XV; Joseph Sambari, *Divrey Yoseph*, in A. Neubauer, ed., *Medieval Jewish Chronicles*, London, 1887, vol. 1, p. 145.

17. Necibe Sevgen, "Nasil Sömürüldük? Sarraflar," *Belgelerle Türk Tarih Dergisi*, 3 (1968), no. 15, p. 64.

18. I thank Bernard Lewis for suggesting this possible connotation which deserves further examination.

19. S.v. "religione," vol. 3, p. 1762.

20. Franciszek Meninski, *Thesaurus Linguarum Orientalium Turcicae, Arabicae, Persicae* . . . Vienna, 1680, vol. 4, p. 4883; second edition entitled *Lexicon Arabico-Persico-Turcícum*, Vienna, 1780, vol. 4, p. 702. I thank Ms. Judith Ann Corrente for obtaining a photocopy of the reference from Meninski's first edition from the Yale University Library.

21. John Richardson, *A Dictionary of Persian, Arabic, and English*, ed. Charles Wilkins, London, 1806, vol. 1, p. 984; Antonio Ciadyrgy, *Dizionario Turco Arabo e Persiano*, Milan, 1832, p. 564.

22. T. X. Bianchi and J. D. Kieffer, *Dictionnaire Turc-Francais*, Paris, 1850, vol. 2, p. 997.

23. Julius Theodor Zenker, *Turkisch-Arabisch-Persisches Handwörterbuch*, Leipzig, 1886–7, p. 876.

24. A. Maliakas, *Lexikon Tourko-Ellēnikon*, Constantinople, 1876, p. 785.

25. A. C. Barbier de Meynard, *Dictionaire Turc-Francais*, Paris, 1886, vol. 2, p. 784.

26. I. Chlōros, *Lexikon Tourko-Ellēnikon*, Constantinople, 1899, vol. 2, 1769.

27. Şemseddin Sami Fraseri, *Kamus-u Türkı*, Istanbul, 1901, vol. 2, p. 1400; Ali Said, *Resimli Kamus-u Osmanı*, Istanbul, 1912, p. 980; compare Diran Kelekian, *Dictionnaire Turc-Français*, Istanbul, 1911, p. 1219.

28. Nihat Erim, *Devletlerarası Hukuk ve Siyasi Tarih Metinleri*, Ankara, 1953, vol. 1, pp. 121–41, particularly 124–5; English translation in J. C. Hurewitz, *The Middle East and North Africa in World Politics, A Documentary Record*, New Haven, 1975, vol. 1, pp. 92–101, particularly pp. 94–5.

29. *Takvim-i Vakayi*, 23, sevvel 1250/22 February 1835, no. 96; French version in Abraham Galante, *Histoire des Juifs d'Istanbul*, 1941, vol. 1, 108. This is not the earliest usage I have seen. A *ferman* issued towards the end of Şaban 1243/March 1828 discusses the Armenians as a *millet*, as does a *ferman* issued towards the end of Safer 1258/April 1842. On the other hand a *ferman* dated end of Rebiülahir 1211/October–November 1796 does not describe the Greeks as a *millet*. The change in terminology and official attitude is illustrated in a *ferman* of the nineteenth century which quotes a decree of the sixteenth century; in a discussion of the Jewish cemetery at Hasköy (beginning Ramazan 1255/mid-November 1839) the Jews are called a *millet*, but in the attached document (dated Sevvel 990/October 1582) they are a *taife*. For these *mühimme defter*s see Ahmet Refik, *Hicri On Üçüncü Asırda Istanbul Hayatı* (1200–1255), Istanbul, 1932, pp. 26–9, 31–3, 12–14, 29–31.

30. A. Şerif Gözübüyük and Suna Kili, ed. *Türk Anayasa Metinleri Tanzimattan Bugüne kadar*, Ankara, 1957, p. 5; English translation in Hurewitz (cited n. 28), p. 270.

31. Gözübüyük and Kili (cited n. 30), p. 8; English tr. in Hurewitz (cited n. 28), pp. 316–317.

32. *Takvim-i Vakayi*, 15 Ramazan 1250/26 January 1835, no. 94.

33. Georgios Sphrantzes, *Memorii 1401–1477, in anexa Pseudo-Phrantzes: Macarie Melissenos Cronica, 1258–1481*, ed. Vasile Grecu, Bucharest, 1966, pp. 234, 446–54; Georgius Phrantzes, *Chronikon*, ed. Immanuel Bekker, Bonn, 1838, pp. 95, 306 (with Latin tr.); *Patriarchike Kōnstantinoupoleōs Historia*, ed. Immanuel Bekker, Bonn, 1838, p. 78–94.

34. *Historia Politikē Kōnstantinoupoleōs*, ed. Immanuel Bekker, Bonn, 1849, p. 27–31 (with Latin tr.) and Sphrantzes (cited n. 33), p. 448, 456 = Phrantzes (cited n. 33) pp. 306–7.

35. Elijah b. Elkanah Capsali, *Seder Eliyahu zuta*, ed. Aryeh Shmuelevitz, Shlomo Simonsohn, Meir Benayahu, Jerusalem, 1975, vol. 1, pp. 120–1, 93, and 98; also see Charles Berlin, "A Sixteenth Century Hebrew Chronicle of the Ottoman Empire: The *Seder Eliyahu zuta* of Elijah Capsali and its Message," in Charles Berlin, ed. *Studies in Jewish Bibliography, History, and Literature in Honor of I. Edward Kiev*, New York, 1971, pp. 21–44.

36. Maghak'ia Ormanian, *Azgapatum*, second edition, Beirut, 1959–61, section 1488, column 2156. I thank Kevork Bardakjian of Harvard University for translating this passage and informing me about matters Armenian.

37. Sphrantzes (cited n. 33), pp. 446–8 = Phrantzes (cited n. 33), 304–7 = English tr. H. T. F. Duckworth in Claude D. Cobham, *The Patriarchs of Constantinople*, Cambridge, 1911, pp. 70–2.

38. For deportation of Jews from Edirne to Istanbul see Abraham Danon, "Documents relating to the History of the Karaites in European Turkey," *Jewish Quarterly Review*, 17 (1926), pp. 168–9. Recent research by Dr. Joseph Hacker of the Hebrew University has suggested that the lamentations of exile composed by Ottoman Jews date not from post-1492, the era of the Spanish exiles, as had been supposed, but from post-1453, the era of the Jewish *sürgün* to Istanbul. I thank Dr. Hacker for informing me of the results of his research on this and other points concerning Ottoman Jewry. The seminar which he conducted at Harvard in the Spring Semester of 1977 taught me much about the sources for the study of the Jewish communities in Salonica and Constantinople and the Ottoman "chief rabbinate."

39. For the problems of such an appointment see Ormanian (cited n. 36), section 1488, columns 2156–7. Ejmiacin and Sis were two established catholicosates within the Armenian Church.

40. Friedrich Giese, ed. *Die Altosmanische Chronik des Aşikpaşazade*, Leipzig, 1929, pp. 133–

4 = German tr. Richard F. Kreutel, *Vom Hirtenzeit zur Hohen Pforte . . . Chronik . . . Aşik Paşa-Sohn,* Graz, 1959, pp. 200–2.

41.   Mik'ayel Č'amč'ean, *Patmution Hayuts,* Venice, 1786, three volumes. There are other Armenian sources which I discuss below; see also chapter 4 below.

42.   Capsali (cited n. 35) and Berlin (cited n. 35).

43.   On the responsibilities and powers of the *contestabile,* the communal leader of Cretan Jewry, see Elias S. Artom and Humbertus M. D. Cassuto, ed. *Statua Iudaoerum Candiae* (in Hebrew), Jerusalem, 1943, vol. 1, pp. 39–41, 48–9; and Charles Berlin, "Elijah Capsali's Seder Eliyahu Zuta," Ph.D. thesis in Near Eastern Languages and Middle Eastern Studies, Harvard University, 1962, pp. 3, 4, 33, and 218.

44.   Excerpts published in Neubauer (cited n. 16). The complete text exists in manuscript at the Bodleian and Alliance Israélite Universelle.

45.   This confusion has given rise to the claim that the chief rabbi sat in the Divan of the Sultan next in pride to the mufti himself and above the patriarch of the "Uncircumcised." The claim is based on Sambari (cited n. 16), vol. 1, p. 138. For more on this claim see the contribution of Joseph Hacker in this volume, chapter 6.

The statement has no basis in the sources or practice of the fifteenth and sixteenth centuries; see H. Z. (J. W.) Hirschberg, "The Oriental Jewish Communities," in A. J. Arberry, ed. *Religion in the Middle East,* Cambridge, England, 1976, 184–6.

46.   For example, Ormanian (cited n. 36), section 1485–6, columns 2151–3.

47.   R. I. Loernetz, "Autor du *Chronichon Maius* attribute à Georges Phrantzes," *Miscellanea G. Mercati: Letteratura e Storia Bizantina,* Vatican City, 1946, vol. 3, pp. 273–311; for continued uncritical use of Phrantzes's work see for example, Şahabettin Tekindag, "Osmanlı Idaresine Patrik ve Patrikhane," *Belgelerle Türk Tarih Dergisi,* 1 (1967), no. 1, pp. 52–5; Selahattin Tansel, *Osmanlı Kaynaklarına göre Fatih Sultan Mehmed' in Siyasi ve Askeri Faaliyete,* Istanbul, 1971, p. 107.

48.   See George Ostrogorski, *History of the Byzantine State,* tr. Joan Hussey, New Brunswick, 1957, p. 417, n. 2.

49.   *Political History = Historia Politikē* (cited n. 34); *Patriarchal History = Patriarchikē Historia* (cited n. 34); for bibliographical details see Theodore Papadopoullos, *Studies and Documents Relating to the History of the Greek Church and People under Turkish Domination,* Brussels, 1952, pp. xviii, xx–xxi.

50.   Georgios Sphrantzes, *Memorii* (cited n. 33), pp. 2–146 = Philippides, tr. (cited n. 34), pp. 21–95.

51.   This work exists in numerous editions; the pages cited deal with post-conquest Constantinople; *Laonici Chalcocandylae Historiarum Demonstrationes,* ed. Eugenius Darko, Budapest, 1927, vol. 2, pp. 147–201 = *Laonici Chalcocandylae Atheniensis Historiarum Libri Deceni,* ed. and tr. (Latin), Immanuel Bekker, Bonn, 1833, 380–441 = *Laonic Chalcocondil Expuneri Istorice,* tr. (Rumanian), Vasile Grecu, Bucharest, 1958, pp. 223–54 = Laonikos Chalkokondyles, *L'Histoire de la Decadence de l'Empire Grec et Establissement de celoy des Turcs,* tr. Blaise de Vigenere, Paris, 1577, pp. 503–79.

52.   Ducas, *Istoria Turco-Bizantina,* ed. and tr., Vasile Grecu, Bucharest, 1958, 275–95 = Doukas, *Decline and Fall of Byzantium to the Ottoman Turks,* tr. Harry J. Magoulias, Detroit, 1975, pp. 231–41.

Doukas mentions Grennadios a number of times, but there is no mention of him after the Capture. See Ducas, ed. Grecu, pp. 315, 317, 323, 329 = Doukas, tr. Magoulias, pp. 180, 204, 208, 210.

53.   Kritovoulos, *Din Domnia lui Mahomed al II - Lea Anii 1451–1467,* ed. Vasile Grecu, Bucharest, 1963, pp. 173–5 = *History of Mehmed the Conqueror,* tr., Charles T. Riggs, Princeton 1954, pp. 94–5.

54.   Konstantinos Paparrhēgopulos, *Historia tou Hellnikou Ethnous apo tōn Neōterōn,* ed. Paulos Karolidos, Athens, 1925, vol. 5, pp. 316; Kritovoulos, tr., Riggs (cited n. 53) pp. vii–ix.

55. See the works and pages (cited n. 51–52); Kritovoulos, ed., Grecu, (cited n. 51), pp. 159–161 = tr., Riggs (cited n. 51), pp. 83–4.

56. See Apostolos E. Vacalopoulos, *The Greek Nation, 1453–1669: the Cultural and Economic Background of Modern Greek Society*, tr. Ian and Phania Moles, New Brunswick, 1976, pp. 103. This work contains the most thorough discussion of the Greek Patriarchate under Ottoman rule available in English.

57. Sphrantzes (cited n. 33), pp. 446–8, 465 = Phrantzes (cited n. 33), pp. 304–7; *Patriarchikē* (cited n. 33), pp. 80–3, 94; *Politikē* (cited n. 34), pp. 27–31. For an examination of the problem of the date of enthronization see Friedrich Giese, "Die geschichtlichen Grundlagen für die Stellung der christlichen Untertanen im osmanischen Reich," *Der Islam*, 19 (1930), pp. 268–71.

58. Donald M. Nicol, *The Last Centuries of Byzantium, 1261–1453*, London, 1972, p. 413; Franz Babinger, *Mehmed the Conqueror and His Time*, tr. R. Manheim, ed. William C. Hickman, Princeton, 1978, pp. 104–105. Steven Runciman, *The Fall of Constantinople, 1453*, Cambridge, England, 1969, pp. 154–6; Steven Runciman, *The Great Church in Captivity*, Cambridge, England, 1968, pp. 165–70. Not all these works accept all three claims, but each accepts at least one. For other, more critical views, see, V. Laurent, "Les Premiers Patriarches de Constantinople sous Domination Turque" *Revue des Etudes Byzantines*, 26 (1968), 229–263 and C. J. G. Turner, "The Career of George-Gennadius Scholarius," *Byzantion*, 39 (1969), pp. 420–455.

59. My impression of Sphrantzes and Pseudo-Phrantzes is that the forgery (i.e., the sixteenth-century polemic masquerading as a fifteenth-century chronicle) is somewhat more hostile to the grand duke than is the contemporary account; compare Sphrantzes (cited n. 33), pp. 16, 64, 84, 87, 90 to *Pseudo-Phrantzes: Marcarie Melissenos* (cited n. 33), pp. 256, 334, 364, 368, 370, 372, 398, 406, 434; see also Margaret Carroll, "Notes on the Authorship of the Siege Section of the *Chronicon Maius* of Pseudo-Phrantzes, Book III," *Byzantion*, 41 (1971), pp. 37–44.

Of course hostility to Notaras appears even in non-Orthodox sources; see Avedis Sanjian, ed., and tr. *Colophons of Armenian Manuscripts*, 1301–1480, Cambridge, 1969, pp. 224–5, 243 and the Western sources used in Runciman, *Fall* (cited n. 58), pp. 226–7. This is a subject which deserves further examination.

60. Kritovoulos, ed., Grecu (cited n. 53), pp. 173–4 = tr., Riggs (cited n. 53). The translation is by Riggs.

61. Gennadios Scholarios, *Oeuvres completes*, ed. L. Petit, X. A. Sideris, and M. Jugie, Paris, 1928–35, vol. 1, pp. 279–80; vol. 4, pp. 228, 265–6.

62. *Versiunea Turceaca a Confesiunii Patriarhului Ghenadie II Scholarius Scrisa la Cererea Sultanului Mehmet II*, ed. Aurel Deceis, Sibiu, 1946; see also A. Papadakis, "Gennadius II and Mehmet the Conqueror," *Byzantion*, 42 (1972), 88–106.

63. Vacalopoulos (cited n. 56), p. 101.

64. Zacharios N. Matha, *Katalogos Patriarchōn*, Athens, 1884, 105; Vacalopoulos (cited n. 56), p. 105, makes the argument.

65. Demetrius Cantemir, *The History of the Growth and Decay of the Ottoman Empire*, tr. N. Tindal, London, 1734, pp. 102–3, n. 17; for a similar story from the time of Patriarch Jeremy, around 1537, see *Patriarchikē* (cited n. 33), pp. 157–68.

66. The passage is not dated though a paragraph just before these lines suggests that the events described took place during the first year of Mehmed's reign. More likely the date is 1454/5 just after one of the deportations of Ottoman Jews to Istanbul. For that date see Danon (cited n. 38), pp. 168–9 which discusses the deportation of Edirne Jewry to Istanbul.

Capsali (cited n. 35), vol. 1, pp. 81–2. I thank my father, W. G. Braude, for improving my translation of this and the following passage.

67. See the contribution by Joseph Hacker to this volume, chapter 6.

68. Samuel de Medina (c. 1500–89) *She'elōt uteshūvot*, Lemberg, 1862, section IV, question 364; tr. in Bernard Lewis, "The Privileges granted by Mehmed II to his Physician," *Bulletin of the School of Oriental and African Studies*, 14 (1952), p. 554. There is a slight difference in terminol-

ogy between my translation and Lewis's, I substitute "warrant of the kingdom" for "by Royal appointment."

69. Gibb and Bowen (cited n. 1), vol. 1, part 2, p. 217.

70. Gibb and Bowen (cited n. 1), vol. 1, part 2, p. 221. Through a typographical error they misspelt Yovakim's (= Hovaghim) name. In their text it is "Horaghim."

71. Č'amč'ean (cited n. 41), vol. 3, p. 500; the English translation is Michael Chamich, *History of Armenia*, tr., Johannes Avdall, Calcutta, 1827, vol. 2, pp. 329–30.

72. The Italian account is Giovanni de Serpos, *Compendio storico di memorie cronologiche concernenti la religione e la morale della nazione Armena suddita dell'Impero Ottomano*, 3 volumes, Venice, 1786. The first edition of Ormanian (cited n. 36) was published in 3 volumes, Constantinople–Jerusalem, 1913–1927.

73. See the contribution by Kevork Bardakjian to this volume, chapter 4.

74. Sanjian (cited n. 59), pp. 325–6.

75. Sanjian (cited n. 59), pp. 304–5, 292–3, 308, 324, 299, 301, 306, 311, 314, 315–6, 318, 320–1, 322.

76. Galabov and Duda (cited n. 7), p. 144

77. Paul Rycaut, *The Present State of the Greek and Armenian Churches*, London, 1679, pp. 391–2; by "Martabet" Rycaut presumably meant "Vardapet," that is *ustadh*, "master," "preceptor," "lecturer," or "doctor," "archimandrite"; see Sanjian (cited n. 59), p. 457. Rycaut's strictures against the Jerusalem Patriarchate do not seem justified, for it had gained recognition some two centuries before the Ottoman conquest, see Avedis Sanjian, *The Armenian Communities in Syria under Ottoman Dominion*, Cambridge, 1965, pp. 95–101.

78. The supremacy of the established Catholicosates of Ējmiacin and Sis over Ottoman Armenians is bolstered with evidence from Başbakanlık Arşiv, Tapu Defter No. 387, reign of Suleyman, town of Kayseri. This document lists Armenian congregations *(cemaat-i Ermeniyan)* of Sis *(Sisyan)* and of the East *(Şarkiyan)*. Ronald Jennings who examined this text suggests that East may refer to Ējmiacin. He also suggests that, since theoretically all Armenians in the empire owed allegiance to their patriarch in Istanbul, these place names must refer to the home-town of the congregation rather than the see of their allegiance. I would argue that since Ottoman Armenians had little or no allegiance to the Istanbul "patriarch," the place names do refer to the see of their allegiance. See Jennings (cited n. 5), p. 30.

79. See above C. E. Bosworth, chapter 1, section 3, pp. 45–46 and A. S. Tritton, *The Caliphs and their Non-Muslim Subjects: A Critical Study of the Covenant of Umar*, p. 88, London, 1930.

The Rise of the
Armenian Patriarchate of Constantinople

KEVORK B. BARDAKJIAN

To the memory of Hayk Berbérian

In his remarkable *History of Armenia* published in 1784–1786, Mik'ayēl
Č'amč'ean thus described the founding of the Armenian Patriarchate of Constantinople:

> . . . Sultan Mēhēmmēt [II], while he was in Prusa [Brusa] earlier, was sym-
> pathetically disposed towards the Armenian nation and the local prelate,
> Bishop Yovakim [Joachim]. Once, as [the Sultan] conversed with him, the Pre-
> late wished that the Lord might make his kingdom the mightiest of all.
> [Thereupon], the Sultan [made a] promise and said: "If I succeed in capturing
> Constantinople, I shall take you there with the leading Armenians and shall
> make you their head." When, a few years after he had captured Constantinople
> and had established his kingdom there, the Sultan happened to go to Prusa, he
> remembered the promise he had made. He brought from [Brusa] to Constantino-
> ple Bishop Yovakim with a number of eminent Armenian families (some
> [sources] say six families), in the year 910 of the Armenian Era [1461]. [The
> Sultan] gave these families dwellings to some inside the city and to others in
> Łalat'ia [Galata], where already many Armenians resided. [The Sultan] also
> brought four Armenian families from Gałatia. [The Sultan] then, with a Royal
> letter, made Bishop Yovakim a prelate naming him *p'at'rik,* that is to say pat-
> riarch; and gave him absolute authority over the Armenians of Greece and
> Anatolia. The Patriarchate in Constantinople has continued to exist ever
> since. . .[1]

Č'amč'ean cited "colophons" and "histories" as his sources but failed to
identify them.[2] Mehmed II's *berat,* if there ever was one, has not survived.
With no authentic documents in existence, in the course of time Č'amč'ean's
statement came to be regarded as an authoritative account to which some
imaginative details were incorporated with little or no corroboration. As a
result, the prevalent view holds that, from the year of its inception, the
Armenian Patriarchate of Constantinople was a universal patriarchate for the

Armenians of the Ottoman Empire, whose authority automatically expanded with the Ottoman conquest of new territories. The establishment of the Armenian Patriarchate of Constantinople has also been seen as a manifestation of the so-called Ottoman *millet* system, the vaguely defined principles of which have been conveniently projected into the distant past. In fact there is no evidence to support either claim and origin of the Armenian Patriarchate of Constantinople is far from clear. The purpose of this article is to trace the rise of the Armenian Patriarchate of Constantinople by examining the extent of its jurisdiction and the nature of its power; and, by looking into some of the subsequent influences, its emergence as a more or less universal Armenian patriarchate. While the *millet* "system" as such is beyond its immediate scope, the findings of this article may also shed some light on the system and, perhaps, on some of the realities of the Greek and Jewish *millets*.

In a series of related articles, the late Hayk Berbérian was the first to question the conventional view concerning the establishment of the Armenian Patriarchate of Constantinople by investigating its earliest history in full detail.[3] Berbérian dismissed the traditional accounts of Mehmed II's friendship with Patriarch Yovakim as mere tales since, he claimed, Mehmed II had never been to Bursa before the fall of Constantinople.[4] Noting that no contemporary historian, Armenian or non-Armenian, recorded the birth of the Armenian Patriarchate of Constantinople and that neither Yovakim (supposedly the first "patriarch" from 1461 to 1478) nor his immediate successors bore the title "patriarch," Berbérian concluded that the rank, with "certain rights," was conferred on the Armenian religious leaders of Constantinople some time in the first half of the sixteenth century; more precisely, between 1526 and 1543, during the reigns of *marhasa* Grigor (1526–1537) and his successor Patriarch Astuacatur (1538–1543), the latter, in 1543, being the first priest ever to call himself the Armenian *patriarck'* of Constantinople.[5] Thus, finding no evidence in early sources and lending no credibility to later and anonymous accounts, Berbérian based his suggestion on the earliest claim to the title. He was aware that the word occurred at least once in an Armenian colophon written in 1480, according to which Mehmed II brought a certain Abraham of Trebizond and a Mat'ēos of Sebastea to Constantinople to install them as "patriarchs" but dismissed this evidence as insufficient to disprove his view.[6]

Berbérian's arguments are generally sound enough and one is tempted to agree with him. After all, the colophon in question may have been the result of a confusion or sheer ignorance and Č'amč'ean's reference to "p'at'rik" may have been his own contribution to the story. But the earliest use of the term "patriarch" can hardly be taken as a solid proof signifying the beginning of the Armenian Patriarchate of Constantinople and no attempt will be made here to date the first occurrence of this term since it was an honorary title. Č'amč'ean himself carefully distinguished between Yovakim's prelacy and his nominal "patriarchate."[7] In the seventeenth century the patriarchate was still recognized as an "honorary seat"[8] and its occupants as "prelates called patriarchs."[9] A close scrutiny of the jurisdiction and power of the patriarch will reinforce this view still further. But first a look at the roots of the patriarchate.

Gibb and Bowen have maintained that

> . . . the Ottoman Sultans did not introduce the *millet* system into their Empire only on the capture of Constantinople, but were already applying its principles to the non-Moslem communities under their rule.[10]

A similar view was expressed, much earlier, by an Armenian historian, Aršak Alpōyačean, who claimed that the Armenians were accorded the status of a religious community under the leadership of a religious head long before the capture of Constantinople.[11] Although Alpōyačean conceded that some "old" Armenian communities, such as Izmir, lay beyond the control of Constantinople, he nonetheless insisted that in 1461 Yovakim was made the "Patriarch of all Armenians of Turkey" (i.e., the Ottoman Empire), whose authority grew with the expansion of the empire.[12] Accordingly, Alpōyačean alleged, the Armenian communities of Bursa, Kütahya, Ankara, Karaman, Sivas, Trebizond and Crimea were all subordinate to the Armenian Patriarchate of Constantinople in Mehmed II's lifetime.[13] There is no proof to substantiate Alpōyačean's view; on the contrary, the evidence against his theory is overwhelming.

There are two colophons referring to Yovakim's position prior to the conquest of Constantinople. The first, written in 1438, recognized him as "Archbishop Yovakim of Constantinople."[14] Whatever the scribe meant by "Constantinople" (it is unlikely that the actual city of Constantinople, then still under Byzantine control, formed a part of this designation), Yovakim's jurisdiction was clearly confined to a limited area, as his title indicates. The second colophon provides some interesting details. It was written in 1447 "in the time of our brave chief-shepherd Sir Yovakim who today is the Bishop of the Province of Pu[r]sa and Constantinople . . ."[15] Needless to say, despite its somewhat unstable borders at the time, the Ottoman Empire certainly extended over a much larger area than Yovakim's domain consisting of Bursa and "Constantinople." Besides, there were other bishops who held independent positions within the community. Thus in 1441 the Armenians of Ankara were led by a bishop who recognized the authority of the Catholicosate of Sis.[16] Later, from c.1458 to 1464 a certain Nersēs was the independent prelate of Ankara.[17] Some time after 1447 but before 1459 Yovakim himself was no longer the bishop of Constantinople (he probably retained the prelacy of Bursa, whence he was shortly to be transferred to Constantinople) and a certain Martiros had replaced him by 1459.[18] The existence, then, of at least four bishops with uncertain territorial jurisdiction, strongly suggests that the Ottomans recognized the Armenian communities separately, an arrangement which was probably based on financial expediency and which remained in effect, it appears, long after Mehmed II's death. For just as Yovakim was made the prelate of Armenians from Bursa, so, almost a hundred and fifty years later, an Armenian bishop was made the head of all Armenians from Erzurum. This occured c.1608 when priests from Erzurum, disenchanted by the taxes imposed on them by the patriarch, decided to form an independent community. With the help of a certain Ěřamat [Ramazan], the *baltacılar kâhyası* ("lieutenant colonel of the corps of halberdiers," Redhouse), the priests obtained a *berat* from Sultan Ahmed proclaiming Bishop Grigor Daranak̇c'i (or Kamaxec'i) as the head of all Armenians of Erzurum who, having fled the Celali rebellions, were now scattered throughout western Asia Minor. With his seat in the Topkapi district of Istanbul, Daranak̇c'i ruled his compatriots for two years in total independence from the Patriarch of all Armenians![19] This arrangement, no matter how temporary, indicates the nonexistence of an Armenian patriarchate for the entire empire and simply suggests that the Armenian communities were recognized as independent groups, distinguished by geographic or administrative division. The case of Constantinople provides further evidence in favor of this suggestion.

Thus, it is significant that fifteenth century Armenian colophons written between 1462 and 1487 in Ankara, Amasya, Sivas, Trebizond and Kafa, make no reference to the Armenian Patriarchate of Constantinople as a higher authority.[20] More important still, colophons written between the sixteenth and eighteenth centuries all recognize the patriarch as the patriarch of "Constantinople," or "the City of Constantinople," or the 'Diocese of Constantinople," but never as the Patriarch of all Armenians, or the Armenians of the empire. The formal Ottoman designation, however, was even more precise; probably something like the Bishop of the *altı cemaat* (six congregations). For, originally, the Armenian community was defined as the "altı cemaat tâbir olunur Ermeni reâyası" (the Armenian subjects known as the six congregations).[21] The expression, found in a *berat* issued in 1764, undoubtedly represents the oldest form by which the community was identified. Found in the same *berat* are definitions such as "Istanbul ve tevabi-i Ermeni patrikliği" (the Armenian Patriarchate of Istanbul and its dependent districts) and "Istanbul ve perankende-i Rumeli ve Anadolu ve tevabi-i Ermeniyan patrikliği" (the Armenian Patriarchate of the scattered communities of Rumeli and Anatolia and Istanbul and its dependent districts),[22] which certainly reflect the gradual expansion of the patriarch's power, but which, it seems, never supplanted the old title. Indeed, as late as 1844, when a new patriarch was to be elected the Porte decreed that the *altı cemaat* elect their new head.[23] The expression *altı cemaat* also squares with some of Č'amčean's anonymous sources who maintained, it will be remembered, that Mehmed II brought six families with Yovakim.[24] The conclusion to be drawn is significant: if Yovakim was proclaimed as the "patriarch" of those transferred from Bursa and Ankara and of the local Armenian population, his "patriarchal" realm could not have gone beyond Stambul, Galata, and, possibly, Scutari.

The next piece of evidence we now turn to is the account of the seventeenth century Armenian historian Grigor Daranak̇c'i, the same priest who headed the Armenians of Erzurum at the turn of the seventeenth century. Daranak̇c'i, who was actively involved in communal affairs in Constantinople, related in 1612 that, having raised the *kabal* (wholesale taxes) jointly, the then Patriarch Zak'aria, a former patriarch, Yovhannēs, and Grigor Daranakc'i himself, divided the "entire country" (i.e., the Ottoman Empire) into three parts: Grigor Daranakc'i was given Rodosto and the Armenian communities that were "dispersed" *(perakende)* in Anatolia; Yovhannēs was given Rumeli with the exception of Rodosto; and Zak'aria, the patriarch, was given "Istanbul with the territories of the old *kabal* of the original *berat*."[25] A year later, in 1613, the three priests repartitioned the empire: this time Grigor Daranakc'i took Rumeli with Galata; Zak'aria, now a former patriarch, was given the "dispersed" Armenian communities of Anatolia "beyond Oskodar" [Üsküdar]; and Yovhannēs, who now was the patriarch, was given "Istanbul and the territories from Sivas to Kafa and [in addition?] K'ot'[ah?]ia."[26]

It emerges from these partitions that Rumeli and the Anatolian *perakende* "beyond Oskodar" and up to Sivas, did not form a part of the original "patriarchal" territories. Kafa could not have been given to the Armenian patriarch by the "original" *berat* of 1461. Trebizond was also highly unlikely to be included in the same *berat;* at any rate the colophons discussed above and other colophons written at the turn of the seventeenth century clearly indicate that Trebizond did not recognize the Armenian Patriarchate of Constantinople.[27] Sivas may have been annexed by Constantinople earlier, but the first formal appointment of a Sivas bishop by Constantinople occurs c.1695.[28] What remains corresponds to the territory inhabited by the *altı cemaat:* Stambul, Galata and, possibly, Scutari.

Daranakc'i's account also indicates, as do countless other sources, that Syria, Cilicia and Western Armenia proper where the bulk of the Armenian people lived were clearly outside of the jurisdiction of the three bishops who claimed to govern the entire Armenian population of the empire. These communities were under the jurisdiction of four religious centers: the Mother See of Ējmiacin, the Catholicosate of Sis, the Catholicosate of Ałt'amar and the Patriarchate of Jerusalem. Gibb and Bowen's assumption that after the incorporation of Ējmiacin in Ottoman dominions in 1514, "the affairs of the [Armenian] *millet* seem still to have been managed as they regard the government . . . by the Gregorian Patriarch of Istanbul" is unfounded.[29] Prior to 1726, the Catholicosate of Ējmiacin dealt with the Ottoman authorities directly,[30] and controlled Eastern and Western Armenia proper. The Catholicosate of Sis exercised its authority in Cilicia and a little beyond: Sis (Kozan), Adana, Zeytun (Süleymanlı), Yozgat, Gürün, Darende, Malatya, Marash, Aintap, Kilis, Aleppo, Antakya and Iskenderun. The Catholicosate of Ałt'amar supervised a few towns (e.g., Hizan) and numerous villages in the southern part of Lake Van. Subordinate to the Patriarchate of Jerusalem were Bethlehem, Jerusalem, Ramla, Jaffa, Beirut, Cyprus, Latakia, Damascus and, until the middle of the nineteenth century, Egypt.

Very little is known of the duties and rights of the early patriarchs of Constantinople. Armenian sources provide so little information concerning

details of taxation that it is not possible to define the patriarch's fiscal responsibilities with any certainty. Most probably, in the original domain of the
"Patriarchate," the *kabal* system was in practice from the outset as
Daranaļc'i's reference to the "old *kabal* of the original *berat*" would suggest,
while in the *perakende* communities, which came under Constantinople later
on, the prelates were responsible for the collection of taxes as Daranaļc'i has
vaguely hinted in his history.[31] Nor is there enough evidence for an approximate assessment of the patriarch's initial authority which must have been
insignificant. But, particularly from the seventeenth century onwards, the
patriarch's nominal jurisdiction began to grow considerably. It is evident
from Daranaļc'i's information that some time before the first partition in 1612,
the Armenian Patriarchate of Constantinople had expanded to include Rumeli
and the "Anatolian *perakende*," a region to the north, and including the
towns of Bursa, Kütahya, Ankara and Tokat. One can confidently assert that
this came about not by imperial edict but gradually, over a long period of
time. No doubt the patriarch, as one whose position according to tradition
was sanctioned by Mehmed II, in the course of time came to be regarded as
primus inter pares, a status which certainly contributed to his future reign
over the entire Armenian population of the empire. Ambitious successors to
Yovakim managed, it seems, to expand their limited jurisdiction by increasing
the amount of *kabal* they could raise. It must have been relatively even
simpler to bring under their control the few, small Armenian communities of
Rumeli and the Anatolian *perakende* first, where the authority of the traditional religious centers (Ējmiacin, Sis, Aļt'amar, Jerusalem) was either lax or
nonexistent. But wresting the traditional territories from these centers was
not so simple. A. Alpōyačean, despite his insistence on the idea of universal
patriarchate from the moment of its creation, did nevertheless admit that it
became a "real" patriarchate only after 1612 by annexing Armenian communities formerly under the control of these centers.[32] The process seems to
have begun later and progressed slowly in the seventeenth century; according
to Pétis de la Croix, in 1695, the Armenian patriarch's jurisdiction extended
from Rumeli to Tokat.[33] The seventeenth century, however, was essentially a
time of turbulence and uncertainty. As has been said, a number of priests
twice divided the patriarchate's territorial jurisdiction by mutual agreement;
in the 1620s a third partition took place, with a "patriarch" for Rumeli and
another for Anatolia;[34] later, laymen performed the patriarchal duties by assuming control over the patriarchate several times in the course of the century;[35] in 1664, with an edict from the Grand Vezir Fazil Ahmed Köprülü, a
former patriarch proclaimed himself Catholicos of all Armenians of the empire;[36] and thirty-four patriarchs, most of whom were corrupt, held office in a
little over half a century (1660–1715).

By contrast the eighteenth century was the most important formative period in the history of the patriarchate. The term of the celebrated patriarch
Yovhannēs Kolot (b. 1678, reigned 1715–1741) ushered in an unprecedented
era of stability and organization. In 1726, having had the new Catholicos of

Ejmiacin elected and consecrated in Constantinople, Kolot submitted the petition for his investiture in the name of the patriarchate—a daring coup which illustrates one of the ways in which Constantinople enhanced its authority; for, following this precedent, Ejmiacin had thereafter to deal with the Porte through the patriarchate.[37] At the same time the patriarchate continued to expand its authority vigorously at the expense of the other Armenian hierarchies, a process which continued well into the nineteenth, but was basically completed in the eighteenth, century.[38] Towards the end of the eighteenth century at least one scribe had ample reason to recognize it as the patriarchate of "all" Armenians.[39] Its prestige was no doubt enhanced when it assumed control over the "Assyrian" *millet,*[40] but its rise as a universal patriarchate was due to a number of other factors which had long since been at work.

As the community grew rapidly, especially from the sixteenth century onwards, some of its more prosperous members acquired influence with the Ottoman government and, consequently, in the community. The so-called Armenian *çelebi*s often used their influence in favor of their protégés in Constantinople or to promote the interests of the community.[41] The Armenian patriarchs of Jerusalem, for instance, who frequently traveled to the Ottoman capital to renew old *berats* or to obtain new ones overruling the governors' unfavorable decisions in the perennial disputes over the Holy Places, could do so only with the assistance of prominent Armenians. These influential individuals often helped obtain *berats* and *emirnames* for bishops and prelates of outlying Armenian communities—a practice which, it seems, had developed into a tradition by the end of the seventeenth century. This not only conferred prestige on the community of Constantinople and its leaders but also set important precedents, which paved the way for future *de facto* jurisdiction of Constantinople over the Armenians of the empire.

At least two additional factors contributed to the ever-growing authority of Constantinople. The first was the rivalry of Sis and Ejmiacin to gain control over the Patriarchate of Constantinople. Since 1441, when the seat of Supreme Catholicos of Armenia was moved from Sis to Ejmiacin, the latter had been expanding its territorial jurisdiction at the expense of the former, whose authority was being limited to Cilicia itself. Although Sis initially managed to control Constantinople, its precarious authority was seriously challenged in the sixteenth and seventeenth centuries and was eventually destroyed in the eighteenth century when bishops loyal to Ejmiacin assumed control of the Armenian Patriarchate of Constantinople.[42] The conflict over the financial management of Armenian churches in Constantinople, between "indigenous" Armenians, who staunchly supported Sis, and "newcomers," most of whom recognized the supremacy of Ejmiacin, considerably influenced the outcome of the dispute. The "newcomers" gradually outnumbered the "local" Armenians and their numerical superiority allied with greater political influence with the Ottoman government, enabled them, more often than not, to secure the election of their candidates as patriarchs. Their position was further strengthened owing to Catholic activities in Constantinople in the seventeenth century. The pro-Latin attitude of the supporters of Sis alarmed the more traditional sections of the community which now supported bishops from Armenia proper who were loyal to Ējmiacin and the doctrines of the Armenian Church.[43] Ējmiacin in its turn had long since recognized the growing significance of Constantinople; after 1726 the latter played an intermediary role between the Ottoman authorities and the Western Armenian dioceses (e.g., Izmir) controlled by Ējmiacin, which was now in hostile territory. Indeed, such was Constantinople's authority in the eighteenth century that it elected several catholicoi for the Supreme Seat of Ējmiacin.

The second factor was the modern Armenian Renaissance initiated by the Mekhitarist Congregation of Venice, founded in 1701. The Mekhitarist monks revived Armenian literature, language and history, set up an extensive network of schools and transmitted Western thought to their fellow countrymen in Armenia proper and elsewhere in the empire.[44] But Constantinople, not Venice, was eventually to assume the leadership of the Armenians of the empire. The individual efforts of Patriarch Yovhannēs Kolot marked the beginning of a cultural revival in Constantinople which, under the formative influence of the Mekhitarists, was to flourish in the nineteenth century. The renaissance wrought profound changes in the community, the most significant of which was perhaps the sense of unity it stirred among the Armenians. The patriarchate came to be regarded as the very symbol of this unity, thus assuming such recognition and authority as never before.

The patriarch's position was further strengthened when Ējmiacin, after submitting to Russian dominion in 1828, ceded the last Ottoman Armenian communities (Izmir, Baghdad) it controlled to Constantinople. Ējmiacin and Constantinople formally regulated their relationship in 1844 and agreed that Ējmiacin should suspend the dispatch of nuncios to Western Armenian communities;[45] that alms for Ējmiacin should be solicited and transferred to Ējmiacin by the patriarch; and that the distribution of Holy Chrism should also be made by the patriarch, as the "permanent nuncio" and representative of the Supreme Catholicos of all Armenians.[46] Within the Ottoman Empire the Catholicosates of Sis and Aḫt'amar and the Patriarchate of Jerusalem retained their local jurisdiction and autonomy but official business with the Porte was conducted via Constantinople. The so-called Armenian Constitution, promulgated in 1863, restricted the patriarch's power within the community but, for the first time, it formally recognized him as the sole representative of the entire Armenian population of the empire.

We may now conclude that, in governing the Armenian community, the Ottomans adopted a system which was already in effect when they arrived in the region:

> . . . the universal practice of the Roman and medieval empires to allow subject communities to retain their own laws and to apply them amongst themselves

under the general jurisdiction of some recognized authority who was responsible to the ruling power.[47]

To this system, which was applied to the Armenian communities individually, no changes were introduced until the nineteenth century; and, so long as the Armenians met their fiscal and political responsibilities adequately, the Ottomans made no attempt to interfere with the internal structure and organization of the community. Therefore, the transformation of the seat of Constantinople from a vicariate into an universal patriarchate was due not to an explicit, or conscious Ottoman policy, but to an evolutionary historical process.

Notes

1. Mik'ayēl Č'amč'ean, *Patmut'iwn Hayoc'* (History of the Armenians), Venice, 1786, vol. III, p. 500.

2. *Ibid.*

3. Cf. Hayk Pērpērean, 1) "Ōsmanean k'ani mě vaweragir Istanpuli hayoc' ekełec'inerēn omanc' masin" (Some Ottoman Documents Concerning Some of the Armenian Churches in Istanbul), *Handēs Amsōreay,* year 75, (1961), cols. 723–732; 2) "Istanpuli hay bnakč'ut'iwně k'ałak'in grawumēn minč'ew Fat'ih Mehmet B.i mahě" (The Armenian Population of Istanbul from the Conquest of Istanbul to the Death of Fatih Mehmed II), *Handēs Amsōreay,* year 76 (1962), cols. 213–227, 405–424; 3) "K. Polsoy hay patriark'ut'ean gawazanagirk'ě ěst Małak'ia dpir Čēvahirčeani" (The List of Succession of the Armenian Patriarchs of Constantinople according to Maghakia Jevahirjian), *Handēs Amsōreay,* year 77 (1963), cols. 325–340; 4) "Kostandnupolsoy hay patriark'neru errord antip c'uc'ak mě" (A Third Unpublished List of Succession of the Armenian Patriarchs of Constantinople), *Handēs Amsōreay,* year 78 (1964), cols. 1–6; 5) "K. Polsoy hay patriark'ut'ean himnarkut'iwně" (The Founding of the Armenian Patriarchate of Constantinople), *Handēs Amsōreay,* year 78 (1964), cols. 337–350, 498–510.

4. Hayk Pērpērean, "K. Polsoy hay patriark'ut'ean himnarkut'iwně" (The Founding of the Armenian Patriarchate of Constantinople), in *Handēs Amsōreay,* year 78 (1964), cols. 338–339. As is known, Armenian, Greek and Jewish traditional sources claim a close friendship between the leaders of these communities and Mehmed II. The earliest and the only evidence (besides Č'amč'ean's later account) suggested to substantiate the Armenian version of this tradition is found in the Hünernâme collection of Ottoman miniatures. In a miniature by Mehmed Bey (cf. *Hünernâme minyatürleri ve sanatçıları,* Istanbul, 1969, plate no. 28) depicting Mehmed II throwing the mace at the serpent pillar in the Hippodrome in Istanbul a figure, clad in what definitely seems to be the traditional attire of Armenian celibate priests, has been identified as Yovakim (cf. Hrant Papazian, *Églises Byzantines transférées aux Arméniens,* Istanbul, 1976, p. 8). Of course, it is not possible to verify the identity of this priest, but one can perhaps reasonably speculate that he represents Yovakim. However, one has to bear in mind that the miniature was painted in the 1580s, at least a hundred and twenty years after Yovakim's appointment in 1461. Furthermore, if the artist considered Mehmed II's acquaintance with Yovakim important enough to be represented in his work,

it is of little or no use to us in determining Yovakim's position or the real nature and extent of his authority over the Armenian community.

5. Pērpērean (cited n. 4), cols. 339–348. It should be noted here that Professor S. Shaw's remarks regarding the origins of the Armenian "millet" are uninformed and contradictory. After stating that the "Armenian Gregorians were given their separate status "during Selim I's Syrian campaign (Shaw, S., *History of the Ottoman Empire and Modern Turkey,* New York, 1976, vol. I, p. 84), Professor S. Shaw reversed his view elsewhere in his *History* (*ibid.*, p. 152) by accepting the traditional date of 1461.

6. Pērpērean (cited n. 4), vol. 10–12 (1964), col. 501.

7. Č'amč'ean (cited n. 1), vol. III, p. 500.

8. [Grigor Daranalc'i], *Žamanakagrut'iwn Grigor Vardapeti Kamaxec'woy kam Daranalc-'woy* (The Chronicle of Grigor of Kamakh), Jerusalem, 1915, p. 176.

9. [Aŕak'el Dawrižec'i], *Patmut'iwn Aŕak'el Vardapeti Dawrižec'woy* (History, by Arakel of Tabriz), 3rd edn., Vaļaršapat, 1896, p. 335.

10. H. A. R. Gibb, and Harold Bowen, *Islamic Society and the West,* Oxford, 1957, vol. I, part II, p. 214.

11. Aršak Alpōyačean, "K. Polsoy patriark'ut'iwnn u Prusayi, Ētirnēi ew Rotost'oyi aŕajnor-dut'iwnnerĕ" (The Patriarchate of Constantinople and the Prelacies of Bursa, Edirne and Rodosto) in T'ēodik, *Amenun tarec'oyc'ĕ,* Constantinople, 1909, p. 209.

12. Aršak Alpōyačean, "Aŕajnordakan vičakner" (Dioceses [of the Armenian Church]), in *Ēndarjak ōrac'oyc' S. P'rkč'ean hiwandanoc'i hayoc',* Constantinople, 1908, p. 291.

13. Ibid. Basing his argument on a colophon written in Philippopolis (Plovdiv) in 1469 (see Babgēn [Kiwlēsērean], *C'uc'ak jeŕagrac' Ļalat'ioy Azgayin matenadarani hayoc'* (A Catalogue of Manuscripts in the Armenian Library of Galata), Antelias, 1961, col. 126, where a Bishop Yovakim has been mentioned, Alpōyačean suggested that the Armenians of the European part of the empire were also subordinate to Constantinople (cf. Alpōyačean, Aršak, cited n. 11, p. 210). As is known, apart from contemporary political events, Armenian scribes also recorded, almost invariably, the names of local religious leaders and the superior Armenian hierarchy to which the local prelate was subordinate. The colophon in question mentions the Catholicos of Ējmiacin and a Bishop Yovakim but does not mention the religious head of the Armenians of Plovdiv, nor does it specify Bishop Yovakim's position or his relation to Philippopolis. What seems to have happened was that in the absence of a local religious leader for the once prosperous Armenian community of Philippopolis, the scribe referred to the Supreme Catholicosate of Ējmiacin and the closest prelate to the East who in the event happened to be Bishop Yovakim (of Constantinople?).

14. *Handēs Amsōreay,* year 38 (1924), cols. 435–436.

15. Xač'ikayan, L. S. (ed.), *ŽE dari hayeren jeŕagreri hišatakaranner* (Colophons of Fifteenth Century Armenian Manuscripts), part III, Erevan, 1967, pp. 409–410.

16. Ibid., p. 398.

17. Ibid., part II, Erevan, 1958, p. 216.

18. Ibid., p. 115.

19. Grigor Daranalc'i (cited n. 8), pp. 127–129.

20. Xač'ikayan (cited n. 15), part II, Erevan, 1958, pp. 51, 228, 265, 278, 389, 433; part III, Erevan, 1968, pp. 69, 75, 99, 253, 268, 398, 447–448.

21. Awetis Pērpērean, *Patmut'iwn Hayoc'* (History of the Armenians), Constantinople, 1871, p. 228.

22. Ibid., pp. 227, 228.

23. Aršak Alpōyačean, "Azgayin Sahmanadrut'iwnĕ, ir cagumĕ ew kiraŕut'iwnĕ" (The Armenian Constitution: its Origin and Implementation), in *Ēndarjak ōrac'oyc' S. P'rkč'ean hiwandanoc'i hayoc'.* Constantinople, 1910, p. 201.

24. Mik'ayēl Č'amč'ean (cited n. 1), vol. III, p. 500.

25. Grigor Daranałc'i (cited n. 8), p. 180.

26. *Ibid.*, pp. 181–182.

27. V. Hakobyan and A. Hovhannisyan (eds.) *Hayeren jeŕagreri ŽĒ dari hišatakaranner* (Colophons of Seventeenth Century Armenian Manuscripts), Erevan, 1974, part I, pp. 293, 428.

28. Yovhannēs Sebastac'i, *Patmut'iwn Sebastioy* (A History of Sivas), Erevan, 1974, p. 76.

29. Gibb and Bowen, (cited n. 10), pp. 226–227.

30. Babgēn Kiwlēsērean, *Kolot Yovhannēs Patriark'* (Patriarch Kolot Yovhannēs), Vienna, 1904, p. 64.

31. Grigor Daranałc'i (cited n. 8), p. 180. As a commercial term, *perakende* also means "retail" (*New Redhouse Turkish-English Dictionary*, Istanbul, 1968, *s.v.*). Although I have rendered the word as "dispersed" (to indicate the separate status of these prelacies and their dispersion in geographical terms as opposed to the territorial unity of the Patriarchate of Constantinople), Daranałc'i almost certainly used the word in its commercial sense. This is an additional indication that the *perakende* initially was not a part of the original domain of the Patriarchate of Constantinople, which paid its taxes wholesale *(kabal),* and that it was incorporated piecemeal into the patriarchate in the course of time.

32. Alpōyačean (cited n. 23), p. 90.

33. Pétis de la Croix, *La Turquie Crétienne*, Paris, 1695, p. 240.

34. Grigor Daranałc'i (cited n. 8), p. 192.

35. In 1641–1650, 1655–1657 and 1657–1659 (cf. Alpōyačean [cited n. 23], p. 110).

36. Małak'ia Ōrmanean, *Azgapatum* (History of the Armenian Church and the Armenians), Constantinople, 1914, part II, col. 2553.

37. Kiwlēsērean (cited n. 30), pp. 64–65.

38. For a detailed description and lists of dioceses and sees absorbed by Constantinople see Alpōyačean (cited n. 12), pp. 289–323.

39. Norayr Połarean, *Mayr c'uc'ak jeŕagrac' Srboc' Yakobeanc'* (A Grand Catalogue of the Manuscripts of St. James Armenian Monastery), Jerusalem, 1972, volume VI, p. 107.

40. On 6 August, 1783, on their own request, the "nation of the Assyrians fell under our [the Armenian Patriarchate of Constantinople] authority" (cf. *Diwan hayoc' patmut'ean* (Archives of Armenian History), vol. X, Tiflis, 1912, pp. 227–228.

41. There are as yet no detailed studies of the Armenian *çelebis*. According to H. S. Anasyan, *XVII dari azatagrakan šarżumnern Arevmtyan Hayastanum* (The Seventeenth Century Liberation Movements in Western Armenia), Erevan, 1961, pp. 58–70, the *çelebis* were mainly moneylenders who operated in Constantinople, as opposed to the Armenian *hocas* who were active in the provinces and were involved in international trade.

42. For a more detailed account, see Alpōyačean (cited n. 23), pp. 102–125.

43. Ibid., p. 119. The Catholicosate of Sis had maintained close ties with Rome during the Crusades.

44. Kevork Bardakjian, *The Mekhitarist Contributions to Armenian Culture and Scholarship*, Harvard College Library, Cambridge, Mass., 1976, pp. 8–18.

45. *Nuirak* in Armenian ("nuncio; deputy", according to M. Bedrossian, *New Dictionary Armenian-English*, Venice, 1875–1879). As personal representatives of the Catholicos, nuncios were assigned to Armenian sees and dioceses usually for a term of three years. A nuncio distributed the Holy Chrism solicited gifts for Ējmiacin and provided spiritual guidance to the community. Also a nuncio acted as an intermediary in local communal conflicts thereby attaining moral and, often, actual power.

46. Alpōyačean (cited n. 12), pp. 270–271. In fact since the war of 1828 Ējmiacin had stopped

the sending of nuncios. With Ējmiacin now under Russian control, the relationship between the Catholicosate and the Patriarchate of Istanbul was affected more than ever before by the traditional antagonism between the two empires and by the opposition of the Western Armenians to *Polozhenie* ("Statute") promulgated in 1836, to regulate the affairs of the Armenian Church in Russia.

47.   Gibb and Bowen (cited n. 10), p. 212.

The Leadership of the Ottoman Jews in the Fifteenth and Sixteenth Centuries

MARK A. EPSTEIN

During the fifteenth and sixteenth centuries there were two types of leadership in the Ottoman Jewish community: traditional leadership as exercised by rabbis of the community and accidental leadership by laymen in the community who were influential in politics and economic affairs. The first type can be divided into two kinds: the leadership of the chief rabbi at Istanbul and the leadership of local rabbis in other communities; the second type is that of prominent physicians, financiers, and politicians. This paper will deal with these three forms of leadership: the central rabbinate, local rabbinates, and that of influential laymen, explaining how each emerged and developed and the ways in which they changed during the period of this study.

The idea of communal independence for religious minorities did not originate with the Ottomans, or even with Islam, though what came to be known in literature and popular usage as the "*millet* system" was one of the largest and most highly developed forms of sectarian self-rule. Such a system was not new for the Jews; they had controlled their internal affairs previously in Christian Europe and in the Islamic world as well. The theoretical bases for rule by rabbis in authority derived from communal consent are to be found in the Talmud.[1]

It remains unclear exactly what were the sources and inspiration from which the Ottomans drew their Jewish policies,[2] and we have little to guide us in determining what factors were at play. Jewish communities existed in the larger Anatolian emirates during the period of the expanding Ottoman frontier state, as well as in the Byzantine Balkans and in the Slavic states. Under the Byzantines, at least as late as the twelfth century, Jewish communities were led by rabbis who were recognized as leaders of their communities by the authorities both in the capital and in smaller towns.[3] It appears that the Ottomans adopted similar policies, at least in their capital cities. The Jews of

Bursa had a quarter of their own, implying a certain measure of autonomy in day-to-day affairs, and they were given access to health and other facilities provided by the Muslim community.[4] With the transfer of most court life to Edirne, a second foundation stone of Ottoman Jewish policy was laid. Presumably as a result of satisfaction in court circles with the role played by Jews in Ottoman life, Jews from Bursa were transferred to the new capital where they were probably assigned a part in the development of the new administrative center. In addition, Jews from non-Ottoman territories in the Balkans, attracted by the intellectual life and economic opportunity in the Ottoman capital, migrated there and joined the existing community which included both the previous Rabbanite and Karaite communities and the more recent arrivals from Bursa.

Already at Edirne the various factions within the Jewish community had rabbis of their own who served as both spiritual and political heads of their congregations. While there is little firm evidence regarding the exact nature of the relationship between these functionaries and the government, it is evident that serving the rabbis was a cadre of officials who acted as administrators for the community. In a sense these officeholders, as well as the rabbis, represented the government because they relieved government officials of responsibility for Jewish affairs. These Jewish officials performed functions which in the Muslim community were fulfilled by the governmental and religious bureaucracies, i.e., the assessment and collection of taxes and the provision of police and court systems to serve their communities. It is in this period that we first encounter Jews with names such as *Subaşı* (captain) and *Başyazıcı* (head scribe), as well as the family name *Beği* (bey).

The foremost official in the Edirne community was Rabbi Isaac Tsarfati. He was the leading rabbi in the city and was the author of an important letter which tells us something of the situation of Edirne Jewry. Tsarfati himself was from Christian Europe and supposedly wrote his letter at the behest of two recent arrivals from there who, upon seeing the prosperity and freedom of the Ottoman Jews, prevailed upon him to write their European coreligionists apprising them of the situation and urging them to migrate. This remarkable letter advised its recipients not only of the pleasant conditions in the Ottoman domains, but described as well the ease of travel to Palestine and the Holy Places, an attraction to those who would make a pilgrimage or choose to be buried there. This appeal was apparently sent in the 1430s.[5]

It is unlikely that such a letter could be sent without the explicit or implicit approval of the Ottoman authorities. Not only was Tsarfati the preeminent rabbi of the capital, but, like other members of the community, he must have had some notion of Ottoman attitudes. In light of the manner in which the Ottomans settled and welcomed Jews in Edirne, the author of this appeal must have been secure in the knowledge that the authorities would be pleased at such a call for Jewish immigrants and would welcome all newcomers. We can safely presume, then, that in the second quarter of the fifteenth century the Jews of Edirne were a community whose contribution to the city and the empire was valued by the authorities, and who felt confident enough in their situation to invite others to join them. They developed a system of self-administration sufficient for their needs, based on the authority of their own leaders and acknowledged by the government.

The conquest of Byzantium by the Ottomans in 1453 is a watershed not only in Ottoman history but, not surprisingly, in the history of the Ottoman Jews as well. In the first years after the capture of the city the Ottomans embarked on a well-known campaign to repopulate the city and to make Istanbul a truly great capital. Among the groups brought to help resettle the city and guide it along this ambitious path were most of the Jews living in Balkan towns under Ottoman rule, and some from Anatolia as well. Jews from more than forty towns, including the majority of the Jews of Edirne, were sent to the new capital. By comparing the list of Jews living in pre-1492 Istanbul[6] with the entries in the cadastral surveys *(tahrîr defterleri)* of the various towns and provinces from which they came, it appears that the Otto-man Balkans were virtually devoid of Jews within two or three years of the conquest of Istanbul. Only a few remnants of the previous communities must have remained. No matter how we assess the ultimate wisdom of the decision to concentrate so many merchants and artisans in the capital at the expense of the provinces, this policy, similar to that by which the Jews of Bursa were transferred to Edirne, necessitated the creation of some system of administra-tion for this community, comprised mostly of newcomers.

Drawing, apparently, on their own previous experience at Edirne and the practice of the Byzantines before them, the Ottomans continued to allow the Jews considerable internal autonomy, and Rabbi Moses Capsali, who had been head of the community under the Byzantines, emerged as the political and spiritual head of the community. It is unclear, however, exactly how much power he actually had, what communities fell under his jurisdiction, and what was his relationship with the Ottoman authorities.

In the period of Capsali's rabbinate a special tax was levied on the Jewish community as a payment for the privilege of having an independent adminis-tration with a rabbi at its head. During Capsali's tenure, or at least late in that period, the tax was recorded as the *"cizye-i râv,"* and Capsali himself was responsible for making the payment, rather than some lesser functionary concerned solely with fiscal affairs. The actual transmission of the money was carried out by a regular governmental messenger-paymaster *(havale)*.[7]

At the time of his appointment, according to the traditional account, Cap-sali was called into the presence of Sultan Mehmet, and the sultan called him *hoca*,[8] and honored him with clothes of gold and silver.This is entirely in keeping with the practice of honoring dignitaries, including non-Muslims and nonsubjects, with robes of honor *(hil^cat)*. Also, it is reported that judicial matters dealing with Jews were sometimes referred to the chief rabbi.[9] On the other hand, the exaggerated claims regarding his power, his role, and the assertion that he occupied a place in the divan and even had precedence over the *Şeyh ül-İslâm* must be viewed with extreme caution, and probably rejected.[10] What does emerge, however, is a picture of a respected functionary who, in the course of nearly forty years in office, must have been called more than once into the presence of the sultan, and on at least one occasion was honored by him, and who, like many other dignitaries, appeared at court on certain ceremonial occasions.

Some controversy has surrounded the question of which communities fell under Capsali's jurisdiction. Within Istanbul, the Karaite community was, insofar as the Ottoman authorities were concerned, granted fiscal independence and, apparently, was able to deal with the authorities through its own functionaries. In the same place where the *cizye-i râv* of Capsali was recorded there is an entry for a payment by the *kethüdâ* (steward, warden) of the Karaites.[11] The prominence of the Karaite community of Edirne before 1453, and their settlement in Istanbul in a quarter named for them suggests that this independence was a carry-over from privileges enjoyed at Edirne. In Istanbul, however, they constituted a small part of the Jewish population, and Capsali's power and influence must have, for this if for no other reason, greatly outweighed that of the Karaites.

Besides the question of the Karaites, the issue of whether Capsali was chief rabbi of Istanbul only or of the entire Ottoman Empire has been the subject of discussion. It is generally held that the office of chief rabbi, as it was known under him and his immediate successor, ceased to exist after the early sixteenth century (see below) and that the various local rabbinic authorities outside Istanbul, who sometimes referred legal questions to the rabbis of Istanbul, were not bound to obey them. However, in light of the evidence that nearly all the Jews in Ottoman territory were settled in Istanbul after 1453, and keeping in mind the Ottoman drive to create a nucleus for the empire in the new capital, no figure in the Jewish community could compare in influence or power with the rabbi of Istanbul in the period of the Conqueror. In addition, there is a text in KK 2411 which reads:

> *dâde mûsâ veled-i 'ilyâ ᶜ cizye-i râv ve metrôpôlîd-i yâhûdîyân-i 'istânbûli 25 R sene-i 885*[12]
> Paid by Moses b. Elijah for the tax on Rabbi and Metropolitan of the Jews of Istanbul the 25th Rebiülahir 885 (= 4 July 1480).

This text raises the question of what "metropolitan" means in the Jewish context. Because there is no hierarchy in Judaism, the term had to be borrowed from Greek usage, though it could have been applied by the Byzantines to the rabbi before 1453. It seems unlikely, though, that the Byzantine authorities, either secular or religious, would consent to honoring a Jew with a title equal to that of a high member of their own clergy. It is more likely that this title demonstrated the status of the Jewish leader in post-1453 Ottoman society. It is unclear whether the phrase *"râv ve metrôpôlîd"* refers to one person or two.[13] What is clear, however, is that the rabbi of Istanbul was recognized by the Ottoman government as the unqualified leader of the Ottoman Jewish community.

Under Capsali the office of chief rabbi reached the pinnacle of its power. As chief legal officer of the community he was granted a bodyguard or small police force which he apparently used to reinforce his own position as well as to administer the affairs of the community. In the exercise of these powers he became involved in controversies both within the Jewish community of Istanbul and with communities abroad, though the limits of his power must have been reasonably clearly defined. For example, a story in the *Seder Eliyahu Zuta* suggests that when Capsali intended to punish some individuals for homosexual activity in which Janissaries were implicated, he could proceed only with the permission of the sultan. In spite of this sanction he is said to have earned the enmity of the Janissaries for his decision, and, the same source reports, during the Janissary uprising after the death of Sultan Mehmet II, the Janissaries made an attempt on Capsali's life.[14]

Another factor which contributed to the remarkable position of the office of chief rabbi in the late fifteenth century was the extremely long tenure of its first occupant. Presuming that Capsali was, as the traditional accounts imply, appointed shortly after the Ottoman conquest of Istanbul, he occupied the position for nearly forty years, well into the reign of Bayezid II. Thus Capsali represents the first type of leadership in Istanbul, as outlined at the beginning of this paper. He was the chief rabbi of the capital and led with the consent of the community and the recognition of the authorities. Toward the end of his tenure, however, the whole structure of the Ottoman Jewish community changed, and with it the chief rabbinate.

The expulsion of the Jews from Spain at the end of the Catholic reconquista in 1492 is a benchmark in Jewish history, and one which had a profound effect on the Ottoman Empire. Many of the exiles from Spain reached Ottoman territory, where they were allowed to settle on favorable terms. There is no indication whether Capsali played any role in persuading Bayezid to allow Jewish settlement, and perhaps Bayezid needed no persuasion. A famous passage in the *Seder Eliyahu Zuta* states that the king of Spain was considered in Istanbul court circles to be a great fool for having enriched an enemy with productive citizens at the expense of his own kingdom.[15] While the statement is often attributed incorrectly to Bayezid himself, it is probably an accurate reflection of the views then current in the Ottoman capital. In the forty years since the conquest of Istanbul the Jews had played an important role in the development of the city, especially of its commerce. Not only did they occupy and run various shops in and around the major markets,[16] they also settled in many quarters near docks and other entrances to the city and played a considerable role in the processing and assessment of goods passing through the customshouses. At times they controlled as well the customshouses in Gallipoli, a major port for incoming goods.[17] Not the least of their important functions was the supervision of mints. It must have been clear that, whatever his conservative religious feelings may have prompted Bayezid to believe about the Jews in general, the Jews of Istanbul had been so important and useful that the arrival of equal their number and more from Spain, either directly or after stops elsewhere, must have seemed a considerable bounty.

Capsali personally was extremely active in the absorption of the new arrivals. While some arrived with funds, others did not. The problems of providing food and shelter, no matter what funds were available, were imposed on his office. During these, for the Jews at least, tumultuous years of the early 1490s, Capsali died and was succeeded in office by Rabbi Elijah Mizrahi, who had been Capsali's assistant in many matters, despite his occasional disputes with the chief rabbi.

Although at the time of his accession to office Mizrahi apparently was appointed under terms similar to those under which Capsali had served, the actual functions of the chief rabbi changed. Within a year or two of his selection, or perhaps even at the time of the actual decision, Mizrahi agreed that he would not play an active role in the fiscal affirs of the community and that he would not carry out the duties related to taxation. By his own account, Mizrahi agreed not to participate in these activities because others had greater prestige at court, and could therefore deal with these affairs more effectively. In addition, Mizrahi is described as being a less forceful personality than his predecessor, and his life was made difficult by personal and financial problems.[18] We also recall that this was the first selection by the Jewish community of a chief rabbi since before 1453, and the drastic changes in the structure of the community and the growth of the power and status of the position must have made clear the need both to cater to the wishes of new elements in the community and, perhaps, to limit the amount of power in the hands of a single individual.

The bifurcation of the secular and religious administrative functions entirely changed the nature of the office of rabbi of Istanbul. While the spiritual leadership of the community was in the hands of Mizrahi, the fiscal and administrative leadership fell to one Rabbi Shealtiel, in the Ottoman documents Salto (Salti in popular Spanish pronunciation) a member of the Sephardic community. He kept the records of the Jewish community, and submitted them to the government for audit and final acceptance. His records include not only the funds paid by the community for their right to maintain an independent rabbinate, for the poll tax, and so forth, but he also submitted reports on the status of incomes and payments of Jewish tax farmers in government service.[19] Clearly, then, this man became the chief source of contact between the central government and the Jewish community as a whole. Due to his position and political connections he became one of the most powerful individuals in the community. The whole Ottoman-Jewish administrative relationship revolved around him, and from his time in office on, the power of the chief rabbi of the city was of far less importance in the eyes of the Ottoman authorities.

Shealtiel's tenure was not without its difficulties. While traditional sources suggest that he was appointed to relieve the rabbi of great burdens and to protect members of the community in their dealings with the authorities and with other groups in Ottoman society, in fact the *kethüdâ*'s own interests and those of his associates often came first. Whether or not he was selected for the job because of his good relations with the government, it was the government which received his primary loyalty. Next came his loyalty to his own welfare, which seems to have been a hallmark of the man's career. A petition to the sultan has survived in which at least one individual complains of irregularities in the disposition of an inheritance, and apparently the *kethüdâ* had a role to play in such affairs as well. The claimant stressed that the whole community was aware of Shealtiel's highhandedness, but that all were afraid to testify or complain against him.[20] Toward the end of Selim I's reign the situation must have become unbearable, as the community, under the leadership of Chief Rabbi Mizrahi, excommunicated Shealtiel and prohibited either him or his sons from carrying out functions having to do with the leadership of the community. He was, however, reinstated at the insistence of the government, with the stipulation that in the future he consult the leaders of the community more fully.[21]

By that time, in spite of the pressure brought to bear by the community, it must have been clear to all that real political power did not rest in the hands of the rabbi of Istanbul and the elected leaders of the congregations. For this reason and others which will be explained more fully below, Mizrahi's successors held a position with considerably less power and status than that which he had inherited from Capsali. When Mizrahi died, in 1526, there was serious debate over the choice of a successor. According to the standard sources, the old congregations and the Iberian Jews, by now an influential force in the community, could not agree on a candidate to succeed Mizrahi. The government grew impatient and declared that the position would simply remain vacant, though, it is pointed out, the assessment of the Rabbi's Tax continued to be collected.[22] Another explanation seems more likely. The power of the chief rabbi, as judge and judicial administrator, was derived from the consent of the community; therefore a candidate opposed by any substantial segment of the population would have difficulties in performing the duties of office. At the same time, the weakening of the office meant that, in light of the growing power of the Sephardic community, the position of the chief rabbi was one of the last trappings of power remaining to the old communities, but of far less significance to the newcomers. In light of what we know of the career of Shealtiel (and so far no information has come to light confirming the date he vacated his office), we can understand that the government was little concerned over who performed these legal functions so long as the work was done. The title or honors allotted to the spiritual head of the Jews were of no importance so long as taxes were paid and the needs of the community fulfilled. This interpretation is supported by an account book listing the payment for Rabbi's Tax late in the sixteenth century where, unlike the entry for the fifteenth century (cited above), we now read:

ᶜan tahvîl-i metrôpôlîd râv-i yâhûdîyân-i istânbûl[23]
(received) toward the account of the Metropolitan for the Rabbinate of the Jews of Istanbul.

This suggests first of all that apparently a century before, but certainly at this time, there was in the Jewish community a functionary known to the Ottoman authorities as metropolitan, i.e., spiritual head for the city, a position equal to that of a Greek bishop, but a rank not equal to that of patriarch, the prime Greek cleric for the whole empire. It also stands witness to the death of the institution of chief rabbinate of the empire, which was indeed the function of the rabbi of Istanbul in the second half of the fifteenth century, thus laying to rest a fiction regarding the power and status of the second chief rabbi. While certain rabbis continued to be appointed as spiritual leaders of Istanbul, albeit with lower rank than Capsali and Mizrahi enjoyed, this marked the *de jure* death of the chief rabbinate of the empire and acknowledged the realities of the situation since the beginning of Mizrahi's tenure. In Istanbul lay leaders had emerged as the prime movers in the community. As we shall see, the situation in the provinces changed as well.

The emergence of provincial Jewish communities and a leadership system in the provincial towns gained momentum in the years after the arrival of the exiles from Spain. The Iberian immigrants, though some had been stripped of their wealth, not only brought their abilities but also a knowledge of Europe and its ways, a knowledge which formed the underpinnings of their cultural life and values well beyond the early years after their arrival. Many were nominal Catholics, and while a large number returned openly to Judaism under the protection of the Islamic state, they brought a way of life which made them a source of difficulty to the Jewish religious authorities. Many of the leaders of the Spanish community were contemptuous of even their own spiritual leaders.[24] In light of these facts we must consider the quarter century in which the Iberian communities established themselves in the Ottoman Empire.

The roots of Bayezid's policy regarding Jewish immigration remain somewhat obscure, but clearly he encouraged the immigration of Jews and their settlement throughout the empire. Many were given official orders which specified the terms under which they might settle in various places.[25] From the few orders which survive, as well as from appeals in which the communities cited the terms of these privileges as the basis for their petitions to the central government, we are able to gain some idea of the conditions under which they settled. They were, depending on the circumstances and the place of settlement, exempted from various taxes, though poll tax *(cizye)* was always charged, whether assessed individually or as a group *(maktuᶜ)*. In many places a tax like the *cizye-i râv* of Istanbul was also charged, though its name was often slightly different: in Salonica *akçe-i-râv*,[26] and later *flôrî-i râv;*[27] at Serres *rüsûm-i râv*,[28] and also *ᶜadet-i-râv*.[29] What is clear, however, is that in each town of any consequence some political system parallel to that in Istanbul was established by which the Jews, governing themselves as an independent community, paid for the privilege of having their own leaders.

The most remarkable system of Jewish self-rule in the provinces was established at Salonica. The Jewish community of that city, which by the early years of Kanuni Süleyman's reign was more than half Jewish, rivaled the Istanbul community in its importance. There, due to the large number of Jews and to the assent of the Ottoman authorities, arose a system of self-rule which even included an element of extraterritoriality. The Spanish and Portuguese Jews, along with smaller groups of Italian and Ashkenazi Jews, forged for themselves a highly developed system in which the congregations, numbering between twenty and twenty-six, were each represented in a municipal Jewish council. Salonica Jews, under the leadership of the council, were granted various tax and customs concessions in exchange for payment of tribute, similar to the practice of Ragusa and certain European powers. This is described in the statutes *(Kânûnnâme)* of Salonica:

> . . . *ve nefs-i Selânîkte ki dâhî güzâr 'ôlâ ve cumhûr-i cemâ'atîle içinde sâkinîn 'ôlsa . . .*[30]
> . . . and for those who reside in the city of Salonica with the mass of the congregations and pay an additional amount . . .[31]

Rabbi Moses Almosnino, who was chosen to lead a delegation to Istanbul in the 1560s in order to obtain confirmation of these privileges, reflects the link of the Iberian Jews with European thought and statecraft when he explains his mission in the following terms:

> . . . *y esta es la causa de mi venida por eleccion de la Republica . . .*[32]
> . . . and that is the reason for my coming to be selected by the Republic. . . .

This choice of language suggests not only the representative nature of the Jewish communal leadership, but also a high level of political sophistication recognized and respected by the community.

The council and the Jewish courts were jealous of their power and had the cooperation of the authorities in protecting their position. One prominent businessman, whose activities included the collective payment of taxes in kind on behalf of the community, incurred the enmity of the council by complaining to the Muslim courts. Noting that he had "cut his relations in that administration," i.e., that he was, or was about to be, excommunicated by the Jewish authorities, the goverment ordered that he be forcibly settled *(sürgün)* in Cyprus.[33]

Clearly the exceptional nature of the Salonica Jewish community was the primary factor in shaping its administrative system. In other towns as well local institutions were developed. In these, however, Jews were a minority of the population and their influence on the towns was correspondingly less important than in Salonica. Certainly, the local congregation or *mahalle* was not comparable in magnificence to the highly sophisticated community of Salonica. The principle, however, was similar. In the census surveys *(tahrîr defterleri)* the head of the community or its chief administrative officer is often noted. In addition to rabbis and teachers we encounter entries for *kethüdâ*,[34] (warden, steward); *nâ'ib*,[35] (deputy); *yayabaşı*,[36] (head of a regiment, usually a military term); *yüz başı*,[37] (captain, also a borrowing from military terminology); and in some cases simply *ser-i mezkûrîn*,[38] (head of the above mentioned). Some of these terms are found in the Ottoman crafts guilds as well as in military usage. In some communities no officer is indicated, but the large number of legal questions forwarded to Salonica and Istanbul by rabbis from smaller towns suggests that, in so far as they had the knowledge and expertise, local rabbis made most of the decisions, and the members of the congregations were active in governing the affairs of the communities.

In the course of the sixteenth century, then, we are witnessing the rise of new, mostly immigrant communities established in towns which were, between the 1450s and the end of the century, virtually devoid of Jews. In some places, such as the Morea, which were not Ottoman territory in 1453, the old communities survived but in the period of Iberian migration were soon outnumbered by the newcomers. In all these places local rabbis or teachers led the Jewish communities, operating in accordance with agreements drawn up by the communities themselves *(haskamot)* and turning to Jewish religious authorities in the largest communities when they needed guidance on particularly difficult problems. For the most part, though, local affairs were the realm of local leaders.

At the same time as these new communities grew and flourished, community leaders emerged who were not part of the rabbinic establishment. Physicians, financiers, and others, by virtue of their position or contacts in government and court circles, were in a position to represent the interests and wishes of the Jewish community to the government. This is not to suggest that they always consented to plead the case of the Jewish community, but certainly the community often approached them with requests for help.

The first Jewish physician who attracts our attention is Hekim Yakub (Jacopo of Gaeta) who, as court physician, was in the unique position of being able to gain intimate access to the sultan and, by the very nature of his work, needed the full trust of his employer. In addition, his European education and knowledge of languages placed him in the forefront of useful advisors. Yakub was already in Ottoman service before 1453 and after the establishment of the Ottomans in the new capital must have risen to great prominence; there was even a quarter of Istanbul which bore his name, *Hekim Yakub Mahallesi*.[39] In addition, he served in capacities other than medical ones, as *defterdâr*, and was raised to the rank of *vezir*.[40] It is difficult to tell, however, just how active he was on behalf of the Jewish community. Ottoman sources comment with disapproval that he brought Jews into the administration,[41] but it appears that later in his career he converted to Islam. His *Vakfiyyeh* gives us some idea that he was a greatly valued member of the highest court circles, as the list of witnesses to the establishment of the *vakif* and his conversion to Islam included former and future Grand Vezirs, Mesih Paşa, İshak Paşa, the *nişancı*

Sinan Çelebi, and so forth.[42] Apparently, Hekim Yakub was first and foremost an Ottoman, but it clearly did not escape notice that he was, at least by birth and well into his career, a Jew. While he may not have been an active advocate for the Jewish community, in official Ottoman eyes he was certainly an example of a valuable citizen who emerged from the ranks of the Jewish community and who, in the end apparently, even perceived the truth of the Islamic revelation. His example serves as an important precedent, an Ottoman Jewish success story.

Other physicians, many of them from Spain, served in court. No doubt the success and loyal service of their Jewish predecessors made it easier for them to gain such prestigious positions. Their influence and importance are clearly reflected in an incident late in the sixteenth century, when all minorities were faced with a rising tide of conservative Muslim opinion. When a Jewish court physician in the palace at Edirne died, the chief physician *(hekim başı)* pressed successfully for appointment of a Muslim to fill the vacant post, due to the large number of Jews and small number of Muslims in such positions.[43]

While not all physicians wielded great influence at court, a figure such as Moses Hamon, Kanuni Süleyman's physician, had great power and prestige, and the Jewish community of Salonica, for example, was assisted by him and other influential Jews in the attempt to have their independent status confirmed by the government. Likewise, with regard to internal problems the intercession of Hamon was enlisted. When an unscrupulous *kethüdâ* in the Jewish community of Salonica became too troublesome for the community to control they appealed to Hamon for help. Eventually, when his letters and requests were insufficient to change the *kethüdâ*'s ways, Hamon arranged to have the man sent to Istanbul and then exiled by government order.[44] It has already been pointed out that his leadership in the community assumed a special importance due to the decline of the rabbinate of Istanbul in the sixteenth century.[45] There were, in addition to the large number of Jewish physicians, dentists, and so forth in the palace service, others with considerable influence, which some used to further the interests of their friends and of the Jewish community.

In addition to the physicians, the businessmen and financiers in the Jewish community were influential. The archetype was, of course, Don Joseph Nasi (Jaoū Miguez), a wealthy Sephardic banker and financier who migrated to the Ottoman Empire and presents a picture of the kind of leader who served both the Ottomans and the Jews. For our purposes here it is not necessary to describe in detail his career or that of his aunt and associate Doña Gracia Mendes. Suffice it to say that after his migration from Europe during Süleyman's reign, having been creditor to both the Spanish and French courts, he became an Istanbul banker, advisor, and tax farmer in the Ottoman administration. After the succession of Selim II, to whom he was extremely close, Nasi was appointed duke of Naxos and the Cyclades with the rank of *sancak beyi*.[46]

Nasi and his aunt were patrons of Jewish learning and founded and supported synagogues in Istanbul and Salonica. Along with Hamon, Nasi was a chief conduit to the government for the Jews and was instrumental in obtaining the confirmation of Salonica's privileges. At the same time, when it suited his interests, he was able to obtain the support of the religious establishment in excommunicating a Jewish rival who had been disloyal to him. Combining this power with his influence at court, he arranged for the man to be exiled to Rhodes.[47] Another account which reflects his immense influence with Selim II is a report that, at Selim's accession, the Greek patriarch approached Nasi and paid him one thousand akça for his intercession to obtain confirmation of the church's privileges.[48]

After Nasi's death there were other important court figures from the Jewish community, but none with an equally great influence and broad network of contacts within and outside the empire, among Muslims and non-Muslims. In spite of the position of other court Jews, the passing of Hamon and Nasi created a vacuum in Ottoman Jewish leadership. They had dominated the Istanbul leadership and had served as representatives for the provincial leaders, and after them the leadership of the community was effectively isolated from the court.

The issue is, of course, not so simple as to revolve around the leadership of a few individuals, no matter what their stature. The increasing role of European traders with their capitulations, though it brought to the Jews positions as agents and translators, also served to remove from their hands certain large investments and weakened their ability to play a primary role in international trade. The growing conservatism of Muslim institutions, or perhaps, better, the revival of attempts to enforce firmly the conditions imposed on non-Muslims in Muslim society,[49] resulted in the weakening of the power of the Jews and caused them to be viewed in the same light as other non-Muslims, which had not been the case up to the late sixteenth century. Economic difficulties not only placed a burden on Jewish tax farmers to produce more wealth for the government by forcing them to undertake unprofitable tax farms, but undermined their prosperity as well. Thus, the period in which the lay leadership of the Jewish community grew weaker and less influential coincided with an assault from many quarters on the position of the Jews.

From these few examples it appears that three different kinds of leaders guided the Ottoman Jewish communities in the fifteenth and sixteenth centuries. In the fifteenth century the rabbi of the capital, first at Edirne and then at Istanbul, guided the community with the approval and encouragement of the Ottoman authorities. The changes in the Istanbul community during the course of that century, and the drive of newcomers to play a more influential role in the community leadership, as well as the contrasting personalities of Rabbis Capsali and Mizrahi, led to a weakening of the power of the rabbinate of Istanbul. In the wake of this and the simultaneous rise of new communities in the Balkans, local systems of leadership outside Istanbul emerged. There each community governed itself, and where questions of Jewish law were in dispute, advice was solicited from Jewish legal authorities in other places. In

Istanbul, a rabbinate continued to exist and deal with internal Jewish affairs, while prominent lay leaders undertook the burdens of liaison with the central authorities, serving both the Istanbul community and other communities in this regard. Each type of leadership had its role, and each developed in response to changes in the status and composition of the Ottoman Jewish communities and their needs.

For the Ottomans a single concern was paramount. They cared only that the communities saw to their own affairs, administered themselves effectively, and paid their various taxes and assessments to the government. In exchange for relieving the government of the duties of administration, the Jews were allowed considerable freedom of action in their personal and economic lives. What makes the case of the Jews special is that, unlike the Christian citizens of the empire, the Jews had no traditional centers or established hierarchy on which the Ottomans could rely as a basis for an administrative system, or on which the subjects could rely as a basis for countering and resisting the Ottoman regime. Though local rabbis had led communities in the past, the Ottoman Jewish communities were moved, resettled, and later swelled by immigration. With each of these changes came a change in the kind of leaders and leadership which stood at the head of the community.

Notes

1. H. J. Zimmels, *Ashkenazim and Sephardim,* Farnsborough, England, 1969, p. 104ff.

2. These were often different from their policies toward Christians, recently described in Karl Binswanger, *Untersuchungen zum Status der Nicht-muslime im Osmanischen Reich des 16. Jahrhunderts, mit einer Neudefinition des Begriffes "Dimma." Beiträge zur Kenntnis Südosteuropas und des Nahen Orients,* vol. 23, Munich, 1977, especially pp. 64–124 and 147–207.

3. Steven B. Bowman, "The Jews in Byzantium, 1261–1453," Ph.D. dissertation, The Ohio State University, 1974, p. 413.

4. Halil İnalcik, "Bursa", *EI,*[2] vol. 1, p. 1334 cites J. Schiltberger, *Bondage and Travels,* ed. J. B. Telfer, London, 1879, p. 40 in regard to health facilities.

5. General historians of the Jews such as Graetz and Dubnow have dated this letter variously at the period after the conquest of Istanbul or after the arrival of the Spanish Jews ca. 1492. Shlomo Rozanes, *Divre Yemei Yisrael beTogarmah,* second ed., Sofia, Jerusalem, Tel Aviv, 1930–45, vol. 1, p. 16 n.29 suggests 1427–30 and Joseph Nehama, *Histoire des Israélites de Salonique,* 3 vols., Paris and Salonica, 1936, vol. 1, p. 117, on the basis of textual evidence, suggests 1430–1440. In any case, it will become reasonably clear from the discussion below of events after 1453 that there is little likelihood of such a letter being sent by Tsarfati after that date. We would at least expect a reference to the conquest, or that the rabbis of Istanbul would have sent the letter.

6. They are listed by congregation in *Başvekâlet Arşivi* (hereafter BVA) *Tapu ve Tahrir Defterleri* (hereafter Tapu), no. 210 and no. 240, the records of the *imaret* of Mehmet II, to which their poll tax was assigned.

7. BVA *Kamil Kepeci Tasnîfî* (hereafter KK) 2411, p. 20, misnumbered as p. 6.

8. Elijah Capsali, *Seder Eliyahu Zuta,* Aryeh Shmuelevitz, ed., Jerusalem, 1975, vol. 1, p. 82. Mehmet Zeki Pakalın, *Osmanlı Tarih Deyimleri ve Terimleri Sözlüğü,* 2nd. ed., 3 vols. Istanbul, 1971, vol. 1, p. 845 refers to Hüseyn Kazim Bey, *Büyük Türk Lûgati,* as giving meanings which include "ihtiyar," aged, elder, chief; "hâkim," governor, judge; "âlim," learned, wise, etc., terms which might well have been applied to a man in Capsali's position.

9. Capsali (cited n. 8), p. 82.

10. On the problem of the sources for this claim see the chapter by Joseph Hacker.

11. BVA KK 2411, p. 20.

12. Ibid., p. 20.

13. This problem will be dealt with below.

14. Capsali (cited n. 8), pp. 128–130 and cited by Rozanes (cited n. 5), vol. 1, pp. 43–44.

15. Capsali (cited n. 8), p. 240.

16. BVA *Maliyeden Müdevver defterleri* (hereafter MM) 19, p. 5b, 25b,ff.

17. BVA KK 2411, p. 1 is but one example.

18. L. Bornstein, "The Structure of the Rabbinate in the Ottoman Empire" (Hebrew), in *East and Maghreb,* ed. by H. Z. (J. W.) Hirschberg with E. Bashan, Ramat Gan, 1974, p. 233 n. 64 cites Mizrahi's *Responsa* no. 14, as does A. Ovadiah, "Rabbi Eliyahu Mizrahi" (Hebrew). *Sinai,* 3 (1939–40), p. 233 n. 289.

19. Topkapi Sarayı Müzesi (hereafter TKS) D 5708.

20. TKS E 12314.

21. Rozanes (cited n. 5), vol. 1, p. 95.

22. Bornstein (cited n. 18), p. 234 n. 72 is the most recent work which cites the *responsum* of R. Samuel de Medina, Section IV, n. 364.

23. BVA KK2287, pp. 125, 33.

24. Abraham A. Neuman, "The *Shebet Yehudah* and Sixteenth Century Historiography," *Louis Ginzberg Jubilee Volume, English Section,* New York, 1945, p. 268 n. 30, pp. 271–272.

25. BVA *Tapu ve Tahrîr defterleri* (hereafter Tapu) 36, p. 139 and published in Nicoară Beldiceanu, "Un Acte sur le statut de la communauté juive de Trikala," REI, 40 (1972), p. 136; also Tapu 607, p. 124 regarding Balyabadra (Patras).

26. BVA MM 15666, p. 1.

27. *Tapu ve Kadastro Genel Müdürlüğü* (hereafter TK) 186, p. 46a.

28. BVA MM 89, pp. 41b, 57b, ff.

29. Ibid., p. 123a.

30. BVA Tapu 403, p. 533.

31. In addition to the physical enclave suggested by *cumhûr,* we may also note that it can be understood as meaning nation or commonwealth, and that it is the modern (nineteenth century) term for republic.

32. M. Almosnino, *Extremos y Grandezas de Constantinopla,* trans. Jacob Cansino, Madrid, 1638, p. 90. The work was completed around 1566.

33. BVA *Mühimme defterleri* (hereafter Müh.) 35, p. 374 no. 951, 17 N 986.

34. BVA Tapu 416, pp. 53–64, regarding Niğbolu (Nicopolis).

35. BVA Tapu 433, p. 480, at Kesterya (Kastoria).

36. BVA Müh. 18, p. 59 no. 120, 25 N 979, at Sofya (Sofia).

37. BVA Tapu 370, p. 483, at Kefe (Kafa).

38. BVA Tapu 494, pp. 84–90, at Edirne (Adrianople).

39. BVA MM 19, p. 19b, and H. İnalcik, "Istanbul," *EI,*[2] vol. 4, p. 226.

40.   Eleazar Birnbaum, "Hekim Ya'qûb, Physician to Sultan Mehemmed the Conqueror," *The Hebrew Medical Journal,* 1 (1961), pp. 241–243.

41.   On Yakub's career and some of these problems see Bernard Lewis, "The Privilege Granted by Mehmed II to his Physician," *BSOAS,* 14 (1952) pp. 551–563.

42.   TKS E 7851.

43.   BVA Müh. 25, p. 83 no. 927, 20 S 981; p. 108 no. 1204, 19 Za 981; p. 116 no. 1273, 26 Z 981.

44.   Rozanes (cited n. 5), vol. 2, p. 63ff.

45.   Uriel Heyd, "Moses Hamon, Chief Jewish Physician to Sultan Süleyman the Magnificent," *Oriens,* 16 (1963), p. 160.

46.   BVA KK 5482, p. 14.

47.   BVA Müh. 22, p. 85 no. 176, 20 S 981; Müh. 27, p. 143 no. 336, 11 N 983; I. S. Emmanuel, *Histoire des Israélites de Salonique,* Paris, 1936, vol. 1, p. 219.

48.   Rozanes, (cited n. 5), vol. 2, p. 97.

49.   Binswanger (cited n. 2), pp. 165–199.

Ottoman Policy toward the Jews and Jewish Attitudes toward the Ottomans during the Fifteenth Century

JOSEPH R. HACKER

It is a common view, accepted by historians of the Jews as well as by historians of the Ottoman Empire, that the Jewish experience in the Ottoman Empire from its very beginning was a calm, peaceful, and fruitful one.

The description in recent historiography is very close to that of the nineteenth century. The Jews, persecuted by almost all the Christian states in Western Europe since the end of the fourteenth century, strove and yearned to settle themselves in a safe land. This promised land was offered to them by the Ottomans, who welcomed the migrating Jews, protected them against oppression, granted them communal autonomy, and tolerated their religious practices. To some extent, they were even the authorities' favorites. On the other hand, the Ottomans, who lacked urban-based craftsmen and professionals—merchants and bankers, doctors and tax farmers—benefited from the Jewish economic activities as well as from the skills and techniques which they brought from their former lands. According to this view, the Jews, out of gratitude to the Ottomans, solidly supported the empire and its rulers, as early as the late fourteenth century. Many migrated to the empire from Christian Europe, and the image of the Ottoman authorities in Jewish historiography has been a very positive one.[1]

It would seem to me that this accepted view of consistently good relations between the Ottomans and the Jews during the fifteenth century should be modified in light of new research and manuscript sources.

In the course of research on the community of Salonica during the fifteenth and sixteenth centuries, I found contemporary Hebrew manuscripts written under Ottoman rule. But in tracing that community back to the fifteenth century I failed to find evidence for its existence between the moment of the city's fall to the Ottomans in 1430 and approximately 1490. It is true that some scholars[2] furnish the names and activities of rabbis from fifteenth-century Salonica, but my examination of the voluminous writings of these men, still in manuscripts scattered in several libraries, revealed that not one was, in fact, from Salonica. Most were from Constantinople, some from Crete, Negroponte, and other places, and the birthplace or residence of others is uncertain. No wonder that in the census of 1478 and in the lists of the capitation tax from 1487 to 1490, Jews from Salonica do not appear.[3] The sole evidence for a Jewish community in Salonica after 1430 are the Ottoman documents dealing with Salonican Jews deported and exiled to Istanbul after its conquest.[4] But these documents do not state explicitly that these Jews were exiled from Salonica proper, and it is possible that these were Jews who originated in Salonica but had left the city prior to their deportation. However, the likeliest reading suggests that they came from Salonica in 1455–1457.

How could it happen that the second city of the Byzantine Empire, a "megalopolis," was abandoned by the Jews just as the tolerant Ottomans came to rule? It seems that there is no way to answer this question without asking a wider one. What was the fate of Byzantine Jewry under Ottoman and Latin rule in the fifteenth century, and how did they react to the Turkish conquests and expansion? What happened to these communities in the turmoil of war and competition between Islam and Christendom? And more specifically, what happened to the Byzantine Jews in Constantinople after its fall?

Unfortunately there has been little research into early Ottoman Jewry.[5] Most of what we do know is based on the following sources: According to Kritovoulos, the Greek historian of Mehmed II who was well informed on Mehmed's policy and deeds after the conquest of Constantinople, Mehmed sent an order to transfer to the city "not only Christians but also his own people and many of the Hebrews."[6] This information is supported by the census of 1455 in Constantinople and by Evliya Çelebi's stories about Istanbul Jewry. Numerous groups of Jewish deportees from Rumelia were settled in the city in 1455 in houses abandoned by Muslims.[7] On the other hand it is also said that during the assault the Ottoman army broke through the walls into the Byzantine Jewish quarter of Vlanga, and devastated it. From then on there is no mention of the Judheca of Vlanga.[8]

Elijah Capsali, a Cretan Jewish scholar, who in 1523 wrote a history of the Ottoman dynasty, tells a different story. While describing the policies and rule of Mehmed II, he says that the Jews were invited by Mehmed to Istanbul and were offered special benefits, and that a special decree was issued on their behalf. Capsali's wording of the decree resembles the decree which Cyrus issued in 538 B.C. permitting Jews to return to their homeland.[9]

Jewish historiography from the sixteenth century onward accepted these facts of Capsali. At the end of the seventeenth century the story was exaggerated by Joseph Sambari's chronicle *Divrey Yosef*,[10] and through the nineteenth-century historian H. Graetz the exaggerated version found its way into modern historiography. Thereafter, the story and its main components were accepted by modern Jewish scholarship. Moreover, historians of the Ottoman Empire accepted these facts, and the relations of the Byzantine-Jewish population with the Ottomans eventually came to seem rosy. It is said that after the fall of Constantinople the Jews were invited to the city, were granted houses, lands, and exemptions from taxes, and became the favorites of the sultan. By Mehmed's initiative a *haham başi,* or chief rabbi, was nominated. This rabbi sat in the *Divan-i Hümayun* and was responsible for assessing and collecting taxes from the Jewish communities in the Ottoman Empire. From then on, the Jews and their communities flourished under Ottoman rule.

There is no need to argue at length that the chief rabbi was neither a permanent nor even a temporary member of the *Divan-i Hümayun,* sitting on Mehmed's right, nor the chief Jewish tax collector. Various Turkish and Hebrew sources from the fifteenth and sixteenth centuries demonstrate the contrary.[11] Furthermore, such an arrangement would be contrary to the prevailing practices of Ottoman administration in the fifteenth century.

However, the first source which ascribes all these positions to the chief rabbi is Sambari, who wrote his chronicle in late seventeenth-century Egypt. Sambari's account of the office of the *Nagid* in Mamlūk Egypt was the object of D. Ayalon's criticism. He has shown convincingly that Sambari's story is not reliable. Though he possessed good sources, he misused them. He frequently exaggerated and confused facts and chronology for no apparent reason. Subsequently, Ayalon's views have been accepted by some, and modified or overlooked by others, but no one working on the history of the Ottoman Empire was aware of Sambari's unreliability.[12]

Furthermore, although it is cited in modern historiography as a well-established fact that the Jews in the Ottoman Empire had a chief rabbi, I failed to find any trace of this fact in contemporary sources. Here again, the first source to mention such a chief rabbi was Sambari. Elijah Capsali, for example, who was related to Moses Capsali, the first alleged chief rabbi, does not mention this fact about him, despite his long and detailed descriptions of his famous relative. Nor is there mention of such a chief rabbi in the Ottoman Hebrew sources of the fifteenth and sixteenth centuries.[13] Thus it appears that the sole established fact about Jewish authority under Ottoman rule is dubious.

From several Romaniot Jewish sources in Istanbul written between 1450–1550 we even have explicit statements about the nature and authority of the so-called "chief rabbis," Moses Capsali and Elijah Mizrahi. In an autograph *responsum* of Elijah Mizrahi from approximately 1498, he discussed Moses Capsali's authority in Constantinople, while the latter was still alive and in charge of communal activities. According to Mizrahi's testimony, Capsali's authority was limited to the city of Istanbul and its neighborhood and it was never exercised or claimed over the Ottoman Empire as a whole.[14] From other sources we know that in the 1480s Capsali was dependent upon the goodwill of the Jewish communities of Constantinople in his very nomination and position.[15]

In the last three decades our information about some Byzantine Jewish communities under Latin rule has been enriched, mainly by archival documents and Hebrew rabbinic sources. Such is the case with the Jewish communities of Crete, Chios, and Negroponte.[16] Unfortunately, the published documents do not contain important data concerning the Byzantine Jewries which came under Ottoman rule during the empire's gradual conquests. But as I was working systematically on Hebrew manuscripts written by fifteenth-century Byzantine Jews from Anatolia, Crete, Negroponte, Rhodes, Mistra and Constantinople, I did find information on the fate of the Jewish communities under early Ottoman rule.

From the new sources it is apparent, too, that after the conquest of Constantinople, the Byzantine Jews were deported by force from the majority of those cities ruled by the Ottomans in which they had been settled. In fact twenty to thirty Jewish communities were removed intact from Anatolia and the Rumelia to Istanbul. For example, from 1456 on, we find all the Karaite dignitaries who had been living in Edirne now living in Istanbul. Moreover, several Karaite sages describe the exile to Istanbul and its aftermath.[17]

In the writings of the Romaniot Jews there appear responses to the fall of Constantinople. And much to our surprise the response was not positive. In fact, Jews in Crete and Rhodes wrote laments on the fall of Constantinople and the fate of its Jewish community. We possess letters written about the fate of Jews who underwent one or another of the Ottoman conquests. In one of the letters which was written before 1470, there is a description of the fate of such a Jew and his community, according to which description, written in Rhodes and sent to Crete, the fate of the Jews was not different from that of Christians. Many were killed; others were taken captive, and children were brought to the *devşirme*. This is the only source, so far known, which mentions the capturing of Jewish children for the Janissary troops.[18] As we know, for example, from a document concerning the Jewish community of Trikala,[19] in Greece, Jews were already exempted from this burden by 1497. Some letters describe the carrying of the captive Jews to Istanbul and are filled with anti-Ottoman sentiments. Moreover, we have a description of the fate of a Jewish doctor and homilist from Veroia (Kara-Ferya) who fled to Negroponte when his community was driven into exile in 1455. He furnishes us with a description of the exiles and their forced passage to Istanbul. Later on we find him at Istanbul itself, and in a homily delivered there in 1468 he expressed his anti-Ottoman feelings openly. We also have some evidence that the Jews of Constantinople suffered from the conquest of the city and that several were sold into slavery.[20]

In contrast to these sources, we have a source on the attitude of the Ottoman authorities toward a Jewish community in the Morea. A Jewish scholar living in Mistra[21] provides us with a short description of the fate of his community during the conquest of Morea by Mehmed II in 1460. According to him it was prohibited by law to subdue or enslave members of the community of Mistra, and they were left in peace. Therefore, it is very likely to assume that Jewish communities from the Balkans had a variety of experiences with Ottoman troops and officials, and we should not look for a common fate of these communities. It was suggested that differences in attitude toward newly conquered cities stem from their different responses to the summons to surrender.[22] It is very likely that this is the reason for the different attitude in this case too, as well as the reason why Mistra and other old communities like Yanina had a different fate, and were not amongst the *sürgün* communities in Constantinople.[23]

The conclusion, based on these new sources and on a reconsideration of other ones, is that between the years 1453 and c. 1470 strong anti-Ottoman attitudes were found among Byzantine Jews. These attitudes prevailed among some Jews who lived under Christian rule and some Jews who lived under Ottoman rule. We may say that these attitudes were a response to the fate of those Romaniot Jews who suffered from the Ottoman conquests and from the Ottoman policy of deportation and compulsory resettlement, which followed the conquests. The deportation and resettlement in Constantinople drew the deepest criticism and for good reason. The outcome of these forced deportations was very grave for Byzantine Jewry. Small in numbers before, now they were plagued and suffered from an economic and cultural crisis. Their freedom was limited and the laws and status of *sürgün* were applied to them.[24] This status still affected their life in the seventeenth century.[25] Moreover, it seems that these Jews, unlike some of the influential Moslems, could not manage to resist and win over local authorities to prevent their deportation. It seems that the majority of the Jews living under Ottoman rule were driven to Constantinople. Constantinople became a melting pot for the Byzantine Jewry and the role played by Moses Capsali in this process was crucial.[26] The Karaites too expressed bitterness and sorrow arising from these new circumstances.[27]

Jewish historiography of the Ottoman Empire and its Jewry, from the sixteenth century on, disregarded these facts and attitudes. Elijah Capsali, who described the conditions of the Jews under Mehmed II, did not mention compulsory resettlement at all, and told nothing about the fate of the Jews of Constantinople after its fall. He too wrote a long and detailed poem on the fall of Constantinople, but his was very favorable to the Ottomans, and he was pleased with the collapse of the Christian Empire.[28] According to his view, the fall of Byzantium and the rise of the Ottomans represented a divine intervention in history on behalf of those who treat the Jews well.

What was the reason for this reversal in attitude?

It appears to me that the answer to this question lies in two main causes. The first is the policy of Mehmed II and his successors towards the Jews; the second is the expulsion of the Jews from Spain in 1492 and from Portugal in 1497 and their reception by Ottoman authorities.

What is known to us about Mehmed's policy toward the Jews?

First of all, we know that the Jews possessed religious autonomy as did other *dhimmī* groups. In addition, it is quite clear that the Jews exiled to Istanbul were permitted to use some of those synagogues which survived the fall of the city in spite of the fact that this was not in accordance with the *shariʿa*.[29]

The policy of the imperial power was to reach the religious and ethnic units through their own authorities and with as little disturbance of their traditional laws and customs as was politically possible. Although there was no chief rabbi over all the Jews of the empire, there was a chief rabbi whose official authority was limited to Istanbul and its constituent communities, and was approved by the Ottoman authorities. Perhaps the *Rav akçesi,* i.e., the Rabbi's Tax, which the Jews paid to the Ottomans, came about as a result of this approval. But it is also possible that this tax was paid in various communities for the privilege of having a rabbi to preside over their own affairs.[30] On the relations between Mehmed II and the Jews we know not a little. Professor Bernard Lewis many years ago published an illuminating essay on Mehmed's Jewish doctor, Jacub Paşa, and the Jewish sources, especially Elijah Capsali, tell detailed stories about Jewish courtiers and their activities in the Porte. It seems that one of the most important figures of those courtiers in the fifteenth century was Yeshaya Messini.[31] This person was deeply involved in communal affairs, he maintained personal connections with Mehmed II, and was involved in various disputes with the Karaite community.[32] From Turkish documents we hear about several Jewish tax collectors during the reign of Mehmed II and Bayazid II.[33] Several Jewish merchants were involved in trading silk, spices, and other goods in Bursa, Istanbul, Gallipoli, and other Ottoman cities.[34] Certain Jews and Karaites gained relatively high positions in the Ottoman bureaucracy.[35] We find Jewish *Subaşıs, Amils, Kahyas,* and other officials. Even though we do not generally know their specific functions, their titles give us some idea of their duties.[36] It is also known that Jews acted as diplomatic envoys between the Ottoman Empire and the Christian powers.[37]

Not by accident did ᶜAşıkpaşazade, who belonged to the men of religion,[38] write bitterly on Mehmed's policy toward the *dhimmī.* The Jews, like the Greeks and Armenians, benefited from the tax exemptions and other favors which were bestowed by Mehmed II upon those who were deported by force to Istanbul, and on those who came there of their own accord after the conquest of the city. It is evident that a small class of Jews rose to wealth and influence in the capital. Our sources reveal a certain tension between this class and other less successful orders of Jewish society, even though these wealthy Jews paid not only their own taxes, but also the taxes of the Jewish poor, who were not able to pay even the *cizye* themselves. In the homilies of the period the sages complained that men spent their entire lives and all their energy in financial enterprises. Elijah Mizrahi reported in one of his homilies, still in manuscript, that the tension between the rabbis and the public was so high that the rabbis of Constantinople decided to have a strike (the only one

known in Jewish history) and stop public teaching and serving the congregations. We must note that the majority of the Jews of Constantinople were not
wealthy, and that the gap between the few who were and the many who were
not was large.

We also know that in 1477, some years before the end of Mehmed's rule,
the Jewish population in Istanbul, according to the census of that year,
reached 1,647 households, or approximately eight thousand people.[39] If we
remember that between 1466 and 1469 Istanbul had suffered a series of
plagues, which ravaged the city and significantly reduced its population,[40] we
must conclude that the Jewish communities were thriving throughout this
period. And, indeed, we know that by the end of the fifteenth century the
Jewish congregations of Istanbul numbered nearly forty.

So much for Mehmed's policies and their effects. The effects of the expulsion from Spain on the Jewish attitude toward the Ottoman authorities were
even more decisive.

Jews from Spain had been trickling into the Ottoman Empire since the end
of the fourteenth century, but they came in significant numbers only during
the last decade of the fifteenth century. Very soon they outnumbered the
Byzantine Jews in the empire. In 1498 they became the majority in Istanbul,
according to Elijah Mizrahi. Their expulsion from Spain was the most critical
and tragic event in Jewish history of the late Middle Ages, affecting not only
Spanish Jewry, the largest and most culturally advanced of the Jewish communities, but also the entire Jewish world. While these exiled Jews were for
the most part prevented from entering Christian lands, the Ottomans welcomed them. Their positive reception at the hands of the Ottomans no doubt
resulted in the widespread Jewish sympathy toward Ottoman authorities. It is
no wonder, then, that Elijah Capsali, writing in 1523, when describing the
reign and deeds of Mehmed II and Bayezid II, was moved to speak only good
about them. According to his view, Christendom was the enemy of the Jews,
and the Ottoman Empire and its rulers were God's scourge sent to punish the
foe. Accordingly, his picture of the Ottomans contained only praise, and the
worst deeds of the sultans were held to be admirable and just. The plight of
Byzantine Jewry deserved no mention. Subsequently, conditions for Jews
improved within the empire and the greater tragedy of Iberian Jewry came to
outweigh all others.

Some conclusions about the case of the Jewish community in relation to the
Ottomans suggest themselves:

1. The Jews, like other inhabitants of the Byzantine Empire, suffered heavily
from the Ottoman conquests and policy of colonization and population transfer.
This explains the disappearance of several Jewish communities, including Salonica,
and their founding anew by Spanish Jewish immigrants.

2. Strong anti-Ottoman feelings prevailed in some Byzantine Jewish circles in the
first decades after the fall of Constantinople. These feelings were openly expressed
by people living under Latin rule and to some extent even in Istanbul.

3. Mehmed II's policies toward non-Muslims made possible the substantial economic and social development of the Jewish communities in the empire, and especially in the capital—Istanbul. These communities were protected by him against popular hatred, and especially from blood libels.

4. This policy was not continued by Bayezid II and there is evidence that under his rule the Jews suffered severe restrictions in their religious life.

5. The friendly policies of Mehmed on the one hand, and the good reception by Bayezid of Spanish Jewry on the other, caused the Jewish writers of the sixteenth century to overlook both the destruction which Byzantine Jewry suffered during the Ottoman conquests and the later outbursts of oppression in the days of Bayezid and Selim.

It is our task to reconstruct a more detailed and critical picture both of the process of development of Jewish history under the Ottomans and of its variety.

Notes

1. H. Graetz, *Geschichte der Juden*, 4th ed., Leipzig, 1897–1911, vol. 8, pp. 206–209, 276–281, 365, 440–449; M. Franco, *Essai sur l'histoire des Israélites de l'Empire ottoman*, Paris, 1897; S. Rozanes, *The History of the Jews in Turkey*, 2nd ed., Tel-Aviv, 1930, vol. 1, pp. 21–25, 30–34 (in Hebrew); A. Galanté, *Histoire dés Juifs d'Istanbul*, Istanbul, 1941, vol. 1, pp. 3–6, 107–118; id., *Documents officiels tures concernant les Juifs de Turque*, Istanbul, 1931, introduction and pp. 32–35, 50–52, 62–64, 162–164; S. Baron, *The Jewish Community*, Philadelphia, 1942, vol. 1, pp. 195–199, 350–351; H. Z. Hirschberg, "The Oriental Jewish Communities," *Religion in the Middle East*, ed. A. J. Arberry, vol. 1, Cambridge, 1969, pp. 146–157, 184–189. This view is accepted by scholars and historians of the Ottoman Empire, including Hammer-Purgstall, Iorga, Babinger, Mantran and others, and A. E. Vacalopoulos who exaggerated it in his various books and articles.

2. Rozanes (cited n. 1), pp. 31–33; I. Emmanuel, *Histoire des Israélites de Salonique*, Thonon-Paris, 1935–6, pp. 51–53; J. Nehama, *Histoire des Israélites de Salonique*, vol. 1, Paris, 1935.

3. O. L. Barkan, "Essai sur les donnés statistiques . . ." *JESHO*, 1 (1957), pp. 35–36; id. "894 (1488–1489) Yili Cizyesin Tahsilâtina âit Muhasebe Bilânçoları," *Belgeler*, 1 (1964), pp. 31–32, 49, 117.

4. On the policy of colonization and repopulation in the Ottoman Empire and especially under Mehmed II, see Ö. L. Barkan, "Les deportations dans l'Empire ottoman," *Revue de la Faculté des Sciences Economiques de l'Université d'Istanbul*, 11 (1949–1950), pp. 67–131; H. Inalcik, "Ottoman Methods of Conquest," *SI*, 2 (1954), pp. 103–129. On the Policy of Mehmed II and Bayezid II and the deportations to Constantinople see H. Inalcik, "The Policy of Mehmed II toward the Greek Population of Istanbul," *Dumbarton Oaks Papers*, 23 (1970), pp. 213–249; id., "Istanbul," *EI*², vol. 4, pp. 224–248; N. Beldiceanu et I. Beldiceanu-Steinherr, "Déportation et pêche à Kilia entre 1484 et 1508," *BSOAS*, 38 (1975), pp. 40–54; R. Mantran, *Istanbul dans le seconde moitié du XVIIᵉ siecle*, Paris 1962, p. 43 sq.

5. On this topic see my forthcoming Hebrew article in *Zion* (a quarterly for research in Jewish history), 46 (1981).

6. Kritovoulos, *History of Mehmed the Conqueror*, tr. C. T. Riggs, Princeton, 1954, p. 93. On the reliability of his account see Inalcik, *DOP* (cited n. 4), pp. 236–241. This is confirmed by the detailed story of J. M. Angiolello. see I. Ursu, Donado da Lezze (sic!), *Historia Turchesca* (1300–1514), Bucharest, 1910; W. Gérard, *Le ruine de Byzance (1200–1452)*, App. A., p. 344.

7. See Inalcik, *EI²* (cited n. 4, p. 238.

8. See for example D. Jacoby, "Les quartiers juifs de Constantinople à l'époque byzantine," *Byzantion*, 37 (1967), pp. 167–227.

9. Elijah Capsali, *Seder Eliahu Zuta*, vol. 1 (ed. Shmuelevitz, Simonsohn, Benayahu), Jerusalem, 1975, pp. 81–83 (in Hebrew).

10. *Divrey Yoseph*, MS. H 130 in the Alliance Israelite Universelle at Paris (three other Mss. known). Portions of the book were anonymously printed in Constantinople (1728) and Izmir (1756).

11. B. Lewis, *Diwān-i Humāyūn, EI²*, vol. 2, pp. 337–339. For documents and information on taxation of Jewish communities in the Ottoman Empire in the fifteenth century, see: M. T. Gökbilgin, *XV-XVI Asırlarda Edirne v Paşa Livası*, Istanbul, 1952; N. Beldiceanu, *Les actes des premiers sultans dans les manuscrits tures . . .* 2 v., Paris-La Haye, 1960–1964; B. Cvetkova, *Fontes Turcici historiae Bulgarica, series XV-XVI*, vol. 3 (16), Sofia, 1972.

12. D. Ayalon (Neustadt), "Some Problems Concerning the Negidut in Egypt During the Middle Ages," *Zion*, 4 (1939), pp. 126–149 (in Hebrew); S. D. Goitein, *A Mediterranean Society*, vol. 2, Los Angeles, 1971, pp. 23–40, 524–530; *id.*, "The Title and Office of the 'Nagid'," *JQR*, 53 (1962), pp. 93–119.

13. B. Lewis, "The Privilege Granted by Mehmed II to His Physician," *BSOAS*, 14 (1952), p. 554 refers to "a chief Rabbi by royal appointment," but it seems to me that we should rather translate the phrase as follows: ". . . They were allowed to have a Rabbi and leader with the permission of the authorities."

14. See my article, "The Institution of the 'Chief Rabbinate' in Constantinople in the Fifteenth and Sixteenth Centuries," (in Hebrew), *Sefunot*, 17 (1981), in print.

15. See for example J. Mann, *Texts and Studies in Jewish History and Literature*, Philadelphia 1935, vol. 2, pp. 302–315 (esp. p. 313).

16. See for example the collections of documents published by F. Thiriet, *Regestes des délibérations du Senat de Venise concernant la Romanie*, Paris-La Haye, 1959–1961; *Délibérations des Assemblées vénitiennes concernant la Romanie*, Paris-La Haye, 1971, vol. 2 (1364–1463) and others, and the research done by D. Jacoby and Z. Ankori on the Jewish communities in Crete, Chios and other Latin ruled colonies.

17. See Mann, (cited n. 15) pp. 292–297; A. Danon, "Documents Relating to the History of the Karaites in European Turkey," *JQR*, NS, 17 (1927), pp. 168–170; *ibid.*, 15 (1925), p. 298; - Z. Ankori, *Introduction to Elijah Bashiatzi's "Aderet Eliahu,"* Ramla, 1966 (in Hebrew).

18. See n. 5.

19. N. Beldiceanu, "Un acte sur le statut de la communauté juive de Trikala," *REI*, 40 (1972), pp. 133, 138.

20. A detailed examination of these and other sources from the fourteenth and fifteenth centuries is included in my article mentioned in n. 5. Some of the well known and famous scholars and philosophers, like Mordechai Comitiano and Shalom Anavi, were held in capitivity, others were reported killed in fires and during the assault.

21. On the Jewish community of Mistra under Ottoman rule see lately Z. Avneri, "The Jews of Mistra," *Sefunot* 11 (1977), pp. 35–42 (in Hebrew); S. Bowman, "The Jewish Settlement in Sparta and Mistra," *Byzantinisch-Neugriechischen Jahrbücher*, 22 (1979), pp. 131–146.

22. Inalcik, *DOP* (cited n. 4), pp. 231–235.

23. See U. Heyd, "The Jewish Communities of Istanbul in the Seventeenth Century," *Oriens*, 6 (1953), pp. 299–305.

24. Beldiceanu (cited n. 4), p. 43ff; *id., Recherche sur la Ville ottomane au XVe siècle,* Paris, 1973, pp. 37, 42–43; Inalcik, *EI*² (cited n. 4), pp. 234–235, 239. A detailed description of this aspect is included in the *Zion* article (cited n. 5).

25. See for example the *Responsa of Solomon ben Abraham Hacohen,* Venice, 1592, (in Hebrew) no. 145; U. Heyd (cited n. 23), pp. 299–314.

26. See n. 14.

27. Mann (cited n. 15), pp. 292–293, 296–299.

28. Capsali (cited n. 9), pp. 75–80. The attitude of the Jews in the Mediterranean to the fall of Constantinople is dealt with in my forthcoming article in *Zion* (see n. 5). In the meantime see J. Hacker, "The Connections of Spanish Jewry with Palestine between 1391–1492," *Shalem,* 1 (1974), p. 120, n. 53; pp. 124–125, n. 65; pp. 146–147, n. 73 (in Hebrew).

29. Inalcik, *DOP* (cited n. 4), p. 234, 237.

30. See n. 14.

31. On Jacub Pasha see n. 13. Yeshaya Messini is not an Italian from Messina, but a Byzantine Jew from Mesene. On the community of Mesene see Heyd (cited n. 23), p. 303. On Yeshaya, see my article, "Some Letters on the Expulsion of the Jews from Spain and Sicily," (in Hebrew) *Studies in the History of Jewish Society . . . Presented to . . . Jacob Katz,* Jerusalem, 1980, pp. 71–73.

32. Mann (cited n. 15), pp. 300–301.

33. See, for example, Gökbilgin (cited n. 11), pp. 93, 148, 151.

34. See, for example, H. Inalcik, "Bursa and the Commerce of the Levant," *JESHO,* 3 (1960), pp. 131–147.

35. See, for example, Halil Sahillioglu, "XV. yüzyil sonunda Osmanlı Darphane Mukataalari," *IFM,* 23, 1–2 (1963), pp. 145–218.

36. See, for example, H. Inalcik, "Bursa XV. asır sanayı ve ticaret tarihine dair vesıkalar," *Belleten,* 24 (1960), pp. 45–102; N. Beldiceanu, *Recherche sur la Ville* (cited, n. 24), s.v. index.

37. See Capsali cited, n. 9); V. L. Menage, "Seven Ottoman Documents . . .", *Documents from Islamic Chanceries,* ed. S. M. Stern, Oxford, 1965, pp. 81–117.

38. Inalcik, *DOP* (cited n. 4), pp. 242–245.

39. See Inalcik, *EI*² (cited n. 4).

40. We have some manuscripts containing eyewitness descriptions of these plagues and their effect preserved in the writings of Jewish scholars from Constantinople.

Foreign Merchants and the Minorities in Istanbul during the Sixteenth and Seventeenth Centuries

ROBERT MANTRAN

The presence of a population alien to the ruling group in Istanbul was not an innovation of the Ottoman period. Due to the role it played as the capital and especially as a great commercial center during the Byzantine period, particularly under the Comneni and Palaeologi dynasties, the city had already known not only colonies from the West—Genoese, Venetians, Amalfitans, Pisans, Catalans, and Provençals—but also from the East—Armenians, Arabs, Turks, Georgians, Jews (the latter under the guise of either Venetian or Genoese subjects.)[1] Contacts between Italians and Greeks or Jews were frequently limited and Venetian Baili had, upon more than one occasion, sought to "naturalize" Jews, Gasmoule (mixed Latins and Greeks), and even Greeks. In fourteenth-century Venetian Romania, the Jewish community was considered to be a separate "nation," the equivalent of a *millet,* and was thereby permanently obligated to pay an annual tax. As individuals or as a collective group, Jews could be subjected to varied taxation.[2] There were also Greeks who, according to legislation of the Baili of Constantinople, were looked upon as Venetians. They were known as the "White Venetians" *(veneti albi).*[3] The same applied to the Genoese, established since 1261 at Galata, where they maintained permanent contact, not only with Greeks, but with other groups of the urban population as well.

Michael VIII Palaeologus and his successors are known to have accorded the Genoese, and subsequently the Venetians, particularly favorable conditions of trade and settlement, which can be called "capitulations." Following the conquest, Sultan Mehmed II, moreover, renewed the privileges granted the Genoese and other Italian merchant colonies.[4]

Furthermore, in his desire to convert Istanbul into an active capital,

Mehmed II took measures to repopulate the city whose Greek population had been transferred to Edirne, Bursa, Plovdiv, and Gallipoli, and whose Jewish population remained in the outskirts of the Balat area. It does not seem likely that other elements of the city's population, who had remained where they were, were driven out. Thus, to repopulate the abandoned areas, Mehmed II invited to Istanbul the Greeks of the Morea, Izmir and Trabzon (after its conquest), the Jews of Salonica, the Armenians of Tokat, Amasya and Kayseri and, naturally, the Turks of Anatolia. He offered them very attractive conditions (free housing, temporary tax exemptions, supply of materials for work, etc.).[5] When voluntary settlement failed, the sultan devised more radical stratagems: selection of forced migrants who had skills in craft and commerce. This procedure was said to have been followed in the sixteenth century by both Selim I, after his conquests of Tabriz, Damascus and Cairo, and by Süleyman I, after his conquests in Balkan and central Europe.

However, in order to make Istanbul prosper, it was not enough to repopulate it or make it the empire's capital and economic center. It was also necessary to make it a center of Mediterranean trade, an entrepôt between the Muslim and Christian worlds. The Ottomans clearly had little experience and few experts in this field. Therefore, they needed those having familiarity with commerce and foreign merchants. Since the Greeks of Constantinople had been expelled, others were brought in to replace them: Greeks from areas in contact with the West, Armenian experts in international trade, and, in addition to the Jews of Istanbul who had remained, the Jews of Salonica. At the very end of the fifteenth century and the beginning of the sixteenth, the expulsion of Jews and Arabs from Iberia brought a number to the Ottoman capital, where they came to strength in craft and commerce and assumed an important position in the empire's financial affairs—e.g., Doña Gracia Mendes and especially Don Joseph Nasi "duke of Naxos."[6] Jews of the Iberian peninsula were joined by Italian Jews as well as a small number of Ashkenazi Jews who had been expelled from central Europe at the end of the fifteenth century. These new arrivals were reinforced in the second half of the seventeenth century by other newcomers from the Ukraine and Poland.[7]

II

The minorities inhabited specified areas of the Ottoman capital. Under the authority and responsibility of their religious leaders, patriarchs or chief rabbis, they lived close to either their church or synagogue, or their work place. Evliya Çelebi has pointed out the areas of settlement of the new immigrants noting that the name of a particular district was often taken or adapted from their place of origin.[8] However, with the exception of an area near Galata, where non-Muslims comprise the majority, minority groups in Istanbul were never established in great numbers. By the end of the fifteenth century, there were in Galata 535 Muslims, 592 Christian, 332 Frank and 62 Armenian households, but no Jews.[9] It is only during the sixteenth and seventeenth centuries that they settled there, and further up the Golden Horn in Hasköy.

In the fifteenth century Galata contained some ten percent of the Istanbul population. During the sixteenth and seventeenth centuries, the population quite possibly stayed the same, but Galata certainly saw its character as a city of Franks and minorities grow. Its Muslims settled in the westernmost reaches—Turks, generally government officials stationed in Galata, and Arabs, either expelled from Spain, or emigrants from Egypt and Syria, settled around the "Arab Mosque" *("Arap cami'i),* the old St. Paul Church. According-ing to Evliya Çelebi, in the mid-seventeenth century Galata numbered seven-teen Muslim districts, seventy Greek districts, three Frankish districts, one Jewish district, and two Armenian districts. He numbered the population at two hundred thousand infidels and sixty thousand Muslims—a count which seems to be quite exaggerated.[10] It is not likely that the Galata (and Pera) populace had reached one hundred thousand. European travelers were struck by the considerable size of the non-Turkish population: "This city (or suburb) is more Christian or Jewish than Turkish";[11] "All the Frankish merchants, i.e., French, British, Dutch, Venetians, Genoese and others, live in Galata because of the residence of their ambassadors, and because their ships land there. Galata also has a large population of Turks, Greeks, Armenians and Jews who have their churches and synagogues."[12] Indeed, while Muslims had three mosques at Galata, the Greeks had numerous churches, the Armenians had three and the Jews had two synagogues; as for the Latins, they had five churches. In the seventeenth century there were 3,080 shops, most of which were owned by Greeks or Franks, eight markets, one oil market, one cotton market, one fishmarket, one customhouse, one weighing-in building for oil, a barracks-station for Janissaries who guarded the city, and 200 cabarets "where all the riffraff of Constantinople assemble."[13] Evliya Çelebi singled out various professional groups: sailors, merchants, craftsmen, carpenters, caulkers, tavern-keepers (either Greek or Jewish), Armenian peddlers and Jewish brokers.[14] Because the port of Galata was the landing area for Frank-ish vessels, there were, in addition to warehouses and shops belonging to Western merchants, shops owned by minority groups—especially shops specializing in ship's stores. One might say that Galata was the port of inter-national traffic, the port whose concern was not provisioning the capital, but export and import. Already by the sixteenth century, one out of every eight provision boats had Galata as its sole destination.[15]

Pera, the suburb which dominated Galata, witnessed during the seven-teenth century the opening of foreign embassies. Greek and Frankish mer-chants had previously built beautiful homes where: "Pera houses are beauti-ful; highly esteemed Greeks are almost exclusively the sole residents";[16] "The houses of Pera are beautiful, especially those belonging to Christian ambassa-dors; they house exclusively Greeks of distinction and esteem who are not inclined to mingle with the populace . . .";[17] "the houses of this entire suburb are beautiful, well-built, and most are made of stone; the suburb also serves as the district of honest people, of Frankish wholesale merchants and venerable Greeks."[18]

Galata and Pera were the points of contact for foreigners and minorities. The foreigners, though few, were an indispensable element in international trade. The minorities participated in a variety of activities; some were merchants, some wholesalers, some shipowners, many of whom were Greeks who seem to have been the most closely involved with the foreigner. The Armenians, numerically small in the fifteenth and sixteenth centuries, did not play an important role. As for the Jews, they monopolized the positions of brokers between the Ottoman administration and foreign merchants, particularly with respect to customs, and taxes collected on merchandise and vessels, etc. They also were bankers and money changers, thus gaining close contact with foreigners.

We know that non-Muslims were active in some of the guilds in Istanbul. To cite only those who dealt with European merchants: traders in leather, hides, and wool, which were exchanged with the West,[19] manufacturers and merchants (Jews) of both parchment[20] and Moroccan leather, whose export was prohibited,[21] fur merchants (Greeks),[22] traders in silk (Armenians)[23] and satin (Jews),[24] jewels (Jews and Greeks)[25] and pearl merchants (Jews).[26] In addition there were the guilds linked to navigation which Greeks dominated, constructing, repairing, equipping, and furnishing, as well as commanding ships and manning their crews.

Without going into exhaustive detail one can say that the minorities were well placed for their contacts with Europeans, for they controlled most of the goods which were used in foreign trade. Commerce was inspected and taxed for the Ottoman treasury. While the tax farmers were generally Turks, between them and the foreign merchants were Jews who acted as brokers, particularly in financial matters.[27] Jews and Greeks also acted as translators which gave them an advantage. The tax farmers and their agents had every interest in the continued development of trade. The inaccessibility of the Ottoman government favored the creation of middlemen who had an interest in the development of foreign trade in the ports of the empire. This system, which the capitulations confirmed and amplified, contributed to the contacts between minorities and foreign merchants.

III

Nevertheless, one must not neglect the human and psychological factors. First, there is the impression that Western traders found it easier to deal with Christians, Greek or Armenian, even if their Christianity differed from that of the West. In addition, marriage between Franks and Eastern Christians came to reinforce the ties of religion and culture.[28] During the sixteenth century Armenians played a minor role, although subsequently their role was enlarged and marriages between Armenians and Franks were not uncommon.

As for the Jews, contacts with them were of a different order. Even when Jews were the objects of a certain disdain—even repulsion—they were still familiar to Westerners. They traded in the West itself and particularly in Mediterranean ports, Livorno, for example, where the British were active.[29] Nonetheless, relations with Jews were limited to commercial and financial matters.

Western merchants, by necessity and by affinity, unquestionably were at ease with minorities. Some of them spoke their language, knew their trade well, and were able to resolve difficulties, foreseen and unforeseen. By contrast, direct contact with Turks was rare. Everything was an obstacle: language, religion, civilization, and in addition a certain mutual contempt. Perhaps the climate of misunderstanding was, to a certain degree, sustained by the minorities who were anxious to maintain their role as indispensable intermediaries.

This notion of indispensability is apparent also in the manner of all Western diplomatic and consular representation, except that of the Venetians. Venice had long been established in the ports of the eastern Mediterranean and in the Ottoman capital. They had their own officials and agents. They had already in place compatriots who were familiar with methods of commerce and dealings with Ottoman authorities. At least in times of peace the Venetians could forego intermediaries. However, in times of war they too resorted to middlemen, most frequently Jews.

The other nations who were able to establish embassies in Istanbul from the sixteenth century onwards had to rely upon local customs. At first, official diplomatic representation was strongly influenced by merchants, since the nomination of representatives—particularly of the English and French—depended on the companies of trade. It was only during the seventeenth century that consuls and ambassadors actually became agents, paid officially by their governments.[30]

In these circumstances, there was nothing unusual in the fact that consuls and ambassadors, both dependent on merchants, followed their practice and also had recourse to middlemen. The dragomans of the French embassy were of local and minority origin (Greeks and then Armenians), but their recruitment was subsequently abandoned, for only French, either from the families who had already settled in the Ottoman capital or from the home country, were used.[31] Dragomans for the consuls in the other ports were usually recruited from minorities, generally Greeks.

In Istanbul the fact that foreigners and many Christians and Jews lived in Galata-Pera, especially from the seventeenth century onwards, facilitated their cooperation. Travel accounts had made a point of noting that this was a district apart from Istanbul. After 1675 the district lost the few Turks[32] it did have when the Galata Saray, training grounds for the *iç oğlan,* the pages who served in the sultan's palace, was shut and its pupils transferred to the other side of the Golden Horn, far from foreigners.[33]

The Turkish disdain for commerce contributed, on the one hand, to the development of foreign settlement in the ports, and on the other hand, to the role of Greek, Jewish and Armenian intermediaries. However, Turks participated in internal commerce. They traded alongside non-Muslim Ottoman subjects (*dhimmī*s) without any difficulty. It was the contact with infidels who were not subject to the sultan's rule—i.e., those belonging to *Dar al-Ḥarb*—which seemed to contradict religious dictates. For the Turks the infidels' coming to Istanbul and the other ports was a mark of their inferiority: the Turk did not lower himself to peddle his wares to the enemy, even if he was at peace with him. According to the Ottomans, the infidel was the one who appealed to the Turk for trade and it was only out of magnanimity that the Turk gave him the authorization to do so—authorization which was not the result of a mutual accord, but rather of a grant by the Turk of limited concessions, at least at the onset, in the capitulations.

This attitude on the part of the Turks encouraged contact between foreigners and minorities, particularly since it was practically impossible for a foreigner to navigate alone and unaided the many bureaucratic way stations along the paths of commerce. As for the Turks, they relied upon Greeks and, above all, Jews, who held official or semiofficial positions within this commercial setup, in the farming of customs duties, for example.

IV

The Jews often farmed the customs tax openly or under cover of a Turkish official. Foreign merchants and ship captains had to deal with them. Moreover, since subjects of the empire were not liable for the same taxes as foreigners, it happened that foreigners, in order to pay less tax, arranged to trade under Jewish names.[34] Similarly consuls or ambassadors would avoid having their names appear on commercial documents so that they would not pay the *cottimo,* a tax imposed by the *Serenissima* on cargo bound for Venice.[35]

The financial situation of some Jews was so strong that foreign merchants, in times of need, would have recourse to them, all the while complaining about their exorbitant rates of interest.[36] Because of these advantages the Jews of Istanbul were able to engage in international trade, particularly since they maintained, directly or indirectly, close relations with the West (note the already cited examples of Doña Gracia Mendes and Don Joseph Nasi). In the seventeenth century Venetian documents even seem to suggest that Jewish families with members in Istanbul and Venice might be answerable to the Bailo—perhaps this was the case with the Francos, the Jesurums, and the Naons. The same family might have subjects of the sultan living in Istanbul and subjects of the Most Serene Republic who settled in Venice. There was nothing extraordinary about this. However, this situation applied only to a few Jewish families, well known to the Venetian authorities; the name of the Naon family, for instance, appeared frequently among the names of Venetian dragomans during the seventeenth century.

Periods of war between Venetians and Turks also benefited the Jews. During the Wars of Candia and the Holy League Venetian merchants were able to continue trade between Venice and Istanbul by using foreign vessels (English and French) and assumed names of Jews (and occasionally Frenchmen) who were certainly compensated.[37] During the seventeenth century the port of Livorno played an important role. Istanbul Jews with relatives and correspondents there and with the assistance of the English and French would use it as a way station in trade between Western Europe and the Ottoman Empire. Of course it must be made clear that those Jews of Istanbul who engaged in international commerce were a small number, that they did not own ships, and that they had either to ship their merchandise on the vessels of others—most frequently English or Venetian—or enter into partnership with foreign merchants.

As for the Greeks, they seem to have been less involved in the administrative aspects of trade. Well-located in the internal market, they were the agents in the provinces for Western merchants, the suppliers of goods from the Black Sea region—an area of trade off-limits to the West—and dealers in forbidden merchandise such as wheat whose contraband trade was centered in the Archipelago.[38] Greeks were also found in the traffic in coins which they bartered with foreigners in the Aegean Islands, Chios and others.[39] The proximity of the large Izmir market was an important factor and, for its part, Istanbul was a center of trade which was not negligible. The Greeks benefited from their ownership of ships and their dispersion throughout the empire. Subjects of the *Grand Seigneur,* nonetheless, they were very close to the Europeans for whom they rendered a number of services in many areas. They sought to gain the privileges which were granted officially only at the outset of the eighteenth century—some of them became protégés *(beratlı)* of Western ambassadors.

As for the Armenians in Istanbul, it seems that at the beginning of the seventeenth century their population had increased substantially. Centuries earlier, in the aftermath of the conquest of Constantinople, some Armenian families had been forced to migrate from Tokat, Sivas, and other cities in eastern Anatolia to the capital. By 1635 their numbers had so risen that Sultan Murad IV ordered those from Kayseri and certain other districts to be sent to their place of origin. Apparently the order was not carried out.[40]

The Armenian influx corresponds to the time when they started to occupy an increasingly important role in Eastern and Mediterranean commerce.[41] Previously they had directed the transit trade with Persia from Erzurum and eastern Armenia, but gradually they established themselves along the route from Persia to Istanbul. They were found in Sivas and Tokat, centers of agricultural production, in Ankara, center for sheep's wool and goats' wool *(tiftik),* in Bursa, center for silk and tobacco, and in Uskudar, the Istanbul bridgehead in Asia and the destination of trade from Anatolia and Persia. Together with European merchants, they played an increasing role in this trade. Certain Armenians reached significant positions in commerce and finance, for their names appear in lists of money changers and bankers. In the eighteenth century they were the most important minority merchants in the capital,[42] but previously, in the seventeenth century, they had close ties with various European merchants, especially the Dutch in Istanbul and Izmir.[43]

The Western powers tried to gain access to the Black Sea for the wheat of the Ukraine, the wood of the Anatolian coast, and the products of eastern Anatolia and Persia. They collided not only with the Turkish refusal of access but also with the monopoly of Persians and Armenians whose well-organized caravans transported to the Ottoman capital Persian silks, Indian linens, and other merchandise which came in enormous caravans of two thousand mules and camels.[44] Here, too, Armenians were the indispensable middlemen for Western merchants. The monopoly in which they participated was not broken until the nineteenth century.

V

Fernand Braudel, in his *The Mediterranean and the Mediterranean World in the Age of Philipe II,* has noted that

> in Turkey the urban bourgeoisie—essentially a merchant class—was foreign to Islam: Ragusan, Armenian, Jewish, Greek, and western. In Galata and on the islands there still survived pockets of Latin culture. . . . Two foreign businessmen were prominent in the Sultan's entourage: one, Michael Cantacuzenos, was a Greek, the other . . . [Joseph Nasi], a Jew.[45]

This observation of Braudel is not incorrect, but it is incomplete. Alongside this merchant bourgeoisie there existed another bourgeoisie, this one administrative, which comprised the high officials of the central administration—grand vezirs, vezirs of the Imperial Divan, chiefs of the army and navy, those in charge of the principal services of the capital, leading religious functionaries, and important dignitaries of the Palace. They profited from the large incomes attached to their positions and from the many revenues, legal and illegal, which were added. They had sumptuous dwellings and, often, numerous attendants. Since they were the most important consumers of local and imported products, they were a major element in commerce. In addition there was a middle bourgeoisie comprised of agents of the central and Istanbul administrations. They constituted a stable class of officials, the vast majority, Turks, although there were certain exceptions: dragoman of the grand vezir (in the seventeenth century the illustrious Greek, Panayotis), a dragoman of the *reis ül-kuttab* (a post occupied during the same period by Alexander Mavrocordato), doctors and surgeons of the Palace, often Jews, and farmers of various taxes and customs duties, also Jews or those who assumed the names of Jews.

This bourgeoisie, different in many respects from the merchant bourgeoisie, contributed to the economic life of Istanbul and the empire. Minority "officials" were also in touch with foreigners for whom they facilitated contacts with high Ottoman officials: e.g., Demetrios Cantemir who made it possible for Grand Vezir Rami Mehmed Pasa to know certain Westerners.

The growing commercial influence of the West during the seventeenth century gave more importance to minority intermediaries and enhanced the role they played especially since the Turks continued to shun international trade. There arose an alliance between the minorities and the Westerners to the detriment of the empire. As middlemen the Greeks in particular sought the protection of a great power to profit from their two-fold position. Some gained wealth and a variety of new contacts. Faced with the inefficiency and stagnation of the Ottomans, they began to consider the possibility of playing a political role. Feeling superior to the Turks, they considered working against their authority, by promoting a "national" resistance based on a "national anti-Ottoman consciousness" which eventually cleared the way to independence. In the eighteenth century the Greeks began the process;[46] the Slavs followed suit. To a large degree counting on the support, open or tacit, of the Western Powers, they persevered. With the blessing of the Powers, this process brought about the independence of the Balkan states, the reforms of the nineteenth century in the Ottoman Empire, and the growing presence— even in the highest positions—of minorities in the administration and government of the Ottoman Empire during the second half of the nineteenth century. The disintegration and the dismemberment of the Ottoman Empire had begun with the economic and later political penetration of Westerners, and was to culminate in the close ties of cooperation which the West established with the minorities who were the ones to gain the greatest advantage.

Notes

1. L. Brehier, *Le Monde byzantin,* Paris, 1950, vol. 3, pp. 85–86; G. Bratianu, *Le commerce genois dans la Mer Noire au XIIIe siecle,* Paris, 1929, pp. 89, 101–105.

2. F. Thiriet, *La Romanie venitienne,* Paris, 1959, pp. 227, 298–301, 406–409.

3. F. Thiriet, *Regestes des deliberations du Senat de Venise concernant la Romanie,* Paris-La Haye, 1961, vol. 3, no. 2994, p. 206.

4. F. Babinger, *Mahomet II le Conquerant et son temps,* Paris, 1954, p. 127.

5. Ö. L. Barkan, "Bir iskan ve kolonizasyon metodu olarak sürgünler," *IFM,* 13(1951–52), pp. 56–78 and references to Aşikpaşazade and Neşri.

6. A. Galante, *Histoire des Juifs d'Istanbul,* Istanbul, 1942, vols. 1 and 2, passim; P. Grunebaum-Ballin, *Joseph Naci, duc de Naxos,* Paris, 1968.

7. A. Galante (cited no. 6), pp. 192–194.

8. Evliya Çelebi, *Seyahatname,* Istanbul, 1898, vol. 1, p. 114.

136   The Early History of the Non-Muslim Communities

9. Topkapi Sarayı Kütüphanesi, Ms no. E 9524 (March 1478).

10. Evliya Çelebi (cited n. 8), p. 431.

11. G. Wheler, *Voyage de Dalmatie, de Grece et du Levant,* Amsterdam, 1689, p. 190.

12. F. Petis de la Croix, *Estrait du Journal de F. Petis de la Croix,* t. I, 169–170.

13. Evliya Çelebi (cited n. 8), pp. 431–432.

14. Ibid., p. 431.

15. R. Mantran, "Police des Marches d'Istanbul au debut du XVIe siecle," *Cahiers de Tunisie,* 14(1956), p. 238.

16. J. Thevenot, *Voyages de M. Thevenot au Levant et en Asie,* Paris, 1664, pp. 51–52.

17. C. Le Bruyn, *Voyage au Levant,* Delft 1700, p. 172.

18. L. d'Arvieux, *Memoires,* Paris 1735, vol. 4, p. 492.

19. Eremya Çelebi, *İstanbul Tarihi. XVII, asirda İstanbul,* Istanbul, 1952, p. 28.

20. Evliya Çelebi (cited n. 8), p. 595.

21. Documents cited by Osman Nuri, *Mecele-i Umur-u Belediye,* Istanbul 1337/1922, pp. 668–669.

22. Evliya Çelebi (cited n. 8), p. 593.

23. Numerous references to this subject in the *Mühimme Defterleri.*

24. Evliya Çelebi (cited n. 8), p. 615.

25. Ibid., p. 571.

26. Idem.

27. W. Lithgow, *The Totall Discourse of the Rare Adventures e Painfull Peregrinations. . . ,* Glasgow, 1906, p. 148; H. A. R. Gibb and H. Bowen, *Islamic Society and the West.* I, *Islamic Society in the Eighteenth Century,* vol. 1, pp. 309–310; vol. 2, pp. 23–24; A. C. Wood, *A History of the Levant Company,* London, 1935, p. 214. Numerous references in the documents of the State Archives of Venice dealing with Constantinople.

28. Y. Debbasch, *La Nation française en Tunisie, 1577–1835,* Paris, 1959, p. 43.

29. R. Mantran, *Istanbul dans la seconde moitié du XVIIe siècle,* Paris, 1962, p. 572.

30. Ibid., p. 547.

31. P. Masson, *Histoire du commerce français dans le Levant au XVIIe siècle,* Paris, 1897, pp. 454–455.

32. Evliya Çelebi (cited n. 8), p. 431, notes.

33. M. Z. Pakalın, *Osmanlı Tarih Terimleri ve Deyimleri Sözlügü,* Istanbul, 1946–1954, s.v. Galata Sarayi.

34. Numerous references concerning the English and Venetians on this subject in the documents in the French and Italian archives.

35. The Venetians used this method arousing the bitter complaint of their *baili.* Compare, for example, Alvise Contarini, *Relazione . . . dagli Ambasciatori veneziani nel secolo decimosettimo,* serie Vª, *Turchia,* Venice, 1871–1872.

36. Alvise Contarini (cited n. 35), p. 387; H. A. R. Gibb and H. Bowen (cited n. 27), vol. 1, part 2, p. 301.

37. Venetian State Archives, Archivio proprio, *passim.*

38. F. Braudel, *The Mediterranean. . . ,* trans. by Sian Reynolds, New York, 1973, Paris, 1949, vol. 1, p. 351.

39. T. Stoianovitch, "L'économie balkanique aux XVIIIe et XVIIIe siècles," These, Paris, 1952, 97.

40. J. von Hammer, *Histoire de l'Empire ottoman,* Paris, 1830, vol. 9, p. 280.

41.   F. Braudel (cited n. 38), vol. 1, pp. 50–51; N. Iorga, *Points de vue sur l'histoire du commerce de l'Orient,* Paris, 1925, p. 23.

42.   T. Stoianovitch (cited n. 39), p. 198ff.

43.   J. Chardin, *Voyages du Chevalier Chardin,* Lyon, 1687–1723, vol. 1, pp. 10–11.

44.   Compare Memoire de Roboly, Archives Nationales, B[1] 375, f° 45.

45.   F. Braudel (cited n. 38), vol. 2, p. 727.

46.   N. Svoronos, *Le commerce de Salonique au XVIII siècle,* Paris, 1956.

III

THE STRUCTURE OF THE NON-MUSLIM COMMUNITIES IN THE EIGHTEENTH CENTURY AND AFTER

8

*Millet*s and Nationality: The Roots of the Incongruity of Nation and State in the Post-Ottoman Era

Kemal H. Karpat

Introduction: The General Picture

The process of nation formation first among Christians and then among Muslims in the Ottoman state in the nineteenth and twentieth centuries was conditioned to an important extent by the socio-ethnic structure and the religious identity engendered by the *millet* system. The newly born states attached themselves to territorial bonds of secular citizenship and historical memories while their group identity, internal cohesion and socio-political values as a nation were determined by their long experience in the *millet* system. Nationality, in the sense of ethnic-national identity, drew its essence from the religious-communal experience in the *millet,* while citizenship—a secular concept—was determined by territory. In effect, the political, social and cultural crises which have buffeted the national states in the Balkans and the Middle East since their emergence can be attributed in large measure to the incompatibility of the secular idea of state with the religious concept of nation rooted in the *millet* philosophy. Thus, in the ultimate analysis, one can say that the dual process of state and nation formations in these areas followed a dichotomous course and created nation-states in which citizenship and nationality remained incongruous and at times conflicting.

It is obvious, therefore, that the study of nation formation in the Ottoman state calls for a study of the *millet* system, not only in order to understand the dichotomy between nation and state, but also in order to evaluate, in depth, the socio-cultural characteristics of the national states in the Balkans and the Middle East born out of the *millet* matrix.

The *millet* system emerged gradually as an answer to the efforts of the Ottoman administration to take into account the organization and culture of the various religious-ethnic groups it ruled. The system provided, on the one hand, a degree of religious, cultural, and ethnic continuity within these communities, while on the other it permitted their incorporation into the Ottoman administrative, economic and political system. An ethnic-religious group preserved its culture and religion while being subject to continuous "Ottomanization" in other spheres of life. It is quite understandable, therefore, why Westerners who traveled through the Ottoman domains in the seventeenth and eighteenth centuries found sharp differences of customs, language, and religion among various regions and communities, but also observed that they were similar in economic, social and political outlook.

The *millet* system was a socio-cultural and communal framework based, firstly, on religion, and, secondly, on ethnicity which in turn often reflected linguistic differences. Religion supplied to each *millet* a universal belief system while ethnic and linguistic differences provided for divisions and subdivisions within each one of the two Christian *millets*. Thus the close affinity between religion and ethnicity which had been the landmark of group identity in the Middle East was preserved and adapted to the exigencies of the Ottoman system in such a way as to make the *millets* a rather unique institution in the annals of social history. Religion, language, community, ethnicity and the family made up the socio-cultural fabric of the *millet* and thus deserve a very brief survey. Religion, which sanctified the communality of the belief system and the supremacy of the family, functioned as a hierarchy of authority culminating in the chief prelate, that is the patriarch, of each *millet* and ultimately in the ruler, the sultan. Language appeared both as a means of communication and as the distinguishing mark of the ethnic subdivisions in the *millet,* although linguistic differences had limited, if any, political significance until about the eighteenth century when the Greek language began to be used as a means to Hellenize the Orthodox *millet.* The Armenian *millet* was spared internal schism not only because of its special structure, but also because there was no effort to spread that language to other subgroups.

The community was the basic organizational unit of the *millet* without which its existence was rather inconceivable. It consisted essentially of people who belonged to the same faith. A community was a religious congregation as much as it was a social and administrative unit. The leadership of the community at the grass-roots level, that is, in the villages and in the town quarters *("mahalle"),* consisted of the representative of the religion, the priest, and the actual administrative head of the community itself, usually a prominent layman living there. The priest acted as the spiritual head of the community and as the intermediary between it and the upper ecclesiastical authorities. The communal leaders at the town level formed the second layer of leadership and enjoyed greater authority and influence, not only because of their connection with the higher Ottoman authorities and their own ecclesiastical heads, but also because of their wealth and their responsibility in collecting taxes and supervising the distribution of state lands to cultivators. They represented the community in its day-to-day dealings with the Ottoman administration and were responsible for order, security, collection of taxes, etc., in the community. Since communication with the members of the community was essential for the primates in order to carry out their obligations, they had to speak the local language and to conform to local customs and traditions.

So the community played a major role as the collective representative and repository of local ethnic, cultural, and linguistic peculiarities. Linguistic, ethnic and religious assimilation occurred on a local basis, rather than on a global one, and was largely voluntary, based on the relative influence of a majority group. It was under Ottoman rule that many Turkish tribes adopted Arabic, Persian, and even Kurdish as their vernacular when living among a larger group speaking such a tongue.

The family was the foundation of the community as well as the chief institution which preserved and transmitted culture. Recent studies have indicated that the family is indeed the chief agent which preserves values and culture and transmits them to the new generations. The *millet* system favored the fusion of the family and the community—the latter can be regarded as an overgrown family—and thus provided a sound basis for the preservation of the grass-roots ethnic identity and customs of a given group.

It is important to note that the Ottomans inherited in the Balkans not states whose populations had developed distinctive political-national allegiances, but rather clusters of urban and rural communities bearing the memory of various ruling dynasties, bitter wars, invasions, and migrations which had ravaged the area from the eighth to thirteenth centuries. The Ottoman government itself consciously eliminated the scions of the old ruling dynasties, not in order to obliterate the political memories of its subjects, but in order to forestall schism and unrest. In sum, the *millet* system emphasized the universality of the faith and superseded ethnic and linguistic differences without destroying them. The policies of the Ottoman government profoundly affected the social and economic life of the community but did not alter its cultural and religious life.

The nation formation process which reached its acute phase chiefly during the second half of the nineteenth century was the consequence of a series of economic and social changes, and of a transformation in the concept of authority, all of which, important as they are, cannot be studied in detail here. Suffice it to mention that the change in land tenure, the administrative reforms and the subsequent new responsibilities given to communal leaders, the rise of propertied groups, and a certain economic vitality gained by some non-Muslim communities undermined the authority of the clergy and enhanced the power of the lay primates.

The disintegration of the traditional *millet*s and communities left the family as the only unit from the old era which retained its structure relatively intact. The family reflected the religious values and the ethnic and linguistic peculiarities of its community and was the chief social unit through which the individual related himself, on a regional basis, to the large, diversified urban communities and ethnic groups. In other words, the individual, freed of the influence of the *millet,* began to develop a sense of identity and belonging in the new socio-political units—urban communities and perceived nations—through the ethnic values, culture, traditions and language preserved in the family. The Ottoman government, on the other hand, instead of following the logical direction of these developments, say, by recognizing the emerging ethnic-religious units as autonomous bodies and incorporating them into some sort of federal or similar structure, imposed upon them, under the impact of pressure of the European powers, a common Ottoman nationality or citizenship without considering whether this nationality could represent and express satisfactorily the religious, ethnic and regional aspirations and the rising national consciousnesses of the various ethnic groups. It is true that the Ottoman government actively supported the reforms of the *millet*s in the 1860s and recognized the religous and cultural peculiarities of each group as part of their religious and cultural rights and freedoms, but this was done without seeking to resolve the incongruity and growing conflict between the developing legal secular concept of state and the idea of nationality rooted in religious identity. In the old days, the *millet*s were able to reconcile the religious, ethnic and cultural characteristics of various social groups within the Ottoman political system as a whole, largely because the political and religious-cultural systems could coexist independently of each other. The idea of the national state, as it emerged among the Ottoman Christians in the nineteenth century, demanded that the political system and the religious-national culture be expressions of each other. One can say that the very essence of the nation-state rests upon the unity of the cultural and political systems. Yet, there is a fundamental difference between the emergence of national states in western as opposed to southeastern Europe. In the West, the nation emerged by stressing its linguistic and cultural peculiarities in order to assert the king's rights against the authority of the Church. In southeastern Europe, the Christians claimed national statehood and independence by asserting their religious differences with regard to the role of the Muslim sultans. Thus religion became the foundation of their nationhood and, despite a variety of other cultural, ethnic and historical factors which helped to define the national identity of the Balkan states, religion continued to color, consciously or subconsciously, their view of the Ottoman state, of the Turks in general and of their own identity in particular.

   The observations made in this paper refer largely to the non-Muslim groups in the Balkans assembled under the Orthodox *millet,* whose transformation preceded that of the other *millet*s in the Near East. The structure and function of what may be called the Muslim *millet,* and especially its political and social outlook, was not different from its Christian and Jewish counterparts. A series of new social, political and economic pressures emerging chiefly in the late nineteenth and early twentieth centuries produced among Muslims different patterns of evolution, without, however, affecting drastically the impact of communities and families in determining the individual's cultural and ultimately political outlook. Some of these ideas will be developed in the next sections.

The Structure of the Early *Millet* System

A cursory survey of the history and composition of the early *millet*s supports the view concerning the relationship between religion and ethnicity mentioned in the previous section. The first major *millet,* the Orthodox, was established in 1454 and, for the first time since the heyday of the Byzantine Empire, the Orthodox Christians were brought together under a single religious authority. Though the election of the patriarch was approved by the sultan, this did not affect the *millet*'s inherent rights and freedoms. In contrast to the situation prevailing during the Byzantine period, the patriarch was not longer the humble servant of the emperor, but a recognized and respected member of the sultan's bureaucracy enjoying full jurisdiction over his followers. The clergy had control over the church organization, the schools, and the legal and court systems. They administered the extensive church properties, which had the same status as the *vakf* property. With such economic power, the Orthodox church enhanced its authority over communities, churches and schools in accordance with its own understanding and interpretation of the original authority invested in it by Sultan Mehmet II (1451–81).

The sultan might have been prompted chiefly by political considerations in giving to the Orthodox *millet* extensive cultural self-rule, probably in order to reward the anti-unionists and allay the fears of the unionists. Indeed, Mehmet II regarded the Papacy and Venice as his main enemies and sought by all possible means to neutralize their influence among the Christians in the Balkans. The establishment of the Orthodox *millet* and the installment of George Scholarius (Gennadios II), the head of the anti-unionist party, as patriarch in 1454 set the model for the other millets. Anyway, the *millet* system was a key element in Mehmet II's legislation which in turn provided the constitutional framework of the Ottoman state, and was formally preserved until the age of reforms. It is of the utmost importance to stress the fact that the rights and freedoms granted by Sultan Mehmet II to the original *millet* were given in perpetuity and thus became inherent in the *millet* itself without being subject to renewal, abolition or limitation.

The Armenian *millet* with its own patriarchate was established in 1461, while the Jewish *millet* was founded later. Thus, the Greeks and Armenians appeared as the dominant Christian groups in the West and East respectively. The patriarchates in Istanbul, notwithstanding the existence of other older Armenian and Orthodox Patriarchates, gained priority because of their location in the capital.

It seems, at first glance, that the special representative status given to the Greeks and Armenians placed these two ethnic groups in a superior position versus the others, but this was in fact not necessarily correct. Until about the middle of the eighteenth century the patriarchs emphasized the universality of the faith and not their respective ethnic origin or language since they could maintain their position in their socially and ethnically diversified *millet*s only by upholding the universal elements of the faith. However, it is important to note that the religious and communal leaders below the higher echelons who maintained day-to-day contact with the community usually belonged to the ethnic group dominant in a given area. Since the upper level of the Orthodox Christian *millet* appeared to be Greek, many observers came to believe that the lower clergy was also largely Greek or had been Hellenized. It is true that the Orthodox church was referred to as "Greek" but until the second half of the eighteenth century the term had no national significance. The lower clergy belonged mostly to the ethnic and linguitic communities they served. For instance, the Armenian Patriarch of Istanbul from 1896 to 1908 described the situation in the following way:

> It was in this manner that the two patriarchs, Greek and Armenian, became recognized as the heads of the two great Orthodox Christian parties in the East; that division was established on the basis of a profession of faith, independently of any consideration of race or nationality. All the orthodox dyophysites, viz., Greeks, Bulgarians, Serbians, Albanians, Wallachians, Moldavians, Ruthenians, Croatians, Caramanians, Syrians, Melkites, and Arabs, became associated, *under their respective chiefs,* with the jurisdiction of the Greek patriarch; while the orthodox monophysites, comprising the Armenians, Syrians, Chaldaeans, Copts, Georgians, and Abyssinians, became subject, *under their respective chiefs,* to the jurisdiction of the Armenian patriarch (italics added).[1]

Harry Luke has also described the situation in clear and precise terms.

> Had a rayah not been a member of this or that millet, he would have had no civil status, would in fact have been comparable to a man of no nationality today, but for the system, the smaller Christian Churches must have been extinguished.[2]

In fact, any infringement upon the ethnic and linguistic integrity of a community, even if done on behalf of religion, could create a reaction and break the unity of faith and undermine the authority of the Church as happened, indeed, after the Orthodox Patriarchate tried to resurrect Byzantium in the eighteenth century through the Hellenization of the existing ethnic churches and religious schools. This policy caused a defensive reaction among non-Greek-speaking Christians, such as the Bulgarians, and led to the establishment of a Bulgarian Exarchate.

   The survival of the ethnic groups in the *millet* was assured and reinforced indirectly by a system of local administration based on rural (village) or town quarter *(mahalle)* communities. The basic organizational unit of the *millet* was, as mentioned, the family-based community, and community meant above everything else a body of persons professing the same faith and in many cases speaking the same language. It was possible for a locality to consist of several distinct communities with their own leaders, although villages tended to consist of a single community.

Initially, after the Ottoman conquest, some Christian chieftains had assumed administrative and military duties extending over entire regions but gradually after the sixteenth century their responsibilities became confined to communal affairs, such as the maintenance of order, collection of taxes, supplying of information to higher authorities, gathering supplies for the army in passage through their region and other duties. Already by the end of the sixteenth century the leading Christian families had either converted to Islam, lost their wealth and prominence, or had migrated elsewhere. The community heads, although in some cases related to the early leaders, seemed in most cases to have come from the lower ranks of the native society. They were known generally as primates or *primkur* according to the prevailing language and administrative precedent, and addressed as *knez, voyvoda, primkur, protogeros,* etc. Later, after Turkish became more widely spoken, some of the titles were changed to *çorbacı* (town head) and *kocabaşı* (village head), etc., in accordance with Ottoman practices. For instance, the term, *kocabaşı,* which can be translated as "big head," derived in reality from the term, *ocakbaşı,* which referred to the head of a hearth or simply of a community. The government and the patriarch relied on the primates and the local clergy in order to communicate with villages and town districts since these communal leaders spoke the local language or dialect and possessed high social or religious status which elicited the respect and obedience of the local people.

The general administrative system of the state in the early centuries also prevented the fusion of various ethnic groups into larger political units. The basic Ottoman administrative unit, the *eyalet,* was very large and cut across ethnic boundaries. For instance, the *eyalet* of Sofia comprised Salonica, Yanya (Jannina), Semendere—just to cite a few of its sixteen *sancak*s that harbored at least a dozen different ethnic groups, including Turks, Greeks, Bulgarians, Vlachs, Serbs, Macedonians, etc. Today the *eyalet* of Sofia is part of Bulgaria, Greece and Yugoslavia.

It was difficult in these circumstances for several related ethnic or linguistic groups to combine into one single social or political unit and establish numerical control over a specific region except for a few areas, such as the Peloponnesus or the Aegean Islands where the Greek settlements were compact. Thus, while the basic *millet* was universal and anational, the small community had distinctive local, ethnic and linguistic peculiarities. The *millet* system therefore produced, simultaneously, religious universality and local parochialism. The balance between religious universalism and ethnic-cultural localism could be maintained as long as the economic and social organization remained intact, social mobility was low and the central government remained strong enough to maintain the status quo. A conflict, however, could develop if the representatives of a *millet* attempted to tailor religion according to the political aspirations of an ethnic group. Conflict could erupt also if various segments of an ethnic or linguistic group broke loose from their communal framework and attempted to reintegrate themselves into larger socio-political units in seeking a new socio-economic and political status and identity.

From an ethnic viewpoint, the *millet* system was a response to the hetero-geneous society in the Balkans. The Ottoman state established its rule in the Balkans over a mosaic of languages and cultures which the Slavic and Turkic migrations in the fifth through eleventh centuries had deposited upon the already existing Greek, Macedonian, Scythian, etc., population of the area.[3] There is no question that the Balkans possessed prior to the rise of the Ottoman state a large number of Turkic groups—such as the Pecheneks, Cumans, Tatars, Karakalpaks, Uz (Oguz), and Seljuki Turks. Some of these had converted to Christianity and had adopted in places the language of the majority while others had remained Muslim and preserved their original lan-guages. This fact is clearly demonstrated by T. Kowalski who found three vocabulary layers—Nordic Turkic, Anatolian and Ottoman—in the Turkish spoken in northeast Bulgaria.[4] The Byzantine Empire, although instrumental in extending Orthodox Christianity throughout much of the Balkan peninsula, was unable to cope with this ethnic diversity and could not produce real unity, as is clearly indicated by the survival of a series of churches identified with specific ethnic groups. It had collapsed because, among other reasons, it had been unable to deal with the ethnic and religious diversity in its Balkan territories and with the social conflicts which fueled it. The Ottomans in-herited this situation and, presumably, were aware of its dangerous implica-tions. Indeed, the struggle among Bayezid's sons, Süleyman, Musa, İsa and Mehmet, early in the fifteenth century, which involved the Muslim and Chris-tian peasantry, the lords of the Balkans, and the Anatolian Turkish nobility had already nearly caused the disintegration of the Ottoman state. The fact is that the feudal system established by Western Crusaders in parts of the Bal-kans, coupled with that of the Byzantines, had transformed much of the ethnic-religious tensions into social conflicts. Catholicism appeared both as a threat to the Orthodox church and as a supporter of the feudal system estab-lished by Western knights, the last of which was brought finally under Otto-man control in 1440.[5] One can further claim that some of the local Greek leaders who had served as intermediaries between the Frankish lords and their own peasantry were more than willing to serve the Ottoman lords in some capacity. Thus Mehmet II, who was familiar with the complex ethnic-religious-social situation in the Balkans, used the *millet* system in order to neutralize these differences and secure a degree of harmony.

The Legal Status of the *Millets* and the Ethnic Groups: Principles and Practice

The constitutional basis of the Ottoman *millet* system was the Muslim concept which recognized the non-Muslim monotheistic believers as the

"Peoples of the Book" and accorded them protection as *dhimmī*s. Although the Ottoman *millet*s remained theoretically within the legal framework of the *dhimmī* concept, in practice their status was determined by the prevailing linguistic and ethnic conditions in the Balkans, as well as by other Islamic principles which gave tacit recognition to linguistic and ethnic differences. Indeed, Islam gave tacit recognition to tribal, ethnic and national groupings, provided that these conformed to the principles of family law and recognized the supremacy of the *umma*. Moreover, the pronouncement "and we have made you into peoples and tribes" (Quran 49:13) can be interpreted as a tacit recognition of the existence of ethnic, linguistic and tribal diversities within the community of believers. The very term *millet* had the meaning of nation but without political connotation. Similar provisions may also be found in the *Surat al-Mā'ida* (5:45–50), which has been interpreted as giving, derivatively, recognition, and even the right of self-determination, to Jewish and Christian minorities.[6]

Obviously, Islam could not support divisions which could threaten the political supremacy and the unity of the Muslim community, *umma* or *ummet,* the latter being the Turkified form of the same. Consequently, it did not regulate ethnic and linguistic divisions in any detail, despite the existence of some *hadith*s on the subject, thus leaving the Muslim ruler considerable freedom to deal with the problem as the situation demanded. The recognition given by the Ottoman government to the Kurds and Turkmen under the label of *kara millet* and *boz millet* can be regarded as an acceptance of ethnic or social differences within the Muslim *ummet*. Consequently, it would be correct to state that the Ottoman rulers relied on *sura*s 5 and 49 of the Quran to recognize the ethnic and linguistic diversity among their non-Muslim subjects. The *millet* system in effect was the outcome of the Ottoman effort to reconcile the ethnic and linguistic realities of their realm with the commandments of Islam.

The paradox of the situation lies in the fact that the *millet* system brought the non-Muslims within a Muslim principle of organization while recognizing their religious and cultural freedom. Organizationally, the Christians were "Islamized" much the same way in which the Ottoman state was "westernized," (or as some Muslims contended, converted to Christian ways) after it began adopting the nineteenth century reforms inspired by the West. I believe that the Ottoman rulers treated their non-Muslim subjects as members of communities with specific ethnic and linguistic characteristics, rather than regarding all of them as part of one uniform *dhimmī* group. I would further argue that the status of the non-Muslims, while theoretically based on Islamic principles including the *dhimmī* concept, in practice came to be determined by the individual's relation to the state. Social ranking in Ottoman society was decided on the basis of service to the state, rather than strictly on religion (the situation of the government and its bureaucracy was different and must be treated separately). The *dhimmī* status began to be applied to non-Muslims chiefly in the nineteenth century after social changes and reforms had undermined the *millet* system and had produced a situation whereby the Ottoman population began to be divided into minorities and majorities chiefly on the basis of their religion. Henceforth the Christians began to be called *raya,* which denoted lower social and political ranking.

The chief distinguishing legal characteristic of the *dhimmī* in the early Islamic states was the special tax levied on them. In the Ottoman state the *haraç* (land tax later converted into a head tax or *cizye* and later in the nineteenth century into *bedel-i askeri* or payment in lieu of military service) was apparently paid only by one third of the *dhimmī* population. Many Christian groups such as the *derbend, dogancis,* and *voynuks,* who performed a variety of services, were exempt from taxes as were their Muslim counterparts. Indeed, Christians in towns such as Kotel, Grabovo, Kalofer, and Klissura, in Bulgaria were tax-exempt because of the services (security, road and bridge maintenance, falconry) performed for the state. Other towns specializing in metal works such as Kratovo, Samakov and Teshevo had a special tax status. (It is interesting to note that from the start these towns played a significant role in the transformation of the Bulgarian miller and the development of a Bulgarian folk culture in the eighteenth and nineteenth centuries.) Non-Muslim females, children, infirm males, the aged and slaves as well as members of prominent families in government service were similarly exempt from the head tax. Consequently, it is extremely difficult to claim that the mere fact of being non-Muslim conferred automatically a *dhimmī* status upon an individual. It is probably more accurate to claim that it was rather the administrative role of the individual which determined his tax status which, in turn, determined his social status both in Ottoman society and in his own *millet.*

An early Ottoman document dealing with this issue establishes beyond a doubt that the *knez* and *primkuran,* that is the local heads of non-Muslim communities, were charged with assisting government officials and notables in collecting taxes, bringing back fugitive land cultivators *(raya),* etc. (According to one explanation the *knez* was the head of the township and *kaza,* while the *primkur* was the head of the village.) They were exempt, because of their services to the state, from taxes *(haraç* and *ispençe)* or from tithes on their own lands *(baştina).* The documents state that "since the aforementioned [*knez* and *primkur*] were engaged in the service of the treasury, the beys should not inconvenience them by taking them to war."[7] Thus, on balance, it seems that tax status among Ottoman subjects was determined chiefly by service to the state rather than religion.

The implications of this basic principle is vital to understanding the evolution of the *millet*s. It meant that since service to the state, and not religion, was basic in determining the payment of taxes and certain social ranking, changes in the functions of the primates were bound to affect their relations with the government and their status and function in their respective community regardless of religion. In fact, that is exactly what occurred in the nineteenth century after the government became increasingly dependent on primates for a variety of services concerning the taxation and administration of non-Muslim communities.

The original *millet* structure was maintained as long as the Ottoman government remained strong enough to fulfill its chief responsibility, namely to assure social harmony by keeping each social group in its place. However, change was inevitable after the classical Ottoman society established in the fifteenth century became subject to a variety of new influences from within and outside. The resulting change affected the hierarchical order in the local communities by giving the communal leaders, that is the notables or primates, a dominant position, and by making language the distinguishing characteristic of the newly-emerging ethnic-national units. Indeed, the transformation of Ottoman society which began early in the eighteenth century helped merge various family-based ethnic and linguistic groups into larger social and economic units which eventually claimed independence and statehood. Consequently, it is appropriate to state that the structural transformation of the traditional community, that is, the basic units of the *millet*s, and the ensuing change in the role and positions of communal leaders, can best explain the transformation of the *millet*s in general, and the nationality process in the Ottoman state in particular.

It has been said that the church helped maintain the ethnic identity of various "national" groups and was instrumental in mobilizing the masses against Ottoman rule during the period of national renaissance. It is obvious that these explanations do not correspond fully to the actual situation. It is probably much more accurate to view the maintenance of the ethnic and linguistic identity of various non-Muslim groups as resulting not from a conscious effort of the church, but as the consequence of the particular organization of the *millet*s, based on communities and the family as the respositories of ethnic culture as explained before. It is interesting to note in this context that all efforts at creating separate groups with a distinct political identity in the Ottoman state as early as the sixteenth century operated within the framework of religion and not secular statehood. For instance, the Uniate secession from the Nestorian Church began in 1551, and was recognized as the Chaldean Church by Pope Julius II in 1553. The Papacy was instrumental also in creating a Syrian Catholic Church through the dissent of a small group from the Syrian Jacobite Church as early as 1662. The Uniate Greek Church was formed at the end of the seventeenth century and its leader attempted to occupy the vacant Patriarchate of Antioch in 1724 but was thwarted by the Ottoman-supported synod in Istanbul. The Maronites, who had all the characteristics of a sub-*millet,* adopted a constitution by 1736 and, enjoying the protection of the Druze chief Fakhr al-Din, and then of Louis XIV, consolidated their position and expanded their influence even into northern Syria (Aleppo). None of these secessionist religious movements had "national" goals or a secularist orientation. Whereas in Europe secularization had been initated by lay rulers who had come to regard the national state as a legitimate area to exert their own authority free of church control, this was not and could not be the case in the Ottoman state where existing linguistic and ethnic identities were deliberately subordinated to religious ones. All this changed in the eighteenth and nineteenth centuries.

The Social Transformation of the *Millets* and the Primates' Ascent to Power

Ottoman society underwent profound changes in the seventeenth and eighteenth centuries under the influence of a series of internal and external economic, political and military factors. I have attempted elsewhere to deal with the causes and changes in the Ottoman social structure after the sixteenth century, largely in order to better explain the nature of change and reform in the nineteenth century, and it is not necessary to repeat that information here.[8] Suffice it to mention that these changes altered the land tenure system, the army, the social arrangement, the communal organization and ultimately the social structure and leadership of the *millets*. The national stirrings among the Ottoman *millets* emerged as a consequence of these structural developments and not chiefly because the ruler and the ruled were of a different faith as posited incorrectly by R. W. Seton-Watson.[9] The differences in faith produced friction only after the *millets* and communities had lost their original structures, a new secular culture had emerged and the differences between the Muslim ruler and the Christian ruled came to be expressed in political terms.

The structural changes which affected the *millet* system were embodied, firstly, in the rise of the rural notables to power, secondly, in the birth of new entrepreneurial-commercial elites in towns, and, thirdly, in the rise of a secular intelligentsia. The structural differentiation assumed social and political significance due in large measure to the fact that the latter two groups rose first among the non-Muslims. These were secular groups whose economic and political demands conflicted with their own church, the organization of the *millet* and with the traditional Ottoman concepts of authority.

The communal leaders' initial rise to power was facilitated after the sixteenth century by their assumption of increased responsibility in the collection of taxes and in the assignment of *miri,* or state lands, to the cultivators. The *ayan*s and the primates replaced the *sipahi,* the cavalrymen who were formerly the provincial representatives of the central government and who had lost their military preeminence to the foot soldiers. Meanwhile, the increased demand for agricultural commodities, both from the Ottoman army engaged continually in wars against the Austrians and Russians, and also from central and western Europe which were then undergoing urbanization, created new opportunities for the rural and town primates to accumulate wealth and gain social status. The celebrated *celep*s, the cattle merchants of Bulgaria, are but one example of these rural groups who achieved social and economic prominence. The power of the notables, both Muslims, that is the *ayan, eşraf* and *derebey*s, and the non-Muslim primates, was enhanced further after the mid-eighteenth century by the disintegration of the central government's authority over most of its territories.

Commercial elites arose in towns as a consequence of the same economic forces which promoted the rise of the communal leaders, with the exception that the primates were engaged chiefly in agricultural production while the merchants dealt with the exchange of commodities. The merchant elite consisted chiefly of non-Muslims after 1800, and these became the favored intermediaries of the European commercial interests because of their wealth and modernist attitudes, especially those engaged in international trade.

The rise of the rural notables is probably the most significant social development in the eighteenth century as far as the *millets* are concerned. The few early studies on the *ayan*s and the *derebey*s have depicted them as opportunistic rebels who took advantage of the government's weakness in order to strengthen their own authority in their respective regions. Recent studies, however, have stressed the fact that many notables drew their influence not only from their position in the community, but also from the ownership of large estates, buildings, and livestock. Many of these estates were operated with hired labor.[10]

The Ottoman government came to accept the *ayanlık,* that is, the area placed under the administrative responsibility of an *ayan,* as an administrative unit in the eighteenth century. Already by 1765 Muhsınzade Mehmet Paşa had decreed that the grand vezir had to approve the *ayan* elected by the population. The decree was abolished but then restored after its author became grand vezir once again. The important relation between ethnic grouping and administrative reorganization of the Ottoman state deserves close study.

In the late eighteenth and early nineteenth centuries the *ayanlık* corresponded to the surface of a *kaza* which became a basic administrative unit after reforms were introduced in the nineteenth century. (See Appendix I.) The *kaza* population often consisted of the people belonging to the same ethnic and linguistic group whereas the old *eyalet*s were of large size and had cut across ethnic boundaries. Consequently some of the new *eyalet*s and *kaza*s in the European regions of the Ottoman state came to consist of non-Muslims. In fact some of the new *eyalet*s were given the name of the predominant ethnic population, such as *Sirb* (Serbian) *eyaleti,* whose capital was at Belgrade. The nucleus of future national states was thus established.

The developments outlined above contained the seeds of ethnic and social conflict. It seems that the office of *ayanlık* was awarded only to Muslims, who thus acquired a rather favored position in the lucrative tax gathering activity and posed a serious threat to the economic interests of the non-Muslim primates. It is therefore understandable why the Greek *kocabaşı*s (village heads) of Morea played such a significant role in the uprising of 1770, only to be confronted and defeated by the army gathered by the Muslim *ayan*s. Whenever suitable to their interests, the Muslim *ayan*s realigned themselves with the government and used its support to enhance their own economic and political positions. The Muslim *ayan*s lived mainly in towns and usually administered their land in absentia, while the non-Muslim primates administered directly and *worked* their own land and often lived in the countryside villages among their kin. The rising economic and administrative power of the *ayan*s and primates and the diversification of their occupational habits and residence further brought the cultural differences between them into the open. The Muslim *ayan*s, in order to assert their autonomy and social position, built in their provincial capitals mosques, schools and *konak*s (mansions), using local artistic motifs or, often, imitating Istanbul architectural and decorative styles and even those of Europe.[11] The mosques of Pasvanoğlu in Vidin (Bulgaria) and of Capanoğlu in Yozgat (central Anatolia) are just two examples of these works. Yet, paradoxically as the reforms enhanced the authority of the central government, the Muslims began increasingly to look to it for status, position and recognition. Consequently a large number of Muslim notables became identified religiously and culturally with the central government even if they opposed it on political grounds.

Meanwhile, the Christian primates tended to identify themselves with their community and its ethnic culture and religion since their chances for upward mobility into the upper ranks of the Ottoman administration were limited. This situation was a determining factor throughout the centuries and forced the primates to seek achievement and social rewards within their own community. Even though the administrative reforms incorporated them into the Ottoman administration in the nineteenth century, this belated measure did not diminish their ethnic and linguistic attachments to their native community. Indeed, the primates played major cultural roles in their communities. Some built churches and monasteries and even schools and provided them with continuous help. The gravestones in the monasteries and churches of Rila and Koprivishita in Bulgaria, just to mention a few sites, contain the names of scores of Bulgarian primates who were instrumental in the cultural development of their towns. The primates also built large mansions and decorated them lavishly, since the building of a large house in one's village or in the nearby town was considered a symbol of achievement, prestige and position. Furthermore, the rich primates made lavish use of native music and dances at the banquets and festivities that took place regularly in their homes. It is true that most of these cultural activities were strongly influenced by models provided by Istanbul and Europe, but they had a rather significant impact in rehabilitating native traditions and generalizing the use of local folk music and dances which often corresponded to the culture of an ethnic group. Moreover, all these activities, ranging from building and decorating houses to playing local music, helped to create and expand the size of local professional groups which more often than not became the craftsmen and folk artists of a specific ethnic and linguistic group. After the establishment of independent states in the Balkans, all this became officially part of the national culture.

All these lay cultural activities were carried out originally under a religious garb. A primate would not start building his house until the priest had blessed *(sfeshtany)* the foundation. A cross would be affixed on the beam of the roof and the dweller would move into the house only after the priest had recited the appropriate prayers and sprinkled holy water in each room. The priest would officiate at weddings, baptisms, and burials. During the festivities the priest would have a place of honor at the table. The other members of the community would ask the priest to perform the same services, usually against a payment in kind or cash. Since the clergy was supported not by a regular salary but by the income derived from religious services, he could at times exploit the believers who revenged themselves by coining sayings such as "a stomach like a priest's" which is still used in the Balkans to describe voraciousness. In sum, the primates played, perhaps unwittingly, an important role in strengthening the association between folk culture, religion and community.

The study of the socio-cultural transformation of the non-Muslim *millets* in the Balkans would be one-sided if demographic and economic changes and the subsequent rise of new elites were ignored. After the annexation of the Crimea by the Russians in 1783, the Serbian and Greek revolts of 1804 and 1821, respectively, and Crimean and Russo-Ottoman wars of 1853 and 1877, the Ottoman territories in Europe and Anatolia became subject to exceptionally important demographic changes. The Muslim Tatars, forced out of Bujak and the Crimea, came to settle in Anatolia and the Balkans while the Kirjalis in the Rhodope Mountains forced many non-Muslims to seek refuge in the valleys and congregate in the towns. The *sipahis* of Serbia and Muslim landlords in Macedonia usurped the Christian villagers' land or subjected them to arbitrary taxation in utter violation of the old Ottoman practices. Bulgarians from Vidin and Lom migrated to Russia, but later returned on ships supplied by the government and many Serbs migrated to Austria-Hungary. Meanwhile, millions of Muslims dislocated from the Caucasus, the Balkans, Wallachia and Moldavia settled in Anatolia. Most of the Gagauzes (Christian Turks) left their homes in Bulgaria (around Varna and Cavarna) and settled in Russia (Moldavia).

The migration into the towns and cities provided the villagers not only with greater freedom of occupational choice, but also liberated them from the authority of the rural primates and the clergy. The expansion of trade and increased demand for agricultural commodities in the nineteenth century further stimulated the growth of port cities and towns creating new employment opportunities. Many of the dislocated people, especially the Balkan Christians, settled in towns and formed new communities different in composition and outlook from the traditional ones. Villagers in turn began to perform seasonal work in cities, a notable example being the gardeners of central Bulgaria, who learned their trade in Istanbul but later went as far as Bucharest and Austria-Hungary to practice their profession. Thus, during the first half of the nineteenth century the rural and urban communities which established closer contacts with each other, and even with foreign lands, became subject to a variety of outside cultural and political influences which sensitized their ethnic and religious consciousness. The new urban communities also produced new merchant and intellectual elites who became instrumental in the reform of the *millets* and the rise of national movements.

The changes in the Ottoman society were reflected in the *millets*. Already by the end of the eighteenth century the primates had acquired greater roles and influence in community affairs than had the clergy. After the abolition of the *sipahis* in 1830, many of the administrative and police functions performed by them were entrusted to the communal heads. The primates' responsibilities now extended even to the administration of religious schools which had been traditionally under religious control and were often financed by revenue from church properties. A series of modern schools, such as the Grabovo chain established by Aprilov, a rich Bulgarian merchant from Odessa, already competed with purely religious schools and eventually limited the latter to the teaching of religious subjects. Thus, one can say that in the nineteenth century changing conditions had forced the primates to become more closely associated with the Ottoman government as its chief local administrators while strengthening their position in their communities. The clergy, in turn, fully aware of the primates' increasing administrative and economic power, often sided with them in settling conflicts with the peasants. The primates' power and their relations with the peasants is perhaps best illustrated in the following lengthy but rather perceptive observation by an eye witness (Mrs. John Elijah Blunt):

> My recollections of Bulgarian social life are to a great extent derived from a three months' stay I made under the hospitable roof of a Bulgarian gentleman, or *Chorbadji,* as he was called by his own people. He was the most wealthy and influential person in the town of . . . where his position as a member of the *meljeiss* constituted him the chief guardian and advocate of the Bulgarian people of the district. . . . I was allowed to study in the midst of the home and family life both of the educated and thinking Bulgarians and of the peasants who daily flocked to the house of my friend from the towns and villages to submit to him their wrongs and grievances, and, as their national representative, to ask his advice and assistance before proceeding to the local courts.
>
> The levees began sometimes as early as six o'clock in the morning, and lasted until eleven. The *Kodjabashi,* or headmen, would come in a body to consult about the affairs of the community, or to represent some grave case pending before the local court of their respective towns; or groups of peasants of both sexes, sometimes representing the population of a whole village, would arrive, at the request of the authorities, to answer some demand made by them, or plead against an act of gross injury or injustice. Whatever the cause that brought them daily under my notice, the picture they presented was extremely curious and interesting. . . . When the interested visitors happened to be the elders of their little communities or towns, they were shown into the study of my host. After exchanging salutes and shaking hands, they were offered *slatko* (preserves) and coffee, and business was at once entered into. At such moments the Bulgarian does not display the heat and excitement that characterises the Greek, nor fall

into the uproarious argument of the Armenians and Jews, nor yet display the finessing wit of the Turk; but steering a middle course between these different modes of action, he stands his ground and perseveres in his argument, until he has either made his case clear or is persuaded to take another view of it. The subjects that most animated the Bulgarians in these assemblies were their national affairs and their dissensions with the Greeks: the secondary ones were the wrongs and grievances they suffered from a bad administration; and although they justly lamented these, and at times bitterly complained of the neglect or incapacity of the Porte to right them in an effective manner and put a stop to acts of unjustice committed by their Mohammedan neighbours and the local courts, I at no time noticed any tendency to disloyalty or revolutionary notions, nor any disposition to court Russian protection, from which, indeed, the most enlightened and important portion of the nation at that period made decided efforts to keep aloof.

When it was the peasants who gathered at the *Chorbadji's* house, their band was led by its Kodja-Bashi, who, acting as spokesman, first entered the big gate, followed by a long train of his brethren. Ranged in a line near the porch, they awaited the coming of the master to explain to him the cause of their visit. Their distinguished-looking patron, pipe in hand, shortly made his appearance at the door, when caps were immediately doffed, and the right hands were laid on the breast and hidden by the shaggy beards bending over them in a salaam, answered by a kindly "Dobro deni" (Good morning), followed by the demand, "Shtosakaty?" (What do you want?). The peasants, with an embarrassed air, looked at each other, while the Kodja-Bashi proceeded to explain matters. Should his eloquence fall short of the task, one or two others would step out of the ranks and become spokesman. It was almost painful to see these simple people endeavouring to give a clear and comprehensive account of their case, and trying to understand the advice and directions of the *Chorbadji*. A half-frightened, surprised look, importing fear or doubt, a shrug of the shoulders, accompanied by the words "Ne znam—Ne mozhem" (I do not know, I cannot do), was generally the first expression in answer to the eloquence of my friend, who in his repeated efforts to explain matters frequently lost all patience and would end by exclaiming "Ne biddy magari!" (Don't be donkeys!)—a remark which had no effect upon the band of rustics further than to send them off, full of gratitude, to do as he had counselled. . . . Disputes between all non-Mussulmans are generally settled by the temporal or spiritual chiefs, and seldom brought before the Courts of Justice.[12]

In sum, the changes in the *millet* surveyed in the preceding sections tend to single out the development of a grass-roots ethnic culture wrapped in religious garb which differentiated, occupationally and ethnically, the communities which formed the Orthodox *millet*. The same changes catapulted the lay primates to a position of authority, wealth and power unknown in the past. The clergy, in fact, were now in the service of the primates, despite the fact that hierarchically they depended on their ecclesiastical heads. Moreover, the primates' frequent conflicts with the local Muslim notables and dissatisfaction with the Ottoman administration forced them to side with and rely upon their own kin. Thus the primates appeared to have acquired a unique position to spearhead the movement of national revival and independence as already claimed by some scholars (Hristov and Bobchev). This was indeed true in a number of cases. However, in many other instances the opposite occurred. The large majority of primates and the upper clergy seem to have sided with the Ottoman government, even after 1856, that is, after Russia promoted Pan-Slavism and acted as the spokesman for the Orthodox Slavs. The fact is that many primates owed their position and power mainly to their association with the Ottoman government rather than solely to their influence in the community as had been the case at the beginning of the century. They were dependent now on the Ottoman government as much as the government was dependent on them since many of them feared their radical nationalist intelligentsia as much as they were suspicious of Russia. It is therefore understandable that the intelligentsia derided the primates as "tools of the Turks" and used the term *corbacı* as synonymous with reactionism and lack of patriotism. In sum, therefore, the rural segments of the Christian *millet*s in mid-century presented a paradoxical picture: their ethnic-religious consciousness and folk culture had developed alongside some of the leaders' interest in maintaining the Ottoman political status quo.

Market Towns, Urban Elites, and
Reform in the Orthodox *Millet*

The new roles assumed by market towns and cities as centers of export for agricultural commodities and distribution of foreign goods, as sources of credit in a rapidly developing market economy, and as sites for new educational institutions gave them a dominant position over the rural communities. Merchants belonging to various non-Muslim *millet*s quickly monopolized the new businesses, such as insurance, transportation agencies, and banking and acquired leadership positions in their communities. They developed business interests and relations with the government, calling for a variety of efficient regulations and prompt services which the Ottoman government was slow to meet. The merchants' court disputes, for example, involving complex economic and commercial matters, could not be easily settled in the religious courts of the *millet*s. Furthermore, the merchants involved in international trade had contacts with Europe and acquired new ideas concerning socio-political organization and different standards of administration and justice. The cash at their disposal gave them financial influence over the villagers far above that of the communal primates. In fact, many primates, or their sons, attracted by the economic opportunities offered by trade, became engaged in urban commercial activities. Moreover, the merchants did not rely on their churches for legitimization or acceptance by the community as was the case with the traditionalist-minded rural primates. Their power lay in trade and wealth, which they used efficiently, whether dealing with the Ottoman government or with their church and community. Finally, the merchants developed a rather secular and enlightened view concerning the relations between church, society and government. They came to regard the clergy, especially the rural ones, as ignorant and uncouth, hardly capable of providing the community with truly enlightened spiritual guidance. Thus the merchants, and to a lesser extent the craftsmen, appeared to belong educationally, philosophically and socially to a world that had little in common with the rural primates, the clergy or even the Ottoman government. This notwithstanding, social pressure, tradition and lack of alternatives forced them to maintain formal ties with the *millet*. However, when the opportunity presented itself, the merchants, craftsmen and intellectuals combined their forces to press for the reform of the *millet*s.

The rise of a new intelligentsia, consisting usually of the sons of merchants and communal leaders, brought the evolution of the *millet* to a new stage.[13] Some sections of the intelligentsia, educated in Europe and especially in Russia, envisaged the history and the future of their own ethnic group, its church, language and culture in a secular-national frame of reference. They visualized their ethnic-religious communities, fragmented into small units within the *millet,* as forming one single nation and labeled its diverse cultural manifestations as part of one single national culture. An imaginary state appeared as the unifying framework. Their secularism, influenced mostly by France, at first antagonized the clergy while their concept of secular nationalism was rejected by the primates and even by the merchants. Yet many members of the intelligentsia were professionals whose services had become indispensable to society, a factor which increased their influence. Others had become teachers and heads of educational institutions in their own communities and indoctrinated many pupils with their views. Their nationalism, consisting of strong doses of Pan-Slavism and Orthodoxy and appealing to ethnic identity and pride, found increasing response among the elites but hardly touched the bulk of the rural population. Nevertheless the intelligentsia's scathing attacks on the clergy, on the state of religion, on the ignorance prevailing among the *millet* members and, finally, their search for and praise of ethnic culture coupled with the use of the press played a significant part in articulating the demands for *millet* reform.

The social, educational and cultural changes within the Orthodox *millet* led to an ethnic awakening which aimed not at political independence and statehood but at building the internal solidarity of the people who spoke the same language and shared the same ethnic culture. But the shift from religion to language as the uniting bond of a community was against the very essence of the *millet*. It meant that allegiance to ethnic and linguistic solidarity conflicted at some level with the allegiance to the *millet* and could undermine its existence. The defensive response to this threat was to generalize the use of the dominant language in the Orthodox *millet* which was also the language of the Church. The existing conditions favored Greek and forced the patriarchate to play a political role which brought schism into the *millet*.

A number of Greek-speaking merchants in Istanbul, due to their leading position in the Orthodox *millet* and connections with the Ottoman government, were the first to attempt an association with the patriarchate to revive the defunct Byzantium. After the establishment of the Phanariote rule in Moldavia and Wallachia in 1711–16, the Phanariote-Patriarchate coalition attempted to Hellenize the non-Greeks in clear violation of the *millet* concept. Already in 1822, during the Greek uprising, the Assembly at Troezen proclaimed that "all inhabitants of the Ottoman Empire who believe in Christ are included in the designation of Hellenes."[14] The Phanariote Pitzipios expressed it better in saying that the "Christian population of the East are composed, as everyone knows, of Greeks and of a large part of those who follow the Greek rite and on that account are designated Greeks."[15] Since the dogma and rules of the Orthodox Church were the same throughout the Balkans, Hellenization implied first and above everything else that Greek would be substituted for the native languages of the various *millets*. Consequently, Greek-speaking bishops were appointed to Bulgarian, Vlach and Serbian dioceses, and religious schools began to use Greek as the language of instruction. Already some Bulgarian and Serbian merchants had adopted Greek as their language of communication and regarded it as the yardstick of refinement and status. As a result, some of the urban elites and primates among the non-Greeks were Hellenized while rural communities remained relatively immune to assimilation except in areas densely populated by Greek-speaking communities.

The imposition of Greek meant that the patriarchate had decided implicitly that language would become the distinguishing mark of the entire Orthodox *millet*. Though the Greek language and liturgy had been confined, until the eighteenth century, mostly to the Greek-speaking population, it had also been used among some Bulgarian and Vlach communities. This had been possible as long as Greek was considered the language of the church rather than the distinguishing characteristic of the Greeks as a superior ethnic group.

The imposition of Greek in church services and the appointment of Greek clergy to Bulgarian and Serbian dioceses made the Slavic languages and the Cyrillic alphabet appear once more as the distinguishing cultural features of the Slavs. The church of Cyril and Methodius, founded in the ninth century next to the Roman and Greek churches, used the Cyrillic alphabet (a modified version of the Greek) to combat the exclusiveness of Greek, Latin and Hebrew and to convert the Slavic tribes to Christianity. The Bulgarians had become part of Christendom after the conversion of King Boris and eventually established their own church under the Assanides (1186–1398). After the fall of the three Bulgarian states under Ottoman rule at the end of the fourteenth century, the archbishop of Ohrid kept the title exarch of Bulgaria until 1767 and used the Bulgarian liturgy in church services. The Serbian church was reestablished during the reign of Süleyman the Lawgiver (1520–1566). Both were closed by 1767 at the instigation of the Greek Patriarchate. Thus, during most of the Ottoman period the Slavic languages coexisted along with Greek as the language of the Orthodox *millet* in the Balkans without causing ethnic conflicts. At times Greek prelates headed the Bulgarian and Serbian churches and even this fact did not create schisms as long as the linguistic and ethnic integrity of various Bulgarian, Vlach or Serbian communities was not directly threatened. In other words, the spiritual supremacy of the Patriarchate of Istanbul and the unity of the Orthodox *millet* remained safeguarded as long as the see upheld the primacy of faith over ethnic and linguistic peculiarities. The Hellenization drive broke this unity by making language the distinguishing mark of an ethnic group and implicitly gave language and ethnicity a higher political priority than religion.

Reaction to Hellenization began in rural and urban communities under the form of protest against the payments extracted by the low and middle-ranking clergy for services rendered to the believers. Some of the money thus extracted went to the upper echelons of the clergy who used it as simony to pay Ottoman officials while a larger part was kept by the prelates. The opposition to Hellenization increased further after merchants, craftsmen and intellectuals in towns and cities acquired leadership positions in their ethnic communities and after schools and the press awakened an interest in the native language and ethnic origin.

The most dramatic example of this reaction, led by the merchant community in Istanbul, was the establishment of a Bulgarian church by Bishop Bosvali in 1851. Istanbul became in fact a major center of Bulgaria's ethnic renaissance. Later, taking advantage of the *Hatt-ı Hümayun* of 1856, the Bulgarian merchants were instrumental in establishing the Exarchate in 1860 which was officially recognized by an Imperial decree in 1870. Thus, the language issue produced a major open break in the very fabric of the Orthodox Christian *millet*.[16]

One could argue that the emphasis placed on language and ethnicity opened the way to secularization and nationalism among the Balkan Christians. Furthermore, one could claim that the language issue provided a useful outlet to air resentments and aspirations by various social groups, including demands for autonomy and independence. While there is some truth in all these views, these should not be confused with nationalism. The latter developed as a political ideology and spread among the Balkan peoples mainly after 1878, and it was promoted by the newly-established independent states to establish internal cohesion and assimilate minority ethnic groups such as the Vlachs. It is essential to point out that the Orthodox Christians were divided into several major ethnic groups which in turn had their own subdivisions. Thus, the Vlachs, or the Aromunes, who spoke a Latin language, the Bulgarians who spoke Slavic and the Greeks were divided into several groups whose dialects, mores and social organization differed considerably from each other, so as to make them appear as different nationalities. The task of the national governments established after independence in these countries was to select a dialect and impose it throughout the realm as the common national language. Incidentally, Turkey did the same by using the Turkish spoken in Istanbul as the standard. It is erroneous therefore to accept the nationalist theses of the

Balkan writers at face value and regard nationalism—as distinct from various movements for autonomy—as having posed a serious challenge to the Otto-man government. In fact, despite frantic efforts by Russian agents and nationalist leaders, the Balkans did not witness grass roots, mass, nationalist uprisings. (The movements in Macedonia after 1878 are not studied here.) It must be emphasized, however, that the socio-cultural transformation of the Ottoman state undermined the *millet* structures and created conditions which facilitated the emergence of larger ethnic and linguistic units. The existence of large ethnic groups which acquired a degree of ethnic consciousness made them easy targets for nationalist indoctrination, although that indoctrination, as mentioned, came chiefly after a series of independent states had been established in the Balkans through the Berlin Treaty of 1878.

Reform of the *Millet* and Nationality

"In the days of the Sultans," wrote the reviewer of Sir Harry Luke's *The Making of Modern Turkey,* "Turkey was less like a country than like a block of flats inhabited by a number of families which met only on the stairs."[17] By the middle of the nineteenth century the walls of the flats had crumbled leaving the *millet*s in a large hall exposed to each other's curious looks. The Serbian and Greek revolts had shown to the Ottoman government beyond a doubt that social grievances had by far the greater impact in determining the subjects' behavior and that the clergy could not contain the dissatisfied, how-ever strong their faith might be. Indeed, the Serbian and Greek uprisings in 1804 and 1821 respectively started essentially as a consequence of social discontent but soon acquired political and national dimensions, especially in the Morea where a variety of influences had sharpened the local Greeks' political consciousness.

The Ottoman government responded to the challenge of social change by initiating a series of reforms intended to strengthen the authority of the central government. It also tried to develop a common secular sense of political belonging. It adopted first, after the *Tanzimat* reforms in 1839, the concept of Ottomanism—that is, the idea of regarding as Ottoman subjects all individuals living in Ottoman territories regardless of their faith and language.[18] In order to achieve further integration, the government recognized the non-Muslims through the reform edict of 1856, the municipality and *vilayet* laws and the right to be represented in the newly established administrative councils. But the representatives in these councils were chosen as individuals rather than as the official spokesmen of their *millet*s.[19] Thus, by 1850 the *millet* members began to be treated already as Ottoman "citizens," although the formal na-tionality law was not passed until 1869. This law, which is often cited as having created a new and modern legal status for Ottoman subjects, was a mere technicality that legalized and clarified further an already established concept.

The Nationality Law of 1869 (art. I) begins by declaring that"every individual born from an Ottoman father and an Ottoman mother, or only from an Ottoman father is an Ottoman subject."[20] In order to understand the special character of this Ottoman nationality which filled a legal and constitutional vacuum it is necessary to review its origin in the *Hatt-ı Hümayun* of 1839. This edict refers to the Ottoman subjects as *"tabaayı saltanatı seniye,"* or Subjects of the High Majesty. The terms *"tabaa"* or *"tebaa"* or *"tabiyet"* literally mean "subject" and "subjection." In Turkish today they mean citizen and citizenship. However, in the 1840s these terms signified the attempt to reconcile the Ottoman concept of the nationality stemming from the *millet* experience with the European idea of citizenship. The term *"tabaayı saltanatı seniye"* expressed only once in 1839 was repeated in various forms three times in the edict of 1856 after the concept of citizenship had gained wider acceptance in the eyes of the government.[21]

In the past all the people, land and goods in the Ottoman state were considered the property of the sultan. The latter exercised his authority by delegating power to his representatives, including the patriarchs, thus preventing direct friction between the individual and the government. The Edict of 1839, on the other hand, theoretically established a new and direct relationship between the individual and the state based on rights and obligations that stemmed from the individual's status as citizen of the Ottoman state. Ottoman citizenship, theoretically intended to cut across religious and ethnic boundaries, undermined the *millet*'s autonomy and self-rule in cultural and religious matters, which had not only isolated various ethnic, linguistic and religious communities from the government, but had also protected them from mutual interference and oppression. Once the corporate status of the *millet* and the segregation of the various groups ended, the relative position of the religious and ethnic groups in the Ottoman Empire toward each other began to be decided on the basis of their numerical strength. Hence they were transformed into minorities and majorities. It was obvious that sooner or later the views of the majority would prevail and its cultural characteristics and aspirations would become the features of the government itself.

Consequently, the Muslim character of the Ottoman government began to acquire a new political significance. The Muslims identified themselves with the government as Muslims and claimed special status and position in society, a process which served merely to bring up further accusations against the government for discriminating and mistreating the non-Muslims. The *millets*, in fact, deprived of their traditional autonomy and functions, had become a source of dissatisfaction and complaint for the Ottoman government, for the European powers and for many members of the non-Muslim communities, albeit for different reasons. The Ottoman government regarded them as obstacles to its own policy of Ottomanization; the non-Muslim urban lay communities complained that the *millets* allowed the clergy and the primates to perpetuate their authority; and intellectuals accused them of delaying the emergence of national consciousness and a secular ethnic culture among their conationals. Thus, paradoxically, the more progressive sections of the non-Muslim groups found themselves allied with the Ottoman government against the old *millet* system.

The *Hatt-ı Hümayun* of 1856 carried a stipulation that the *millet*s should be allowed to reform themselves.[22] However, they were unable to do so and consequently the Ottoman goverment, prodded by the European powers, finally initiated the reform itself. The Armenian *millet* which was beset by factionalism and fear of conversion to Catholicism and Protestantism (an Armenian Protestant *millet* was formed in 1850) finally was reformed in the 1860s.[23] The Greek *millet,* which rightly feared that the reform would further deprive it of the claim to represent all the Orthodox Christians, finally produced its reform constitution in 1860 and 1862. The Jewish *millet* produced a new constitution in 1865 although the actual reform was not carried out because it was superfluous.

The key feature of the *millet* reform was to allow laymen, mainly merchants and craftsmen, to participate in the election of their patriarchs and in the administration of the reconstituted *millet*. Roderic Davison, who has dedicated considerable space to the study of the *millet*s, credits these reforms with having introduced the rudiments of representative government among minorities, of having strengthened their national consciousness and of having served as models for the Ottoman Constitution of 1876.[24] Actually, the *millet* reform was the last step in the liquidation of the old *millet* system. The reforms did indeed bring about the internal reorganization of the *millet*s, but at the same time *recognized implicitly that the government was the source of their rights and freedoms* (italics added). The sultan formally granted to the *millet*s, through the edict of 1856, all the rights and privileges given to them by his predecessors. However, the sultan demanded also that the *millet* proceed *"with my high approval and the supervision of my high Porte* (italics added) to the examination of their present immunities and privileges. . . . The powers given to the Patriarchs and bishops of Christian rites by Sultan Mehmet II and his successors, *shall be harmonized with the new position which my generous and goodwilling intentions assured to these communities*[25] (italics added). The edict issued further directions concerning the election of the clergy and their remuneration in the form of salaries, the building and repair of religious establishments and then proceeded to proclaim equality among the races and religions.

In the old days rights and freedoms were inherent in the millet itself and could not be restricted or changed at will. Now these rights and freedoms, even though expanded and guaranteed, were entrusted to the government. The reform also made the *millet*s increasingly subject to governmental control and regulation. In 1880 Ahmet Cevdet Paşa tried to secularize the *millet*s' religious courts by introducing a single procedure. Moreover, overlooking the objections of the clergy, the government recognized the right of the individual members of the *millet*s to appeal to state courts even in cases involving inheritance and wills which had been under the jurisdiction of the old *millet*s' religious courts. Furthermore, the government extended its control over the *millet* schools by examining their textbooks and curricula in accordance with the Educational Law of 1869, despite bitter complaints and the protest resignation of some patriarchs. It was quite obvious that the *millet* reforms had restricted the jurisdiction of the clergy to the performance of religious duties, and consequently the government felt free to extend its authority over the nonreligious activities of the community. In effect, the reforms had transformed the *millet* into simple confessional groupings dealing strictly with religious matters. Indeed, by the end of the century there were about nine *millets* which represented practically all the non-Muslim religious denominations. In the past the number had remained constant at three non-Muslim *millets*.

The expansion of governmental authority did not stem from the government's express desire to curtail the freedoms of its Christian subjects but from a logical and unavoidable incompatibility between the concept of a centralized unitary form of government and the idea of corporate autonomy which the reformed *millets* desired to retain, despite the fact that their members were now first and above everything else Ottoman citizens whose rights and obligations were determined by the government. The non-Muslims found themselves torn between the need to conform to Ottoman law, in order to take advantage of its benefits, and the desire to preserve the privileges granted to them under the old *millets*. In fact, they did not hesitate to complain that their rights and freedoms were violated by the Ottoman government by referring to the privileges granted to them under the old *millet* system and with the backing of European powers often succeeded in evading the provisions of the law and their responsibilities as citizens. The Muslims, on the other hand, had no one to ask for protection and blamed the Christians and the European powers for their plight. The ensuing resentments degenerated into religious conflicts between Muslims and non-Muslims and reached a climax during Abdülhamid II's reign when the government bowed to the majority's wishes and embarked upon a policy of reforms which reflected the Muslims' cultural and religious aspirations and their own version of modernity. But the cultural legacy of the old *millets* survived both among Muslims and non-Muslims even after they reorganized themselves into nation-states, at least by appearance. They regarded the nation as though it were a religious community while claiming language as its distinctive national characteristic. Consequently, nationality, despite claims to the contrary, came to be determined first by religious affiliation and then by language. A "Turk" can be anyone who belonged to the Muslim *millet* during the Ottoman time. The Muslim Bosnians, Pomaks, Albanians, or Greeks can migrate and settle in Turkey without being able to speak one word of Turkish. "Greek" means any Orthodox Christian including any Turkish-speaking Karamanli who regarded himself as Greek. The Bulgarian government, despite its atheism, discriminates against its Muslim citizens, including Bulgarian-speaking Pomaks, because of their religion. The examples can be multiplied *ad infinitum* to prove that the *millet* legacy has weathered time and reforms and has been imbued in the culture and behavior of former Ottoman nationalities.

The twin concepts of "nation" and "state" which were naturally integrated into each other in Western Europe had no basis for success in the Ottoman state or in its successor states. The nation was considered a religious community and consequently most of the successor states as indicated here remained faithful to this principle in their understanding of a nation. The territorial state on the other hand is defined in secular terms as a national political entity which paradoxically enough is the homeland of other nations that often feel dominated and oppressed by the majority nations. In essence the two concepts are so opposed to each other as to make their reconciliation impossible, except by fully secularizing the nation, or by imbuing the state with the spirit of the nation. Israel alone seems to have attempted to establish a certain harmony between the nation and the state, but her ability to maintain it indefinitely is doubtful.

In sum, centralization, unified administration, and the reforms including the concept of citizenship, created a set of new relations between the individual subjects and the government and the *millets*. The new relations implied that the loyalty and the allegiance of the subjects belonged to the government which, in turn, would secure them rights, freedoms and services by conforming as much as possible to the subjects' cultural, political and ideological expectations. Obviously the new relationship called for a new organizational framework which ideally would have taken into consideration the corporate traditions of organization, that is the *millet* system, under which the Ottoman peoples had lived for centuries.

The alternative model of reorganization was the nation-state supplied by Western Europe. This model was imposed on all the Ottoman peoples by their leaders regardless of their historical experience and political culture. Each major ethnic group—Serbian, Greek, Bulgarian, and later Turkish— sharing a kindred language was assembled arbitrarily in a given territory and forced to accept a national identity chosen by the self-appointed "national" leaders. If one of these groups escaped somehow from being assimilated by the majority it did not fail to assert its collective personality when the situation permitted. I shall choose one well-known controversial example to illustrate this point. In the 1870s a substantial number of people living in Macedonia spoke a dialect close to the Bulgarian. Consequently, if Macedonia had been given to Bulgaria as decided in the San Stefano Treaty of 1878 that land would have become Bulgarian. The Serbians tried unsuccessfully to assimilate them. Finally after World War II Yugoslavia recognized the Macedonians as a distinct nationality. The same is true for the Albanians and for the Muslim Bosnians whose identities were ignored by the Yugoslav regime prior to World War II. The examples could be multiplied to indicate how the Ottoman *millet* helped maintain the ethnic and linguistic identity of various groups and how some of the national states established after 1878 ignored those differences while other states were compelled to recognize them under the modern principle of federalism. Indeed, if the turbulent history of Serbia and its subsequent metamorphosis into a unitary, and then federal, Yugoslavia were to be studied in depth, one would discern there both the influence of the *millet* system and a possible solution which the Ottoman government might have used to solve its nationality problem in the nineteenth century.

APPENDIX I

OTTOMAN VILAYETS, SANCAKS, *AND* KAZAS
APPEARING IN THE SALNAME *FOR 1900 (H. 1318, R. 1316)**

Vilayets *and* Special Districts *("Liva")*		Number of Kazas	Number of Nahiyes	Number of Villages
1	Hicaz (Hejaz)	*vilayets*	5	3	13
2	Yemen	"	27	54	6,339
3	Basra	"	10	29	210
4	Bağdat (Baghdad)	"	17	34	47
5	Musul	"	15	22	3,331
6	Halep (Aleppo)	"	21	54	3,476
7	Suriye (Syria)	"	18	13	1,072
8	Beyrut (Beirut)	"	16	43	3,057
9	Trablusgarp (Tripoli-Libya)	"	17	22	—
10	Hüdavendigâr (Bursa)	"	26	49	3,450
11	Konya	"	25	32	1,939
12	Ankara	"	21	19	2,765
13	Aydin	"	35	50	2,787
14	Adana	"	15	21	1,632
15	Kastamonu	"	18	27	4,045
16	Sivas	"	21	227	3,042
17	Diyarbekir	"	14	57	3,177
18	Bitlis	"	13	30	2,107
19	Erzurum	"	20	79	2,617
20	Mamuretülaziz (Elaziğ)	"	14	70	1,890
21	Van	"	13	9	1,594
22	Trabzon	"	18	24	2,738
23	Cezayiribahrisefit (Aegean Archipelago)	"	15	18	297
24	Girit (Crete)	"	—	—	—
25	Edirne	"	33	117	1,995
26	Selânik (Salonica)	"	23	16	1,860
27	Kosova	"	23	16	3,211
28	Yanya (Janina)	"	15	10	1,597
29	İşkodra (Scutari-Albania)	"	8	10	476
30	Manastir (Bitolia)	"	22	24	2,003

				Number of Kazas	Number of Nahiyes	Number of Villages
1	Kudüs (Jerusalem)	*special*	*sancak*s	3	2	328
2	Bingazi (Bengazi-Libya)		"	4	9	—
3	Zor		"	4	4	149
4	Izmit		"	4	10	938
5	Kale-i Sultaniye (Dardanelles)		"	5	8	498
6	Çatalca		"	2	1	95
7	Cebel-i Lübnan (Mount Lebanon)		"	8	40	931
	Total			568	1,253	65,706

*The list does not include the number of administrative units in the *vilayet*s under foreign occupation or declared autonomous, although legally, these were considered still under Ottoman suzerainty: Egypt (occupied by Great Britain, 1882); Bosnia and Herzegovina (occupied by Austria, 1878); Tunisia (occupied by France, 1881); Bulgaria (autonomous in 1878); Eastern Rumelia (autonomous but annexed by Bulgaria in 1885); Sisam (Samos) island. Crete is listed but without its administrative dependencies. Turkish spelling adopted.

Notes

1. Malachia Ormanian, *The Church of Armenia* (London, 1955), p. 61.

2. Sir Harry Luke, *The Old Turkey and the New* (London, 1955), pp. 96–97.

3. K. H. Karpat, "Gagauzların Tarihi Menşei ve Folklor'undan Parçalar," *I Uluslarası Folklor Kongresi Bildirileri,* Ankara, 1976, pp. 163–178.

4. Tadeus Kowalski, *Les Turcs et la langue turque de la Bulgarie du nord-Est* Cracow, 1933.

5. For this idea I am relying on the works of D. Jacoby, K. M. Setton, and Halil Inalcik. See, for instance, K. M. Setton, "Catalan Society in Greece in the Fourteenth Century," *Essays in Memory of Basil Laurdas* (Thessaloniki, 1975), pp. 241–285.

6. Muslim thinkers and jurists such as al-Tabari, Sufyan al-Thari, Abu-Ubayda have elaborated on this issue based on various *hadith*. See Roy P. Mottahedeh, "The Shu'ubiyah Controversy and the Social History of Early Islamic Iran", *IJMES,* 7 (1976), pp. 166 ff. Although the recognition accorded to a people grouped together by reason of common residence or birth lineage refers chiefly to Muslims, this extends by analogy to other peoples of the book.

7. See TKGM—Kuyudu Kadime, 57—Defter-i mufassal-ı Liva-i Vidin, folio 10v.–11r. Photocopy in Dusanka Bojanič, *Turski Zakoni I, Zakonski IZ XV I XVI Veka Za Smederevsku, Krusevacku I Vidinsku Oblast,* Belgrade, 1974, p. 124. On the *dhimmi* see H. A. R. Gibb and H. Bowen, *Islamic Society and the West,* London, 1957, vol. 1, Part 2, p. 253.

8. Kemal H. Karpat, *An Inquiry into the Social Foundations of Nationalism in the Ottoman State* (Princeton, 1973). For the administrative division of the Ottoman domains in Europe see P. L. Inciciyan (H. D. Andrasyan, ed.), "Osmanlı Rumelisi Tarih ve Coğrafysı," *Güney Doğu Avrupa Araştırmaları Dergisi,* 2–3 (1973–1974), pp. 11–18. The original work was published in 1804.

9. He also wrote "The first opposition to Turkish domination in the Balkans was on behalf of Orthodoxy and looked to distant Tzar as the champion of the orthodox faith." R. W. Seton-Watson, *The Rise of Nationality in the Balkans,* (London, 1918), p. 7.

10. An important study on this problem is by Yuzo Nagata, *Muhsin-Zade Mehmed Paşa ve Ayanlık Müessessei,* Tokyo, 1976, and "Some Documents on the Big Farms *(Çiftliks)* of the Notables in Western Anatolia," *Studia Culturae Islamicae* (Tokyo, 1976).

11. For additional information see G. Renda, *Batılılasma Doneminde Turk Resim Sanatı 1700–1850* (Ankara, 1977).

12. Stanley Lane Poole, *The People of Turkey: Twenty Years' Residence Among Bulgarians, Greeks, Albanians, Turks, and Armenians,* vol. 1 (London, 1878), pp. 15–18. For additional information on primates see Ami Boue, *La Turquie d'Europe,* 4 vols. (Paris, 1840). For a work dealing almost exclusively with the role of the communities and primates in the formation of national consciousness see Hristo Hristove, *Bulgarskite Obsciny Prez Vyzrazdaneto* (Bulgarian Communities During National Revival; Sofia, 1973).

13. Much of this succinct information is well known. Space prevents me from going into the details of this vital subject. I should, however, acknowledge my gratitude to Drs. Thomas Meininger and Milenko Karanovich whose Ph.D. dissertations provided original information on the educational history of Bulgaria and Serbia. Both dissertations were submitted to the University of Wisconsin, Madison.

14. Luke (cited n. 2), p. 81. See also the works of Steven Runciman on this subject.

15. Ibid.

16. The Bulgarian church represents a clear instance when a schism in the Orthodox Patriarchate was caused by language conflict. Other churches became independent as the consequence of the establishment of a political authority identified with a national group. The Russian church became independent in 1589, the Polish in 1594, after its union with Rome, the Montenegrin became *de facto* independent in 1766, the Croatian in 1690, those of Hungary and Dalmatia in the seventeenth century, the church of Greece in 1850 and those of Serbia, Romania, and Cyprus became independent in 1878. However, the Serbian and Romanian churches had already been freed of Greek domination in 1815 and 1821 respectively. See George Young, *Corps de droit ottoman* (Oxford, 1905), vol. 2, p. 12, ns. 1–10.

17. Luke (cited n. 2), p. 8.

18. Karpat (cited n. 8), pp. 75 ff. The Ottoman subjects going abroad were being issued passports as early as 1844 which were, in fact, the counterparts of a document used for interior travel known as the *mürur tezkeresi.* The latter is the predecessor of the *nüfus tezkeresi* and of the *nüfus cuzdanı* which today are the basic documents proving Turkish citizenship. The Ottoman censuses conducted in the nineteenth century, in addition to counting the population, had the purpose of issuing to each Ottoman subject a *tezkere.* Registration or *kayid* in the *Nüfus Sicilli* was regarded both as a population count and as proof of citizenship on the basis of which the subjects' responsibilities in matters of taxation and military service were assessed.

19. See Kemal H. Karpat, "The Ottoman Population Records and the Census of 1881/82–1893," *IJMES,* 9 (1978), pp. 237–274.

20. See text in Young (cited n. 16), vol. 2, pp. 226ff.

21. Roderic H. Davison, *Reform in the Ottoman Empire* (Princeton, 1963), p. 56, n. 14. See also Niyazi Berkes, *The Development of Secularism in Turkey* (Montreal, 1964), pp. 96–98, 150–154.

22. Davison (cited n. 21), pp. 114–135. Also Karpat (cited n. 8), pp. 88ff, and Steen de Jahay, *De la situation legale de sujets ottomans, non-musulmans,* (Brussels, 1906).

23. For the Porte's attitude towards the conversion of the Armenians to Catholicism, see Ahmet Refik, *Hicri Onucuncu Asırda Istanbul Hayatı, 1200–1255,* (Istanbul, 1932).

24. Davison (cited n. 31), p. 135.

25. Young (cited n. 16), vol. 2, pp. 4–5.

9

The Dual Role of the Armenian *Amira* Class within the Ottoman Government and the Armenian *Millet* (1750–1850)

Hagop Barsoumian

Introduction

The Ottoman government administered the Armenian population of the empire as one of the two Christian *millet*s. Although all members of the *millet* were legally *zimmi*s, or non-Muslim subjects (*gâvur* in popular terminology), they were not treated even handedly by the Ottoman rulers. Not only were the clergy a class apart, but also there existed within the Armenian *millet* a class known as the *amira*s who enjoyed a separate, privileged status. This paper will focus on their dual role in the administration of the empire, on the one hand, and as power brokers within the Armenian *millet,* on the other.

The word *amira* is derived from the Arabic *emir,* meaning prince or commander.[1] It was used by Armenians to designate a group of wealthy leaders of the community who were favored by the Ottoman government in a variety of ways. The determining factor in acquiring this honorific appellation was wealth, coupled with influence within the Ottoman government.[2] Although the word *amira* was not an official Ottoman designation of rank, an examination of the history of the Armenian *millet* will demonstrate that they in fact functioned as a class with special powers and privileges.

The first use of *amira* as an honorific title dates from 1559, when an Iskender *amira* is mentioned in the sources.[3] From this date until the mid-eighteenth century, however, this was less frequently in use than other honorifics applied to prominent individuals, such as *hoca, çelebi* and *mahdesi.*[4] The individuals who were so labeled were often contemporaries, and the distinctions among them are vague, except that the *çelebi*s tended to live in Istanbul while most of the *hoca*s were found in the provinces. There is no consensus among Armenian historians as to whether any of the latter three constituted a class,[5] but there is almost universal agreement in describing the *amira*s as a class, with its own special interests and outlook. This outlook encompassed its role in the empire and in the administration of the internal affairs of the Armenian *millet.*

From the 1750s on, and especially after the 1780s, the use of the title *amira* increases while all the others decline. It is not my intention here to speculate about the possible relationships within these categories, but rather to concentrate on the origin of the *amira*s, and on their function as intermediaries between the Ottoman government and the Armenian population of the empire.

Geographically, the origins of *amira*s were diverse. Of the nearly one hundred sixty-five individuals who were designated as *amira*s, approximately half had migrated to Istanbul from the town of Akn (Egin in Turkish, presently Kemaliye).[6] Of the others, many came from Van, some from Sebastia (Sivas) and a few from as far away as Persia; others rose from the ranks of the long established Armenian population of Istanbul. There seems to be no identifiable common factor uniting them, except that the majority had made a small fortune and perceived ways of putting their capital to the best possible use in Istanbul. The sources of such capital were diverse: those from Akn were frequently *sarraf*s while the group deriving from Van tended to be goldsmiths. Others were merchant-entrepreneurs, and this is especially true of the *amira*s who came from Persia. Whatever the origin of their wealth, the individuals who came to be perceived as *amira*s were able to use their wealth to attain positions of responsibility. There were a few exceptional cases, however, in which the title *amira* was used to describe individuals who rose thanks to technical skills, were appointed to high positions such as director of the gunpowder mill *(barutcu başı),* and then amassed wealth.

Role in the Ottoman State

The *amira*s made their presence strongly felt in two spheres of economic activity, those of government finance and industry. Perhaps the single most lucrative and prestigious profession pursued by the majority of *amira*s during the century under discussion was that of *sarraf,* the Ottoman designation for a banker or moneylender who was primarily involved in the *iltizam* taxation system. The majority of fee-paying *sarraf*s were Armenian.

Although there were some Jewish and Greek *sarraf*s, the privilege to practice the trade was granted with overwhelming frequency to Armenians. Western contemporary accounts, along with Armenian historical sources, confirm the domination of the profession by the Armenians. The nineteenth-century court historian, the *vak'anüvis* Ahmet Cevdet, names two prominent Armenian *sarraf*s and implies that the others were also predominantly drawn from the same ethnic group.[7]

These *sarraf*s played a pivotal role in Ottoman *iltizam* taxation. According to the *iltizam* system of tax farming, the right to collect taxes from imperial or state-owned lands, in Ottoman terminology the *hass-i hümayun,*[8] was sold at auction to the highest bidder. The successful bidder had to have the guarantee of an Armenian *sarraf*, for the sum that was bid had to be deposited in the state treasury, either immediately as a lump sum or in installments. In order to obtain the financial support of a *sarraf* the bidding *paşa* needed "a note of hand from his former banker, declaring that all his demands had been satisfied".[9] The government would hold responsible the *sarraf* and not the *mültezim,* the actual tax collector, for the payment of the debt to the state treasury. Even if the *mültezim* was wealthy, the government still required that he have the guarantee of a *sarraf*.[10] The *sarraf*, as banker, would provide the *mültezim paşa* with the necessary capital and the guarantee for payment. In addition to the interest on the money loaned, the *sarraf* was entitled to a commission or agency on the sale of commodities given in lieu of cash by taxpaying villagers, thus acting both as a banker and merchant.[11]

Because of the size of the capital required, only very wealthy individuals could enter into the profession in which it was possible to reap such sizable profits. These were *"hazine sarrafları,"* treasury *sarraf*s, who were *kuyruklu,* literally, "tailed," meaning licensed or privileged. They tended to accumulate great wealth rather quickly. The wealth of the richest *sarraf* could reach one million pounds sterling, according to one Western source.[12]

Some of the *sarraf*s, in addition to their profession as bankers in the *iltizam* system, were also jewelers and goldsmiths (*kuyumcu* in Turkish). Most of them served the palace, providing members of the sultan's family with jewelry and other gold ornaments. According to a Turkish historian, the *kuyumcu başı,* chief goldsmith, and all the goldsmith *sarraf*s were Armenians.[13]

An Armenian *sarraf* or his family held the responsible and sensitive position of superintendent of the mint (*darphane* in Turkish). The income of the mint was also farmed out at auction. Although the *amil,* the intendent of finance or collector of revenues,[14] was responsible for the collection of income, the actual operation of the mint remained under the control of a state-appointed employee, titled the *emin,* who was responsible for the supervision of the mint. Another appointee, the *sahib-i ayar,* saw to it that all technical and legal requirements were met, and acted as the director of operations. Finally, the *ustad,* or *usta,* managed the minting process.[15] All these appointive positions were entrusted to Armenians who thus held the operational and managerial control of the mint.

After 1757 a member of the prominent Duzian family held the position of *nazir* or *emin,* superintendent of the mint. According to Süleyman Sudi Efendi, who was familiar with its operations, the founders of the modernized mint were Hagop Duzian or Düzoğlu, as the family was known in governmental circles, and Mihran Bey Duzian, his relative and successor.[16] Except for the interval from 1819 to 1832, during which Harutiun *amira* Bezjian was the superintendent, the Duzian family held the supervision of the mint till 1880, thus keeping the control of this institution like a dynastic privilege.

A good indication of the complete control of the mint by the Armenian superintendent and his immediate subordinates is the fact that the records of the mint were kept in Armenian.[17] In addition to high-level personnel, most of the employees, especially those with technical skills, were Armenian.[18] While these employees received lifetime appointments from the government, the *darphane emini* himself, the collector of revenues, held the responsibility for only a limited period of time.

Evidence of the extent of the influence of the *sarraf amira*s in Ottoman finances is the creation of an official association of *sarraf*s in 1842, the Anadolu ve Rumeli Kumpanyası, with governmental sanction and encouragement. The association with its two divisions was responsible for the collection and remittance of the revenues of the whole empire to the treasury. Each division consisted of six Armenian *sarraf*s; one division was assigned to Rumelia and the other to Anatolia. This association, headed by an Armenian *sarraf*, proved to be a short-lived experiment; due to irregularities, European competition and lack of efficient organization, it was eventually dissolved.[19]

The *sarraf*s flourished until the Crimean War when they were gradually supplanted by European capitalists and banks.

In 1836 a British resident of Istanbul observed: "These people [the Armenians] are the greater artificers of Turkey, and the few factories established in the empire are generally conducted by them."[20] Recently an American historian, analyzing the efforts of the Ottoman government to create an industrial base in and around the capital, stated that "management of the entire Istanbul complex together with supporting mines, farm, sheep-ranch and the Hereke and Izmit ventures were headed by one family—the Dadians."[21] As the Duzians were masters of the mint, so the Dadian *amira*s had the privilege of managing the two gunpowder mills. In 1795 Sultan Selim III rewarded Arakel *amira* Dadian for his technical innovations at the old gunpowder factory at Ay Stefano (or San Stefano, now Yeşilköy) with an appointment as its superintendent, *barutçu başı* in Turkish.[22] As the position was hereditary, his sons succeeded him, the elder holding the title of *barutçu başı*. Upon the latter's death in 1832, the third son, Hovhannes, who was "more experienced in industrial management than was any other Ottoman subject,"[23] inherited the position. Hovhannes, the most talented of the family members, in addition to his managerial skills, was an inventor and innovator. In 1827 he devised a new machine for the piercing and rifling of the barrels of muskets, then a device to polish them. The following year he built three machines for the manufacture of muskets, four others for spinning, and a few years later a water pump.[24]

To improve his technical knowledge, Hovhannes traveled to Europe three times. He founded many new state industrial enterprises. To cite a few: in 1840 he supervised the construction of a silk mill at Hereke and an iron smelting foundry at Ay Stefano; in 1842 a tannery at Beykoz; in 1844 two factories for the manufacture of *çuha* (broadcloth) at Izmit; in 1845 a cotton factory, again at Hereke, and one small and one large iron smelting foundry at Zeytinburnu.[25] Other members of the family continued this innovative management of Ottoman industry. To name only one, Hovhannes's son, Nerses-Khosrov, who was a mechanical engineer, built a railroad track on the Strait of Bosporus in 1847, the first in Turkey.[26] The administration and management of all these factories and enterprises were exclusively in the hands of the Dadians. Although interesting, the enumeration of all the major and minor innovations that the Dadians either invented or adapted from European samples is beyond the scope of this paper. The family seems to have had a monopolistic privilege in the Ottoman government's early industrialization efforts. The only exceptions we can find in the records are the cases of Hagop *çelebi* Duzian who built a paper mill at Izmir,[27] and that of the Kavafian family, which constructed and managed a shipyard in Istanbul.[28]

Of the great merchants, only those connected with the palace were named *amira*. These merchant-*amira*s, whom the Ottoman government called *bazirgân*, officially appointed purveyor, provided the palace with various necessities. In addition to performing this function, many of these *bazirgân-amira*s served the army, assuming responsibility for its provisions, while others were involved in general trade. Many controlled a single trade route or specialized in a particular commodity. Throughout the 1780s and 1790s, for example, Garabed *amira* Manougian's fleet dominated shipping between Istanbul and Russia, enabling him to amass a great fortune.[29] In the 1750s, Hovsep (Yusuf) *Çelebi*, as *bazirgân*, enriched himself nearly monopolizing the importation of watches from England, and controlling their distribution and sale throughout the empire.

The *bazirgân-amira*s are a much more limited phenomenon than the *amira*s engaged in finance and industry. The sources are silent about their activities after 1800.

A unique position within the class recognized by the Armenians as *amira*s is that of certain families of architect-builders, of whom the Balians are by far the most prominent. Sultan Ahmet III's *mimar başı* or chief architect was Meldon Arabian or Araboğlu, and the position was later held by another Armenian, Sarkis Kalfa. However, it was the Balian family which monopolized the position from 1750 to the last quarter of the nineteenth century. The Balians built numerous palaces, mosques, public buildings and garrisons, as well as most of the factories set up by the Dadian *amira*s. The Armenian community of Istanbul appears to have held this family of *amira*s in exceptionally high regard, for reasons that have more to do with their philanthropic and political activities within the Armenian *millet* than with wealth.

*Amira*s, then, were capitalist-entrepreneurs *par excellence*; as bankers their capital was essential for functioning of the Ottoman financial structure. In the *iltizam* taxation system their dual role of *sarraf*, as banker providing capital and as merchant selling commodities given in lieu of cash, was indispensable. Their vital importance and usefulness is frequently lost in intemperate attacks on the usurious rates of interest they charged. However, there have been some contemporary and modern Turkish historians who have recognized that the *sarraf*s helped keep the fragile system going. One modern Turkish historian asserts that "the roles that the *sarraf*s played during the times of need of the state are truly great."[30] Cevdet Paşa, the contemporary historian, was more critical of the *mültezim*s than the *sarraf*s; he called the former "that group of bankrupt and rude men, who went to the provinces and, in order to collect higher taxes for the *iltizam,* tormented the poor."[31]

As for the influence of the *amira*s, according to one contemporary Western historian, it was decisive and enormous, for "they can reduce any Turkish governor to the condition of a private individual."[32] This assessment of their economic power is exaggerated, if not misleading, for this same observer noted that "the bankers have no power of their own, they have no distinct influence . . . they are wholly deprived of all political importance."[33]

The *amira*s' importance and power were determined by their financial capacity and economic skill. They were subject to the same political vicissitudes as the *paşa* with whom they were dealing. If the *paşa,* whose political patronage the Armenian *sarraf* enjoyed, was elevated in the Ottoman hierarchy, the prestige and influence of the *amira* were also raised; however, if the former was disgraced, exiled, or executed, the same fate awaited the *amira,* except in some cases, when through bribery he was able to save his life. Many a *sarraf* and *bazirgân-amira* lost both his wealth and life. It is sufficient to cite two such instances: Yagub *amira* (Hagop Hovhannesian), Sultan Ahmed III's *bazirgân başı,* was beheaded in 1752, while Kasbar *amira,* a well-known *sarraf,* was hanged in Istanbul in 1821.[34] The most notorious among numerous cases was that of the Duzians, who held the twin positions of superintendent of the mint and chief goldsmith. In 1819 four male members of the family were hanged and their extensive properties and great wealth confiscated.[35]

The contradictory remarks already cited about the power of the *amira*s, and the precariousness of their individual fate, attest to their problematic and exceptional status. Whereas many historians and political scientists have thought it would be axiomatic that great wealth will be translated, by one means or another, into political power, this is wholly negated by the example of the *amira*s. Even within the Middle Eastern context, where the wealthy leaders of other *millet*s were also virtually powerless, the *amira*s were an extreme case, with their combination of remarkable wealth and influence within their *millet* and none outside it. Their great wealth was precarious; it could be, and was sometimes, seized by the sultan on any pretext. Though they received the outward signs of prestige, they could be stripped of all of them with the greatest of ease. The list of the glittering tokens of power they were allowed seems impressive: *sarraf-amira*s were accorded the privilege of wearing special garb distinguishing them from both Muslim and non-Muslim *raya*s, common people.[36] Some, like the Balians, could ride horses and keep a retinue of servants. Most had easy access to the palace, and could gain frequent audience with the sultan. At least one *sarraf,* Bezjian *amira,* was so close an advisor and companion of Mahmud II that the latter visited him at his bedside when the Armenian *amira* was ill.

Yet all this was a fragile structure of appearances which could not conceal from them, and should not conceal from modern historians, the powerlessness of these enormously wealthy individuals, whom their Armenian compatriots, at least, perceived as a class.

Role in the Armenian *Millet*

When we turn our attention to the role of the *amira*s in the Armenian *millet*, we are confronted with a complete reversal: here, they were always very powerful, and from 1810 to 1845 it would not be an exaggeration to say that they were all-powerful. The center of all aspects of Armenian life was the patriarchate, located in Istanbul. The patriarch was both the spiritual and civic leader of the entire Armenian population of the empire.[37] *Amira*s were in effective control of the patriarchate. The influential ones installed their nominees on the patriarchal chair, or dismissed them at will.

The *amira*s were able to use their control of the patriarchate, and the prestige which their proximity to the Porte gave them within the Armenian community, to guide the development of many institutions and to delay the rise of others which might challenge their authority within the *millet*.

*Amira*s were instrumental in the cultural revival of the Armenian people. In 1790, thanks to the financial generosity and efforts of Mkrdich *amira* Mirijanian, the first Armenian secular school was opened in the Kum Kapu district of Istanbul. From then on, next to each Armenian church in the capital, a school was established either by an individual *amira* or a group of *amira*s. In 1831 the first school for girls was set up in the Samatia district. *Amira*s not only provided the initial financial funds for the construction of these schools, but also endowed them with income-producing properties which paid for their day to day operation.

In addition to schools, some *amira*s created cultural societies for the propagation and encouragement of literature and the publication of periodicals. Hovhannes *çelebi* Duzian, in 1812, established the Aršaruneac[c] Society which, in the same year, started the publication of the periodical *Ditak Biwzandean* [Byzantine Observer] and a number of books.[38] His son, Hagop *çelebi* Duzian, gave financial support to the publication of the journal *Ewroba* [Europe], published in Vienna. Many *amira*s sponsored the publication of a number of books, mostly of a religious, didactic or pedagogic nature. In 1790 Shnork *amira* Mirijanian set up a printing shop at Kum Kapu,[39] while Mkrdich *amira* Jezayirlian began to finance the education of Armenian students in European universities.

Perhaps the most historic step in the cultural endeavors of *amira*s was their decision, in 1836, to establish a secondary school, known as *Jemaran*. This school was to be an object of dispute and discussion in the Armenian community in Istanbul, which eventually culminated in the adoption of an internal constitution for the entire *millet*.

In the motives for the cultural activities of *amira*s one may discern, besides pride and self-glorification, a concerted effort to educate the common people.

Their intention was to increase the literacy of the Armenian people, both in order to assist them in acquiring Western technical skills and professions, and also to encourage the spread of Armenian literature and general culture.

In the spirit of the times, *amira*s were devoted to religious charities and philanthropy. Many an *amira* sponsored the construction of a church, and a few of them, like the Dadians, the Balians and Bezjian, built several. Indeed, the Dadians went so far as to build a church for the Greeks who lived in Makri Köy and worked in their factories. The cost of some of these charities were astronomical. In 1828 Bezjian defrayed half of the reconstruction expenses of the burned-out patriarchate at Kum Kapu, which amounted to three million *kuruş.*[40]

*Amira*s initiated the establishment of several hospitals in Istanbul. As early as 1743, a hospital was built at Narlı Kapu, but the outstanding institution of this kind, which is still functioning today, is the large St. Saviour National Hospital, created mainly thanks to Bezjian *amira*. The financial burdens the *amira*s were able and willing to shoulder were astonishing. For example, the yearly contribution of the Dadians to just one of their many charities, the National Hospital, amounted to a sum between fifty thousand and sixty thousand *kuruş.*[41]

Financing these educational and charitable institutions was important, but even more important was obtaining the necessary *ferman* (imperial permission) for the erection of the buildings. It was an extremely difficult, troublesome and expensive undertaking. Even permission for the repair of churches was very difficult, sometimes impossible to obtain; a *ferman* permitting the construction of a new church could take years to acquire and cost immense sums of money. Yet, thanks to their access to the palace, as well as to the administrative hierarchy of the government, *amira*s were able to obtain the *ferman*s. Many churches as well as schools, and the great National Hospital, were built during Mahmud II's reign, in part due to his tolerance toward the non-Muslims, especially the Armenians, and partly thanks to the unfailing efforts of the *amira*s.

Based on their economic capacity and their easy access to the Ottoman government, the *amira*s become for awhile the unchallengeable leaders of the Armenian *millet*. They never hesitated to use their financial generosity to preserve and further their influence and control over the *millet*.[42] Evidence of their priorities can rarely be found in Armenian contemporary sources, which generally extol their charities and devotion, but the writings of American missionaries, who viewed the internal affairs of the Armenian *millet* with a more critical eye, contain much revealing information. In 1836, by imperial order, thousands of Armenian youngsters, "from eight to fifteen years of age,"[43] were collected from "Karin [Erzurum] and Sebastia [Sivaz], and other parts of Anatolia, to work in Constantinople at the *iplikhane* [spinning mill], the imperial shipyard, the factory manufacturing sails, and at [the foundry] forging hot iron; it was ordered to give them only clothing and bread, and no salary."[44] According to contemporary American missionaries stationed in

Istanbul, some of these youngsters converted to Islam to avoid suffering and separation from their parents. The missionaries, in their collective letter, complained that

> there is no one who dares present such a case as that of those Armenian boys to the government. The bankers [*sarraf-amiras*] dare not do it themselves, lest they should no longer remain bankers; and they object to the priest's [i.e., the Patriarch] doing it himself; or sending in any of these numerous complaints and petitions which have come to him from the interior, lest the blame should fall on themselves. And thus national religious interests become sacrificed to [the] monied interest of the nation; and the people suffer.[45]

The Armenian historian who reported this same incident was a former secretary of the patriarchate and was therefore well informed. He too laments: "No one among our leaders was able to remove this troublesome danger from our nation; we ask Lord's assistance to them and to us."[46]

Even as late as 1871, this Armenian writer dared not openly criticize the *amira*s, but was satisfied to repeat a pious imploration. The American missionaries, on the other hand, do blame the "bankers" for not intervening and protesting against the measures ordered. In this incident one may observe not only the *amira*s' silence, but also their ability to silence the patriarch, too. In their eyes, the security of their economic interests far outweighed the gains that any attempted intervention might produce.[47] This was typical of the *amira*s' leadership of the Armenian *millet*. As the historian Varandean put it: "[The *amira*s were] humble servants when with the Turkish grandees, and arrogant and commanding [while] in their own milieu."[48] In fact, the patriarch and his subordinate bishops were nothing but "tools" in the *amira*s' hands.[49]

Whatever abuses the *amira*s may have committed, they functioned as defenders of the Armenian Apostolic Church, the patriarchate and of the status quo of the *millet,* which was threatened by the efforts of Catholic priests and Protestant missionaries who began to gain converts in the eighteenth and nineteenth centuries. Conversion was a political issue within the Ottoman Empire: the French, and to a lesser degree the Austrian, ambassadors championed the Catholic cause; the British diplomats defended Protestantism, while the Armenian national church had no foreign power to support it. However, the Ottoman policy was to stabilize the *millet* system by supporting the patriarchate, and the *amira*s were the cutting edge of this policy. Their own values and interests within the *millet* were in perfect accord with Ottoman policy, and this coincidence made the *amira*s formidable opponents. Even the powerful French ambassador in Istanbul feared their enmity, as reported in his letter to the foreign minister concerning his efforts to advance the cause of Catholicism:

> ... *éviter* ... *le double inconvenient d'attirer gratuitement sur moi suel l'inimité fort redoutable des sarafs arméniens et de tous les turcs influens qu'ils ont su gagner à leur cause. ...*[50]

Clearly, the Armenian *sarraf-amira*s must have enjoyed the full support of Ottoman governing circles in their opposition to Catholic and Protestant inroads.

However, by themselves, the *amira*s were not strong enough to obstruct Catholic propaganda and incursions in the Armenian *millet,* for, in 1830, due to heavy diplomatic pressure by the French, supported by the British, Mahmud II was obliged to grant the status of a separate *millet* to Armenian Catholics.[51] In fact, a number of the *amira*s had converted to Catholicism earlier. The well-known Duzians were staunch Catholics, though they feared to profess their Catholicism openly. As a matter of fact one of the reasons of the hanging of four members of the Duzian family in 1819 was the discovery of their conversion to the Catholic faith.[52]

Until 1846 the patriarchs were selected by the *amira*s, without regard to the opinion of either the church hierarchy, or the *esnaf*s and other civic groups. The *sarraf-amira*s formed a separate front which resisted the sharing of power even with the group of technocrat-*amira*s, which was composed of the *mimar başı* family (Balian), *barutçu başı* family (Dadian) and their supporters. All of the latter were favorably inclined toward reform, hoping to curb and diminish the power of the *sarraf*s within the *millet.* It was the rivalry of these two groups that made possible the eventual victory of the progressive elements who advocated the adoption of a constitution for the Armenian *millet.*

The constitutionalists, known as *lusavoreal* (the enlightened), represented the young, educated generation, which was imbued with progressive, democratic principles and doctrines. In the opposing camp was the group of traditionalists and conservatives, composed of the *sarraf-amira*s and their adherents, called *xavareal* (obscurantists). The conflict between these two antagonistic groups was not only political, it was also cultural, economic and social.

As the constitutional movement grew stronger, demanding democratic measures—such as representation in the *millet* organizations—the *amira*s formed a united front. However, the promulgation of the two imperial edicts, especially the Hatt-i Hümayun of 1856, combined with the power and popularity of the progressive elements, proved to be too strong for the *amira*s to oppose. Grudgingly, they endorsed the constitution, more to block the radical elements from positions of power in the new system than out of genuine conviction in favor of the constitution.

Conclusion

This attempt to portray the dual role of the *amira* class leads us to certain paradoxes, which however are resolved when viewed in a larger frame. We are confronted with a class which had a complex and vital *function* in the financial and economic administration of the Ottoman Empire, but lacked any real *power* in that sphere. Conversely, it had both an important function and enormous power within the Armenian *millet,* but these were at the service of the state, and did not enable the *amira*s to generate policy on their own. Modern Armenian historians, such as Leo, have asserted that "*amira* capital [ism] constituted a purely Turkish institution, whose *raison d'être* emanated from the essential nature of the Turkish Islamic state."[53] This is a fundamentally accurate evaluation, and again one that seems paradoxical when we consider the immensely useful role of the *amira*s in the cultural revitalization of the Armenian *millet.* To many outside observers this role seemed paramount, and at least one contemporary Greek historian chastised his own countrymen by citing the example of the *amira*s:

> *Les Fanariotes songent à eux, les arméniens* [speaking of the *sarraf*s and other wealthy notables] *songent à leur nation; ils ont établi entre eux une espèce de solidarité qui contribue au bonheur de la grande famille. Les Fanariotes ne regardent jamais la Grèce; l'armènien a toujours les yeux fixés sur sa patrie.*[54]

This paradox disappears in turn when we understand the cultural and educational role of the *amira*s as the result of an essentially conservative vision. They hoped to preserve the integrity and specific religious-cultural profile of their *millet,* because their own function within the multireligious and multiracial empire was predicated upon their role as intermediaries between the state and the Armenian *millet.* To conserve the *millet* was to conserve the Ottoman Empire, and this in turn guaranteed their own position within the status quo. Thus, what modern nationalist Armenian historians regard as a revolutionary step, namely, the emphasis on the Armenians' separate identity, was perceived by the *amira*s as a reasonable conservative policy.

The trajectory of the rise and fall of the *amira*s is a direct response to the needs of the Ottoman state, in which they had a dual role to play. We can resolve the functional paradoxes and the contradictory viewpoints of historians about the financial, political and cultural activities by which the *amira*s sought to fulfill these two roles if we begin to understand the monolithic and rational nature of *amira* conservatism as central to its own view of its interests and mission. That mission was defined by the Ottoman state as controlling both its financial-economic system and the Armenian *millet.*

Notes

The first part of this paper, about the economic role of the amira*s in the Ottoman state, is based on a paper read at the XI Annual Meeting of the Middle East Studies Association, held in New York, November 9–12, 1977.*

Except for the proper names in the text, Armenian titles of books and articles in this section as well as words in the text are transliterated according to the Hübschmann-Meillet-Benveniste system.

1. H. Ačarean, *Hayoc' Anjnanunneri Bararan* (Dictionary of Armenian Proper Names), vol. 1, Beirut, 1972, p. 120.

2. Biwzand K'ēč'ean, *Patmut'iwn S. P'rkč'i Hiwandanoc'in Hayoc' i K.polis* (History of the St. Saviour Armenian Hospital in Constantinople), Constantinople, 1887, p. 49.

3. Aṙakel M. K'ēč'ean, *Akn ew Akǹc'in, 1020–1915* (Akn and Its Inhabitant [sic]), vol. 1, Bucharest, 1942, p. 60.

4. *Mahdesi* is derived from Arabic *mukaddes,* meaning sacred, holy, and is equivalent to the Arabic term *hajji* or the Turkish *hacı.* It denotes one who has made the pilgrimage to Jerusalem. *Hoca* and *çelebi* are Turkish words.

5. For a discussion of this subject, as well as the meaning of these titles see H. S. Anasyan, *XVII Dari Azatagrakan Šarżumnern Arevmtyan Hayastanum* (XVIIth Century Liberation Movements in Western Armenia), Erevan, 1961, pp. 59–63; also Y. C. Siruni, *Polis ew ir Deré* (Constantinople and Its Role), vol. 1, Beirut, 1965, pp. 489–494.

6. Mkrtič' Barsamean, and Aṙakel K'ēčean, *Akn ew Aknčik* (Akn and Its People), Paris, 1952, pp. 203–222.

7. Ahmet Cevdet, *Tarih-i Cevdet,* vol. 1, Istanbul, 1871, pp. 159–163, and vol. 11, pp. 45–46; Armenian trans. A. X. Safrastyan, tr., *Turk'akan Ałbyurnerě Hayastani, Hayeri ev Andrkovkasi Myus Žołovurdneri* (Turkish Sources about Armenia, Armenians and the Other Peoples of Transcaucasia), vol. 1, Erevan, 1961, pp. 237–243, and 300–302.

8. For a detailed explanation of the term see Mehmet Zeki Pakalın, *Osmanlı Tarih Deyimleri ve Terimleri Sözlüğü,* vol. 1, Istanbul, 1971, pp. 770–771.

9. David Urquhart, *Turkey and Its Resources,* vol. 1, London, 1833, p. 108.

10. Pakalın (cited n. 8) vol. 1, p. 793 ("Hazine sarrafları").

11. R. Walsh, *A Residence at Constantinople,* vol. 2, London, 1836, p. 430.

12. Urquhart (cited n. 9) p. 109; Y. G. Mrmérean, *Masnakan Patmutiwn Hay Mecatuneru 1400–ēn 1900* (Partial History of Armenian Magnates), Istanbul, 1910, p. 118.

13. Pakalın (cited n. 8) vol. 2, p. 334 ("Kuyumcubası").

14. *New Redhouse Turkish-English Dictionary,* Istanbul, 1974, p. 57.

15. H. Inalcik, "Dar al-Darb", *EI²,* vol. 2, p. 118.

16. Pakalın (cited n. 8), vol. 1, p. 396 ("Darphane").

17. Jan Reychman and Ananiasz Zajaczkowski, *Handbook of Ottoman-Turkish Diplomatics,* The Hague, 1968, p. 29.

18. Hovhannēs Tēr Petrosean, "Hayeru Satarě Turk Mšakoyt'in ew Tntesut'ean" (The Contribution of Armenians to Turkish Culture and Economy") *Arew* (Cairo), 30 November 1976, p. 3.

19. Awetis Pērpērean, *Patmut'iwn Hayoc'* (History of the Armenian People), Constantinople, 1871, p. 276; Małakia Ormanean, *Azgapatum* (Armenian History), vol. 3, 2nd ed., Beirut, 1961, pp. 3734–3735; Y. G. Mrmérean, "Hayk i Kostandnupolis" ("Armenians in Constantinople") *Verjin Lur* (Istanbul), 5 June 1921, p. 4. None of these sources give the date of the dissolution of the organization.

20. Walsh (cited n. 11), vol. 2, p. 431.

21. Edward C. Clark, "The Ottoman Industrial Revolution", *International Journal of Middle East Studies,* 5 (1974), p. 70.

22. Ep'rem Połosean, *Tatean Gerdastané* (The Dadian Dynasty), Vienna, 1968, p. 28.

23. Clark (cited n. 21), p. 70.

24. Połosean (cited n. 22), pp. 52–65; *Arśaloys Araratean* (Smyrna), 19 March 1848, p. 2.

25. Anna Naguib Boutros-Ghali, *Les Dadian,* Archag Alboyadjian, tr., Cairo, 1965, pp. 146–147.

26. Poḷosean (cited n. 22), p. 158–162.

27. K'ēč'ean (cited n. 3), p. 170.

28. Hayk Ḷazaryan, *Arewmtahayeri Soc'ial-Tntesakan ev K'aḷak'akan Kac'ut'yuné 1800–1870 tt* (The Social-Economic and Political Condition of Western Armenians, 1800–1870), Erevan, 1967, p. 207.

29. Mrmérean (cited n. 19), p. 71.

30. Pakalın (cited n. 18), vol. 1, p. 793.

31. Cevdet (cited n. 7), vol. 4, pp. 235–238; Safrastyan (cited n. 7), vol. 1, pp. 278–279.

32. Urquhart (cited n. 9), vol. 1, p. 108.

33. Ibid., p. 112.

34. Pērpērean (cited n. 19), p. 175; K'ēč'ean, (cited n. 3), p. 207.

35. Gabriel Ayvazovski, *Patmut'iwn Osmanean Petut'ean* (History of the Ottoman State), vol. 2, Venice, 1841, p. 519; AE Correspondence Diplomatique, Turquie, vol. 232 (July 1819–December 1820), p. 108.

36. Arsen Bagratuni, *Azgabanut'iwn ew Patmut'iwn Nśanawor Anc'ic' Aznuazarm Tann Diwzeanc'* (Genealogy and History of Major Events of the Noble Duzian Family), (1856, manuscript at the Mekhitarist Library, Venice), p. 299; K'ēč'ean (cited n. 3), p. 301.

37. For a detailed analysis of the importance and functions of the patriarchate and the strength of the patriarch see, in English, Leon Arpee, *The Armenian Awakening, A History of the Armenian Church, 1820–1860,* Chicago, 1909; in Armenian, among various sources, Aršak Alpoyaćean, "T'urk'ioy Hayoc' Patriark'ut'iwné" ("The Armenian Patriarchate of Turkey"), *Éndarjak Orac'oyc' Azgayin Hiwandanoc'i* (Comprehensive Calendar of the National Hospital), Istanbul, 1908.

38. Vahan Zardarean, *Yiśatakaran* (Memoir), Cairo, 1933–1939, no. 2, p. 70.

39. Vahram Torgomean, *Eremia Ć'elepii Stampoloy Patmut'iwn* (Eremia Çelebi's History of Istanbul), vol. 1, Vienna, 1913, p. 202.

40. *Ibid.,* p. 491.

41. *Éndarjak Orac'oyc' Azgayin Hiwandanoc'i* (Comprehensive Calendar of the National Hospital), Istanbul, 1900, p. 113.

42. Ḷazaryan (cited n. 28), p. 400.

43. *American Board of Commissions for Foreign Missions,* Mission to Armenians, Constantinople, vol. 1, 1838–1844, no. 114 (Harvard University, Houghton Library, Cambridge, Mass.), 7 Jan. 1839.

44. Pērpērean (cited n. 19), p. 261.

45. American Board (cited n. 43).

46. Pērpērean (cited n. 19), p. 261.

47. Biwzand K'ēč'ean (cited n. 2), p. 84, claims that Hovhannes Bey Dadian informed Mahmud II of the sufferings caused by the forced collection of Armenian youngsters "and asked the sultan to abrogate the order. The sultan was not only surprised but angry . . . With his well-known love for justice he ordered the cessation of these misdeeds." K'ēč'ean does not mention the source of his information nor the year the alleged conversation takes place. Such a good deed would hardly have escaped the attention of Pērpērean, an earlier and well-informed historian. Furthermore, had the order been reversed, the missionaries writing in the year of Mahmud's death would have heard of the abrogation and witnessed its execution.

48. Mikayel Varandean, *Haykakan Śarźman Naxapatmut'iwn* (History of the Period Preceding the Armenian Movement), vol. 1, Geneva, 1912, p. 234.

49.   Ašot Hovhannisyan, *Nalbandyané ev Nra Žamanaké* (Nalbandyan and His Times), vol. 1, Erevan, 1955, p. 351.

50.   AE (cited n. 35), vol. 284 (octobre–decembre 1841), p. 14.

51.   The granting of this status took place in the aftermath of a lost war, the Russo-Turkish war of 1828–1829.

52.   Ayvazovski (cited n. 35), p. 519.

53.   Leo, *Xojayakan Kapitalé ew Nra K'alak'akan-Hasarakakan Deré Hayeri Mej* (Khoja Capitalism and Its Political-Social Role Among the Armenians), Erevan, 1934, p. 246.

54.   Marc-Philippe Zallony, *Essai sur les Fanariotes,* Marseille, 1824, p. 252.

10

The Greek *Millet* in the Ottoman Empire

RICHARD CLOGG

The *Millet-i Rum,* or "Greek" *millet,*[1] in the Ottoman Empire, embracing as it did all the Orthodox Christian subjects of the sultan, reflected in microcosm the ethnic heterogeneity of the empire itself. It contained Serbs, Rumanians, Bulgarians, Vlachs, Orthodox Albanians, and Arabs, while the strictly "Greek" element itself, although firmly in control of the *millet* through its stranglehold over the Ecumenical Patriarchate, the Holy Synod, and the higher reaches of the Orthodox ecclesiastical hierarchy, was by no means homogeneous. A Greek of Epirus, for instance, would have had much difficulty in comprehending one of the Greek dialects of Cappadocia,[2], while a Greek of Cappadocia would have experienced equal difficulty in understanding the Greek of Pontos, which in the view of one authority was by 1922 well on the way to forming a distinct "daughter language."[3] Moreover the Greek spoken in many areas of the empire, but more particularly in the Kayseri region, was so heavily penetrated by Turkish as to be intelligible only to those with a knowledge of both languages. Its body, as R. M. Dawkins put it, had remained Greek but its soul had become Turkish.[4] Many "Greeks" spoke only Turkish which they wrote with Greek characters, and for whom a substantial literature was published in the eighteenth, nineteenth, and early twentieth centuries, ranging from translations of Confucius to the novels of Xavier de Montepin.[5] The bulk of these *karamanlı* Christians were concentrated in the region of Kayseri, but they were also to be found in western and northwestern Anatolia and there were scattered communities in the Crimea and European Turkey. Even in the Ottoman capital in the late eighteenth and early nineteenth centuries there were few among the Greek population who could understand the Holy Scriptures or ecclesiastical encyclicals written in Greek.[6] In many quarters of the city, among them Samatya, Kumkapı, Narlıkapı and Yedikule, the "Greek" populations were almost wholly Turkish-speaking.[7]

Towards the end of the period under review Turkish nationalists, among them Şemseddin Sami, began to expound the view that these Turkish-speaking Orthodox Christians were not in fact Greeks at all but Turks.[8] They habitually referred to themselves not as Greeks but as "Christians" or as "Christians who inhabit the East" ("Anadol etrafında sakın olan Hırıstıyanlar").[9] Matters were further complicated by the existence in İstanbul (especially in Topkapi) and in the Orthodox eparchies of Nicaea, Nicomedia and Chalcedon of communities of Armenian-speaking "Greeks," who employed the Greek alphabet to write Armenian.[10] A further element of ethnic ambiguity without the *Millet-i Rum* was afforded by the Crypto-Christians, who outwardly subscribed to Islam but secretly adhered to the tenets and practices of Orthodox Christianity. Substantial numbers of these Crypto-Christians were to be found in southern Albania, in Crete, in Cyprus and, above all, in Pontos, where their numbers ran into many thousands. The year after the *Hatt-ı Hümayun* of 1856 the Cypto-Christians of Pontos petitioned the ambassadors of Great Britain, France, Austria, Russia and, significantly, Greece that they be allowed to register officially as Christians. With considerable reluctance the Ottoman authorities allowed them to be recorded in the tax registers as apostatized Muslims. Some twenty-thousand Crypto-Christians thereupon registered in the tax registers under two names, one Christian, one Muslim. Only after 1910 were they fully recognized as Christians.[11]

In addition to the very considerable degree of ethnic differentiation there was also a very wide range of social differentiation. The polyglot primate of the Phanar had little in common with the Turcophone tavernkeeper of Niğde, the Bulgarian milkman of Istanbul with the Vlach muleteer of the Pindos, the Romanian peasant with the prosperous Greek bourgeois of Izmir. Given such ethnic and social differentiation this paper cannot hope to offer a systematic analysis of the history of the *millet* from its inception in the fifteenth century until its collapse in the confused aftermath of World War I. Instead it will concentrate on aspects of the *Millet-i Rum,* which are either little known or are misunderstood, both when the *Millet* could be most accurately categorized as Orthodox and when it had acquired a more exclusively Greek character. A certain concentration on the Greek element is justified by the fact that the Greeks were always the dominant ethnic group in the *Millet-i Rum,* just as the *Millet-i Rum* itself appears to have enjoyed a tacit precedence over the other *millets.*

The basic structure of the *Millet-i Rum* is sufficiently well known not to need rehearsal here. The wide-ranging jurisdiction in both civil and ecclesiastical matters devolved upon the Orthodox church through the *millet* system is well and succinctly stated in the complaint of Bishop Theophilos of Kampania in his *Nomikon* of 1788: "In the days of the Christian Empire (alas) . . . prelates administered only the priesthood and ecclesiastical matters and did not intervene in civil matters. . . . Now, however . . . provincial prelates undertake secular lawsuits and trials, in connection with inheritance, with debts and with almost any aspect of the Christian civil law."[12] This wide-ranging civil as well as religious authority, which, as Theophilos rightly noted, was wider than that enjoyed by the Church in the Byzantine Empire, was exercised over the Orthodox Christians of the empire by the Ecumenical Patriarchate, the Holy Synod and the provincial metropolitans and bishops who, until the latter part of the nineteenth century, were almost always Greeks or Hellenized Orthodox who showed scant respect for the linguistic and cultural susceptibilities of their non-Greek flocks. A characteristic example was Ilarion of Crete, during the 1830s Metropolitan of Tyrnovo, who became a symbol of Greek ecclesiastical tyranny to fledgling Bulgarian nationalists.

The Greek stranglehold over the upper levels of the Orthodox hierarchy was consolidated during the course of the eighteenth century with the suppression, at the instigation of the Holy Synod in Istanbul, of the Serbian Patriarchate of Peć in 1766 and of the Bulgarian Archbishopric of Ohrid in 1767,[13] a move which was paralleled by the establishment of Greek hegemony over the Patriarchate of Antioch, where between 1720 and 1898 the patriarchal throne was occupied exclusively by Greek prelates. In the 1760s a Syrian contender for the throne of Antioch was rejected by the Ecumenical Patriarchate in favor of one Daniel of Chios for fear "lest some of the Arabs come in and . . . extinguish the bright flame of Orthodoxy".[14] Moreover, this Greek hegemony over the higher reaches of the Orthodox Church, not only over the "Great Church of Christ" in Istanbul itself but also over the patriarchates of Alexandria, Jerusalem and Antioch, was strengthened by the financial dependence of the other patriarchates on Constantinople. For much of the eighteenth and indeed nineteenth centuries the patriarchs of Jerusalem and Antioch, financially dependent on the Ecumenical Patriarch, actually resided in Istanbul and participated in the deliberations of the Holy Synod.[15] Greek hegemony and financial control over the Church was accompanied by a situation of endemic corruption in the conduct of its affairs. The jibe of an Armenian ("a famous banker but honest nonetheless") that "you [Greeks] change your patriarch more easily than your shirt" was sufficiently near the mark to make its recipient, the eighteenth century chronicler Athanasios Komninos Ypsilantis, feel uncomfortable.[16]

In the seventeenth century the office of Ecumenical Patriarch changed hands fifty-eight times, the average tenure in office being some twenty months. The shortest patriarchate was that of Kallinikos III who in 1757 died of joy on hearing the news of his election. Despite the fact that, theoretically, a patriarch had life tenure it was by no means unknown for a patriarch to hold the office on more than one occasion. Dionysios IV Mouselimis was five times patriarch between 1671 and 1694. An English traveler, Sir George Wheler, pinpointed in the late seventeenth century the root cause of this corruption. The patriarchs, he wrote, buy their "dignity dear, and possess it with great hazard."

> Yet so ambitious are the Greek Clergy of it, that the Bishops are always buying it over one another's Heads, from the Grand Vizier . . . as soon as they are

promoted, they send to all their Bishops, to contribute to the Sum they have disbursed for their Preferment . . . Again, the Bishops send to their inferior Clergy; who are forced to do the same to the poor People. . . .[17]

In this undignified scramble for preferment lay members of the Greek community of Istanbul as well as Ottoman officials were heavily involved. The ecclesiastical imposts and the venality that accompanied them were, of course, deeply resented by all the sultan's Orthodox subjects and by none more than the Greeks themselves among whom there was a saying that the country labored under "three curses, the priests, the cogia bashis [*kocabaşıs*], and the Turks."[18] The Greeks, no less than other Orthodox Christians, experienced the oppression of the ecclesiastical hierarchy in full measure, and this goes far to explain the widespread anticlericalism that existed at a popular level as well as among the nascent intelligentsia in the decades before independence.[19]

The great majority of the members of the *Millet-i Rum* had far more dealings with their own ecclesiastical authorities than they had with their Ottoman overlords, and undoubtedly a new dimension was added to the bitterness and resentment felt by the non-Greek members of the *millet* when their oppressors were not only extortionate but Greek to boot. It is, of course, a commonplace that the national movements of the Christian peoples of the Balkans were a response not only to Ottoman hegemony but also to Greek ecclesiastical and cultural oppression. Yet just as historians of the emergent Balkan nations have tended to paint an overly black picture of Ottoman rule, so they have tended to gloss over the more positive aspects of this parallel Greek ecclesiastical and cultural hegemony. Rigas Velestinlis (1757–1798), the protomartyr of Greek independence, has for instance been denounced as a Greek chauvinist for envisaging Greek as the official language of his projected multinational republic, a kind of restored Byzantine Empire with republican in the place of monarchical institutions which was to arise from the ashes of the Ottoman Empire. It would be governed, as in Byzantium, by an elite that was Greek by culture if not necessarily by race. In the context of the late eighteenth century Balkans such an insistence on the unifying potential of Greek language and culture was not as "chauvinistic" as it might appear. Greek was the commercial *lingua franca* of much of the Balkan mercantile bourgeoisie, whose emergence was such a significant development in the *Millet-i Rum* in the eighteenth century.[20]

Moreover, up until the period of Greek independence there was a widespread admiration for, and indeed in many cases a determination to acquire, a facade of Greek culture on the part of many non-Greek Orthodox Christians. This was indeed acknowledged by Paisii Khilandarski, the progenitor of Bulgarian nationalism, in his Slavo-Bulgarian history *(Istoriia Slavenobolgarskaia)* compiled in 1762. In a famous passage he attacked the Graecophilia of the emergent Bulgarian bourgeoisie and urged them to employ the Bulgarian language and to interest themselves in the glories of Bulgaria's past. "There are those," he wrote, "who do not care to know about their own Bulgarian nation and turn to foreign ways and foreign tongue . . . but try to read and speak Greek and are ashamed to call themselves Bulgarians."[21] It was not, however, until the 1820s that a serious reaction began to set in among the nascent Bulgarian intelligentsia against Greek ecclesiastical and cultural domination. Even then, as late as 1860, a Bulgarian, Grigor Părličev (Grigorios Stavridis ex Akhridos), won an important literary prize at the University of Athens. It was only after a disgruntled rival had denounced him as a Bulgarian that Părličev began to consider himself to be Bulgarian rather than Greek and refused a scholarship to Oxford which was offered on the condition that he retain an "Hellenic" consciousness.[22] Among humbler elements in Bulgarian society it was not until the 1850s that ethnic antagonism became pronounced. The cloth guild of Plovdiv, for instance, was obliged at this time to divide into separate Greek and Bulgarian organizations.[23]

In the 1760s, however, Paisii Khilandarski was very much a voice crying in the wilderness. Although he argued that the Greeks had no monopoly over learning and culture, many of his Bulgarian compatriots thought otherwise. In this connection it is worth noting that by the time the first Bulgarian book was published in 1806, the Greeks had established a strong publishing tradition dating back to the sixteenth century. During the first two decades of the nineteenth century alone well over thirteen-hundred titles in Greek for a Greek readership were published, some in editions of several thousands of copies. Those who could afford to sent their children to acquire a veneer of Hellenic culture at the burgeoning Greek academies of Ayvalık (Kydonies), Izmir (where Dimitrije Obradović, one of the leading figures of the Serbian national revival, also studied), Chios, Istanbul (The *Megali tou Genous Skholi* at Kuruçeşme),[24] etc. Learned culture in the Danubian principalities, dominated by the princely academies of Jassy and Bucharest, was, in the eighteenth century, very largely Greek in inspiration.

The view of the extreme Hellenizers among the non-Greek Orthodox found expression in Daniel of Moschopolis' *Eisagogiki Didaskalia* printed in Istanbul in 1802, a rudimentary tetraglot Greek, Rumanian, Bulgarian and Albanian lexicon, designed to facilitate the learning of Greek by those benighted enough not to possess it as a native language. Characteristically, Daniel prefaced the work with the following verses:

> Albanians, Vlachs, Bulgarians, speakers of other tongues, rejoice,
> And prepare yourselves all to become Greeks.
> Abandoning your barbaric language, speech and customs,
> So that they may appear to your descendants as myths.
> Do honour to your Nations, together with your Motherlands,
> By making your Albanian and Bulgarian Motherlands Greek.[25]

Daniel of Moschopolis, significantly, was himself a Vlach and his attitude was by no means untypical. Moreover, Modern Greek frequently acted as a filter through which the learning and literature of the West percolated to the other members of the Orthodox *millet,* particularly in the Balkans but also in the Arab world.[26]

If a knowledge of Greek and of Greek culture in the eighteenth and early nineteenth centuries, at least, was widely disseminated among the nascent Balkan intelligentsia (the major exception being the Serbs, whose basic cultural orientation was toward Hapsburg central Europe), then the unlettered masses of the Orthodox *millet* also shared a common corpus of ballads hearkening back to the glories of their past, and to their defeats at the hand of the Turks, to the battle of the Kossovo plain and to the taking of Constantinople. Perhaps more significantly, they shared a corpus of messianic beliefs foretelling eventual liberation.[27] The Greeks' subscription to the notion of a "xanthon genos," a fair-headed race widely interpreted as the Russians, as their future liberators was paralleled by the belief among Orthodox peasantry of southern Syria in the early years of the nineteenth century that the hour approached when a "yellow King" *(al-malik al-asfar)* would deliver them from the Muslim yoke.[28] The reverses experienced by the Ottomans during the Russo-Turkish war of 1768–1774 occasioned great excitement in the Orthodox world, for had not the Oracles of Leo the Wise foretold that three hundred and twenty years after the fall of Constantinople the Turk would be expelled by God from the City and from Europe? Credence in such oracles was no by means confined to the illiterate masses of the Orthodox population.[29] Moreover, the disappointment felt by the Orthodox when the Treaty of Küçük Kaynarca (1774) brought with it no visible improvement in the lot of the Orthodox *raya* did not diminish belief in the prophecies and oracles.[30] Rather their nonfulfilment was rationalized as a sign of God's displeasure at the sins of the Orthodox community. During the Greek War of Independence itself a reliable eye witness in Izmir reported that in May 1821, on the eve of the feast of St. Constantine, Greeks of the "lower orders" had been openly congratulating themselves in the bazaars on "the approach of the morrow, as the day appointed by heaven to liberate them from the Ottoman yoke and to restore their Race of Princes to the throne and possession of Constantinople." This delusion had resulted in the shooting of sixteen Greeks in reprisal.[31]

Until the early decades of the nineteenth century, then, there was little antagonism between different ethnic groups within the *Millet-i Rum,* whose intelligentsia for the most part shared a common faith, a common admiration for Greek culture and whose masses remained steeped in the thought world of what Nicolae Iorga termed *Byzance après Byzance.* Such antagonism as there was, was focused on Muslims, Jews and non-Orthodox Christians. An Orthodox cleric, Konstantinos Oikonomos o ex Oikonomon, in preaching a sermon in 1819 in Ayvalık, an almost exclusively Greek populated town in Anatolia, congratulated its inhabitants on the good fortune of their autonomy and the fact that the population was composed of Orthodox Christians of the same race—for the presence of Jews and other heterodox races in the other parts of Asia and of Greece, he declared, had frequently been the occasion of fights and disturbances.[32] Antagonism between Jew and Greek was longstanding and particularly virulent. According to the memoirs of a Phanariot primate, Nikolaos Soutzos, at the beginning of the nineteenth century a Jew entering one of the predominantly Orthodox villages on the Bosphorus, Arnautköy, was in a danger of a beating,[33] while it was regarded as particularly galling that the corpse of the Ecumenical Patriarch Grigorios V should have been handed over to a Jewish mob after his execution in 1821. Relations between the two communities were not enhanced by the Orthodox practice of burning (and sometimes shooting at) an effigy of Judas Iscariot on Good Friday, nor by periodic accusations that the Jews engaged in the ritual murder of Christian children at Passover.[34]

Hostility was also felt by Orthodox Greeks toward Gregorian Armenians, but the most deeply-rooted Orthodox prejudice was directed against Latin Catholicism. Antagonism between Orthodox and Catholic periodically erupted into violent clashes, which could result in relatively low key violence, as that in Izmir in May 1818 between Orthodox Greeks and Levantine Catholics, or in actual killings, as did a major riot in Aleppo between Orthodox and Uniates in the same year. The death toll on this occasion was eleven.[35] These intercommunal antagonisms, however, did not inhibit periodic collective demarches by leaders of the different communities to the Ottoman authorities. An example of such intercommunal cooperation occurred in 1742 when a disastrous fire in Izmir was blamed on the "tradimento" of the *kadi*. Four representatives each of the Jewish, Greek, and Armenian communities were dispatched to make representations to the Porte.[36]

The particularly bitter prejudice of the Orthodox against the Latins had its roots, of course, in resentment at Latin attempts, during the declining years of the Byzantine Empire, to blackmail the Orthodox into submission to Rome as the price for assistance in warding off the Ottoman threat. In the last days of the empire a high official declared that he would rather see the turban of the Turk rule in Constantinople than the Latin mitre.[37] Such attitudes were a commonplace among the Orthodox of the Ottoman Empire. The classic formulation of the view that the Ottoman Empire was part of the divine dispensation, created to defend the integrity of Orthodox Christianity, was advanced by the Patriarch Anthimos of Jerusalem. In this *Patriki Didaskalia* (Paternal Exhortation) published at the press of the Ecumenical Patriarchate in Istanbul in 1798, Anthimos went so far as to argue that God had inspired in the heart of the sultan of the Ottomans an inclination to chastise Christians who deviated from their faith so that "they have always before their eyes the fear of God."[38]

The attitude of *ethelodouleia,* voluntary submission to the powers that be, which the leaders of *Millet-i Rum* manifested in their dealings with the Ottoman authorities, was increasingly resented toward the end of the eighteenth century by the more ardent spirits among the Orthodox. The initial onslaught on the power and pretensions of the *millet* leaders came from Greeks who, with their growing network of commercial ties with Western Europe and with their cultural ascendancy within the Orthodox *millet,* were more susceptible to nationalist and rationalist currents emanating from Western Europe. The principal target of these embryonic nationalists were the elites of the Orthodox *millet,* the bureaucratic caste of the Phanariots, with their lucrative monopoly of power and its economic perquisites in the Danubian principalities, the increasingly prosperous mercantile bourgeoisie, the *kocabaşıs,* or primates, and the ecclesiastical hierarchy. All these groups were seen as being comfortably wedded to the existing Ottoman *status quo;* all were, in the words of an early nineteenth-century Greek satire, "slaves to tyranny."[39] The higher ranks of the ecclesiastical hierarchy were the objects of particular obloquy. The anonymous author of one of the most remarkable documents of the movement for Greek independence, the *Hellenic Nomarchy,* published in Italy in 1806, attacked the corruption and flamboyant life-styles of the higher clergy in the bitterest tones, but he reserved special venom for their willingness not only to acquiesce in the continuance of Ottoman rule but to seek to justify it as part of the divine dispensation.[40]

The small Greek nationalist intelligentsia which posed the first major threat to the integrity of the *Millet-i Rum* was, for the most part, not centered within the jurisdiction of the *millet* itself, but within the world of the Greek diaspora of central and western Europe, France, Italy and southern Russia that had emerged during the course of the eighteenth century. Recent research has thrown up the remarkable statistic that a mere seven percent of the two hundred or so books, for the most part of an improving nature, published by subscription for a Greek readership between 1749 and 1832, were ordered by subscribers in areas that were subsequently to form part of the independent Greek state.[41] The intellectual ferment that preceded the outbreak of the Greek War of Independence was largely centered in the diaspora, as indeed were efforts to bring about the emancipation of the Greeks through more dynamic means. The *Philiki Etairia* or "Friendly Society" that laid the organizational framework for the outbreak of the Greek revolt in 1821 was founded in Odessa in 1814 by three impoverished émigré Greeks. It subsequently drew the bulk of its membership from the Greek communities of southern Russia and the Danubian principalities and not until the eve of the revolt did it attract any wide membership within the areas (Morea and Rumeli) in which the revolt was to meet with success. The efforts of the conspirators to attract the support of the other Balkan Orthodox peoples met with scant success. There was little inclination to assist the Greeks to overthrow the Ottoman yoke and thereby strengthen the Phanariot hold over their country, as the response of Tudor Vladimirescu and his followers in the Danubian principalities indicated.

When hostilities did break out in 1821 it was inevitable that reprisals should be taken by the Ottoman authorities against the *millet başı,* Gregory V, members of the Orthodox hierarchy, and against leading lay members of the *Millet-i Rum.* For they had manifestly failed in their primary duty, that of ensuring the fidelity and obedience of the Orthodox community to the sultan, in return for which they had been granted such wide-ranging authority over

Orthodox Christians in both ecclesiastical and civil matters. The Ecumenical Patriarch Gregory V was himself fully aware of his obligations, and he was executed not, as is still sometimes maintained,[42] because of his refusal to denounce the insurgents, but despite the fact that he had denounced them. In March 1821 Gregory V and the Holy Synod, acting with the authority of the Greek *koinon* of Istanbul, issued a number of encyclicals denouncing Ypsilantis as "reckless, arrogant and vainglorious" and the *hospodar* of Moldavia, Mikhail Soutsos, who had given him encouragement as an "ingrate monster."[43] No doubt Gregory V was subject to pressure from the Ottoman authorities, yet there is no evidence to suggest that his denunciations of the insurgents were anything but sincere. His condemnation of the revolt was entirely consistent with the attitude taken by the patriarchate at earlier moments of crisis. Moreover, it must have appeared to the leaders of the *millet* that Ypsilantis's enterprise was doomed to fail and that it could only result in massive reprisals against Orthodox Christians who had taken no part in the conspiracy. Gregory's uncompromising opposition to the revolt, however, neither saved his own life nor stood in the way of his being officially canonized in 1921, on the centenary of his death, as an "ethnomartyr."

It was the emergence of an independent Greek state in 1830 which rendered inevitable the eventual demise of the *Millet-i Rum,* although it was formally to survive for almost another century.[44] For only some three-quarters of a million of the approximately two million Greeks under Ottoman rule were contained within the frontiers of the new Greece, and for much of the first century of its independent existence the entire *raison d'être* of the Greek state was the redemption of the "unredeemed" Greeks of the Ottoman Empire, even if sizeable numbers of these Ottoman Greeks were quite happy to accept the existing *status quo.* The classic expression of the *Megali Idea,* the Great Idea of bringing all the Greeks of the Ottoman Empire within the confines of a single state is that of Ioannis Kolettis, a Hellenized Vlach, in a speech before the Constituent Assembly in Athens in 1844:

> The Kingdom of Greece is not Greece. [Greece] constitutes only one part, the smallest and poorest part. A Greek is not only a man who lives within this kingdom but also one who lives in Jannina, in Salonika, in Serres, in Adrianople, in Constantinople, in Smyrna, in Trebizond, in Crete, in Samos and in any land associated with Greek history or the Greek race. . . . There are two main centres of Hellenism: Athens, the capital of the Greek kingdom, [and] 'The City' [Istanbul], the dream and hope of all Greeks.

In the rump of Greece created through Great Power mediation in 1830 the Greeks had acquired their Piedmont. An immediate blow to the power of the Ecumenical Patriarchate was the creation of an autocephalous Church of Greece in 1833, which was only recognized by the partriarchate in a synodical *tomos* of 1850, which confirmed a church constitution for Greece of a severely Erastian kind. In the 1830s, too, the patriarchate was forced to accept the *de facto* autonomy of the Serbian Church, together with the Serbianization of its hierarchy, in the wake of Milos Obrenović's acquisition for Serbia of a substantial degree of autonomy. The collapse of the Phanariot regime in the Danubian principalities also hastened the Rumanization of the Orthodox Church in Rumania. This was reorganized in 1859, and its autocephalous existence was formally recognized by the patriarchate in 1885. The Ecumenical Patriarchate also found its hegemony under increasing challenge in the patriarchates in the Arab lands. In 1843 a lengthy dispute developed between the sees of Jerusalem and Constantinople following the advancement of a claim by the Holy Synod of Jerusalem to elect its own patriarch without the participation of the Synod of Constantinople. The greatest blow, however, to the ecumenical pretensions of the Patriarchate of Constantinople was the establishment in 1870 of the Bulgarian Exarchate.[45] This was followed by the imposition by the patriarch of an anathema on the Bulgarian Exarchate in 1872, which was only lifted in 1945, and from whose imposition the patriarchates of Antioch and Jerusalem significantly dissented. The provision that dioceses could place themselves under the jurisdiction of the exarchate provided that two-thirds of their members voted to do so inaugurated forty years of bitter strife involving Bulgarians, Serbs and Greeks in Macedonia.

All these developments contributed to the transformation in the later nineteenth century of the *Millet-i Rum* from a grouping that embraced all Orthodox inhabitants of the empire into one that was largely, but still by no means exclusively, ethnically Greek. For the patriarchate engaged in a tacit conspiracy with the Ottoman authorities to deny the existence of an Albanian ethnic identity, claiming all Orthodox Albanians as Greeks. As late as 1892 Archbishop Philaretos of Kastoria in a pastoral letter denied the existence of an Albanian language,[46] while the patriarchate showed itself equally determined to maintain its grip on the Vlachs of European Turkey who in the late nineteenth century were increasingly the target of Rumanian propaganda.

The diminution of the power of the hierarchy of the Orthodox Church over the non-Greek members of the *Millet-i Rum* in the nineteenth century was paralleled at the center by an increase in lay influence in the administration of the *millet*, a consequence of the *millet* reforms that followed the *Hatt-ı Hümayun* of 1856. Although there had traditionally been some lay element in the election of a patriarch, power had essentially been concentrated in the hands of the *gerondes*, the senior metropolitans in the twelve-man Holy Synod. At the urging of some of the leading members of the Istanbul Greek community three lay members had been already added to the Holy Synod in 1847 at the behest of the Porte. The major reforms in the *Millet-i Rum* were elaborated by a provisional national assembly, consisting of seven metropolitans together with lay representatives from Istanbul and the provinces which met between 1858 and 1860. The reforms proposed, which were neither as wide-ranging nor as "democratic" as those introduced into the Armenian *millet*, were enshrined in a series of "General Ordinances" *(Genikoi Kanonismoi)*, presented to the Porte in 1862 and ratified the following year.[47] In contrast to the proposals for the Armenian *millet*, there was no provision for a general assembly of the "nation" in permanent session. Such an assembly, with a large lay majority, was to be summoned only for the election of a patriarch. The patriarch was to administer the *millet* with the advice of the Synod, whose membership was now to be open in rotation to all metropolitans, and a mixed council elected from among the Greek population of Istanbul alone. The mixed council, with both lay and clerical members, was charged with the administration of community finances, education, hospitals, orphanages and like matters. The new reforms were not welcomed by the Orthodox hierarchy, which had been equally discomfited by the provisions in the *Hatt-ı Hümayun* of 1856 which had sought to remedy a major source of ecclesiastical corruption by substituting fixed salaries for the traditional ecclesiastical imposts.[48]

As Roderic Davison has pointed out, the *millet* reforms did not, as the Ottoman authorities had hoped, promote the concept of *Osmanlılık* among the non-Muslims of the empire. Rather, by diminishing ecclesiastical control, they undermined a powerful factor making for loyalty to the Ottoman state.[49] Moreover, the *Tanzimat* reforms in general, and the great reforming decrees, the *Hatt-ı Şerif* of Gülhane of 1839 and the *Hatt-ı Hümayun* of 1856, in particular, despite the unevenness of their application,[50] contributed substantially to the remarkable economic and demographic resurgence of the Greeks of the Ottoman Empire after the setbacks of the 1820s.[51] They also encouraged the substantial migration of Greeks from the independent kingdom to the Ottoman Empire which began to develop very soon after independence and was to accelerate during the course of the nineteenth century. The primary motive of this emigration was economic, for the Ottoman Empire offered far greater scope for entrepreneurial talent than did the impoverished and restricted markets of the independent state. Moreover, this emigration was a feature of all levels of Greek society. In 1875, for instance, the Greek minister to the Porte complained to the demarch of Ermoupolis in Syra of the very large numbers of women and girls who migrated to the cities of the Ottoman Empire in search of work as domestic servants, in the process running the risk of "moral degradation, religious seduction, the loss of all feeling of nationality and dignity, the danger of total catastrophe."[52]

Partly as a consequence of migration from the islands of the Aegean, partly as a result of unusual demographic growth, the Greek presence in Western Anatolia increased dramatically in the course of the nineteenth century. According to the British consul in the city, C. Blunt, the Muslim population of Izmir declined from eighty thousand in 1830 to forty-one thousand in 1860, while during the same period the Greek presence increased from twenty thousand to seventy-five thousand.[53] The town of Ayvalık which had been devastated and depopulated in 1821 had by 1896 acquired an almost exclusively Greek population of thirty-five thousand.[54] In the second half of the century railway construction provided a further boost to Greek settlement. The archaeologist William Ramsay had found only one Greek when he visited Sarayköy in 1881. By the time of his next visit, in 1894, the Greek population had risen to four hundred and fifty. The line from Aydin to Afyonkarahisar had opened in 1882.[55] Many competent observers noted how much more fertile the Greeks were than the Turks. The economist Nassau Senior attributed this to the effects of conscription, from which the Christian populations of the empire were exempt until 1908, and to the fact that Turkish women "of the lower classes try very mischievous means to avoid having many children."[56] Abortion and "the shocking prevalence of unnatural crime amongst the Mussulmans" were also advanced by Consul Blunt as significant factors in explaining the low rate of Turkish population growth in the *vilayet* of Aydın in a passage of his report which was censored in the official printed version.[57] One estimate, that of A. Synvet, as reliable as any, put the number of Greeks in Asia Minor c. 1875 at 1,188,094, with an additional 230,000 in the capital.[58] This last figure accords with a figure of 236,000 for the Greeks of the capital (as against 597,000 Turks) in 1897 given in another reliable source.[59] The Greek population of European Turkey amounted to a further million and a half. In the large commercial centers of the empire there was also a large, if fluctuating, population of citizens of the Greek Kingdom. In 1859 there were some forty-five hundred Greek subjects in Izmir alone, more than in Piraeus, the port of the Greek capital.[60] The Greek populations of the rural areas of Anatolia and European Turkey were principally farmers, traders, and small shopkeepers. In the large urban centers of the empire, however, Greeks were well represented in banking, shipping, railways, manufacturing, commerce, and the free professions.[61] Bankers such as Christaki Efendi Zographos amassed huge fortunes and lavishly endowed educational and other community establishments. Greeks also figured prominently in the Ottoman bureaucracy and, despite the fact that the War of Independence had destroyed Phanariot influence in the conduct of Ottoman diplomacy, the Ottomans continued to place considerable reliance on Greeks for the conduct of their foreign affairs. The first Ottoman ambassador to the Greek Kingdom, Mousouros Paşa, was a Greek as, of course, was Alexander Karatheodori Efendi, who became deputy foreign minister. There was also a sizeable Greek urban working class and, at the turn of the century, Greeks played an influential role in the incipient working-class movements of the Ottoman Empire.

By the second half of the nineteenth century, then, the Greeks had largely regained the economic, and to a somewhat lesser degree, the political influence in the affairs of the Ottoman Empire which they had enjoyed prior to 1821. The existence of the Greek Kingdom, however, in providing an alternative focus for the loyalties of the Ottoman Greeks was to create tensions within the *Millet-i Rum* that were ultimately to bring about its collapse. In the middle of the nineteenth century, Abdolonyme Ubicini, an acute observer of the Ottoman Empire, detected two basic parties within the Greek *millet*. The one, much the largest and led by the Phanariot elite, government functionaries, the lay dignitaries of the patriarchate, wealthy merchants, and the higher clergy, was firmly attached to the *status quo*.[62] Pavlos Karolidis, a leading intellectual of the Ottoman Greek community and a Greek deputy in the reconstituted Ottoman parliament of 1908, summarized the basic, though seldom explicitly articulated, aspirations of this first group, as expressed by the influential Greek newspaper of Istanbul, *Neologos,* during the reign of Abdülaziz. The "Great Idea" of the Greek nation was the propagation throughout the Ottoman Empire and the East "through the protection of the Ottoman state" of Greek education, Greek life and civilization. From an economic point of view the Ottoman Empire already constituted a Greek state, since all economic life and many public works were carried out either by Greeks or by Greek capital. Greek and unbiased foreign observers seeing these things, the newspaper continued, deplored the hostile policy of Greece towards the Ottoman Empire, believing the Hellenization of the Ottoman state to be a simple matter of time.[63] Although expressed with characteristic hyperbole such attitudes were by no means uncommon among both Greeks of the empire and Greeks of the kingdom.[64]

The second party analyzed by Ubicini consisted of the protagonists of Hellenism, that is to say, the supporters of the irredentist policies of the Greek state that were regularly manifested at times of crisis for the Ottoman Empire, e.g., 1839–40, 1854, 1878, culminating in the Greco-Turkish war of 1897. The medical, legal and literary professions, according to Ubicini, tended to favor "Hellenism", which was "confined to the precincts of colleges and drawing rooms."[65] But, as is the way with nationalist movements, the influence of the Hellenists soon began to transcend the colleges and literary salons of Greek society in Istanbul.

The two parties shared one basic common objective, namely, instilling a sense of Greek consciousness in those members of the *Millet-i Rum* who even in the later nineteenth century thought of themselves as Christians rather than Greeks. Numerous educational, literary and cultural societies, known as *syllogoi,*[66] sought to "Hellenize" the Orthodox populations of Macedonia and Anatolia. In Istanbul alone, circa 1878, there were some twenty such *syllogoi,* the most important of which being the Greek Literary Society *(O en Konstantinoupolei Ellinikos Filologikos Syllogos),* which alone founded some two hundred Greek schools throughout the empire. One of the *syllogoi* most active in the "re-Hellenization" of the Orthodox populations of Anatolia was *O Syllogos ton Mikrasiaton i Anatoli.* Founded in 1891, the *Anatoli* was supported by banks in Greece, by the municipality of Athens, by the university, by subventions from the Greek state and from the prosperous Greek communities of Egypt. The basic objective of the *syllogos* was to educate young Greeks from Anatolia, either in the university or theological colleges of Greece or in the numerous Greek schools of Istanbul and Izmir. One of the basic intentions of the society was that, once graduated, the holders of these scholarships should return to their native communities to enable their fellow villagers to become superior to those of other races and to retain this superiority.[67]

The phenomenon of teachers trained at the very fount of Hellenism, the University of Athens, seeking to impart, with varying degrees of success, their nationalist fervor to their Ottoman Greek brethren was a common one in the nineteenth century. Ubicini, in mid-century, wrote of Greek teachers "haranguing from their professorial seats against the government, and openly making their lectures the vehicle of sedition." In a number of Greek schools in the capital he had found portraits of the emperor of Russia opposite those of Christ.[68] After disturbances at the Great School of the Nation *(Megali tou Genous Scholi)* in Kuruçeşme in 1849 the Porte had prohibited Greek nationals from teaching in any part of the empire. This prohibition was not very vigorously enforced, however, and, in any case, by this time there was a steady flow of Ottoman Greeks graduating at the University of Athens and able to carry on the burden as apostles of Hellenism. In a further, and also rather ineffectual, measure to minimize Hellenic propaganda among the Greeks of the empire the Porte introduced censorship of books imported from abroad. In 1894 the teaching of Turkish was made compulsory in all schools of the empire. But otherwise Greek attempts at "re-Hellenization" met with relatively little opposition from the Ottoman authorities.

Indeed, the Orthodox hierarchy on occasion showed itself to be more apprehensive about these Hellenizing efforts than did the Ottoman authorities themselves. One traveler was told by a Greek of İsparta, called Serefedinoğlu, that the Orthodox bishop of Antalya was opposed to the establishment of Greek schools among his Turcophone flock for fear of corrupting their Orthodoxy.[69] Although by the end of the nineteenth century there were well over four thousand schools within the authority of the *Millet-i Rum,* it is clear that the efforts of these nationalist zealots met with relatively little success in the interior of Anatolia. Despite the fact that it was urged that the first duty of Orthodox parents was to imbue their children with "the divine language of Plato and Aristotle,"[70] one Ottoman Greek author lamented at the end of the century that the Orthodox inhabitants of Kayseri region had not the faintest idea about Greece, Athens and the Parthenon.[71] Indeed these apostles of Hellenism proved incapable of stemming the transition from the use of Greek to Turkish that occurred in a number of the Orthodox communities of central Anatolia during the course of the nineteenth century.[72]

In the coastal regions of the empire, however, and in particular in the great urban centers, where there were in any case substantial concentrations of Hellenic subjects, these efforts to inculcate a sense of identity with the irredentist aspirations of the Greek Kingdom met with greater success. In 1866 Namık Kemal criticized "the impertinence of local Greeks in singing songs in their cafés that had as leitmotiv the extermination of the Turks."[73] A speech given in Trabzon in 1865 to a Greek audience to celebrate the accession of King George I of the Hellenes ended with the stirring peroration: "Come, sovereign, the peoples of the East await you . . . and like . . . the Greek Alexander, implant civilization in barbarized Asia. . . . Long Live George I King of the Hellenes! Long Live the Greek nation! Long Live the Protecting Powers!"[74] On the very eve of the Greco-Turkish war of 1897, the Orthodox priest of Salihli, a small town near Izmir, publicly prayed for the "most pious

King George and Queen Olga, their heir Constantine and for the trampling underfoot of their every enemy."[75] At the time of the war Greek clerks and employees openly left Istanbul to fight for Greece, returning seemingly unmolested, at the conclusion of hostilities. When the hundreds of Greeks who had abandoned Mersin on the outbreak of hostilities began to flock back, they were required to sign a document renouncing Greek nationality. Those who refused were afforded protection by the British consulate which upheld the Greek minister to the Porte's claim that since the document had been signed under duress it had no validity.[76]

The irredentist intrigues of the Greek Kingdom in the nineteenth century, culminating in the war of 1897, combined with ceaseless Hellenic propaganda emanating from the same source posed an increasing strain on the loyalties of the Ottoman Greeks and inhibited the development of any genuine commitment to the principle of *Osmanlılık*. A real enthusiasm for the principle was briefly evoked in the flurry of excitement with which the Ottoman Greeks, as indeed the Greeks of the kingdom, greeted the Young Turk revolution of 1908 and the restoration of the constitution, whose original proclamation in 1876 had also been greeted with wild enthusiasm by the Greeks.[77] The reaction in the Ecumenical Patriarchate, however, was much less enthusiastic, for the proclamations of equality among all the subject peoples of the empire were seen as posing a threat to the traditional privileges of the patriarchate. In particular it was feared that its jurisdiction in educational matters throughout the *millet* would be challenged. The threat to the traditional autonomy enjoyed by the *millet*, coupled with the introduction of compulsory military service for non-Muslims, raised the dread specter of assimilation. Soon after the revolution the patriarch expressed his private regrets to the Grand Vezir, although he was forced by demonstrations within the Greek community of Istanbul to express public support for the restoration of the constitution.[78]

Twenty-four Greek deputies were elected to the Ottoman parliament in the elections of 1908, after blatant meddling in the electoral process by Greek consular officials who made it quite clear to Ottoman Greek voters which candidates enjoyed the favor of the Greek state. Turkish suspicions as to the basic loyalties of the Ottoman Greeks had been further enhanced by the announcement on 6 October 1908 of the Cretans' resolution to unite with Greece. On the same day Austria had announced its decision to annex Bosnia-Hercegovina, and on the previous day Bulgaria had formally renounced Ottoman suzerainty. The Committee of Union and Progress responded to the unilateral Cretan declaration of *enosis* by inspiring a commercial boycott of the Greeks. This was mainly directed at the Greeks of the kingdom and large numbers of Greek nationals were deported from the empire. The boycott lasted until the outbreak of the Turkish-Italian war in September 1911. Mutual antagonism between the Young Turks and the Ottoman Greeks increased as the former increasingly stressed Ottomanization of the minorities and as the Greek legation stepped up its attempts to influence the Greek deputies in the Ottoman parliament. The legation, indeed, continued to press for the formation of a "Greek" political party within the Ottoman parliament. Sixteen out of the twenty-four Greek deputies were induced to join this caucus. Those who refused, some of whom were members of the Committee of Union and Progress, were subsequently denounced by Greek diplomatic officials as being "anti-national." With the dissolution of the Ottoman parliament in 1912, the Committee of Union and Progress began to make more conciliatory overtures towards the patriarchate and the Greek "party" but the legation-sponsored Political League ensured that the Greek "party" supported the *Hürriyet ve İtilâf Fırkası*. Some Greek deputies continued to campaign on behalf of the Committee of Union and Progress, but the new parliament had only fifteen Greek deputies. The increasingly rampant nationalism of the Committee of Union and Progress, combined with the continued readiness of the majority, although by no means all, of the Ottoman Greek leadership to look to the Greek Kingdom for guidance made the prospect of any real partnership based on equality of rights increasingly remote. Such faint hopes as did exist were finally shattered when in October 1912 Greece joined Serbia, Bulgaria, and Montenegro in the scramble for European Turkey. The consequences of the First and Second Balkan wars for the Greek populations of the Ottoman Empire were, not surprisingly, far more serious than those of the war of 1897. Moreover, national antagonisms were exacerbated by the massive influx of refugees from European Turkey, and the Ottoman authorities tolerated the harassment of Greeks on the west coast of Anatolia as a bargaining counter with Greece over possession of the Aegean islands. On the eve of World War I Venizelos the Greek prime minister, anxious to secure Ottoman recognition of Greek sovereignty over Mitylini, Chios and Samos, negotiated an agreement with the Porte for a voluntary exchange of the Moslems of Greek Macedonia and Epirus for the Greeks of Turkish Thrace and the *vilayet* of Aydın. Turkey's entry into World War I, however, prevented the ratification of the agreement.[79] But its negotiation did ease the position of the Anatolian Greeks which, however, worsened with Greece's entry into the war on the side of the Entente in 1917.

The formal demise of the *Millet-i Rum* should perhaps be dated to March 1919, on the eve of the Greek occupation of the west coast of Asia Minor, when the Ecumenical Patriarchate formally released the Ottoman Greeks from their civic responsibilities as Ottoman citizens, although the Ottoman government had earlier sent Ahmet Riza, the president of the Senate, to call on the patriarch to express its goodwill towards the Ottoman Greeks.[80] Thus, almost a century after the outbreak of the Greek War of Independence the privileged status of the *Millet-i Rum* was unilaterally abrogated by its temporal and ecclesiastical leader. What is most surprising, perhaps, is that the *Millet-i Rum,* should have survived for so long after the creation of an independent Greek state.

Notes

1. The term "Orthodox *millet*" (*Ortodoks milleti*) is occasionally met with in the Greek sources but is used only concerning the Turkish speaking *karamanlı* Christians. The title page, for instance, of the *Didaskalia Khristianiki tis Orthodoxou imon Pisteos . . . Talim Mesihi Ortodoks . . . imanımızın . . .* printed in Bucharest in 1768, records that it was printed "at the new press of the Orthodox *millet* (*Ortodoks milletin yeni basmahanesinde*)." The Greek title page refers to the press "tou Orthodoxou Genous ton Romaion."

2. Cf. Carsten Niebuhr, *Reisebeschreibungen nach Arabien und andern umliegenden Ländern*, ed. J. N. Gloyer and J. Olshausen, Hamburg, 1837, vol. 3, p. 128. The definitive study of the idiosyncratic Greek of central Anatolia is R. M. Dawkins, *Modern Greek in Asia Minor. A Study of the dialects of Silli, Cappadocia and Pharasa . . .*, Cambridge, 1916.

3. R. M. Dawkins, "Notes on the Study of the Modern Greek of Pontos," *Byzantion* 6 (1931), pp. 396, 389. Cf. P. M. K., "Peri Marianoupoleos," *Pandora*, 16 (1866), p. 534.

4. Dawkins (cited n. 2), p. 198. N. S. Rizos, *Kappadokika . . .*, Istanbul, 1856, p. 100; Skarlatos Byzantios, *I Konstantinoupolis, i perigraphi topographiki, arkhaiologiki, kai istoriki tis perionymou taftis megalopoleos*, Athens, 1869, vol. 3, p. 596. This penetration extended to the written language as this passage from the eighteenth century chronicle compiled by Athanasios Komninos Ypsilantis, sometime *kapıkâhyası* to the hospodar Grâgorios Ghikas, indicates: "O veziris Dervis-Mekhmet-passas genomenos veziris evthys ekame kekhagiapein ton Masalatzi Ibraim ephendin, prolabontos defterdarin eita kai kekhagiapein; meth'on ekame ton Laleli-Mustafa-efendin; meth'on ton Derendeli." *Ekklisiastikon kai politikon ton eis dodeka vivlion . . . itoi ta meta tin Alosin*, Istanbul, 1870, p. 557.

5. A convenient survey of the literature in *karamanlıca* may be found in Janos Eckmann, "Die karamanische Literatur", in J. Deny et al., eds., *Philologiae Turcicae Fundamenta*, Wiesbaden, 1964, vol. 2, pp. 819–835. Sévérien Salaville and Eugène Dalleggio, *Karamanlidika. Bibliographie analytique d'ouvrages en langue turque imprimés en caractères grecs*, vol. 1, 1584–1854, Athens, 1958, vol. 2, 1851–1865, Athens, 1966, vol. 3, 1866–1900, Athens, 1974, is indispensable.

6. Manouil Gedeon, "To kirygma to Theiou Logou en ti ekklisia ton kato khronon." *Ekklisiastiki Alitheia*, 7 (1888), p. 200. See also Gedeon in *Ekklisiastiki Alitheia*, 22 (1902), p. 178 and *Eikasiai meta erevnan kodikon Konstantinoupoleos*, Athens, 1935, pp. 4–5. The enormous output, stretching over more than seventy years after 1870, and much of it scattered in rare periodicals and newspapers, of Manouil Gedeon, the historian *par excellence* of "i kath'imas Anatoli," has recently been listed by Kh. G. Patrinelis in *Dimosievmata Manouil Gedeon. Analytiki anagraphi*, Athens, 1974. A selection of Gedeon's more important articles has been reissued, Alkis Angelou and Philippos Iliou, eds. as *I pnevmatiki kinisis tou Genous kata ton 18 kai 19 aiona*, Athens, 1976.

7. A favored burial ground of the *karamanlıs* of Istanbul was at the monastery of the Zoodokhos Pigi, Balıklı. "Some of the inscriptions in *karamanlıca* that still survive have been published in my "Some Karamanlidika Inscriptions from the Monastery of the Zoodokhos Pigi, Balıklı, Istanbul," *Byzantine and Modern Greek Studies*, 4 (1978), pp. 55–67. See also Semavi Eyice, "Anadolu'da 'karamanlıca' kitâbeler (Grek harfleriyle Türkçe kitâbeler)," *Belleten. Türk Tarih Kurumu*, 39 (1975) pp. 25–58.

8. Şemseddin Sami, *Kamus-ül-A'lam*, Istanbul, 1890–1900, vol. 1, pp. 396–397 and also his article 'Türklük' in *Ikdam*, 20 March 1899, cited in David Kushner, *The Rise of Turkish Nationalism 1876–1908*, London, 1977, pp. 52–53. This is not the place to discuss the involved question of the ethnic origins of the *karamanlides*, on which a large literature exists.

9. *Kolay iman nasihatı cem olunmuş Ekklisamızın türlü Daskaloslarından . . .*, Venice, 1806, p. 18. Dimitrios Alexandridis published his Turkish-Greek lexicon in Vienna in 1812 "pros khrisin ton en ti Anatoli oikounton Khristianon."

202   Non-Muslim Communities in the Eighteenth Century

10. Gedeon, "To kirygma" (cited n. 6), p. 200 and S. A. Khudaverdoglou-Theodotos. "I Tour-kophonos elliniki philologia, 1453–1924," *Epetiris Etaireias Vyzantinon Spoudon,* 7 (1930), pp. 301–302. A Greek of Simferopol complained in 1817 that many of the numerous Greeks of southern Russia were in danger of losing or had lost their mother tongue in favor of Russian, *Ermis O Logios,* January, 1817, pp. 11–12. See also K. A. Palaiologos, "I en ti Notio Rossia Ellinismos," *Parnassos,* 5 (1881), p. 613.

11. N. P. Andriotis, *Kryptokhristianiki Philologia,* Thessaloniki, 1953, p. 12; R. Janin, "Musulmans malgré eux, les Stavriotes," *Echos d'Orient,* 97 (1912), pp. 501–503; O. Blau, "Querrouten durch die pontischen Alpen," *Zeitschrift für Allgemeine Erdkunde,* 10 (1861), p. 378. On the Crypto-Christians in general see N. E. Milioris, *Oi kryptokhrystianoi,* Athens, 1962, R. M. Dawkins, "The Crypto-Christians of Turkey", *Byzantion,* 8 (1933), pp. 247–275 and Stavro Skendi, "Crypto-Christianity in the Balkan area under the Ottomans," *Slavic Review,* 26 (1967), pp. 227–246.

12. Cited in N. J. Pantazopoulos, *Church and Law in the Balkan Peninsula during the Ottoman Rule,* Thessaloniki, 1967, pp. 44–45. On the juridicial basis of the Orthodox Church in the Ottoman Empire there is a large literature. Among the more useful works are H. Scheel, *Die staatsrechtliche Stellung der ökumenischen Kirchenfürsten in der alten Türkei. Ein Beitrag zur Geschichte der türkischen Verfassung und Verwaltung,* Berlin, 1943; C. G. Papadopoulos, *Les privilèges du patriarcat oecuménique (communauté Grecque Orthodoxe) dans l'Empire Ottoman,* Paris, 1924; Steven Runciman, *The Great Church in Captivity: A Study of the Patriarchate of Constantinople from the Eve of the Turkish Conquest to the Greek War of Independence.* Cambridge, 1968; L. Hadrovics, *Le peuple Serbe et son église sous la domination Turque,* Paris, 1947; J. Kabrda, "Sur les bérats des métropolites orthodoxes dans l'ancien Empire ottoman au xviiie siècle," *Izvestija na Balgarskoto Istoriohesko Druzhestvo,* 15–18 (1940), pp. 259–268; A. Schopoff, *Les réformes et la protection des Chrétiens en Turquie 1673–1904,* Paris 1904. A convenient summary of the "constitution" of the Orthodox *millet* in the Ottoman Empire after the mid-nineteenth century *millet* reforms is contained in L. Petit, "Règlements generaux de l'église orthodoxe en Turquie," *Revue de l'Orient Chrétien,* 3 (1898), pp. 405–424, 4 (1899), pp. 227–246.

13. On the Patriarchate of Peć, see Hadrovics (cited n. 12), passim; on the archbishopric of Ohrid see A. P. Pechayre, "L'Archevêché d'Ochrida de 1394 à 1767," *Echos d'Orient,* 39 (1936), pp. 183–204, 280–323; prompted by the publication of Ivan Snegarov, *Istorija na okridskata arkiepiskopija patriarchija (1394–1767),* Sofia, 1932.

14. J. M. Neale, *A History of the Holy Eastern Church: the Patriarchate of Antioch,* London, 1873, pp. 193–194, cited in Robert M. Haddad, *Syrian Christians in Muslim Society. An Interpretation,* Princeton, 1970, p. 65.

15. James Dallaway, *Constantinople Ancient and Modern,* London, 1797, p. 380; H. A. Ubicini, *Letters on Turkey,* London, 1856, vol. 1, p. 125.

16. Ypsilantis, *Ta Meta tin Alosin,* pp. 519–520.

17. Sir George Wheler, *A Journey into Greece . . . in Company of Dr. Spon of Lyons,* London 1682, p. 195. As an anonymous chronicler of the early nineteenth century put it, as soon as the news that a see was vacant had reached Istanbul, clerics "like crows around a corpse" rushed "not to the bosom of Mother Church, but into the courts of worldly nobles, of impious princes, of the eunuchs of concubines, servilely beseeching, kissing the hems of their robes, proferring gifts . . ." Mount Athos, Panteleimon Codex 755. I am grateful to Dr. Leandros Vranousis for allowing me to consult this manuscript. On the state of the patriarchate in the eighteenth century see T. H. Papadopoullos, *Studies and Documents relating to the History of Greek Church and People under Turkish Domination,* Brussels, 1952.

18. William, Gell, *Narrative of a Journey in the Morea,* London, 1823, pp. 65–66. For a striking example of the kind of behavior that brought the Orthodox Church into popular disrepute see William Turner, *Journal of a Tour in the Levant,* London, 1820, vol. 3, pp. 509–510.

19. I have discussed this phenomenon in my "Anti-Clericalism in Pre-Independence Greece c. 1750–1821," in D. Baker, ed., *The Orthodox Churches and the West,* Oxford, 1976, pp. 257–276.

20.   This indeed was a principal factor in encouraging the Hapsburg authorities, in whose domains they were particularly active, to classify these Balkan Orthodox merchants indiscriminately as Greek, a tendency against which Traian Stoianovich has given a salutary warning, "The Conquering Balkan Orthodox Merchant," *Journal of Economic History,* 20 (1960), p. 309. For a Hapsburg document recording as "Greeks" many manifest non-Greeks, see P. K. Enepekides, *Griechiesche Handelsgesellschaften und Kaufleute in Wien aus dem Jahre 1760 (Ein Konskriptionsbuch). . . .,* Thessaloniki, 1959.

21.   Quoted by M. V. Pundeff, "Bulgarian Nationalism"; in P. F. Sugar and I. J. Lederer, eds., *Nationalism in Eastern Europe,* Seattle, 1969, p. 101.

22.   I am grateful to Dr. Peter Mackridge for material on Părličev.

23.   R. J. Crampton, "The Social Structure of the Bulgarians in the First Half of the Nineteenth Century," in Richard Clogg, ed., *Balkan Society in the Age of Greek Independence,* London, 1981, p. 187.

24.   Veselin Beshevliev, "Der Widerhall des neugriechischen Sprachkampfes und der neugriechischen Literatur im Bulgarien des vorigen Jahrhunderts," in *Ed. J. Irmscher, Probleme der neugriechischen Literatur,* vol. 2, Berlin, 1960, p. 49. See also Stojan Maslev, "Die Rolle der griechischen Schulen und der griechischen Literatur für die Aufklärung des bulgarischen Volkes zur Zeit seiner Wiedergeburt" in Johannes Irmscher and Marika Mineemi, eds., *O Ellinismos eis to exoterikon. Über Beziehungen des Griechentums zum Ausland in der neueren Zeit,* Berlin, 1968, pp. 339–395 and M. Stoyanov, "Les syndromites bulgares de livres grecs au cours de la première moitié du XIXe siècle," *Byzantinisch-neugriechische Jahrbücher,* 19 (1966), pp. 373–400.

25.   *Eisagogiki Didaskalia, periekhousa lexikon tetraglosson ton tessaron koinon dialekton, itoi tis aplis Romaikis, tis en Moisia Vlakhikis, tis Voulgarikis, kai tis Alvanitikis . . . ,* Istanbul, 1802 preface. Another Macedonian Vlach G. Rozia, declared that he had written his *Exetaseis peri ton Romaion i ton onomazomenon Vlakhon* (Inquiries concerning the Romans or Vlachs as they are called) Pest, 1808, in Greek because he considered modern Greek to be a link among the Balkan peoples.

26.   Mīkhā'il Mishāqa (1800–1888) recalled having come among his uncle's books an Arabic translation of Anthimos Gazis' *Grammatiki ton filosofikon epistimon,* itself a translation of Benjamin Martin's *The Philosophical Grammar . . . ,* a popularization of Newtonian science first published in 1735, see A. Hourani, *Arabic Thought in the Liberal Age 1798–1939,* London, 1962, pp. 58–59.

27.   On millenarian ideas among the South Slavs of the Ottoman Empire see Traian Stoianovich, "Les structures millénaristes sud-slaves aux XVIIe et XVIIIe siècles," *Actes du Premier Congrès International des etudes balkaniques et sud-est europeennes,* Sofia, 1969, vol. 3, pp. 809–819. A fascinating account of the various prophetic beliefs circulating among the Greeks, and in particular that of the "Emperor turned into marble," is contained in N. A. Veis, "Peri tou istorimenou khrismologiou tis Kratikis Vivliothikis tou Verolinou (Codex Graecus fol. 62–297) kai tou thrylou tou 'mamaromenou vasilia," *Byzantinisch neugriechische Jahrbücher,* 13 (1937), pp. 203–244.

28.   J. L. Burckhardt, *Travels in Syria and the Holy Land,* London, 1822, p. 40, cited in Haddad (cited n. 14), p. 84; cf. F. W. Hasluck "The Crypto-Christians of Trebizond," *Christianity and Islam under the Sultans,* Oxford, 1929, vol. 2, pp. 471–472.

29.   Even Ioannis Pringos, a merchant of Zagora who had prospered mightily in Amsterdam and who is often cited as the epitome of the "progressive" bourgeois chafing at the restraints imposed by the Ottomans on the amassing of profit, was firmly convinced in the early 1770s that it was only a matter of time before God drove the impious Hagarens from Europe, N. Andriotis, "To khroniko tou Amsterdam," *Nea Estia,* 10 (1931), p. 846 ff. Nicolae Cercel (Nikolaos Zertzoulis), a Vlach from Metsovo, who directed the *Academia domnească* in Iaşi in Moldavia, a man who had studied for seven years in Western Europe and was the translator of Newton into Greek, was also the author of learned commentaries on the Oracles of Leo the Wise, see Ariadna Camariano-

Cioran, *Les academies princières de Bucarest et de Jassy et leurs professeurs*, Thessaloniki, 1974, pp. 599–604.

30.   Ypsilantis (cited n. 16), p. 534 and Kaisarios Dapontes, "Istorikos katalogos andron episi-mon (1700–1784)" in K. N. Sathas, ed., *Mesaioniki Vivliothiki*, Venice, 1872, vol. 3, pp. 119–120.

31.   Letter of 2 June 1821 of Consul Francis Werry in Izmir to the governors of the Levant Company, P(ublic) R(ecord) O(ffice) SP 105/139.

32.   Kostantinos Oikonomoos, *Logos Kydoniakos B'. Peri agapis patridos* . . ., Athens, 1837, p. 18.

33.   P. Rizos, ed., *Mémoires du Prince Nicolas Soutzo, Grand-Logothète de Moldavie 1798–1871*, Vienna, 1899, p. 10.

34.   See, for instance, Jacob Landau, *Jews in Nineteenth Century Egypt*, New York, 1969, pp. 215–217, 225–226, 289–290. A Greek attack on the Jewish quarter of Izmir in 1872, prompted by rumors of ritual murder at Passover, resulted in the death of two Jews. See E. J. Davies, *Anatolica; or, the Journal of a Visit to some of the Ancient Ruined Cities of Caria, Phrygia, Lycia and Pisidia*, London, 1874, p. 245. See also Lucy M. J. Garnett, *Greece of the Hellenes*, London, 1914, p. 12.

35.   Journal of William Jowett, 10 May 1818, Church Missionary Society Archives C. M/E 3; Philpin de Rivière, *Vie de Mgr. de Forbin-Janson, missionaire, évêque de Nancy et de Toul primat de Lorraine, fondateur de la Sainte-Enfance*, Paris, 1891, pp. 104–110; H. L. Bodman, *Political Factions in Aleppo, 1760–1826*, Chapel Hill, North Carolina, 1963, ix.

36.   Markos Antoniou Katsaitis, "Secondo viaggio da Corfù à Smirne l'anno 1742," in Ph. Phalbos, *Dyo taxidia sti Smyrni 1740 kai 1742*, Athens, 1972, p. 77.

37.   Ducas, *Historia Turco-Byzantina (1341–1462)*, ed. V. Grecu, Bucharest, 1958, p. 329. Cf. D. M. Nicol, "The Byzantine View of Western Europe," *Greek, Roman and Byzantine Studies*, 8 (1967), pp. 334–335. The archimandrite Kyprianos in his *History of Cyprus* printed in Venice in 1788 noted that the Greeks of the island preferred to be subject to the Ottomans rather than a Latin power "because so far as concerned their rites and customs, they escaped the tyranny of the Latins," *Istoria khronologiki tis Nisou Kyprou*, Venice, 1788, quoted in C. D. Cobham, *Excerpta Cypria*, Nicosia, 1895, p. 251. Nikodimos Agioretis in his great *Pidalion*, a standard commentary on the canon law of the Orthodox Church, argued that now that Divine providence had set up a mighty guard, in the shape of the Ottoman Empire, against the haughty pretensions of the Latins, there was no longer any need not to apply the canons of the Eastern Church with full vigor, . . . *Pidalion tis noitis nios, tis mias, agias, katholikis, kai apostolikis ton Orthodoxon Ekklisias* . . ., Leipzig, 1800, p. 36. One reason that the great majority of the Arab Orthodox Christians of Syria were prepared to accept Greek control of the Patriarchate of Antioch until the latter half of the nineteenth century is that the Greeks afforded the best defense against Uniate proselytism, see Haddad (cited n. 14), p. 64.

38.   I have translated the complete text of the *Didaskalia Patriki* in my "The Dhidhaskalia Patriki' (1798): An Orthodox Reaction to French Revolutionary Propaganda," *Middle Eastern Studies*, 5 (1969), pp. 102–108. A Rumanian translation of the *Didaskali Patriki*, the *Invăţatură părintească*, was published in Iaşi in 1822 as a response to Alexandros Ypsilantis's invasion and to Tudor Vladimirescu's revolt. On the response of the Ecumenical Patriarchate to the ideas of the French Revolution and of the Enlightenment, Ariadna Camariano, "Spiritul filosofic şi revolu-ţionar combatut de Patriarchia Ecumenică şi Sublima Poartă," *Cercetări Literare*, 4 (1941), pp. 114–136 and *Spiritual revoluţionar francez şi Voltaire in limă greaca şi romînă*, Bucharest, 1946, are extremely useful.

39.   K. Th. Dimaras, "To keimeno tou Rossanglogallou," *Ellinika*, 8 (1962), pp. 189–199. For a translation of this text, which appears to have served as the model for *Mati Bolgariya*, a Bulgarian poem in similar genre, see my *The Movement for Greek Independence 1770–1821. A Collection of Documents*, London, 1976, pp. 96–106.

40.   *Elliniki Nomarkhia, itoi logos peri eleftherias*, Italy, 1806, pp. 185–186.

41. Philippos Iliou, "Pour une étude quantitative du public des lecteurs grecs á l'Époque des Lumières et de la Révolution (1749–1842)," *Actes du premier congrès international des Ètudes balkaniques et sud-est européennes,* Sofia, 1969, vol. 4, p. 480.

42. E. g., by Runciman (cited n. 12), p. 406.

43. G. G. Pappadopoulos and G. P. Angelopoulos, *Ta kata ton aoidimon protathlitin tou ierou ton Ellinon agonos ton Patriarkhin Konstantinoupoleos Grigorion ton E,* Athens, 1865, vol. 1, pp. 235–241.

44. The acquisition by Serbia of an autonomous status before the Greeks was by no means such a serious threat to the *Millet-i Rum* for Serbia's irredentist aspirations were less embracing than those of the Greeks.

45. For the ferman instituting the Bulgarian Exarchate see George Young, *Corps de Droit Ottoman . . .,* Oxford, 1905, vol. 2, pp. 61–64.

46. Stavro Skendi, *The Albanian National Awakening, 1878–1912,* Princeton, 1967; pp. 137–138. On Greek relations with the Albanians at a crucial period in the Albanian nationalist movement see Kondis, *Greece and Albania 1908–1914,* Thessaloniki, 1976.

47. *Genikoi kanonismoi peri diefthetiseos ton ekklisastikon kai ethnikon pragmaton ton ypo ton Oikoumenikon Thronon diatelounton Orthodoxon Khristianon Ypikoon tis Autis Megaleiotitos tou Soultanou,* Istanbul, 1862.

48. E. Engelhardt, *La Turquie et le Tanzimat ou histoire des réformes dans l'Empire ottoman depuis 1826 jusqu' à nos jours,* Paris, 1882, p. 142.

49. Roderic Davison, *Reform in the Ottoman Empire 1856–1876,* Princeton, 1963, p. 131ff.

50. Nassau Senior, the economist, was told during the winter of 1857–1858 by the British consul at the Dardanelles that "the influence of the *Hatt-i Humayoon* did not extend 160 miles from Contantinople," *A Journal Kept in Turkey and Greece,* London, 1859, p. 159. A detailed account of one particular instance of the misapplication of the *Hatt-ı Şerif* of Gülhane is given in a long dispatch by the British vice-consul in Trabzon, J. J. Suter, to Viscount Ponsonby, British ambassador to the Sublime Porte, 16 April 1841, P.R.O. F(oreign) O(ffice) 1975/173.

51. In the Pontos area alone approximately a thousand new Orthodox churches were built in the forty years after the *Hatt-ı Şerif* of Gülhane, see A. A. M. Bryer, "The Pontic Revival and the New Greece", in Nikiforos P. Diamandouros et al., eds., *Hellenism and the First Greek War of Liberation (1821–1830): Continuity and Change,* Thessaloniki, 1976, p. 184. See also Halil Inalcik, "Application of the Tranzimat and its Social Effects," *Archivum Ottomanicum,* 5(1973), pp. 97–128.

52. A. Miliarakis, *Ypomnimata perigraphika ton Kykladon nison kata meros, Andros Keos,* Athens, 1880, pp. 149–150. A. W. Kinglake, in *Eothen, or Traces of Travel Brought Home from the East,* London, 1844, p. 74, reported such migrations as early as 1835, which seemed to show that on the whole the Greeks preferred "groaning under the Turkish yoke," to the honor of "being the only true source of legitimate power, in their own land."

53. *Accounts and Papers,* 68(1861), p. 531. Blunt drew attention to the way in which, following the *Hatt-ı Hümayun* of 1856, Christians were rapidly buying up Turkish landed property in the *vilayet* of Aydın.

54. G. Tsitsitis, "Peri Kydonıon," *Xenophanis,* 1(1896), p. 243.

55. W. Ramsay, *Impressions of Turkey during Twelve Years' Wanderings,* London, 1897, pp. 131–132.

56. Senior (cited n. 50), p. 164.

57. Whatever the reasons for the high rate of Greek population growth, it enabled Eleftherios Venizelos to argue in 1920 *a propos* the Greek occupation of the *vilayet* of Aydin that "owing to the breeding qualities of the Greeks his Smyrna population before the end of the century would exceed the total population of the Turkish Empire." Quoted in M. Llewellyn-Smith, *Ionian Vision. Greece in Asia Minor, 1919–1922,* London 1973, p. 121.

58.   A. Synvet, *Les Grecs de l'Empire Ottomane, Étude statistique et ethnographique*, Istanbul, 1878, pp. 4–5.

59.   Vedat Eldem, *Osmanlı İmparatorluğun iktisadı şartları hakkında bir tetkik*, Ankara, 1970. p. 55, cited in Kemal Karpat, "The Social and Economic Transformation of Istanbul in the Nineteenth Century," *Istanbul à la jonction des cultures balkaniques, méditerranéennes, slaves et orientales, au xvie–xixe siècles*, Bucharest 1977, p. 431.

60.   G. K. Typaldos, *Anatolikai epistolai. Smyrni, Aigyptos, Palaistin*, Athens, 1859, p. 2.

61.   In 1896, for instance, Greeks controlled 156 out of a total of 214 businesses in Samsun, see Bryer (cited n. 51), p. 189.

62.   Ubicini (cited n. 15), p. 236f.

63.   *Sympliroma eis K. Paparrigopoulon, Istoria tou Ellinikou Ethnous*, Athens, 1904, vol. 6, part 2, p. 393, cited in D. A. Zakythinos, *I Politiki Istoria tis Neoteras Ellados*, Athens, 1965, p. 52.

64.   G. K. Typaldos, in mid-century, for instance, wrote that in the Ottoman Empire one can already see "on the one hand the rapid and extraordinary progress of the Greeks, on the other, and even more rapid and extraordinary decline of the Ottomans, who today are reduced to being but feeble shadows of their barbarous past (cited n. 60), p. 5.

65.   Ubicini (cited n. 15), p. 239.

66.   On the activites of the Greek *syllogoi* in the Ottoman Empire see Tatiana Stavrou, *O en Konstantinoupolei Ellinikos Philologikos Syllogos; to Ypourgeion tou Alytrotou Ellinismou*, Athens 1967; Albert Dumont, "Des syllogues en Turquie," *Annuaire de l'association pour l'encouragement des études grecques en France*, 8(1874), pp. 527–538; Queux de Saint-Hilaire, "Des syllogues grecs en Orient et en Europe et du progrès des études littéraires dans la Grèce de nos jours," *Annuaire de l'association pour l'encouragement des études grecques en France*, 11(1877), pp. 288–322; S. I. Papadopoulos, "Eisagogi stin istoria ton Ellinikon Philekpaideftikon Syllogon tis Othomanikis Aftokratorias kata ton 19on kai 20on aiona," *Parnassos*, 2nd. ser., vol. 4(1962), pp. 247–258.

67.   N. E. Milioris, "O Syllogos ton Mikrasiaton i 'Anatoli,'" *Mikrasiatika Khronika*, 12(1964), p. 348. *Anatoli* published an annual yearbook, *Xenophanis*, which is a mine of information on the Orthodox communities of Asia Minor.

68.   Ubicini (cited n. 15), p. 194. The foundation of Greek schools in the Turcophone communities of the Kayseri region in the mid-nineteenth century was in the view of the acting British consul, J. H. Skene, the result of Russian subsidies but there is little evidence for this, see Dispatch of 21 July 1851, P.R.O. F.O. 195/338.

69.   Davies (cited n. 34), p. 147.

70.   M. Georgiadis, "Anakoinosis peri tis Kilikias katholou kai Adanon," *Xenophanis*, 1(1896), p. 279.

71.   IoakeimValavanis, *Mikrasiatika*, Athens, 1891, p. 27.

72.   P. Karolidis, *Glossarion sygkritikon ellinokappadokikon lexeon, itoi i en Kappadokia laloumeni elliniki dialektos kai ta en afti sozomena ikhni tis arkhaias Kappadokikis glossis*, Izmir, 1885, pp. 36–37, and S. Krinopoulos, *Ta Phertekaina ypo ethnologikin kai philologikin epopsin exetazomena*, Athens, 1889, p. 14. One serious obstacle to the diffusion of Greek was the insistence by its proponents on teaching not the spoken *dimotiki* but the archaizing *katharevousa*, then the intellectual fashion in the Greek Kingdom. The Greek taught in the Kayseri region at the end of the nineteenth century was, according to one Hellenizer, "free of the foreign usages, mutilated words and barbarous phrases with which the language of the uneducated free Greeks is unfortunately replete," S. B. Zervoudakis, "Dianoitiki anagennisis en Kaisareia Kappadokias," *Xenophanis*, 1(1896), p. 83.

73.   "Bir Mülâhaza," *Tasvir-i Efkâr* (1 October 1866) cited in Şerif Mardin, *The Genesis of Young Ottoman Thought. A Study in the Modernization of Turkish Political Ideas*, Princeton, 1962, p. 27.

74.   Periklis Triandaphyllidis, *I en Ponto Elliniki Phyli, itoi ta Pontika,* Athens, 1866, pp. 15–18. Triandaphyllidis was a schoolmaster from Pontos who had studied at the University of Athens.

75.   T. I. Ioannidis, "Anamniseis apo to Salikhli," *Mikrasiatika Khronika,* 8(1959), p. 379.

76.   Aubrey Herbert, *Ben Kendim. A Record of Eastern Travel,* ed. Desmond MacCarthy, London, n.d. (?1923), p. 273; A. F. Townshend, *A Military Consul in Turkey. The Experiences and Impressions of a British Representative in Asia Minor,* London, 1910, p. 102.

77.   For an interesting eyewitness account of the impact of the Young Turk revolution on the polyglot population of Salonika see Avraam Benaroya, *I proti stadiodromia tou Ellinikou Proletariatou,* Athens, 1975, p. 41. Benaroya, a Jew from Vidin, was active in the early development of the socialist movement in Salonika. Within a month of the restoration of the constitution a socialist newspaper, *O Ergatis: Ephimerida gia tonergatiko lao,* in an appropriately "hairy" form of demotic Greek, was being published in Izmir. Interestingly, the newspapers' owner, Mehmet Mecdet, was a Turk who had been persecuted under Abdülhamit II for his progressive views.

78.   I am much indebted to the University of London M.A. thesis of Catherine Boura, "The Young Turk Revolution and the Greeks of the Ottoman Empire, 1908–1912" (1976) for information on this period.

79.   Llewellyn Smith, (cited n. 54), pp. 31–33.

80.   I owe this information to Alexandros Alexandris who is writing a University of London Ph. D. thesis on the Greek community of Istanbul after 1918. In October 1919 the patriarchate forbade Ottoman Greeks to participate in the forthcoming elections for the Ottoman parliament on the ground that they were no longer Ottoman subjects; see Clair Price, *The Rebirth of Turkey,* New York, 1923, p. 147.

Jewish Communities in Turkey during the Last Decades of the Nineteenth Century in the Light of the Archives of the Alliance Israélite Universelle

BY PAUL DUMONT

The main objective of the Alliance Israélite Universelle[1] created in 1860 by a group of French Jews, was to work for the emancipation of Jewish communities scattered throughout the world and to struggle against the discrimination from which Jews suffered in many countries. Stress was laid at the very beginning on the necessity to organize schools. In the opinion of the leadership of the Alliance, the moral and material progress of Jews was necessarily linked to a radical renovation of instruction: it was only modern education, based on linguistic, scientific, and technical studies, that could save Jewish communities from misery and obscurantism.

The first school of the Alliance in Ottoman Turkey was founded in Edirne, in 1867. At the beginning of the seventies, other establishments followed: Salonica, Izmir, Hasköy, Balat, Galata. Within a few decades, nearly fifty schools were established throughout the country. These different institutions were all linked to a Central Committee in Paris. Thence came directives and subsidies. There converged the reports of regional committees, the petitions of communities, the letters of schoolmasters, the school's accounts, etc. All this administrative red tape referred principally to the life of the schools. Timetables, programs, administrative and financial problems constituted each year the subject matter of detailed reports. Furthermore, the correspondents of the Alliance were entrusted with the task of studying local ways and customs and of reporting to headquarters on the economic and social situation of the communities. The Central Committee attached great importance to these reports. In fact, based upon them, decisions were made about the distribution of subsidies, the establishment of new schools, and the adjustment of programs to specific local needs.

The schoolmasters of the Alliance carefully observed the environment in which they lived and were in most cases remarkably well informed. Whenever they felt it necessary they gave lengthy explanations on matters which, in their opinion, deserved special attention. Their letters, carefully preserved in the Archives of the Alliance, provide today a valuable source for those who are interested in cultural, economic and social history of Jewish communities of Turkey.

Ninety-six files, each filled to the brim with a thousand documents—such is the by-product of over half a century of the existence of the schools of the Alliance on Turkish territory. This figure does not take into account the archives concerning the cities of Remelia lost during the Balkan wars: Salonica, Kavalla, and Serrès. A systematic study of this material would doubtless fill many gaps in our knowledge of the recent past of Jews in Turkey. This, however, is a strenuous study which no one seems to have undertaken until now. As far as I am concerned, I have merely glanced through a few files, just a first inspection to determine the outlines of this abundant source.

The letters and reports which provide the material for my study concern in most cases the communities of Izmir, Bursa and Istanbul. But I have also made use of data pertaining to other localities including Aydın, Tire, and Silivri. My intention was not to draw up a series of local monographs but, on the contrary, to give a general image of the situation of Jews in Turkey during the last decades of the nineteenth century. This explains why, in addition to the archives of the Alliance, I have made use of certain complementary sources. In particular, I drew on the numerous works of Abraham Galanté, which are known to constitute a rich mine of information.[2] I have not taken up here the specific case of Salonica which would deserve a special examination by itself. I have also excluded the communities of the Oriental provinces which are comprised in the territories of now independent countries. That is to say, I limited my work to the communities that were established within the geographical limits of the present Turkish republic.

A Reality Painted in Dark Colors

When reading the correspondence of the schoolmasters of the Alliance, one is impressed by the recurrence of certain words: poverty, misery, distress. If we are to take these reports into account, only a few communities escaped these evils. The community of Bursa was, it would seem, one of those exceptions: many of its members were poor, but each family was fortunate enough to own the house in which it lived.[3]

Elsewhere, it sufficed to wander through a Jewish quarter to be aware of the extent of extreme destitution of its inhabitants. Dark and tortuous alleys, dilapidated houses, cramped and unsanitary living quarters, such was at the end of the nineteenth century the characteristic aspect of most of the "ghettoes" of Turkey. In certain Anatolian towns, in Izmir and in Aydın for instance, an important part of the Jewish population lived in *cortijos,* vast enclosed yards where dozens of families were herded together. Sometimes these families, each confined to a single small room, comprised ten to fifteen members. Here misery, promiscuity, and dirt reached their peak. For example, one of the numerous rabbis of the city of Aydın lived with his wife, their children, and the family of his married son in a slum of three-by-four meters, with a single room, at once bedroom, kitchen, and washroom. It is there that he received his pupils, there that believers came to read the *Tikon Hatsot* (midnight prayer vigil), while the *rabissa* was getting on with housework.[4] The situation was very similar in the *cortijos* of Izmir. And when, each Friday, the clerk of the Muslim landlord came with his suitcase to collect the rent, numerous lodgers could but sob and implore for a delay in payment of the debt.[5]

In Istanbul, a great metropolis with a population around 1900 of nearly a million, including more than fifty thousand Jews, the well-to-do group seemed comparatively more important than in Anatolia. The "rich"—bankers, traders, and members of learned professions—had their own quarters, which often were quite pleasant; Pera, Kusgunçuk, Haydar Paşa, Kadiköy. But the two most characteristic Jewish suburbs of the Ottoman capital, Hasköy and Balat, looked like a network of half-ruined hovels and there misery was more hideous than anywhere else. Balat, whose narrow alleys sheltered some ten thousand Jews, had even then the dubious distinction of being one of the foulest smelling localities of the Golden Horn.[6]

Many theories have been voiced to explain this decay of the Jewish communities of Turkey: exorbitant taxes, all kinds of crimes committed against them by Janissaries (plunder, arson), and the absence of forceful and respected leaders among Jews. Naturally, stress has also been laid on economic factors. Whilst until the beginning of the eighteenth century Jews still played an important part in the Ottoman economy, they had been progressively pushed into the background and superseded in all the decisive sectors (trade, banking, manufacture, crafts, and learned professions) by Armenians and Greeks. Their lack of interest in manual work put them at a further disadvantage as regards their Christian competitors, reputed for their skill in numerous crafts.[7]

Jewish ghettoes meant misery, but also overpopulation. In the correspondence of the schoolmasters, poverty and proliferation of the species appear practically always together, closely related to each other. It would seem that families of eight, ten or even fifteen people living under the same roof, were not exceptional, especially in smaller towns, such as Silivri, Aydın or Tire.[8] If we are to believe the schoolmasters, the factor responsible for this state of things was largely the practice of early marriages, a custom of longstanding among Oriental Jews. In many localities, most of the young girls married at thirteen or fourteen. Young men waited a little longer but, even so, they often were married and had a family before eighteen. In 1884 S. Pariente, the director of the Izmir school, reported upon a case of a grandfather twenty-nine years old.[9] These early marriges were not only a factor of overpopulation. They were also held responsible, in accordance with the then current theories, for a certain "degeneration" of the race. For instance, according to Pariente, the irregular features, the dark coloring, the thick stature, the heavy and dragging gait of the Jews of Tire at the beginning of the eighties were mainly due to the great number of marriages at too young an age.[10]

Unfortunately, the documents of the Alliance yield but little precise data on the demographic evolution of Turkish Jews. From the different figures at our disposal, and especially from official statistics, it appears that most of the communities achieved a comparatively high population increase in the last decades of the nineteenth century, but it is very difficult to go beyond elementary conclusions.[11] A few examples illustrate in a spectacular manner the general trend. In Bursa the official census of 1883 counted 2,179 Jews. Three years later the director of the school in this city noted an increase of nearly 600 persons, that is, an unbelievable rate of 8 percent per annum. This expansion was to continue into the twentieth century, reaching its peak of 3,500 persons around 1900.[12] The same astonishing increase is observed in Silivri, a small agricultural town on the Marmara, some 70 kilometers from Istanbul. In 1896, there were 1,200 Jews. In August 1901 there were 1,584 people forming 329 families (which, by the way, amounts to a very reasonable average of five persons per family). Six years later, the number of families grew to 400 and that of individuals to a total of 2,024.[13] Within a period of ten years, the Jewish population of the town had practically doubled! In large cities, such as Izmir and Istanbul, the demographic evolution of the Jewish community is more difficult to establish because of the overabundance of contradictory estimates.[14] However, here again, the statistics show a definite increase. According to the *Bulletin de l'Alliance Israélite Universelle,* there were 40,000 Jews in Istanbul in 1886; this figure increased to 65,000 by 1904. For the same period, the Jewish population of Smyrna grew from 20,000 to 35,000 persons.

There is reason to believe that this increase was largely due to demographic growth within the Jewish community and also (especially during the last years of the century) to the developing commercial and—to a degree—industrial centers located on the coast and on other major crossroads of economic penetration. Nevertheless, we must also take into consideration Jewish emigration from the Balkan countries and from Russia. It is common knowledge that the last decades of the nineteenth century were in this respect a very stormy period. Every time a conflict arose between the Ottoman Empire and the neighboring states, Jewish refugees in great numbers flocked to Turkish territory. Thus, for instance, thousands of Bulgarian Jews came to Edirne and Istanbul at the time of the Russo-Turkish war of 1877.[15] A similar, though smaller, movement took place when Eastern Rumelia was annexed by Bulgaria in 1885.[16] Conflicts between Turkey and Greece, at the end of the century, also resulted in large migrations. To these refugees driven by wars toward Turkey were added successive waves of emigrants fleeing the anti-Semitic policy of Rumania and Russia. The archives of the Alliance note the periodic arrival of small groups of a few hundred individuals, particularly in Izmir and Istanbul. As an example, we can mention the case of some two thousand Jews ousted from Russia on the pretext that they were Ottoman subjects who came to Istanbul during the summer of 1892 completely destitute.[17] Rumanian emigration was particularly important at the end of the century. In 1899 and in 1900 hundreds of Rumanian Jewish families drifted toward Turkey, which had been described to them as a kind of Eldorado. They were hoping to create agricultural colonies there.[18]

Nevertheless, one should not overestimate the impact of these waves of emigration upon demography. Doubtless, in certain cities (Istanbul, Izmir, Aydın), groups of refugees contributed to an increase of Jewish population, but this contribution does not seem to have been very significant. As a matter of fact, many of the emigrants merely passed in transit through Turkey. Even if at the beginning certain families had intended to settle in European Turkey or in Anatolia, they often gave up the idea and joined the great migratory currents toward the United States, Canada, South America, Palestine, or certain African countries. In spite of their innate hospitality, the poor and overpopulated Jewish communities of Turkey were, in general, unable to receive the newcomers and hastened to direct them toward other points of possible resettlement. It even happened that emigrants were invited to return to their countries of origin. Thus, immediately after the Congress of Berlin Jews who fled the Russo-Turkish war were driven back toward Bulgaria where they had been authorized to retrieve their possessions.[19]

Naturally, the increase of mouths to feed was a great burden for the Jews of Turkey. It would seem that toward the end of the nineteenth century, communities consciously decided to limit births in a more efficient manner than in the past. For instance, the schoolmasters of the Alliance noted during this period a distinct decrease in the number of premature marriages in certain localities. We can suppose that the propaganda of the Alliance and of its local representatives in favor of a reasonable birth rate was beginning to be effective.

But demographic balance was also reestablished, in a most cruel way, by the great epidemics which from time to time eliminated the less resistant individuals. Chronic malnutrition and deplorable hygiene in certain Jewish quarters made them very vulnerable to the great scourges of the time: plague, cholera, smallpox, diphtheria, typhoid, and childbed fever. In large cities, such as Izmir or Istanbul, such epidemics were more frequent and more deadly than elsewhere. The "suspect illness" that broke out in Izmir in 1893—the word cholera was carefully avoided—was doomed to remain in the memory of local Jews, like the great plague of 1865, as one of the most terrible calamities that ever struck their community.[20] Neither were small localities immune from danger. The cholera epidemic which broke out in Bursa in 1894 was, it would seem, just as deadly as that of Izmir.[21] In this same city, in November 1900, four to five children died of smallpox every day in the Jewish community.[22]

On the other hand, from the eighties, the demographic surplus began to be absorbed, though very gradually, by emigration. At first few people left, but the letters which they sent from Argentina, from the United States, from the Congo and other places inspired many other young people over the years to follow in their steps. It is difficult to evaluate this emigration exactly, but we know that towns such as Istanbul provided at the dawn of the twentieth century important contingents of emigrants who established themselves in different countries of the New World and Africa as well as in certain European cities. For example, according to the *American Jewish Yearbook*, nearly eight thousand Jews from Turkey migrated to the United States between 1899 and 1912.[23]

Besides poverty and overpopulation, the schoolmasters in their reports never failed to mention ignorance as one of the principal evils from which the Jewish communities suffered. In their opinion, the lack of adjustment of traditional education to the needs of modern life constituted one of the most important causes of the backwardness of the Jews compared with the advance of the Greeks and Armenians. Stressing the fact that after several years of study, children could barely do the four mathematical operations or translate into Ladino a limited number of religious texts, they insistently denounced the ineffectiveness of the education dispensed by the *Talmud torahs* and sometimes even attacked the rabbis themselves. For instance, here is how A. Löwy, one of the members of the Anglo-Jewish association, presented the situation of the rabbinic schools in Istanbul at the beginning of the nineties:

> Constantinople, unhappily, contains as many as twenty-eight Talmud Torahs. These are the nurseries in which the deplorable misery of the rising generation of Jews is perpetuated. More than 2,500 boys between ages of four and twelve are huddled together in seventy to eighty rooms, which, with few exceptions, are extremely filthy and insanitary. The poor children, whose school-hours are from 8 o'clock to 5 pm, present an exceedingly unhealthy appearance except perchance some little fellows who have recently been received in these dens of wasted childhood.
>
> Many of the sallow countenances are ominously marked by large dark rings round the lusterless eyes. The destitution of these ill-fed and ill-clad children is still more aggravated by the self-told tale of their mental neglect. The jovial freshness of youth gives way forever to premature debility. In a forbidding attitude stands before these children their illiterate teacher, whom some of his patrons may have promoted to this post, on finding that he could not make headway as a dealer in petty wares. He holds in his hand the rod of punishment, and visits upon the helpless children the sins of his own incompetency. The elder boys are made to recite mechanically, in a choral sing-song, the Pentateuchal portion of the week. In chorus they translate parts of the portion of the Law into

the Judaeo-Spanish dialect, but they are not taught how the precepts of the Bible should be used to improve the heart and straighten the conduct of life.[24]

This aggressive attitude of the members of the Alliance toward the traditional schools (due in part to the fact that the *Talmud torah* competed with the "new style" schools established by the Alliance) is seen everywhere. It would seem that the rabbis of Izmir, Bursa and Aydın were not much better—from the Alliance's view—than those of Istanbul.

Unfortunately, we did not find in the archives of the Alliance data allowing us to establish with precision the level of instruction of the Jewish population of Turkey. For instance, what was the percentage of illiteracy within different communities? In the present state of our research we cannot reply to this question. It is reasonable to think, however, that thanks to the *Talmud torahs,* and in spite of all the defects of these institutions, persons who could read and write represented a rather high percentage of the total population. The development of the Ladino press in Izmir and Istanbul in the last decades of the nineteenth century is significant in this respect.[25]

The Alliance's criticism of traditional education was not so much that it let the children wallow in illiteracy as that it supplied them with knowledge that was useless or at least insufficient. Outside the Jewish quarters, of what use could be the rudiments of Ladino and Hebrew taught in the *Talmud torah?* To have a chance of "becoming a somebody," one should possess additional knowledge. To begin with, the Jews had to learn the official language of the country—Turkish. Naturally enough, everybody in the community could speak it (with an accent that kept the displayers of *Karagöz* happy*) but those who could read and write it were extremely rare. For instance, during the eighties in Aydın, in a community of some three thousand individuals, there were only two Jews who could read and write Turkish. These two young men, indispensable to their coreligionists, served as translators and lawyers.[26] In Bursa, in 1886, the only Jew who could boast of some knowledge of Turkish—a clerk of the cadastral survey—had left the town to establish himself in Kassaba, a locality near Izmir. In large cities, the situation was probably less dramatic but nevertheless worrying enough. According to the Rev. A. Löwy, in Istanbul, in 1886, there were only sixty-six Jewish children who were being taught Turkish in primary schools.[27] The schoolmasters of the Alliance considered this widespread ignorance of the official language as one of the principal impediments to the progress of Jewish communities in Turkey. But though they constantly struggled to introduce Turkish into primary and secondary schools, the results were for a long time very slight. It is interesting to note that the different periodicals published in the course of the last decades of the nineteenth century with the object of promoting the use of the Turkish language among the Jews (the *Ustad* and the *Messerat* of Izmir, the *Zeman*

Karagöz: a shadow-play Punch and Judy show, had a stock character, the Jew, who spoke with an easily mocked accent.

and the *Ceride-i Lisan* of Istanbul, etc.) were printed not in Arabic but in Hebrew characters. Were it otherwise, these periodicals would have touched only a small elite and would have been unable to survive.

Misery, demographic disequilibrium, ignorance: a reality painted in dark colors. Nevertheless, we know that the last decades of the nineteenth century, represented for the Jews in addition, a period of change and of progress. During the reign of Abdülhamid II, the Jewish bourgeoisie of large towns became more established; certain "ghettos" were cleansed (particularly in the aftermath of the great fires that devastated Jewish quarters); remarkable results were achieved in education; and the acceleration of economic life brought about a certain mobility among the most heavily handicapped classes. The schoolmasters of the Alliance could not avoid noting these numerous transformations, to which we will duly revert. Why then had they this tendency to underscore the negative elements of the situation? Probably because they knew that by pointing out these evils they were working for their elimination.

The Socio-Professional Profile of Jewish Communities

Now we must try to elaborate on the above outline. Naturally, the Jewish communities of Turkey were not composed of paupers alone. In Izmir, for instance, D. Cazès, the director of the Alliance, noted that out of a total of about three thousand five hundred families, about a thousand households were destitute. Nevertheless the Jewish population of the city belonged essentially to the "middle class." D. Cazès classified in this category brokers, merchants, small traders, craftsmen, in short all those who, without actually being in easy circumstances, were more or less provided for. About a hundred families who engaged in trade and had some means composed the "higher class." Finally, D. Cazès set apart a class of "parasites," comprising some five-hundred families of rabbis. In his opinion, these people dressed up in rabbinic costumes endeavored to "deceive fanatics and old women" and lived only on gifts in cash and kind which they managed to extract from their coreligionists.[28] Thus, it appears that the Jewish community of Izmir had a diverse character: it had its "bourgeoisie," its middle strata, its people in reduced circumstances, its profiteers, and its subproletariat. Naturally enough, elsewhere, particularly in Istanbul, the situation was more or less similar. The schoolmasters of the Alliance were always impressed by the considerable economic and social disparities that they observed around them and which they found shocking.

The documents of the Alliance—at least those that we have had the opportunity to consult—give unfortunately only a dim picture of the socio-professional stratification of the Jews. The schoolmasters who reported their impressions to the headquarters limited themselves in most cases to general information (of the type that we have noted in connection with Izmir) and rarely gave detailed figures. Nevertheless, for some towns we do have precise information.

To begin with, we will examine the case of Silivri, a small town near Istanbul. At the dawn of the twentieth century, this small town surrounded by fields and pasture land was, essentially, an agricultural center. Its cereals, wool, raw skins, poultry, eggs, and cheese were sold in the market of the capital. Silivri was also known for its excellent yogurt which had the reputation of prolonging the life of its consumers. Women and children were engaged in making lace exported by the traders of Istanbul to France and Germany. In 1907, the population of this locality was of 7,486 people, of which 2,024 were Jews, 2,019 Greeks, 1,950 Muslims, 950 Armenians, and 543 miscellaneous.

About 400 homes were grouped in the Jewish quarter. We know the socio-professional division of the population—at least in part—thanks to the statistics drawn up by A. Confino, director of the school of the Alliance at Balat.[29] According to this document, at the beginning of the twentieth century, there was only one Jew at Silivri with significant wealth (50,000 francs). The Jewish community also counted a dozen "notables," wholesalers and cloth merchants, with assets between 200 and 500 Turkish liras. Besides these people who constituted the top of society, A. Confino counted 130 peddlers, 50 boot cleaners, 40 water carriers, 20 grocers, 12 tinkers, 4 butchers, 3 jewelers, 2 cobblers, 2 moneychangers, 1 leather merchant, 1 glass cutter, 7 cloth merchants, 3 hairdressers, 3 wineshop keepers, 2 government clerks, 1 mason, and 1 casemaker. Most of these people had no capital whatsoever and lived from hand to mouth, earning enough for the bare necessities of their family. The figures given by A. Confino refer only to 282 homes. Presumably, the 120 chiefs of families not accounted for belonged mostly to the category of daily workers who drew their income from odd jobs, varying according to seasonal fluctuations of the labor market. They worked for the craftsmen and merchants of the town, or for the agriculturists of the hinterland.

Assuming that they are trustworthy, these data serve to stress the tenuousness of the Jewish "bourgeoisie" of Silivri. The people who managed to emerge from among the needy crowd, the "notables" according to the term used by A. Confino, constituted less than 3 percent of the Jewish population of the town. Evidently, this very low percentage should in no case be extrapolated (also it might be appropriate to view it with some suspicion), but it does illustrate a state of things which the numerous correspondents of the Alliance dwell upon.

It was only in large cities—not surprisingly—and in certain economically privileged areas that people in easy circumstance formed a group of some importance. Thus, in Bursa at the end of the nineteenth century, Jewish traders in silk or in cloth, haberdashers, moneychangers, and moneylenders occupied a whole sector of the bazaar and most of these businessmen had rather important assets varying from 500 to 1,000 Turkish liras.[30] Rich Jews were also numerous in Tire, a most prosperous agricultural center, situated about a hundred kilometers west of Izmir. They owed their wealth mostly to the damage inflicted in France by phylloxera, since the principal produce of Tire was raisins, greatly appreciated in the market of Marseilles. Some of them dealt also in the export of cotton, cereals, and figs, or else imported manufactured objects which they sold either locally or in the neighboring towns. In 1884 the patrimony of the Danons, the leading family of Tire, amounted to over half a million francs. Specifically, this family had a *çiftlik* of 2,500 hectares which it rented to Muslim villagers. Several other traders of the town had purchased vineyards and land suitable for growing wheat which provided them with significant incomes.[31] Toward the end of the nineteenth century, the development of tobacco culture prompted some Jews of Tire to venture into this industry. In 1888 J. Levi founded a factory for cigarette paper; a few years later two members of the Danon family, who had obtained a concession from the *Régie,* organized a tobacco-packing enterprise.[32] Finally, there was the community of Aydın where there was, as in Tire, a large enough group of importers of manufactured goods and of traders in agricultural products—cotton, figs, cereals, raisins, valonia (a dyestuffs), wool, and skins—alongside a large "proletariat." Some of these traders had farms, vineyards or plantations of fig trees whose exploitation was turned over to Turkish or Greek farmers. The industrial sector was represented by a soap factory belonging to the firm of D. Levi and also by an important cotton-gin owned by Barki,[33] one of the most respected families of Aydın.

Nevertheless, it is important to stress that even in the prosperous towns such as Bursa, Tire, or Aydın, the majority of Jews belonged to the lowest rungs of the social ladder. Let us examine again the example of Silivri. Considering the most widespread trades, we note that practically 60 percent of the chiefs of households exercised an ambulant activity, which required only insignificant investment. At the top of the list, the grocers alone (5 percent of the chiefs of households) could boast of a small shop and a little capital. The representatives of other professions—peddlers (32 percent of the chiefs of households), boot cleaners (12.5 percent), water carriers (10 percent), tinkers (3 percent)—could set aside only enough money for Sabbath feasting. Water carriers had to satisfy their needs and those of their families with a daily income of thirty to forty centimes. Tinkers and especially peddlers were certainly better off—some of them earned the equivalent of two to three francs a day. Nevertheless, their lot was in no way an enviable one. It is difficult to understand the presence of so many boot cleaners in Silivri, all the more so since many inhabitants of the town went barefoot. Confino himself underlines the strangeness of this situation. Probably they were speculating on an eventual tendency of their compatriots toward displays of finery.

According to the reports of the schoolmasters of the Alliance, this dominance of ambulant crafts prevailed in most Jewish communities of Turkey. Toward the end of the nineteenth century, the typical Jew was not a banker, a moneychanger, or a cloth merchant but certainly a peddler. This extraordinary development of Jewish peddling is linked to the fact that at the time the case or the bale of a peddler constituted, in many instances, the only "shop" of manufactured goods available to villagers (and especially to village housewives). Under such circumstances, peddling constituted a trade which, if not very profitable, was at least more profitable than most of the others accessible to Jews. However, one had to enjoy steady health to engage in peddling, for it was not easy to walk ten leagues a day, with a heavy bale full of different goods on one's back. Most of the Silivri peddlers left town, sometimes with their children, early on Sunday morning and returned only on Friday evening to spend the Sabbath with their family, while others returned only for major religious holidays. The work of the peddler was not only to go from village to village offering his bric-a-brac of manufactured goods. He was also expected to bring back to town wheat, corn, barley, poultry, eggs and fruit received in exchange for his goods and endeavor to sell them on the market.

Those who did not have the necessary physical stamina for peddling turned to other professions considered less straining: they became porters, water carriers, and window cleaners. There was thus a range of ambulant or semi-ambulant crafts, such as that of tinkers or cobblers, which were the favorite of lower class Jews. By dint of hard work some of these disadvantaged people succeeded in saving a little money which was generally invested in commercial activities (ragpicking, ambulant sale of fruit and vegetables, and groceries).

On the other hand, in certain regions, particularly in the *vilayet* of Izmir, a great number of Jews were seasonal laborers, engaged for the harvest of agricultural export products, such as grapes, figs, valonia and nuts. Side by side with this agricultural proletariat, a Jewish proletariat of mills and factories began to form. There is reason to believe that most of the Jewish chiefs of enterprises preferred to recruit their staff from among their coreligionists. Jewish workers were especially numerous in tobacco factories. These factories located in different points of the Ottoman Empire—notably Istanbul, Salonica and Izmir—were great users of labor and became important centers for worker agitation. It is mainly through them that unionization developed among the Jews of Turkey. Besides these tobacco workers there existed in Istanbul, toward the beginning of the twentieth century, about 500 unqualified Jewish occasional laborers in some ten cigarette-paper factories, most of which belonged to Jews. Among other enterprises that called upon Jewish labor, special mention should be made of several textile factories in the *vilayet* of Izmir and also of the silkworm nurseries and the spinning mills of Bursa which employed around the year 1900 nearly 200 Jewish girls.[34]

As in many other countries, the industrial proletariat was composed mainly of women and children. In tobacco factories, for instance, women and children represented more than 50 percent of the total labor staff (in Istanbul these were often young girls of the Ashkenazi community of Galata). Women did not work in factories only: they were laundresses, servants, and nurses. Furthermore, in agricultural regions, they participated, side by side with men, in certain seasonal activities: gathering figs, harvesting and drying grapes, and collecting nuts. It would seem, however, that the part assigned to women in the family economy varied considerably from one town to another. In Izmir, for instance, outside work for women was usually considered as unseemly and, according to one of the schoolmasters of the Alliance, certain women preferred to starve at home or go out begging rather than accept work as servants or laundresses.[35] But, on the other hand, in Silivri most of the women and girls worked. When a Jewish family of Istanbul needed a strong, conscientious and cheap servant girl, it turned to Silivri or Rodosto (Tekir-dağ). Silivri was also an important center of lacemaking, and this activity employed more than 200 young girls who worked full time—twelve to fifteen hours a day—for a taskmaster in Istanbul.

The Jewish community of Silivri, with its cohorts of mercilessly exploited lacemakers, water carriers, boot cleaners, and peddlers, seems to offer the image of a polarized society: on one side a handful of households well pro-vided for, on the other a mass of destitute and needy people. This, however, is certainly an extreme case. In most of the other communities in Turkey, especially in large cities, the intermediate strata were, as we have already stated above, numerically much more important.

We can take as an example the case of the Jewish community of Balat on which we have precise information. On the basis of data from the matricula-tion register of the school of the Alliance which describe some 600 chiefs of families, A. Navon established four great socio-professional categories. As everywhere else, the most important group—more than half of the people—were chiefs of households who had nothing but their manual labor: workers in cigarette-paper factories, servants, window cleaners, merchants of fried food, and boatmen. But though Balat was the poorest Jewish quarter of the capital, the group of small merchants there was far from insignificant. A. Navon placed in this category about 200 druggists, dealers in secondhand clothes, tavernkeepers, and ragpickers, estimating their "fortune" at about fifty Tur-kish liras. On the other hand, fifty-four chiefs of families (that is 9 percent of the individuals under consideration) possessed assets of 2,000 to 10,000 francs: thirteen moneychangers, seventeen cloth merchants, eight ironmon-gers, fourteen traders, one jeweler, and one livestock merchant. A little be-low this leading group, A. Navon noted a category of craftsmen composed of forty-four persons: twenty-two tinkers, eight cobblers, three tailors, six car-penters, two masons, two bookbinders, and one typographer.[36]

Though we have no precise statistics, we can assume that in other Jewish quarters of Istanbul, the middle classes were even better represented. Never-theless, even if in general Jews of the capital seemed to enjoy a relatively satisfactory situation, it is necessary to underline that in the contest for pros-perity they were well behind Christians. Thus, for instance, out of the 1,015 large handicraft and "industrial" enterprises noted by the *Indicateur oriental* at the end of the nineteenth century, only thirty-one were owned by Jews. In the learned professions (architects, lawyers, doctors and engineers), we find the same disproportion: sixty Jews as against 1,052 Christians. it is only in the financial and commercial sectors that Jews succeeded to a degree in competing with Christian rivals (178/1323).[37]

These data by themselves should not be taken as completely accurate since the *Indicateur oriental* supplied only limited information. But they do allow us to acquire some idea of the general trend. Even allowing for the fact that, in Istanbul, Jews were much less numerous than Christians (about 50,000 persons against over 300,000), we must note that the disparity between the Jewish community and the various Christian communities was an important one.

At the end of the nineteenth century, we find the same difference in most of the towns of Turkey: in Bursa, where the silk industry was almost entirely in the hands of Armenians and Greeks; in Izmir, where Christians were well ahead in the various sectors of urban economy; in Silivri where the essential production of local agriculture and handicraft was held by the Greek element. Many other examples could be cited. However, Jews were gradually beginning to catch up with Christians. As we have seen, they invested more and more in well-chosen industrial sectors (cigarette-paper factories, spinning mills, brickmaking, and tobacco-packing factories) and those among them who drew their income from commerce could expect prosperity from the growth of economic relations between Turkey and the West. On the other hand, Armenians and Greeks, who had greatly contributed to the development of native handicraft, had to face the invasion of European manufactured goods and were therefore in a less desirable position. In short there was an inkling of a trend toward a redistribution of assets among the minorities. The political developments also played a role in this process since relations between the Ottoman government and the Christian subjects of the empire were deteriorating.

Relations Between Communities

There are but few countries, even among those which are considered the most enlightened and the most civilized, where Jews enjoy a more complete equality than in Turkey. H. M. the sultan and the government of the Porte display towards Jews a spirit of largest toleration and liberalism. In every respect, Abdul-Hamid proves to be a generous sovereign and a protector of his Israelite subjects. . . . The unflinching attachment of Jews to His Person and to the Empire is the only way in which they can express their gratitude. Thus, the Sultan, as well as his officials know that Jews are among the most obedient, faithful and devoted subjects of Turkey.[38]

Such are, in 1893, the opening sentences of the annual report on the Jews of Turkey in the *Bulletin de l'Alliance Israélite Universelle*. We find similar appreciations (and not only in the organs of the Alliance) throughout the last decades of the nineteenth century. While in Russia, Rumania, and most of the Balkan states, Jewish communities suffered from constant persecution (pogroms, anti-Jewish laws, and other vexations), Jews established on Turkish territory enjoyed an altogether remarkable atmosphere of tolerance and justice. Guarantees solemnly granted minorities by the *Hatt-ı Şerif* of Gülhane and confirmed by the constitution of 1876 were not empty words. The measures adopted during the reign of Abdülmecid to ensure the security of persons and property had, on the whole, attained their purpose.

Nevertheless, on closer examination, the increase of anti-Semitic incidents in Turkey during the second half of the nineteenth century is striking. Though the Ottoman government never failed to punish the guilty parties, the antagonism between communities remained intense. In most towns of Rumelia, as well as Anatolia, Muslims, Jews, and Christians lived in apparent harmony, often intermingled in the same quarter. But the slightest spark sufficed to ignite the fuse. Whenever a young Christian disappeared at the approach of Passover, Jews were immediately accused of having kidnapped him to obtain blood necessary for the manufacture of unleavened bread. Threats and violence followed close behind the suspicions and generally things ended with a boycott of Jewish shops and peddlers.

It is especially with Greeks that the Jewish communities had a bone to pick. But anti-Semitic prejudice was also frequent among Armenians and Bulgarians. Furthermore, as a general rule, when an incident occurred, Christians, without regard to their particular ethnic or religious affiliation, forgot their own quarrels and formed a bloc against Jews. In the region of Izmir, where the Greek population was particularly cohesive, the correspondents of the Alliance, from the 1870s onward, reported anti-Jewish upheavals practically every year. These upheavals were usually based on the blood libel. Similar disorders were frequent in certain cities of Rumelia, in the islands (Crete and Rhodes) and even in Istanbul in spite of the presence of the central government.[39]

Often the disturbances lasted no more than a day or two, but this only added to the sudden violence of the conflagration. Thus, in Haydarpaşa, during the riots of April 1885, caused by the discovery of a polluted cross on the doorstep of a Greek grocer, the windows of most of the Jewish houses were broken and passersby were stoned in the streets. The minister of war, Osman Paşa, had to intervene in person and order the arrest of a hundred persons in order to stop the disorders.[40] In some cases, it took several weeks for the situation to become normal again. For instance, in April 1872, the discovery of a Christian child's body in a sewer provoked such a fury among the Greeks of Izmir that the *vali* was obliged to protect the Jewish quarter with police. Disorders lasted over a month and as a result several Jews were killed and many more wounded. On 24 May, the secretary of the local committee of the Alliance wrote the central office that since thousands of Jews were prevented from working they were threatened with famine. It was only at the beginning of June that, with the help of the Orthodox metropolitan, Turkish authorities finally succeeded in reestablishing peace and Jewish peddlers could again go into Greek quarters.[41] In 1874 the riots in

Urla (a village about forty kilometers from Izmir) were just as dramatic. Though the so-called victim—a young Greek girl—eventually reappeared, Jews were persecuted and boycotted for several weeks. Here again the governor of the province was obliged to order Orthodox priests to preach peace and goodwill in their churches.[42]

These disorders nearly always had a religious basis. It was usually at the approach of great Jewish or Christian holy days that accusations of ritual murder were made and riots broke out. During Easter week, the recital of the death of Jesus never failed to awaken the fury of Christians. At the least provocation, the "Murderers of the Savior" were pursued, insulted, and eventually beaten up. Naturally, such outbursts of anti-Semitism cannot be explained by solely religious motives. Suspicions against Jews were also due to the fact that most of them exercised ambulant trades. In the eyes of the sedentary population, Jewish peddlers, ragpickers, tinkers and cobblers seemed just as dangerous as Gypsy sellers of charms and fortune-tellers. They were charged with spreading epidemics, suspected of carrying in their bales stolen goods, and were accused of abducting children. When some incident occurred in a locality, the scapegoat was always the same: the accusations were directed at a band of Gypsies or a Jewish ragpicker who had wandered through some time earlier.

It is striking to note that numerous anti-Jewish riots were accompanied by boycott. As soon as some trouble occurred, Christians forbade Jews access to their quarters and stopped trading with Jewish bazaar merchants. A simple phenomenon? These "penalties" were, in fact, the direct expression of a growing anxiety among Greeks and Armenians faced with competition that ceaselessly encroached upon them. It would be an exaggeration to see in the intercommunal conflicts of the end of the nineteenth century nothing more than a reflection of economic rivalries, but this aspect of the question must nevertheless be stressed. As already stated, the reemergence of anti-Semitism among the Christian populations of Turkey, from the sixties onward, was certainly linked—at least in part—to the slow but steady progress of Jews in certain key sectors of the Ottoman economy (export of agricultural products and raw materials, import of manufactured goods and, to a lesser degree, light industry).

Naturally the disorders that occurred from time to time were a violent and occasional form of intercommunal rivalry. Ordinarily the rivalry was manifested in other ways: mockery, insults, and various vexations. In certain towns, Christians increased their efforts to prevent Jews from gaining access to crafts. The most significant example of this was the silk craft at Bursa which was almost entirely in the hands of Greek and Armenian women. In 1899 the Jewish community had to undertake numerous steps with the inspector of the Public Debt to obtain the right to spin and weave silk at home. When this permit was finally granted, the weaving workshop created by the school of the Alliance met with incessant difficulties: under the pressure of Greek weavers, most of the silk traders refused to support the project, women who were hired by the school to act as monitors left the workshop one after another, looms were sabotaged, goods were soiled or torn. In spite of all these obstacles, the experiment was pursued and the workshop functioned through several years. But the women trained as weavers and spinners by the Alliance continued to meet with open ill-will on the part of Christian workers.[43] The example of silk workshops in Bursa is certainly an excessive but not an isolated case. Though Jews and Christians often worked together in the same offices and workshops, it also happened, not unfrequently, that Greek and Armenian employers refused to accept young Jews as apprentices. They generally justified themselves by referring to the problem of the Sabbath which deprived them of their Jewish workers for two consecutive days, Saturday and Sunday.

Relations between Jews and Muslims were, on the whole, much more satisfactory. Naturally, we must not take the reports of the teachers of the Alliance too literally: at the time of Abdülhamid, it was decidedly more risky to complain of Turks than of Armenians or Greeks, but there is no doubt that Muslims of Rumelia and of Anatolia, even if they tended to despise to a certain extent the *çıfıt*, were much more tolerant than Christians.

Though the belief in the blood libel was quite prevalent among Turks (according to a correspondent of the Alliance, the sultan himself "was not altogether convinced that the accusation against the Jews of the use of blood in unleavened bread was pure slander"[44]) serious incidents based on such prejudice were extremely rare. The documents which we examined, covering a period of thirty years, note only two or three cases of anti-Jewish riots in Muslim quarters.[45] In general, the feelings of ill-will that certain Muslim elements nourished against Jews were expressed by quibbles and minor vexations.

Only in eastern Anatolia apparently (restricting our discussion to the territory of modern Turkey) did Jews and Muslims have problems. In Diyarbakır, Urfa, Siverek, Mardin and several other cities of this region, Kurds continuously attacked Jewish communities, forcing them to pay taxes and contributions in addition to those already exacted by the Turkish authorities.[46] The slightest tendency to resist was immediately suppressed with blood. Jews were crushed with scorn and had to accept all sorts of humiliations. Thus, for instance, when rains were delayed in spring or late in autumn, Kurds went to Jewish graveyards, dug up newly buried corpses, cut off the heads and threw them in the river to appease Heaven's wrath and bring on rain.[47] In spite of the complaints of Jews to the Turkish authorities, the perpetrators of such misdeeds remained, as was to be expected, undiscovered.

Toward the end of the nineteenth century, the insecurity in the Kurd country was so great that Jewish peddlers could no longer venture outside the cities. The communities of the *vilayet* of Diyarbakır fell into misery and diminished year after year. Thus, whilst in 1874 the town of Siverek situated on the Urfa road counted about fifty Jewish families, three decades later Joseph Niégo, entrusted with a mission in Asia Minor by the Jewish Colonization Association, found only twenty-six households, totaling about 100 persons.[48] Similarly, the 500 Jews who, according to Vital Cuinet, constituted the community of Mardin toward the end of the nineteenth century, were all gone by 1906. At that time, there remained in this town only one Jew, who had the task of guarding the synagogue. He was very much liked by the population because of his talent for fortune-telling. He could foresee the future and, if need be, avert the evil eye.[49] In the *vilayet* of Diyarbakır the Jewish community of Nusaybin was the only one to escape depopulation. According to J. Niégo, at the beginning of the twentieth century there were still 180 Jewish families in this locality and some of them were quite prosperous.

Those who could leave preferred Palestine, or, as a second choice, towns such as Mosul or Urfa. Located about forty kilometers from the proposed route of the *Baghdadbahn,* in the center of a fertile plain, Urfa seemed destined for a brilliant future and was an attractive center for the Jews of the Kurdish districts. In 1906, 56 out of 191 Jewish families established in this town (that is about 30 percent) originated from localities in the Diyarbakır province.[50]

Disturbances comparable to those which affected the life of Jewish communities of eastern Anatolia occurred also in other *vilayet*s of the empire's periphery. But in Rumelia and on the Aegean coast of Asia Minor, contacts between Jews and Muslims presented, as we have already underlined, fewer problems. As a general rule, although the many anti-Jewish incidents noted by the teachers of the Alliance might give us a different impression, we should not overestimate the importance of intercommunal disagreements which at regular intervals troubled the climate of goodwill that Turkish authorities endeavored to maintain. The incidents between Jews and Christians or, more rarely, between Jews and Muslims proved, of course, the existence of strong antagonisms—antagonisms stimulated by national ferment and by the redistribution of wealth in certain sectors of the Ottoman economy—but such occurrences had, of course, nothing in common with the anti-Jewish riots that took place at about the same time in Russia, Rumania and certain Balkan states. When, in April 1892, the Jews of Turkey celebrated the fourth centenary of the day when their ancestors driven away from Spain had found an asylum in the lands of the sultan, it was with expressions of sincere gratitude that the regional committee of the Alliance thanked Abdülhamid for the protection which Jews enjoyed in Turkish territory.[51]

Conclusion: The Strategy of the Alliance

In the foregoing, we have tried to examine what can be gleaned from the archives of the Alliance regarding the Jewish communities of Turkey in the last decades of the nineteenth century. Were we to summarize the state of things in one word, we would probably use the rather anachronistic term—underdevelopment. It is a fact that, in comparison with the other minorities of the country, Jews seemed behind the times, hindered by poverty, obscurantism and inertia. What were the solutions suggested by the Alliance? This is the question to which we shall now endeavor to reply.

We have already stressed the fact that according to the Alliance, the struggle against the social and economic backwardness of the Jewish communities had to start with the organization of a modern system of education. New generations had to be introduced to secular knowledge (mathematics geometry, physics, history, and geography). They also had to receive a solid instruction in languages. The first place was allocated to French, the language of civilization *par excellence*. On the other hand, the Jews of Turkey had to learn how to read and write Turkish, so as to be able to gain access to public employment. The teaching of Hebrew and the Bible was to be pursued. This teaching had to be freed from all scholastic preoccupations that encumbered the message transmitted by the traditional *Talmud torahs*. Whilst endeavoring to maintain Jewish ritual and doctrines, the teachers of the Alliance had the duty to fight superstition, prejudice and formalism.[52]

At the end of the nineteenth century, the establishments of the Alliance had already accomplished remarkable work in their schools. In important cities like Istanbul, Salonica and Edirne, school attendance was over a thousand pupils per year. Elsewhere, in middle size towns such as Bursa, Canakkale, and Aydın, the average was about 200 to 400 boys and girls in school. Naturally, children who attended the schools of the Alliance represented only a small part of the student-age population—for instance in Balat, the *Talmud torah* continued to teach at the end of the seventies more than 700 boys, whereas the school of the Alliance had only 120 pupils[53]—but these advanced elements, bearers of an ideal of innovation and progress, were nevertheless in a position to impart a decisive stimulus to the Jewish communities of Turkey.

Thanks to the Alliance, the number of Jews who could read and write French increased considerably within a few decades. This "Francisation" of the Jewish communities (illustrated, especially after 1908, by the multiplication of periodicals in French in Salonica, Istanbul and Izmir) did not only favor the propagation of French "civilization" in Turkey but also allowed a great number of Jews to participate more effectively in the economic life of the country. Indeed, it is mainly in French that correspondence was conducted between Ottoman firms and their customers or suppliers abroad. Knowledge of French was also indispensable in order to obtain a job with one of the banks or with some great company, such as the Tobacco Régie.

Substantial results were also attained in the study of German. In 1876, the Alliance created in Galata a German-Jewish school—the Goldschmidt school—for the Ashkenazi Jews who lived in this quarter of Istanbul. Certain Yiddish-speaking families used also to send their children to Protestant German schools. Thus there developed a group of Jews of German culture who later were the first to benefit from the intensification of German activity in Turkey.[54]

(Let us note that those who preferred to learn English had the possibility of attending British mission schools which supplied not only free instruction but also, in winter, clothing and shoes. In Izmir, the majority of pupils of the Scotch schools were Jews. They were proportionately so numerous that their Christian comrades tended to speak Ladino rather than their native tongue during school recess.).

Paradoxically, in spite of the importance attached by the Alliance and by part of the local Jewish intelligentsia to the teaching of Turkish, in this sector the results were small. In Istanbul, in 1890, the boys' school of Hasköy was the only establishment that taught some rudiments of the official language of the country. In provincial towns the situation was even less encouraging. Most of the teachers of the Alliance educated in France were not equipped to teach Turkish and schools had to apply to native masters who required higher salaries or proved to be incompetent. Under the circumstances, Jewish children who wanted to learn Turkish had generally but one recourse: to register with government schools. Only after the revolution of 1908 did Turkish gain in Jewish schools, in part because the Committee of Union and Progress strictly required such instruction.

Besides this civilization by book learning, which was effective at the beginning of the eighties, the Alliance endeavored to organize professional apprenticeship to redirect Oriental Jews toward manual work. The idea had been launched in 1873 by the director of the Tangiers school after he had noticed that about half of the pupils of his establishment had no future whatsoever in spite of the education they received. At about the same time, identical fears had been expressed by the director of the Volo school who suggested the same solution as his colleague in Tangiers:

> The trouble is that all those children are very poor; they are very little interested in education provided they have something to eat. . . . Among the pupils that had entered the school last May, there are ten or twelve, aged thirteen to sixteen, whose parents are submerged by poverty. I thought that it would be a good thing to teach these children some craft. I would place them with employers and they would learn to be shoemakers, tailors, carpenters, smiths, etc. I would take care to make with these employers contracts that should guarantee the physical and moral condition of apprenticeship. I would go and visit them in workshops at least once a week and finally I would give them a lesson in the morning before they go to work, and another lesson in the evening.[55]

In Turkey, apprenticeship organizations were created in Istanbul, Izmir and Salonica, as well as in some towns of lesser importance such as Bursa and Edirne. Furthermore, many schools, in particular those for girls, were endowed with workshops, which avoided the problem of outside placement, always a little risky. We have already mentioned the weaving workshop of the Bursa school. Workshops of the same type were created wherever the circumstances were favorable and the sale of goods produced by pupils (cloth, lace, clothing, and furniture) proved in many cases quite profitable. Income thus obtained allowed the schools to subsidize their general programs of instruction.

The effort made for the apprenticeship program produced excellent results on the whole. Thus, for instance, in Istanbul Abraham Galanté counted in 1915 nearly 500 craftsmen trained by the Alliance.[56] Comparable results were attained in Izmir, Salonica and several other provincial towns.[57] The Alliance endeavored to dissuade its pupils from engaging in "easy" and unprofitable crafts such as tin or shoe-mending and to direct them toward crafts that required a degree of technical skill: carpentry, cabinetwork, clock-mending, jewelry, electricity, and mechanics. In many cases these were expanding trades which had escaped the crisis of the traditional crafts and which could eventually lead to a position in light industry. The success in this field must not however be overestimated. In spite of the ardent propaganda of the Alliance in favor of manual crafts, Turkish Jews continued to prefer, at the end of the nineteenth century, trade. Whatever the opinion of the promoters of the apprenticeship organizations on this point, this very definite partiality for commerce—either large or small—was not a bad choice. In the economic conditions of the time, prospects were certainly better in trade than in the handcrafts or industry.

Among the principal strategic choices of the Alliance we must also mention the apprenticeship of agriculture. Teachers never failed to read to their pupils passages of the Bible that recalled the joys of rustic life. They extolled the days when Jews lived in Palestine and drew abundant crops from this "land of milk and honey."

In Anatolia, Jews engaged in agriculture were only a small minority: a few families scattered here and there. In certain areas (Tire, Aydın, Nazilli, and Manisa) notables invested in vineyards and in *çiftliks* but the actual work was almost always performed by Christian and Muslim farmers. Jewish seasonal workers who drifted towards the countryside at the time of harvest were all of urban origin. They displayed no interest whatsoever in agriculture and hurried to return to town at the end of the season.

Under such circumstances, it was naturally exceedingly difficult to swim against the tide. The Alliance had devoted its efforts to the "ruralization" of Jews since the beginning of the sixties, and had already obtained in this field indisputable success, particularly in Palestine. In the eighties it started to examine seriously the creation of agricultural colonies in Anatolia. A first group of settlers (they were emigrants from Russia) was established in the neighborhood of Aydın in 1888.[58] Later on, several other colonies were created, in general near large towns or along railway lines. Stress was laid, at the same time, upon the need to organize agricultural training for local Jews. With this object in view a piece of land was acquired in 1890 at Burnabat, near Izmir to serve as the site of an agricultural training program for children of Izmir workers.

Nevertheless, despite the fact that the Alliance considered Turkey a country with great potential for Jewish agricultural colonization, most of these efforts at "ruralization" ended in failure. Established as a general rule on lands of poor quality—granted, true, free of charge by the sultan—the settlers had no experience whatsoever at agricultural work and they had, further-more, to overcome the rigors of the climate. Thus, for instance, at Beylik Ahır and Sazılar, two settlements along the railway of Anatolia, settlers con-tended not only with the infertility of the land, aggravated by several consecu-tive years of drought, but also with marsh fever, very widespread in Anatolia at that time. Before they could found a lasting establishment, they were decimated by illness and poor nutrition. In spite of its modest beginning, the experience of Burnabat was the only one that gave really satisfactory results. The success of this school encouraged the Jewish Colonization Association at the beginning of the twentieth century to purchase a large *çiftlik* of 28,000 dunams, some one hundred kilometers from Izmir, where about fifteen families from Russia were settled. This estate, named Or-Yehuda, recruited about fifty pupils and became a model institution providing modern agricul-tural training. It can be supposed that had this effort been pursued, a certain number of Jews of Turkey would have taken to agriculture. The war, how-ever, thwarted the hopes of the Jewish Colonization Association. From 1914, Or-Yehuda began to wither. The occupation of Western Anatolia by the Greek army in the spring of 1919 was the *coup de grace*.[59]

The failure of agricultural colonization dims, somewhat, the accomplish-ments of the alliance. But this failure was more than offset by triumphs in education and craft apprenticeships. On the other hand, we must underline the fact that undisputable progress was achieved in another field to which the alliance attached a great importance, that of communal solidarity.

Jews of Turkey, like most of their coreligionists scattered throughout the world, had numerous structures of mutual help and brotherhood: communal administration, charitable associations, and corporative organizations. The promulgation in 1864 of the Organic Statute of the Istanbul community—a statute that was gradually adopted with some modification by most of the other communities of the country—had, up to a certain point, allowed the collectivities to reinforce their control on the management of communal busi-ness. Nevertheless, in numerous cities much remained to be done. Communal resources were in general insufficient and assistance associations functioned slowly. Furthermore, certain communities—particularly, in large towns— were divided by grave internal quarrels: rabbinic rivalries, misunderstandings between Ashkenazi and Sefardi Jews, and revolts by the simple taxpayer against the *gaballeros* who were entrusted with the levy of communal taxes.[60]

The ardent propaganda of the alliance and its representatives for solidarity helped from the seventies on to alter the situation radically. In a few decades, scores of associations of mutual assistance were created, new hospitals were organized in great urban centers, considerable amounts of the largesse of European donors were channeled toward Turkey. These manifestations of brotherhood caused not only an improvement in the plight of the most disad-vantaged strata. They also helped reduce socioeconomic antagonisms which, since the sixties, troubled the life of some communities. Thus, it is certainly thanks to the ideas of union and concord propagated by the alliance and by other societies of similar inspiration that the tax wars pitting Istanbul Ashkenazis against Sefardis were somewhat reduced in the eighties.[61] In other towns, in Izmir in particular, internal strife sometimes took longer to abate, but toward the end of the century constant appeals for peace began to bring results.

In conclusion, we should note that the various programs of the alliance in order to alleviate the economic and social backwardness of the Jewish communities of Turkey proved, on the whole, very effective. On the eve of the First World War, Narcisse Leven, one of the founders of the alliance, was able to present a triumphant balance sheet of the work accomplished during a few decades by schools, apprenticeship organizations, and charitable associations spread throughout the Orient by his organization:

> If we compare Jewish communities to what they were less than forty years ago, we note the rapidity of their progress. At that time, hardly a few men favoured by fortune emerged from among the others and enjoyed a certain consideration. The mass remained sunk in misery and resigned to vegetate. Let us glance today at the same communities. . . . Everywhere appear aspirations for a new life, for the welfare provided by skillfully directed work.[62]

Naturally, and Narcisse Leven underlined it himself, there remained at the dawn of the twentieth century much to be done yet. Solidly anchored within the Jewish population, destitution, apathy, obscurantism were far from being completely eradicated. All the more so as the circumstances were not favorable for a brilliant "take off." But henceforth time worked for the children of Israel: the impulse was given.

Later, changes become more noticeable. The progressive elimination of Christian competition resulting from the policy of "Turkization" of the country adopted first by the Committee of Union and Progress and later by the Kemalist government, the reduction of demographic pressure within Jewish communities thanks to mass departures for Western Europe and the New World, and the considerable profits of certain tradesmen during the years of war: all these factors helped upset the older way of life.

APPENDIX I

JEWISH POPULATION OF CERTAIN OTTOMAN TOWNS 1880–1908
(expressed in thousands)

	1880	1885	1890	1895	1900	1905	1908
Turkey of Europe							
Edirne	15	12	15	15	15	17	17
Istanbul	40	40	40	40	40	65	65
Dimotika					0.9	0.9	0.9
Monastir					6	6	6
Rhodes					3	4	4
Salonica	30	30	36	45	60	75	90
Asia Minor							
Aydın				3	3	3.5	3.7
Bursa		2.45	3	3	3.5	3.5	3.5
Kassaba					0.85	1.05	1.1
Çanakkale	2	2	2	2.73	2.7	2.9	3
Manisa				2	2	1.7	2.1
Izmir	25	25	25	23	25	35	35
Tire					1.2	1.5	1.5
Syria							
Aleppo	10.2	10.2	10	10	10	12	12
Beirut	1.2	1.2	3	3	3	3	5
Haifa		0.8	1	1	1	1.3	1.6
Damascus		8	8	10	10	12	12
Jaffa				3	3	3.5	5
Jerusalem		15	25	30	40	40	40
Safed					6.5	7	7
Tiberias					4	7.7	7
Mesopotamia							
Baghdad	30	26	30	35	40	40	45

Source: *Bulletin de l' A. I. U.*

APPENDIX II

SCHOOLS OF THE ALLIANCE IN TURKEY (1908)

Town	Total Jewish Population (according to the Alliance)	Boys' School		Girls' School	
		Date of foundation	Number of pupils (1908)	Date of foundation	Number of pupils (1908)
Edirne	17,000	1867	1,106	1870	551
Aydın	3,700	1894	222	1904	90
Bursa	3,500	1886	335	1889	150
Kassaba	1,100	1887	79		
Kavalla	1,800	1905	112	1905	127
Constantinople	65,000				
Balat		1875	359	1882	352
Galata		1875	235	1879	352
Kusguncuk		1879	178	1880	201
Goldschmidt School		1879	250		
Hasköy		1874	454	1877	372
Ortaköy		1881	269	1882	215
Çanakkale	3,000	1878	206	1888	146
Dimotika	900	Mixed school founded in 1897 182 pupils			
Gallipoli	2,500	Mixed school founded in 1905 219 pupils			
Janina	3,500	1904	413	1904	142
Manisa	2,100	1892	186	1896	126
Monastir	6,000	1895		1903	142
Rhodes	4,000	1901	180	1902	175
Rodosto	1,500	1904	199		
Salonica	90,000	1873	461	1875	437
Popular school		1897	270	1897	225
Izmir	35,000	1873	312	1878	351
Popular school		1898	219		
Serres	1,200	Mixed school founded in 1901 114 pupils			
Üsküp	1,300	1902	167	1905	104

Source: *Bulletin de l'A.I.U.*, 1908, pp. 151–176.

APPENDIX III

APPRENTICESHIP ORGANIZATIONS IN 1908 (BOYS)

Town	Date of Foundation	Crafts	Total Number of Apprentices
Aydın	1901	2 joiners, 1 tanner, 1 zinc-worker, 1 wood-sculptor	5
Edirne	1878	5 joiners, 2 cabinet-makers, 2 upholsterers, 1 turner, 1 case-maker, 2 painters, 3 smiths, 5 founders, 5 wheel-wrights, 3 stove-maker-tinkers, 2 broom-makers, 2 typographers.	33
Bursa	1893	3 painters, 3 founders, 1 coppersmith, 1 smith, 2 typographers, 3 joiners, 2 case-makers, 1 embroiderer.	16
Constantinople	1871	10 cabinet-makers, 4 chimney-builders, 1 gilder, 2 painters, 3 clock-menders, 5 jewelers, 1 sculptor, 1 marble-cutter, 4 mechanics, 1 goldsmith, 4 upholsterers, 2 turners, 4 typographers, 1 engraver.	43
Janina	1905	5 joiners, 6 smiths-mechanics.	11
Kirk Kilise	1897	1 smith, 1 tailor.	2
Manisa	1893	2 wheel-wrights, 1 smith, 1 turner, 1 joiner, 1 cabinet-maker.	6
Rhodes	1902	3 joiners, 2 smiths	5
Rodosto	1896	2 joiners, 1 bootmaker, 1 cobbler	4
Salonica	1877	4 cobblers, 1 wheel-wright, 4 case-makers, 1 chair-maker, 3 smiths, 22 joiners, 7 marble-cutters, 1 goldsmith, 7 wood-sculptors, 3 upholsterers, 3 typographers, 1 cooper, 1 dryer	58
Izmir	1878	1 smith, 4 joiners, 5 sculptors, 1 turner, 1 cooper, 7 founders, 3 mechanics, 1 cobbler, 3 typographers, 1 clock-mender	27

Source: *Bulletin de l'A.I.U.*, 1908, pp. 177–181.

APPENDIX IV

YOUNG GIRLS' WORKSHOPS (1908)

Town	Date of foundation	Number of apprentices
Edirne	1890	22
Bursa	1898	15
Constantinople	1908	8
Salonica	1887	350
Izmir	1884	56

Source: *Bulletin de l'A.I.U., 1908.*

APPENDIX V

AN EXAMPLE: JEWISH HANDICRAFTS IN EDIRNE (1897)

Crafts	Set up in Business by Family		Set up in Business by the Alliance		Total	Weekly Income (francs)	
	Head	Apprentice	Head	Apprentice		Range	Average
Tailors	78	54	5		138	20 to 46	27
Tinsmiths or Stove-setters	44	25	1		70	6 to 10	9
Sheep-shearers	60				60		
Bricklayers or unskilled laborers	60				60		
Confectioners	25	30	1		56	15	15
Cheesemongers	44				44		
Cobblers	12	18	7		37	6 to 15	10
Seamstresses	15	20			35		
Oriental style tailors	31				31		
Book-binders	7	15	1		23	7	7
Cap-makers	5	15			20		
Stove-setters	9	9	3		21	6 to 10	8
Distillers	19				19		
Locksmiths or stove-setters	7	4	1	3	15	6	6
Cabinet-makers			12	3	15	6 to 42	19
Carpenters	6		4	5	15	8 to 18	11
Window-glass setters	7	7			14		
Restaurant-owners	13				13		

	Set up in Business by Families		Set up in Business by the Alliance			Weekly Income (francs)	
	Head	Apprentice	Head	Apprentice	total	Range	Average
Pharmacists	5	4	1	1	11		
Clock-sellers			6	4	10	10 to 100	40
Hairdressers	6		3		9	10 to 30	20
Bakers-confectioners	7		1		8		
Dyers/cleaners	7				7		
Case-makers	3		3	1	7	8 to 60	28
Upholsterers	3		3	1	7	6 to 30	15
Felt-makers	2			3	5		
House-painters	4		1	1	6	20	20
Chandlers	5				5		
Coppersmiths	1		1	3	5	15	15
Cartwrights			2	3	5	6 to 15	10
Blacksmiths/coppersmiths			2	3	5	6 to 20	14
Gilders/frame-makers	1		2	1	4	12 to 20	16
Scale-makers	1		3		4	6 to 50	20
Smelters				4	4	6 to 12	8
Joiners			3	1	4	15 to 30	22
Wet-coopers			2	1	3	5 to 10	7
Typographers	1		1	1	3	16	16
Shirt-makers			2		2		
Calligraphers			2		2	20	20
Mechanics			3		3	10 to 48	29
Saddlers/Harness-makers	1			1	2		
Clog-makers			1	1	2		
Chair-makers	1		1	1	3		
Cutlers			1		1		
Makers of Trimmings	1				1		
Photographers	2				2		
TOTAL	493	201	79	42	815		

Source: *Archives of the A.I.U.*, France, XVI-F (27), Report of S. Loupo of 3.X.1897.

APPENDIX VI

The following documents are samples that give an idea of the information that can be found in the Archives of the Alliance. These two letters had been addressed to the president of the organization in Paris, the first one by the director of the Izmir school, the second by the director of the school in Bursa. They are drawn respectively from files Turkey I-C 1 and Turkey XV E. The translation from French is mine.

(A)

City of Smyrna
Boys' school
Signed: A. Benveniste

Smyrna, the 5th May 1892

Sir,

Not far from our school, there is a quarter called "Kidjidjis," the principal and the most frequented thoroughfare of which is inhabited by Jews, whereas the adjacent streets, all of them solitary, are occupied exclusively by Turkish dwellings. Within restricted spaces there are houses for rent belonging to rich Turks; they comprise eighty to one hundred small rooms, each one inhabited by a whole family in regrettable promiscuity: the father, the mother and the children sleep in the same and only room. Some of these rooms are clean and the tenants even cultivate flowers in pots at their doorstep; they take good care of them and are very pleased—especially the women—to wear in their hair the flowers raised by themselves. Other lodgings are in a pitiful state. In some cases poor crippled and gouty creatures lead there a miserable life. An old mother and sometimes sisters do the laundering for richer people and it is the product of this work that covers all the household expenses—expenses that must be very small and reduced to the bare necessities since a laundress receives no more than seventy centimes for a whole day of hard and tiring work. I would add that actually, very often, especially in winter, some of these poor people go to bed without any food.

They pay their rent as best as they can. Expenses for objects of utmost necessity are curtailed so that this payment might be made as regularly as possible. Lodgings are rented at four to seven francs a month, rent paid weekly. Every Friday an employee of the landlord comes with a suitcase for a fruitful collection. Then tragi-comical scenes take place: moans, entreaties of the tenants who do not have the means to settle their arrears and are threatened with eviction without respite or mercy, vociferous and sometimes coarse insults from the rent-collector. Some insolvent and dishonest tenants arrange to be warned of the arrival of the rent-collector and hide themselves in a cupboard or under a bench where they await his departure; if he asks where they are, the answer is that no one knows or else that they are traveling and are expected to come back Sunday afternoon. Everybody laughs at this trick, Saturday is gaily spent and the same game is played again the next week. In the end, it happens that tenants owe a half year's rent and one morning the owner loses patience and drives them out, allowing them to remove the shapeless rags which are all they have. If they are really destitute they ask the Community for a shelter and are lodged in some slum of the immense estate owned by the Community. If there is no room, they look for lodgings in another house where the smallness of rents corresponds to that of rooms.

The population living in these caravansarays is exceedingly ignorant and fanatical. Many of the inhabitants cannot even read Hebrew prayers. The young men, numerous enough and inclined to laziness and idleness are the "pallicares" of the quarter. They drink and after their nocturnal orgies they come home drunk, breaking the shop windows and using knives from time to time. They are the plague of the whole quarter. Consequently, brawls are frequent and women often side with them. After having lived in the "Kidjidjis" for two years, I can say that not a Saturday afternoon passes without noise and confusion and without the police being obliged to intervene to reestablish order. In truth, I must add that the good policemen of this country are also a little afraid of these toughs whose reputation is well established; if they take them by the scruff of the neck to the nearest police station, they hurry to set them free half an hour after. Their conscience is at peace: they have done their duty. I know a Jew who had half murdered a Greek woman with a knife. Four months later he returned home and since then walked calmly the streets like a man with nothing on his conscience, whereas he should have been condemned to several years hard labor.

Two months ago, I learned with curiosity and surprise that these young men decided under some unknown influence to mend their ways and to adopt a better life. Inspired by one of them, they formed a small charitable association composed solely of young men too well-known in the quarter. This association had regulations written in square characters on large pieces of cardboard hanging on the walls of the assembly room so that the members might at any moment learn their duties. The association had a most philanthropic object: help to confined women. The idea was excellent because this quarter had greatly suffered two years ago from an epidemic of child-bed fever which had carried away so many young mothers because of lack of timely care. Furthermore, members were forbidden to frequent taverns and threatened with a fine should they do so. All had to be present in the evening on the premises of the association. No one was to be absent when the roll was called. It was a somewhat strange sight to see all these bad boys sitting in a circle on mats, squatting in a Turkish manner, religiously silent, smoking their cigarettes like Indian chiefs at a war council. No one spoke out of turn and the most learned gave them some advice in his language, exhorting them to adopt good ways, or reading passages of a book in Judeo-Spanish. As you see, this was a charitable institution which, at the same time had an aim of improved morality. Unfortunately, like many good things in this Oriental country, the association lived only three months. The trimester of temperance and good conduct seemed a century to these young people who bolted as quickly as they could to return to their old habits of vagrancy and misconduct. Drive away nature and it gallops back.

To retrieve completely a nation, education must reach deep levels of society. Our moral regeneration depends therefore upon the good functioning of Talmud torahs and the introduction in those establishments of able teachers acquainted with new methods. The execution of this project has already begun and great progress has been accomplished in this new direction.

Pleace accept the expression of my devoted sentiments.

Abr. Benveniste.

(B)

[The first sheet is missing]   Brussa, 31/XII/1900
Albala

... Whilst busy with our boys, I did not lose from sight the necessity to teach a craft to our poor little girls. As soon as I arrived at Brussa, I was impressed by the great number of Jewish women workers in the silk spinning-mills. I am being assured that there are nearly 200 of them. When enquiring about their salary, I learned that it varied between Frs. 0.40 and 1 franc per day. But the spinning-mills are open only five months out of twelve, and Jewish workers are obliged to stop working two days a week. It is to be noted that most of these girls work only to collect a small dowry; once married they no longer go to spinning-mills, as they are kept at home by housework and the numerous children to be brought up. I must add that work at the spinning-mills, in an unwholesome atmosphere, very often does not suit the enfeebled constitution of our young coreligionists, many of whom are also repulsed by the corrupting promiscuity of the factories in which women workers live. Many young girls engage in sewing but they hardly earn enough to live on.

On the other hand, the pupils of our school cannot all establish themselves as seamstresses and many among them are not destined to spinning-mills. I undertook therefore to teach them a craft which they would follow at home and which would allow them to earn their living whilst having enough time to deal with household occupations. It is with this object in view that I founded at school a silkweaving workshop.

You know that cocoon nursing is the most precious resource of this *vilayet* which develops this production every year. On the Brussa market 1,900,000 kilos of fresh cocoons are sold yearly. Not long ago, Brussa was tributary of Europe for silkworm seeds. Today not only does it not import seeds but it sells important quantities of its own production to Russia, Persia, and Turkestan. A great part of the cocoons are shipped to Lyon and to Milano; the rest is spun locally. During these last years silk spinning has developed considerably in Brussa where about thirty spinning-mills exist today. Spun silk is destined in major part for export. The silk that is not exported is supplied to the local industry for scarves, gauzes and other light articles, highly reputed throughout the Orient. Weaving of these silk goods occupies 500 women workers, almost all of them Greek. In each Greek house there is a weaving loom. In general it is the women and young girls who work. They are paid not daily but by the piece. A piece is composed of 100 to 120 meters of cloth and is paid twelve, nineteen, or twenty francs, according to the quality and the width of silk cloth. Working two to three hours in the evening, a good worker can finish three pieces a month. If a family has two weaving looms you can see what an excellent income this means.

In the past, silk weaving was exclusively in the hands of Greeks; then Armenians and finally Turks began to work at it. It is only Jews who were jealously kept off this industry that provides an honest livelihood to hundreds of families.

You know already in what circumstances we have undertaken the creation of our workshop that we opened last March with a little capital of 400 francs advanced by our loan fund. You know the relentless hostility of the Greeks, their underhanded intrigues to ruin our enterprise, how for about three months I was unable to find a teacher for the workshop. When I enrolled one who was attracted by a large salary, she soon left us because of the threats of the corporation coalesced against us. Finally, you are not unaware that I managed to interest in our work a silk merchant, Tewfik bey, whom I took care to bind to us by a contract for one year. With his help I could thwart all the intrigues and overcome all the obstacles. In three months our workshop developed rapidly. We have at present four looms occupying six apprentices. We have not yet passed the period of groping. Naturally, our beginner-apprentices spoil the work and we have to compensate Tewfik bey for the damage to the silk that he supplied us with. But these difficulties were foreseen and I am pleased to have had no more trouble. On the other hand, our young workers are making perceptible progress. I hope to double between now and Passover the quantity of looms, and the workshop will then be amply self-sufficient. But unfortunately we are lacking space. The vast hall that we have built this year is large enough to contain up to ten looms. If we use this hall as a workshop, what are we to do to have a refectory? During the warm season, which here lasts more than six months, there would be no difficulty: children would eat in the covered playground. But during the cold winter weather, where shall we put the children for their meals? This is the question that I am endeavoring to solve.

On the whole, since I am in Brussa, I have raised to seventeen the number of apprentices. They are classified as follows: two smiths, two painters, two carpenters, one shoemaker, one typographer, one coppersmith, one seamstress, one silk warper (woman), and six weavers (women). Out of these seventeen, I found work for fifteen and my aim has been mainly to satisfy the employers by providing them only with strong and well-disciplined workers. As regards the silk workshop, I devote all my efforts and my inventiveness to ensure its success because in the not too distant a future we can expect from it most rejoicing results. When silk weaving will be implanted among our Brussa coreligionists and when each family will have one or two looms, a marked improvement will have been made in the precarious conditions of their difficult existence.

Please accept, Sir, the assurance of my devoted sentiments.

M. Albala

Notes

1. Numerous works have been devoted to the history of the Alliance Israélite Universelle. For a general view, see in particular Narcisse Leven, *Cinquante ans d'histoire. L'Alliance Israélite Universelle (1860–1910)*, 2 vol., Paris, 1911–1920, and André Chouraqui, *Cent ans d'histoire. L'Alliance Israélite Universelle et la renaissance juive contemporaine (1860–1960)*, Paris, 1965.

2. The most interesting works of Abraham Galanté in the field covered by our study are his *Histoire des Juifs d'Anatolie*, 2 vol., Istanbul, 1937–1939, and also his *Histoire des Juifs d'Istanbul*, 2 vol., Istanbul, 1941–1942.

3. *Arch. of the A.I.U.*, Turkey I-C 1, letter of Matalon dated 28.IV.1886.

4. *Arch. of the A.I.U.*, Turkey I-C 1, report of Pariente, April 1884. Part of this report has been published in the *Bulletin de l'A.I.U.*, no. 8(1884) pp. 50–56.

5. *Arch. of the A.I.U.*, Turkey, I-C 1, letter of A. Benveniste, 5.V.1892.

6. For the description of Hasköy and Balat toward the middle of the nineteenth century, see in particular Dr. Witlich, "Les Israélites de Constantinople," *Archives israélites*, September 1856, pp. 1–12. See also the pages devoted to these quarters by N. Leven (cited n. 1), vol. 2, pp. 155–171.

7. Though somewhat chaotic, the works of Galanté give a good general idea of the historic evolution of Jewish communities on the Turkish territory. With regards to the situation of different *millets*, see for instance the account of R. Davison, *Reform in the Ottoman Empire. 1856–1876*, Princeton, 1963, pp. 52–80 and 114–135.

8. Among the numerous documents pertaining to this problem preserved in the *Arch. of the A.I.U.*, we must particularly call attention to a long report of V. Gerson (Turkey, I-C 1, December 1894) which provides a very precise description of the matrimonial customs of Oriental Jews.

9. *Arch. of the A.I.U.*, Turkey, I-C 1, report of Pariente, April 1884, p. 2.

10. Ibid.

11. The numerous discussions which have already taken place concerning the demographic evolution of the Ottoman Empire in the nineteenth century are far from having exhausted the subject. The official documents recently brought to light by certain historians give an indication of the general tendency but they must, nevertheless, be corroborated.

12. *Arch of the A.I.U.*, Turkey I-C 1, report of Matalon dated 28 April 1886. See also A. Galanté, *Anatolie* (cited n. 2), vol. 2, p. 195.

13. *Arch. of the A.I.U.*, Turkey I-C 1, reports of Nabon (Sept. 1901) and of Confino (7 August 1907).

14. As regards Istanbul, see for instance the different figures supplied by A. Galanté, *Istanbul* (cited n. 2), vol. 1, p. 70. In the case of Smyrna, the data at our disposal are even more fanciful. See A. Galanté, *Anatolie* (cited n. 2), vol. 1, p. 15.

15. *Arch. of the A.I.U.*, Turkey I-C 6, letters of Fernandez and Salomon. Further to this important file, see also the *Bulletin de l'A.I.U.*, 2nd semester 1877, pp. 7–22.

16. *Bulletin de l'A.I.U.*, no. 10(1886), pp. 21–23.

17. *Bulletin de l'A.I.U.*, no. 18(1893), p. 39. See also N. Leven (cited n. 1), vol. 2, pp. 428–431.

18. *Arch. of the A.I.U.*, Turkey, II-C 8, report on the situation of Jewish colonies of Anatolia. 31.X.1900. For a general view concerning the Rumanian emigration, see also N. Leven (cited n. 1), vol. 2, pp. 438–444.

19. *Bulletin de l'A.I.U.* (1879), pp. 16–17.

20. *Bulletin de l'A.I.U.*, no. 18(1893), pp. 38–40. In connection with the plague of 1865, which seems to have killed thousands of people, see A. Galanté *Anatolie* (cited n. 2), vol. 1, p. 202.

21. Ibid., vol. 2, p. 217.

22. *Arch. of the A.I.U.*, Turkey, XV E, letter of Albala, 26 November 1900.

23. Rev. de Sola Pool, "The Levantine Jews in the United States," *American Jewish Yearbook*, 15(1913/14), p. 208. This author gives in connection with Jews of Turkish origin settled in the United States the following figures:

Year	Emigrants originating from European Turkey	Emigrants originating from Turkey of Asia
1899–1902	190	297
1903–1905	413	284
1906	252	209
1907	588	330
1908	379	256
1909	346	344
1910	953	435
1911	723	454
1912	760	621
	4,604	3,230

24. A. Löwy, *The Jews of Contantinople: A Study of their Communal and Educational Status* (reprinted from the Nineteenth Annual Report of the Anglo-Jewish Association), London, 1890, p. 5.

25. For a general view concerning the Jewish press of the time, see the already mentioned works of Galanté.

26. *Arch. of the A.I.U.*, Turkey, I-C 1, report of Pariente, April 1884.

27. A. Löwy (cited n. 24), p. 9.

28. *Arch. of the A.I.U.*, Turkey I-C 1, report of Cazès, dated 10.X.1873, pp. 1–2.

29. *Arch. of the A.I.U.*, Turkey, I-C 1, report of Confino, dated 7.VIII.1907.

30. *Arch. of the A.I.U.*, Turkey, I-C 1, report of Matalon, dated 28.IV.1886, p. 3.

31. *Arch. of the A.I.U.*, Turkey I-C 1, report of Pariente, April 1884, p. 5. See also A. Galanté, *Anatolie* (cited n. 2), vol. 2, pp. 32–34.

32. Ibid., vol. 1, p. 34.

33. *Arch. of the A.I.U.*, Turkey, I-C 1, report of Pariente, April 1884, pp. 13–14. A. Galanté, *Anatolie* (cited n. 2), p. 136.

34. *Arch of the A.I.U.*, Turkey XV E, letter of Albala, 19.I.1900. For a general view, however very incomplete, of the place occupied by Jewish enterprises in Ottoman industry, see for instance, besides the works of Galanté, the statistics published by A. G. Okçün, *Osmanlı Sanayıı. 1913–1915 yılları sanayı istatistiki,* Ankara, 1970.

35. *Arch. of the A.I.U.*, Turkey, I-C 1, report of Cazès, 10.VIII.1873, p. 4.

36. *Arch. of the A.I.U.*, Turkey, II-C 8, "Quelques notes sur les professions manuelles de Constantinople," report de Navon, dated 15.I.1900.

37. We base ourselves on the study of A. Navon, ibid.

38. *Bulletin de l'A.I.U.*, no. 18(1893), pp. 38–39.

39. We cannot give here an exhaustive inventory of these disorders. For a general view, see N. Leven (cited n. 1), vol. 1, pp. 149–152, 233–236, and 387–390. See also the different information published in the *Bulletin de l'A.I.U.*

40. *Arch. of the A.I.U.*, Turkey, I-C 6, letters of Fernandez, April 1885. See also the *Bulletin de l'A.I.U.*, no. 9(1885), pp. 24–25.

41. *Arch. of the A.I.U.*, Turkey, II-C a, letters of V. P. Argi, May–June, 1872. See also A. Galanté, *Anatolie* (cited n. 2), vol. 1, pp. 186–187.

42. N. Leven (cited n. 1), vol. 2, p. 234.

43. *Arch. of the A.I.U.*, Turkey XV E, letters of Albala, 1898–1904.

44. *Arch. of the A.I.U.*, Turkey, I-C 6, letter of Bloch, 12.IV.1887.

45. It is thus, for instance, that on 29 May 1884, a Muslim woman whose child had disappeared excited the whole quarter of Kulaksız (Istanbul) against the Jews under the pretext that her child was hidden in the synagogue where the Jews intended to slaughter him. The chiefs of the Jewish community tried in vain to convince the crowd of the falseness of this accusation. The crowd persisted in its claims and threatened to break down the door of the synagogue if it were not allowed to proceed to a search. Finally the child was found. He had been playing near a tannery and had fallen asleep. Concerning this incident, see the *Bulletin de l'A.I.U.*, no. 8 (1884), p. 10.

46. *Bulletin de l'A.I.U.*, no. 21 (1896), pp. 52–55.

47. *Bulletin de l'A.I.U.*, no. 31 (1906), p. 94.

48. *Arch. of the A.I.U.*, Turkey, II-C 8, report of Niego, dated 17.VII.1906. The letters of Niego have been published in the *Bulletin de l'A.I.U.*, No. 31 (1906), pp. 85–103.

49. *Bulletin de l'A.I.U.*, no. 31 (1906), p. 95.

50. Ibid., p. 191.

51. *Bulletin de l'A.I.U.*, no. 17 (1892), p. 47.

52. As regards the educational doctrines of the Alliance, see for instance N. Leven (cited n. 1), vol. 2, pp. 27–29.

53. Ibid., vol. 2, p. 162.

54. Ibid., p. 166.

55. Ibid., p. 291.

56. A. Galanté, *Istanbul* (cited n. 2), vol. 2, p. 72.

57. Listed in the appendix are statistics of the apprenticeship organizations in 1908.

58. *Bulletin de l'A.I.U.*, no. 13 (1888), pp. 74–75; no. 19 (1894), pp. 46–51.

59. As regards the estate of Or-Yehuda, see in particular A. Galanté, *Anatolie* (cited n. 2), vol. 2, pp. 117–120.

60. For a general view of the conflicts within the Jewish communities of Turkey in the nineteenth century, see the numerous works by Galante.

61. A. Galanté, *Istanbul* (cited n. 2), vol. 2, pp. 202–210.

62. N. Leven (cited n. 1), vol. 2, p. 556.

12

The *Millet* System and Its Contribution to the Blurring of Orthodox National Identity in Albania

Stavro Skendi

Albania has not only passed through various occupations by foreign powers, but has also experienced unusual confessional changes. After the schism of 1054, she was divided into a Catholic north and an Orthodox south. Westerners from across the Adriatic invaded Albania and attacked the Byzantine Empire. Her territory became the battleground between East and West. Whenever the Western armies were successful, the boundaries of the Eastern Church receded; whenever Byzantium was victorious, its frontiers expanded. Church power followed the vicissitudes of the political power. With these oscillations and the mixed composition of the population of the cities, the Orthodox-Catholic conflict still did not take a violent form.[1]

With the arrival of the Ottomans, a third religion was introduced in Albania: Islam. The Ottomans invaded that country for the first time in 1385. They were invited by an Albanian feudal lord of the central part, Charles Thopia, who, distrusting Venice and fearing the domination of a ruling house in the north, the Balshas, asked for Ottoman support. In the battle that ensued the Ottomans were the victors. Other invasions followed, in 1394–1396 and in 1429, when the Ottoman armies reached as far as the Adriatic Sea.[2]

At the outset the Ottomans chose to be tolerant in religious matters. They allowed the Albanian feudal lords to maintain their positions, on condition that they pay the *haraç* (tribute), send their sons as hostages to the sultan's court, and furnish auxiliary troops. In a register of *timar*s in southern and middle Albania for the years 1431–32 only 30 percent were held by Turks from Anatolia, the rest were held by Christian Albanians.[3] There were *timar*s in the hands of Christians even during the reign of Mehmed II.

It seems local conditions influenced the Ottomans to pursue a conciliatory policy toward Albania before Skenderbeg's time: warlike inhabitants, inclined to rebellion; across the Adriatic was the Catholic West, and Venice, a potential enemy, was in possession of a significant part of the Albanian coast; the Albanian feudal lords who were small and independent had led an amphibious life between Catholicism and Orthodoxy.[4] Besides, a military state like that of the Ottomans offered a wide field of opportunities for their warlike qualities. The interest of the Ottomans in that country had been primarily in recruiting support, irrespective of religion.

But in 1443 Skenderbeg revolted and declared his independence. He was joined by other Albanian feudal lords, and a series of wars took place until the end of the fifteenth century, when the country was completely conquered by the Ottomans. Then a great apostasy followed as well as a great exodus of the population to the southern part of Italy. During the subsequent four centuries, the propagation of Islam pursued a slow and uneven process, with apostatic bursts, opposed at different periods in the Catholic north and in the Orthodox south, which were separated more or less by the Shkumbi River.

In 1453 Mehmed II conquered Constantinople. Being Muslims, the Ottomans believed that the distinctive feature of a people was its religion rather than its nationality. In the Quran and the Divine Law *(Sharīᶜa* or *Şeriat),* which derived from it, they found the rules of behavior for Muslim communities. With this religious-political outlook, the Conqueror organized formally the Ottoman state in a series of parallel non-Muslim religious communities, called *millets,* recognizing as the head of each one its spiritual leader *(millet başı).* Of all the *millets* the largest and most important was the *Rum millet*: (Greek *millet)* with its head the Patriarch of Constantinople.

Already before the fall of Constantinople, toward the end of the fourteenth century, the Ottomans had invaded Macedonia. They recognized the Church of Ohrid, which, founded as a patriarchate by the Bulgarians in the heyday of their empire, was reduced to the Archbishopric of Ohrid by the Byzantines. The Ottomans not only preserved it, but it was the first and earliest Orthodox church that entered as a whole in their state structure and began to expand its power.[5] The Orthodox churches, whether it was the Archbishopric of Ohrid or the Patriarchate of Constantinople, lent themselves well to the structure of the Ottoman state: territorially, they were organized into well-defined dioceses; administratively, they had a distinct hierarchical order. When the Union of Florence was declared in 1439, the Archbishopric of Ohrid did not accept it,[6] for it was in the interest of the Ottoman state to keep the Orthodox and Catholic worlds separated. On the other hand, the Church of Ohrid lived on good terms with the various ethnic groups over which it reigned—Albanians, Serbs, Wallachians.[7] Mehmed II subordinated it to the Patriarchate of Constantinople. From the end of the sixteenth century the leading positions of the high clergy were occupied by persons of Greek nationality, while the simple clergy were composed of natives.[8] This explains the existence of an ancient document in the Albanian language but written in Greek characters. While other scholars considered it to be of the fourteenth century it is from the fifteenth–sixteenth century. It is a fragment of the gospel according to St. Matthew, often read during the passion week in the Orthodox church and expected to be understood by the congregation.[9] On Albanian territory there were three metropolitan sees during the existence of the Archbishopric of Ohrid.[10]

The Orthodox *millet* was under the leadership of the patriarch for civil as well as religious matters. Under the Ottomans he acquired more power than he had as a spiritual chief alone in the Byzantine Empire. He became a political head vested with fiscal, judicial, and administrative powers. The same power was exercised by the high clergy, his representatives in the provinces, who intervened in worldly affairs. The *berats* (decrees) issued by the sultan to the patriarch and the high clergy in the provinces did not differ from each other, except that the patriarchal *berats* contained defined geographical extent of jurisdiction.[11]

In juridical matters the bishops were the counterpart of the Muslim judge or *kadi*. As the *kadi* heard cases between Muslims or between Muslims and non-Muslims, according to the *Şeriat,* the bishop heard cases between the Orthodox, on the basis of the canon law or the civil law of the Byzantines, as recorded in the manual of Constantine Armenopoulos (1320–1380), a jurist from Salonica. In Albanian territory, it is likely that the customary law of the regions was in many instances applied. Bishops were not allowed to judge criminal cases. Everywhere cases of marriages, divorce, and wills among the Orthodox came within their exclusive jurisdiction. Usually the bishops acted as arbitrators among people who preferred their judgment to that of anybody else. Their unofficial authority extended beyond their acknowledged duties. The notaries, who prepared official documents, such as deeds or wills, for the people, were, as a rule, ecclesiastical officials under the bishop's control.[12]

For the administration of the parts of the country inhabited by the Orthodox, the government had its own Ottoman agents. Parallel to them, however, there were the representatives of the native Orthodox people. The communes, whether they were a town or a cluster of villages, elected their own officials, who were known as elders, *archons*, or *demogerons*, the last two terms adopted from the Greek. As in Greece, so in Albania, there were also some autonomous villages called *kephalokhōria* (head-villages). These men did not merely administer the affairs of their respective communes, but once a year they met with the Turkish authority of the district as an advisory assembly, one or two members of which were elected as an executive council of the Ottoman authority. These were the primates or notables, or the *koca başıs*. With this system the Orthodox reduced the contact with the Ottomans and enjoyed greater local autonomy. But the real rulers of the Orthodox people, whether in Albania or Greece, were the high clergy, the unofficial advisers and defenders.[13]

The liturgy in the Orthodox southern part of Albania was, as of old, in Greek. The Albanians had not been able, like their neighbors the Bulgarians and the Serbs, to create a state and an autocephalous church, which could use Albanian as a church language. Witness the Greek service which the Orthodox Albanians who emigrated to southern Italy carried with them. When, under the influence of the Vatican, many of them became Uniates, they maintained it. Only recently, after World War II, the Italo-Albanians were allowed to translate the liturgy into

Albanian. It was the time of ecumenism. On the other hand, the Ottoman Turks, while giving a blow to the previous cultural life, were not in a position to replace it from the beginning by their Islamic culture. The feudal class of *sıpahi*s and those who served Islamic faith in Albania, who would be the bearers of Islamic culture, were in general of Albanian origin and very few knew Turkish, Arabic, or Persian. Islamic culture in Albania began to be spread mainly during the seventeenth century, when conversions increased the number of Islamic believers, especially among the Catholics of the north.[14]

It fell upon the Patriarchate of Constantinople to come to the assistance of the Orthodox Albanians against the spread of Islam. Considering itself the heir of the Greek-Byzantine Empire, it demanded of the faithful that they learn Greek as a language of both liturgy and instruction. Through the teachers prepared on Mount Athos, it strove to impose the learning of Greek on the Albanian believers.[15] Its teachers preached that their children should be taught Greek, "for our Church is in Greek and our race is Greek. And if you don't learn Greek, my brother, you cannot understand what our church says. It is better to have a Greek school in your place than to have fountains and rivers."[16] As a consequence, the Orthodox church and clergy became the bearers of Greek culture in Albania.

Under their direction, Greek elementary schools were opened during the seventeenth century in towns and monasteries, as for instance, in the region of Zagorie and the province of Himarë. The funds for the schools were collected from the faithful and from the guilds of Orthodox craftsmen.[17] Other Greek schools are mentioned in the eighteenth century: in Vlorë (Valona) in 1741 and in Korçë in 1723. They increased after the middle of the eighteenth century, owing particularly to the Greek monk-teacher Kosmas Aitōlos (1714–1779), who is believed to have founded more than two hundred elementary schools in southern Albania. He traveled extensively and preached tirelessly. He even went as far as Durrës (Durazzo) and Krujë (Croya), which is an indication that there were Orthodox in those regions. But the center of his activity was Berat (Belegrada, in church language; in Turkish it was called Arnavud Belgrad) where in 1779 he fell a martyr to his faith.[18] The increase in schools was also encouraged by the Russo-Turkish Treaty of Küçük Kaynarca (1774), when the situation of the Orthodox in the Ottoman Empire was improved, as Russia, liberally interpreting the treaty, claimed the protection of the Orthodox subjects of the sultan.[19]

Two centers of Greek culture exercised strong influence on the Orthodox Albanians: Voskopojë (Moschopolis), in the south, near Korçë, and Janinë (Iōnnina or Janina) in northern Greece. In Voskopojë there were no Muslim inhabitants and the authority of the Ottoman government was not directly felt. Its population was principally Vlach and Albanian, and it had grown to more than forty thousand in the middle of the eighteenth century. A Greek school which was opened in 1720 attracted students from other districts of Albania and Macedonia.[20] Voskopojë had become an important intellectual and commercial center. It carried on trade with the West, mainly with Vienna, Leipzig, Venice, Budapest, and Cluj (Klausenburg).[21] In 1774 a school called "The New

Academy" was founded there, which emulated the best Greek high schools of the time. A substantial number of books, especially ecclesiastical, were printed in Voskopojë and distributed in the Orthodox Christian world, enhancing the city's prestige.[22]

But the prosperity of Voskopojë did not last long. In 1767 the Patriarchate of Constantinople suppressed the Archbishopric of Ohrid which had become its rival in the Balkans. Two years later, in 1769, during the Russo-Turkish war, the people of Voskopojë manifested their sympathy for Russia and supported the Himariots, who, in the same year, revolted against the Turks.[23] The Ottoman government found the occasion to incite the *derebeys* (feudal despots whose power rested on bands) around Voskopojë against it. They attacked and destroyed the city.[24] On the other hand, the Patriarchate of Constantinople took steps against the remaining inhabitants to achieve cultural hegemony. The teachers of the past were replaced by those linked to the patriarchate so that the spirit of the "New Academy" would favor its interests.[25] In the dedication of his *Tetralingual Dictionary* master Dhanil (also known as Daniel of Moskhopolis), a monk who was representative of the Greek-Orthodox tendency, exhorted his Albanian, Vlach, and Bulgarian students "to give up their barbarian languages," and learn Greek, which is "the mother of wisdom."[26] Toward the end of the eighteenth century Voskopojë was reduced to a village of four to five hundred houses and the "New Academy" could not any longer continue its activity.[27]

When Voskopojë began to decline, Janinë emerged as a Greek cultural center near Albania. It opened a secondary school (gymnasium), called *Zōsimaia Skholē*, which was famous all over Greece. It was frequented not only by Orthodox Albanians but also by Muslim Albanians, like the brothers Frashëri, who played a prominent role in the Albanian national awakening toward the end of the nineteenth century.

While in the Catholic north there were several autonomous units where the customary law of the mountains was in force, in the Orthodox south there was only one autonomous unit—the district of Himarë, south of Vlorë. The Himariots had obtained that autonomy after a long resistance to the armies of Bayezid II in 1492 and they preserved it with ups and downs for many centuries. According to the agreement, the sultan would not send Ottoman authorities to govern the district of Himarë, and the Himariots would enjoy the right to rule themselves on the basis of their own traditional laws, have their own courts, and freely bear their weapons. On their part, the Himariots promised not to revolt and to pay only the *haraç* (tribute) as a token of submission. They were also obliged to dispatch soldiers whenever the sultan was engaged in war; by 1868 their number did not exceed one thousand men.[28]

The conditions which prevailed in the south during the first centuries of Ottoman occupation were not harsh on the Orthodox. The Ottomans were at the height of their power and feared no intervention from an external Orthodox Christian power. The Patriarchate of Constantinople had become an associate institution in the state system of the empire. It was in its interest when the Ottoman Empire expanded, for when new Orthodox lands were annexed in the

Balkans they as a rule fell under the religious jurisdiction of the patriarchate. Under such circumstances, there appeared to be no reason for apostasy. So long as the Orthodox were not dangerous, they could be milked better than "the true believers," and conversion *en masse* was in no one's interest.[29] If the Orthodox Albanian embraced Islam, he did so mainly for exemption from taxation and worldly advantages. The ignorance and illiteracy of the clergy were contributing factors. But the ignorance of the Orthodox priest was not as important as that of the Catholic, since the traditionalism of Orthodoxy did not need a rational theological culture. The force of religious convictions among the Orthodox was not dictated by the understanding of dogmas, but by the unshaken belief that they had inherited from their ancestors the true faith and that they had to preserve and transmit it unchanged.[30] The traditionalism of the Orthodox church was a great force against conversion to Islam.

Islamic pressure on the Orthodox Christians began with the decline of the empire and the outbreak of the Russo-Turkish wars of the eighteenth century. The officials in the provinces were corrupt and avid to enrich themselves at the expense of the population. In order to defend themselves, many Orthodox converted to Islam. In 1768 the Ottomans declared war on Russia. Alexis Orlov was entrusted with the task of organizing an insurrection among the Orthodox of the Balkans, in the name of Orthodoxy, in order to divert troops from the principal theater of operations in Moldavia and Wallachia. When his enterprise failed, the Ottomans made reprisals against the Orthodox. Regarding them as allies of Russia, they used pressure to Islamize them.[31]

The conversions were more numerous around the city of Berat, where Muslims lived near Orthodox Christians. Since the visit of Evliya Çelebi (1670), Berat had been predominantly Muslim: nineteen of its thirty quarters were Muslim. Many of its Orthodox quarters were compelled to apostatize, and a great number of churches had ceased holding services, for there was a lack of priests.[32] Since Russia entered the scene as an enemy of Turkey, the Ottoman authorities began to suspect the loyalty of the Orthodox, for it was on the basis of religion that the distinction was made.

During the Greek War of Independence (1821–1829), the Orthodox Albanians who joined forces with the Greeks were those who lived in Greece proper, whether in continental Greece or on the islands, and who descended in general from the Albanians who had emigrated there toward the end of the fourteenth century. The Orthodox inhabitants of Albania proper did not participate in that conflict. Apart from the fact that they were surrounded by Muslims and any revolt on their part would be doomed, they possessed an Orthodox but not a Greek national consciousness.

Following the establishment of the Greek state, both church and school worked more for the Hellenization of the Albanian Orthodox population. The high clergy whether in Durrës, Berat, Gjirokastër, or Korçë, although dependent on the Constantinople Patriarchate, which had been reconciled to the Ottoman regime, were nationalistic-minded Greeks. During the Greek Revolution several Orthodox prelates had been active, and the patriarch in Constantinople had been executed.[33] This contributed to the mutual hatred between Greeks and Ottomans. On the other hand, the policy of the Greek state began to become more expansionistic to liberate the Greeks who were under Ottoman rule. The so-called "Great Idea" *(I Megali Idea)*, which was to be shattered in Anatolia in 1922, was gaining force. The Greek schools among the Orthodox Albanians were increased, better organized and equipped with better teaching personnel than before. The programs were those of the Greek state, and the textbooks came directly from Athens. The history that was taught was that of ancient Greece, Byzantium, and the Greek War of Independence; and in literature, there were patriotic excerpts in prose or poetry, as for instance, the poem by Rigas Pheraios (or Velestinlis), a hero of the War of Independence, who compared Ottoman rule to "slavery." History and literature were geared to extol what was Greek and to inspire hatred against the Muslims, who were synonymous with Turks. For the Greeks the Orthodox Albanians were Greek; Albanians were by definition Muslim. They called the latter *Tourkalvanoi* (Turkish Albanians). As for the Catholic Albanians, they were seldom mentioned—they were few and lived far from the confines of Greece.

Indicative of the new tendency of Hellenization were the names the Orthodox gave to their children at the baptism. Earlier, the names the Orthodox carried were biblical, like *Josif* (Joseph), *Benjamin* (Benjamin), *Emanuel* (Emmanuel), *Jakov* (Jacob), or of saints, like *Dimitri* (St. Demetrius), *Nikolla* (St. Nicholas), *Jorgji* (St. George), *Jani* (St. John), with their feminine counterparts, *Dimitra, Gjorgjia* or *Jorgjia, Joana*—all deriving from good all-Orthodox names. With the introduction of Greek mythology and history in the schools, a new set of names made its appearance: *Irakli* (Hercules), *Jason* (Jason), *Odhise* (Odysseus), *Antigoni, Elektra, Agamemnon, Sokrat* (Socrates), *Themistokli, Perikli, Aristotel*. The names of the Christian saints continued to be employed; the biblical names were used less. For those who bore pagan names, mythological or historical, the church had seen to it that a special day be devoted to their collective celebration, All-Saints day.

With the *millet* system, the use of Greek was reinforced in the liturgy and all other religious services among the Orthodox. It was intensified by the multiplication of schools and the new programs of the Greek state. Efforts were made to develop pro-Greek sentiments. An ethnic minority, the Orthodox Albanians, different from the Greeks, were compelled, by entering the *Rum millet,* to forego use of their own language and their own folk culture, and to forget their ancient past. The more Orthodoxy and the Greek school were interwoven, the more their ethnic identity was blurred.

Among the Balkan Slavic Orthodox nations there has been an identity of religion and nationality. The Serbs had formed a powerful state in the late Middle Ages; they had also created an autocephalous church, which later was promoted to the Patriarchate of Peć. After the fall of Serbia, the Serbian church was subordinated to the Archbishopric of Ohrid until 1557, when it was resurrected as the Patriarchate of Peć to be incorporated in the Patriarchate of Constantinople in 1766. At the popular level, however, the Serbian church continued its role as a symbol of national unity and as the propagator of national mythology.[34] It had created its own liturgy in the Serbian language and thus prevented the Patriarchate of Constantinople from intervening and imposing its Greek liturgy. Bulgaria had also been a very strong state in the Balkans at the time of Tsar Simeon and his immediate successors. It had founded an independent church with its headquarters in Ohrid. When Bulgaria was reborn as a state under the Assenids, she also created a patriarchate in Tyrnovo to be abolished in 1393 at the fall of that city to the Ottomans. Following the conquest of Constantinople, the Bulgarian church was incorporated in the Greek Patriarchate. For centuries the Bulgarian people were dominated ecclesiastically and culturally by the Greeks.

There is a certain similarity between the Orthodox Albanians and the Orthodox Bulgarians. Although the Bulgarians had created an ecclesiastical language—the Old Church Slavonic—and the Albanians had not been able to, Church Slavic receded to some forlorn monasteries when the Greek ecclesiastical dignitaries began to arrive. They had no interest in Slavic liturgy or Bulgarian culture, and soon these were forgotten. In the towns, especially in those on the Black Sea, there was constituted a relatively educated Greek upper class respected by the well-to-do Bulgarians, above all the merchants. Already in the seventeenth century in Tyrnovo a considerable part of the Bulgarian notables had been Hellenized.[35] Hellenization had progressed through church and school. It was against the Greek culture which dominated them that the Bulgarian nationalists revolted in the first half of the nineteenth century, as a preparation for political independence.

In Albania the field for the penetration and development of Greek culture was more open. Not only did the Patriarchate of Constantinople prevent the opening of Albanian schools, but the Ottoman government also prohibited their functioning, though the population of Albania, both Christian and Muslim, spoke Albanian at home and in public. It was in the interest of both if the people did not become aware of their national origin. Schools in Albanian were not permitted even after the proclamation of the *Hatt-ı Hümayun* (imperial rescript) of 1856, which promised equal treatment in education to all the peoples of the empire.[36]

In the course of centuries the Orthodox in Albania, on account of conversions, diminished substantially, and the Muslims increased. The Albanian Muslims did not come from Anatolia; they were Albanian Christians who had embraced Islam. On the basis of a register of *timars,* from approximately 1510 (912 A.H.) there were in the district of Vlorë 1,206 Muslim as against 14,304 Christian families, and in the district of Gjirolastër (Argyrokastro) 53 Muslim and 12,257 Christian families.[37] In 1912, when Albania won her independence, these ratios were likely the reverse.

In the movement for the development of Albanian consciousness an important role was played by the Italo-Albanians. Living in separate communities as Uniates, they had preserved the language, customs, and traditions of their fatherland. Since several of them descended from the ruling families of Albania which had fought against the Turks, they also preserved the memories of the glories and defeats of their forefathers. They praised in songs the resistance of the Albanians to the Ottoman invaders and the exploits of their national hero of the fifteenth century, George Kastrioti Skenderbeg, although such songs remained unsung in Turkish-dominated Albania. The Albanians of Italy were also able to create an Albanian literature with nationalist tendencies and to found schools for their own education, and in 1794 they possessed an excellent institution, Collegio di San Demetrio Corone, in Calabria, where the Albanian language was taught.[38] There were no Greek schools and there was no Greek church to hinder the use of written Albanian.

The formation of the Albanian League, commonly called the League of Prizren, the city in Kosovo where it first convened, gave an impetus to nationalist cultural trends within Albania and the Albanian settlements abroad. It was founded at the time of the Congress of Berlin (1878), with the tacit consent of the Ottoman government, in order to protest the decisions of the Great Powers detrimental to Albanian territory. It was a union of representatives of all three religions in Albania, but the Muslims were most active, not only because they constituted the majority of the Albanian population but also because they were more directly concerned. The League of Prizren also signaled the first blow against the Hellenization of the Orthodox.

While the league was actively opposing with arms the encroachments upon Albanian territory, a cultural-educational society called the Society for the Printing of Albanian Writings was created in September 1879 in Constantinople, with the aim of promoting publications in the Albanian language. They sought to enliven the strongest link among the three religions of the country—language. It was headed by Sami (Şemseddin) Frashëri, and its membership was composed of adherents of the three faiths. The signatures to the constitution of the society show that the charter members were prominent Albanians. The Society for the Printing of Albanian Writings strengthened the work of the Albanian League; it may even be said that it was its cultural branch.[39]

In the preamble of its constitution the society stressed enlightenment through one's own language:

> All enlightened nations have been . . . civilized by writings in their own language. Every nation that does not write its own language and has no works in it is in darkness and barbarian. And the Albanians, not writing their own language and having no works in their own language, are in the same state. . . . Therefore, those who think and see this great calamity are also aware of the great need to write their language and read works in it.

The society then declared that it would publish educational works written originally in Albanian or translated from foreign languages; it would found branches wherever there were Albanians, and it would open schools in Albania, if the financial situation permitted.[40]

The consciousness of national identity began to manifest itself also among the Orthodox who emigrated abroad. Albanian emigration to foreign lands, particularly to Rumania, Bulgaria, Egypt, and the United States started toward the end

252 Non-Muslim Communities in the Eighteenth Century

of the nineteenth century. The immigrants came from the south and were as a rule Orthodox. In Rumania and Bulgaria they came into environments which were not pro-Greek because of unpleasant memories of Phanariot rule, and in reaction to Hellenizing propaganda among the Vlachs of Macedonia and of the Rumanian Pindus Mountains and, the Hellenizing influences of church and school for many centuries in Bulgaria. The Albanian Orthodox immigrants began to free themselves from Greek cultural influence and direct their attention to Albanian language and culture, although not totally untinged by Christian Orthodoxy. Most of the immigrants in Rumania were small businessmen and most of those in Bulgaria were workers, stonecutters and masons. They were active in forming societies and publishing journals and papers. It was hard, perhaps impossible, for them to work in Albania, where the well-to-do coreligionists—lawyers, physicians, businessmen—pursued a pro-Greek policy. The immigrants in Egypt were predominantly from southern Albania and lived in Cairo, Alexandria, and the cities of the Nile Delta. There were not only wealthy businessmen among them but also intellectual patriots, like Thimi Mitko, Spiro Dine, Çajupi, and others; the first two have given us collections of folklore and the third is considered one of the best Albanian poets. They were fewer in number than their compatriots in Rumania but more broad-minded, partly because they lived in a rather cosmopolitan environment. As the country was ruled by an Albanian Muslim dynasty,[41] the colony also comprised Muslim Albanians. The Orthodox Albanians who emigrated to Egypt could not very well get rid of Greek influences. The Greeks in the Egyptian cities, toward the turn of the century, were numerous and had a developed cultural life. They seemed to have exercised considerable influence on the Albanians, whom they claimed as members of their own family, on the basis of a supposed common Pelasgian origin. This created confusion in the ranks of the Orthodox Albanians.[42] Among the societies which existed in the various countries there were exchanges, but not well organized.

Among the immigrations in foreign lands, the one that distinguished itself was that of the United States. It emerged at the outset of the twentieth century. Gradually it grew, and became the most important of all the Albanian settlements abroad. The immigrants were from the south, chiefly from the district of Korçë, which maintained supremacy even later when others from Gjirokastër began to arrive. They were mainly Christian Orthodox and settled for the most part in Massachusetts, with Boston as a center. The immigrants on the whole became uneducated and unsophisticated factory workers. The Albanian leaders, however, enjoyed in America a freedom of action which they could never find in any other country. Conditions in the United States were very favorable for the work of the Albanian leaders. Their activity was made easier because the Albanians in America, living among so many other ethnic minorities, became more conscious of their national identity. Although the immigration was mixed, the opposition between the ruling Muslims and the ruled Christians which existed in the Ottoman Empire no longer prevailed here. Besides, the economic opportunities enabled the immigrants to support the national movement financially.

Societies were created in various cities of the United States and several newspapers were published. The most important publication was the weekly *Kombi* ("Nation"), founded in Boston in June 1906, which laid the cornerstone of the national movement. It supported the program of the nationalist leaders in Albania and abroad which at this time was chiefly cultural. It emphasized the demand for the use of the Albanian language and the opening of Albanian schools.[43]

What the Albanians lacked was an autocephalous church, particularly since church and schools were intermingled. The establishment of such an Albanian Orthodox church had been one of the main objectives since 1880. Sami Frashëri rated it next to the Albanian language in importance. He urged the Albanians to free themselves of their dependence on the Greek, Bulgarian, and Serbian churches—especially the Greek church—and create their own church with Albanian priests and a liturgy in Albanian.[44] As it was impossible to reach this goal in Albania, because of the opposition of the Patriarchate of Constantinople and the Ottoman government, an attempt was made to introduce only the Albanian language in the church services. When this failed, the patriots turned their thoughts to the constitution of an Albanian church outside Albania and Turkey. Bucharest seemed at the moment best suited for this purpose.

The founding of an Albanian Orthodox church failed in Bucharest, but it was successful in the United States. On 22 March 1908 the first liturgy in Albanian was celebrated in Boston. An incident expedited it which is indicative of the bitter struggle of Hellenization of church and school against the emerging Orthodox affirmation of Albanian national consciousness. In 1907 a young Albanian died in Hudson, Massachusetts, and the local Greek priest refused to officiate for the funeral services on the grounds that the young man was an Albanian nationalist and as such "automatically excommunicated." No other Orthodox priest being available in the neighborhood, the deceased was buried without any religious service. The incident provoked indignation among Orthodox Albanians of Massachusetts, who called a meeting and decided to have an Albanian priest ordained. They invited Fan S. Noli—later he became prime minister of Albania and bishop of the Albanian Orthodox Church in America—to undertake this mission, and he hastened to accept it. Platon, the Russian archbishop of New York, ordained him as a priest at the age of twenty-six.[45]

The creation of the Albanian Orthodox Church in America was a powerful incentive to the growth of Albanian national feeling. With the introduction of Albanian in the liturgy, the church assumed a national character. Fan S. Noli translated the service from Greek and used it immediately after his ordination. The function of the Albanian Orthodox Church did not remain religious; it also became patriotic. As a religious institution, it interested only the Orthodox Albanians. As an institution established in order to detach them from the Patriarchate of Constantinople, whose policy was to Hellenize them and unite them with Greece, it acquired a broader and national significance. This second aspect of the Albanian Orthodox Church of America concerned not only the

Orthodox Albanians but also their Muslim and Catholic compatriots. The activity of the Albanian colonies in the United States was intensified in the period following its establishment.[46]

While in the colonies Albanians, particularly Orthodox Albanians, were active in affirming their national identity, in Albania proper Albanian patriots were seeking to open Albanian schools. It was not an easy task. They were confronted with the policy of separation of the Porte, with which the Patriarchate of Constantinople concurred. The latter power opposed the Albanian language and schools because they ran contrary to its centuries-old and recently renewed program of Hellenization. There were some Albanian schools established in Korçë and its surroundings; they were alternately opened and closed. This was due, on the one hand, to the influence which certain Albanians could exercise in the Ottoman capital, and on the other, to the domestic policy of the Porte, which oscillated between reform and conservatism in response to European pressure. An attempt was made by a prominent member of the society *Drita* ("Light") in Bucharest to introduce the teaching of the Albanian language in the existing Orthodox Greek schools in Korçë. He discussed the matter with the metropolitan and his council (*demogerontia*), but the Patriarchate of Constantinople refused to introduce Albanian in the schools of the Orthodox communities.[47] The patriots in Albania were confronted with another difficulty: they could not raise funds for the support of the schools. The pro-patriarchate party falsely accused them of raising funds for the *comitadjis,* who were in revolt against Ottoman rule. But the most important obstacle the nationalist-minded Orthodox had to face was that the Albanian schools were technically at a serious disadvantage: they could not compete with the superior Greek culture. Moreover, while the Greek schools had long been established in the south, Albanian education was still in its infancy. However, the strong fight waged by the Albanian patriots in defense of the Albanian schools in Korçë gave a new stimulus to the national movement.

The creation of Albanian schools gave urgency to the question of texts, and in turn, to that of a common alphabet. The alphabets which were employed until then—that of the Catholic north, Hahn's or Kristoforidhi's, those of the Italo-Albanians, and others—were restricted in scope and were inconvenient. Sami Frashëri then devised a new alphabet on the basis of the Latin script with certain Greek characters and some of his own invention for sounds which the Latin alphabet could not convey. The Constantinople Society for the Printing of Albanian Writings adopted it, and in 1879 the first *ABC* was published. It spread widely in a brief time since several educational books were printed in it. The reports of the Austrian consuls in Albania show that by 1905 the Constantinople alphabet was used by the majority of the population, Orthodox and Muslim. The books used in the few Albanian schools in the south were printed in the alphabet of Constantinople, which was also adopted by various publications of the Albanian colonies. They were published mainly in Bucharest.

The writing of the Albanian language, which had been banned for centuries, was allowed after the success of the Young Turk revolution. But no progress could be made without Albanian schools and without a uniform alphabet. The two questions—school and alphabet—were inextricably connected.

Toward the end of 1908 (14–22 November) an alphabet congress was held in Monastir (*Bitola*) in order to decide on a unified national alphabet. It was organized by the Albanian Club of that city and was attended by delegates from other Albanian clubs and societies, towns and schools, both from Albania proper and from the colonies abroad. Some of the prominent delegates were Midhat Frashëri, president of the club of Salonica and editor of *Lirija* ("Freedom"); Pater Gjergj Fishta, representing the Catholic society of Shkodër *Bashkimi* ("Union"); and Sotir Peci, an Orthodox from Korçë, editor of the newspaper *Kombi* ("Nation") in the United States. After speeches by the various delegates, each one of them became aware that it was most important to achieve national unity. A committee was chosen to decide on the common alphabet. It resolved that the two—the Constantinople (mixed Latin, Greek etc.) and the new Latin alphabet—would be the only ones to be used and all Albanian schools were obliged to teach both to their pupils. The congress approved of the resolution.[48]

The decision on the alphabet question was an important step toward the unification of education and the union of the Albanians. Although not an ideal solution, which would have been a single alphabet, it was a wise one. The Constantinople alphabet could not have been discarded, for it had a long tradition and had been widely spread. As time advanced, the Constantinople alphabet receded until it finally fell into disuse and there remained only the Latin alphabet. The Young Turks tried to prevent the use of the Latin alphabet, for they wanted to obstruct the growth of national consciousness among the Albanians. They too became aware of the unifying force of the alphabet. With the adoption of the Latin alphabet Albania abandoned both Greece and the Orient and turned toward the West.

The next important question, both in order to fight Hellenization and to bring the people more closely together, was a unified language. Sami Frashëri had stressed it when he wrote toward the end of the nineteenth century: "The Albanian language should be undivided and unified, just as Albania herself should be, for many dialects bring about separation and aloofness."[49] But this took a long time to attain.

With the declaration of Albanian independence (28 November 1912), the Orthodox *millet* of the country officially was united with the Muslims—there was national identity between the rulers and the ruled. Yet at times the mentality of the *millet* system continued to linger and blur the issues. In the course of years, however, the schools became all Albanian and the Orthodox Church of Albania proclaimed its autocephaly. It was the end of Hellenization and the *millet* system.

Notes

1.   M. Sufflay, *Srbi i Arbanasi* (Serbs and Albanians), Belgrade, 1925, pp. 85–89, 94; Cf. also *Idem.*, "Die Kirchenzustände in vortürkischen Albanien. Die orthodoxe Durchbruchszone im Katholischen Damme." in L. von Thallóczy et al., eds., *Illyrisch-albanische Forschungen,* Munich and Leipzig, 1916, vol. 1, pp. 190–191.

2.   C. Jireček, *Geschichte der Serben,* Gotha, 1918, vol. 2, p. 128.

3.   H. Inalcik, "Timariotes chrétiens en Albanie au XVe siècle après un registre de timars ottomans", *Mitteilungen des Oesterreichischen Staatsarchivs,* 4 (1952), pp. 120, 123.

4.   About the disposition of the Albanian feudal lords, see N. Iorga, *Geschichte des osmanischen Reiches,* Gotha, 1918, vol. 1, p. 261.

5.   E. Grafenauer, B. Djurdjev, J. Tadić, eds., *Istorija Naroda Jugoslavije* [(History of the People of Yugoslavia), Belgrade, 1960, vol. 2, pp. 56, 61.

6.   I. Snegarov, *Istorija na Okhridskata Arkhiepiskopija-Patriarshija ot' Padaneto i pod' Turtsite do Neinoto Unishchozhenie* (1394–1767 g.) [(History of the Ohrid Archbishopric-Patriarchate from the Fall under Turkey to its Disappearance (1394–1767)], Sofia, 1932, p. 8.

7.   A.-P. Péchayre, "L'Archevêché d'Ochrida de 1394 à 1767. A propos d'un ouvrage récent", *Echos d'Orient,* 39 (January-March, 1936), pp. 193, 188.

8.   Grafenauer et al., eds. (cited n. 5), vol. 2, p. 57.

9.   G.Schiró, *Storia della letteratura albanese,* Milan, 1959, pp. 69–70.

10.   Grafenauer (cited n. 5), vol. 2, p. 56; cf. also I. Konidari, *The Greek Church as a Civilizing Force in the History of the Balkan Peninsula* (in Greek), Athens, 1948, p. 179; I. Snegarov (cited n. 6), p. 160, also gives the eparchies which were constituted in Albania through the fifteenth and the beginning of the sixteenth century.

11.   K. Amantos, "The privileges of Islam in Favor of Christians" (in Greek) in *Hellnika* (Athens), 9 (1936), pp. 156–157.

12.   Cf. J. A. Petropoulos, *Politics and Statecraft in the Kingdom of Greece, 1833–1843,* Princeton, N.J., 1968, pp. 24–25.

13.   Ibid., pp. 27–30

14.   State University of Tirana: *The History of Albania* (in Albanian), Tirana, 1959, vol. 1, p. 372.

15.   IBid., pp. 373–374.

16.   Dim. Garouphas, "Kosmas Aitōlos: The Saint of the Race. The Teachings Which Remain Still Alive Among the People of the Mountains and of the Struggle" (in Greek), *Macedonian Life,* vol. 150, year 13 (November 1978), p. 38.

17.   State University of Tirana (cited n. 14), p. 374.

18.   T. E. Evanghelidès, *Education under Turkish Rule* (in Greek), Athens, 1936, pp. 102, 129–130, 137, 173–176, 187, 194. Cf. also A. E. Vakalopoulos, *History of Modern Hellenism* (in Greek), Salonica, 1973, vol. 1, pp. 363–371.

19.   Cf. J. C. Hurewitz, *Diplomacy in the Near and Middle East, a Documentary Record, 1535–1914,* Princeton, N.J., 1956, vol. 1, p. 54.

20.   State University of Tirana (cited n. 14), p. 414.

21.   Ibid., p. 415.

22.   Vakalopoulos (cited n. 18), vol. 3, pp. 320–321; State University of Tirana, (cited n. 14), pp. 414–415.

23.   Ibid., p. 415.

24.   Ibid., pp. 417–418.

25. Ibid., p. 413.

26. A. E. Vakalopoulos (cited n. 18), vol. 4, pp. 321.

27. State University of Tirana (cited n. 14), p. 418.

28. Ibid., pp. 318–320.

29. F. W. Hasluck, *Christianity and Islam under the Sultans*, Oxford, 1929, vol. 2, p. 469.

30. Cf. L. Hadrovics, *Le peuple serbe et son église sous la domination turque*, Paris, 1947, p. 22.

31. T. W. Arnold, *The Preaching of Islam*, London, 1913, p. 115.

32. Cf. G. Babinger, *Ewlijâ Tschelebi's Reisewege in Albanien*, Berlin, 1930, p. 19; Konidarē (cited n. 10), pp. 178–179.

33. Petropoulos (cited n. 12), p. 41. However, on this see Volume I, chapter ten by Richard Clogg.

34. M. B. Petrovich, *A History of Modern Serbia, 1804–1918*, New York and London, 1976, p. 13.

35. Cf. S. Skendi, "The Emergence of Modern Balkan Literary Languages—a Comparative Approach," in G. Reichenkron and A. Schmaus, eds., *Die Kultur Südosteuropas, ihre Geschichte und ihre Ausdrucksformen*, Wiesbaden, 1964, pp. 309–310.

36. See text in Hurewitz (cited n. 19), p. 151.

37. Inalcik (cited n. 3), p. 132.

38. Cf. A. Scura, *Gli Albanesi in Italia e i loro canti tradizionali*, New York, 1912, p. 75; A. Galanti, *L'Albania*, Rome, 1907, p. 234.

39. S. Skendi, *The Albanian National Awakening, 1878–1912*, Princeton, N.J., p. 119.

40. Ibid., p. 120.

41. The founder of the Egyptian dynasty was an Albanian, Muhammad c Alī.

42. See Skendi (cited n. 39), pp. 152–154.

43. Ibid., pp. 159–161.

44. S. Sami Bey Frashëri, *Was war Albanien, was ist es, was wird es werden?* (Aus dem Türkischen übersetzt von A. Traxler), Vienna and Leipzig, 1913, p. 49.

45. Metropolitan F. S. Noli, compiler, *Fiftieth Anniversary of the Albanian Orthodox Church in America, 1908–1958*, Boston, 1960, pp. 104–118.

46. See Skendi (cited n. 39), pp. 162–164.

47. Ibid., pp. 133–134.

48. For the struggle for national schools and national alphabet, see ibid., pp. 366–390.

49. State University of Tirana (cited n. 14), vol. 2, p. 154.

IV

THE ROLE OF CHRISTIANS AND JEWS IN OTTOMAN LIFE DURING
THE NINETEENTH CENTURY AND AFTER

------------------------------ 13 ------------------------------

The Transformation of
the Economic Position of the *Millet*s
in the Nineteenth Century

CHARLES ISSAWI

Introduction

The rise and decline of the *millets* is one small aspect of a vast process. In the nineteenth century a worldwide market was formed; it was made possible by the industrial and transport revolutions, the mass emigration of tens of millions of Europeans and Asians to other continents, the outflow of a large amount of European capital and the establishment of an international network of trade and finance. In the countries thus affected by Europe's thrust, foreign or minority groups played a very important role as intermediaries between Western capital and the local population: Chinese in Southeast Asia, Indians in Burma and East Africa, Lebanese in West Africa and so on. The liquidation of the European empires, the ending of the predominance of Western capital and the intensification of local nationalism spelled the downfall of these groups, just as the rise of English, French, and other nationalisms in the late Middle Ages had led to the expulsion of the Jews and Lombards, who had played a similar part.

In the Middle East—Turkey, Egypt, the Levant and, to a lesser extent because of its late and slow development, Iran—the function of the *millets* was essentially that of middlemen between the Muslim masses and the forces that were transforming them, i.e., European capital and enterprise and modernizing Middle Eastern governments. More specifically, the *millets* performed three roles. First, they were an entrepreneurial petty bourgeoisie of traders, moneylenders, brokers, and commissioners, linking the large European importers, exporters, and banks with the indigenous farmers, craftsmen, petty traders, and other producers and consumers. Secondly, along with some Europeans, they staffed the liberal professions, whose skills are required by a developing society: physicians, pharmacists, engineers, architects, lawyers (in the Western-type courts set up in Turkey and Egypt) and stockbrokers. Lastly, they formed a large part of the salaried middle class employed by the government or by the large European enterprises such as banks, railways, public utilities, and industries; and a perhaps even larger part of the skilled urban working class.

Needless to say, in the performance of these functions, some members of the *millets* acquired great wealth and power as high government officials, merchants, bankers, industrialists, and even landowners, but the vast majority remained in the ranks of the petty bourgeoisie or lower.[1] Not surprisingly, their influence grew along with European economic and political power in the Middle East and the concurrent efforts of the Middle Eastern governments to reshape society on Western lines and began to decline—either immediately before, or more generally, just after the First World War—when Middle Eastern society began to produce Muslims capable of carrying out these middle-class functions and when growing nationalism demanded the replacement of foreigners or members of minority groups by ethnic Turks, Egyptians, Iraqis, or Persians.

I

From the very beginning of Islamic civilization, Christians and Jews had been prominent in such urban activities as medicine, trade, moneylending, and handicrafts.[2] Occasionally, one group had enjoyed a brief period of great influence and prosperity. Thus in the sixteenth century Jewish immigrants from Spain and Portugal played a leading part in medicine, banking and, occasionally, diplomacy. Their knowledge of European languages, their training in Iberian or Italian universities and their contacts with coreligionists and others in Western Europe gave them a decisive advantage over all other groups, Muslim or Christian. The books in Greek, Latin, Spanish, Italian, and Hebrew that poured out of the presses they set up, starting in 1494 in Istanbul, bear witness to their intellectual activity.[3] In Iran in the seventeenth century Armenians "dominated the Persian external trade and much of the internal commerce," their activity stretching from Europe to India.[4] But such prominence was exceptional; generally speaking, in most handicrafts Muslims were either the majority or a strong minority, most local or regional trade was in Muslim hands and the Eastern trade—which until perhaps as late as the end of the eighteenth century was distinctly larger than the European—was dominated by Muslims.[5]

Developments in the late eighteenth and nineteenth centuries changed all this. A survey of the situation at the beginning of this century, when the influence of the *millets* was at its peak, reveals a very different picture. In most parts of the Middle East they played a leading role in the economy. In Turkey, the Greeks, Armenians and Jews, in that order, dominated the urban sector and controlled a considerable part of the rural. The predominance of non-Muslims in finance is shown by the fact that of the 40 private bankers listed in Istanbul in 1912 not one bore a Muslim name. Of those that could be identified with a reasonable degree of confidence, 12 were Greeks, 12 Armenians, 8 Jews, and 5 Levantines or

Europeans. Similarly, of the 34 stockbrokers in Istanbul, 18 were Greeks, 6 Jews, 5 Armenians and not one was a Turk.

As for the provinces, in the European parts there were 32 bankers and bank managers: of those identifiable, 22 were Greeks, 3 Armenians, 3 Jews and 3 Levantines or Europeans. In the Asian parts (excluding the Arab provinces in which many Arab, particularly Christian, names were to be found) there were 90 bankers. Of those that could be identified, 40 were Greeks, 27 Armenians, 6 Levantines or Europeans, and 2 Turks (in Eskişehir and Harput).[6]

A similar situation prevailed in industry, though here one cannot be as precise since many establishments, especially the larger ones, were listed under the names of the firm, not the owner. Turkish Muslim names appear much more frequently than in finance, but still constitute a small minority. In the silk industry, Armenian names prevail and in the cigarette paper industry, Jewish. In the other branches of industry, the predominance of Greeks is very clear.[7] According to a calculation by Tevfik Çavdar, the capital of 284 industrial firms employing 5 or more workers was divided as follows: Greeks 50 percent, Armenians 20, Turks 15, Jews 5 and foreigners 10, and their labor force: Greeks 60, Armenians 15, Turks 15 and Jews 10 percent.[8]

In foreign trade the share of the *millets* was also overwhelming. A list of the large importers of textiles in Istanbul in 1906 shows 28 Armenian names, 5 Turkish, 3 Greek and 1 Jewish. In 1910, of 28 large firms in Istanbul importing Russian goods, 5 were Russian, 8 Muslim, 7 Greek, 6 Armenian and 2 Jewish, and almost all large traders with Russia in the eastern provinces were Armenians.[9]

A detailed breakdown for 1912, based on various yearbooks, is given by Indzhikyan,[10] whose totals are (in percentages):

	Number	Turks	Greeks	Armenians	Others
Internal Trade	18,063	15	43	23	19
Industry and Crafts	6,507	12	49	30	10
Professions	5,264	14	44	22	20

In agriculture Muslims—Turks in Anatolia, Arabs in the Asian provinces—were predominant but the *millets* also played an important part. Figures on shares of landownership or the output of different crops are lacking but the following remarks, by an acute observer, are suggestive:

> Cereal cultivation in western Asia Minor is in large measure in Greek hands, in central Anatolia almost exclusively in Turkish, in Armenia predominantly in Armenian, and in other parts in Arab hands. In fruits and cash crops, the leading role in western Asia Minor is played by the Greeks, further east by the Armenians, and to a small extent in Palestine by the Jews. In the growing of mulberries [for silkworm breeding] the leading groups in western Asia Minor are the Armenians and the Greeks, in Syria the Christian Arabs.[11]

It may be added that in the most rapidly expanding sector of agriculture, cotton, the main thrust came from the *millets*. In the Izmir region, cotton farms belonged "mostly to Greeks, but also to Turks." While in Adana, of the large landowners using modern methods, "few are pure Turks, but rather Greeks, Armenians, Syrians and so on."[12] Greek predominance was even more pronounced in cotton growing, spinning and weaving, and cotton oil pressing in Adana. Thus, whereas the Muslims accounted for the bulk of the traditional grain crops, the *millets* developed and controlled the more valuable cash crops exported to foreign markets.

Whereas in Turkey the two leading *millets*, the Greeks and Armenians, were even more indigenous than the Turks, in Egypt the oldest non-Muslim community, the Copts, played a minor part in the economy. That their average economic level was higher than that of Muslims is shown by the fact that, shortly before the First World War, although forming only 6 percent of the population, they claimed that they paid 16 percent of the land tax[13]—and land was by far the greatest source of wealth and income. Scattered data support this contention and indicate that during the second half of the nineteenth century Copts bought large amounts of land and invested in irrigation pumps, cotton gins, and other machinery and, particularly in Upper Egypt, ranked among the largest landowners.[14] Prominent Coptic landowning families included Khayat, Dos, Bushra Hanna, Wisa, Sarofim, and Bulus. Copts were also prominent among the directors of land development companies.[15] Their higher educational level (see below) explains the disproportionately large share of Coptic government officials, 45 percent of the total, particularly marked in such departments as finance, interior, and railways.[16] Copts were also—and have continued to be—well represented in the professions and included many of Egypt's most prominent lawyers, physicians, engineers, scholars, and journalists.[17] In the first half of this century they supplied many leading politicians, such as Butrus Ghali, Sinot Hanna, Georges Khayat, Wasif Ghali, Makram Ebeid, and Saba Habashi. They also continued to pursue their traditional handicrafts, notably goldsmithery. But in modern industry and finance they played only a minor part: a list of 1,406 company directors in 1951 shows only 4 percent had Coptic names.[18] Overall, their economic position was distinctly better than that of Muslim Egyptians, as witnessed by the fact that of the over one thousand persons who had the unwelcome distinction of being sequestrated in 1961 6 percent bore Coptic names—a proportion relatively much larger than that of Muslims (55 percent) but far smaller than that of Jews (4), Syrians or Lebanese (22), Greeks or Armenians (9) and Europeans (4).[19] "During the 1940s, Copts became middlemen, entering the business of contracting or export-import. In recent years some Copts from the leading families have gone full cycle, becoming tradesmen, but on the level of the high-fashion couturier shop in Cairo's new Hilton Hotel."[20] But they were neither innovators in modern business nor in control of any important economic sector.

Second only to the Copts in antiquity and much less influential politically, the Jews played a far more prominent economic role. Perhaps the most striking illustration of this is the fact that as late as 1951, after nearly thirty years of attempts to Egyptianize the economy and after the Arab-Israeli War of 1948 had severely shaken their position, Jews still formed 18 percent of company directors, a figure that had fallen to 5 by 1960.[21] Jewish families such as Cattaui, Mosseri, Menasce, Suares, Rolo, and Harari, most of whom had been resident in Egypt since the beginning of the nineteenth century or before, played an important part in the foundation and administration of Egypt's leading banks: National Bank, Crédit Foncier, and others. Although individual ownership of land by Jews was small,[22] they provided much of the capital and most of the directors of some leading land development companies, notably Kom Ombo Company.[23] Together with some more recent immigrants from Europe, such as Mandelbaum and Horowitz, they established industries like sugar refining and cigarettes.[24] Two of Cairo's three principal department stores, Cicurel and Chemla, were Jewish-owned as were several somewhat smaller ones. Jews constituted a large proportion of stockbrokers,[25] insurance agents, and the personnel of banks and leading business firms. They were very well represented in the professions, notably medicine, law, and the foreign language press. Lastly, in the period before the First World War, some had risen to high positions in the Egyptian civil service, e.g., Blum, Seligman, Harari, Adeh, and Biyalos.[26] But the majority of Jews were of modest means—petty traders and employees—and a small number were extremely poor.

The same was true of the Syro-Lebanese community, which was roughly equal in numbers to, but less affluent than, the Jewish. It included some very large landowners such as the Sidnawi, Sursuq, Lutfallah, Karam, Chedid, Sa'b, Zogheib, Khlat, Eid, Kahil, and other families, most of whom had acquired their land in the years 1882–1914.[27] In 1951 Lebanese and Syrians constituted 11 percent of company directors, a figure that had risen to 13 by 1960.[28] Starting in the 1920s, they founded some rather large firms in the textile and other industries (e.g., Rabbath, Tagher). They supplied a large number of professional people—lawyers, physicians, engineers, stockbrokers—though few of the very top rank. Many attained high posts in the Egyptian civil service, while in the Sudan they formed an indispensable link between the highest British officials and the lower rank Sudanese; such families as Shuqayr, Atiyah and Isawi contributing several top administrators.[29] But the greatest impact of the Syro-Lebanese was on the press. "Out of 166 papers published in Cairo between 1828 and 1900 about 36 were owned by men whose names were recognizably Syrian; out of 188 between 1900 and 1914, about 21 were Syrian. In Alexandria, there were 31 Syrian newspapers out of 61 between 1873 and 1900, and 7 out of 27 between 1901 and 1914." Similarly for periodicals, in Cairo 28 out of 130 started between 1848 and 1900 and 12 out of 161 between 1900 and 1914, while in Alexandria, "9 out of 23 periodicals started between 1881 and 1900 had Syrian editors and 6 out of 34 between 1901 and 1914."[30] It should be added that their publications included both the two leading newspapers, *al-Muqaṭṭam* and *al-Ahrām,* and the two most prestigious and influential journals, *al-Muqtaṭaf* and *al-Hilāl.*

The political and administrative power enjoyed by Armenians under Muḥammad ᶜAlī and his immediate successors, which culminated in the premiership of Nubar Paşa and the cabinet or undersecretary posts of Tigrane, Yacoub, Artin, Boghos Nubar, and others,[31] had disappeared by the First World War, no doubt helped by the substitution of Arabic for Turkish (which was spoken by many Armenians) as the official language. This was not offset by an increase in economic power. Some of the larger cigarette factories (e.g., Matossian) were owned by Armenians, as were several smaller factories and workshops in shoemaking, metalwork, and other industries. They had few company directors —under 2 percent in 1951 and less in 1960.[32] The amount of land owned by Armenians was very small. In some professions, such as medicine, engineering, and pharmacy, they were quite well represented. But the enormous majority consisted of petty traders, small employees, skilled craftsmen, and industrial workers.

Unlike the Copts, Jews, and Syro-Lebanese, the Greeks were never in a position to influence Egyptian politics or contribute to Arabic culture, though they can boast of modern Alexandria's most distinguished son, the poet Cavafy, and did produce a large number of minor scientists as well as prominent physicians, engineers, and lawyers in the Mixed Courts.[33] But their influence on the country's economic development from the early days of Muḥammad ᶜAlī until the Second World War was probably the greatest and most widespread of any *millet*. More than any other community, they operated at every level of Egyptian society except the government bureaucracy, from high finance and large-scale cotton exporting to village grocers, petty traders and moneylenders, and industrial workers. It may be added that they played much the same role in the Sudan, which they had first penetrated in the middle of the nineteenth century and reentered literally on the heels of the British army of reconquest, to Lord Cromer's amazement and slight amusement.[34] However, in the Sudan, Greeks were far less prominent in the upper layers.

Starting at the top, in 1951 Greeks constituted 7 percent of company directors;[35] fifty years earlier the ratio must have been still higher.[36] Greeks founded, or played a major part in establishing, many of Egypt's earliest banks: Anglo-Egyptian Bank, 1864, Banque d'Alexandrie, 1872, Banque Générale around 1880. Such leading families as Salvago, Benachi, Rhodonachi, Zervudachi, Zafiropoulo, Zarifi, and others were also instrumental in creating the National Bank and the Land Bank.[37] In cotton exporting Greeks, including, in addition to the above families, such firms as Choremi, Benachi, Gregusci, Andritsakis, and Casulli—some of them founded in the 1860s—accounted for nearly a quarter of the quantity shipped. Most of the balance was exported by British and other European houses.[38] Greeks were no less well represented in other branches of import-export trade and when, in 1883, the Alexandria General Produce Association was formed, 15 of the 24 founding members were Greeks, including names like Ralli and Sinadino.[39]

Greeks were also active in various branches of internal trade, more particularly in purchasing cotton from the smaller farmers and delivering it to the exporters in Alexandria. Indeed from the dissolution of Muḥammad ᶜAlī's monopolies, in the late 1840s, until after the turn of the century, they almost monopolized the business, but were gradually subjected to a double squeeze by the large banks on the one hand and small Egyptian and other traders on the other.[40] During the same period they acquired a good deal of land, by purchase or foreclosure for debt. Thus in 1899 Averoff willed 1,160 *feddans* to the Greek community[41], and there were even larger landowners.[42] They played a leading part in the development of long staple cotton, commemorated by such varieties as Sakellarides, Zagora, Yannovitch, Pilion, and Casulli, introduced vine growing (Gianaclis), and were active in dairy and poultry farming.[43] In industry, they were prominent in cotton ginning, controlling one quarter of Egypt's gins in 1929 and introducing noteworthy improvements in the closely linked oil pressing, as well as in tanning, alcohol, beer, soft drinks and various food processing industries. They also dominated both the manufacturing of cigarettes, which they introduced in the 1860s, and its export (Gianaclis, Kyriazi, Melachrino, etc.).[44] Lastly, mention should be made of their active part in construction work, hotels and Nile transport.[45] And Greeks were well represented among the employees and skilled workers not only of Greek but of other firms.

The peculiarity of Lebanon is that here alone Christians not only secured a commanding early lead in the nineteenth century but managed to keep it until the 1970s. Already in the eighteenth century their superior education and French connections (see below) had enabled them to move ahead in both the embryonic bureaucracy and the expanding trade with Europe. The collapse of the French trading network in the Levant, during the revolutionary and Napoleonic wars, left a vacuum into which they eagerly stepped and Muhammad ᶜAlī's rule created further opportunities for both Europeans and Lebanese Christians. But the remarkable fact is that the latter soon took over in Lebanon's two main activities: silk production and foreign trade.

Silk in Lebanon was grown mainly by Maronite farmers and, starting in 1836, reeled by up-to-date French and British establishments. But already by 1846 there were five silk-reeling plants "à l'européenne" owned by Lebanese— almost certainly all Christians—"in the plains of Beirut and the lower reaches of the Mountain."[46] And in 1862 the French consul stated that of 44 silk-reeling plants, 33 belonged to natives—the vast majority Christians—who owned 1,350 out of the 2,200 pans in use.[47] It may be added that by the 1850s silk had come to account for over one half of Lebanon's gross agricultural output.[48] By 1870 foreign firms were only 15 percent of the total and by 1910 3 percent.[49] This local Christian lead was maintained until the demise of silk cultivation, following the destruction of mulberry trees during the First World War and growing competition from Japanese silk and rayon. In 1931 an observer could state: "Lebanese industrialists have set up improved *(perfectionnés)* establishments that produce a good quality silk bought by Lyon. We may mention, as a model of the kind, the filature of M. Naccache, in Beit Mery."[50]

The same was true of trade. In 1826 the French consul stated that out of 34 commercial firms dealing with Europe, 15 belonged to local Christians and 6 to Turks, i.e., Muslims. By the late 1840s, the Lebanese seem to have taken over much of the foreign trade from the British and French, and here too the Christians were an overwhelming majority. A list of the 29 firms engaged in direct trade with England in 1848 shows only 3 Muslim and no Jewish names; the others consisted of Maronites (e.g., Naqqash, Eddeh, Dahdah), Greek Orthodox (Sursuq, Bustros, Trad) and Greek Catholics (Medawwar, Misk). Lebanese Christians had also established agencies in London, Manchester, and Marseille.[51]

This situation persisted during the next hundred years or more. The development of Lebanese trade after the First World War was accomplished mainly by Christians, as was the promotion of tourism (Sursuq, Qasuf, Jbeili),[52] the establishment of a far-flung financial network and, later, the laying of an industrial base (Cortas, Esseili, Tamer). Christians continued to be disproportionately represented in the civil service, the professions, and intellectual activities, all of which naturally resulted in their earning distinctly higher incomes than Muslims or Druzes. Thus according to the 1971 National Fertility and Family Planning Survey, the average annual family income of Catholics (80 percent of whom were Maronites) was LL 7,173, of non-Catholic Christians (65 percent Greek Orthodox and 29 Armenian Orthodox) LL 7,112, of Sunnis 5,571, of Shi'is 4,532 and of Druzes 6,180, the national average being LL 6,247; the percentage of families in each group earning less than LL 1,500 was 6%, 8%, 15%, 22%, 11% and 12% respectively. The percentages in the two top occupational groups, professional/technical and business/managerial, were 23%, 27%, 20%, 15%, 23% and 22% respectively.[53]

The situation was somewhat different in Syria. It is true that in the main commercial center, Aleppo, from the sixteenth century on, Europeans traded "chiefly through the intermediary of the native Christians and Jews," including Armenians.[54] In the late eighteenth century the role of minorities in Aleppo "as bankers and moneylenders was vital."[55] In 1840, speaking of geographical Syria, Bowring could state:

> The Mussulman population are seldom associated with the progress of arts or industry, and, though possessing the influence which belongs to the ruling authorities, are rarely instrumental in the creation of capital or the diffusion of civilization. Most of the commercial establishments are either in the hands of the Christian or Jewish population

and, more specifically, "the principal moneylenders and traffickers in specie, throughout the East, are the Jews."[56] But the figures he gives on the firms engaged in foreign trade show that the Muslim share in Aleppo was not insignificant while in Damascus it was preponderant; they may be tabulated thus, keeping the original spelling:[57]

Denomination	Number of Firms	Capital (millions of piasters)	Main House
Aleppo			
Muslim	85	8.5–10	Agi Wosa Muaket
Christian	30	14 – 18	Fathalla Cubbe
Jewish	10	2 – 2.5	Abderachman Asim, Aga Bagdadi, Mahomet Said
Damascus			
Muslim	66	20 – 25	Hadji Hussein Chertifchi
Christian	29	4.5 – 5.5	Hanah Hanouri
Jewish	24	16–18	Mourad Farhi, Nassim Farhi

Both Christians and Jews played a significant part in handicrafts, and a preponderant part in a few, but Muslims formed a large majority in most branches.

In the course of the next hundred years, the commercial power of the Jews declined and that of the Christians increased, but the Muslims continued to be very active in trade. And when, after 1945, Syria began to industrialize, it was Muslim traders rather than Christians who played the main part. The main group, the Khomasiyya of Damascus, consisted entirely of Muslim merchants, who also formed the majority in the second largest Damāscene combine, although it was headed by a Christian, Sahnawi. The Aleppo industrialists were all Muslims: Mudarris, a large landowner, Hariri and Shabarek, both the latter being traders.

For Iraq, one fact is clear: trade and finance were dominated, to an extent unknown elsewhere, by Jews. Longrigg puts the matter bluntly: "In Baghdad, with a city community of some 50,000, they almost outnumbered the Sunni Arabs and exceeded the Christian, Persian and Turkish minorities combined. With their agents in Manchester, Bombay, and Paris they had so far the supremacy in commerce and foreign trade that Muslims were often forced into partnership, while Christian merchants had been largely driven from the field."[58] This statement may be confirmed by some figures. A list of exporters in the United Kingdom in 1907 dealing directly with Persia and the Persian Gulf shows 12 Jewish names, 5 British, 2 Muslim, 1 Christian Arab, and 2 uncertain.[59] Similarly, a list of the main establishments in Iraq engaged in import-export trade around 1908 shows 7 foreign names, 5 Jewish, and 1 Muslim.[60]

A distinction must, however, be made between import trade, centered on Baghdad, and export trade, centered on Basra. The former soon passed into local hands. In 1839–40 two British firms were established in Baghdad and as late as 1857, in spite of the arrival of two Greek and one Swiss firms "except the two British firms . . . there are no foreign merchants who are engaged in the direct trade with Europe."[61] But the business was soon taken over by local firms, at first Persian and Jewish and then almost solely Jewish.[62]

In 1879 "the Jewish Mercantile Community of Baghdad have nearly all the trade with England in their hands whereas the native Christian merchants trade mostly with France. There are only two English merchant firms in Baghdad."[63]

Trade with Britain was many times as great as that with France. A few years later a British consul declared: "The wealth of Baghdad is rapidly passing from the Mohammedans to the Christians and Jews"[64] while another stated: "The Jews are the largest traders in Baghdad but there are also many native Christian and Muhammedan merchants."[65] Finally, in 1909, a list of importers who had branches in England showed 19 names, of importers who bought through Commission Houses 30, and of bankers 5; all were Jewish.[66] The Jewish business community included such internationally famous names as Sassoon, Zilkha, Haskiel and Kadoorie.

In the provinces the situation was somewhat different. At Gumtara in 1891 the government put orders for grain with two Jewish and one Christian merchant, at Samawa with one Jewish and one Muslim, at Diwāniyya with two Muslims, and at Dighara with two Muslims.[67] At the Shiʿī holy city of Karbala in 1882 there were no Christians except one or two government clerks; "a few families of Jews monopolize, as usual, the money-dealing of the place."[68]

The situation in Basra was also different, but then "Baghdad has a decided mercantile predominance over Basra which, apart from the date and grain export trade, is merely the ocean port of Baghdad."[69] In the 1870s, export of dates was carried out by 6 European and 6 local firms, most of the latter being Muslim, and the same was broadly true of grain and wool.[70] A petition of Basra merchants in 1891 was signed by 5 Britishers, 3 Muslims, 2 Greeks, and 1 Syrian, and in 1908 there were 2 Greek firms.[71]

This structure of export and import markets continued until the Second World War, except that in both the Muslim share increased.[72] Throughout the period landownership and agricultural production remained in the hands of Muslims.

II

An explanation of the economic ascent of the *millet*s can start with two general remarks. First, as observed by various social scientists from Sir William Petty to Alexander Gerschenkron, a minority that is excluded from certain avenues of power, like the army, church, and politics, tends to concentrate on and excel in business and the professions—in other words, the Avis complex. Secondly, minorities are clannish. They help, hire, promote, and do business with each other, to the great annoyance of the surrounding majority. But these explanations are insufficient for the Middle East: firstly, because there were other minorities, such as the Shiʿīs, Nusayrīs, Kurds, and others who did less well than the Sunnī Muslims; secondly, because the success of the *millet*s was relatively greater than that of similar minorities in other parts of the world. Five further factors may be mentioned: participation in expanding sectors; foreign protection; a favorable situation following various reforms in the Ottoman Empire and Egypt; superior education; and help from coreligionists outside the region.

The *millet*s participated actively in those sectors of the economy that expanded most rapidly in the nineteenth and twentieth centuries: foreign trade with Europe and the Americas, the various branches of finance, mechanized transport, export-oriented agriculture, and modern industry. By the last decades of the nineteenth century some 90 percent of Middle Eastern trade was with Europe and the United States, and the formerly predominant Eastern trade had dwindled to a trickle.[73]

This change had been accompanied and facilitated by a marked shift in trade routes, from caravans to steamships; particularly important was the diversion caused by the opening of the Suez Canal. All this seriously hurt such inland towns as Kayseri, Konya, Diyarbakır, Erzurum, Aleppo, Damascus, and Mosul, where Muslim traders had been predominant. Conversely, it greatly benefited such ports as Salonica, Izmir, Beirut, and Alexandria, where *millet*s were an important minority, or even a majority, of the population. Even where caravan trade continued, it tended to shift its route to a closer port. Thus the Tabriz trade from the 1830s on made for Trabzon rather than Aleppo, Izmir, or Istanbul and was soon captured by foreign or minority firms;[74] similarly the trade of Mosul turned away from Aleppo and toward Baghdad and Basra.[75]

Already by the eighteenth century many minority groups were active in the trade with Europe. A French report of 1784 states: "Formerly, the Armenian and Greek cloth merchants formed an association, through which they made all their purchases, thus imposing their terms on the French. The Grand Signor has destroyed this association by severe penalties."[76] In the 1820s Armenian merchants established their bases in European countries. "In the 1860s the Armenian colony in Manchester already consisted of 30 families; these firms opened branches in Istanbul and Izmir."[77] The Greeks were no less active, monopolizing certain branches. "One third of the members of the Ottoman Chambers of Commerce consisted of Greek firms and organizations. In the Commercial-Industrial Chamber, founded in 1884, Greeks retained a majority until the Balkan Wars." The role of Jews was far smaller, but quite significant.[78]

In Syria the Christians, starting as interpreters for the French and other consuls and merchants, soon struck out on their own and by the beginning of the eighteenth century Melkites controlled a large part of the trade and shipping between Syria and Egypt.[79] When the French commercial position in the Levant was ruined by the Revolutionary Wars and Napoleon's expedition to Egypt, Syrian Christian and Jewish firms took over part of its business.[80] The same trade established the basis of the Syrian community in Egypt, some of whose members also became middlemen between European importers and the Mamlūks.[81] Similarly, during the French occupation and the first years of Muḥammad ᶜAlī's reign, the Greeks in Egypt both increased in numbers and engaged in shipping and trade with the eastern Mediterranean—activities that prepared them to take full advantage of the subsequent expansion of trade with Europe.[82]

The result of these developments may be seen in a list compiled by Bowring of the 72 merchant houses in Alexandria in 1837.[83] Of the identifiable names, forty-three were European (British, French, Austrian, Tuscan, and Swiss), fourteen Greek, five or six Syrian, four or five Jewish, two Maltese and one Armenian. Of the twenty-seven in the last five groups, seventeen were protégés of European countries other than Greece. Only two were Muslims, a Tunisian, and a Turk. The business of the minority firms was still very small compared to that of the big European houses, but the Muslims hardly entered the picture at all. And for a long time the process was cumulative: the profits made in foreign trade could be used to buy real estate in the expanding seaports, where values and rents were rising rapidly.

The *millet*s were even better placed in finance. The famous Galata bankers were Levantines, Greeks, Armenians, and Jews, and during the first half of the nineteenth century they dominated the field. Most of the *sarraf*s came from the *millet*s. In Turkey the Armenians were particularly influential,[84] but the Jews also played an important part until 1826.[85] All this led to important international contacts: "The Rayahs who lend their money secretly at an exorbitant profit, have no method of placing their fortunes when they retire from trade. This inconvenience has induced many rich Greeks, Armenians and Jews to place money in the foreign Funds and even to follow it into Italy, Germany, France and Russia."[86] In Egypt the *sarraf*s had been, since the Arab conquest, Copts. But the customs were held by Jews until the second half of the eighteenth century when they were replaced by Syrians[87] or Copts.[88] Under Muḥammad ʿAlī Greeks and Armenians joined their ranks.[89] In Syria and Iraq, Jews and Christians were also well represented among the *sarraf*s, and sometimes engaged in bitter rivalry.[90]

All this meant that the *millet*s were well placed to found small private banks, some of which attained considerable importance in the second half of the nineteenth or first half of the twentieth century, e.g., Zilkha, Suares, Trad, Tepeghiosi. They were also able to serve as agents or employees of European banks, insurance companies, brokerage houses and other institutions.

The other growing branches may be briefly examined. Minority members soon became local agents of the French, Austrian, Russian, British, and other shipping lines serving the eastern Mediterranean. Others, like the Sursuqs in Beirut, supplied the ships with coal. As regards the railways and river steamers, except for a few concessions in Syria and Palestine which were soon sold to foreign interests, the minorities had little part, but they supplied a large share of their technical and skilled personnel. Thus in Iraq the only large government enterprise, the Saniyya steamboats, was ably headed by a Jew, Sasoon. When he resigned in disgust he was succeeded by an Armenian, Sirop.[91] And it may be noted that the two engineers sent by the Baghdad Railway to northern Iraq in 1911 were Greek and Armenian.[92]

The decline of the handicrafts, due to European competition, ruined many members of the *millet*s, but probably a far larger number of Muslims. In the founding of modern factories, however, the minorities showed much more enterprise and skill until the First World War. In addition to the data given above, mention may be made of the Armenians, notably the Dadians, who managed the various factories established by the Ottoman government in the 1830s, and some private entrepreneurs like the *sarraf* Jezairli (Jezairlian) who set up silk filatures in Bursa.[93] Greeks and Armenians also worked many coal mines in the Zonguldak area. Greeks, Armenians, and Jews, as well as Muslims, opened workshops for carpetmaking in the Izmir region. Such activities were often financed by capital accumulated in foreign trade, moneylending, or tax collecting.

Most of these developments could not have taken place without the foreign protection enjoyed by so many *millet* members. In the eighteenth century and much of the nineteenth, property was very insecure in the region, being subject to arbitrary taxation and high risk of confiscation. Some scholars have seen much merit in this situation, as a dispenser of rough justice, an accelerator of social mobility and a provider of government revenues, but it was hardly conducive to private enterprise, innovation and investment. Girard saw this clearly. Ottoman subjects had no protector for their trade in their own ports, but were subject to exactions which "n'avaient de bornes que celles de l'avidité des exacteurs." That is why almost all foreign trade was carried out by foreign nations.[94]

Quite a large number of Christians and Jews, but not Muslims, got around these obstacles by acquiring a *berat* from a foreign power. As shown so clearly by Robert Haddad[95] for the Christian Syrians, this enabled them to pay lower customs duties than unprotected Ottoman subjects, avoid part of the arbitrary taxes levied by local authorities and in addition acquire much greater immunity from the Maltese and other corsairs who preyed on Ottoman shipping. In Turkey, *berats* had originally been issued to embassy interpreters recruited from the *millets*, but by the end of the eighteenth century each mission had begun "to rear up its own interpreters" and no longer needed Ottoman subjects. "Those invested with *berats* therefore turned the protection to purposes of trade. The most opulent among the Greeks, Armenians, Jews, etc., in Constantinople and in the provinces made it a point to obtain a protection."[96] Hence although, as noted before, the Eastern trade, including that between Istanbul and Egypt, was in the hands of Muslims, some of whom were very rich, that with Europe, both maritime with England, Holland, France, and Russia and overland with Austria, was dominated by Greeks and Armenians.[97] A note in 1802 from the Porte to the British minister stated explicitly that Muslim traders were "a very small number" compared to *rayas*.[98] Selim III tried hard to end the abuses arising from the excessive issuance of *berats* and to foster Ottoman trade and shipping but had no success.[99]

In Egypt it is worth noting that in 1837 all but one of the 72 Alexandrine merchants listed above had either foreign citizenship or protection. In Aleppo, 19 Jews were granted British protection between 1848 and 1861, and by 1881 their number had risen to nearly 40; it may be presumed that most of them were engaged in trade.[100] Christian *protégés* of France, Austria, Russia and other countries, also largely in trade, were probably much more numerous. In Damascus in 1863 the consul reported that "British subjects and their *protégés* were then the chief moneylenders there."[101] As for Iraq, in Baghdad in 1844 "a considerable proportion of the native merchants connected with the Indies, Syria and Constantinople enjoy the protection of the English, French and Russian governments."[102] Here, as in Aleppo, the British extended their protection mainly to Jews and the other Powers to Christians. In 1850 a list of British *protégés* in Baghdad showed 7 Jews, all merchants trading with India and 4 Christians, one of whom was a trader.[103] By 1890, "with the exception of Sir Albert Sassoon, the whole of the Sassoons are British born subjects. Sir Albert Sassoon, by naturalization and Firman is a British subject—he used to sit in the Legislative Assembly of Bombay."[104]

The mobility and security provided by foreign protection may be illustrated by the history of the Thaddeus family. Their ancestor, David, emigrated from Isfahan to India. His son Kevork, born in Surat in 1747, became in 1778 "linguist and broker of the English factory at Basra" and died in 1807. His son, Thaddeus, succeeded him in his post but in 1832 took his family to Bombay where he died in 1842. In 1843 Rawlinson brought Thaddeus's two sons, George and John, to Baghdad, to serve in the Residency where they were joined in 1845 by their brothers, Yaqub and Gabriel, who were still serving in the Residency in 1894. George died in 1892 and John, having become a landowner and a Turkish subject, had been dismissed but all other descendants were British subjects.[105] The obverse is illustrated by the following remark by the very knowledgeable Resident at Baghdad, Kemball, in 1862. Pointing out that the steamboat run by Lynch and Co. was in "constant occupation," had "full cargoes," and was "universally appreciated," he continues:

> "The example set by Messrs. Lynch and Co. would be immediately followed by the Native Speculators were they not deterred by the curse of the Sukhreh which is in constant operation in this Province and which would subject their vessel to be at all times diverted from her commercial voyages whenever the Government might require her services to supply the place of a damaged bridge boat or to carry stores, fodder, grain and troops from one point of the River to another. From this curse, experience has shown that a Foreign Flag could alone protect them.[106]

Ten years earlier his predecessor, Rawlinson, had stated that Turkish officials were so arbitrary that it was impossible for any native merchant to do a proper job as agent of a British firm unless he enjoyed British protection, and asked that such protection be granted to an Armenian in Basra.[107]

By the middle of the nineteenth century foreign protection of minorities had greatly widened. Not only holders of *berat*s but all aggrieved members of *millet*s within reach of a foreign consul looked to him for protection and redress. At the same time the Ottoman government was attempting to remove some of the disabilities from which its non-Muslim subjects suffered, and Muḥammad ᶜAlī carried this policy much further. Moreover, in their efforts at modernization, both governments needed every ounce of local talent available, and since the minorities were already much more educated and westernized their role in administration and policymaking greatly increased.

The result was an odd combination of privilege and discrimination. In Egypt Christians and Jews were treated remarkably well and so, on the whole, were Greeks and Jews in Anatolia—except, of course, for the atrocities committed by both sides during the Greek War of Independence. In eastern Anatolia the

Armenians were "ruthlessly exploited and oppressed" by the Kurdish Beys, sometimes with the connivance of the local authorities.[108] In the Fertile Crescent intercommunal relations were more tense. The struggle in Lebanon was more or less between equals, but the anti-Christian riots in Aleppo in 1850 were not; nor were the pillaging and killings at Ma^{c}lula in 1850–51;[109] nor above all were the Damascus massacres of 1860, in which some five thousand Christians died. But, under international pressure, these incidents were followed by severe punishments and nothing comparable took place even during the tense period of the 1875–78 wars, although the British consuls reported several incidents of killing and pillaging in Aleppo and its region (but not in Damascus), and the visit of a British naval squadron to Syrian waters was deemed salutory.[110] Except for the apprehension caused by occasional blood libels, such as the one in Damascus in 1840, the Jews in Syria were left undisturbed. In the Mosul region, however, the eight thousand Jews were "subject to tyranny of the worst kind"[111] while "the atrocities practised by the Kurds upon the Christians are revolting to humanity."[112] In 1867 Jews in Arbeel were killed and robbed with impunity[113], and in 1899–1900 Christians in the region also suffered.[114] The attitude of the Muslims of Mosul toward Christians and Jews was described in 1909 as "that of a master towards slaves whom he treats with a certain lordly tolerance so long as they keep their place. Any sign of pretention to equality is promptly refused."[115] This attitude was not unknown in other towns, and on the whole the minorities learned to keep their place, thus avoiding major incidents.

But while the situation of the minorities was not enviable, their economic position was becoming much more favorable. First, their taxes were reduced, as shown by the following judgment on the effect of the *Tanzimat* on Erzurum, made in 1845:

> The Armenian Agriculturist formerly often paid 20 per Cent, while the Mohamedan paid only 5, or at most 10 per Cent; and it frequently happened, besides, that the latter, by favor, was exempted altogether from the Tax. This year, however, both classes have paid equally their legitimate 10 per Cent, and the Tax has been fairly levied. Free quarters on the Christians and forced labour are both prohibited by the Tanzimat; but, until Essat Pasha's time, the abuses continued; they probably will be abolished hereafter. The property of the inhabitants of the Town has been three or four times assessed, but always so unfairly, that the valuation has been rejected. At last, it was asked what the Mussulmans could bear and what the Christians. The answer given was, that the former (consisting of 9,000 families) could contribute 75,000 piastres or £750; and the latter (1,000 families), 32,000 piastres or £320; this sum, the Armenians had usually paid for Salian, while the Turks had never contributed at all. The Government, then, ordered that the Mussulmans should pay 75,000 piastres, and the Christians 35,000; but it abated from the two 10,000 piastres, and directed the Chiefs of the nations to distribute the tax justly and conscientiously among their coreligionists. The Turks here took, however, the whole abatement on their own contribution; so that they pay 65,000 piastres— £650, and Christians 35,000—£350.[116]

Secondly, minority members were increasingly employed by the government.

"The Egyptian government made the same use of Syrian Christians as it customarily made of Coptic Christians in Egypt, employing them all over Syria as tax collectors," and appointing the Bahri brothers to head the finance departments of Damascus and Aleppo.[117] This was a mixed blessing since tax gatherers are seldom liked. The same happened to Armenians, Greeks, and Jews in Turkey. In Lebanon, Volney had already noticed that, thanks to their higher literacy, the Maronites had become "what the Copts are in Egypt; I mean, they are in possession of all the posts of writers, intendants and kiayas among the Turks."[118] Thirdly, the increasing modernization of Ottoman and Egyptian legislation and the establishment of courts based on Western principles helped the minorities who were more at ease with them and able to take fuller advantage of their provisions. Particularly important was the Ottoman Land Code of 1858 and its counterparts in Egypt; allowing free transfer of land, it made possible the accumulation of vast holdings by Christians and Jews in Anatolia, Egypt, and Syria through purchase or foreclosure for debt.[119]

But the most important advantage resulted from the exclusion of the *millet*s from the army, viz., their exemption (in return for payment of a special tax) from conscription to which Muslims were increasingly subjected. This, together with the removal of restrictions on land purchase and other forms of discrimination and oppression which had impeded them, put *raya*s in a very advantageous position to compete with Muslims. A few examples from Anatolia are illustrative:

In Erzurum in 1848: "The Armenians have more hands, the Mussulman youth being taken for military service. The Mussulmans do not hire labour and they are unable to cultivate the extent of land they possess."[120] In Biga in 1860: "Their [Christians'] pecuniary means being larger than those of the Mussulmans, they are constantly purchasing property from the latter. I understand however that formerly Christians were restricted from so doing; but the prohibition as regards this province was abolished some years ago, mainly through the instrumentality of Mr. Consul Calvert."[121] In Izmir: "The Christian races are . . . buying up the Turks." Before the Decree of Gülhane, the large Turkish landlords "lived by a system of oppression and plunder which was put a stop to by the Hatt." The Turks, handicapped by conscription, "fall into the hands of some Christian usurious banker (Armenian, Greek or occasionally European) to whom the whole property or estate is soon sacrificed."[122] Relative freedom from conscription also helped the Lebanese Christians under Muhammad ʿAlī. "Financially, it is possible to observe them in the 1820s as serfs of such Druze Shaikhs as Abu Nakad and at the end of the Egyptian period as the chief moneylenders to the same shaikhs."[123] Moslems were fully aware of this factor: "The Mussulmans of Beyrout and I believe generally of Syria express an opinion that if they are to be treated on a footing of exact equality with their Christian fellow subjects, it is unjust that they alone as a class should give their flesh and blood for the conscription but that the Christians equally with themselves should furnish recruits for the army."[124] Conscription was not applied to non-Muslims until the eve of the First World War.

The matter was put succinctly by a British diplomat and scholar in 1900: "But when force does not rule, when progress, commerce, finance and law give the mixed population of the Empire a chance of redistributing themselves according to their wits, the Turk and the Christian are not equal; the Christian is superior. He acquires the money and land of the Turk, and proves in a lawcourt that he is right in so doing."[125]

The help provided to the *millet*s by their coreligionists abroad was twofold: business contacts and opportunities and education. The Greeks, and to a lesser extent the Armenians, in Western Europe and Russia certainly facilitated the trade of their Middle Eastern coreligionists with these countries. The Jews of Livorno, and elsewhere, performed the same function and so, to a far smaller extent, did the Lebanese in America and the Parsees in India. But a still greater service was the opening of schools by these foreign groups for the local communities: the Greek and Armenian schools in Turkey and the Alliance Israélite schools in all parts of the region. The Syrian Christians were even more fortunate in having numerous Italian and French Catholic, American, British and German Protestant, and Russian Orthodox schools, starting in the early nineteenth century. The Copts also greatly benefitted from the mission schools opened in Egypt in the nineteenth century.

The use made by the *millet*s of this opportunity, and the results achieved, may be illustrated by some figures. In the Ottoman Empire in 1896 there were 31,000 pupils in Muslim middle *(rüşdiye)* schools, compared with 76,000 in non-Muslim and 7,000 in foreign (the vast majority being non-Muslims), and 5,000 in secondary *(idadiye)* compared with 11,000 and 8,000. It is true that in elementary *(ibtidaiye)* schools Muslims far outnumbered the others, but the education received in them was of very little value.[126] As early as the 1870s the Greeks in Istanbul alone had 105 schools with 15,000 pupils[127] and the Armenians were not behind, frequenting in addition to their own schools those of the Catholic and Protestant missionaries.[128] In Egypt the Greeks opened their first school in 1843 and soon had a wide network.[129] Jewish schools, opened by immigrants from Europe, also date from the 1840s,[130] and the Syrians and Armenians had theirs, too. As a result, in the 1907 census the literacy rate for Jews was 44 percent, that for Copts was 10, and for Muslims only 4 percent. The contrast was even more striking in Iraq, where the Christians and Jews had their local missionary and Alliance schools—most of which were attended by members of the other religion as well—while the Muslims were almost unprovided for. In Mosul, for example, the 90,000 Muslims had "practically no education at all . . . even amongst the members of the great families there are very few indeed who can express themselves in Turkish and, so far as I am aware, there is only one Muslim in the whole city who knows a European language, viz., Daud Chelebi, dragoman to the German vice-consultate. This gentleman is also the only one who has visited Europe." In contrast the 9,000 Christians had about 2,000 children (some no doubt from nearby villages) in missionary schools and the 4,000 Jews had an Alliance school.[131]

Two aspects of this educational headstart may be noted. First, the minorities learned European languages, which equipped them to deal with the new social structures that were coming into being. A search by the British consular authorities in Syria in 1878 for interpreters produced the following results: in Beirut, 53 persons were named as knowing at least Arabic and English, 10 knew French as well, and one in addition Italian and Turkish; of these 4 were foreigners, 6 Druzes and all the rest Christians. In Damascus, 10 knew English and Arabic and 4 also knew French, 1 Italian, 1 Spanish, and 3 Turkish; all were Christians. In Jerusalem, 9 persons—6 Jews and 3 Christians—knew English and Arabic, and most of them knew several languages, including Turkish, French, Italian, and Greek. And in Aleppo, one of the dragomans knew English, French, Italian, Arabic, and Turkish, while the other was described as an even "better linguist"; both were Christians.[132]

The other aspect is concentration on professional education. "Although the Copts make up only 6 percent of the population, they produced 21 percent of the law graduates, 19 percent of the engineering, 15 percent of the medical, and 12 percent of the teaching graduates between 1886 and 1910."[133] The same was broadly true of other *millet*s and explains their predominance in the professions and as employees of large enterprises. It is perhaps superfluous to add that the minorities felt much more affinity with Western culture than did Muslims and absorbed it with almost no reservations.

III

The downfall of the *millet*s may be briefly described. Essentially, it was due to the fact that they had been too successful, absorbed too large a share of the fruits of economic progress and, to make matters worse, began to forget the traditional wisdom of their fathers and to take seriously the dangerous slogans "Liberty, Equality, Fraternity." In the latter they were abetted by foreign well-wishers, or interested parties who naturally let them down in their hour of need.[134] Many were even more shortsighted and actively collaborated with the occupying powers, from whom they had in the past sought protection.

With his usual sweep, Berque states: "Who profited thereby, apart from the colonizers? Here and there we find partial indications: some middlemen—Jewish, Syro-Lebanese, Coptic, very occasionally Muslim, turning the import trade to their best advantage; some pashas, associated with the interests of those in power; an occasional landowner, acquiring mechanized pumps and setting himself up as a bourgeois lord of the manor; on a humbler level the village *'umdas* and shaikhs."[135]

Of course this was not so—the level of living of the Egyptian masses rose,[136] education spread and a remarkable intellectual and social awakening took place. But to most Egyptians, squeezed between the rich foreigners on the one side and the Greek, Jewish, or Syrian moneylender on the other, the description would have seemed accurate. Eliot makes the same point about Turkey: "One may criticize the Turkish character, but given their idiosyncracies, one must admit that they derive little profit from such blessings of civilization as are introduced into their country. Foreign syndicates profit most, and after them native Christians, but not the Osmanli, except insofar as he can make them disgorge their gains.''[137] This was achieved in the horrendous events of 1895–1923, which disposed of practically all the Armenians and Greeks. Many Jews left of their own accord, and the remaining minority members were finally finished off by the *Varlık Vergisi* of 1942.[138]

In Egypt the economic position of the foreigners and minorities remained strong until after the Second World War, as the figures given above indicate. But from the late 1930s the government tried to squeeze them out, by stimulating a local bourgeoisie and insisting, quite properly, that books be kept in Arabic (which most had not bothered to learn) and that preference be given to Muslims—and to a lesser extent Copts—in hirings. After 1946 many foreigners and minority members, seeing the storm signals, left the country. The 1948 Arab-Israeli War undermined the position of the Jews, and the 1956 war destroyed it, along with those of the French and British. The nationalizations and sequestrations of 1961, which crippled the Egyptian bourgeoisie, finished off foreign interests and those of the Syrians and remaining Jews. Copts have also come under great pressure.[139]

The development of Zionism in Palestine had increasingly adverse effects on the position of Jews in Iraq, and the 1948 war led to a mass exodus. The same occurred, to a lesser extent, in Syria. In the latter, Christians, who were disproportionately represented in business and the professions, suffered correspondingly from the upheavals, nationalizations and sequestrations that have occurred since 1949. In Lebanon the current civil war, whatever its outcome, will probably end Christian predominance. The golden days of the *millet*s are gone.

Notes

1. In a memorandum of 27 February 1910, printed in Elie Kedourie, *Arab Political Memoirs,* London, 1974, p. 267, the dragoman of the British Consulate in Baghdad classified the Jewish community of that city as: 1) rich and well off—bankers, merchants—5%; 2) middle class—petty traders, retail dealers, employees—30%: 3) poor—60%; 4) beggars—5%. My impression is that the Armenian, Jewish and Syro-Lebanese communities in Cairo and Alexandria were somewhat better off (i.e. a larger proportion fell in the top two brackets), and the Jewish communities in Damascus and Istanbul worse off—for the latter, see A. Sussnitski, in *Allgemeine Zeitung des Judentums,* Berlin, 3, 12 and 19 January 1912. An indication of the condition of the Armenians of Istanbul in the 1860s is given by the fact that when an attempt was made to raise money for religious purposes only 3% were able to contribute 75 piasters (say $3.50), although such statements must be taken with a large pinch of salt. O. G. Indzhikyan, *Burzhuaziya osmanskoi imperii,* Erevan, 1977, p. 154.

2. And not only in Islam. "At the end of the [fifteenth century], Joseph Bryennius sadly recorded that medical practice was entirely in the hands of Jews," Steven Runciman, *The Last Byzantine Renaissance*, Cambridge, 1970, p. 92.

3. Abraham Galanté, *Turcs et Juifs*, Istanbul, 1932, pp. 94–101.

4. R. W. Ferrier, "British Persian Relations in the Seventeenth Century, Ph.D. Thesis, Cambridge University, quoted in Charles Issawi, *Economic History of Iran*, Chicago, 1971, p. 57. A monopoly in Persian silk in Aleppo was established in 1590–1632 by the Armenian Khocha Petik, whose commercial network covered Anatolia, Persia and India, Avedis Sanjian, *The Armenian Communities in Syria under Ottoman Dominion*, Cambridge, Mass., 1965, pp. 48–49. See also Niels Steensgaard, *The Asian Trade Revolution of the Seventeenth Century*, Chicago, 1973, pp. 378–385.

5. In Egypt in 1783, trade with Europe was put at only 236 million *paras*, compared with 1,373 million for North Africa, the Ottoman Empire and the Red Sea; except for some of the trade with Syria the latter was in Muslim hands, André Raymond, *Artisans et Commerçants au Caire*, Damascus, 1973, vol. 1, p. 193. In Iran, too, trade with Central Asia, Transcaucasia, the Ottoman Empire and India in 1800 far exceeded that with India and Europe by the East India Company and other European groups and was mainly in Muslim hands, Issawi (cited n. 4), pp. 130–135, 262–267. In 1825, Damascus alone bought 18,500,000 piasters "worth of Asian goods, mainly brought by caravan from Baghdad, or more than twice as much as all Syria then bought from Europe. There was a brisk trade with Mecca. . . . Thus, in the years before the Egyptian invasion such international trade as there was was primarily an Asian trade." William R. Polk, *The Opening of South Lebanon*, Cambridge, Mass., 1963, p. 162, citing Boislecomte. In Iraq, at the beginning of the nineteenth century, trade in Asian goods was almost certainly larger than in European, and most of the latter came to Baghdad by caravans from Syria and Turkey, Charles Issawi, *Economic History of the Middle East*, Chicago, 1966, p. 136. For Muslim economic activity in Ottoman Empire, see Kemal Karpat, *An Inquiry into the Social Foundations of Nationalism in the Ottoman State*, Princeton, 1973 and Halil Inalcik, "Capital Formation in the Ottoman Empire," *JEH*, 29(1969), pp. 97–140 and Ronald Jennings, "Loans and Credit in Early Seventeenth Century Ottoman Judicial Records," *JESHO*, 16(1973), pp. 168–217.

6. Marouche and Sarantis, *Annuaire Financiere de Turquie*, Pera, 1912, pp. 137–140.

7. A. Gündüz Ökçün, *Osmanli Sanayi*, Ankara, 1970, *passim*.

8. Cited by Indzhikyan (cited n. 1), p. 166. This book is a rich source of information on the economic activity of the minorities.

9. Ibid., pp. 206–209.

10. Ibid., pp. 211–214.

11. A. J. Sussnitzki, "Zur Gliederung wirtschaftslicher Arbeit," translated in Issawi (cited n. 5), p. 117.

12. W. F. Brück, "Türkische Baumwollwirtschaft," *Probleme der Weltwirtschaft*, No. 29, Jena, 1919.

13. Report of Coptic Congress, cited by Kyriacos Mikhail, *Copts and Moslems under British Control*, London, 1911, p. 29. Some estimates are even higher. Thus Ramzi Tadros, *Al-Aqbāt fī al-qarn al^{c}ishrin*, Cairo, 1910/11, cited in Doris Behrens-Abouseif, *Die Kopten in der aegyptischen Gesellschaft*, Freiburg in Breisgau, 1972, p. 48, puts Coptic holdings at about one-fifth of the cultivated area and states that 26 families owned 20,000–30,000 *faddans*.

14. Gabriel Baer, *A History of Landownership in Modern Egypt*, London, 1962, pp. 63–64, 137–138.

15. Ibid., pp. 129–131.

16. *British Parliament, Accounts and Papers*, Egypt, no. 1, 1911, p. 8; in a few of the more technical departments, Copts were prominent until very recently: in the Department of Mechanical Power of the Ministry of Rural Affairs in 1959, Copts "comprise 20 percent of the personnel"; but in the ministry as a whole they formed only 13 and in the Ministry of Foreign Affairs under 2 percent. Edward Wakin, *A Lonely Minority*, New York, 1963, pp. 43–44.

17. See two interesting autobiographies: Naguib Mahfouz, *The Life of an Egyptian Doctor,* Edinburgh, 1966 and Salāma Musā, *Tarbīyat Salāma Musā,* Cairo, 1947; both men began their activity before the First World War and continued it after the Second.

18. Charles Issawi, *Egypt in Revolution,* London, 1963, p. 89.

19. Ibid., pp. 89–90. This had also been true at the beginning of the century; speaking of the "bourgeoisie of businessmen" that was growing up in Cairo and Alexandria, Berque notes "a few" Muslims but "many Copts such as Bushtur, Hinaya Shinuda, Andraus Bishara and others" Jacques Berque, *Egypt: Imperialism and Revolution,* New York, 1972, p. 243; see also p. 200 for the career of the merchant-industrialist Wisa Buqtur.

20. Wakin (cited n. 16), p. 28.

21. Issawi (cited n. 18), p. 89.

22. Berque (cited n. 19), pp. 227, 244.

23. Baer (cited n. 14), pp. 130–131.

24. Jacob M. Landau, *Jews in Nineteenth Century Egypt,* New York, 1969, pp. 13–15.

25. The first chairman of the Cairo Stock Exchange, in 1872, was A. Cattawi, and the tradition proved durable, Berque (cited n. 19), p. 99.

26. Landau (cited n. 24), pp. 11–12.

27. A. H. Hourani, "The Syrians in Egypt in the Eighteenth and Nineteenth Centuries," *Colloque international sur l'histoire du Caire,* Cairo, 1964, pp. 226–227.

28. Issawi (cited n. 18), p. 89.

29. See biographical details in Richard Hill, *Biographical Dictionary of the Sudan,* London, 1967. In 1932, out of the total of qualified government personnel, 4,793, there were 913 British, 520 Egyptians, 164 Syrians, 2,913 Sudanese and 71 others, Anthony Sylvester, *Sudan under Nimeiri,* London, 1976, p. 48. These figures reflect the massive retrenchment of non-Sudanese personnel; earlier the figure for Syrians was distinctly higher.

30. Hourani (cited n. 27), pp. 226–227.

31. Lord Cromer, *Modern Egypt,* New York, 1908, vol. 2, pp. 219–225.

32. E. I. Politi, *Annuaire des Sociétés egyptiennes par Actions,* Alexandria, 1951; *Egyptian Stock Exchange Yearbook,* Alexandria, 1960.

33. Athanase G. Politis, *L'Hellénisme et l'Egypte moderne,* Paris, 1929–30, vol. 2, pp. 401–490.

34. Cromer (cited n. 31), vol. 2, p. 250.

35. Politi (cited n. 32).

36. See list for 1929 in Politis (cited n. 33), vol. 2, pp. 291–294.

37. Ibid., vol. 2, pp. 260–266; this list excludes branches of Hellenic banks operating in Egypt, e.g. Banque d'Athènes, Banque d'Orient, etc., see ibid., vol. 2, pp. 266–278.

38. Ibid., vol. 2, pp. 230–243.

39. Ibid., vol. 2, pp. 213–219.

40. Ibid., vol. 2, p. 223.

41. Ibid., vol. 1, p. 290.

42. See list in ibid., vol. 2, pp. 103–107 and Baer (cited n. 14), p. 121.

43. Politis (cited n. 33), vol. 2, pp. 97–159.

44. Ibid., vol. 2, pp. 304–374.

45. Ibid., vol. 2, pp. 56–68, 374–379.

46. Dominique Chevallier, *La Société du Mont Liban,* Paris, 1971, p. 220; in previous centuries other communities had also grown silk on a large scale, information kindly supplied by Professors Bernard Lewis and Adnan Bakhit.

47.   MAE, CC, Beirut, VII, f. 354.

48.   Charles Issawi, "Lebanese Agriculture in the 1850s," *American Journal of Arabic Studies,* 2(1973), pp. 66–80 and Chevallier (cited n. 46), chapter 14.

49.   Toufic Touma, *Paysans et institutions féodales chez les Druses et les Maronites du Liban du XVIIᵉ siècle à 1914,* Beirut, 1971, p. 372, and more generally, pp. 366–373 and Ismail Haqqi, ed. Lubnān: mabāhith ʿilmiyya wa-ijtimaʿīyya, Beirut, 1970, vol. 2, pp. 487–530.

50.   Raymond O'Zoux, *Les États du Levant sous mandat français,* Paris, 1931, p. 275.

51.   CC, Beirut, vol. 1, fol. 398 and see list in Charles Issawi, "British Trade and the Rise of Beirut, 1830–1860," IJMES, 8(1977), p. 98; also Chevallier (cited n. 46), p. 206.

52.   For the period before 1914 see *Lubnān* (cited n. 49), pp. 521–544.

53.   Joseph Chamie, "The Lebanese Civil War: an Investigation into the Causes," *World Affairs,* Winter 1976/77, for a breakdown of businessmen by religion, see Yosif A. Sayigh, *Entrepreneurs of Lebanon,* Cambridge, Mass., 1962, p. 70.

54.   Avedis Sanjian (cited n. 4) pp. 47–51.

55.   Herbert Bodman, *Political Factions in Aleppo, 1760–1826,* Chapel Hill, 1963, p. VIII.

56.   John Bowring, *Report on the Commercial Statistics of Syria,* New York, 1973, pp. 7, 25.

57.   Ibid., pp. 80, 94.

58.   Stephen Longrigg, *Iraq: 1900 to 1950,* London, 1953, pp. 10–11.

59.   *Kelly's Directory,* quoted in FO 195/2243.

60.   See Issawi (cited n. 5), pp. 184–185 for details.

61.   Kemball to Redcliffe, 26 December 1857, FO 195/577.

62.   Muḥammad Salman Ḥasan, *Al-taṭawwur Al-iqtiṣādī fī al-ʿIrāq,* Beirut, n.d., p. 263.

63.   Trade Report 1878/79, FO 195/1243.

64.   Plowden to St. John, 11 February 1881, FO 195/1370.

65.   Trade Report 1884, FO 195/1509.

66.   Ramsay, Note, FO 195/2308.

67.   Muston to Consul General, 18 September 1891.

68.   Tweedie, Diary, FO 195/1409.

69.   Crow to Barclay, Memorandum, 8 January 1907, FO 195/2242.

70.   Ḥasan (cited n. 62), pp. 139–152.

71.   Petition of 20 June 1891, FO 195/1722 and Crow to O'Conor, 18 January 1908, FO 195/2274.

72.   Ḥasan (cited n. 62), pp. 139–152.

73.   For figures on Turkey see Vedat Eldem, *Osmanlı İmparatorluğun İktisadi şartları hakkında bir tetkik,* Ankara, 1970, chapter 9; for Egypt see Ministry of Finance, *Annuaire Statistique,* Cairo, 1910; for Iran see Issawi (cited n. 4), chapter 3.

74.   Issawi (cited n. 4), pp. 92–116.

75.   Ḥasan (cited n. 62), p. 262.

76.   See Issawi (cited n. 5), pp. 31–32.

77.   Indzhikyan (cited n. 1), p. 186.

78.   Ibid., pp. 157–158. Greek migration to England began in the 1830s; by the 1850s there were 55 Greek firms in Manchester, including Ralli Brothers—see Issawi (cited n. 4), p. 104—and 14 in London and by 1870 there were 167 in Manchester, see S.D. Chapman, "The International Houses: the Continental Contribution to British Commerce, 1800–1860," *Journal of European Economic History,* 6(1977), 5-48. The Jews missed an earlier opportunity in the sixteenth and seventeenth centuries. As late as the 1670s a French visitor stated that there was no "noteworthy family or foreign merchant who did not have a Jew working for them, either to appraise merchandize and judge its

quality, or to serve as interpreter or inform them of what was happening. . . .The other Oriental nations, like the Greeks, Armenians, etc. do not have this talent and do not attain their skill." But the reaction caused by the messianic claims of Sabbatai Ṣevi (in 1666) caused the Jewish community to turn its back on modern learning and to reduce its participation in outside activities. See M. Franco *Essai sur l'histoire des Israélites dans l'Empire Ottoman,* Paris, 1897 p. 115. However, on this point see also the introduction to Volume I, p. 24–26.

79. Robert Haddad, *Syrian Christians in Muslim Society,* Princeton, 1970, p. 40.

80. William Polk, (cited n. 5) p. 73, citing Boislecomte.

81. Hourani (cited n. 27), pp. 222-23.

82. Politis (cited n. 33), vol. 1, chapters one and two.

83. J. Bowring, "Report on Egypt and Candia," *UK Accounts and Papers,* 1840, vol. 21, pp. 80–82. In Cairo, out of 55 large firms, 15 were European, 10 Greek Catholic (Syrian), 6 Greek Orthodox and 24 "Turkish."

84. See Vartan Artinian, "A Study of the Historical Development of the Armenian Constitutional System in the Ottoman Empire, 1839–1863," Ph.D. Thesis, Brandeis University, 1969, pp. 18–19.

85. For the fierce struggle in 1815–26 between the Jewish *sarrafs,* who were linked to the Janissaries, and their Armenian rivals, and the tragic death of all the protagonists, see Franco (cited n. 78), pp. 133–140. By 1831 Slade could say "The Armenians are the chief bankers of European Turkey, having supplanted the Jews in that dangerous but lucrative employment in consequence of possessing superior honesty or rather inferior knavery." Adolphus Slade, *Records of Travel in Turkey, Greece, etc.,* London, 1854, p. 434.

86. Ainslie to Carmarthen, 10 January 1786, FO 78/6.

87. Hourani (cited n. 27), pp. 222–223.

88. Stanford Shaw, *The Financial and Administrative Organization and Development of Ottoman Egypt,* Princeton, 1962, p. 103.

89. Politis (cited n. 33), vol. 2, p. 279.

90. See Polk (cited n. 5), pp. 134–135.

91. Newmarch to Stronge, 29 April 1904, FO 195/2218; despatch FO 195/2340.

92. Despatch November 1911, FO 195/2369; for the role of Greeks and Armenians in the Ottoman agricultural bureaucracy, see Donald Quataert, "Ottoman Reform and Agriculture in Anatolia," Ph.D. Thesis, UCLA, 1973, pp. 64–128.

93. For the Dadians, see Edward Clark, "The Ottoman Industrial Revolution," *IJMES* 5(1974), pp. 65–76; for Jezairli and others, Indzhikyan (cited n. 1), pp. 160–171 and Report for 1851/52, FO 78/905.

94. Girard, "Mémoire," in *Description de l'Egypte,* Paris, 1809–22, vol. 17, p. 373.

95. Haddad (cited n. 79), pp. 32–49.

96. Report 24, April 1806, FO 78/50.

97. Board of Trade, 17 September 1790; Traian Stoianovitch, "The Conquering Orthodox Merchant," *JEH,* 20(1960), pp. 234–313.

98. FO 78/36.

99. Stanford Shaw, *Between Old and New,* Cambridge, Mass., 1971, pp. 177–179.

100. Note of 22 July 1876, FO 195/1113 and Wilson to Goschen, 11 May 1881, FO 78/3535. Perhaps even more important was the appointment of local consular agents. In a letter to the minister of foreign affairs of 20 March 1836 (CC Beirut, 2), the French consul in Beirut, Guys, pointed out that this innovation had begun in Egypt and been introduced into Syria under Muhammad ᶜAli; the Ottoman government had forbidden and punished such practices. "Since the dearest wish a *raya* can have is that of becoming a consul, there is no doubt that in future everything will be done to secure such a place."

101.   Cited by Polk (cited n. 5), p. 224.

102.   Rawlinson to Aberdeen, 25 April 1844, FO 78/574.

103.   List, 16 September 1850, FO 195/334.

104.   Livingstone to Tweedie, 15 August 1890, FO 195/1722.

105.   Mockler to the Wali of Baghdad, 18 January 1894, FO 195/1841. Armenian connections with India and other parts of Asia were very old. Armenians had played an important part in the trade of India, Indonesia and the Philippines in the seventeenth and eighteenth centuries—see Holden Furber, *Rival Empires of Trade in the Orient, 1600–1800* (Minneapolis, 1976) *passim.*

106.   Kemball to Bulwer, 10 September 1862, FO 195/717.

107.   Rawlinson to Redcliffe, 2 November 1853, FO 195/367.

108.   M. S. Lazarev, *Kurdistan i Kurdskaya Problema,* Moscow, 1964, pp. 32–37.

109.   See Antoine Rabbath, *Documents inédits pour servir à l'histoire du Christianisme en Orient,* Paris, 1910, vol. 2, pp. 167–85. Needless to say, the Syrian Christians often behaved foolishly when they felt protected against the Muslims. "The Christians of Damascus, who were horribly tyrannized by the Turks of this city and who now feel protected, are perhaps taking too great an advantage of the fortunate change that has taken place in their political existence. It is a fact that they miss no occasion to defy the Muslims and that this bluster has deplorable consequences for them in spite of the support of the authorities and the armed forces." Guys to Broglie, 3 June 1832, MAE, CC Beirut, 1 bis.

110.   Various despatches in FO 195/1113.

111.   Rassam to Ponsonby, 10 August 1841, FO 195/228.

112.   Rassam to Canning, 29 July 1843, ibid.

113.   Kemball to Lyons, 10 August 1867.

114.   Agent Mosul to Consul General, 11 January, 24 February and 1 July 1899, FO 195/2055 and 4 December 1900, FO 195/2074.

115.   Notes on the city of Mosul, FO 195/2308. More generally, for the indignities and vexations, or worse, suffered by Christians, see Consular Reports from Aleppo, Beirut, Damascus, Jerusalem, and Mosul, FO 195 series.

116.   Report on Trade, FO 78/654.

117.   Polk (cited n. 5), p. 135; H. Lammens, *Syrie,* Beirut, 1921, vol. 2, p. 156.

118.   C.F. Volney, *Travels Through Syria and Egypt,* London, 1788, vol. 2, p. 32.

119.   Issawi (cited n. 5), pp. 71–90; Baer (cited n. 14), pp. 7–12, 63–70.

120.   Report on Trade, FO 78/796.

121.   Reply to Questionnaire, FO 78/1525.

122.   Ibid., FO 78/1533.

123.   Polk (cited n. 5), p. 137.

124.   Eldridge to Elliot, 7 February 1876, FO 195/1113.

125.   Sir Charles Eliot, *Turkey in Europe,* New York, 1965, p. 153.

126.   *Istatiskik umumi idaresi,* Istanbul, 1316/1898.

127.   A. Synvet, *Les Grecs de l'empire Ottoman,* Istanbul, 1878, pp. 32–33.

128.   Artinian (cited n. 84), chapter 3.

129.   See Politis (cited n. 33), vol. 1, chapter 5, for details.

130.   Landau (cited n. 24), p. 71.

131.   Notes on the city of Mosul, FO 195/2308.

132.   Various despatches in FO 195/1201. Already, around 1830, Slade (cited n. 85), p. 288, had noted: "Some of the Greeks here [Philippopolis] spoke German tolerably. The most useful European language in Turkey is Spanish. All the Jews talk it, impurely certainly, but quite well

enough for interpretation; indeed their Spanish, such as it is, is their household language, Hebrew being considered classical. Moreover, Spanish is the chief ingredient of the lingua franca.''

133.   Donald M. Reid, ''Educational Career Choices of Egyptian Students, 1882–1922,'' *IJMES*, 8 (1977), 349–378; note also ''In the late 1940's, the proportion of Copts in Egyptian schools above the elementary reached one in four.'' Wakin (cited n. 16), p. 27.

134.   An incident related by the British consul in Baghdad illustrates an attitude that was becoming widespread among all the *millet*s: ''When a Jew (an Ottoman subject) named Salih bashi, who had been arrested for forcible resistance of the town authorities, was brought before the proper tribunal (or perhaps before H.E. the Wali) to be interrogated, he refused to answer unless the Foreign Consuls were present, an attitude on his part, as may easily be imagined, not calculated to mollify the Government.'' This and similar incidents led the United States consul to say it was ''The Baghdad Government rather than the Jews who stood in need of support.'' Tweedie to Ambassador at Constantinople, 17 November 1889, FO 78/4214. As against that, ''The French Consul has been rather posing as the Protector of the Christians, but I think he would be much wiser if he told them that he was in no position to protect them, which is the truth, and advized them to be very careful in their behaviour.'' Ramsay, Confidential Memorandum, 21 April 1909, FO 195/2039. As regards the painfully acquired wisdom of the fathers, the following story came to me from a highly trustworthy source. In 1943 General Catroux, feeling that France's position in Syria was becoming shaky, invited a delegation of Armenian notables in Aleppo. He explained that their situation would be perilous if France left and reminded them of the 1915 massacres and other horrors. A long silence followed, broken by the eldest and wisest Armenian, ''If I understand you right, you are seeking our help. But if you need our help, you must be in a very weak position. And if you are in such a position, it would be very unwise of us to offer you our help.''

135.   Berque (cited n. 19), p. 190.

136.   The most observant and scientifically minded Egyptian of his time, ᶜAlī Pasha Mubārak, writing in the early 1870s, had no doubts regarding both the population growth and the improvement in living conditions that had taken place since Muhammad ᶜAlī. See *Kitab Nukhbat al-fikr fī tadbīr Miṣr* Cairo, 1297/1880, p. 184. For the rise in mass consumption in 1885–89 to 1910–12, see Issawi, (cited n. 5), p. 365, and the sources cited there.

137.   Eliot (cited n. 125), p. 153.

138.   See Bernard Lewis, *The Emergence of Modern Turkey*, London, 1961, pp. 291–296.

139.   Wakin (cited n. 16), pp. 43–49.

14

Trade and Merchants in Nineteenth-Century Trabzon: Elements of Ethnic Conflict

A. ÜNER TURGAY

The expansion of European trade into the Black Sea after the Küçük Kaynarca Treaty of 1774 was the chief factor affecting Trabzon's economic development. This development unleashed a series of social changes among which demographic mobility and urbanization occupy an important place. Furthermore, the economic and social changes affected the various segments of Trabzon's population according to their religious and ethnic identity and conditioned to some extent their relations with Russia and other major European nations as well as with the Ottoman government.

The Anglo-Ottoman Commercial Convention of 1838 and various trade agreements with other powers soon after gave great impetus to European trade in Ottoman markets. By then, however, a fundamental change had already occurred in the ethnic composition of the Ottoman merchant class. Foreign trade in the Ottoman provinces in general and in the Black Sea region in particular, which had been dominated earlier by Muslim merchants, fell slowly under the monopoly of non-Muslim Ottoman merchants, chiefly of Greek and Armenian origin. During this transition a marked change also became apparent in the relations between foreign powers and the Christian Ottoman subjects. Already feeling morally bound to their coreligionists in the Ottoman Empire, the European powers also identified their own political and economic interests with those of the non-Muslim Ottoman subjects. Russia, having secured through the Küçük Kaynarca Treaty legal rights to represent the interests of the Orthodox Ottoman subjects at the Porte, buttressed her relations with the Orthodox by establishing ties with them. Britain, the major trading partner of the Ottomans, similarly preferred to establish commercial contacts with non-Muslim Ottoman merchants by using them as intermediaries in trade with the Ottoman state.

Throughout the nineteenth century, as international competition in the Ottoman markets increased, preference, explicit in formal legal arrangements, often without the Ottoman government's consent, reinforced the somewhat informal relations existing between non-Muslim Ottoman subjects and foreign powers. These Ottomans, mainly merchants, while often serving the economic interests of the European powers, came to control Ottoman foreign trade almost exclusively, and became the chief beneficiaries of it. Many of them maintained their economic positions by relying on European powers and Russia for protection.

By the end of the nineteenth century, most of the Ottoman state had experienced considerable economic growth. Paradoxically, this growth helped divide the Muslim and non-Muslim Ottoman subjects into two increasingly hostile groups. Ultimately, it undermined the multiethnic, multireligious foundations of the Ottoman Empire. In other words, while foreign trade was largely responsible for having stimulated the growth of the Ottoman economy and the modernization of its cities, the same economic factor was responsible for intensifying social differentiation among the various ethnic groups in the state, particularly in the port cities. Indeed, the sum of these economic developments and subsequent social changes was to stimulate ethnic consciousness on the side of both the Muslims and the Christians. In fact, the non-Muslim merchants, anxious to express their economic power in political terms, effectuated constitutional and structural changes in their respective *millet* systems.

This chapter will deal with the economic development of Trabzon and the factors which affected the changes in the ethnic composition of its merchant class during the nineteenth century. It will also examine relations of the city's merchants with the European powers, including Russia, and the attitudes of Muslim and non-Muslim merchants toward each other. Here, economic development is defined as the growth of foreign and transit trade and subsequent establishment of various institutions that serviced trade. The merchant class includes only those who operated from the city, indigenous as well as newcomers. Muslim merchants were, with few exceptions, Turkish.

Despite the military losses and political setbacks of the seventeenth century, the Ottoman Empire retained its economic vitality and it could indeed point to its trade in the Black Sea when measuring its success. This was the result of the state's ability to preserve the economic unity of the Black Sea region. Paradoxically, Ottoman political failures—particularly against Austria and especially after the Passarowitz Treaty in 1718—helped increase its trade. This created, in turn, a strong merchant class consisting of Muslims and non-Muslims alike. In the Black Sea the Ottoman merchants, chiefly Muslims and a few Greeks, controlled the entire trade despite increasing attempts by European powers to open this trade to their own merchants and ships. Evliya Çelebi, a keenly observant Ottoman traveler of the seventeenth century, had reported that there were eight thousand people in Istanbul, operating from two thousand shops and stores, who were specifically engaged in Black Sea trade supplying the needs of the capital by bringing cereals, rice, salt, honey, wax, tallow, butter, leather, and hides from the ports of Wallachia, the Crimea, and northern Anatolia. Henry

Grenville, the British ambassador and the chief officer of the Levant Company in Istanbul (1762–1765), commenting on the prosperity of the Black Sea trade, observed, "the trade of the Black Sea is so lucrative that one could consider nothing lost if of three ships, one returned safe and sound."[1]

The merchants of Trabzon also benefited from the liberalization and intensification of the interregional and international trade. Many Trabzon merchants and shipowners carried the produce of the region, such as hazelnuts, beans, fish, copper, and ship masts, as well as some Persian goods and Russian iron, to Istanbul. Their trade with the capital, the Crimean ports, and Wallachia and Moldavia provided them with a return cargo consisting chiefly of cotton cloth, hardware, paper, and foodstuffs.[2]

During the eighteenth century, as in the earlier centuries, European countries made repeated representations to the Porte requesting shipping and trading rights in the Black Sea for their own merchants, but the Ottomans repeatedly refused. It was with the Treaty of Küçük Kaynarca in 1774, following the Ottoman defeat by Russia, that the Black Sea was opened to Russian merchant ships. Article XI of the treaty provided "free and unmolested navigation" rights to Russian ships in the Black Sea and permitted "the subjects of the Russian Empire to carry on their commerce in her [the Ottoman] possessions on land as on sea, even as far as to sail on the Danube River." Also important, and with long-lasting repercussions, was Article VII of the treaty, which permitted "the Minister of the Imperial Court of Russia to represent on every occasion the cause of the church constructed at Constantinople . . . as well as the cause of those who serve the church. . . . "[3] In the following century this provision would offer easy pretext for the tsar's government and his consuls in the Ottoman territories to interfere in the Porte's affairs, indeed in the affairs of the provinces, especially in commercial matters. Commercial privileges granted to Russia were soon extended to the other European nations. First Austria in 1784, then England in 1799 and France in 1802 obtained the right to ply the waters of the Euxine.[4]

The loss of the control of the Black Sea trade had a profound impact on the economy of the Ottoman state. New trade and shipping patterns that developed deprived the Ottoman merchants of substantial income.[5] Equally important was the gradual change in the composition of the Ottoman merchant class. The merchants of the Black Sea ports had been predominantly Muslims, with a few Greeks, Armenians, and Jews. But in the decades that followed, Greek merchants began to acquire an upper hand in the Black Sea trade, some establishing themselves at Russian coastal towns.[6] This advantageous position of the Greek merchants was aided by the favorable treatment they received from the Russian tsar; the support they secured from the Phanariote rulers of Wallachia and Moldavia, supplemented by favorable legislation issued by these rulers directed toward the concerns of commercial groups; and the emigration of many Muslim merchants from northern Black Sea ports after the expansion of Russia into that region.

The Adrianople Treaty in 1829 gave victorious Russia distinct political and economic advantages. The complete emancipation from restrictions of Russian, and subsequently other European, navigation and trade in the Euxine and through the Straits helped accelerate these nations' commercial development in that region.[7] The Black Sea was no longer a scene of intense political and commercial rivalry between the Russians and the Ottomans, but became a very important region for the economic interests of every major European power.

The impact of the treaty was felt in Trabzon immediately. Its trade showed profound changes both in the quantity and composition of goods imported and exported. In 1828, for instance, its exports and imports were valued at 217,500 rubles and 1,105,000 rubles respectively. In 1830, a year after the treaty was concluded, Trabzon's exports more than doubled to reach 752,000 rubles, while imports totaled 5,270,000 rubles and consisted of woolen cloth, sugar, coffee, iron manufactures, as well as some luxury goods such as rum, porcelain, and cut glass.[8]

Before 1832 a considerable volume of the trade between Europe and Persia by way of the Black Sea centered on the Russian port of Redout Kale at the mouth of the Phasis. This resulted from the exemption granted by the *ukase* of October 8, 1821, to the Russian provinces to the south of the Caucasus, which freed these provinces from the duties charged on commodities in other parts of the empire; foreign goods were admitted at the lower duty of 5 percent. All the goods from Leipzig, for instance, were carried by land to Odessa and from there forwarded to Redout Kale across the Black Sea. From this port the goods were sent to Tiflis and Erevan and then distributed over the adjacent areas in Armenia, northern Persia; and the eastern Ottoman provinces. This traffic was handled almost exclusively by the Armenian merchants who first appeared as an important commercial group in Odessa in 1823 and began extensive business transactions in Leipzig in the following years. In 1824 the Armenian merchants brought more than 600,000 French francs worth of European manufactures from Leipzig. In 1825 their purchases rose to 1,200,000 francs and in 1826 to 2,800,000 francs.[9] In January of 1832, however, the Russian government, to encourage native manufacturers of cloth and to limit the imports of British and French goods into this region, decided to apply to the port those customs regulations and duties prevailing in other parts of the empire. Tiflis, about 220 miles inland from the Black Sea coast, was made the center of the customs administration. These regulations, coupled with the Russian blockade of the Circassian and Georgian coasts starting in 1831, forced a change from Redout Kale-Tiflis-Caspian Sea-Persia to a southern course, the Trabzon-Erzurum-Tabriz route.

Because of these actions by Russia and because the geographical location of Trabzon contributed to lower transportation costs for goods bound for Persia, the importance of Trabzon as a trading center continued to increase. In 1830 about five thousand packages valued at £250,000 were imported and forwarded to Persia; in 1834 about twelve thousand packages valued at £600,000 were similarly received and forwarded; by 1835, the number of packages increased to 19,327 with a total value of £996,350.[10]

Tabriz was the terminal point for the bulk of the European goods shipped through Trabzon and Persian merchants, along with a few Armenians, handled most of this trade in the mid-1830s while the city's commerce prospered.[11] In 1837, however, drastic changes occurred; the imports of Tabriz fell to approximately 12 million rubles from about 40 million in the previous year. The overconfident Persian merchants had extended themselves beyond their means and could no longer meet their debts to European firms. Consequently several major Persian merchants both in Istanbul and Tabriz went bankrupt. Their places were taken most often by Russian, Greek, and Armenian merchants. Indeed, some Greeks from Istanbul moved to Tabriz and established trading houses, gradually taking control of an important portion of the city's foreign trade. Efforts by the Persian merchants to obstruct them were unsuccessful. Tellingly, most of the Greek merchants had assumed Russian consular protection. In addition, Russian customs authorities, while affording minimum formalities to Russian, Greek, and Armenian merchants trading between Persia and Russia, started causing unnecessary delays to Persian merchants, particularly to those who carried British goods.[12]

These developments also affected the trading community in Trabzon. As the activities of the Armenian and Greek merchants of the Russian Black Sea ports and Tabriz increased, the position of the non-Muslim Ottoman merchants— Armenians and Greeks—in Trabzon, acting as intermediaries, became increasingly important. Some established partnerships with their kinsmen in Tabriz; others frequently traveled to Istanbul to supervise in person large orders coming from the Persian market. Meanwhile, these merchants attracted the increasing attention of both the Russian and the British consuls at Trabzon, who naturally saw them as sole agents of European trade. The legations viewed these merchants as indispensable if they were to expand the trade of their respective countries into the eastern Ottoman provinces and northern Persia.

In the 1830s, two developments further stimulated Trabzon's trade: the establishment of steamship services to Trabzon and the signing of the Anglo-Ottoman Commercial Convention of 1838. In 1836 the first steamer, a British one, began service on the Istanbul-Samsun-Trabzon route. This pioneer effort was followed in 1837 by the establishment of an Ottoman steamship line on the same route. Soon afterward, Austrian, French, and Russian companies followed suit. The success of each line often depended, however, upon the political events and economic policies of their respective governments.[13]

During the last two decades of the century, as the number of nations trading with and through Trabzon increased, new lines extended their services to this port, and by the late 1890s ten companies serviced Trabzon. Two significant developments, however, took place in the process. First, vessels under sail, unable to compete with the steamers, lost a large share of their business. After the Crimean War (1853–1856), the Greek owners of a number of these vessels found it more profitable to operate between the small ports along the Russian coast, chiefly carrying grains and sailing under the Russian flag. A few left Trabzon for the Aegean Archipelago, carrying olives, currants, citrus fruits, and tobacco, and sailed between the islands and Izmir and Salonica, flying Greek colors.[14] The vessels owned by the Muslim captains confined their operations to the transport of inexpensive bulk goods such as wood, charcoal, and sand.[15] Second, except *Idare-i Mahsusa* (formerly the *Osmaniye* Company) which employed a Turk, and the Deutsche–Levant Line, represented by a local Swiss agent, every steamship company, European or other, appointed non-Muslim Ottomans as agents at Trabzon. A semiofficial publication of 1896–1897 listed the following companies and representatives:[16]

Company	Agent
Deutsche-Levant Line	Hochstrasse and Company
The Danoise	M. Khidichian
The Ege	Phostiropoulos
Austrian Lloyd	A. Sassi
Messageries Maritimes	Boyadighi
General Italian Navigation Co.	A. Mahokian
Pan-Hellenic Company	N. D. Constantinoff
Paquet Company	M. Missir
Russian Navigation Co.	E. Serafimow
Russian Black Sea Company	Phostiropoulos

Similar appointments were in effect at Samsun and other Ottoman Black Sea ports.[17] Despite creating some hardship and dislocation for the owners of sailing vessels, the expansion of steamship lines to Trabzon benefited the region's trade, while offering new economic opportunities chiefly to non-Muslim Ottoman commercial agents.

The Anglo-Ottoman Commercial Convention, which was signed in 1838, indeed set the tone of the Ottoman commercial policies for the rest of the century. It removed all Ottoman monopolies, allowed British merchants to purchase goods anywhere in the Ottoman domains, and imposed duties of 5 percent on imports, 12 percent on exports, and 3 percent on transit.[18] Soon after, trade agreements based on similar terms were signed with other major European powers and Russia.

The convention gave great impetus to British trade in Ottoman markets. Other foreign powers trading with the Ottomans also made outstanding advances. It furthermore allowed Ottoman agriculture to realize its full potential by lifting monopolistic restrictions. This agreement did, however, open the way to the decline and dislocation of Ottoman industries and handicrafts, especially in the second half of the century. In years to come these changes would profoundly affect the trade at the Ottoman ports as well as the general economy of the state.

The favorable effects of the convention were felt early in Trabzon. In 1838 Trabzon closed the year with a total trade value of £1,858,287,[19] whereas during the five-year period from 1846 through 1850 yearly imports and exports averaged over £1,700,000 and £500,000 respectively. Goods destined for Persia, mostly British-made manufactures, still made up the major portion of the imports; in exports, the share of the local produce increased, though it did not match the value of Persian goods shipped from Trabzon.

The Crimean War markedly affected Trabzon's trade; many needs of the Allied armies in the Crimean peninsula were supplied through this port. In 1855 the total value of imports reached a record £2,432,160 while exports exceeded those of the previous year by £53,047.[20] Immediately after the war, the trade of Trabzon continued to expand. In 1857 and 1858 imports totaled £3,293,422 and £3,750,529 respectively, though exports dropped from £1,483,334 to £1,228,794, chiefly as the result of a declining demand in Europe for Persian silk.[21] Incoming trade was stimulated also by increased steamship activity.

In the 1860s and 1870s Trabzon's trade decreased and then leveled off (see Appendix 1 at the end of the chapter). Factors such as the silkworm disease, which broke out in Persia in 1864 and lasted several years, and the fall of European demand for Persian cotton after the American Civil War ended, certainly caused a decrease in Trabzon's trade volume. More than these, however, two developments during this period permanently undermined the importance of the Trabzon-Erzurum-Tabriz route. First, the opening of the Suez Canal in 1869 greatly reduced the sailing time between Europe and the Persian Gulf and attracted a considerable portion of Trabzon's trade, especially the British trade, to the new route. Second, the building of an alternate route by Russia in the Caucasus specifically for the purpose of diverting the Persian transit trade to her own territories altered the direction of the Persian-European trade.[22] Pressing demands on the Ottoman budget, coupled with the reduction of the transit duties to 1 percent in 1869, in accordance with the 1861-1862 trade agreements, left little incentive for the Porte to undertake any costly competition with the Poti-Tiflis road.[23] In the last two decades of the nineteenth century, Trabzon's trade gradually declined.[24] The British, the prime users of the Trabzon-Erzurum-Tabriz route, and a number of other European countries continued to carry their manufactures, albeit at reduced volumes, through Trabzon to northern Persia and the eastern Ottoman provinces in exchange for the produce of these regions.

In the nineteenth century, the European powers exerted increased political and economic influence on the Ottoman Empire. At the same time, based on political, economic, and religious considerations, they assumed protective roles regarding the Christian Ottoman population. As Europeans initiated broader economic and technological changes, the economic influence and control of Christian elements in the Ottoman Empire expanded. These groups became increasingly involved in the commercial activities of the state, as intermediaries between the European interests and the local population. A knowledge of Western languages was also necessary for conducting foreign trade and many urban Greeks and Armenians learned to speak French or English.[25] These factors, besides personal connections in the major trading centers of Europe, provided the Armenian and Greek Ottoman traders with sure opportunities to assume prominent positions in foreign trade.

A very special relationship developed between the non-Muslim Ottoman subjects and the European powers—Russia included. These countries viewed

Greek and Armenian merchants not only as valuable intermediaries to extend their own economic interests but also as means to fulfill their political ambitions. Thus, major European countries, through their legations, provided various means of support to Christian Ottoman subjects, chiefly to merchants.

This general situation in the Ottoman Empire, that is the economic dominance of non-Muslims and the protection afforded to them by European powers, was clearly reflected in Trabzon. According to a British document dated 1884, the foreign trade of Trabzon had clearly come under the domination of Greek and Armenian merchants (see Appendix II). Of the fourteen major commission agents in the city, three were Persian, one was Swiss, and the rest were Greek and Armenian. Out of thirty-three exporters, only three were Turkish, exporting, incidentally, foodstuffs, hazelnuts, and tobacco to Istanbul—that is, dealing with traditional produce in a domestic market. The Swiss firm Hochstrasse and Company exported similar products to Europe; the remaining exporters were again Greeks and Armenians. Among the sixty-three major importers a similar situation prevailed. Aside from the two local associations (the tailors' and the shoemakers' societies), only ten Turkish merchants were involved in the importation of European goods. A large portion of the British trade passed through the Armenian and Greek commercial houses and agencies in Istanbul.[26] These large firms extended considerable credit to their kinsmen residing in Trabzon and facilitated shipments to that port with minimum requirements, thus providing a competitive advantage to merchants of these ethnic groups.

A similar situation existed in professional services that catered to foreign trade. Until the last decade of the nineteenth century the use of insurance was very limited in Trabzon. Some major European insurance companies, such as Manheimer Transport Veroicherungs Gesellschaft, the Helvetia, and the Lloyd Suisse, had been represented in the city by local professional men, chiefly Greek lawyers. Toward the end of the century, however, as some bulk goods gave way to more delicate and expensive European manufactures and machinery, and as new nations began trading with Trabzon, more companies opened offices in the city. Since the insurance business was new to the general public, a few Europeans, acting as agents, at first worked in partnership with local merchants who could easily communicate with other exporters and importers and were familiar with conditions peculiar to the locale. Later when these Europeans left Trabzon for Izmir and Istanbul for superior economic opportunities, ownership of the insurance agencies passed to their local partners. By mid-1894 these fourteen insurance companies were represented at Trabzon:[27]

Company	Agent
Marine Insurance Company of London	J. Enepekoglou & Sons
North British Mercantile and Northern Company	Agop Shvarsh
The Patriotic Insurance Company	A. Sciandaphylidis
The New York Life Insurance Company	S. Ekmedjian
Cie. Gle. de Dresden	A. Mahokian
Manheimer Transport Veroicherungs	Boghos O. Marimian
La Foncière et Union de Paris	A. Sciandaphylidis
Ottoman Insurance Company	Imperial Ottoman Bank
Helvetia	Hochstrasse & Company
Lloyd Suisse	Hochstrasse & Company
British Lloyd	Hochstrasse & Company
La Badoise	Nourian Brothers
La Maritime Belge	Boghos O. Marimian
Cie. Francfortaise	Boghos O. Marimian

Except Hochstrasse and Company, which represented two Swiss firms and one British firm, and the Ottoman Bank, which acted as an agent for its own insurance subsidiary, the agents were non-Muslim Ottomans.

In 1895 and 1896, as new insurance companies opened offices in Trabzon, they too employed non-Muslim Ottomans as agents:[28]

Company	Agent
Assicurazioni Generali di Trieste	A. Sassi
Balkan	Sahatdjian & Sons
La Nationale d'Athènes	S. Yorghanteli
L'Alliance de Berlin	P. Grammaticopulo
La Providentia	N. P. Haldeopoulo
Manchester	G. Ch. Mouzenides
Marine Insurance Company of London (a new office)	J. Enepekoglou & Sons

Hence, within a short time after its introduction into the economic life of Trabzon, the industry was managed chiefly by the members of Greek and Armenian communities. Once again Muslim merchants and agents were excluded from an important economic opportunity.

In extending protection to Christian Ottomans, European diplomats and consuls in major Ottoman cities abused privileges granted to them through capitulations. They extended the rights accorded to their own nationals to some non-Muslims Ottoman subjects for political and economic aims and interfered in the proceedings of the Ottoman tribunals. The most common form of abuse was the issuance of *berat*s of protection or, in many cases, passports. Here they created a special privileged class—the protégés—and through capitulatory concessions, helped them obtain tax exemptions and preferential treatment in business transactions. This practice, especially intensified during the Crimean War, spread throughout every province of the Ottoman Empire after the war, "so that thousands of native-born Christians in all chief centers of commerce" came under the protection of European powers.[29] In addition, many Ionian and Maltese Greeks and Armenians from Persia traveled and conducted their business with British and Russian passports respectively.[30] This protection policy was largely inspired by commercial interests. The desire of the Europeans to protect those people who served them, even though their interests conflicted with those of the Ottomans, increased the scope of this wardship.

A similar situation had also existed in Trabzon since the 1830s, intensifying in the 1850s. In 1836, for instance, a few years after the establishment of the British consulate, there were five people under British protection besides the consul, including two Greek merchants. In 1844 the number increased to thirty-two and included several merchants from the Ionian Islands, as well as a few Maltese, and local Greek traders and shopkeepers.[31] In 1855, however, the number of people under the protection of the British consul at Trabzon increased to sixty-seven and also included a few Greeks who had moved to Trabzon from their native Greece (see Appendix III). Reporting for the neighboring port of Samsun to the Foreign Office in November 1856, Consul Guarracino included forty-three names on his list, excluding families, ten of which were Armenian and Greek Ottomans, and summarized the protection policy thus:

> Consular authorities of France protect the Roman Catholic Rayahs as a matter of right; in other respects foreign consuls pursue much the same system as we do—they protect all Turkish subjects employed in the Consulates or acting as mercantile agents for European houses.[32]

In Trabzon, the British consul also extended his protection to a group of Italian subjects, who numbered thirty-seven in 1868, "by a temporary, but frequently renewed arrangement," as well as "Officious Patronage, rather than Protection" to a group of Wallachians residing in the city.[33] In general, however, the British consuls at Trabzon exercised caution in granting protection to these groups as well as to local residents, usually seeking the approval of the Ottoman authorities and always obtaining the permission of the embassy in Istanbul. In the late 1870s, for instance, when the Persian and Armenian residents of the city asked for British protection because they were partners in some London and Manchester firms, the request was adjudged "a very objectionable arrangement" and was thus denied.[34]

The Russian consul at Trabzon, on the other hand, as reported by the British consul, availed himself "of every opportunity, to extend his protection"[35] to all foreigners, particularly to Greek and Armenian residents of the city. The abuses of their diplomatic privileges by the Russian consuls were evident as early as 1820s. Particularly after the Russo-Ottoman War of 1828–1829, the tsar's consuls at Trabzon and Erzurum, along with the commanders of the Russian forces that occupied Kars, Beyazit, and Erzurum during the war, concentrated their efforts to entice the non-Muslim Ottoman subjects to emigrate to Russia and issued certificates putting them under Russian protection.[36]

The practice of extending protection or issuing passports to local Greek and

Armenian Ottomans by the Russian consul in Trabzon continued in the 1840s. In May 1848 the British consul F. J. Stevens, in his special dispatch to Stratford Canning, confirmed the latest occurrences of such and explained a routine procedure that was followed:

> A number of the Christians belonging to this town [Trabzon], more especially from the Greek Community, have within the past few months become Russian subjects, and I understand that a large number are on the eve of obtaining similar protection. The Christians here are all more or less traders with Georgia, and after a short residence at Redout Kaleh, and other places on that coast whither they resort to trade, procure Russian passports. Their chief object in changing their nationality, is to facilitate their affairs, and many for the sake of evading the payment of taxes here. Some of them first obtain Wallachian passports, and these are afterwards exchanged for those of Russia, a matter easily accomplished. It is impossible not to consider this business as a great abuse, and detrimental to the Turkish Government, which should take some decisive measure to put a stop thereto. If this is not done, every Rayah here will belong to Russia in the course of a few years.[37]

The Crimean War temporarily slowed down or stopped these arrangements.[38] In the years that immediately followed, however, the Russian authorities in Georgia and the consul at Trabzon continued to grant passports to non-Muslim Ottomans in Trabzon, in many instances urging them to receive protection. In October 1858, Consul Stevens reported that it was "impossible to state accurately the number of natives of Trebizond who have resorted to Russian protection within the last two or three months, but it can be fairly calculated at two hundred, chiefly individuals from the commercial and working classes."[39] Indeed, in February of the same year, Stevens, "through the kind aid of respectable Greeks and Armenians," had obtained a list of those who acquired Russian passports within eighteen months after the Crimean War and sent it to his embassy with the following remark:

> The Greeks and Armenians whose names I have given may be considered as less than half of those in Trebizond possessing documents of the description already mentioned . . . it must be also recollected that my list refers only to persons in Trebizond and its immediate vicinity, without reference to crews of ships and coasting boats and the emigrants from the interior, nor those going to Russia from the numberless ports and roadsteads along this coast . . . the arduous exertions of the Russian Consul to obtain subjects, know no bounds. . . . The Greek and apparently also the Austrian Consuls aid and assist their Russian colleague— especially the first named, whose Government has lately granted several passports to Turkish subjects in Trebizond and its vicinity—some of the holders obtained them by visiting some parts of Greece and others from the Greek legation at Constantinople.[40]

The list shows several interesting facts. Of the eighty-nine Greeks listed, forty-two were merchants or traders, thirteen were merchants' clerks or servants, six were shopkeepers, and one was a moneychanger; the rest were, for the most part, involved in occupations requiring skilled labor—master mariners, stone-cutters, tailors, and tinners. Of the 116 Armenians listed, seventy-seven were merchants, six were storekeepers, nine were sailors or boatmen. The rest were clerks, servants, a coppersmith, and so forth. Also, most of the people, both among the Greeks and Armenians, fell within the age groups of twenty and forty (average age: 28.8). Apparently the non-Muslim Ottomans who enjoyed Russian protection in Trabzon were, in general, young, skilled in a specific trade and often merchants with knowledge of various commercial transactions and well-established contacts, and with capital. The Ottoman Empire was evidently being deprived of the full potential of a very important segment of its population. Russia, by extending her protection, was in fact providing the Greeks and Armenians in Trabzon with various capitulatory privileges and thus enhancing their domination of the city's economic life.

This practice enabled the Russian consulate at Trabzon to collect substantial fees. Interestingly, the consular fees were fixed according to the "classes of merchants," indicative of Russia's expectations that applicants would be chiefly merchants:[41]

	Silver Rubles
A. For all visas granted by Russian authorities to Ottoman subjects (going to or coming from Russia)	1½
B. For certificates of oath and cost of passport	
first-class merchant	700
second-class merchant	410
third-class merchant	100
For mere resident	5
C. An annual fee for every person who took the oath as residents, whether they were in Russia or abroad	3

For the Christian Ottoman subjects under protection the advantages they secured by obtaining Russian passports far outweighed these fees. For the Russians, these passports also served their long-term interests in the Ottoman Empire. With so many non-Muslim Ottoman subjects under her protection Russia acquired additional pretexts for involving herself in the affairs of the Porte as well as in the operations of the local governments, particularly in commercial matters. Also, Russia was gradually gaining the allegiance of that portion of the Ottoman population under its protection while alienating them from their own government.[42]

The Porte, however, made serious efforts to check the issuance of passports to its subjects by foreign powers. On January 27, 1852, it sent a note to every foreign legation in Istanbul, declaring it would no longer recognize such protection unless extended to Ottoman subjects working in the service of the embassies or consulates. In September 1860 a similar memorandum was issued stating that the new protégés would be subject only to Ottoman jurisdiction and could leave the state if they wished within three months after their declaration of a change of nationality.[43] Both these notes, however, were ineffectual.[44] A memorandum of April 24, 1862, which requested that the foreign legations settle the problem with the Porte in terms agreeable to both sides, led to the regulation of August 9, 1863. This defined the relations between Ottoman subjects and foreign powers, strictly limiting the extension of protection in the future.[45] The regulation checked the practice to a degree, but it was only after the issuance of the Nationality and Naturalization Law of January 19, 1869, which was not to be applied retroactively, that the arbitrary extension of protection was brought under control. Nevertheless, Russia still invoked the practice wherever possible.[46]

Despite the efforts of many Armenian and Greek merchants in Trabzon to secure foreign protection, there is no evidence that the Porte or local government attempted to curtail the economic activities of these groups. For instance, the collection of duties on tobacco for the 1851–1853 period was entrusted to a Greek Ottoman merchant, Vassilio Fengirmenzipulo; in 1854 another local merchant, Dimitri Çarvinsky, assumed this responsibility.[47] Similarly, in the early 1860s revenues in Trabzon, "of several branches, the most indeed, of Public Dues and Taxes,"[48] were collected by the Armenian Ottoman subjects. Actually, in the late 1850s, several non-Muslim residents of Trabzon, merchants and otherwise, received decorations sent by the Istanbul government.[49] Though the protection by foreign powers of its subjects, merchants and nonmerchants alike, irked the Porte, its relations with them, especially in economic matters, remained undisturbed.

Relations between the Muslim and the non-Muslim merchants in Trabzon, on the other hand, presented a different picture. The Muslim merchants, subject to higher taxes than their protected non-Muslim counterparts and often drawn into the jurisdiction of consular courts in commercial disputes, were not only annoyed but actually lost considerable leverage in the economic life of the city. The superiority the Greek and Armenian merchants who held Russian passports displayed, transformed the Muslims' initial mild annoyance into firm resentment. There were cases, indeed, in which funds owed a Muslim merchant were denied by a non-Muslim debtor on the mere grounds of his carrying a foreign passport.[50] The situation in nearby Samsun dramatizes the general conditions. On August 6, 1858, the British Consul Guarracino made this report:

> The number of Greeks styling themselves Russian subjects increases daily, and their insolence and arrogance towards the Turks become at times unbearable. . . . The Russian consul's mode of protecting these new Russian subjects is at times very exasperating to the Turks—so much so, that the Pasha has on more than one occasion said to me that he is obliged to employ every means in his power, in order to be on his guard, and to prevent some unpleasant catastrophe happening to the Christians in the Place. These are no doubt serious remarks to make, but I must confess, that taking into consideration the Russian Agent's way of acting, and other incidents, which have occurred in this neighborhood, in connection with the Russian protected Rayahs, I should not feel astonished if the Turkish population lost command of itself some day.[51]

As similar reports reached Istanbul from Erzurum[52] and elsewhere, a group of

Muslim merchants at Trabzon expressed their discontent in a petition to Mehmet Ragıp Paşa, the governor of Trabzon, on February 19, 1858. Their commendatory statements on the *Hatt-ı Hümayun* of 1856 was followed by these remarks:

> Since some time back, the non-Mahomedans residing at Trebizond have surpassed the equality and turn a superior face to the Mahomedans, who though they reluctantly accept this, cannot satisfy them (the Christians) and when they have any business with anyone, they reply that they are holders of Passports and we may say also oppose the authorities and in every case touch the honor of Musulman subjects.
>
> We the undersigned . . . since many years established as Merchants and pursuing an honorable path and trading constantly with them (the Christians) have seen their wish, by their conduct, to trample upon Mahomedan Subjects and but for our business, property and connections in this Town, we would have all been driven to emigration—not being able to suffer any longer the repeated attempts to touch our honor. . . .
>
> We therefore humbly pray, that proper measures may be adopted for saving our honor and adjusting these matters.[53]

The document shows how strongly the Muslim merchants felt. They were frustrated because of economic inequity, and, perhaps more importantly, they were beginning to view the whole situation as a threat to their honor, a sensitive personal and social issue.

The petition prompted the governor to send a circular the next day to the heads of the Greek and Armenian Orthodox and Protestant communities. Ragıp Paşa diagnosed the problem as a "matter capable of creating a public perturbation" and asked the leaders to issue "stringent instructions" to their communities, "requiring them to abstain from such unbecoming acts . . . towards their Mussulman fellow subjects, in a manner reconcilable with the dictates of humanity, justice and good feeling, as a fellow citizens and neighbors."[54] Thus, not only the British consul at Samsun but the governor of Trabzon as well was seriously concerned over the implications of granting passports to non-Muslim Ottoman merchants.

In a joint letter the following day from the bishops to the governor, malfeasance on the part of the non-Muslims that would demean the person or position of any Muslim was categorically denied. The letter further stated that some members of their community were disturbed because "the offensive epithet of *Giavur* has again been used without restraint in the streets and in certain meetings." Emphasizing the efforts of the Christian community in maintaining good relations with the Muslims, the leaders continued:

> The complaint brought against us has filled us with grief and sorrow . . . the expressions used in your Excellency's letter respecting the disturbance of the public peace coupled with a complaint that is unfounded has caused agitation, the more so when it is considered that the complaints are Mussulmans of the higher class. If they are animated with such sentiments, what must be those of lower sphere. . . .[55]

Whether the non-Muslim officials were unaware of the situation, or, whether they just chose to deny it, is not clear. In either case the correspondence distinctly shows the growing rift between Muslim and non-Muslim segments of the population in general and the increasing tension between the merchants belonging to these groups in particular in Trabzon. But as long as the Porte could not prevent the issuance of passports to its non-Muslim subjects, the situation remained the same. The governor of Trabzon could not institute strict measures independent of the central government.[56] Although after 1869 much of this abusive practice was checked, the seeds of discontent had been firmly planted among the Muslim population.

The resentment created by this situation and later reflected in the political events of the late nineteenth and early twentieth centuries could well be assessed as one of the important factors in the conflicts between the different ethnic groups. Indeed, in January 1868, after traveling through Erzurum, Kars, Ardahan, Amasya, Çorum, and Yozgat districts, the British consul of Trabzon, investigating complaints that the Christian Ottoman subjects were being oppressed by the "government officials and by some fanatic Muslims," exonerated the local administrations and the Muslim population from charges and summarized his observations as follows:

> Not on the coasts only, but in the centermost interior, the very supposed focus of Mahometan fanaticism, by the manner in which the Christians of those districts flaunt their ostentatious wealth in splendid houses, gay dresses, and all the ornament of prosperity, a manner wholly incompatible with anything of that oppression so much talked of for them at a distance. Among the Mahometan population these conditions are sadly reversed. It is a mistake, though not an unfrequent one, to attribute the evident prosperity of the Christians in Turkey, by comparison with the Mahometans, to some greater energy on their part, industry, and other virtues. Truth is, that in vigour, in probity, and in steady work the Mahometans are, as a rule, decidedly ahead of their Greek and Armenian fellow countrymen. But the former have been and are systematically overburdened, not to say oppressed, while the latter, under protection of their advantageous position in the Ottoman Empire, have been enriching themselves for the last half century, mainly by questionable speculation. . . . As matters now stand, the Ottoman Government lies under the very serious charge of oppressing its Mahometan, in favor of its Christian subjects. I regret to have to confirm the charge.[57.]

A few weeks later, writing from Trabzon to Lord Lyons at the British embassy in Istanbul on "the treatment of the Greek and other Christian subjects of the Sultan," the consul stressed the point the governor of Trabzon had made a decade earlier:

> It is precisely in these same quarters [where the complaints originate], and among the Greek and Armenian populations, that foreign, and especially Russian, influence and intrigue are most real and active, rendering the Christians hereabouts habitually restless, and exciting the suspicions of the Mahometans. And should at any time some general manifestation of illwill or outbreak, though of that there is at present no sign, occur, such influence and intrigue, and no other, will be the cause. . . . The complaints of the Christians, and especially of the Greeks, here at least, are unjust. They do not aim at equality, which they have already got, but at mastery.[58]

Reports of this nature, besides fostering an awareness of the increasing Russian influence among non-Muslim Ottoman subjects, perhaps induced British diplomats in Istanbul to show minimum resistance in 1869 when the Porte issued the laws dealing with nationality.

The non-Muslim Ottoman merchants, while receiving the support and protection of European powers, opposed the establishment of European-manned offices which could have broken their near-monopoly over foreign trade and economic life of Trabzon. They were able to do so because of their strong social basis. On several occasions, European firms attempted to establish branch offices in the city. They were hindered in their efforts, however, by the opposition of local Armenian and Greek merchants. The British consul made this clarifying report in 1871:

> I know of only two European commercial houses—the one Swiss, the other German-Swiss—that have to any degree succeeded in honourably holding their own; and even they have only been enabled to do so by means of continued Consular support and protection—a protection without which not merely the scanty direct, but the much larger indirect, British trade in these harbours would, as matters stand, be seriously impaired, if not checked altogether.[59]

Two years earlier he observed the pressures the Armenian and Greek traders exerted on the Turkish and European merchants who wanted to engage in large scale foreign and domestic trade, and said this:

> It is precisely the unwillingness to enter into competition with Armenians and Greeks that has hitherto confined the only European house (a Swiss one) established at Trebizond to commission and agency business, instead of trading on their own account. . . . The only thing that renders trading possible is precisely that which is most often and most unjustly complained of, namely, the Turkish Presidency and elements in the Tribunal of Commerce. Were that element withdrawn, and the direction of affairs left solely in the hands of the native Christians, all commerce would come to a speedy end, from a sheer impossibility of trust and credit.[60]

This situation stood in the way of establishing a more advanced capitalist system in Trabzon.

The development of economic activity and the ethnic composition of merchants in Trabzon during the nineteenth century should be viewed in conjunction with demographic changes in the city. An English traveler visiting Trabzon in 1813 estimated the city's population at fifteen thousand people, consisting mostly of Turks and some Greeks and Armenians, followed by Lazes, Tatars, and Circassians.[61] After Trabzon regained its importance as a trading center—particularly after the Adrianople Treaty in 1829—new opportunities in the city attracted people from the neighboring provinces. By 1835, Trabzon's population practically doubled to between twenty-five and thirty thousand inhabitants. Of these figures twenty to twenty-four thousand were Muslims, thirty-five hundred to four thousand Greeks, and the remaining fifteen hundred to two thousand Armenians. Among the Muslim population, the Turks composed a great majority, followed by Lazes, Tatars, Circassians, Kurds, and the Persian merchants residing in Trabzon.[62]

The Crimean War was responsible for causing important demographic changes in Trabzon. While the port became a major supply center for the Ottoman armies in the Crimea and the eastern Anatolian provinces, the volume of trade increased and the commercial activity in the city reached its peak. To provide the services the city's intensive trade necessitated, many people from the neighboring towns and villages moved into Trabzon. In 1855–1856, the region suffered a serious drought. Food shortages resulted, particularly in the villages, forcing many farm workers to migrate to the city.[63] By the end of 1856 the total population of Trabzon had risen to about seventy thousand.[64] The immigrants included many Greeks and Armenians who lived in nearby towns as well as a substantial number of Turks from the villages. Most of the Armenians and Greeks entered new occupations and provided diversified services in the large trading houses of their kinsmen. The Turks, on the other hand, were mainly employed by the building trades. The Crimean War created a rich class, chiefly non-Muslim merchants, and the lavish spending of these merchants stimulated the rapid growth of the city. Large reserves of accumulated capital were placed into the building of warehouses, inns, and large private homes. In January 1857 the British consul at Trabzon made this observation:

> Trebizond locally has materially improved: The three years' war threw a great quantity of gold into the place, and several of the chief Traders have been benefitted. Buildings are daily rising, the town assumed a remarkable extension, the natives are better clothed and live better, and although the poor have been thinned by suffering and privation, strangers from all parts fill up the gap.[65]

Many Turks among the immigrants were also employed at minimal wages in public projects, such as the betterment of the Trabzon-Erzurum road and the repair of bridges financed by the local government. In the following years, however, many of these migrant workers returned to their villages and once again occupied themselves with subsistence farming while some moved to Istanbul to put their newly acquired skills in construction to use in the capital.

After Trabzon's trade began leveling off at the end of the Crimean War, its population decreased. In 1860 the population of the city was 55,700 and consisted of forty thousand Turks and Muslims of other ethnic origins, ten thousand Greeks, thirty-six hundred Armenians, fifteen hundred Europeans or people "enjoying European protection," and six hundred Persians.[66] Less than ten years later, when Trabzon's trade began to decline, the British consul in the city reported the population as over thirty-four thousand with the following composition:[67]

	Male	Female	Total
Turks	8,175	10,763	18,938
Greeks	3,280	3,241	6,521
Armenians	2,913	2,989	5,902
Tatars			800
Others:			
Persians			320
Wallachians			80
French (some engineers and small shopkeepers)			51
Russians (mostly Armenian and Greek-Ottoman subjects with Russian pseudo-passports purchased at Odessa)			342
Italians (mostly druggists)			51
Austrians			29
British (a Maltese family; not including the staff of the consulate)			5
Greeks			92
Misc. (pack-horse drivers, sailors, etc.)			1,000
		Total	34,131

During the rest of the century the population of the city remained steady. In 1891, Vital Cuinet estimated Trabzon's population at thirty-five thousand, with nineteen thousand Turks, eighty-two hundred Greeks, six thousand Armenians, and thirteen hundred others.[68]

In the nineteenth century two distinct population trends could be observed in Trabzon. First, changes in the size of the population were directly related to the volume of trade at the port. During the years when trade was intense, new opportunities attracted the inhabitants of the towns and villages around Trabzon into the city. Many of the newcomers, however, left as the trade stabilized. Second, although every segment of the population had risen by over 100 percent by the peak trading years, the Turks, involved mostly in supporting services, were the first to leave the city during the years of commercial decline. This can be attributed to the marginal nature of their services. Lack of employment forced them to return to their previous occupations in the interior or to seek opportunities elsewhere. Of the non-Muslim immigrants who had moved to Trabzon, those from the neighboring towns, with better educational and trade backgrounds, remained in the city; those coming from the rural areas, however, could no longer support themselves once the commercial activity at Trabzon had decreased. These trends indicate that economic opportunity and ethnic affiliation provided, to a good degree, a basis for community formation in Trabzon.

The European powers, in order to strengthen their own political and economic positions in the Ottoman Empire, supported the Christian Ottoman population in general and non-Muslim merchants in particular, causing social and economic imbalance in Ottoman society. Also, this interference gave a new direction to the development of the Ottoman economic structure, later influencing the sociopolitical system. The dominant position of the non-Muslim merchants in the economic life of Trabzon and the subsequent high social status attained by them led to divisions that were undoubtedly stronger than those based on religious differences. Conceivably, these merchants, in the eyes of the Turkish-Muslim majority, were identified with their respective ethnic communities in general, thereby broadening the prevalent resentment. This situation should be viewed as an important contributing factor to the conflicts between different ethnic groups and the motivations of political organizations during the events of the late nineteenth and early twentieth centuries in the Trabzon region.

The middle class, albeit rather small, which existed in the urban Ottoman society in the nineteenth century, was mostly composed of non-Muslims who had limited access to the Ottoman political system. Their direct political influence was mainly confined to those developments within their respective *millets*. The fact that this middle class could not effectively participate in the policymaking of the central government frustrated its ability to effect political change and at least indirectly encouraged it to continue to concentrate its energies in that area which it could influence—trade. At the same time, the Muslim elite which did have political power had fallen behind in this same, important aspect of economic life. Thus, each group became alienated from the other and reinforced its own position. Because of this situation and the fact that there were no institutionalized means for the merchants to communicate with the government, the Porte did little to adjust its policies to reflect the economic realities of the modern world.

Later, the control of commercial activities by non-Muslim groups stimulated the development of nationalistic economic policies by the Young Turks. The dramatic decrease in the size of this merchant class in Turkey as a result of political events in the early twentieth century—especially after the Greek-Turkish population exchange in 1924—created a vacuum of entrepreneurs and necessitated the establishment of etatist programs in the early decades of the Turkish Republic.

The economic development in Trabzon, that is, its opening to foreign trade and its integration into the network of world markets, as well as the growth of the city, was not an isolated process in the nineteenth century. Other Ottoman port cities such as Izmir, Beirut, and Salonica, indeed a number of port cities in Asia, Africa, and Latin America, where European industries obtained raw materials in return for manufactured goods, became subject to a similar process. In many of these cities the Europeans also used ethnic groups traditionally engaged in trade as intermediaries, sometimes transplanting them from other places which they had earlier colonized. In Trabzon, however, as in the Ottoman Empire in general, the European control over non-Muslim merchants was limited since these domains were not colonized and the Ottoman government, still politically viable and modernizing its institutions, was anxious to incorporate the non-Muslims into its social and economic system. The broad and strong social basis which these merchants had in the Ottoman Empire, and which helped them resist total

European domination of economic life, was also a reason for a deeper division among communities and made it inevitable that economic and social problems be identified with religious and ethnic affiliations.

During the nineteenth century, in ꞓ ᵢntrast to the composition of the merchant class in the major urban centers, the ꞓ ᵣovincial landowning class in the Ottoman Empire was predominantly Muslim, and, in Anatolia, Turkish. Hence, it is essential that a complete study of socioeconomic differentiation in the Ottoman society in relation to the *millet* system make this urban-rural distinction. This is particularly important since political, economic, and social forces which effected change were expressed differently in urban and rural areas through agents of diverse interests, thus subjecting them to a different modernization process.

APPENDIX I

GENERAL TRADE OF THE PORT OF TRABZON FROM 1856 to 1900

	Exports			
	To the United Kingdom	*To Other Countries*	*Five Years*	
Half-Decades			*Total*	*Average*
	£	£	£	£
1856–60	564,100	5,432,500	5,996,600	1,199,320
1861–65	500,000*	4,500,000*	5,000,000*	1,000,000
1866–70	376,000	3,620,400	3,996,400	799,280
1871–75	466,800	3,206,900	3,673,700	734,740
1876–80	207,500	2,328,800	2,536,300	507,260
1881–85	265,000	3,032,400	3,297,400	659,480
1886–90	322,600	2,723,000	3,045,600	609,120
1891–95	253,500	2,809,600	3,063,100	612,620
1896–1900	134,600	3,120,800	3,255,400	651,080
Total	3,090,100	30,774,400	33,864,500	6,772,900

	Imports			
	From the United Kingdom	*From Other Countries*	*Five Years*	
Half-Decades			*Total*	*Average*
	£	£	£	£
1856–60	14,997,100	1,535,400	16,532,500	3,306,500
1861–65	7,000,000*	4,000,000*	11,000,000*	2,200,000
1866–70	3,880,800	2,209,000	6,089,800	1,217,960
1871–75	4,362,300	2,753,900	7,116,200	1,423,240
1876–80	3,986,900	2,399,100	6,386,000	1,277,200
1881–85	4,474,500	3,647,300	8,121,800	1,624,360
1886–90	4,148,700	3,188,000	7,336,700	1,467,340
1891–95	3,336,000	3,783,600	7,119,600	1,423,920
1896–1900	2,719,100	3,960,500	6,679,600	1,335,920
Total	48,905,400	27,476,800	76,382,200	15,276,440

*Based on a comparison of one year with another.

Source: FO 526/12.

APPENDIX II

LIST OF TRABZON MERCHANTS DEALING IN FOREIGN TRADE
(AS OF DECEMBER 1884)

Commission Agents

Ballassarian, M.	Anatolia
Constantinoff, D. J.	Persia
Dernersessian, M.	Anatolia
Hadji, Mirza Baba	Persia
Hadji, Djavad	Persia
Hadji, Mehmed Hassan	Persia
Hochstrasse and Co.	Anatolia; agent for Lloyd's, Imperial Ottoman Bank, etc.
Inebegoglou fils	Persia
Khedechian and Khoubesserian	Persia; agent for Reliance Insurance Company of New York
Makkokhian, A.	Anatolia and Persia
Marimian, B. O.	Persia; agent for Manheimer Insurance Company, etc.
Triandaphilides, A.	Anatolia; agent for La Fonciere Insurance Company, etc.
Efremides, A. C.	Lawyer
Kedikoglou Lazar Effendi	Lawyer

Exporters

Arnaoudoglou Brothers	Nuts, beans, tobacco, salt fish (anchovies)
Aznavorian Brothers	Nuts, beans, porpoise oil
Boyadjidhis, P.	Bones, horn scrapings, rags
Caprielian Brothers	Skins, tobacco, nuts, beans, walnut loupes, wool
Captanian, M.	Cereals, beans, nuts, linseed, linen stuffs
Cacoulides, P.	Nuts, tobacco, maize
Caragheuzian Brothers	Boxwood, walnut loupes
Carvonides, Georges	Nuts, tobacco
Constantinoff, D. G.	Skins, beans, tobacco, cereals, nuts
Davidian, G.	Skins, tobacco, wax, linseed, beans, nuts
Dernersessian, M.	Beans, nuts
Diradourian Brothers	Cereals, nuts, beans, walnut loupes
Djermakian, G.	Guts, porpoise oil
Efremides, L. P.	Nuts, beans, tobacco, cereals, wax, porpoise oil, etc.
Ghiurekian, S.	Beans, nuts, cereals
Hadji Ali Halfouz Efendi	Wheat, nuts, tobacco
Hochstrasse and Co.	Nuts, tobacco, beans, etc.
Khedechi, Yartan	Linen stuffs
Lemlioglou Brothers	Nuts, beans, tobacco, raisins, wax, cereals, etc.
Makhokhian, A.	Nuts, beans
Marmarian, S.	Tobacco, beans, maize, nuts, skins
Melides, S.	Nuts, cereals, tobacco, linseed
Missir, O.	Skins, beans, nuts, maize, tobacco

Nourian Brothers	Beans, skins, nuts, maize, linen stuffs
Pareghentanian, S. J.	Beans, nuts, skins, maize, hair
Parigoris, Th.	Nuts, salt fish (anchovies)
Sahatdjian, H. Boghos	Boxwood
Salihoglou, Ali Hafouz	Nuts, tobacco, beans
Sarafian, B.	Beans, nuts, guts
Sassi, A.	Porpoise oil, nuts
Saoulides, C.	Tobacco
Triandaphilides, A.	Maize, beans, nuts, tobacco, porpoise oil, etc.
Vartabedian Brothers	Nuts, maize, beans

Importers

Arabian, Maranian	Manchester goods, Aleppo goods, yarn bagging, metals, etc.
Arabian Brothers	Manchester goods, Aleppo goods, fezes
Arghiropoulos, D.	Colonial wares, bags, shot, steel
Arnaoudoglou Brothers	Colonial wares, flour, metals, gold thread, jewelry
Boyadjidhis, P.	Fancy goods, perfumery, hosiery, etc., cloth
Calpakdjides Brothers	Manchester goods (especially prints)
Capayanides, G.	Colonial wares, tea, soap, candles, metals, etc.
Caprielian Brothers	Colonial wares, bags
Captanian, M.	Flour, bags
Cariofili Brothers	Manchester goods, yarn
Casfikis, D.	Cloth, spirits and wine, grocery
Condozi, Constantinoff	Grey goods, Aleppo goods, bags and bagging
Congalides Brothers	Colonial wares, metals, olives, oil, fruits, etc.
Constantinides, D.	Drugs, spices, haberdashery, hardware
Derhampartzoumian Brothers	Leather and shoemakers' articles
Djermakian, G.	Matches, scythes
Djoulfazoglou, Hadji Hussein	Grey goods, Aleppo goods, tea, metals
Efremides, P. L.	Flour, petroleum, indigo, hides
Elefteriadhi, Lefter	Gold thread and laces, haberdashery
Fetvadjian Brothers	Cloth, fezes, fancy goods, hardware, etc.
Goondoubzade, Vehbi Effendi	Grey goods
Hamamdjizade, H. Ismail	Manchester goods
Hekimian, J.	Spirits, wine, beer, provisions, empty bottles, etc.
Israelian, Nigoghos	Sewing machines
Kazandjioglou Brothers	Manchester goods, Russian cotton manufactures
Khedechian, Caloust, and Cie.	Manchester goods
Khederian, Artin	Fezes, tassels
Kytrides, Anesti	Crockery and glassware, hardware
Kytrides, Gregoire	Grocery, looking glasses, lamps, bedsteads
Lemlioglou Brothers	General goods, colonial wares, metals, salt, etc.
Makhokhian, A.	General goods, colonial wares, metals, bags, candles, etc.
Marengo, J. B.	Apothecary
Marengo, J. N.	Apothecary
Meghavorian Brothers	Silken and woollen stuffs
Melides, S.	Sugar, spirits, matches

Metaxa Brothers	Manchester goods, bags, wax-cloth, fezes
Missir, O.	Colonial wares, cochineal, bags, leather, etc.
Mikaelian, O.	Jewelry, watches
Nourian Brothers	Aleppo goods, raw cotton
Pareghentanian, S. J.	Hides, cereals
Petropoulos, P.	Cereals
Sarafian, B.	Matches, steel
Serassi and Elefteriadi	Manchester goods (especially prints)
Serdarzade Salih Effendi	Yarn
Shoemakers' Society	Leather and shoes, etc.
Sirinopoulos, Y.	Grey goods
Sofianopoulos, L.	Colonial wares, fruits, soap, starch, paper
Taghmazian	Aleppo goods
Tailors' Society	Cloth, haberdashery, etc.
Terzopoulos, V.	Aleppo goods, yarn
Tchairoglou, P.	Crockery and glassware, lamps, hardware, etc.
Tigdaban, Vahid and Akif Effendi	Manchester goods
Tirakian, Garabed	Window glasses, lemons and oranges
Triandaphilides, A.	General goods, colonial wares, rice, tea, metals, etc.
Tzouliadis, G.	Flour, biscuits, and macaroni
Vafiadis, Mourad	Colonial wares, chemicals, dyes, paints, window glasses
Vafiadis Brothers	Bags and bagging
Vartabedian Brothers	Grey goods, colonial wares
Velissaridhi Brothers	Cloth, fezes, fancy goods, haberdashery
Xifilino and Sofiano	Bookseller and binder, printer, stationer
Yanicapani, Panajoti	Silken and woollen stuffs, velvets
Yelkendjizade Brothers	Flour, maize
Zimplinides Brothers	Manchester goods

Source: FO 526/10

APPENDIX III

PEOPLE ENJOYING BRITISH PROTECTION IN TRABZON DURING 1855–1857

Name	Country	Profession
1. Dionisio Valiano	Zante	Merchant
2. G. Cunduri	Ionian Isles	Merchant
3. Basilio Glizzo	Cerigo	
4. Nicolo Dimitropolo	Zante	
5. Giogio Cimiri	Cerigo	
6. Demitrio Demitropolo (Wife and Daughter)	Zante	
7. Gerasimo Giorgopulo	Ionian Isles	
8. Gerasimo Amide	Ionian Isles	
9. Giuseppe Portelli	Malta	Doctor
10. George Karavan	Moldavia	

11. C. G. Dapolo	Greece	Carpenter
12. Arditi Fortuni	French protege	Merchant
13. Michel C. Caires	Greece	Merchant
14. Stav. Stavrinaki (Wife and Daughter)	Greece	
15. A. D. Paleologue	French protege	Merchant
16. Alex. Petrochilo	Greece	
17. Fotio Kalfoglu	Wallachia	Merchant
18. Dimitri Panopolos	Greece	
19. C. Sobeiszezansky	French protege	Doctor
20. G. Cagnioli and Wife	Sardinia	Doctor
21. Padre Fiorenzo	France	Capucin
22. Paolo Calmati	Sardinia	Merchant
23. Fiornini Maritekopulo	Greece	Carpenter
24. Gerasimio Cuvrelo	Ionian Isles	Captain
25. Giovanni Thorosini	Greece	Agent
26. Manoli Dorzie	Ionian Isles	Agent
27. Aloise Cuviello	Ionian Isles	Agent
28. N. Dorzie	English subject	French Adm. Employee
29. Parasceva Giogiadi	Greece	Merchant
30. Paolo C.	Sardinia	Merchant
31. Const. Laskari	Greece	Merchant
32. Dionisio Valiano	Ionian Isles	Merchant
33. Nicola Bogiajoglu	Moldavia	Merchant
34. Constantin Ivannu	Greece	Merchant
35. Constantin G. Benpualy	Greece	Merchant
36. Arditi F.	France	Merchant
37. Michel Kardura	Greece	Merchant
38. Kirkor Shahnazuroff	Russia	Inn keeper
39. Henry James Ross	England	Vice-Consul/Merchant
40. Vienzo Caslia	Malta	Merchant
41. Stefanos Calmatty	Sardinia	Merchant
42. Jean Kyriacides	Greece	Merchant
43. Moussour Gustani	Tarsus	
44. Ohannes B. der Sarrafyan	America	Priest
45. G. Ponzetto	Sardinia	Merchant
46. Purri Cofsini	France	Merchant
47. D. Dimitropulo	Ionian Isles	Merchant
48. A. Forniri	Sardinia	
49. N. Xanthopulo	Greece	Merchant
50. Giogio Malano	Ionian Isles	Shopkeeper
51. Anastasio Postolis	Ionian Isles	Physician
52. Rainesio Gregorio	Sardinia	Baker
53. Haralambo Gergopulo	Ionian Isles	Merchant
54. Dionisio Valiano	Ionian Isles	Merchant
55. Panagin Sansonio	Ionian Isles	Merchant
56. P. Cairio	Greece	Merchant
57. Constantino Johanidi	Greece	Merchant
58. Joseph Ziglinski	France	Doctor

59. Theodori Gilbert	France	
60. Ercole Vandoro	Ionian Isles	Trader
61. Guisseppina Portelli and two children	Britain	Widow
62. Mikhail Voligios	Ionian Isles	
63. Gregorio Reno	Corfu	
64. Caralambo Sansonio Marulli	Ionian Isles	Trader
65. Panagin Marulli	Ionian Isles	Trader
66. Adolphie Arnair	France	Agent
67. Haralambo M.	Ionian Isles	Trader

Source: FO 526/5.

Notes

1. Henry Grenville, *Observations sur l'état actuel de l'Empire Ottoman*, Andrew S. Ehrenkreutz, ed., Ann Arbor, 1965, p. 53.

2. The trade between Trabzon and Wallachia and Moldavia started as early as the thirteenth century and increased considerably in the following centuries. An Italian monk, Niccolo Barsi da Lucca, traveling in Moldavia in 1634, emphasized the quantity and quality of goods from Istanbul and Trabzon exchanged for butter, cheese, and other foodstuffs. Constantin C. Giurescu, *Le voyage de Niccolo Barsi en Moldavie*, Paris and Bucharest, 1925, pp. 38–40. Other seventeenth-century travelers, such as the Swedish consular agent Johann Mayer in 1651 and Evliya Çelebi in 1659, described the activities of the merchants from Trabzon in these provinces. Dimitri Cantemir, one of the *voyvoda*s of Moldavia, described the active trade of Trabzon merchants at Galatz, mostly Muslim, with envy. Indeed at Jassy, in the mid-eighteenth century, the merchants from Trabzon displayed their goods on the street named after them—"rue trebizondine." See the article by the same author, "Les relations des pays roumains avec Trebizonde aux XIVᵉ-XIXᵉ siècles," *Revue Roumaine d'Histoire*, 13 (1974), pp. 241–243 and notes 19–20.

3. For the full text of the Küçük Kaynarca Treaty, see Fred L. Israel, *Major Peace Treaties of Modern History, 1648–1967*, New York, 1967, vol. 2, pp. 913–919. Abdurrahman Şeref Efendi, the last official Ottoman historian (1908–25), viewed the Treaty of Küçük Kaynarca as the treaty most detrimental to the Ottoman state. See his *Tarih-i Devlet-i Osmaniye*, Istanbul, 1894–97/1312–1315, vol. 2, p. 196. Perhaps the most apt remark on the treaty was made by the Austrian envoy to Istanbul, Baron Thugutt, who said: "The Ottoman Empire becomes henceforth a kind of Russian province . . . events now passing in this empire will in the future exercise the greatest influence on the policy of all other states, and will give rise to endless troubles." Reports of Baron Thugutt, August 17, and September 13, 1774, cited by A. Sorel in *The Eastern Question in the Eighteenth Century: The Partition of Poland and the Treaty of Kainardji*, London, 1898, pp. 250–251.

4. See Halil Inalcık, "Imtiyāzāt," *The Encyclopedia of Islam* (EI²), vol. 3, p. 1186, and X. de Planhol, "Karā Deniz," *EI²*, vol. 4, p. 574.

5. The Ottoman government, aware of the importance of the Black Sea trade and in control of the Straits, exercised certain prerogatives, for instance, the practice of preempting grain from foreign ships passing through the Bosphorus. Indeed, during wars this practice was applied to other essential

items such as iron, olive oil, soap, potash, and coffee. This was not done arbitrarily, however. The government, when in need, would preempt only that portion of grain deemed necessary—generally not more than half of any ship's load—and this amount would be purchased for cash at prices then in effect in the Ottoman market. In 1813, for example, the Russian Ambassador Italinski accepted a compromise whereby a maximum of one-half the Russian grain passing through the Bosphorus could be preempted in Istanbul. In that year the Porte bought, for cash, grain from several Russian ships at the price of five *kuruş* per *kile*. Başbakanlık Arşivleri (hereafter cited as B. A.). *Hatt-ı Hümayun,* Nos. 46102 and 46102A.

6. Some of these merchants assumed Russian citizenship. This situation drew the immediate attention of the Ottoman government. In the 1790s, it sent a number of imperial edicts to the governors and *kadı*s of the Ottoman provinces along the southern Black Sea coast prohibiting emigration. In 1799, for instance, the *kadı* of Trabzon acknowledged to the Porte that he had received and communicated to the people the *ferman* that prohibited the emigration of the Ottoman subjects to the Crimea. B. A., *Cevdet-Dahiliye,* No. 10804.

7. Article VII of the treaty specifically once again provided for free and unrestricted trading and navigation rights to Russian subjects. The same article, moreover, granted that all these privileges be expressly extended to all nations with commercial relations with Russia. Israel (cited n. 3), vol. 2, p. 936. The Ottomans at first were hesitant to extend the benefits of the treaty to nations other than Russia. The treaty was signed in September 1829, but not until December, for example, did the Porte agree to allow British ships carrying every kind of produce to pass through the Straits.

8. Jules Hagemeister, *Essai sur les resources territoriales et commerciales de l'Asie occidentale,* St. Petersburg, 1839, p. 185.

9. Xavier Hommaire de Hell, *Travels in the Steppes of the Caspian Sea, the Crimea, the Caucasus, etc.,* London, 1847, p. 17.

10. James Brant, "Journey Through a Part of Armenia and Asia Minor, in the Year 1835." *The Journal of the Royal Geographical Society of London,* 6 (London, 1836), p. 189.

11. In the Tabriz trade for the years immediately following the Adrianople Treaty, it is of special note that the value of imports reaching the city almost tripled from 15,346,536 rubles in 1833 to 40,090,084 in 1836. The great bulk of the goods were of British origin brought by Persian merchants to Tabriz from Istanbul. In 1834, for instance, the Persian merchants brought to Tabriz from the Ottoman capital, via Trabzon, 14,976,144 rubles worth of merchandise out of Tabriz's total imports of 17,937,986 rubles; goods valued at 1,506,218 rubles were directly imported from Russia; 180,000 was imported from England and other places by foreign merchants—mostly Austrian and Russian—residing in Tabriz; 478,232 rubles worth of diverse merchandise was brought in by Russian merchants from Leipzig, England, and France; and 176,000 rubles worth of goods were carried by Russian merchants from Istanbul. In the following year, the value of imports from Istanbul handled by the Persian merchants doubled to 28,286,240 rubles. I. Berezin, *Puteshestvie po Sievernoi Persii,* Kazan, 1852, vol. 2, Appendix 3.

12. Public Records Office. FO 60/107.

13. During the Crimean War, for instance, Russian and Ottoman ships lost their carrying trade to the Austrian and French companies. British ships, receiving no subsidy from London, could not compete with other nations' lines.

14. During the Greek Revolution a large number of vessels were destroyed. Although small shipyards on the islands built a good many of them in the years that followed, concentration was not as heavy as at the port of Trabzon. Also, the variety of produce in the region could accommodate the use of more vessels. Steamers, naturally, offered competition in the Aegean also. Toward the end of the century, "the problem was solved by the purchase and operation . . . of old steamships discarded by Western firms." L. S. Stavrianos, *The Balkans Since 1453,* New York, 1958, p. 299. Interestingly, this practice developing at the end of the nineteenth century was followed, particularly after the Second World War, by some Greeks who would form shipping empires.

15. It is noteworthy that many small open vessels with engines *(takas)* carrying such loads in Turkey today are owned and manned by people of the Black Sea coast.

16. *Annuaire Oriental du commerce, de l'industrie, de l'administration et de la magistrature,* Constantinople, 1903, vol. 2, p. 1646. On agencies, also see *Trabzon Vilayeti Salnamesi,* Trabzon, 1900/1318, pp. 170–173; F.O. 526 Turkey 11 (the appointment of Migirditch Khedechian as an agent of the newly established Danish Line in March 1888); FO 526/13. (the appointment of D. Georgantelli Brothers as agents for the Holland-American Line in September 1894).

17. At Samsun, the list of agents included the following names: Theodore J. Arzoglou, Algardi, Henri Cortanze, I. J. Marcopoli, J. Joannides, J. Hekimian, Y. A. Dervichyan, etc. At this port, the *Idare-i Mahsusa* was also represented by a Greek resident, M. Sevastikoglou. At Giresun, Georges Mavrides, E. Pappadopoulo, T. Genna, M. Pysolian, Alexi Kypriotti, S. C. Papadopoulos, G. Pisani; at Ordu, Afendoul Pouloulides, D. Gregoriades, M. Vostantik, G. P. Coucoulidis, Pandeli Ioannidis, Boghos Tchildjian, Agop and Hrand Kubdjian; and at Tirebolu, G. P. Mavrides and H. Boyadjian represented various steamship companies. *Annuaire Oriental* (cited n. 16), pp. 1649–1650. On Samsun, also see FO 526/14.

18. Before the expiration date (1834) of the effective tariff, British merchants and consuls often advocated the abolition of Ottoman monopolies. In his report of June 4, 1833 to Lord Ponsonby, for instance, the British vice-consul at Trabzon, James Brant, expressed a common concern and suggested "The renewal of our Tariffe with Turkey next year will be an opportue moment for Your Excellency's intervention, to protect British commerce from the venations of the Government [Ottoman] and Custom. . . ." And in his year-end report, he echoed the same message:

> It would be very desirable if the opportunity which the approaching renewal of the British Tariffe with Turkey may afford could be availed of the claim a removal of all restrictions as to Exports, the difficulty of effecting returns in Produce, forming the greatest disadvantage under which our Trade at the present labours.

FO 195/101. For the analysis of the 1838 Convention, see Charles Issawi, *The Economic History of the Middle East, 1800–1914,* Chicago and London, 1966, pp. 38–39.

19. FO 78/367.

20. Great Britain. The House of Commons, *Accounts and Papers,* vol. 38 (1857), Session 2, p. 775, and FO 524/5. Trabzon's exports for 1854 totaled £668,691. This figure, however, includes £397,518 worth of species passing through Trabzon; of this amount, £288,518 belonged to Persian merchants, and the rest was sent to Europe by local accounts. FO 195/433.

21. FO 195/597.

22. Aware of the importance of the European-Persian trade and its political implications, Russia, in the second half of the nineteenth century, made every effort to divert the Persian transit trade from Trabzon to its own ports and from there through Tiflis to Tabriz. Russia had already taken untoward steps to undermine the Ottoman economic position after the Treaty of Adrianople. Early in 1846, Viceroy Vorontzov prevailed on the Russian government to reopen passage to Persian merchants through Transcaucasia, subjecting their goods to lower rates of duty. In March of the same year, the British consul at Trabzon made this report to his embassy in Istanbul:

> The Russian Consul here has received a Circular from the Governor General of Georgia, announcing that the Russian Government has reduced the Quarantine on passengers and Goods entering Russia from Persia by the stations at Gumri, Akiska and other places on the frontier. . . . The object of Russia is to endeavour to deprive Turkey of the benefit of the Extensive Transit Trade with Persia which passes through this town, and adding to her own resources.

FO 195/261, from British consul at Trebizond to Stratford Canning, March 14, 1846. As Russian political and economic interests expanded in Georgia and the Caucasus, the tsar's government increased its efforts to alter the direction of the European-Persian trade. Late in the summer of 1865, Russia began the construction of a railroad between Poti and Tiflis. After a brief interruption in 1866, because of the Abkhaza uprising in the Caucasus, construction was resumed. In the fall of 1872 the line was in operation over a distance of 280 *versts. The Levant Herald* (Istanbul), October 25, 1872, p. 174, col. 4–5. For reports on the early stages of the construction, see the April 20, 1867 issue of the same newspaper. In addition, the Tiflis Railroad Company, which was supported by the Russian government, established special rates for goods transported between Poti and Tabriz. The establishment of Russian steamship service on the Caspian Sea soon after helped divert the bulk of the Persian transit trade, particularly their export trade, to Russian Georgia. The examination of the trade figures of Trabzon immediately thereafter reveals that exports, from £827,213 in 1872, dropped to £783,430 in 1873, and to £696,833 in 1874 and to £598, 073 in 1875. FO 195/1110.

23.   The Ottoman government, however, especially in the 1860s, made various attempts to improve the condition of the Trabzon-Erzurum-Tabriz route. See B. A., *Cevdet-Nafia,* No. 1773; B. A., *Irade-Meclis-i Mahsus,* No. 1207; B. A., *Irade-Meclis-i Vâlâ,* No. 22469. For the allocation of over 31,000 *kuruş* in 1865, for instance, to improve the Trabzon-Erzurum section of the road, see B. A., *Cevdet-Nafia,* No. 31.

24.   See Charles Issawi, "The Tabriz-Trabzon Trade, 1830–1900: Rise and Decline of a Route," *International Journal of Middle East Studies* 1 (1970), pp. 18–27.

25.   See Eugene Mittwoch, "The Economic Significance of the Language Question in Turkey," *Archiv für Wirtschaftsforschung im Orient,* 1 (1916), pp. 317–343.

26.   [The British trade] is conveyed in foreign bottoms, and passes through foreign houses and agencies, mostly Armenians and Greeks, at Constantinople. A consequence of this is that the prices of the goods themselves, whether export or import, are considerably raised, to the sole advantage of the brokers and agents in Galata; while the countries at either extremity of the commercial line—namely Persia on the one side and England on the other—are proportionately losers.

Accounts (cited n.20), 66(1871), p. 739. In his 1874 report to the Foreign Office on the British trade in the Ottoman domains, Consul Locock, in particular reference to Trabzon, wrote:

It appears that in consequence of this utter absence of the English element, the merchandise passes both at the ports themselves and at Constantinople through the hands of native traders, agents, or brokers, mostly Greek or Armenian . . . notwithstanding the progress it has made, to a certain extent "crippled, overweighted, and distorted by the commissions, extra charges, and sometimes adulterations," to which it is subject at the hands of these middlemen.

Ibid., vol. 6 (1874), p. 1075.

27.   FO 526/13.

28.   *Annuaire Oriental* (cited n. 16), p. 1645.

29.   Sir Edmund Hornby, *An Autobiography,* Boston and New York, 1938. Sir Edmund was sent to Istanbul as the British commissioner of the Ottoman Loan in 1855, and two years later was appointed judge of the British Supreme Court there. Writing around 1856, he said:

These protected Ottoman subjects were looked upon as the subjects of Russia, if they were of the Greek faith; of Italy and France and Austria if they were of the Roman faith; and of England and Germany if Protestants. All the powers abused the privileges they assumed, i.e. of granting protection—none more so than the Russians, French, the English; the latter having acquired a protection over the Ionian Islands granted passports right and left, so that many thousands more than the whole population of the seven islands placed themselves under British protection in the Levant, whilst as many so-called Italians registered as Maltese, to say nothing of genuine Greeks and Armenians who managed to get English passports under one pretence or another. . . . "

Ibid., pp. 92–93. In 1860, the American legation estimated the number of Ottoman subjects in Istanbul that enjoyed foreign national status at around fifty thousand. *The United States National Archives, Legations, Dispatches, Turkey,* vol. 16, Williams to Cass, September 17, 1860.

30.   Charles Thomas Newton, the British vice-consul at Mytilene in 1852 wrote: "The advantages of British protection in a Turkish court are so obvious, that the Ionians are the object of general envy among the Christian subjects of the Porte. The desire to possess a British passport is so strong that every sort of ingenious device is practised in order to obtain one." See his *Travels and Discoveries in the Levant,* London, 1865, vol. 1, pp. 76–77. The returns covering 1851 only, submitted by the British consul general in Istanbul, showed the following:

British subjects	368
Natives of British India	6
Natives of Malta	703
Natives of Gibraltar	9
Ionians	2,840
Protected by Her Majesty's embassy	39
Total	3,965

FO 78/976.

31. FO 97/405; FO 526/15.

32. FO 881/768. For a petition submitted to the French consul at Trabzon by the Armenian Catholic bishop on February 18, 1858, asking for French protection over all his coreligionists residing in Trabzon, see FO 195/597.

33. The list of the Italian subjects, 37 with their families, includes a surgeon, a doctor, a pewterer, a shopkeeper, writers, "man-of-all-work," etc. No number is given for the Wallachians. In a separate partial listing containing mostly the names of Greeks and Armenians who assumed British protection, the following notation is made: "All these men are well to do; the Traders are chiefly in Corn and Grain; the shopkeepers of Manchester goods, on a largish scale for Trebizond." FO 195/812.

34. A confidential "Memorandum on the Question of granting British Protection to Persian Subjects in Persia, and to Turkish Subjects in the Ottoman Dominions (including Egypt), when Partners in British Mercantile Houses in England," July 6, 1880, FO 881/4686.

35. FO 195/597.

36. Indeed, Russian officials persuaded a large group of Armenians from Erzurum and Kars to emigrate to Georgia. The Ottoman government agreed to pay the emigrants 410,000 *kuruş* in two installments, yearly, for their land and property left behind. B. A., *Hatt-ı Hümayun*, Nos. 36840 and 36840A. Later, many of these emigrants returned to Erzurum with Russian passports. At the start of the Crimean War, they were asked to choose "between their expulsion from Turkey or their renunciation of Russian protection. Since most of them held property and had other interests in this country they eagerly embraced the latter alternative and were accordingly enrolled in the Registers of the Patriarchate at Constantinople as Ottoman subjects, the Armenian Patriarch himself becoming Guarantee to the Porte for their future conduct and loyalty." FO 195/493.

37. FO 524/8. On this, also see FO 195/294.

38. Soon after the war started, attempts were made by a group of Armenians—those engaged in the Trabzon-Erzurum-Tabriz trade—to secure Persian protection. The Ottoman government, however, issued strict orders to prevent this. B. A., *Irade-Hariciye*, No. 6207.

39. FO 78/1396.

40. FO 195/597.

41. Ibid.

42. On May 27, 1858, the British consul at Trabzon reported a rather interesting incident:

> I have the honour to report for your Lordship's information the arrival here on the 22nd Instant of the Russian steamer "Kertch" of the Burthen of about 250 Tons and 80 or 90 Horse power, being the first boat of a new line of communication between Trebizond, Poti, Redoot Kaleh, Soukoum Kaleh, Anapa, Kertch, Theodosia, Sevastopol, Eupatoria and Odessa. This vessel left on her return voyage on the 24th Instant.
> While in port she was visited by nearly two thirds of the Christian population of Trebizond, a fact worthy of remark, considering the insignificance of the vessel, when compared to so many fine Steam Vessels which visited Trebizond almost unnoticed during the late Russian War.

"Report from Consul Stevens to the Earl of Malmesbury, Trebizond, 27th May, 1858," FO 78/1396. The event clearly indicates the interest of the non-Muslim residents of Trabzon in the technology displayed by Russia, and reminds the writer of the interest shown by the Turks during the visits of the American ships to Turkish ports in the late 1940s and early 1950s.

43. P. Dislere and R. de Mouy, *Droits et devoirs des français dans les pays d'orient et d'extrème orient,* Paris, 1893, p. 45, and G. Pélissié du Rausas, *Le régime des capitulations dans l'empire Ottomane,* Paris, 1905, vol. 2, p. 36.

44.   On August 27, 1862, the British consul at Trabzon reported that, "The abuse of granting Russian Nationality to foreigners has of late become extensive on this side. . . ." FO 195/78.

45.   Some of the points defined in this regulation were: the number of Ottoman subjects to be employed by foreign legations; that no Ottoman subject could act as consul or vice-consul for any European nation; protection of those employed at the embassies, consulates, and so forth would not be granted to the families of the employees; that the regulation was not retroactive. See Pierre Arminjon, *Etrangères et protégés dans l'empire Ottoman,* Paris, 1903, vol. 1, pp. 325–330.

46.   Although Russia was among the powers consenting to this law, for instance after the 1877–78 Russo-Ottoman War, the Russian authorities again started granting passports to many Armenian Ottomans in eastern Anatolia. On February 24, 1879, the British Consul Biliotti made this report:

> The Armenians who passed on Russian territory during the last war, all those who return to Turkey for the purpose of disposing of their property and go back to Russia, or with the intention to remain in Anatolia, are provided with Russian passports, and considered as subjects by the Consul General of that Nation. This circumstance giving a rise to continual discussions between the Russian and Turkish authorities at Erzeroom.

FO 195/1238. Also, when the war broke out, Russian subjects were required to leave the Ottoman domains. Many of these people were Greek and Armenian merchants, carrying Russian passports. Upon their return in 1878, they filed suits, asking for damages against the Porte, at the Russian embassy in Istanbul. A special commission formed for this purpose at the embassy rendered favorable judgment in all cases and compensations were paid by the Ottomans. Many cases involved Greek and Armenian residents of Trabzon and included names such as: Hagop Gasparow, Yorghi Machkolidis, Iorgi Ionai Papadopoulos, Kosma Iani, Mikhali Theodoroff, Levteri Gheorghion, Boghos Meghavorian, Haralambo and Anesti Ziottoglou, P. D. Psomiades, Stavros Sarieroglou, Carabed Aivazoff, etc. For the details of these claims, see *Requêtes présentées par les sujets russes à la commission instituée à l'ambassade impériale de Russie à Constantinople,* Constantinople, 1910.

47.   FO 195/448.

48.   FO 195/953.

49.   B. A., *Irade-Hariciye,* No. 8268 [decoration to Artin Arzuman, the dragoman of the British consulate at Trabzon]; B. A., *Irade-Dahiliye,* Nos. 27532 and 28786; B. A., *Irade-Hariciye,* Nos. 8464 and 8681 [decoration to Ilya, a Greek member of the Administrative Council in Trabzon]; B. A., *Irade-Hariciye,* No. 11110 [*Mecidiye* decorations to Hoça Aleksan (a Catholic) and to his son Kirkor, merchants of Erzurum]; B. A., *Irade-Dahiliye,* No. 36608 [decorations to Kerkyan Istefan and Arslanzade Ohan Efendi, merchants in Trabzon].

50.   In 1862, for instance, the British consul at Trabzon observed such a case and brought it to the attention of the governor. He reported that the debtor, "on being applied to for payment, boasted of the high protection he was enjoying and in an insolent tone denied the Pasha's right to conduct the case . . . similar cases are being frequent occurrence—indeed it is common practice here, for Rayahs when they find themselves in trouble to pass over to Russian protection with the express purpose of screening themselves from the ends of justice." FO 195/728.

51.   FO 78/1396. In an earlier report dated June 10, 1858, to Stratford Canning, Consul Guarracino said: "I must also report to you that in the Greek churches here every Sunday, prayers are read for the preservation and welfare of the Emperor of Russia and all the Members of the Imperial Family." FO 195/597.

52.   During the Crimean War, some of the Armenian merchants of Erzurum under Russian protection were also temporarily granted Austrian protection. FO 195/410.

53.   FO 78/1396.

54.   "From the Pasha of Trebizond, Circular to the Armenian *Vekil,* February 20, 1858," FO 195/597.

55.   "From the Bishops of the Greek and Armenian and Armenian Catholic Churches in Trebizond to Governor Ragip Pasha, February 21, 1858," Ibid.

56.   Two days before the submission of the petition by the Muslim merchants to the governor,

Consul Stevens sent a report to the British embassy in Istanbul stating: "I know from himself [the governor] that he considers he has been badly treated by the Porte, which has in several instances failed to support him in his discussions with the Russian Consulate. During a private conversation I held with him one day, we talked of the Pasha of Batoom, and my remarking that he was a friend of the Russians, he replied, 'What will you have him do? Were he to oppose them, he would not be supported.' " From Consul Stevens to Charles Alison, Esq., February 17, 1858, FO 195/597.

57.   From a report entitled "On *the relative position of Christians* and *Mahometans,* in the Eastern Provinces of the Ottoman Empire," January 30, 1868. FO 881/1592.

58.   FO 195/812.

59.   *Accounts* (cited n. 20), 66 (1871), p. 740.

60.   Ibid., vol. 59 (1868–1869), p. 355. The Tribunal of Commerce referred to by the consul was one of the institutions established during the *Tanzimat* period. In 1840, *ad hoc* courts to deal with commercial disputes were established under the newly created Ministry of Commerce, following a new commercial code prepared under Reşit Paşa and based on French models. In a few months, facing strong opposition of the conservative-religious groups, these courts were closed. In 1850 when Reşit Paşa's Commercial Code was promulgated, its administration was delegated to the Tribunals of Commerce, to be established in every province. See Hıfzı Veldet, "Kanunlaştırma Hareketleri ve Tanzimat," in *Tanzimat,* Istanbul, 1940, pp. 196–197; and *Düstur,* Istanbul 1289/1872, pp. 445–465. In 1858, the commercial tribunals were reorganized, and in 1860, they were combined with mixed courts (with Muslim and non-Muslim members). See Roderic H. Davison, *Reform in the Ottoman Empire, 1856–1876,* Princeton, 1963, pp. 55–56. E. Hertslet, in his confidential report to the Foreign Office, dated April 29, 1880, entitled "Memorandum on the Establishment of the 'Tidjaret' or Commercial Tribunals, in Turkey," wrote that: "In June 1850, Sir S. Canning recommended the Porte to establish Mixed Tribunals of Commerce and Civil Judicature in all parts of the Turkish Empire where a sufficient number of individuals qualified to take part in them might be found, and Lord Palmerston approved of his Excellency having done so." FO 881/4232. After its merger with the mixed courts in early 1860, the composition of the tribunal in Trabzon was also changed (now including Turks, Greeks and Armenians) and remained so until the end of the century. In 1895, for instance, its members included: Ibrahim Hakkı Bey-president, Çulhazade Kadri Efendi and Yorgi Mihalapulo-permanent members, Serdarzade Salih Efendi and Nuryan Alko Efendi-temporary members. *Trabzon Salnamesi,* Trabzon, 1313/1895, p. 128. In 1900, the membership of the Tribunal of Commerce consisted of the following: Mehmet Seyfi Efendi-president, Mehmet Efendi and Karabet Efendi-permanent members, Tahsin Efendi and Yordanaki Efendi-temporary members. *Trabzon Salnamesi,* Trabzon, 1320/1902, p. 129.

61.   John MacDonald Kinneir, *Journey Through Asia Minor, Armenia, and Koordistan, in the Years 1813 and 1814,* London, 1818, p. 341.

62.   James Brant (cited n. 10), p. 190.

63.   In November 1856, the British consul at Trabzon, F. J. Stevens, reported that: "A great number of Families have thrown themselves on Trebizond, from Towns and Villages of the interior, driven therefrom for want of Bread." F O 195/528.

64.   *Accounts* (cited n. 20), vol. 38 (1857), Session 2, pp. 775–776.

65.   F O 524/5.

66.   *Accounts* (cited n. 20), vol. 58 (1862), p. 191. Often included in the Muslim population—though no specific numbers are given—were groups of Ottoman subjects from the Balkans living in exile in Trabzon. In 1850, for example, such a group of Albanians residing in Trabzon secured the permission of the Porte to visit Mecca on a pilgrimage. B. A., *Irade-Meclis-i Vâlâ,* No. 5418.

67.   *Accounts* (cited n. 20), 59 (1868–1869) p. 338. In regard to ninety-two Greeks listed under "Others," the consul reported: "These are, I believe, no less fictitious than the Russians [Ottoman subjects of Greek origin, carrying Russian passports]."

68.   Vital Cuinet, *La Turquie d'Asie,* Paris, 1892, vol. 1, p. 44.

The *Millet*s as Agents of Change in the Nineteenth-Century Ottoman Empire

RODERIC H. DAVISON

It is logical, for two reasons, to ask whether the non-Muslim *millet*s were agents of change in the Ottoman Empire in the nineteenth century. The first is that members of these *millet*s had, in various ways, considerable contact with Europe. They associated with European merchants and diplomats, often working for or with them. The connection with Europe through coreligionists outside the empire was often easy, certainly easier for them than for Muslims, whose religious ties tended toward the East rather than the West. There were Greek, Armenian, and Jewish merchants in European countries, sometimes considerable colonies of them in major ports and trade centers. Some of the *millet* members had schooling in Europe. Some others had Western missionary schooling at home. The hypothesis that the *millet*s would serve as agents or channels of Westernization in the Ottoman Empire appears, then, to have some basis. The second reason is that the nineteenth century seems to have been a period of more rapid social and political flux than were the preceding centuries. Political, economic, and intellectual pressures were eroding the stratifications of society. In this process, the status of *millet*s and of their members was altered and their internal structures were changed. Again it is not illogical to suppose that Western influences would work on the *millet*s as they sought to change their forms and to improve their status, and that some of the Western influence would in turn be transferred to Turkish society. Do these suppositions conform to the evidence?

In pursuing this inquiry, the historian should bear in mind three caveats. First, moral judgments must be held in abeyance. It cannot be assumed, as Europeans commonly did, that Westernization was an automatic good. Nor can it be assumed, as Europeans also often did, that the non-Muslims of the Ottoman Empire operated on a higher moral plane than the Muslims. Arminius Vambery rightly remarked, in the heated days of the Ottoman Empire's great crisis of 1876, that all Near Eastern peoples had essentially the same morals.[1]

Second, the historian must be prepared for the possibility that the influence of *millet*s, even if proven, may not rank high among the many agents of change then at work. These include: the impact of military defeats inflicted on the Ottomans, especially by Russia, between 1768 and 1833; the development of a group of top-level Ottoman military and civil officials, and finally of a professional class, who knew French and Western ways; the political pressures of the European powers; and the economic dominance of Europe in the Near East.

Third, the evidence may be sparse. Much information about the histories of non-Muslim *millet*s, and about their situation at any given time, is available, but information about so potentially vast and yet so subtle a subject as the influence of local non-Muslim groups on Muslims is likely to be slim. How often can one expect a Turk to say, "We do thus and so, or we adopt this view, because of the Greek example"? And how often can one expect even an outsider to observe, "The Muslims have taken this Westernism from the Gregorian Armenians, and that from the Catholic Armenians, this from the Ashkenazi Jews and that from the Sephardim"? Some speculation will be necessary.

One further prefatory statement needs to be made about the nature of the term *millet*. Three closely related, yet distinguishable, meanings have been attached to the term. The first, and most common, meaning of *millet* is a community of people, a collection of individuals, who get their identity from a common religious affiliation. In this sense *millet* has also been used for the *umma*, the people of Islam—the *millet-i Islamiye,* which Cevdet Paşa said was equated in the popular mind to the *millet-i hâkime,* the ruling *millet*.[2] For this paper, however, the term *millet* will throughout refer only to one or more of the non-Islamic *millet*s, the *millel-i mahkûme,* the ruled *millet*s, as Reşid Paşa once called them, who together with the Muslims made up the traditional *millel-i erbaa* of the Ottoman Empire, the four religious communities: Muslims, Greeks, Armenians, Jews.[3]

In addition to denoting a group of people belonging to the same religious confession, the term *millet* has also at times been used as an adjective, to denote primarily the body of doctrine and practice common to one of these confessions: *millet* worship, *millet* ritual, and *millet* law, especially the law of civil status.

The third use of *millet* has been to refer to a formal organization of the religious community: its ecclesiastical hierarchy; its clerical or judicial organs; its constitution; its partial autonomy as recognized by the Ottoman sultans. Use of the term in this sense for periods before the nineteenth century has recently been questioned unless careful qualifications and restrictions are added. Halil Inalcik has pointed out that the post-*Tanzimat* connotation of the term cannot be applied to earlier periods and that assertions of legal autonomy for *millet*s are exaggerations, despite the allocation of some administrative powers to the *millet*s.[4] Benjamin Braude has reported that before the early nineteenth century the term *millet* was not normally used by the Ottoman government to refer to the non-Muslim religious communities. Furthermore he suggests the delegation by Mehmed II of authority over such a community to a patriarch or rabbi is greatly exaggerated.[5] In this paper the term will be used, when referring to the structure of a non-Muslim community, in its nineteenth-century sense. Most of my evidence comes from the middle two quarters of that century.

The three connotations of the word *millet* indicate three possible ways in which non-Muslim influence, and through them Western influences, might have reached the Muslim community. Probably the most important one is the influence of individual Ottoman subjects who were members of one *millet* or another. These Ottoman subjects would not be acting as formal or even informal representatives of any *millet,* but simply as individuals who took actions, undertook enterprises, made recommendations, elaborated ideas, or wielded power that affected Ottoman Muslim society and government.

A second path of influence would be, in theory, the influence of *millet* religious belief or doctrine, or of *millet* forms of worship and ritual, or of *millet* laws of civil status, on the religious beliefs or ritual or civil status laws of Muslims. At first this sounds like a far-fetched possibility. But there was so much syncretism and symbiosis among the variegated peoples of the Ottoman Empire—the kind of mixtures and survivals that modern folklorists report and Hasluck wrote of—that the possibility cannot be excluded, although most of the syncretism probably dates from far earlier times.[6] In the nineteenth century American Protestant missionaries in Istanbul and in Anatolia did occasionally encounter surprising inquiries about Christianity from Turks of various inchoate sectarian movements, from Bektashis, even from some orthodox *ulema,* and occasionally they rejoiced in a brisk sale of their New Testaments to Turks.[7] But these events do not indicate any direct *millet* influence on Turks in religious matters. Further, so far as law is concerned, the objections of most of the *ulema* to the adoption of French Western-style law and courts and to the acceptance of non-Muslim testimony were so vigorous that, *a fortiori,* such influence from the *millets* would seem to be most unlikely.[8] Any consideration of this second possible path of *millet* influence, and through it, of Western influence on Turks, is therefore arbitrarily excluded from this discussion.

The third path for *millet* influence, and through it Western influence, on Muslim society and government would be the action or example of the *millet* as a structural entity. This might include the influence of the *millet* educational organs, of written *millet* constitutions, and of *millet* members who were representatives of their *millets* as entities to various Ottoman political bodies. Occasionally it may be difficult to distinguish between the influence of a *millet* member as an individual and the influence of a *millet* member acting as a *millet* representative, but this is not a serious difficulty.

To begin, then, what evidence can be pieced together to show that individuals, who were members of *millets* in the Ottoman Empire, acted as agents of change within that empire and helped to bring in Western influences?

The most obvious, and most superficial, aspect of Westernization was clothing. Non-Muslims more easily adopted European dress than Muslims, especially in the Western seaboard cities. It appears that Armenians may have done this more readily than Greeks, though this assertion is subject to correction.[9] The use of Western forks, chairs, and bedsteads followed. So did the use of alcohol and the proliferation of liquor stores.[10] These habits spread to Turks in the seaboard cities, especially to upper-class Turks, in the period following the Crimean War. It is difficult, however, and perhaps impossible, to distinguish the influence on Turks of *millet* members who adopted European ways from the direct influence of Europeans. There was a social spectrum or continuum in the Ottoman Empire, graded roughly according to decreasing connection with the West: Europeans resident or visiting in the empire, Levantines with European citizenship, Levantines without such citizenship but enjoying European protection, ordinary Levantines, *millet* members with foreign passports or protection, *millet* members without foreign protection, Turks of the coastal cities, Turks of interior cities, village and tribal Turks. (*Millet* members in the interior do not seem to fit neatly into the spectrum, but most probably were close to Turks of the interior cities and villages.) Western habits may, in some cases, have been passed along this chain. In other cases they may have jumped directly from Europeans resident in Istanbul to Istanbul Turks. They may even have jumped directly from Parisians to Turks who visited Paris. A common Turkish criticism of nineteenth-century Turkish Westernizers, however, was that voiced by Ziya Gökalp early in the next century: that the Turkish leaders of the *Tanzimat,* the Western-influenced reform movement launched by the Gülhane decree of 1839, took most of their knowledge of Europe from the Levantines of Beyoğlu.[11]

The chain of influence is even harder to trace specifically since the mid-nineteenth century was a time when the old regulations setting apart non-Muslims from Muslims were rapidly falling into desuetude. Outward signs like the color of a Christian's or a Jew's house or shoes, the distinctive style of his headdress, the rule of his dismounting from a horse on meeting a Muslim, the upper limit of three pairs of oars in his Bosporus *kayık,* were disappearing. Non-Muslims and Muslims were therefore harder to differentiate, whether in European habit or not.[12] It may seem logical that the adoption of European costume and other customs by some of the non-Muslims would make Muslims more familiar with Western ways, and more likely themselves eventually to adopt some. Such a causal relationship would, however, be difficult to demonstrate. There was certainly, at the time, some resistance among ordinary Turks to European ways as exemplified in the non-Muslim communities. During the severe cholera outbreak of 1865 it was reported that "the Turk finds the cause of the plague in a . . . breaking down among his own people of those former habits of dress which distinguished them from the (so-called) infidel among them."[13]

Non-Muslim social gatherings, a more delicate matter than costume, also sometimes included Muslims, even on occasion the sultan. Abdülmecid shattered precedent by attending the Greek Orthodox wedding of Istefanaki Vogorides's daughter to Photiades Bey in 1851 or 1852, and in 1856 by attending a ball given by Stratford de Redcliffe, where *millet* members were present along with European diplomats. The *Paşa* of Edirne in 1868 ordered Turkish officers to dance the quadrille at his soirées with Christian ladies in décolleté.[14] Such social mixing was undoubtedly confined to small official and upper-class circles.

In cultural pursuits of more intellectual content the influence of *millet* members is easier to establish. This is particularly true for the development of modern theater in Istanbul, where Armenians played a leading role in the mid-nineteenth century, both as producers and as actors. A Syrian Christian, Mikhail Naum, took over an Italian theater in 1844 and in 1858 produced the first play known to have been publicly performed in the empire in Turkish, though the actors were Armenians. The more important Gedikpaşa Theater, where Namık Kemal's *Vatan* and other plays by Turks, as well as European plays translated by Turks and successful Molière adaptations by Ahmed Vefik Paşa, were staged, was operated by Güllü Agop (Agop Vartovyan), again with Armenian actors, whose Turkish pronunciation was sometimes execrable. By the 1870s the Gedikpaşa Theater employed some Turkish actors (though, of course, no actresses as yet). Other theaters were also operated by Armenians, including Dikran Çuhaciyan, whom Metin And calls "the father of opera and musical plays in Turkey."[15] The close cooperation of Turks and Armenians in bringing Western dramatic forms to upper-class Turkish audiences marks an important milestone in cultural Westernization, despite the jaundiced sarcasm of the New Ottoman writer Ziya who charged that the *Tanzimat* elite were indulging in immoral superficialities: "building theatres, attending dances, not being jealous of one's wife, going about without ritual (ablution) purity."[16]

The burgeoning Turkish journalism of the 1870s also saw similar cooperation of Westernizing Turks and non-Muslims. Teodor Kasap (Theodore Cassape), an Ottoman Greek, edited *Diöjen,* which published some of Namık Kemal's articles, and later *Istikbal* and *Hayal. Ibret,* the newspaper that Namık Kemal edited in 1872–73, and in which he advocated various modes of Westernization, was owned by an Armenian, Sarafian.[17] The principal Westernizers of the press and the theater were Turkish journalists and playwrights—Gedikpaşa Theatre had a directing committee of Turkish literati—but *millet* members lent valuable assistance. Further, Syrian Christian and other Arab Christian writers, like the school of Butrus al-Busānī, influenced the Westernization of thought and institutions among Arabs in the Ottoman Empire.[18] In another, more technical, field of communications, non-Muslims also shared with Turks in spreading Western techniques, working in telegraph offices. Some of the newly instituted telegraph stations in Anatolia in the 1870s had Armenians as directors.[19]

The profession of translator from Western languages (principally French and Italian, with the former rapidly becoming dominant in the nineteenth century) was one for which members of non-Muslim millets seemed to have a natural advantage. Of course, Greeks had for years occupied the office of translator of the imperial divan. But when this monopoly was abolished after the Greek revolt of 1821, some members of the *millets* continued to serve as translators in the newly established Translation Bureau (*tercüme odası*). It is probably unfair to count among them the first two directors of the new office: Bulgaroğlu Yahya Efendi was a convert to Islam from Greek Orthodoxy, while his successor, Hoca Ishak Efendi, is generally thought to have been a convert from Judaism.[20] But

Greeks and Armenians who were not converts to Islam also worked in the *tercüme odası*. Zenob Manasseh was an early one, Alexander Karatodori and Krikor Efendi were later ones. Their role in transmitting knowledge of the West to Turks included the translating not only of documents for the Sublime Porte, but of Western newspaper articles as well. Furthermore, they helped to teach French to the growing number of Turks who were trained in the Translation Bureau.[21] Krikor was also a French teacher at the medical school, translator at the War Ministry, and author of a textbook on French grammar for Turks.[22] The translating of Western books into Turkish by *millet* members may not have been common, but it did occur. One example is the geography, written in French by a young Turk serving in the Ottoman embassy in London in the 1790s, which was translated into Turkish by Yakovaki Efendi, a Greek who was chargé d'affaires in the Ottoman embassy in Vienna and printed at the press in Üsküdar in 1804–05.[23]

Millet members also sometimes served as dragomans for Western embassies and, even more often, for Western consulates in the Ottoman Empire. As interpreters of oral communications and as translators of documents, they were obvious channels of Western ideas (and often demands) to Ottoman officials. Whether they were anything more than a channel, i.e., whether they were an important influence in their own right, is questionable, partly because of the position they occupied, and partly because of the unsavory reputation that dragomans as a group acquired, as a "curse" or as "Levantines" in the pejorative sense of that term.[24]

In the areas of dress, drama, journalism, and translation, then, the role of the individual non-Muslim seems at times to have been that of a channel for Western ideas or concepts, at times that of a filter. Sometimes it may also have been that of a buffer or barrier, as in the case of the Turkish regret at the growing lack of distinction between Muslim and non-Muslim clothing.

All three of these roles—channel, filter, buffer—seem to be observable in the economic sphere as well, where non-Muslims also were active as agents of change. Individual non-Muslims, like individual Muslims, could be the channels or filters for Western ideas. For example, the Armenian Agop Efendi, who went to Paris as an interpreter for Reşid Paşa's embassy, observed European industrial methods. When thereafter Agop went to Bursa, and saw all the mulberries, he used his acquired information to write a book on a new way to make silk and increase prosperity.[25] The many *millet* members engaged in the import and export trade with European merchants often were given diplomatic passports or protection by European powers, and increased in numbers after 1774.[26] In addition to bringing Western goods into the empire, they must certainly have introduced some Western business concepts and practices, and were probably aligned with Europeans in pressing the Porte for secular, Westernized commercial law and commercial courts.

In agriculture non-Muslims seemed to prosper more than Muslims in the third quarter of the nineteenth century. The reasons are not clear and require more investigation. One, certainly, was that the whole burden of military service fell on Muslims; non-Muslims paid a *bedel* amounting to twenty-eight piasters (5/10d) per capita in lieu of service, whereas a Muslim who wanted to buy out had to pay roughly forty-five to ninety liras, which peasants could not afford. It may also have been that some of the non-Muslims were more enterprising and used more progressive methods. From many sections of Anatolia it was reported that the Turkish population was declining, while the non-Muslim population was rising and getting richer. In Diyarbakır whole quarters of the city had changed from Turkish to Christian; "Armenians, Jacobites, and Protestants are continually buying Turkish houses, but never does it happen that a Turk buys a Christian house." Outside of Harput "land is slowly passing into the hands of the Christians," in this instance because "heartless Turkish landlords" who oppressed their tenants had been forced to sell to repay debts to wealthy Armenian lenders. In the Amasya region the Greeks were richer than the Turks, better able to buy justice in the courts, and were as well armed as the Turks but fiercer. In Rodosto, in Thrace, Greek moneylenders were doing the Turks out of their landed property.[27] These prospering Christians were obviously agents of change for their own economic advantage; whether the change was anything but disaster for Turks, or brought them any Western benefit, it is hard to say. Yet the non-Muslims might act as an irritant, to spur Muslims on to change for their own benefit. In Seyidi Gazi, the *müdür's divan efendisi* complained that no *raya* lived in that town of 3,000 houses; at least 200 houses ought to be Christian, he said, because they are skilled in agriculture and crafts and their example would spur the Muslims.[28]

The big *sarraf*s of the capital, often known as "the Galata bankers," occupied a special place in the Ottoman economy and in the political scene as well. All were non-Muslims. They wielded great power as lenders to the Porte and its various ministries, as money managers for leading *paşas,* as foreign exchange brokers, and as tax-farmers. In the nineteenth century Greek *sarraf*s were still prominent, but Jewish *sarraf*s had been eclipsed in influence by Armenians. Because of their wealth, their frequently exorbitant rates, their willingness to use political pressure and bribery, their contribution to squeezing the last tax-piaster out of the peasant, *sarraf*s acquired an evil reputation, perhaps worse than they deserved.[29] Although the importance of *sarraf*s dwindled slightly after the Crimean War, when the Porte found that it could tap the European money market directly through the sale of Ottoman bonds, it continued great throughout the century. One of the European/Levantine financiers of Istanbul was heard to say openly in the Treasury Ministry in 1871 that "when Zarifi, Christaki and Agop Efendi want to carry through a transaction, that deal has to be made *no matter what.*"[30]

As part of the establishment, the *sarraf*s were often conservative rather than a force for change. They resented attempts to abolish tax-farming and helped to defeat them. But they could also be a force for change and Westernization. Although proof is not in hand, I suspect that Armenian *sarraf*s may have suggested the first issue of paper money *(kaime)* to the Porte in 1840.[31] On occasion, they cooperated with European merchants and bankers in trying to maintain an orderly market for bills of exchange and for the paper money. When improvident government and palace spending brought the Porte near bankruptcy, as it strained to pay the coupons on its European bond debt, some of the same *sarraf*s were appointed to cooperate with European bankers and top Ottoman officials on an imperial commission to find measures to bail out the government. Among these *sarraf*s were two of those just mentioned: Kristaki Zografos Efendi and Agop Köçeoğlu Efendi.[32] Further study of the *sarraf*s' economic and political activities and of their role as possible agents of Westernization might be rewarding. Some, at least, were on the side of the angels at crucial moments. Kristaki Zografos and Agop Köçeoğlu, along with a small group of Turks including Namık Kemal, were intimates of Prince Murad, the hope of reformers as heir-apparent to Sultan Abdülaziz.[33] Zografos, as banker for Prince Murad (later Murad V) and his mother, is said to have distributed money in *medrese*s at Midhat Paşa's direction, helping to incite *softa*s to demand the deposition of the reactionary Grand Vezir Mahmud Nedim in 1876.[34] When, later in that same year, Sultan Abdülhamid promulgated Midhat Paşa's constitution, a parade of Galata Bourse members and *sarraf*s marched to the sultan's palace and to Midhat's *konak* to thank them.[35] Possibly the *sarraf*s were celebrating simply what they hoped was the end of the chaotic and financially irresponsible government, but it may be that they were also genuine partisans of Western-style parliamentary government.[36]

Millet members, again as individuals, played an important role in various offices of the central Ottoman government. This was particularly true in the Foreign Ministry in post-Crimean days. A few cases, picked at random from the third quarter of the nineteenth century, will serve to illustrate. Agop Efendi was chargé d'affaires in Paris in 1859. Takvor Efendi, in the ministry's Bureau of Foreign Correspondence, was also translator/editor of the French edition of the *Code Civile Ottoman*. In 1875 Ruben Karakaş, working in the same correspondence bureau, asked to be assigned to Paris as second secretary of embassy. The Grant Vezir, approving the memorandum, sent it to Artin Efendi, undersecretary of the ministry, who sent it to Serkis Efendi, the secretary-general of the Foreign Ministry, who sent it to the foreign minister. All those here named, below the rank of foreign minister, were Armenians. Serkis was a key man in the ministry, and even served as foreign minister *ad interim* in August 1867. In November 1875 another Armenian, Artin Dadian Efendi, was also interim or acting foreign minister.[37]

Greeks also were prominent. If one examines Ottoman diplomatic dispatches for 1867, for example, one finds that the Ottoman ambassadors in the capitals of the major powers were Musurus (London), Cemil (Paris), Hayder (Vienna), Aristarchi (Berlin), Comnenos (St. Petersburg), Rustem (Florence). Of the six, three were Greeks, two were Muslim Turks, and one (Rustem) an Italian. In addition, the post in Athens, next most important in the scale of Ottoman diplomatic concern, was held by a Greek, Photiades.

These men were all part of the establishment. They held influential positions. Does that mean that they were agents of change, of Westernization? In one way, they were agents against change. Every one was a strong defender of the Ottoman Empire against European encroachment or minority separatism. In that sense, every one was a conservative. But they were all, in addition, strong supporters of the *Tanzimat* brand of Westernization, and in that sense were agents of change even though not initiators. They were not, of course, working for Turkish nationalist goals, but for Ottoman goals. It is this pluralistic aspect of Ottoman diplomacy that modern Turks have often reacted against. In the early days of the nationalist movement one Turk wrote with pride of the new Turkish diplomats, comparing them to the earlier Ottoman group, to which his father had belonged: "When my father was appointed to his first important diplomatic position, his counselor was Pangiris Bey, a Greek, and his first secretary Ohannes Bey, an Armenian."[38]

Other departments of the central Ottoman government also had non-Muslims in their employ by the middle or later nineteenth century. In 1876 the Turkish author of a pamphlet promoting constitutionalism and a parliament to represent all ethnic elements of the empire pointed out that already there was no civil department of government without Christian officials.[39] A number of them were of families traditionally linked to Ottoman state service—the Düzian (Düz) family who supplied directors for the mint, the Dadian family whose members had run the powder works, the Vogorides and Karatodori (Carathéodory) families whose members had filled various administrative positions.[40]

Others were new. Some rose to top positions. Krikor Agaton, an Armenian, became minister of public works in 1868. Garabed Artin Davud Paşa, a Roman Catholic Armenian who had been governor of the Lebanon, later occupied the same ministerial post for a time. In the first ministry appointed by Sultan Abdülhamid after the exile of Midhat Paşa in early February, 1877, Kostaki Adossides Paşa was undersecretary of the interior, Ohannes Çamiç Efendi was minister of agriculture and commerce, and Ohannes Efendi Sakisian was undersecretary of public instruction.[41]

At least, Agaton and Davud were genuine modernizers, active agents of Westernization, and perhaps the other three were also; all certainly were influential. A special mention should be made of Krikor Odian Efendi, a determined Westernizer, who was close to Midhat Paşa for a dozen years or so as adviser, as director of political affairs ("foreign minister") for the Tuna *vilayet*, and in other posts.

In the areas so far mentioned—theater, journalism, translation, commerce, finance, diplomacy, and central government administration—it is incontrovertible that non-Muslims, as individuals, occupied influential positions. In some of these areas it is obvious that they were agents for Westernization. But how important their influence in this regard actually was must remain a matter for speculation. The *millet* members were cooperating with Turks working in the same areas. Many of these Turks were also agents of Westernization, had their own direct contacts with Europe and Europeans, and undoubtedly would have proceeded along the same lines had there been no non-Muslims working with them. This is probably true for the rather nebulous areas of costume, as well.

Parisian modes came to a few upper-class Istanbul women through the influence of visiting members of the Egyptian ruling family, as well as through other channels. Some of the *alafranga çelebiler,* the "Westernized gentlemen" of the major cities and of the bureaucracy, wore European-style clothes because of their own experiences in the West, their own contacts with Europeans, or because Sultan Mahmud II had decreed that his officials should wear the *istanbulin* and tight trousers along with the fez.[42] Until more evidence is accumulated, the degree of influence that individual non-Muslims exerted on the process of Westernizing change cannot be accurately judged.

Non-Muslims were also, in mid-nineteenth century, participants in various government bodies, not just as individuals, but specifically as representatives of their *millets.* This representation was an important aspect of the Administrative Council (*Idare Meclisi*) instituted at local levels in 1840 by Reşid Paşa.[43] But the tendency of the Christian and Jewish members of these local councils was, when they did possess influence, to exert it in favor of the *status quo.* They represented generally the wealthier class and the clergy, not the common man.[44] Officials sent out from Istanbul tended to be more progressive than the local notables who sat on the councils and do not appear to have been a force for Westernization. The same seems generally to have been true in local councils after application of the *vilayet* law of 1864, despite improvements in the system of electing members.[45]

In councils of the central government, the situation was somewhat different, for the non-Muslims who had seats there were hand-picked from among the best educated and most prominent members of their *millets.* They were members of the Ottoman bureaucracy and closely tied to *Tanzimat* statesmen. The non-Muslims first appointed to the chief council that deliberated on new regulations, the Supreme Council of Judicial Ordinances, in 1856 were a Dadian, a Düzian, a Vogorides, and Halim *fils,* a Jewish *sarraf.*[46] When that body was superseded by the Council of State in 1868, eleven members (out of thirty-eight) were non-Muslims, again all of them prominent, though a few were from major provincial cities and were not Istanbul residents. The likelihood is that most of them, like most of the Muslim members of the councils, were Westernizers, but it is not apparent that they exerted a leading influence in the councils in that direction.[47]

The verdict must be the same for the non-Muslims who were elected to seats in the first Ottoman Parliament of 1877–1878. Like their Muslim confrères, they represented varying political views, but were generally critical of the ministry and even of Abdülhamid II. This can be represented as a liberal, perhaps a Western, characteristic of parliamentary politics, but this is not necessarily the case. Most of the deputies did seem to have the reformer's instinct, tempered by feelings of patriotism during the Russo-Turkish War.

On one question the Christian deputies did take a more Western and progressive view than the Muslims. The Christians opposed the inclusion in a new press law of a prohibition of humorous journals, while Muslims were generally willing to accept this restriction, which related to Abdülhamid's fear of cartoon and satire. But enough liberal Muslims joined the Christian deputies to strike out the prohibition. On another matter, however, the Christians took a decidedly conservative, and in fact anti-Western, view. When one of their number, Vasilaki Efendi of Istanbul, proposed that Christians should do military service, and cited various advantages that the empire would derive therefrom, he got no support from other Christian deputies. And when a civic guard was created and non-Muslims were invited to enroll, Christian deputies were unenthusiastic. The impression given was that Christians would prefer paying a tax to serving in the armed forces.[48] It should be recognized that the Christians and Jews who sat in the two sessions of Parliament were not there, technically, as *millet* representatives. Like the Muslim deputies, they were elected solely as Ottomans. And in the Chamber of Deputies, most debates and votes were not along sectarian lines. But care was taken in the electoral process to see that non-Muslim representatives were elected. Furthermore, as deputies, the non-Muslim could not totally shed their sectarian identity, however much they might feel and act as Osmanlis. They had, in effect, a dual character, and in a sense they still represented their *millets*.

When one considers the *millet* as a form of organization, a constitutional structure, one can find a continuous thread of influence in the nineteenth century from Western example through *millet* organization to Ottoman organization. The Western influences were Anglo-Saxon and French. The *millet* structure that best absorbed these was the Armenian. The Ottoman institutions that showed evidence of some influence coming through these channels were the new *vilayet* system, under the law of 1864–1867, and the constitution of 1876. The channels were not simple transmission lines, however, but filters.[49]

In each of the three major *millets* there was a social upheaval and a cultural renaissance in the nineteenth century. As well-educated laymen, other than the great merchants and bankers, sought a voice in what had been an oligarchic *millet* structure controlled by the wealthy and the higher clergy, they absorbed Western ideas. A number of the coming generation of Armenian leaders had lived and studied in Paris and had seen the Revolution of 1848 and the Second Republic. In addition, Protestant missionaries in the Ottoman Empire had sponsored the formation of a Protestant *millet,* composed largely of Armenians, which obtained formal recognition with an imperial *ferman* in 1850. The *millet*'s organization was lay controlled, democratic, and on Anglo-Saxon lines. A comment by the American missionary H. G. O. Dwight in 1860 is instructive, even with its Protestant bias. ''A silent, though deep and thorough revolution is going on in the minds of the Armenian people in regard to their civil rights,'' he wrote. The Armenian patriarch, said Dwight, formerly nearly absolute, has been ordered by the Porte to form a lay committee to supervise the civil affairs of the *millet*. This committee recently proposed rules for doing business copied from the Protestant *millet* rules, which were based on popular sovereignty, and had been printed in Turkish and Armeno-Turkish. ''So far as I know, nothing of this sort had ever appeared in any of the languages of Turkey before.'' The patriarch did not like these rules. But recently the members of the committee signed an open letter to the patriarch which was published in the leading Armenian newspaper of Istanbul, *Massis,* threatening to resign if the rules were not kept. "To have a letter like this over responsible signatures, addressed, through a public paper, to the Patriarch of the Armenians, is certainly a novel thing; but it shows clearly how things are tending here." Dwight added, "I will just say here that the same thing is going on in the Greek community."[50] By 1863, after a number of vicissitudes, the Armenian *millet* had a constitution providing for lay control of an elected assembly as the keystone of its *millet* government. The constitutions of the Greek and Jewish *millets,* also made in the early 1860s, were less complete in their reforms, but went in the same direction.

When the new statute for administration of Ottoman provinces, the *vilayet* law, was drawn up in 1864, its provisions for indirect election to provincial councils bore a resemblance to the electoral provisions of the Armenian *millet* constitution. Whether the influence here was direct, or not, I do not know, but some of the top statesmen, especially Fuad Paşa, had been concerned with each. When the Ottoman constitution of 1876 was drafted, the connecting links were clearer. For one thing, the example of the elected general assemblies of the *millet* constitutions was probably influential. Namık Kemal, the New Ottoman writer, worked on the constitution drafting committee; he had as early as 1867 remarked that the assemblies of the Christians could serve as an example for a chamber of deputies.[51] Further, of the twenty-eight members of the constitution drafting committee, six were Christians—three Armenians, three Greeks.[52] One of the Armenians was Krikor Odian, who had earlier been one of the authors of the Armenian *millet* constitution. Odian, as had been noted, was close to Midhat Paşa, the chairman of the constitution committee, and certainly in the preceding years had contributed something to the shaping of Midhat's ideas about parliamentary government. The editor of Odian's speeches and letters says further that when Midhat was grand vezir on a previous occasion (1872), he used to dine at Odian's house at least once a week, and there talked with other Armenians, including Serviçen (Serovpe Viçenyan), who like Odian had been a member of the committee that drafted the Armenian millet constitution.[53] The Ottoman constitution of 1876 was, of course, the product of other major influences, both European and domestic, which the Turks primarily responsible for its existence brought into the discussions and the drafting. But some of the Western influence that contributed to that momentous document flowed through the filter of the Armenian *millet* constitution.

It is interesting to note that Ziya Gökalp, about fifty years after the *millet* constitution had been completed, castigated the *Tanzimat* statesmen not only for allowing and encouraging *millet* organization, but also for intending to organize a Muslim *millet* on the same basis. In fact, Ziya asserts that a Muslim community was set up on the Christian/Jewish model in Edirne, but fortunately, he says, it was never extended to the other provinces. I know nothing of this Muslim *millet* of Edirne. If Ziya's report is accurate, it would be rewarding to study this sort of change stimulated by the non-Muslim *millets.* Ziya blames Âli Paşa, in particular, for conceiving of the Ottoman Empire in terms of *millets*—a confederation of cults.[54] But here Ziya probably misconstrues Âli and other *Tanzimat* statesmen. They were perched on both horns of a dilemma. They did confirm the rights of *millet*s, in part owing to European pressures. But at the same time they tried to secularize those *millet*s and to transform the Ottoman Empire into a more secular state made up not of autonomous cults but of individual Ottoman subjects.

One other aspect of organized *millet* life had an impact on Turkish thinking. This was education. Traditionally, there were no secular schools, but only religious schools, and each *millet* had its own. Non-Muslim schools certainly did not as a rule serve as examples for Turkish schools, though Osman Ergin, the historian of Turkish education, points to two cases where this was true, or possibly true. One was the *Darüşşafaka,* the part-time school for orphans, poor children, and guild *(esnaf)* apprentices, created by thoughtful Muslims on the model of non-Muslim schools in Istanbul. The other was the *Mektebi Osmanî* in Paris, a school established about 1857 to care for Turks sent from the military schools in Istanbul for further education. Its establishment may have been suggested in part by the fact that Mehmed Ali had established a school for young Egyptians in Paris, and in part by the fact that there was an Armenian school, the *Muradian Mektebi,* there also.[55]

But the major influence of *millet* schools on Turks was probably that they forced Turks to think about improving their own literacy rate. A litany of complaints by educated Turks in the later nineteenth century points out that non-Muslim children could outperform Muslim children in reading and writing. Ziya Paşa said that a ten-year-old Armenian or Greek schoolboy usually could write, and read a newspaper, while a fifteen-year-old Turkish schoolboy rarely could write a two-line note or read the *Takvim-i Vekayi*. The fault is not with our children, whose natural capacity is as great as that of Armenian, Greek, and Jewish children, said Ziya, but with our educational system.[56] The newspaper *Basiret* voiced similar complaints, and even suggested that the minister of education should severely control Greek and Armenian schools.[57] Süleyman Paşa, a leader in military education, said that the whole *millet-i islamiye* needed educational progress.[58] Ahmed Midhat, writing about Turkish educational progress in 1877, was painfully aware of educational progress among Greeks, Armenians, Jews, and Bulgarians.[59] The *millet* schools were not, however, a channel, and probably not even a filter, for Western influence on Turkish education. They seem more to have been an irritant, or a spur, to better performance by the Turks, who sought out French school models rather than *millet* models. But as an irritant, the non-Muslim *millet* still functioned as the agent of change.[60]

The evidence so far presented has shown that the *millet*s were, in some fields of human endeavor, and to varying degrees, agents of change, in the role of channels, filters, or irritants. But it is important to ask whether this was the major characteristic of *millet*s or whether they were not also agents of conservatism and the *status quo*. The answer is obvious: the *millet*s were also conservative, probably much more so than they were agents of change. This subject could be examined at length, but a few considerations may suggest why *millet* conservatism was probably the rule. Any society, to begin with, seems to be in majority conservative. The bulk of Serbs, Bulgars, Greeks, Albanians, Romanians, Armenians, etc., were peasants, remote from Western influence. They may have sent delegations to Istanbul to ask redress of local grievances, or may on occasion have risen in revolt, but probably by nature they were not innovative. The Armenian and Greek clerical hierarchies, and the Jewish rabbinate, in the second place, were usually conservative. The term "obscurantist" is often applied to them. One has only to listen to the impassioned words of Adamantios Korais— "now we are governed by scoundrels and stupid men as well as by an ignorant clergy who are even worse than our foreign tyrants the Turks"—[61] to learn the sentiment of the minority of *millet* members who *were* progressive and Westernizers. The famous story about what the Greek metropolitan of Izmit said when the Ottoman reform decree of 1856 had been read and put back in its red pouch is illustrative of a mentality long current in *millet* hierarchies: "God grant that it not be taken out of this bag again."[62] Further, there was often lay mistrust of priests and rabbis as extortionate.[63]

In the third place, some Westernizing reform measures of the nineteenth century were opposed by influential *millet* groups, quite naturally so in protection of their own interests. The attempted abolition of tax-farming was opposed by the *sarrafs*, who were pleased to see the experiment in direct state tax collection fail. It was also opposed by non-Muslim and by Turkish peasants, who found the inexperienced new state collectors more demanding.[64] The various proposals that non-Muslims do military service, sharing this burden with the Turks, were regularly opposed by the non-Muslims, despite their wish for theoretical equality. There *were* a few Ottoman non-Muslims in the armed services—it is startling to learn that two Armenians in 1862 attained the rank of general—but conscription of non-Muslims was never achieved in the nineteenth century.[65]

There is another way in which *millets* may have worked against change and Westernization, although involuntarily. They may have acted as a buffer between Turks and the West. By accepting Western ways more readily than Muslims, the non-Muslims may, by the very fact that they were non-Muslims, nonmembers of the Islamic *millet,* have deterred Muslims from accepting the same ways. I cannot think of a particular Western product or concept which was rejected by Ottoman Muslims in the nineteenth century simply because the Ottoman non-Muslims did accept it, but there may well be such. The adverse Turkish reaction would be rooted in religious reasons, and in the general prejudice against *bidat,* especially against innovation that comes from infidel origins. Had the brimmed Western hat been universally accepted by Ottoman non-Muslims, its rejection by Muslims might be explained in terms of anti-*millet* reaction. But such was not the case. The brimmed hat was rejected by Turks, evidently as blasphemous and *bidat,* but because it was a symbol of the Western Christian world, not because it was a symbol of the *millets*; the *millets*, Greeks partly excepted, had been shifting to the fez which Muslims wore.[66] Again, the refusal of Turks to accept printing in Turkish before 1727 seems unrelated to the fact that Jews, Armenians, and Greeks had presses in Istanbul, although the refusal was rooted in religious reasons—and also, it seems, in the opposition of calligraphers.[67] There was, nevertheless, an undercurrent of resentment on the part of liberal and Westernizing Ottoman Turks against Ottoman non-Muslims that could well have led to the rejection of Western innovation simply because it found favor among the *millets*. The undercurrent of resentment was fed from three sources: dislike of the *millet* members' recourse to foreign diplomatic protection and privilege; dislike of the *Hatt-ı Hümayun* of 1856 as a "ferman of concessions" *(imtiyaz fermanı)* for non-Muslims; and annoyance that the *millets* were often wrapped up in their own affairs and seemed little concerned with the empire's welfare.[68] The role of the non-Muslim *millets* that Bernard Lewis speaks of as a "cushion" embodies some of this buffering action, though it embodies perhaps more of what I have called a "filter."[69]

The greatest conservatism of the *millets* was, finally, their mere continued existence as separately defined communities. Had the concept of a secular Ottoman citizenship gained wholehearted support from non-Muslims and Muslims, a new age would have dawned. But the religious distinctions that had existed from the earliest times continued into the nineteenth century, and even were reinforced in the 1860s by the reform of the *millet* structures. The conservatism of separate religious identity then developed, paradoxically, into the most explosive agency for change that the modern world has known. When Greek Orthodox subjects became Greek nationalist rebels, and when Serbs, Romanians, and others followed suit, the Ottoman Empire was torn apart. The non-Muslims' roles in promoting change as channel, filter, and irritant, and in retarding change as buffer, were all in the end eclipsed when they took up the role of revolutionary nationalists. As nationalists, the non-Muslims were greater purveyors of change than ever before. Finally nationalism, a modern Western invention, was communicated to the Turks themselves. In part they received it directly from Europe. But in part they received it from the non-Muslims of the Ottoman Empire, both by contagion and by revulsion.

Notes

1. Hermann Vambery, "Der Kreuzzug im neunzehnten Jahrhundert," *Augsburger Allgemeine Zeitung,* no. 225, 12 August 1876. This observation carried with it, of course, an implication of European superiority, although Vambery specifically noted Western faults as well.

2. Cevdet Paşa, *Tezâkir,* ed. Cavid Baysun, Ankara, 1953–1967, vol. 1, p. 68. The same language is used by Ahmed Refik in "Türkiyede Islahat Fermani," *TOEM* 14:4 (81) (1 Temmuz 1340), pp. 195–196.

3. Resid's memorandum in Cevdet (cited n. 2), p. 79. Nineteenth-century recognition of Latin, Catholic Armenian, Protestant, and other *millets* expanded the number.

4. In *Belleten*, 28 (1964), p. 791, reviewing Roderic H. Davison, *Reform in the Ottoman Empire, 1856–1876*, Princeton, 1963. He calls for investigation in depth of the *"millet* system" from early times.

5. Benjamin Braude, "Myths and Realities of the Ottoman Communal System Before the *Tanzimat,"* MESA Conference Paper, New York, 11 November 1977.

6. See F. W. Hasluck, *Christianity and Islam Under the Sultans,* ed. Margaret M. M. Hasluck, 2 vols., Oxford, 1929.

7. Records of the American Board of Commissioners for Foreign Missions (hereafter, ABCFM), now on deposit in the Houghton Library, Harvard University, contain references to such events, scattered among the more usual reports of indifference to their mission work, or of opposition to it.

8. Cevdet (cited n. 2), vol. 1, p. 63. The *ulema* said that the alteration of the fundamental laws of a *millet* (here the Islamic *millet*) would be equivalent to the destruction of that *millet*.

9. David Porter, *Constantinople and Its Environs,* New York, 1835, vol. 1, p. 138; Karl Braun-Wiesbaden, *Eine türkische Reise,* Stuttgart, 1876, vol. 2, p. 210; United States National Archives, State Department Records (hereafter USNA), Turkey, no. 14, Spence (Constantinople, to Marcy), 28 Nov. 1856.

10. Henry Harris Jessup, *Fifty-Three Years in Syria,* New York, 1910, vol. 1, pp. 119–120. USNA also contains reports on the alcohol problem.

11. Uriel Heyd, *Foundations of Turkish Nationalism,* London, 1950, p. 75. Ziya may have been thinking of *millet* members as part of the Levantine society there. The "freshwater Franks," Levantine or *millet* members with European citizenship or protection, were often associated with Greeks, Armenians, and Jews: cf. Refii-Şükrü Sulva, "Tanzimat Devrinde İstikrazlar," *Tanzimat,* Istanbul, 1940, vol. 1, p. 265. Süleyman Paşa, *Hiss-i inkılâp,* Istanbul, 1326/1908, p. 5, associates Beyoğlu Europeans with Greeks and Armenians.

12. Cf. Davison (cited n. 4), p. 50 and references there. Cyrus Hamlin, *Among the Turks,* New York, 1878, p. 371, notes that one Christian, Istefanaki Vogorides, prince of Samos and *kapıkethüdası* of Moldavia, had been allowed four pairs of oars in the 1830s.

13. ABCFM, vol. 284, no. 173, E. E. Bliss (Constantinople) to Anderson, 26 Aug. 1865.

14. Hamlin (cited n. 12), p. 371; Stanley Lane-Poole, *The Life of the Right Hon. Stratford Canning,* London, 1888, vol. 2, p. 215; Albert A. E. Dumont, *Le Balkan et l'Adriatique,* Paris, 1874, p. 120 ff. I am guessing that the ladies in evening gowns were Ottoman rather than foreign Christians.

15. Metin And, *A History of Theatre and Popular Entertainment in Turkey,* Ankara, 1963–64, pp. 66–71, 112–113; François Alphonse Belin, "Bibliographie ottomane," *Journal Asiatique,* série 6, 18 (Aug.–Sept. 1871), p. 126; Y. G. Çark, *Türk devleti hizmetinde Ermeniler, 1453–1953,* Istanbul, 1953, pp. 278–279.

16. In *Hürriyet,* no. 41, 22 Zilhicce 1285/5 April 1869, reprinted in İhsan Sungu, "Tanzimat ve Yeni Osmanlılar," *Tanzimat* (cited n. 11), vol. 1, p. 814.

17. Mithat Cemal Kuntay, *Namık Kemal,* Istanbul, 1944–56, vol. 1, pp. 586–591, and vol. 2, Part 1, p. 721; *Le Stamboul,* 10 Feb. 1877; *Levant Herald,* 10 April 1873. Kasap had spent about fourteen years in Paris, most of them as secretary to Alexandre Dumas père.

18. See, for example, Albert Hourani, *Arabic Thought in the Liberal Age,* London, 1970, p. 55 ff., and index s.v. "Christians"; Shimon Shamir, quoting from Palestinian Christian editors in "The Impact of Western Ideas on Traditional Society in Ottoman Palestine," in Moshe Ma'oz, ed., *Studies on Palestine during the Ottoman Period,* Jerusalem, 1975, pp. 507–514.

19. Frederick G. Burnaby, *On Horseback through Asia Minor,* London, 1877, vol. 1, pp. 70, 268.

20. Osman Ergin, *Türkiye maarif tarihi,* Istanbul, 1939–43, vol. 1, pp. 57–60. Abraham Galanté (Bodrumlu), *Histoire des juifs d'Istanbul,* Istanbul, 1941, vol. 1, p. 23, says that İshak was known to Jews as the Haham of the Tershane, from the district of Istanbul where he lived, but Carter V. Findley, "The Foundation of the Ottoman Foreign Ministry," *IJMES* 3 (1972), p. 402 and nn. 4, 5,

finds the evidence conflicting and summarizes Faik Reşat Unat's case against the surmise that Ishak was a convert.

21. Andreas David Mordtmann, *Stambul und das moderne Türkenthum,* Leipzig, 1877–78, vol. 1, p. 141, and vol. 2, p. 177; Findley (cited n. 20), pp. 401–404.

22. *Journal Asiatique,* série 5, 16 (Oct.-Nov. 1860), 325–336. Hoca İshak also taught at the military engineering school, in mathematics, and wrote a four-volume work on the mathematical and natural sciences: Avram Galanti (Bodrumlu), *Türkler ve Yahudiler,* second ed., Istanbul, 1947, p. 130; Abdülhak Adnan Adıvar, *Osmanlı Türklerinde ilim,* Istanbul, 1943, pp. 196–197.

23. Ibid., pp. 188–189.

24. Cf. Sir William White's words, quoted in B. H. Sumner, *Russia and the Balkans 1870–1880,* Oxford, 1937, p. 236: British embassy dragomans were "all Levantines of a very bad type and suspected of being corrupt"; Howard A. Reed, The Destruction of the Janissaries, Princeton University Ph.D. thesis, 1951, p. 98 and n. 8: "There are three scourges to beware of in Turkey: fires, the plague, and dragomans"; Ziya's comments in *Hürriyet,* no. 55, 2 Rebiülahir 1286/12 July 1869, in Sungu, *Tanzimat* (cited n. 11), vol. 1, pp. 789–792.

25. Fatma Aliye, *Ahmed Cevdet Paşa ve zamanı,* Istanbul, 1332/1914, p. 45. She says that Agop wrote in Armenian, and Cevdet Paşa put the manual into Turkish for him. I fail to understand why Agop did not write the Turkish himself.

26. Üner Turgay, "International Trade and Great Power Pressures: Trabzon in the 19th Century," MESA Conference Paper, New York, 10 November 1977.

27. ABCFM, vol. 284, no. 289, H. G. O. Dwight (Diyarbekir) to Anderson, 22 May 1861; ABCFM, Eastern Turkey Mission 1, no. 121, Allen (Harput) to Clark, 13 Dec. 1872; Henry F. Tozer, *Turkish Armenia and Eastern Asia Minor,* London, 1881, pp. 41–42; Dumont (cited n. 14), pp. 15–16. On the *bedel,* James Baker, *Turkey,* New York, 1877, pp. 384–386.

28. A. D. Mordtmann, *Anatolien, Skizzen und Reisebriefe (1850–1859),* Hannover, 1925, p. 539.

29. Charles MacFarlane, *Turkey and its Destiny,* Philadelphia, 1850, vol. 1, p. 463, and vol. 2, pp. 177–184, 472–474; Juchereau de St. Denys, *Histoire de l'Empire ottoman,* Paris, 1844, vol. 2, p. 16 and n. 1. Radical Armenians lumped Armenian *sarraf*s with clergy and *aga*s as oppressors (perhaps worse than Turks) of their own people; Frédéric Macler, *Autour de l'Arménie,* Paris, 1917, p. 253, condensing from Varandian, *Haykakan Charmjan Nakhapalmouthiun,* Geneva, 1912–14, vol. 2.

30. Başbakanlık Arşivi (Istanbul) (Hereafter BBA), Yıldız tasnifi, kısım 18, evrak 525/321, Garabed Karakaş, (Caracache) to Sadık Paşa, Istanbul, 1/13 April 1871.

31. Roderic H. Davison, "The First Ottoman Experiment with Paper Money," in Halil Inalcik and Osman Okyar, ed. *Türkiye'nin Sosyal ve Ekonomik Tarihi (1071–1920)* (Papers of the First International Congress on the Social and Economic History of Turkey, Hacettepe University, 1977), Ankara, 1980, p. 244.

32. Foreign Minister to United States Minister, no. 6, 29 Rebiulahir 1265/24 March 1849, USNA, Notes and Translations from the Sublime Porte, 1848–1849, and enclosure; USNA, Turkey, no. 26, Goodenow (Constantinople) to Fish, no. 17, 23 April 1874.

33. Kuntay (cited n. 17), vol. 2, part 1, p. 738.

34. Ahmed Rasim, *Istibdaddan hakimiyeti milliyeye,* Istanbul, 1342/1924, vol. 2, p. 126, n. 2.

35. *Levant Herald,* 26 December 1876.

36. One avenue of influence from the West is important, but I shall not attempt to explore it here, even though many non-Muslims worked in it: the Ottoman Public Debt Administration. See Donald C. Blaisdell, *European Financial Control in the Ottoman Empire,* New York, 1929.

37. *Levant Herald,* 27 October 1876; BBA, Yıldız tasnifi, Kısım 18, evrak 525/570; Haus-Hof-und Staatsarchiv (Vienna), Politisches Archiv XII/88, 22 August 1867; Public Record Office (London), Foreign Office 78/2390, Elliott (Constantinople) to Derby, no. 745, 12 November 1875.

38.   Mufty-Zade Zia, "How the Turks Feel," *Asia* 22 (1922), p. 861.

39.   Esad Efendi, *Hükümet-i meşrute,* Istanbul, 1293/1876, reprinted in Süleyman Paşa zade Sami, ed., *Süleyman Paşa muhakemesi,* Istanbul 1328/1910, pp. 86–87.

40.   Çark (cited n. 15), pp. 51 ff. and 75 ff.; Ergin (cited n. 20), vol. 1, 57–58, n. 3.

41.   Çark (cited n. 15), pp. 199–201; Mordtmann (cited n. 21), vol. 1, p. 72; *Levant Herald,* n.d., encl. in USNA, Turkey, no. 31, Maynard (Constantinople) to Fish, no. 30, 20 February 1877. See the list of Christian officials in Hamlin (cited n. 12), pp. 371–375.

42.   Fatma Aliye (cited n. 25), p. 84; Bernard Lewis, *The Emergence of Modern Turkey,* 2nd ed., London, 1968, p. 102.

43.   Halil Inalcik, "Tanzimat'ın uygulanması ve sosyal tepkileri," *Belleten,* 28 (1964), pp. 623–636.

44.   Reports of British consuls on local government councils in 1860 from widely scattered places within the empire confirm the conservative nature of the non-Muslims: Great Britain, House of Commons, *Sessional Papers,* 1861, vol. 67, "Reports . . . Conditions of Christians in Turkey."

45.   Davison (cited n. 4), pp. 166–167.

46.   Ibid., p. 93 and n. 39. Cavid Baysun in Cevdet (cited n. 2), vol. 1, p. 177, indicates that the Armenian Gregorian member was Ohanes Tingirian rather than Ohanes Dadian. Tingirian (Tingiroğlu Ohanes) was a wealthy tax-farmer whom Çark (cited n. 15), p. 69, further identifies as Fuad Paşa's *sarraf.* Baysun may be thinking of Tingirian's membership on the successor body, the Council of State, in 1868.

47.   Council members listed by name and *millet* in PRO, FO 195/893, no. 160, a printed list of 1 May 1868. There were four Armenian Catholics (a great overrepresentation), three Greek Orthodox, two Jews, one Armenian Gregorian, and one Bulgarian Greek Orthodox.

48.   Robert Devereux, *The First Ottoman Constitutional Period,* Baltimore, 1963, pp. 186–226, based on Hakkı Tarik US, *Meclis-i meb'usan 1293:1877 zabıt ceridesi,* 2 vols., Istanbul 1940–1954. The Armenian *millet* Assembly approved Armenian enrollment in the guard, but the *millet* Council decided that no Armenians would serve, Devereux, p. 225, n. 94.

49.   Davison (cited n. 4), chapter 3 and portions of chapters 5 and 10.

50.   ABCFM, vol. 284, no. 260, Dwight (Constantinople) to Anderson, 28 February 1860. The editor of the newspaper *Massis* was Garabed Utujian, one of those Armenians who had had experience in Paris.

51.   In his "Answer to the *Gazette du Levant*" in Kuntay (cited n. 17), vol. 1, p. 185.

52.   List of members in Devereux (cited n. 48), pp. 259–260.

53.   Mikael Kazmarian, ed., *Krikor Odian,* Constantinople, 1910, vol. 1, p. xiv.

54.   Ziya Gökalp, *Turkish Nationalism and Western Civilization,* ed. Niyazi Berkes, New York, 1959, pp. 206–208, 223.

55.   Ergin (cited n. 20), vol. 2, pp. 405–412, 379–381; Richard L. Chambers, "Notes on the *Mekteb-i Osmani* in Paris, 1857-1874," in William R. Polk and R. L. Chambers, eds., *Beginnings of Modernization in the Middle East,* Chicago, 1968, pp. 313–329.

56.   In *Hürriyet,* no. 5, 7 Rebiulahir 1285/27 July 1868, and no. 54, 25 Rebiulevvel 1285/5 July 1869 (sic) (the second Hicrî year should probably be changed to 1286), in Sungu (cited n. 16), p. 841. The *Takvim-i Vekayi,* it might be pointed out, would not be an easy test. A pamphlet of 1867 contains similar sentiments, but might have been written by a European rather than a Turk: summary in *Levant Herald,* 1 May 1867.

57.   Mordtmann (cited n. 21), vol. 1, pp. 148–149, citing an article entitled "We are wasting our time," in *Basiret,* February (n.d.) 1873. Further articles are quoted, pp. 149–150, comparing Christian largesse in school support to Turkish niggardliness.

58.   Süleyman Paşa (cited n. 11), p. 16.

59.   Ahmet Midhat, *Üss-i inkilâp,* Istanbul, 1294–95/1877-78, vol. 1, p. 119.

60. Some of the *millet* schools may not have been of good caliber. Even the Alliance Israélite schools, supported by lavish gifts from abroad, may have been superficial (some Turkish students did attend these Alliance Israélite schools). See the criticism by a Galician Jew, Naphtali Herz Imber, visiting Istanbul in 1882: "Leaves from My Palestine and Other Diaries," in Daniel Carpi and Gedalia Yogev, eds., *Zionism,* Tel Aviv, 1975, p. 303. Cf. Abdolonyme Ubicini and Pavet de Courteille, *État présent de l'Empire ottoman,* Paris, 1876, pp. 209–211, on the schools and their foreign support.

61. Stephen G. Chaconas, *Adamantios Korais,* New York, 1942, p. 28. There were, of course, some clergy who were reform-minded and even leaders of change.

62. Edouard Engelhardt, *La Turquie et le Tanzimat,* Paris, 1882–84, vol. 1, p. 142.

63. "Reports . . . Conditions of Christians in Turkey" reflects this. In 1879 the Jewish community of Baghdad asked the *vali* to remove their *haham başı* for "bribery and embezzlement." David S. Sassoon, *A History of the Jews in Baghdad,* Letchworth, 1949, p. 157 ff.

64. Stanford J. and Ezel Kural Shaw, *History of the Ottoman Empire and Modern Turkey,* Cambridge, 1976–1977, vol. 2, pp. 95–96; H. W. V. Temperley, *England and the Near East: The Crimea,* London, 1936, p. 166.

65. The Armenians were officers employed in the war and navy ministries. Although they were made *mir-liva,* "general of brigade," presumably they commanded desks rather than troops. Alphonse Belin, *Étude sur la propriété foncière . . . en Turquie,* Paris, 1862, p. 55, n. 3.

66. Niyazi Berkes, *The Development of Secularism in Turkey,* Montreal, 1964, pp. 123–126.

67. Lewis (cited n. 42), pp. 41, 50–51; Berkes (cited n. 66), pp. 39–41.

68. Namık Kemal in *Hürriyet* no. 4, 30 Rebiulevvel 1285/20 July 1868, in Sungu (cited n. 16), pp. 795–796; Ziya in *Hürriyet* no. 15, 18 Cemaziülahir 1285/5 October 1868, cited, ibid., p. 797; Süleyman Paşa (cited n. 39), p. 76.

69. Lewis (cited n. 42), pp. 62–63.

The Acid Test of Ottomanism:
The Acceptance of Non-Muslims
in the Late Ottoman Bureaucracy*

CARTER V. FINDLEY

For centuries the Ottoman sultans insisted with considerable rigor that those who entered their service adhere to the state religion. All who became members of the ruling class, with but occasional exceptions, were Muslim by the processes of their recruitment and training if not by birth; and only such individuals were properly "Ottoman" *(Osmanlı)*. During the nineteenth-century era of reform, by contrast, both the architects of imperial policy and the pioneers of political ideology formally committed themselves to egalitarian principle. With this they espoused an expanded concept of Ottomanism as a composite imperial "nationality" intended to embrace and attract the loyalty of all populations of the empire without distinction. The concept of the state as fundamentally Islamic did not change, but the old dichotomy of rulers and subjects, at least by implication, was effaced. The origins of these changes lie in factors such as doubts about the ability of the empire to survive, the positive attraction which the ideas of European liberalism had begun to exert on the thinking of Ottoman reformers, and the insistence of the European powers on reform as the price for their support of the empire.

The underlying principles and general outlines of the egalitarian reforms have in recent years been studied in some detail. We shall accordingly take up only one specific question about these measures, but one to which the success of the whole program was particularly linked. This question concerns the extent to which the sultans and statesmen of the period managed to implement their newly proclaimed principles within the ranks of government servants and thus satisfied one obvious prerequisite for the credible projection of the same principles over

*The research on which this paper is based was assisted by grants from the American Research Institute in Turkey and the Joint Committee on the Near and Middle East of the Social Science Research Council and the American Council of Learned Societies.

the vast complexity of Ottoman imperial society. We shall briefly consider this question as it relates to the entire governmental apparatus of the day. Then, for a more precise measure of the changes of the period, we shall focus on the Ottoman Foreign Ministry and on the detailed information in its personnel records.[1]

To appreciate what happened in the wake of the egalitarian reforms, it is really necessary to begin by noting that there had always been some kind of non-Muslim presence in, or more often on the flanges of, the Ottoman ruling class. In the early days of conquest in Europe, for example, there had been Christian cavalrymen. At the height of the empire, there had been Jewish financiers and physicians, influential at court if few in numbers. From the mid-seventeenth century on, what has been called the Phanariot Greek *noblesse de robe* acquired an eminence which reached its height with the Phanariot monopoly over the princely thrones of Moldavia and Wallachia (1711–1821). By the early nineteenth century Armenians were serving as financiers *(sarrafs)* and in the Imperial Mint and Powder Works. What was true of non-Muslims in Istanbul was surely more so in some outlying regions, especially the Christian vassaldoms of the Balkans. The non-Muslim presence was perhaps also stronger in capacities which were no more than semiofficial, such as those of tax-farmer, architect in government employ, or craftsman or purveyor of goods to the Palace.[2]

In all such cases, however, several traits stood out. One of these was the marginality of the non-Muslims to the ruling class and its norms. Non-Muslims in "official" or "semiofficial" positions were few in numbers, both absolutely and by comparison with the non-Muslim officials of the later nineteenth century. Prior to the reforms of the nineteenth century the very fact that these men retained their identity as non-Muslims signified that they had not gone through the processes of recruitment and training by which individuals traditionally became part of the ruling class. This meant in turn that the non-Muslim "officials" usually had no more than limited mastery of the cultural patterns characteristic of the ruling elite, particularly of that arcane Arabo-Perso-Turkish pastiche which served as the official medium of communication. The more or less technical capacities in which the non-Muslims usually appeared suggest that it was their cultural marginality which made them useful to the state in the first place.

Marginality and religious distinctness also tended to find expression in what amounted to the confinement of the non-Muslims in enclaves on the edge of the ruling class. This pattern recalled the enclavement of the larger non-Muslim communities into the general framework of the Muslim state in some form of what we may term semiautonomous confessional communities. Certainly in the case of the Phanariots the development of an official enclave with an internal structure and dynamic of its own became quite clear. We note this especially with the development of a distinctive Phanariot *cursus honorum* including university study in Italy, perhaps the posts of "Agent at the Porte" *(kapı kahyası)* for the princes of Moldavia and Wallachia, then the translatorship of the Imperial Fleet, that of the Imperial Divan, and finally the two princely thrones themselves.[3]

Western observers were impressed by the splendid style which the leading figures in this Phanariot enclave were in position to assume, but also by the ambiguity of their status in relation to the sultan. A non-Muslim from a different community summed up this ambivalence succinctly in a petition submitted in 1825 by referring to himself as *zimmi kulları,* a phrase implying that he was in the "protected status" *(zimmet, dhimma)* of a non-Muslim member of the subject classes and at the same time was also a slave *(kul)* of the sultan, as members of the ruling class were conventionally termed.[4] Not only were the non-Muslim "officials" marginal to the high culture of the ruling class, then, but their position in relation to the Muslim elite resembled a replication in miniature of the pattern by which the life of the non-Muslim communities was generally organized under the aegis of the Islamic state.

In the nineteenth century the bases on which non-Muslims were affiliated with Ottoman government service began to undergo change for a variety of reasons. Some of these changes resulted from the growth of separatist nationalist feeling among various of the subject nationalities. The position of the Greeks, for example, was profoundly shaken by the outbreak of the Greek Revolution in 1821. This fact in itself then stimulated the expansion of the Armenian presence in official circles. Reforms which the state itself enacted, particularly through the two great reform decrees of 1839 and 1856, also made a fundamental difference, and they did so in a more positive sense.

To be more precise, the first of these documents, the Gülhane Decree of 1839, initiated the process of egalitarian reform but in terms which were not well enough elaborated to have material impact on government service. Including such specifics as guarantees for life, honor, and property, a demand for regularization of tax-assessment and military conscription, and a promise of due process of law, this decree added a general provision that "the Muslim and non-Muslim subjects of our lofty Sultanate shall, without exception, enjoy our imperial concessions."[5] Some practical improvements followed the promulgation of this decree, but they do not appear to have included any dramatic change in the access of non-Muslims to official position, unless we so interpret the inclusion of representatives of the non-Muslim communities in the local administrative councils set up in 1840.[6]

Toward the end of the Crimean War, however, and in an effort to gain European goodwill, the Ottomans did begin to go into specifics as to how egalitarianism should be applied. In 1855 there was an announcement that non-Muslims should be admitted to military service through the grade of colonel, to civil service without limit of grade, and that the poll tax traditionally emblematic of the subordinate, protected status of non-Muslim subjects should be abolished.[7] The Reform Decree of 1856 then took up these same points along with many other details. It proclaimed, for example, that ". . . all the subjects of my empire, without distinction of nationality, shall be admissible to public employments, and qualified to fill them according to merit, and conformably with rules to be generally applied. . . ."[8] The same decree also expressly affirmed the liability of non-Muslim subjects to military recruitment but permitted the sending of substitutes or the purchasing of exemption. The development of general rules on conditions of official service really did not follow as the decree of 1856 promised, but available evidence indicates that it was essentially in the wake of that decree that the non-Muslim presence in Ottoman government service—at least in some parts of it—began to grow significantly in size and to alter in character.

Although the principles enunciated in 1855–1856 went into specifics as to the parts of government service into which non-Muslims were to be admitted, it is thus appropriate to begin our investigation of subsequent developments by inquiring where non-Muslims in fact assumed places in official ranks during the decades that followed. Here we shall leave aside the semiofficial extensions of the non-Muslim presence, a field in which the most important innovation would have been the appearance of non-Muslims in the various representative bodies, particularly the Parliament of 1877–1878 and the later ones of the Young Turk period.[9] Instead, we shall look only at the four branches into which we may regard Ottoman officialdom proper as being divided in this period. These are the religious establishment, the military, the palace service, and the civil bureaucracy.

The lack of any mention of the religious establishment in the statements of 1855–1856 obviously reflects the fact that non-Muslims could not take a place in the religious establishment of a Muslim state, although there was a tendency to think of the religious leaders of the non-Muslim communities as holding a kind of semiofficial status. This tendency was nothing new; yet it found some new expressions in this period, such as the listing of the heads of the various communities in a special section on "religious leaders" in the government yearbooks or the inclusion of these leaders *ex officio* in various representative bodies.[10] The possibility of any more thoroughgoing "bureaucratization" of the non-Muslim religious leadership does not appear to have been considered.

In the military, too, while occasional non-Muslims continued to appear as they had for some decades already in special capacities such as the military medical service, and while some Greek sailors were enlisted in the 1840s, non-Muslims clearly preferred to take advantage of the provision about purchasing exemption. Seeing Islam as the main factor in motivating men to risk their lives for the state, Muslims shared this preference. The purchasing of exemption from military service thus soon became institutionalized as a special tax on non-Muslims, a tax assessed and collected just as the old poll tax had been.[11] There appears to have been no further effort to draft non-Muslims before 1909, when the exemption tax was abolished and non-Muslims, together with the formerly exempt residents of certain towns, were proclaimed liable to conscription. Thereafter, non-Muslims did enter military service, some pursued careers as officers, and occasional later laws reasserted the obligation to serve. There were other measures, however, which again authorized the purchase of exemption in certain instances, and most non-Muslims surely continued to prefer this.[12] In this branch of government service, then, the pronouncements of 1855–1856 produced but slight effect.

In contrast, parts of the palace service seem to have been easier of access or more attractive, not only for artists, craftsmen, and merchants, but also for men who actually became palace functionaries and administrators. Non-Muslims do not appear to have assumed places in the immediate entourage of the sultan. Still under Abdülhamid the role of Armenian experts in the administration of the Privy Treasury, then a large and wealthy organization, was marked.[13]

Where the non-Muslim presence became most pronounced, however, was in the fourth branch, the civil bureaucracy. Indeed, a survey of sources such as the government yearbooks of the period suggests that when we speak of non-Muslims in official service, we are practically speaking of non-Muslims in the growing roster of ministries, councils, courts, local administrative agencies, embassies and consulates which comprised the Ottoman civil bureaucracy of the nineteenth century.

To look more closely now at the non-Muslims in the Foreign Ministry, one of the most influential and organizationally most developed of the civil-bureaucratic ministries, will tell us a great deal more about the extent to which the promises of egalitarian reform became a reality. To assess the data which the personnel records of the ministry offer on this score, we shall posit that full equality would have entailed two elements. The first is equal access to office for members of the various ethnic or religious groups. The second is equal reward for equal work. These may be anachronistic criteria to apply in a sense. They are perhaps implicit in the relevant passage of the Reform Decree of 1856, but Ottoman statesmen do not appear to have defined any particular standards, let alone such exacting ones, for the realization of egalitarian principles. If determination to demonstrate complete achievement of equality was missing, however, the criteria of equal opportunity and equal reward can still serve as standards by which to measure even limited progress in that direction. To assess how much change did occur, we shall therefore apply these criteria in examining selected items from the data which the personnel records offer on the topics of background and training, modes of employment and problems of reward and punishment.

The official personnel records *(sicill-i ahval)* system, set up at the beginning of the reign of Abdülhamid II (1876–1909), functioned regularly until 1908 and fitfully thereafter. Since the records on each individual were retrospective, the files include a great deal of information predating the creation of the system, although naturally the further back one looks in time, the thinner this becomes. My own research has enabled me to recover files on 366 officials who were associated with the Foreign Ministry and whose recorded careers spanned at least fifteen solar years, a number which I arbitrarily selected as a means by which to separate real careerists from non-careerists.[14] During the years 1850–1908, on which we shall concentrate, we find that of these 366, the numbers in service simultaneously in any given year ranged between 24 in 1850 and 310 in 1891. Of the 366, 107 (or 29 percent) are identifiable as non-Muslims. The number of non-Muslims serving simultaneously ranged from 7 in 1850 to 93 in 1892, the increase after 1856 being gradual.

Looking at the documents more closely, we realize that the staff of the ministry actually contained groups and subgroups of several different kinds. First, since this was an era of educational and cultural innovation as much as of egalitarian reform, the personnel of this and other ministries was taking on a pattern of differentiation along lines of educational or cultural orientation as much as of ethno-religious identification. Particularly since the Foreign Ministry placed a great premium on that proficiency in French which contemporary Ottomans tended to identify as practically the sum total of intellectual modernity, we shall need in speaking of the personnel of the ministry as a whole to distinguish three main groups: traditionalistic Muslims who lacked proficiency in this critical language, modernist Muslims who had such proficiency, and non-Muslims, of whom virtually all possessed this skill. Within these three larger groups there were at times also significant subgroupings. The only type of these which needs concern us here consists of the different ethnic or religious communities among the non-Muslims.

Perhaps in keeping with the egalitarian official spirit of the times, the questionnaires which formed the basic document in the personnel files normally did not include any requirement that the respondent identify the community to which he belonged.[15] Consequently, in identifying the various types of non-Muslims in the Foreign Ministry, we have to rely chiefly on the names which the individuals gave for themselves and their fathers and on such other unequivocal information as voluntary mention of *millet* membership. Certain other types of data, such as those on languages known or types of schools attended, provide additional but not in themselves conclusive evidence. The result of having to rely on such data in distinguishing non-Muslim subgroups is inevitably less than optimal precision. We usually cannot distinguish Uniates among Armenians and Greeks, for example; nor can we always distinguish the various denominations of Arab Christians. If there are cases where an individual's apparent identity masks his real pedigree, these pass unnoticed. It is possible that some non-Muslims remain undetected or incorrectly assigned. It also proves easier to make identifications in terms of ethnicity, as defined chiefly in linguistic terms, rather than in terms of the religious divisions which were still more basic to Ottoman concepts of social organization. In any case, the data in the records enable us to conclude with probably no more than a very small margin of error that we have 107 non-Muslims consisting of 30 Greeks, 52 Armenians, 12 Jews among whom were representatives of the Sefardi, Ashkenazi, and Karaite communities, 7 Arab Christians with family roots in Syria and Lebanon, and 6 men whose origins lay in European lands outside the Ottoman Empire. Some of these last were definitely foreigners who had gone into Ottoman service; some were Latin Catholic Levantines.

The presence of these subgroups already begins to tell something about the question of equality of access. While the Foreign Ministry alone was too small for matters to be otherwise, it is clear for a start that nothing like all the

TABLE 16-1   COMPARISON OF THE REPRESENTATION OF VARIOUS NON-MUSLIM GROUPS IN THE FOREIGN MINISTRY AND IN THE POPULATION OF ISTANBUL

	MUSLIM	NON-MUSLIM	Greek	Armenian	Jewish	Arab Christian	European Origin	No. of Officials / Total Male Pop. of Istanbul (Ottoman Subjects)	Total Population of Istanbul
Representation in Foreign Ministry	71%	29%	8%	14%	3%	2%	2%	(366)	
Census of 1844[a]	55%	45%	17%	25%	4%	?	?	(477,820)	(866,000)[b]
Census of 1893[a]	49%	51%	23%	21%	5%	?	1%	(407,609)	(873,565)
Census of 1897	55%	45%	22%[f]	15%	4%	?	2%	?	(1,052,000)[d]

[a] Data for 1844 and 1893 include separate totals for males and females and also give figures for "foreign citizens." In addition, the figures for 1844 distinguish "residents" of the city and "non-residents." The latter category consists of males without families in the city and is so defined as to indicate that most of these men were Ottoman subjects. Since only males served in the bureaucracy, and since the vast majority of bureaucrats were Ottoman subjects, only the figures for male Ottoman subjects, including the "non-resident" category for 1844, have been used in computing percentages for 1844 and 1893. The source cited for the census of 1897 does not show breakdowns by sex, however. Consequently, for purposes of comparison with the figure used as the base in computation of percentages for that year, the total population of the city, for both sexes, also appears in the last column at the right of the table.

[b] Not counting non-Ottoman subjects.

[c] Listed as "Orthodox," thus including non-Greeks and omitting Greek Catholics.

[d] Rounded to nearest thousand in the source. This source gives no breakdown by sex; percentages for this year are thus for the entire population of each non-Muslim community.

Sources of Census Data:
  Data for 1844 from M. A. Ubicini, *Letters on Turkey: An Account of the Religious, Political, Social, and Commercial Condition of the Ottoman Empire; The Reformed Institutions, Army, Navy etc.*, trans. Lady Easthope, 2 vols., London, 1856, vol. 1, p. 24.
  Data for 1893 from Kemal H. Karpat, "Ottoman Population Records and the Census of 1881/82-1893," *IJMES*, 9 (1978), p. 274.
  Data for 1897 from Vedat Eldem, *Osmanlı İmparatorluğunun İktisadi Şartları Hakkında bir Tetkik*, Ankara, 1970, p. 55.

population groups of the empire are represented here. Indeed, the data on place of birth reveal that, with the chief exception of the men of European origin, what the non-Muslims of the Foreign Ministry really represent is the non-Muslim population of Istanbul. Among non-Muslim officials of the ministry, as more or less equally among their Muslim colleagues, three-fourths were Istanbul-born. Among the Armenians the proportion was closer to 90 percent, and even among the Arab Christians it was better than half. Even if we narrow the frame of comparison to the capital city alone, however, it does not necessarily follow that the non-Muslims had achieved representation within the ministry in proportion to their strength without. While some of the figures perhaps reflect no more than the vagaries of Ottoman census data, Table 16-1 illustrates this point by comparing the size of various personnel elements within the Foreign Ministry with the size of the corresponding elements of the population of Istanbul according to three censuses of the period.

What can explain this underrepresentation? In the case of particular non-Muslim subgroups, it must relate in part to fluctuations in their political fortunes. This would have been true of the Greeks in general after the 1820s although vestiges of their old eminence did linger about Greek officials of later dates. Similar problems beset other non-Muslim subgroups at other times. The total absence from the Foreign Ministry of some of the smaller minority groups is also a factor. Otherwise, in an age when service in the bureaucracy was still—as Muslim and non-Muslim alike knew—almost the only way to participate in political life, and when the statesmen who conceived the egalitarian reforms explicitly interpreted equality to mean admission of non-Muslims into the bureaucracy,[16] further explanation is required. Probably the key point here must be that the sultans and statesmen of the Islamic Empire, far from having a conscious determination to achieve complete equality of opportunity, were reluctant in certain respects to make full use of bureaucratic patronage in their efforts to consolidate non-Muslim loyalties. Given that the scope of patronage was limited at best in relation to the complexity of Ottoman society, such reluctance points to the ultimate lack of realism of the reformers' attempt to use the bureaucracy as a mechanism for political mobilization of the non-Muslim population in support of the empire.

Another part of the data on background and training provides both a further insight into this reluctance and an indication of the uncertainty which eventually beclouded the political situation of non-Muslim bureaucrats. Presenting median years of birth and first appointment, Table 16-2 brings out the point that although the non-Muslims were in some sense a "new group" in the civil bureaucracy of the late nineteenth century, they were not a "young group" as compared even with the more traditionalist of their Muslim colleagues. The one exception in this respect was the Jews, who stand out clearly as the last of all groups and subgroups to enter government service. The dates in Table 16-2 indicate, then, that one factor in the underrepresentation of non-Muslims was that their entry into the civil bureaucracy was a transitory phenomenon, the passing of which was already apparent by the latter part of the reign of Abdülhamid, while the

TABLE 16-2   MEDIAN YEARS OF BIRTH AND FIRST APPOINTMENT

	MUSLIM I	MUSLIM II	NON-MUSLIM	Greek	Armenian	Jewish	Arab Christian	European Origin
N	(115)	(144)	(107)	(30)	(52)	(12)	(7)	(6)
Median Year of Birth	1856	1860	1851	1845	1851	1865	1851	1821
Median Year of First Appointment	1873	1879	1871	1869	1871	1885	1871	1842

Note: In this and subsequent tables, the headings Muslim I and Muslim II refer to`traditionalist Muslims (those lacking proficiency in French) and to modernist Muslims (those claiming such proficiency), respectively.

recruitment of Muslims, especially the growth of the modernistic sector of Muslim officialdom, displayed a stronger and more persistent trend.

Comparison of the birth years and years of first appointment shown in Table 16-2 also points to another fact relevant to the assessment of the conditions governing the access of non-Muslims to bureaucratic position: education. The fact that non-Muslims of all subgroups tended to be one or more years older than their Muslim colleagues at first appointment implies that the non-Muslims were more highly educated. The implication is then corroborated by the fact that the non-Muslim officials almost unfailingly had the proficiency in French which characterized only one group, amounting to barely over half, of the Muslims. The nineteenth-century Ottoman educational "system" was so changeable and unclear in its organizational traits that a comprehensive analysis of the data on education cannot find a place here. There are, however, certain points which stand out as relevant to our theme.

Where schools attended are concerned, we find that while non-Muslims took advantage of the new Ottoman schools created in this period to a markedly lesser degree than did their modernist Muslim colleagues, still it was the non-Muslims who led in study at European institutions at the lycée and university levels. Table 16-3 illustrates this point by extracting from the data on education those pertaining to three major types of upper-level educational opportunities: the Galatasaray Lycée (1868), including the School of Law founded there in 1874; lycée-level institutions in Europe, including ones founded there by some of the Ottoman non-Muslim communities; finally European universities and other institutions of comparable level. Readers conversant with Ottoman educational history will question the omission from the table of the School of Civil Administration (*Mülkiye Mektebi,* 1859), much favored by Abdülhamid. In fact, its contribution to the training of the men of the Foreign Ministry was small, amounting to perhaps fewer than 5 percent of the traditionalist Muslims, fewer than 10 percent of the modernist Muslims, and none at all of the non-Muslims.

The figures dramatize the role of the French-inspired Galatasaray, the first

TABLE 16-3   STUDY BY FOREIGN MINISTRY OFFICIALS IN SELECTED TYPES OF
EDUCATIONAL INSTITUTIONS
(in percent)

	MUSLIM I	MUSLIM II	NON-MUSLIM	Greek	Armenian	Jewish	Arab Christian	European Origins
N	(115)	(144)	(107)	(30)	(52)	(12)	(7)	(6)
Galatasaray Lycée	6	25	14	17	13	25	14	17
Lycée-Level Institutions in Europe	1	2	22	23	21	—	14	67
University-Level Institutions in Europe	—	6	15	27	13	—	14	17

Ottoman lycée, in the formation of the modernist Muslim segment of the civil bureaucracy, the correspondingly marked role of European institutions in the preparation of the non-Muslims, and the low but uneven frequencies with which officials of various groups and subgroups went on to university-level institutions, of which there were none—at least in any modern sense—in the empire before 1900.[17]

As in other cases, there are striking differences among the non-Muslim subgroups. For example, the fact that a quarter of the Jews studied at Galatasaray, while none at all studied in Europe, is perhaps another sign of the "newness" of this group of officials as well, more generally, as of the cultural backwardness of Ottoman Jewry as compared with the Christian communities.[18] The unusually high percentage of the men of European origin who studied in European lycées, in contrast, is presumably a reflection of the origins of these men or of their families. Finally, the fact that the Greeks outstripped all others in study at European universities is one of a number of signs of the extent to which the Greeks retained something of the elitist aura of the old Phanariots, from whom some of this subgroup were in fact descended.

To look beyond questions of institutions to measure the quality of education is difficult. The data make clear, certainly, that there was a profound crisis of discipline in schools of all types. Not only were the schools in a state of organizational and curricular flux, but most students either saw no point in completing the curricula of the schools they attended or saw no point in reporting the receipt of a diploma if they got one. To attempt to assess the diffusion of the more modern types of education in this period, we can investigate the files for indications of a variety of modern skills, ranging from relatively modest ones such as telegraphy or stenography to more advanced ones such as law and medicine. This line of inquiry is, however, unrewarding. Among both modernist

TABLE 16-4   *EXTENT OF CLAIMS TO PROFICIENCY IN SELECTED LANGUAGES*
(in percent)

	MUSLIM I	MUSLIM II	NON-MUSLIM	Greek	Armenian	Jewish	Arab Christian	European Origins
N	(115)	(144)	(107)	(30)	(52)	(12)	(7)	(6)
Turkish	99	99	78	77	85	92	57	17
Modern Greek	1	2	31	93	4	8	—	33
Armenian	—	1	34	—	69	—	—	—
Spanish	—	—	7	—	4	42	—	—
Hebrew	—	—	3	—	—	25	—	—
Arabic	6	6	6	3	2	8	57	—
French	—	100	96	97	98	83	100	100
Italian	—	4	30	40	25	8	29	67
English	1	6	19	27	15	8	14	33
German	—	1	17	27	12	17	—	33
Russian	1	1	5	3	6	8	—	—
Rumanian	1	—	3	3	2	8	—	—
Serbo-Croatian	—	—	3	—	4	8	—	—
Bulgarian	—	1	2	3	—	8	—	—
Albanian	1	—	—	—	—	—	—	—

Muslims and non-Muslims, one quarter of the respondents record some attainment of this type, with no marked difference as to level of qualification or orientation, except that legal training was more apt to be in Ottoman law among the Muslims and in European legal systems among the non-Muslims. Presumably, what we are encountering here is the Ottoman expression of an assumption then prevalent in other countries as well: that diplomacy and administration were callings for which the generalist was qualified, with no specialized training deemed necessary.

A real difference among the two modernist groups appears, however, in the knowledge of languages. The questionnaire used in creation of the personnel files asked the respondent to name the languages he knew and to rate himself in terms of whether he could use the written form of the language for official purposes *(kitabet etmek)* or merely speak it *(tekellüm)*. The weaknesses of a system of self-rating are obvious enough in a matter of this kind, although the concept of *kitabet,* linked in Ottoman minds to the level of literacy required to use Ottoman Turkish in the official style, did imply a high standard. At any rate, if we can assume the incidence of error and prevarication to be more or less equal in the self-ratings of officials of all types, we can draw some interesting conclusions.

In general terms, we note that while somewhat over 60 percent of both the groups of Muslim respondents indicated that they had some knowledge of at least three languages, including their native tongue, almost exactly half of the non-Muslims claimed some knowledge of five languages or more. Examining claims to proficiency in a variety of languages, Table 16-4 gives a more precise idea of where the expertise of the non-Muslims lay.

To a degree, obviously, the wider proficiency of the non-Muslims had to do with languages distinctive of their various subgroups. Here in passing we note signs of differing levels of cultural development within the various non-Muslim communities: more than 90 percent of the Greeks claimed proficiency in Greek;

TABLE 16-4   *EXTENT OF CLAIMS TO PROFICIENCY IN SELECTED LANGUAGES*
(in percent)

	MUSLIM I	MUSLIM II	NON-MUSLIM	Greek	Armenian	Jewish	Arab Christian	European Origins
N	(115)	(144)	(107)	(30)	(52)	(12)	(7)	(6)
Turkish	99	99	78	77	85	92	57	17
Modern Greek	1	2	31	93	4	8	—	33
Armenian	—	1	34	—	69	—	—	—
Spanish	—	—	7	—	4	42	—	—
Hebrew	—	—	3	—	—	25	—	—
Arabic	6	6	6	3	2	8	57	—
French	—	100	96	97	98	83	100	100
Italian	—	4	30	40	25	8	29	67
English	1	6	19	27	15	8	14	33
German	—	1	17	27	12	17	—	33
Russian	1	1	5	3	6	8	—	—
Rumanian	1	—	3	3	2	8	—	—
Serbo-Croatian	—	—	3	—	4	8	—	—
Bulgarian	—	1	2	3	—	8	—	—
Albanian	1	—	—	—	—	—	—	—

not quite 70 percent of the Armenians claimed proficiency in Armenian; four out of seven Arab Christians could make such a claim about Arabic; but fewer than half the Jews could in Spanish and only a quarter in Hebrew. Yet the superior linguistic attainments of the non-Muslims clearly went beyond these "minority languages." To a slight extent, it was a matter of knowledge of the Balkan tongues which appear at the foot of the table. Chiefly, however, it was a matter of diversity in the major European languages, and not just French alone. Certainly in Italian, English, and German, we find anomalously high percentages of non-Muslims claiming proficiency, especially for the Greeks, the best-educated of our non-Muslims, and the men of European origin. The figures in Table 16-4, it should also be recalled, represent only claims to proficiency. If we included men claiming limited knowledge of the same languages, the percentages would in most cases increase considerably.

What is curious about this linguistic proficiency of the non-Muslims is the suggestion that even after the egalitarian reforms, it was still a peculiar form of expertise, not so widely encountered among Muslims, that had a lot to do with gaining these men their places in the bureaucracy. Indeed, a certain persistence of the old marginality of the non-Muslims becomes quite clear from the contrast between the greater numbers of languages they knew and the fact that an appreciable element of these men were still not proficient in Ottoman Turkish. This was true of some 22 percent of the non-Muslims. Once again, there are noteworthy differences among the various subgroups, and these differences appear to correspond in a roughly inverse way to the degree of Westernization then characteristic in each community. To the extent that we can rely on the percentages for the smaller subgroups, we note that the Jews were the most proficient in Turkish and the least so in French. Then, in decreasing order of proficiency in Turkish we have the Armenians, Greeks, Arab Christians, and men of European origin. The questionnaires in the personnel files also provide qualitative evidence at times of limited mastery in the main language of government, for there are obvious errors in some cases and at least one individual of European origin who eventually lost a position on account of his ignorance of Ottoman.[19]

Overall, then, the data on background and training tell an important part of the story about the extent to which the Ottoman reformers of the later nineteenth century in fact achieved equality of opportunity in the Foreign Ministry. Compared to their formerly much smaller numbers, non-Muslims had taken advantage of the mid-century concessions to the extent of coming to form almost a third of the personnel of this particular ministry, even though only a few non-Muslim groups were represented and not in proportion to their strength in the population at large. Signs of cultural marginality lingered among these men, and we sense that their generally superior educational attainments had a lot to do with their appointments. Yet, the old cultural marginality had at least diminished in the sense that the Westernist orientation which almost unfailingly characterized the non-Muslims was one that now also characterized the more dynamic sector of

Muslim officialdom.[20] To judge from the dates of first appointment, the non-Muslim influx into the civil bureaucracy was to be a transitory phenomenon; but for the time being, it seems, the non-Muslims had gained in relative prominence and in centrality to the life of the civil bureaucracy.

To move on now to the data on the career records of the non-Muslim officials will make it possible to gain a clearer picture of the extent and limits of the non-Muslims' movement into the mainstream of civil-bureaucratic life. Here we must begin by recognizing that the nineteenth century was a time of transition between an older, patrimonial concept of the state and a new concept of the state as a rational-legal order.[21] The realization of equality in conditions of employment was hindered not only by the tradition of inequality and by the patrimonial emphasis on arbitrariness in the use of power. In addition, there were also the social patterns, particularly the kind of patron-client relationships, characteristic of what I have elsewhere described as the "model of the patrimonial household." These patterns amounted in practice to the "personnel policy" of the late traditional empire. The elaboration of the kind of rationally structured and legally defined personnel system which could alone assure that equality would become a reality in the day-to-day workings of the bureaucratic system had been called for in the Reform Decree of 1856 but did not really begin to occur even on paper before the 1880s, its application in practice only beginning after that and on a fragmentary and inconsistent basis.[22] As a result, the non-Muslim officials whom we are studying operated in an environment where the old types of personality-centered factionalism and clientage were still of paramount importance and where full equality in conditions of service could only exist to the extent that such phenomena could produce it. As Table 16-5 shows, the personnel records contain evidence of this fact.

The table records individuals who, at any time during their careers, served in four of the more important of the central bureaus of the Foreign Ministry in Istanbul and in four categories of consular and diplomatic positions. Officials who had more than one of these types of experience have been counted once for each type they recorded. To interpret the information in the table, it will help to look first at the four central bureaus, then at the four categories of consular and diplomatic posts. It is advisable also to compare percentages only within rows, as differences in the size of a given bureau or service-category naturally influenced the percentage of any group that could serve there.

Among the four central bureaus, the Translation Office *(Bab-ı Ali Tercüme Odası)* is the famous one, founded in 1821 upon the abolition of the Greek Dragomanate and long regarded as the seedbed of the modernist Muslim elite. What we refer to here as the Foreign Correspondence Office *(Tahrirat-ı Hariciye Kalemi)* was an offshoot of the Translation Office, founded at the end of the Crimean War to handle correspondence in French, the Turkish Correspondence Office *(Mektubi-i Hariciye Kalemi)* having been set up about a decade earlier to handle correspondence in Turkish. The Office of Legal Counsel *(İstişare Odası)* appeared only in the 1880s and had the mission of advising the entire Ottoman government in international law.[23]

TABLE 16-5   SERVICE BY FOREIGN MINISTRY OFFICIALS IN SPECIFIC
OFFICES OR TYPES OF POSITIONS
(in percent)

	MUSLIM I	MUSLIM II	NON-MUSLIM	Greek	Armenian	Jewish	Arab Christian	European Origins
N	(115)	(144)	(107)	(30)	(52)	(12)	(7)	(6)
Translation Office of the Sublime Porte	24	42	15	20	13	8	—	33
Foreign Correspondence Office	6	23	46	20	69	17	43	33
Turkish Correspondence Office	41	16	—	—	—	—	—	—
Office of Legal Counsel	6	14	7	7	8	8	—	17
Major Western Diplomatic Posts	4	33	21	20	19	—	43	67
Other Diplomatic Posts	8	39	36	47	31	17	29	83
Major Western Consular Posts	3	14	13	3	19	8	29	—
Other Consular Posts	21	30	50	53	46	75	43	17

Note: These figures are based on preliminary analysis of the data and are subject to future recomputation.

The figures in Table 16-5 bear witness, first, to the association of the modernist segment of the Muslims with the Translation Office. The lower but still substantial percentage of traditionalist Muslims serving in the same office is explicable in terms of the fact that some of these men did have at least limited knowledge of French, that persons with limited qualifications could perform tasks such as copying or filing and that translators operating solely in Arabic and Persian were at times also attached to this office. What is more suprising is the limited association of non-Muslims with service in an office for which they possessed the requisite skills.

This, indeed, is a sign of the influence in the Foreign Ministry of the patrimonial traditions of factionalism and clientage. For if the Translation Office was a bastion of the modernist Muslim elite, including the leading statesmen of the *Tanzimat* and their protégés, it was the Foreign Correspondence Office which came closest to playing the same role for non-Muslims, or more exactly for the Armenians, of whom more than two-thirds served in this office at some point in their careers. This fact can be traced to the appointment of Sahak Abro Efendi, a prominent Armenian closely associated with the leading statesmen of the *Tanzimat,* as one of the first directors of the office and the consequent transformation of the office into an Armenian enclave.[24] After the tenure of Sahak Abro (c. 1857–1867), the office continued to have Armenian directors at least into the mid-1880s,[25] only gradually losing its Armenian character thereafter.

Of the Turkish Correspondence Office, in turn, there is no need to say more than that it, too, was a "ghetto," although for a different reason. For this bureau became the natural place of concentration for Muslims who lacked the linguistic skills required for service in most other parts of the ministry. Presumably as a consequence of this fact, none of our non-Muslims recorded service in this office.

The evidence on the Office of Legal Counsel, finally, gives scant indication of the prestige, and thus the size, which it took on in the Hamidian patronage system. In fact, comparison of what these records imply to have been the modest size of the office with the scores of individuals assigned there by 1908[26] yields one sign of the extent to which Abdülhamid padded bureaucratic rolls with men who were not really career officials but whom he sought by such means to reduce to the obligatory docility of clientage in relation to himself. In our personnel records, the clearest sign of the status attributed to the office is that the group most in evidence there was the modernist Muslims, although the smallness of the percentages again reflects the limited extent to which technical skills, going beyond linguistic proficiency, had yet begun to be appreciated.

For the central offices as a group, then, we note that while there was usually some mixing of Muslim and non-Muslim officials, still each of the major personnel groups was particularly associated with a given office. The uneven distribution of the non-Muslims and the modernist Muslims between two offices for which the required qualifications were identical, a disparity largely explicable in terms of patronage patterns, is particularly striking.

To go on now to the data on the four categories of consular and diplomatic positions, what we have identified as the major Western diplomatic and consular posts are those located in the offices of the major powers of the day: the United Kingdom, France, Germany, Austria-Hungary, and Russia (excluding consular posts in the Black Sea area). Consular and diplomatic posts in the smaller European states, outside Europe, and around the periphery of the Ottoman Empire fall into the "other" categories, their chief common characteristic being that they were less desirable posts to occupy and could at times be held by individuals who lacked the linguistic qualifications required to function successfully in the major Western posts.

Where the three major personnel categories are concerned, the data in the table at first glance suggest that the employment records of modernist Muslims and non-Muslims were more alike in the consular and diplomatic services than in the central offices, the contrasting relegation of the less well-qualified Muslims to peripheral positions being clear. Yet, there are again differences to note between non-Muslims and modernist Muslims. For example, an inspection of the actual records suggests that the apparent similarity in places of service for members of these two groups masks a tendency among heads of consular and diplomatic missions, the composition of whose staffs was in good measure a matter of their choice, to surround themselves with sons or other dependents usually drawn from their own group or subgroup. A comparison of one mission with another might thus yield a pattern of quasi-segregation like that found in some of the central offices.[27]

In addition, even in the data included in Table 16-5, there are unmistakable signs that the position of the non-Muslims was not as good on balance as that of the Muslim modernists. In the four categories of consular and diplomatic positions which we have distinguished, we note that the non-Muslims were clearly less well represented than the modernist Muslims in the most desirable category, the Western diplomatic positions, and clearly more strongly represented in the least desirable category, the "other" consular posts, the only one of the four categories in which any notable percentage of traditionalist Muslims appeared.

This disparity no doubt signifies that any Muslim misgivings about employment of non-Muslims had particularly to do with positions of prominence. Yet considering the marked differences in the representation of individual non-Muslim subgroups in the various categories of consular and diplomatic posts, more was involved than that. Indeed, it almost seems as if the smaller the representation of the subgroup in bureaucratic ranks, the more apt its members were to appear in the most desirable posts. A contemporary source reinforces this impression, suggests a reason for it, and thus reveals another shortcoming of egalitarian reform.

A German ambassador, Joseph-Maria von Radowitz, blamed the problem on what he described as the vulnerability of Christian Ottoman diplomats to intrigue. Writing in 1890 in comment on the possibility that one of our officials of European origin, Edouard Blacque Bey, might be appointed as Ottoman representative in Berlin, Radowitz referred to problems experienced previously when a Greek held the same post and argued that it would be preferable on account of this vulnerability to have a Muslim. But then Radowitz added an important qualification: "To be sure, it has almost always been a question of Greek and Armenian rayahs [as non-Muslim ambassadors]. The only Christian diplomat in high position at this time who does not belong to one of these nationalities, Rüstem Paşa, rightly figures in contrast as one of the best *(tüchtigsten)* and most reliable of Turkish ambassadors."[28]

In the second half of the nineteenth century Greeks and occasionally Armenians were at times able to hold on in diplomatic positions for decades on end. In Istanbul members of these communities were among the non-Muslims who rose to be foreign minister on four occasions between 1878 and 1919, and an Armenian was undersecretary for foreign affairs for many years.[29] Nonetheless, such individuals episodically displayed a vulnerability which was no doubt linked to the "intrigues" Radowitz cited but which also seems to have reflected contemporary perceptions about the loyalty of the various non-Muslim communities to the empire. The great advantage of what appear in our tables as the weakly represented non-Muslim subgroups is that Ottoman Muslims associated little if any separatist nationalist threat with them. This was true of the Jews although most of those under study got no further than minor consular positions. It was also true of both the Arab Christians and the men of European origin, subgroups which included several heads of consular and diplomatic missions. Among these were the very Rüstem Paşa and Edouard Blacque Bey of whom Radowitz wrote. An Italian born in Germany and educated in Paris, Rüstem had been in Ottoman service ever since the 1830s, had headed many diplomatic missions as well as serving from 1872 to 1882 as governor of Lebanon, and was thus indeed a non-Muslim whom the paranoid Abdülhamid could feel "safe" in using in the West to foster the image of Ottoman progress and egalitarianism.[30] A similar trust could be placed in Blacque Bey, the Germanophile son of a French journalist who had entered Ottoman service in the days of Mahmud II (1808–1839).[31] More or less the same was also true of the French-born Morel Bey, whose career record makes clear that he was a protégé of Rüstem Paşa,[32] or of Nihad Paşa, born Severin Biliński, sometime Polish landowner and revolutionary who ended his career as Ottoman representative to the autonomous Bulgarian principality created after the Russo-Turkish War.[33] Among the Arab Christians were others who could be regarded in similar light, especially when, as in the case of Nikola Gadban Efendi, they also figured as members of the espionage network centered in the palace.[34]

With the data in Table 16-5, then, we gain additional insights into the problem of equality of opportunity and begin to gain others into the question of equality in access to reward. The growth in the size and centrality of the non-Muslim presence in the civil bureaucracy had clearly entailed the assumption by non-Muslims of positions which were no longer peculiar to them but were qualitatively little different from those held by Muslims with similar skills. Clearly, too, officials of both types now worked together in many settings. Yet, just as traces of the old marginality still appeared in the educational records of the non-Muslims, elements of the old patterns of clientage and enclavement persisted in their employment, a fact more or less inevitable as long as no serious effort at rationalization and regularization of personnel policy occurred. There was seemingly also a tendency, at least in the Hamidian period, to discriminate among the various non-Muslim subgroups on the basis of estimates of their fidelity to the state, while non-Muslims generally do not seem to have gained access to the most desirable positions with the same frequency as did the modernist Muslims. A finer scrutiny of data on conditions of service, as for example on the placement of individuals within given agencies, would assuredly add further nuances to this picture. The lack of a systematic personnel policy makes it difficult to classify such data for analysis; but in the field of reward and punishment, such nuances become measurable even despite this lack.

To illustrate this point, it will suffice to select several types of data pertaining to salaries, compensation by noneconomic means, certain disadvantages which formed a normal part of conditions of service, and what we may in a broad sense term punitive action. Table 16-6 illuminates the first of these topics by presenting median monthly salaries in *kuruş*,[35] computed year by year, for each of the major personnel groups and for three categories of non-Muslims. On account of the sometimes small numbers of cases—and it should be remembered that not all members of any personnel group were ever in service in any one year—we are here combining the Jews, Arab Christians, and men of European origin into a single category of "other" non-Muslims. For the same reason, we are arbitrarily excluding from the table all statistics computed for the major groups in years when there were not at least 25 members of the group in service, as well as all statistics computed for the non-Muslim subgroups in years when the number in service fell below 10; hence the missing figures in certain columns. The figures should not be taken as possessing scientific accuracy, either. The frequency of certain digits and combinations of digits reflects nothing more than the method of interpolation used in computing these statistics from bracketed data. The appearance of anomalously small salaries, similarly, does not mean that half the officials in a stated category earned no more than that, but rather that something near half of them were in the unpaid apprentice status in which Ottoman officials characteristically began their careers. Finally, given the irregularity of salary payments, it would be unwise to assume that the medians of the salaries which Ottoman officials actually collected matched those in Table 16-6. What these figures do provide, however, is an indicator of the "priorities" of those who disposed of the power to determine nominal compensation levels. The indicator is the more valuable in that there was virtually no reliable, explicit statement of policy on this question during this period.

Looking at the table with these considerations in mind, we find that a year-by-year comparison of the medians for the three major personnel groups provides a new kind of insight into the centrality of the position which non-Muslims had now assumed in the bureaucracy. For example, median salaries for non-Muslims exceeded those for traditionalist Muslims in 32 years out of 46, equaling salaries for the latter group in 1 year, and falling below in 13. Even in comparison with the modernist Muslims—a more logical comparison since they and the non-Muslims resembled each other more strongly in terms of qualifications and service records—we find that the median salaries for the non-Muslims

*TABLE 16-6   MEDIAN FOREIGN MINISTRY SALARIES (*KURUŞ *PER MONTH)*

Year	MUSLIM I	MUSLIM II	NON-MUSLIM	Greek	Armenian	Other
1860	14					
1861	14					
1862	15					
1863	216		14	1049	5	
1864	237		16	1066	7	
1865	324		999	1049	349	
1866	509	2149	17	1024	8	
1867	529	2524	18	1049	8	
1868	462	3199	19	1074	9	
1869	474	3074	1062	1149	699	
1870	549	3074	999	1049	11	
1871	574	3049	1009	1049	574	
1872	587	18	699	999	15	
1873	599	2049	30	949	17	5
1874	549	24	33	949	18	5
1875	549	1299	33	1499	18	1399
1876	582	1074	1082	1499	18	1949
1877	562	999	1074	1249	974	1399
1878	599	974	899	1082	20	1899
1879	832	1124	1249	1449	21	2749
1880	799	1266	1149	1274	20	2749
1881	699	1207	1899	2012	1499	2749
1882	712	1241	1932	2019	1499	2799
1883	699	1974	1549	1999	1899	1049
1884	799	1999	1749	2019	1699	1074
1885	687	2008	1899	1549	1932	1082
1886	599	1549	1932	1949	1999	1062
1887	624	1349	1916	1949	1949	1199
1888	721	1071	1587	1999	1924	9
1889	705	1043	1566	1949	1949	10
1890	716	1059	1587	1999	1899	1016
1891	662	1032	1537	1999	1799	949
1892	666	1149	1274	2019	1249	1024
1893	762	1066	1549	2049	2016	999
1894	778	1166	1516	2039	2012	999
1895	760	1166	1566	2024	2019	949
1896	794	1582	1474	1999	1749	999
1897	812	1782	1069	1074	1449	916
1898	949	1774	1024	999	1374	949
1899	1043	1832	957	10	1324	949
1900	1116	1882	993	10	1449	937
1901	1199	1892	1032	9	1649	749
1902	1449	2024	1249	949	1799	899
1903	1399	2149	1349	1199	1799	1099

TABLE 16-6   MEDIAN FOREIGN MINISTRY SALARIES (KURUŞ PER MONTH)
(Continued)

Year	MUSLIM I	MUSLIM II	NON-MUSLIM	Greek	Armenian	Other
1904	1449	2324	1449	999	1849	1099
1905	1449	2449	1674	1049	1849	1199
1906	1512	2499	1699	999	1849	
1907	1512	2632	1799	1099	1882	
1908	1524	2674	1809	1049	1999	

Note: These figures are based on preliminary analysis of the data and are subject to future recomputation.

were higher in 17 years. In this case, however, the Muslim group was ahead more often, in 26 of the 43 years for which our figures permit comparison. Comparison of the medians for the three major personnel groups thus indicates that where salaries were concerned, the position of the non-Muslims was now in fact an intermediate one of advantage in relation to the traditionalist Muslims but disadvantage in relation to the modernist Muslims. By the same token, this element of disadvantage also provides another indication of how far the non-Muslims remained from achieving full recognition of their qualifications.

Comparison of the various non-Muslim subgroups, to the extent that these are distinguished in the table, adds important nuances to this picture. The lingering elitism of the Greeks finds particularly strong expression in the fact that median salaries for Greek officials were higher than those for modernist Muslims in 23 out of 43 years. The less brilliant record of the Armenians, presumably reflecting their more recent influx into the bureaucracy and their somewhat lower educational level, expressed itself in a contrasting picture, with median salaries higher than those of the modernist Muslims in only 13 years and lower medians in 30 years out of 43. It is particularly noteworthy that the median salaries of both Greeks and Armenians, if for different reasons, were invariably lower than those of the modernist Muslims from 1897 on. In the case of the Greeks, we sense the effects, very strongly marked through 1901, of the Greco-Turkish War of 1897. In the case of the Armenians, the corresponding issue would be the troubles of the mid-1890s. Among our "other" non-Muslims, finally, the picture is consistently more negative, with members of this category enjoying higher median salaries than the modernist Muslims in only 8 years—and never after 1882—out of 33 years for which the figures permit comparison. Inspection of the records on these men indicates that those who achieved high levels of compensation were mostly of European origin. The extreme seniority of this subgroup (cf. Table 16-2) would thus help to explain the relative earliness of the years in which those who appear in Table 16-6 as "other" non-Muslims outstripped the modernist Muslims in median salary-levels.

Of the various noneconomic forms of compensation—ranks, decorations, etc.—in use in the late Ottoman bureaucracy, the ranks will suffice here to illustrate the extent to which data on these kinds of reward corroborate and amplify the picture which emerges from Table 16-6. Not every official received a rank; yet there was by mid-century a civil rank table of nine grades defined in ascending order as the fifth rank, the fourth, the third, the second rank second class, the second rank first class (also called *mütemayiz* or "distinguished"), the first rank second class, the first rank first class, the "superior" rank *(balâ),* and the rank of vezir. Table 16-7 presents the records of the different categories of officials in the achievement of these ranks.

If we add the percentages shown in the various columns of the table, beginning with the highest rank and working backward from it, we find that 58 percent of the traditionalist Muslims achieved the second rank first class *(mütemayiz)* or better. Among the modernist Muslims, by contrast, a slightly larger proportion, 64 percent, achieved the next higher rank, the first rank second class, or better. For the non-Muslims, the rank in which the median falls is again the second rank first class, but the proportion which had achieved that or higher rank, at 56 percent, is this time marginally smaller than in the case of the traditionalist Muslims. To explain this seeming anomaly, we recall the low general level of systematization in the compensation system and note that the percentage of non-Muslims who received no rank at all—a phenomenon of which the significance is not always clear—was higher than the corresponding proportion for any other of the major groups. At any rate, the information on ranks confirms what we have already seen with the salary medians at least in the sense that the non-Muslims, however much they resembled the modernist Muslims in qualifications and services performed, clearly did not equal them in access to reward.

The data on the ranks achieved by members of the non-Muslim subgroups add to this picture and confirm inferences already mentioned in the analysis of service records. Here we note that in both the two largest subgroups, the Greeks and Armenians, most members had again attained the second rank first class or better, the proportion being higher for the Armenians, surprisingly, than for the Greeks. The weakest of the subgroups in terms of achievement of high rank was clearly the Jews, the subgroup which had entered the bureaucracy most recently and seemingly possessed the least in the way of educational or other advantages. Of these men, 50 percent held no rank, while the ranks of the others varied between the third and the second class of the first rank. The signs which we noted in our discussion of career records of a tendency to prefer non-Muslims from the smaller communities not associated with any separatist threat seem to find confirmation again in the case of the Arab Christians, of whom 57 percent rose to the first rank second class or better—a record almost as good as that of the modernist Muslims—and more still in the case of the men of European origin. They excelled all the other personnel categories which we have distinguished in that fully half of them rose to the two highest of civil-bureaucratic ranks. Of course the smallness of the numbers of cases under study means, here as elsewhere, that the percentages shown for the Jews, Arab Christians, and men of European origin cannot be regarded as more than rough indicators.

For non-Muslims, as in some senses for all officials, however, the most

TABLE 16-7   HIGHEST RANK ATTAINED
(in percent)

N	MUSLIM I (115)	MUSLIM II (144)	NON-MUSLIM (107)	Greek (30)	Armenian (52)	Jewish (12)	Arab Christian (7)	European Origin (6)
None; Unclear	9	4	16	20	10	50	—	—
Fifth Rank	—	1	—	—	—	—	—	—
Fourth Rank	7	2	2	—	4	—	—	—
Third Rank	10	9	13	10	12	8	43	17
Second Rank Second Class	16	5	13	17	12	25	—	—
Second Rank First Class	22	15	12	13	15	—	—	17
First Rank Second Class	18	20	19	17	23	17	14	—
First Rank First Class	13	23	13	13	15	—	14	17
"Superior" Rank (Balâ)	4	9	8	7	6	—	29	33
Vezirial Rank	1	12	4	3	4	—	—	17
TOTAL	100	100	100	100	100	100	100	100
This percentage .... of this group or subgroup held this rank or higher	58 II/1	64 I/2	56 II/1	53 II/1	64 II/1	50 III	57 I/2	50 Balâ

important qualifications that need to be made about the workings of the official reward system pertain to the corresponding problem of punishments and to the rather surprising difficulties which the Ottomans experienced in maintaining an effective differentiation of the two. What we mean by this begins to become clear from certain disadvantages which, thanks to the economic weakness of the state and the lack of any thorough systematization of conditions of service, formed a normal part of bureaucratic life at the time. For example, not only did many officials, in this as in many Western bureaucracies, experience an initial period of unpaid service, but many endured periods out of office without benefiting from the system of unemployment stipends *(mazuliyet maaşı)* which did formally exist. Salary cuts were undertaken occasionally for reasons of economy but

TABLE 16-8   INCIDENTAL PROBLEMS OF OFFICIAL SERVICE

	MUSLIM I	MUSLIM II	NON-MUSLIM	Greek	Armenian	Jewish	Arab Christian	European Origin
N	(115)	(144)	(107)	(30)	(52)	(12)	(7)	(6)
Median Length of Initial Unpaid Service (in years)	2.8	2.1	2.2	2.2	2.1	3.0	4.0	.0
Median Number of Years out of Office without Unemployment Stipend	.0	.0	1.0	1.5	1.5	.0	.0	.0

never, so far as the personnel records show, with unfailing or impartial impact on all officials. Bureaucrats might also experience a drop in salary simply because of a change of position, a fact which might signify not demotion but only the disorderly state of the salary system. Another problem about which reformers of the Young Turk years complained was that earlier personnel practice did not recognize the possibility that an official might need to be removed from a position for reasons which were no fault of his own. If two officials could not be exchanged, one would simply be dismissed. Presumably many periods out of office, including many of those endured without an unemployment stipend, thus reflect nothing more than administrative necessity.

Efforts to tabulate the manifestations of problems of these kinds do not always yield clear results. Still, as Table 16-8 shows, elements of the kind of pattern that we have already detected in the assignment of salaries and ranks are at times discernible. It is perhaps enough to say that once again the non-Muslims prove to be in an intermediate position, at best, among the three major personnel groups. Among the non-Muslim subgroups, the pattern of relative advantage and disadvantage varies in a way which again underscores the lack of systematization. To some degree, however, all subgroups experienced problems of the types shown, the one exception being the men of European origin. Their apparent exemption may reflect no more than the small number of cases; alternatively, like their relatively high salaries, this may reflect the added inducements required to attract and hold such men in Ottoman service.

Indicative of aspects of the personnel system that were punishing in effect but presumably not intended expressly for that purpose, problems of the kind documented in Table 16-8 obviously do not exhaust the question of punishments. A look at the evidence which the personnel records offer on disciplinary problems that did lead to overtly punitive action is thus in order. This look will provide further insights into the ineffectiveness of the Ottoman system in maintaining a meaningful distinction of reward and punishment, as well as our final and most telling evidence on the limits of egalitarianism.

The kinds of incidents with which we must deal in assessing the frequency of overtly punitive action are complex and variable in detail. It is nonetheless difficult in inspecting the records to escape the impression that non-Muslims were more "accident-prone" than their Muslim colleagues and that this vulnerability increased over time. Indeed, if we go through the files looking for cases in which officials were subject to various forms of disciplinary action ranging from censure to prosecution and conviction, we find that while only some 10 percent of the traditionalist Muslims had any such experience, 19 percent of the modernist Muslims did and 22 percent of the non-Muslims did. Among the non-Muslim subgroups, the Arab Christians and men of European origin— fortunate in this respect as in others—experienced no such occurrences. In contrast, 23 percent of the Greeks, 25 percent of the Armenians, and a full third of the Jews were subject to such incidents.

The heterogeneity of the incidents which provoked punitive action makes it difficult to proceed further by quantitative means; yet certain characteristics of the data seem clear. Some incidents were really products of the low state of official discipline and the historic failure of sultans and statesmen to find effective ways to cope with that problem, a failure clearly connected in part to the inadequacy of the compensation system. For example, we note frequent cases of nonattendance, overstaying leaves, or refusing to accept assignments.[36] A lot of officials got away with this kind of behavior. Very confusing incidents also tended to arise when, in the confined atmosphere of a consular or diplomatic mission, personal relations degenerated into accusations and recriminations which the ministry in Istanbul, despite sometimes strenuous efforts, would be hard put to resolve.[37] Where alleged abuses were of sufficient gravity to warrant investigation or prosecution, the creakiness of Ottoman justice, compounded by things like the difficulties of communicating with remote localities, usually reduced the entries in the personnel records to inarticulate confusion. At times it seems that justice was done and offenders punished.[38] Still, the efficiency with which the Porte disposed of problems of this type was low, and the consequences of this fact were only aggravated by one peculiar by-product of the often-cited shortage of qualified official manpower. For the ministry continued to take back and reassign men who had lost their positions for disciplinary reasons, thus in effect rewarding unsatisfactory service when it could not effectively or consistently reward the contrary.[39]

From the entries in the personnel records it is certainly possible to see at times that non-Muslim officials benefited from efforts which their Muslim colleagues made at fairness and impartiality in the disposition of disciplinary problems.[40] Still, the "accident-proneness" was there, implicitly reflecting the fact that non-Muslims were subject not only to the same kinds of problems as all other officials, but also to other doubts and suspicions that emerged increasingly as faith in the viability of the Ottomanist synthesis of nationalities—a synthesis to which the official commitment to egalitarianism was directly tied—began to erode.

Sometimes the reticence of the officials responsible for the keeping of the personnel records in fact leaves us guessing as to whether it is the effects of this erosion that we observe. We read of one Armenian, for example, who lost his post as secretary of embassy in Brussels in 1905 on account of "certain causes and circumstances" *(bazı esbab-u-ahval)*[41] and of a Greek dismissed from the office of consul at Antwerp in June 1908 because of "some special [or personal] circumstances" *(bazı ahval-i hususiye)*.[42] In other cases the records are more explicit. One Greek official serving as foreign affairs director of the Province of Baghdad lost his position in May 1914 on the ground that "his being in contact with foreigners would entail difficulties in confidential matters" *(ecnebilerle münasebette bulunması mahremane hususatta müşkülâta tesadüf bahisle . . .)*.[43] Another Greek lost his place as consul in Liverpool in June 1905 when the Foreign Ministry received the express order from the Palace Secretariat to appoint a Muslim instead.[44] Explicit avowal of such a motive is rare in these records, and the fact that the order came from the palace marks the decision more or less clearly as an expression not of civil-bureaucratic initiative but rather of the sultan's pan-Islamic policy, the implications of which for the conduct of relations with the British Empire were manifold. Still, such a case is impossible to overlook. While there would be a tendency during the early Young Turk years to reemphasize the official employment of non-Muslims, this incident throws an added and poignant light on that transitoriness which we have already detected in the non-Muslim presence in civil-bureaucratic ranks.

On balance, then, the data on compensation corroborate the implications already noted in discussion of service records to the effect that the non-Muslims had become a sort of central or intermediate element within the overall social fabric of the civil bureaucracy. There are signs, to be sure, that members of some of the smaller non-Muslim subgroups enjoyed a position which could better be described in some respects as one of preferment. These exceptional cases aside, what is more significant is that the intermediate position of most non-Muslims comported important elements of disadvantage, compounded by the generally malfunctional character of the compensation system. We sense this element of disadvantage particularly in the relative lack of proportion between compensation and level of qualifications and more still in the vulnerability of the non-Muslims to various forms of punitive or at times even discriminatory action.

With reference to official service in general or to the Foreign Ministry in particular, it is not difficult—especially by present-day standards—to draw a negative picture of the efforts of the Porte to meet what was in fact an acid test of egalitarian Ottomanism. To speak only of branches of government service in which change was promised, we note particularly significant problems in the fulfillment of the promises about military service. In the civil bureaucracy, as represented by the Foreign Ministry, there were other problems in the lack of any general systematization of conditions of service, the consequent persistence of elements of the old patterns of marginality and enclavement, the limited scope to which the various non-Muslim communities found equal access to official positions, the even more imperfect realization of equality in reward and, above all, the circumstances attendant on the eventual erosion of the non-Muslim presence.

To say no more than this, however, would be to overlook the positive implications of one of the few important efforts made in the Middle East of the nineteenth century to implement a key element of the liberal political philosophy with which the modernist statesmen and thinkers of the era were so fascinated. In some respects, certainly, very significant changes did occur. Compared to the ambiguous status of the non-Muslim "officials" of the prereform period, the mere fact that the presence of non-Muslims in government service had received legal recognition on a basis of egalitarian principle was in itself of considerable value. Together with the relative effacement of the old cultural marginality of the non-Muslims, a phenomenon linked in turn to the rise of a Westernist Muslim elite, the legal changes had made it possible for non-Muslims to move to an unprecedented degree into the mainstream of Ottoman bureaucratic life. With the beginning of the appointment of non-Muslims to positions such as those of bureau chief, ambassador, or even minister, as with their appearance in representative bodies, non-Muslims had also begun to acquire a new influence in the conduct of administration and in policymaking. The very fact that officials of different communities were beginning to collaborate and, in civil-bureaucratic ranks as in the Parliament, at least to some degree to develop a fund of mutual respect reflects the extent to which egalitarianism really had begun to take root in Ottoman minds.[45] In view of considerations like these, the fact that the standing of the non-Muslim bureaucrats was in some respects an intermediate one can be regarded, not as a sign of the failure of reform, but as a measure of progress in what was bound at best to be a process of change over time. In this perspective it would even make sense to compare the results which the Ottomans achieved in a given period after 1855–1856 with those which other societies have realized within comparable periods after becoming committed to policies of egalitarian reform.

Such a comparison would extend far beyond the limits of this discussion but would be extremely useful in helping us to arrive at a fully balanced assessment of the record of the Ottoman reformers. If made with societies which have achieved a successful record in egalitarian change, however, the comparison would surely also direct our attention back to the fundamental fact that such reform cannot produce lasting effect without an underlying basis of social cohesion such as the nineteenth-century attempt at the redefinition of Ottomanism could not produce. The failures of the egalitarian reforms which we have studied here relate to this fact more than any other. The positive gains can only fully be appreciated when we recall that they were achieved in spite of this problem.

Notes

1. On the experiences of Armenians in provincial service, see also Mesrob K. Krikorian, *Armenians in the Service of the Ottoman State, 1860–1908*, London, 1977.

2. Traian Stoianovich, "The Conquering Balkan Orthodox Merchant," *Journal of Economic History*, 20 (1960), pp. 269–273 on the *noblesse de robe;* cf. Bernard Lewis, *The Emergence of Modern Turkey*, second ed., Oxford, 1968, pp. 14–15, 31–32, 53, 62, 454–455; M. Franco, *Essai sur l'histoire des Israélites de l'Empire ottoman depuis les origines jusqu'à nos jours*, Paris, 1897, passim; Y. G. Çark, *Türk Devleti Hizmetinde Ermeniler, 1453–1953*, Istanbul, 1953, pp. 39ff.; Steven Runciman, *The Great Church in Captivity: A Study of the Patriarchate of Constantinople from the Eve of the Turkish Conquest to the Greek War of Independence*, Cambridge, 1968, pp. 360ff.; also Théodore Blancard, *Les Mavroyéni: histoire d'Orient (de 1700 à nos jours)*, 2 vols., Paris, 1909, passim; and Alexandre A. C. Stourdza, *L'Europe orientale et le role historique des Maurocordato, 1660–1830*, Paris, 1913, passim.

3. C. Findley, "The Legacy of Tradition to Reform: Origins of the Ottoman Foreign Ministry," *IJMES*, 1 (1970), p. 338 n. 1; idem., *Bureaucratic Reform in the Ottoman Empire: The Sublime Porte, 1789–1922*, Princeton, 1980, ch. 3; Runciman (cited n. 2), pp. 360ff.

4. *Başbakanlık* Archives (Istanbul), Cevdet Collection, *Hariciye* 6033, petition of c. 29 Safer 1241/1825 from Zenob Manas; cf. Çark (cited n. 2), pp. 137ff.

5. J. C. Hurewitz, *The Middle East and North Africa in World Politics: A Documentary Record*, second ed., New Haven, 1975, vol. 1, p. 270.

6. Roderic H. Davison, "The Advent of the Principle of Representation in the Government of the Ottoman Empire," in William R. Polk and Richard L. Chambers, eds., *Beginnings of Modernization in the Middle East: The Nineteenth Century*, Chicago, 1968, pp. 98ff.; on the general effects of reform, cf. Halil Inalcık, "Application of the Tanzimat and its Social Effects," *Archivum Ottomanicum*, 5 (1973), pp. 97–127, and Mark Pinson, "Ottoman Bulgaria in the First Tanzimat Period—the Revolts in Nish (1841) and Vidin (1850)," *Middle Eastern Studies*, 11 (1975), pp. 103–146.

7. Lewis (cited n. 2), p. 337.

8. Hurewitz (cited n. 5), vol. 1, p. 317.

9. Davison (cited n. 6), 106ff.; Robert Devereux, *The First Ottoman Constitutional Period: A Study of the Midhat Constitution and Parliament*, Baltimore, 1963, pp. 216–226, 261–282; Çark, (cited n. 2), pp. 113, 234–239.

10. On the religious leaders, see e.g., *Salname-i devlet-i aliye-i osmaniye*, Istanbul, 1315/1897, pp. 604–615; ibid., Istanbul, 1326/1908, pp. 1034–1048; on non-Muslim religious leaders in provincial administrative assemblies, see Davison (cited n. 6), p. 99; İlber Ortaylı, *Tanzimattan Sonra Mahalli İdareler (1840–1878)*, Ankara, 1974, pp. 58–62.

11. Lewis (cited n. 2), pp. 337ff.; Roderic H. Davison, "Turkish Attitudes Concerning Christian-Muslim Equality in the Nineteenth Century," *American Historical Review*, 59 (1954), p.

859; idem., *Reform in the Ottoman Empire, 1856–1876,* Princeton, 1963, pp. 94–95; Çark (cited n. 2), pp. 222–229; Paul Fesch, *Constantinople aux derniers jours d'Abdul-Hamid,* Paris, 1907, p. 250.

12.   *Düstur,* second series, 12 vols., Istanbul, 1329/1911–1927, vol. 1, pp. 420–431, law of 24 Receb 1327/August 1909; ibid., vol. 6, pp. 912–913, 926, 1331–1332, temporary laws of 11 Ramazan-17 Zilkade 1332/August–October 1914; ibid., vol. 8, pp. 250–251, law of 19 Safer 1334/Jan. 1916; ibid., vol. 8, pp. 375–376, 378–381, laws of 3 Rebiülahir 1334/Feb. 1916; Stanford J. Shaw and Ezel K. Shaw, *History of the Ottoman Empire and Modern Turkey,* II: *Reform, Revolution, and Republic: The Rise of Modern Turkey, 1808–1975,* Cambridge, 1977, p. 100; personal communications with Avigdor Levy and Feroz Ahmad, January 1978.

13.   Çark (cited n. 2), pp. 156–165; cf. *Salname* (cited n. 10) (1326/1908), pp. 140–151.

14.   The bulk of these files are in the *Hariciye* Archives (Istanbul), *Sicill-i Ahval* Collection, where we find one envelope for each individual, normally including the original of the autobiographical questionnaire on which the system was based. I have supplemented these files with those of certain other individuals who are missing in the *Hariciye* collection but are known to have been associated with the Foreign Ministry. These additional files are found in the *Başbakanlık* Archives, *Dahiliye Sicill-i Ahval Defterleri,* passim. For reasons having to do with the way the records were kept, the cases found in this collection are mostly men of high rank. In subsequent notes we shall identify files from the Foreign Ministry personnel records simply by the letters ''SA'' plus the envelope number; those from the *Başbakanlık* collection, by the letters ''DSA'' plus the volume and page numbers.

15.   Personal observation makes this clear, although the instructions for the maintenance of the records at times demanded the contrary: *Düstur,* 1st series, 8 vols. and various supplements, Istanbul and Ankara, 1289/1872–1943, vol. 5, p. 966, instructions of 19 Şaban 1304/1887, art. 2, calling for mention of *millet*-affiliation.

16.   Şerif Mardin, *The Genesis of Young Ottoman Thought: A Study in the Modernization of Turkish Political Ideas,* Princeton, 1962, p. 19, n. 16.

17.   Osman Ergin, *Istanbul mektepleri ve ilim, terbiye ve san'at müesseseleri dolayısile Türkiye maarif tarihi,* Istanbul, 1939–43, vol. 3, pp. 997ff.

18.   On this problem and the reasons for it, see Lewis (cited n. 2), pp. 62, 454–455.

19.   SA 258, Henri Armaon (?), dismissed for this reason on 20 Safer 1310/1892.

20.   On the formation of the new, Western-oriented Muslim elite, which amounts essentially to the leading element among the Muslims proficient in French, see Findley, *Bureaucratic Reform* (cited n. 3), chs. 4 and 5.

21.   Cf. Max Weber, *Economy and Society: An Outline of Interpretive Sociology,* ed. Guenther Roth and Claus Wittich, 3 vols., New York, 1968, vol. 1, pp. 212–299; vol. 3, pp. 901–1069.

22.   Findley, *Bureaucratic Reform* (cited n. 3), ch. 1 on the ''model of the patrimonial household;'' chs. 6 and 7 on personnel regulations.

23.   Ibid., chs. 5 and 6 on the history of these offices and the justification for the translations used here for *Tahrirat-ı Hariciye* and *Mektubi-i Hariciye.*

24.   DSA, IV, 178; Çark (cited n. 2), pp. 130–132.

25.   E.g., SA 124, file of Saferzade Neşan Safer Efendi, director of the office, 1881–1884.

26.   *Salname* (cited n. 10) (1326/1908), pp. 240–245, lists almost sixty men for the office; the yearbook listings are almost never exhaustive.

27.   In the official personnel records, patron-client networks are usually perceptible only in part. Among Greeks with diplomatic experience, the records on members of the Aristarchi (SA 504), Karaca (DSA, II, 1030), Karatheodory (SA 30, 42), Musurus (DSA I, 684), and Photiadi (SA 4) families include evidence of links of this kind within the family. Among Arab Christians a comparable example appears with the family of Franco Paşa, former governor of Lebanon (SA 66, 173). A clear case among the men of European origin, but without the element of kinship, lies in the parallelism between the careers of Rüstem Paşa (DSA, II, 100) and Morel Bey (SA 434).

28. Auswärtiges Amt, Türkei 162, Band 2, Radowitz to Caprivi, 16 May 1890 (on microfilm in US National Archives, T 139, roll 394).

29. To mention only heads of diplomatic missions whose files are among those under study, we have Yahya Karaca Paşa (a Greek, DSA, 2, 1030, representative to Sweden and the Netherlands, 1881–1894), "Etienne" Karatheodory (SA 30, in Brussels, c. 1875–1900), S. Musurus (DSA, 1, 684, in London, 1902–1907, his father having been ambassador there from 1850 to 1885), and Yusuf Misak (or Hovsep Misakyan; SA 36, at the Hague, 1900–1913). The non-Muslim foreign ministers were Alexander Karatheodory Paşa (1878–1879), Sava Paşa (1879–1880), Gabriel Noradounghian (1912–1913), and Yusuf Franco Paşa (1919); see *Dişişleri Bakanlığı Yıllığı, 1964–1965,* ed. Hâmid Aral, Ankara, n.d., p. 14. The long-time Armenian undersecretary was Artin Dadian Paşa (SA 435). On Misakyan, Noradounghian, and Dadian, cf. Çark (cited n. 2), 147–56.

30. DSA, 2, 100.

31. DSA 1, 1016; pro-German feeling mentioned by Radowitz, Auswärtiges Amt, Türkei 162, Band 2, to Caprivi, 16 May 1890.

32. SA 434.

33. SA 5.

34. SA 332.

35. Information on the monetary system of the period may be found in George Young, *Corps de droit ottoman,* 7 vols., Oxford, 1905–06, vol. 5, p. 1ff.

36. Ohan Bağdadlıyan (SA 31), career apparently terminated 26 Safer 1313/Aug. 1895 due to prolonged absence in Europe; and Moise Hanail (SA 128), career apparently terminated 17 Rebiülevvel 1317/July 1899 when he refused to accept reassignment. For the sake of brevity, we shall in this and subsequent notes cite only cases of non-Muslims who experienced disciplinary problems; it should be noted that there usually were members of both the Muslim groups who also had problems of the same kinds.

37. Sarkiz Balian (SA 170), incident of 1316–1317/1898–1899 involving conflicting reports on his services in Montenegro; Gürci Cemil (identifies himself as Jewish, SA 513), removed in Şaban 1323/1905 from a consular post in Greece because of conflict between himself and the consul-general.

38. Krikor Hâkimoğlu (SA 68), another consular official accused of misdeeds in Montenegro, but exonerated; Tavik (?) Besim (identifies himself as Jewish, SA 212), convicted of embezzlement and unsuccessful in appeal.

39. Dimitraki Lefteriadi (SA 722), reappointment of Ramazan 1322/1904; Dimitraki Theodosiadi (SA 313), reappointments of Rebiülahir 1304/1890 and Receb 1317/1899; Tade Andonian (SA 331), reappointment of Cemaziülevvel 1321/1903; Minas Aram Bağdadlıyan (SA 45), reappointment of Safer 1317/1899; Rupen Davud (presumed Armenian, SA 164), thrice dismissed for negligence or incompatibility with superiors and twice reappointed.

40. Krikor Hâkimoğlu (SA 68); file includes detailed evidence on his exoneration following dismissal as consul at Podgorica on allegations of negligence and misconduct.

41. Mihran Kavafian (SA 39), entry of Şaban 1323/1905.

42. Alexander Dosios (SA 505).

43. Nikolaki Faler (SA 270).

44. Pandeli Logaris (SA 9). At the time of the dismissal of Krikor Hâkimoğlu (SA 68—cf. nn. 38 and 40) from the consulate at Podgorica, the argument was advanced that the consul there should be a Muslim. The reason was that there were Muslims in the vicinity who were Ottoman subjects. Krikor Efendi was accused of not having served their interests, and his exoneration followed a report from the ambassador in Cetinje, Ahmed Fevzi Paşa, indicating that he had done so zealously.

45. For an example of such respect, see the portrait of Artin Dadian Paşa in Galib Kemali Söylemezoğlu, *Hariciye Hizmetinde Otuz Sene,* 4 vols. Istanbul, 1949–1955, vol. 1, pp. 54–55. Cf. Devereux (cited n. 9), pp. 222–226.

Minorities and Municipal Reform in Istanbul, 1850–1870

Steven Rosenthal

A study of the beginnings of urban modernization in Istanbul provides much insight into the attitudes of the non-Muslim minorities of the capital toward Ottoman reform in general. The growth of a Western conception of urban administration owed much to minority influence. The foundation in 1857 of a European-style municipality took place in Galata, the area of the capital inhabited primarily by foreigners and non-Muslims. The new municipality, administered by a municipal council composed of Greeks, Armenians, and Jews, was designed to introduce modern urban administration and amenities to Galata. If successful, the system would be extended to the rest of the capital. Given the large measure of autonomy accorded the municipal council, an examination of the impetus, direction, and success of the municipality illuminates the role of the non-Muslim minorities as cultural mediators and as real or potential instruments of Ottoman regeneration.

The district of Galata had long been a non-Muslim stronghold. Sharing the European side of the Bosphorus with the old city of Stambul, Galata was cut off from that seat of empire by the muddy and slow moving waters of the Golden Horn. Galata's sheltered harbors, slow currents, and deep water dockages had made it a natural site for maritime commerce with Europe. Even before the Turkish conquest the suburb had been the seat of the Genoese commercial colony whose activities had gradually sapped the Byzantine Empire of its economic vitality. After 1453 Galata had retained its foreign and commercial character. Although after the sixteenth century Muslims increasingly established themselves in Galata and in the overlooking district of Pera, they always remained a distinct minority.[1]

When in the seventeenth century Galata became the site of the European diplomatic legations its non-Muslim character was reinforced by the capitulations. The newly arrived diplomats and merchants refused to be tried by *kadis'* courts; foreigners on Ottoman soil were granted the privilege of extraterritoriality by which they were not subject to any legal jurisdiction save that of their home country.[2] For crimes committed in the sultan's realm the new inhabitants could be tried only in their own embassy. Originally intended to safeguard the small European diplomatic and merchant community against perceived and actual abuses of the Ottoman legal system, extraterritoriality was soon given by the European embassies to members of the non-Muslim minorities. First the man who occupied the vital post of embassy translator was given the privilege, then the merchants who supplied the legation. From here it was only a short step to selling embassy protection to anyone who could pay for it.[3] In the era before the Crimean War when the Great Powers had competed for the role of guardian of the empire's religious minorities, embassy protection had been extended to almost anyone. Since foreign "protective citizenship" helped free a non-Muslim from the arbitrariness of Ottoman officials and from the venality of *millet* tribunals, vast numbers of Armenians, Greeks, and Jews obtained embassy protection.[4] By 1858 the foreign domination of Galata was demonstrated by the fact that approximately half of the suburb's inhabitants were not subject to indigenous legal institutions.

The district's population in 1882 was put at 237,293.[5] It was the second most populous district after Fatih, containing fully one quarter of Istanbul's population of 875,000.[6] Galata's population was extremely heterogeneous. Although half, or 111,000 persons, were listed as foreign subjects, the vast majority of these were not European expatriates but protected Ottoman citizens. The number of Muslims living in the district of Galata represented only between one-fifth and one-fourth of its total population and less than one-seventh of the Muslim population of the entire city. Also living within the district were 17,589 Greeks, 29,559 Armenians, and 22,865 Jews not enjoying consular protection and respectively comprising one-twelfth, one-ninth, and one-tenth of Galata's population.[7] Fully half the Jews of Constantinople were concentrated in Galata. The much larger Greek and Armenian populations were more dispersed. One-fifth of Constantinople's 159,511 Armenians and only one-eighth of its 182,847 Greeks were domiciled in Galata.[8] In addition to these major *millets* 3,338 Armenian Catholics lived within the district as did smaller numbers of Armenian Protestants and Latin Catholics.[9]

This heterogeneous population lived in eighty-eight neighborhoods *(mahalle)* usually containing twenty-five hundred to three thousand persons, although neighborhoods as large as fifteen thousand also existed in Pera, the area above Galata proper which became a part of the Galata municipal district.[10]

In spite of much change and imprecision, a few residential patterns can be ascertained within the district. Armenian and Greek neighborhoods intermingled around the Galata tower and continued down toward the commercial section below.[11] Armenians were also concentrated in Pangalti above the eastern part of Pera bordered by the Great Field of the Dead. Many Muslims lived in small, self-contained houses in the ravines behind Pera along the border of Kassım Paşa, and in the area of Tophane east of Karaköy.[12] Some of the most important Muslim neighborhoods were Tershane, Azapkapı, Galatasaray, Firoz Bey and

Ayaz Paşa. This represented a distinct change in the residential pattern of Galata and reflected economic developments brought on by the 1838 Anglo-Turkish commercial treaty and by the Crimean War. Muslims had originally occupied the central parts of the suburb, but the great influx of non-Muslims had for years been driving them to the peripheries of Galata and even across the Horn and the Bosphorus. The European expatriates and consular protégés who had originally occupied the base and brow of the hill of Galata were rapidly occupying its slopes. A map prepared by the German Stolpe between 1857 and 1861 graphically demonstrates this evolution. On both the east and west sides of the Galata tower, the Muslim population increases in proportion to the distance from the district's center. Higher rents for tenants, soaring living expenses, Muslim xenophobia, and above all, the prices non-Muslims were willing to pay for land and houses had increasingly induced Muslim proprietors to sell out and move to places more congenial to their sensibilities.[13] As former Muslim neighborhoods in the center of Galata had become Christianized by the end of the Crimean War, the conversion process was extended to such peripheral areas as Halil Paşa, halfway between Taxım and the west end of Pera, and Tophane. The most exclusive non-Muslim residential neighborhood remained the Tomtom Mahal, where the stone houses of bankers and merchants vied with the nearby embassies in size and pretention. But for the vast majority of Galata's population the high price of land and the high cost of building meant that houses were usually small, cramped, and crowded. Most dwellings were constructed of wood, and were usually two-storied with a balcony extending out over the street. The severe land shortage was manifested by the fact that this small dwelling typically served as the home for about fifteen people.[14]

Land use patterns also help to reveal the character of the district. Logically, shipping and the wholesale trade dominated the harbor area around the Golden Horn, along with establishments catering to the needs of the transient maritime population. The retail trade and cafés of the Grand Rue, the diplomatic work of the embassies, and the domestic life of the private residences comprised the business of Pera above. At least one hundred banks and commercial concerns, the total number of these establishments in Constantinople, were located in Galata, demonstrating the near monopoly that Christian minorities possessed in these activities.[15] For local trade the district possessed one hundred twenty-two of the city's four hundred eighty-three *hans*, or large commercial buildings.[16]

Other factors emphasized the district's semi-European orientation. The only pieces of state land *(miri)* in the district were a plot at Kapı Kuli, the Galatasaray Palace, the artillery barracks, and the artillery factory at Tophane.[17] Of the 188 advanced Muslim religious schools *(medrese)* in Constantinople, only one was located in Galata.[18] The existence of over fifty churches and synagogues reflected the predominantly non-Muslim population.[19]

The non-Muslim population was extremely diverse and was composed of all classes. According to a survey taken in the late 1860s, based in part on information furnished by the famous Ottoman intellectual, Ahmet Vefik Efendi, 13,500 Ottoman artisans lived within the district. These included 4,500 Greeks,

3,200 Armenians, 1,500 Jews, the rest being classified as Arabs or Bulgarians.[20] These were organized into 140 guilds with Greeks and Jews predominating in the tailors' guild and Armenians in the goldsmiths'.[21] Under the impetus of European commerce these guilds had been seriously and in most cases fatally weakened. In addition, many European craftsmen had taken up residence in the district. By 1870 these European artisans had reached 8,500 in number and were mostly from Italy and central Europe.[22]

Ahmet Vefik Efendi's information was corroborated by a similar inquiry conducted by the British consulate during the same period. The British found that except for Galata there were 120,000 guild members within the entire city.[23] This figure when subtracted from the 133,000 guild members given by the census for all the city yields a number compatible with that of the original estimate. Assuming the 1860s figures to be approximately correct, at least half of the Greek males and one-fifth of the Armenians were members of craft guilds. The very high proportion of Greeks who were guild members may reflect that community's predominance in the numerically important guild of boatmen. The percentage of Armenians belonging to a guild was greater within Galata than outside the district's borders. This may reflect the building boom that followed the Crimean War since many Armenians were connected with the construction trade. Only about one-tenth of Galata's male Jews were guild members. Many eked out a living as itinerant hawkers and peddlers.

Of the communities residing within the district of Galata, the Jewish *millet* showed the greatest numerical correspondence between men and women over all age groups.[24] This probably indicates that it was the most stable and least geographically mobile community in the district. The numerical correspondence between male and female Armenians was only slightly less stable. The gap between the numbers of Greek men and women in the district was much greater, again reflecting the large numbers of semitransient Ionians employed in the shipping trade.

It was the non-Muslim embassy protégés of Galata who were most affected by commercial developments during the Crimean War era and whose enhanced economic and social status led them to demand reform of the administration of the capital. Traditional urban administration neither recognized the city as a corporate entity nor provided for a governmental apparatus separate from that of the Imperial administration as a whole.[25] This nonspecialized city administration was adequate so long as the level of urban activity calling for governmental intervention and coordination remained comparatively low. But the economic and social change stemming from the effects of the Anglo-Turkish commercial treaty of 1838 gave rise to new demands that the old institutions were ill equipped to handle.[26] Much of the vast increase in trade passed through Istanbul, and it was the foreign and non-Muslim merchants and bankers of Galata, the European section of the city, who possessed the facilities and the European contacts to obtain the bulk of this new commerce. A new class of Ottoman merchants arose composed of foreigners, and Ottoman Greeks and Armenians. It was they who were responsible for the flight of non-Muslims from the center of the district. The ornate stone houses they built on former Muslim-occupied property reflected their desires to be thought of as Europeans and the attempt to create an environment in accord with their aspirations. Such desires soon transcended personal domiciles. As early as 1846 two Galata businessmen opened an opera house, and a few years later a philharmonic society was formed.[27] A clear attempt at social differentiation through the direct imitation of Europe occurred in 1849 when Galata's first private club, the Casino de Pera, opened its doors. The casino, occupying the old British embassy building, was filled with all the accepted trappings of bourgeois elegance, including, as a newspaper noted, "overstuffed furniture, a billiard table and immense gilded mirrors."[28] Cafés were built along the main commercial street and a French restaurant opened next to the convent of the Mevlevi Dervishes, which itself became an obligatory stop for the ever increasing numbers of European tourists. It was from within this atmosphere that domestic demand for municipal reform arose. Galata's lack of municipal services and amenities and its unpaved and at times impassable streets were not in accord with European standards and inhibited commerce and social life. For the emerging bourgeois a program of municipal reform would strengthen Galata's European image, and help rationalize economic relations. Most important, if coupled with the development of Western municipal conceptions of self-rule, such a program would help the non-Muslim merchants to break out of the political straitjacket of the *millet* system and gain political influence more in accord with their economic power.

What emerges from this portrait of Galata is a sense of ethnic diversity, entrepreneurial activity, and cultural interaction. The suburb's multitude of nationalities, religions, and social classes reflected the heterogeneity of the empire as a whole. The reconciliation of the emerging national aspirations of these subject *millet*s with the traditional concept of the Ottoman state posed the chief domestic problem of Ottoman administration in the nineteenth century. The concentration of such diversity into the limited area of Galata, the resulting urban problems of congestion, crime, and disease, the influence of the foreign embassies through direct pressure and indirect example, and the ambitions and pretensions of the emerging European and native bourgeoisie exemplified the problems of Imperial administration and gave them a special urgency.

The events surrounding the Crimean War provided additional impetus toward municipal reform. The capital's inability to cope with the influx of British and French troops, the problem of inflation and food shortages, and constant complaints from the Allies concerning lack of urban amenities induced the Ottoman government to create a new ministry, the City Prefecture.[29] Although the prefecture was based upon its French namesake and had theoretical responsibility over "guild supervision, the cleanliness and embellishment of the city, and the general assurance of the good condition of the streets and bazaars,"[30] its efforts were largely limited to the well-trodden paths of commercial regulation. This failure to exercise initiative was a great disappointment to the economic and political aspirations of the capital's new minority elite who noted that the new administration had not included any non-Muslims. With the encouragement of a member of the Ottoman administration the merchant community created an ad hoc "*İnitizam-i Şehir* Commission" (Commission for the Regulation of the City) to agitate for municipal reform.[31] Its members included Antoine Alléon, a French subject permanently residing in Istanbul who often performed financial services for the sultan, especially negotiation of loans and currency exchange.[32] He was reputedly the richest man in the city. Avram Camondo was another extremely wealthy financier and was the leader of the reform wing within Istanbul's Jewish *millet*.[33] He was a French protected citizen. Ohanes Migerdich and David Revelaki were Armenian and Greek businessmen, the latter a British protégé. Noncommercial members included an Ottoman citizen who was a member of the Porte's translation bureau and the Austrian General Stein.[34]

The granting of official status to the commission marked the government's realization that municipal reform was explicitly dependent "on the knowledge of Ottoman and foreign families long resident in the city familiar with foreign ways." The commission was explicitly given the task of producing a set of municipal regulations which would "serve as a model for the New Administration."[35] After a two-year period of study and experiment marked by delay, the commission voiced its dissatisfaction and demanded the creation of a new urban framework.[36] "Although a municipal commission has been formed by the government, since its tasks have not been properly defined it has not achieved the hoped for results and it is clear that up to this point it has lacked the capacity to do anything. Such a commission must be instituted on a firm basis as is done in other countries." The merchants now demanded a municipal treasury, the right of taxing, and the power to administer all areas of municipal concern independently of the central government. A new non-Muslim confidence brought on by wartime gains is evident in the last line of the merchants' memorandum: "In the case that the government does not accept our view and grant the power and responsibility we request, the commissioners will consider it their obligation to resign."[37] By entrusting urban reform to the most Western component of the population, the government had unwittingly encouraged new demands the implication of which could revolutionize political relationships between the Muslims and minorities of the empire.

The demands of the Galata merchants reached the High Council of Reform at a most opportune time. The Crimean War was over. The influence of the British and French had reached new heights. The Treaty of Paris (1856) had recognized the Ottoman Empire as a member of the Concert of Europe. The institution of a program of municipal reform would therefore simultaneously meet the longstanding complaints of the Allies, demonstrate the empire's capacity for internal regeneration, and help establish its credentials as a bona fide member of the European community. The last was particularly important, for the British embassy never tired of badgering the Turks concerning the necessity of establishing representative institutions.

The external and internal pressure was effective and the response of the government marks a watershed in the municipal history of the Ottoman Empire. The High Council's language clearly demonstrated its dependence upon the previous commission. "In every place the affairs of reordering and similar affairs of cities or sets of districts should be left to an administration composed of its inhabitants. And although the previously mentioned *İntizam-i Şehir* Commission was formed to do something along these lines it was unable to do anything because this fundamental rule was neglected in the fixing of its tasks."[38] The government drew up a new code of regulations which envisaged no less than the eventual reform of the entire administration of Istanbul. The first efforts at reform, however, would be restricted to the municipal district of Galata which also would include Pera. The reasons for beginning the reform in the European section of the city were stated by the government in its announcement of the founding of the Sixth Municipal District.

> Since to begin all things in the above-mentioned districts would be sophistry and unworthy, and since the Sixth District contains much valuable real estate and many fine buildings, and since the majority of those owning property or residing there have seen such things in other countries and understand their value, the reform program will be inaugurated in the Sixth District.[39]

The announcement went on to state that if the work of this model district were to prove successful, the new municipal system would be extended to the other districts, which until such a time would continue to be administered by the prefecture.

The High Council could have listed many other reasons for choosing to begin the first thoroughgoing attempt at municipal reform in Galata. Most obviously, the *İntizam-i Şehir* Commission had been almost exclusively composed of residents and merchants of that suburb, and had concentrated much of its reform efforts there. Most of the experiments in paving and street cleaning had taken place in the European part of the city. The Grand Rue de Pera had been the scene of Istanbul's first public gas lighting. Other, more general factors made Galata the ideal location in which to inaugurate European-style reform. The absence of resident Muslim notables *(ayan)* and the comparatively small number of guild members minimized potential resistance from these two repositories of Islamic tradition. Moreover, the religious authorities had always considered Galata to be an infidel area and could not raise objection to Westernizing reform among the *gâvurs* (infidels). The district was blessed not only with the asset of a Christian population presumed to be familiar with and predisposed toward European municipal usages, but also with an absence of many of the factors which had inhibited secular reform elsewhere in the empire. By choosing Galata as their starting point the High Council of Reform had ensured that the municipal experiment would be entrusted to non-Muslims under the most favorable conditions possible within the Ottoman domain.

Within the new district the basic governmental mechanism was to be a Municipal Council composed of owners of property within the district. Four "foreign" property holders, either native Europeans or Ottoman protégés of the embassies were appointed to the council not as regular members but as "advisers."[40] The six regular members of the new council, also chosen by the grand

Vezir, were required to own property within the district worth one hundred thousand piasters. Foreign advisers, perhaps reflecting the economic advantages of protective citizenship, were required to own property worth five hundred thousand piasters.[41] Despite these differences in nomenclature and qualifications the powers and duties of both members and advisers were identical and the term seems to have been employed solely as a means of smoothing over the unsettling implication of rule by Christian foreigners in an area also inhabited by Muslims. Member, adviser, Ottoman citizen and the occasional native European all represented the same community of interest. All were of the same class of merchants who had composed the *İntizam-i Şehir* Commission. The choice of Antoine Alléon and Avram Camondo as "advisers" ensured a continuity in personnel as well as in spirit. The other advisers were Septime Franchini, an Italian protected citizen, and Charles Hanson, a native Englishman.[42] The regular members included two Greeks, an Armenian, two Muslims and Theodore Naum, a Protestant who had built Galata's opera house a decade earlier.

The powers and responsibilities given to the Municipal Council were considerable. The director *(müdür)* of the district was appointed by the grand vezir and would supervise the Municipal Council and serve as intermediary between it and the central government. The basic responsibilities of the Municipal Council were very broadly conceived and later expressed as "everything touching the welfare of citizens."[43] It received jurisdiction over market regulation, roads, sewers, streetlighting, and the right to regulate professions and commercial occupations not organized into guilds.

The powers given the Municipal Council for the performance of these duties were extensive. It was empowered to determine its jurisdiction by writing its own basic regulations. It could pay municipal bills, and prepare budgets which would be submitted to the government and published every six months in the local newspapers. Although extraordinary expenses were subject to the approval of the central government, daily expenses were to be administered directly by the council. Most important of all, the council was given the power to levy a maximum tax of 2 percent on the income of property. According to the fundamental regulations of the district promulgated a short time later, the proceeds from this tax would be devoted to the cost of running the district.[44] For extraordinary expenses such as the building of roads and sewers, the District Council was authorized to levy a 3 percent extraordinary tax on the income of all property in the neighborhood where the work was taking place.

Although it had considerable powers the model district was not a true municipality. Linked to the Grand Vezir's office the municipality had no corporate identity. It lacked a true police force, though it soon instituted a municipal court. These weaknesses notwithstanding, council membership represented a remarkable advance in the political power of its non-Muslim members. The council realized the need for gradualism and seemed well satisfied with its new powers. The legal implications of the municipal experiment were explicitly recognized and the council's hopes for the future were revealed in its first report.

Since we will derive no special benefit from the execution of these articles, we have only been motivated by the desire to be useful to the Sultan in view of the long time that we have received the hospitality of the Ottoman Empire. And since the granting of citizenship will mark one of the great days in the history of the empire, we will work with all of our power to assure the good execution of these regulations.[45]

Whatever the connotations of "citizenship," municipal reform was explicitly linked in the minds of its minority adherents with the political reorganization of the empire.

Despite the hopes of the council, the minority-directed municipality failed to reflect or encourage the growth of precisely those civic virtues which were indispensable to the growth of a real sense of citizenship. For this the council's own conceptions were to blame. Its *haut bourgeois* members used their new power not to effect the physical or social reorganization of the district but to rationalize existing economic and social relationships through the improvement of streets and the provision of municipal amenities. It was the streets in the center of the district where the council members owned houses or businesses that almost exclusively received the benefits of widening, leveling, refuse collection, and in some cases gas lighting. The council's commercial orientation and sense of priorities was further demonstrated by the fact that its two largest expenditures were for the erection of a commercial building *(han)* in the wharf area and for a carriage road linking the wharf with the area of retail commerce in Pera. Its European pretentions were shown by its publication of a sophisticated sanitary code, copied from the French, which was impossible to enforce,[46] and by abortive plans to publish a municipal journal devoted to "general questions of political economy."[47] Such "reform" had little relevance to the poor Greek and Armenian populations of the district and even less to most of Galata's Muslim inhabitants. When the council concerned itself with such people at all it did so from an exclusively commercial perspective. In the interest of free trade the council abolished guilds within the district but sought to charge former guild members license fees that were far higher than they had previously paid to the *esnaf*.[48]

Despite the council's narrow focus the first two years of the municipality were marked by concrete achievement and ever increasing plans and ambitions. The members of the council basked in the approval of both the general population and of official organs of government. The British ambassador, while deeming some of the council's policies as contrary to the capitulations, was forced to concede that "it [the council] has done in less than a year more for Pera than had been done for centuries."[49] The Porte, flattered by such praise, seemed well content with this new indication of the empire's modernity and European orientation. In 1859, the Grand Vezir congratulated the council on "the direction of the many good works being daily accomplished."[50] Minority direction of the experimental municipal district seemed to be a resounding success and the Porte now considered extending the local councils to the other districts of the capital.

In actuality the material achievements of the foreign dominated municipal council served as a facade concealing poor planning, financial mismanagement, and the strong possibility of internal corruption. The district's extensive capital improvements had been based upon government grants and loans, the repayment of which was dependent upon the collection of the property tax. But the minority character of Galata could be an obstacle as well as an encouragement to municipal innovation. In Galata resistance to the Ottoman tax collector had been long elevated to the level of a moral principle and the Municipal Council had underestimated the force of old habits. Despite their satisfaction with the improvements brought about by the municipality, most householders took advantage of their protective foreign citizenship to refuse to pay the property tax. Rumors of graft and other forms of municipal corruption also discouraged payment.[51] By mid-1860 the municipality had run short of funds and initiated a vicious circle of cutting back services which in turn prompted further refusal to pay the tax.[52] The largest individual investment of the council, the *han* in the wharf area of Karaköy, remained unfinished and became a symbol of poor planning and the focus of new charges of cronyism and corruption.[53]

The first council had served its three year term and it was hoped the appointment of new members would revive public support. The new council was chosen by May 1861 and had the same minority composition as its predecessors. Its advisers were an Austrian citizen, a Greek protégé of the Russians, Alléon for the French, and an Italian merchant under British protection.[54] The council could do little but make appeals for payment and attempt to examine the legality of all claims to the foreign protection which shielded the recalcitrants. But appeals and threats failed and all municipal work was halted. In late 1862 the council's debts had reached five million piasters and the municipality was bankrupt.[55] One of the earliest supporters of the municipal experiment, the influential *Journal de Constantinople,* now accused the council of being a toy of the rich who hid behind the capitulations to avoid paying their own property taxes.[56]

The *Levant Herald,* which had formerly viewed the foundation of the original council as a panacea for the problems of both the capital and the empire, now condemned the municipal experiment in the most scathing terms. The *Meclis,* it stated, "was assumed to represent Pera, which looks down upon Stamboul from its supposed pinnacle of superior administrative intelligence. But if these illustrious 'ediles' had been Turkish officials . . . the result of their wisdom could hardly have been more disastrous than they have been."[57] The newspaper failed to understand how the council, composed of individually successful merchants and bankers, could fail so miserably as a collective body and attributed the district's bankruptcy to graft and dishonesty. "The district offered all of the pleasures of gambling with none of the risks."[58] If the speculations failed, the Ottoman government would assume the responsibility.

The newspaper's evaluation was overly harsh. Poor planning and corruption had existed in substantial measure, but the refusal of foreign and protected minority citizens to support the municipality with the property tax had also been a major cause of its failure. The embassies, especially the British, feared that the new Municipal Council might provide grounds for the removal of European legal privileges. But it was not only the desire to protect the capitulations that prevented the embassies from supporting the municipality by taking coercive measures against European citizens and protégés who refused to pay their rightful taxes. The European attitude toward the Municipal Council was also a product of the European perception of the non-Muslims who comprised it.

The Greeks, Armenians, and Jews who comprised the majority of the Municipal Council were termed Levantines by native Europeans and were heartily disliked by the diplomatic community. Levantines, although born and brought up in the East, considered themselves to be genuine Europeans, a claim which was resented by European foreigners, who usually saw the Levantine as the product of Oriental civilization. One traveler expressed the popular European view of Ottoman civilization in a description of the city of Izmir. "From the Frank Quarter extend back irregular, narrow and filthy lanes inhabited first by Greeks, next by Armenians and Jews, and last by the Turks. Turktown, as it is called, is built partly on the acclivity of the hill. In the popular usage, Turktown includes all but the Frank Quarter."[59] Another observer was more explicit in detailing Levantine claims and the European reaction to them. "In my rapid definition of European society I must not omit to mention that the Perotes or natives of Pera consider themselves as much Franks as if they had been born and nurtured on the banks of the Thames or the Seine, and your expression of amusement at this very original notion would inevitably give great offense."[60]

When Levantines were, in fact, perceived by Western Europeans as distinct from Turks, it was doubtful that even this distinction was a flattering one. The Levantine was viewed, justly or unjustly, as exclusively concerned with the pursuit of wealth, and as an enthusiastic practitioner of the dissimulation and bribery that were a part of contemporary Ottoman society. If the Turk was to be distrusted, the Levantine was to be despised for his presumed dishonesty and for his pretentions to European superiority. Sir Stratford Canning, longtime British ambassador to the Porte, advised a member of his staff in the following terms: "Don't assume that men like Ali or Fuad Paşa are trying to cheat you, but always assume that everyone below their stamp is not only ready and willing to cheat you but is actively doing so especially if he is a Christian."[61] Given these attitudes it was not surprising that the embassies should have looked upon the beginning of Levantine political power with "jealousy and mistrust" and have refused despite their continuous proclamations of the necessity of Ottoman internal reform, to give the Municipal Council that measure of support which might have saved it from bankruptcy.

The bankruptcy of the district determined the subsequent course of the municipal experiment. Although the central government had basked in the praise elicited by even a limited reform program, it henceforth associated municipal autonomy with extravagant expenditure. Hoping to obtain the best of both worlds, the government now retained the council but took direct control of the municipality by appointing Server Efendi, a regular government official, as director and by shifting most power to him.[62] The secretary general of the district, previously elected from among the council members, was now also appointed by the Porte.[63] Henceforth the Ottoman administration was responsible for the planning and implementation of municipal reform, and the Municipal Council was gradually reduced to the status of an advisory body. It is indicative of the Porte's active role in the municipality that from this time onward communications to the embassies are signed not by the secretary general but by the Ottoman foreign minister. Since it was now in a position to prevent abuses the Porte felt secure enough to respond to the continuous demands that the council be chosen by the inhabitants of the district. In July 1863 all owners of property within Galata subject to two thousand piasters annual tax were invited to municipal headquarters to choose twelve of their number as council members. It is not certain whether there was a direct election or the owners merely communicated their preferences to the central government. The Porte's influence may be indicated by the fact that although there were four foreign advisers as before, half of the eight regular members were now Turkish Muslims and at least two of these were government officials.[64] Whatever the precise mechanism, in view of the Porte's determination to control the district, the new procedure was a substitution of form for substance.

Notwithstanding its failure to make the council a truly representative and powerful body, the surprising success of the Turkish-run municipality implied that the institution of a viable program of reform had not been beyond the capability of the original minority council. With less funding than its predecessor the administration of Server Efendi was able to carry out a broad program of reform that benefited all classes within the municipality. Beginning in 1864 it extended municipal services to all parts of Galata, dug wells, built public parks and promenades, and provided a free hospital for the poor.[65] The work of economic rationalization was continued as the municipality constructed new and larger port facilities and demolished the ancient walls that had impeded communication between the upper and lower portions of the district.[66] After a year of Ottoman administration of Galata, the *Journal de Constantinople* could note with astonishment that "the work of reforming the capital is acutally proceeding."[67] As a result the municipality was able to collect 1,500,000 piasters in property tax by 1867. While substantially less than the 5,000,000 for which the district had been assessed, this was far better than the insignificant amounts collected before 1864.[68] By the end of 1865 the restoration and extension of municipal services had bred a whole new set of demands. Relieved of the necessity of agitating for urban services the inhabitants of Galata again agitated for the broader aspects of municipal reform. An editorial in the *Levant Herald* expressed the continuing aspirations of many of the district's minority inhabitants when it noted:

> With the best disposition in the world to make generous acknowledgement of the Council's services in the past couple of months, we are unable to perceive in its actions a single proof of the advance of municipal organization or one resulting advantage which this side of the Horn has enjoyed over Kismet ruled Stamboul. . . . Until the constitution of the Council is reinforced up to the level of a

provincial *Meclis* in which the elective principle and its implied responsibility to the electorate are implicitly recognized, it is futile to speak of this Pera board as other than a mere governing bureau.[69]

But the fact remained that it was a "governing bureau" of the Porte and not the semiautonomous council of minority members that had been responsible for the transformation of the district. Once circumstances had compelled the Porte to take an active role in municipal reform it was able, contrary to European expectations and stereotypes, to meet urban needs far more effectively than had the non-Muslims who had directed the previous councils of Galata. A probable reason for this success is that the Porte did not simply imitate European conceptions and priorities but placed its own distinct interpretation upon the Western notion of active governmental intervention on behalf of the city. In this sense the tenure of Server Efendi represented the wedding of the new idea of government responsibility for municipal development to the traditional Islamic concept of charity previously manifested by *vakıf* and by informal donations of the well-to-do on behalf of the poor.

Without pushing the findings of this study too far, the difference between the minority and Turkish experience of municipal reform has interesting implications for the perception of the *Tanzimat* era as a whole. In creating the original Municipal Council the Porte had provided a test of one of the major premises of Ottoman Westernizing reformers, namely that the granting of substantial autonomy combined with reform would promote a sense of Ottoman solidarity and loyalty among the non-Muslims of the empire. The minority members' conduct of the Municipal Council between 1858 and 1863 was hardly calculated to give credence to this hope. During this period the provision of substantial power, autonomy, and money to the municipality not only failed to encourage the growth of the concept of Ottoman citizenship but also failed to promote in some council members even rudimentary feelings of loyalty toward the central government. The exceedingly loose manner in which the first *Meclis,* composed of individually successful Armenian, Greek, and Jewish businessmen, expended public funds demonstrated at the very least a nonrecognition by the council of its responsibility to the community. The inflated cost of municipal projects lent credence to the contention that the council, far from attaining its high aims, became simply another instrument of Levantine corruption. The degree to which the Municipal Council failed to exercise the responsibilities of citizenship serves to illuminate another aspect of the problems facing Ottoman political reform.

The reaction of the general public to the innovations of the experimental district had even more serious implications for the fulfillment of general *Tanzimat* programs and ideals. Many within the district recognized and appreciated the advances in public works and in provision of urban amenities brought about by the municipality. But this approval was not even translated into meaningful support for the municipality, let alone into loyalty to the Ottoman state. Most property owners took advantage of their embassy protection and simply refused to pay the new municipal tax. Some, especially householders on smaller residential streets, were disturbed by the failure of the district to provide services in their area of residence. But for the vast majority the nonpayment was simply the result of long-ingrained habit. In an area of the city where resistance to the Ottoman government was almost an involuntary reflex it was unthinkable to pay one's taxes if one could use one's foreign protection to avoid doing so. Since those holding foreign protection comprised the wealthier elements of the population, this was especially disastrous and demonstrated that the minority middle class were no more disposed to give their support to the Ottoman government than were the *haut bourgeois* merchants.

The success of most property owners in employing their foreign citizenship to avoid paying municipal taxes points up the crucial role of the foreign embassies in determining the attitudes of the city's non-Muslim Ottomans. On the one hand, by granting protective citizenship to Ottoman Christians, they provided an alternative source of security and loyalty, and reduced the motivation of non-Muslims to work for the genuine reform of Ottoman society. Moreover, the system of foreign protection served to create secular *millets* which further fragmented the population in a manner inimical to the growth of a sense of community and citizenship. Within the Municipal Council the Porte itself contributed to this tendency when it insisted that each of the Great Powers be represented on the council by one of its protégés. The embassies' influence upon Ottoman minorities thus undercut the patriotic basis of the municipality and their specific refusal to allow collection of the property tax helped seal the doom of the municipal experiment.

If the Municipal Council of Galata did not live up to its potential as an instrument of reform its shortcomings were a precise reflection of the limits and difficulties of the entire *Tanzimat* reform movement. Of all contemporary Ottoman reform bodies the original Municipal Council of Galata was perhaps the best equipped in terms of knowledge of Europe and availability of personnel and funds to carry out a successful and lasting program. It was also distinguished by its community of interest with the Ottoman state. The maintenance of their commercial privileges and the prosperity of the council members both rested upon the continued existence of the empire. The fact that even this elite minority council, predisposed to reform and rejuvenation, could not work in a disinterested manner indicates the difficulty, if not the impossibility, of promoting non-Muslim loyalty and creating a genuine Ottoman citizenship. In this sense, to the historian the failures of the Municipal Council of Galata are as important as its successes.

Notes

1. Robert Mantran, *Istanbul dans la seconde moitié du XVIIᵉ siecle*, Paris, 1963, p. 73. Evliya Çelebi, who visited Galata in 1638, counted eighteen neighborhoods inhabited by Muslims, seventy by Greeks, three by Franks, one by Jews, and two by Armenians. Evliya also counted 1,160 streets and 3,080 shops. *Seyahatname*, Istanbul, 1314/1898, vol. 1, pp. 431–432; also in Joseph von Hammer's English translation, London, 1800, pp. 51–52.

2. On the capitulations see Nassim Sousa, *The Capitulatory Regime of Turkey: Its History, Origin and Nature*, Baltimore, 1933.

3. For an example see Great Britain Public Record Office, F.O. 195/39, Ali Paşa to Bulwer, 24 April 1862.

4. *Journal de Constantinople*, 11 January 1860.

5. "Dar as Saadat ve Bilad-i Selese Nufus Sayımı," p. 13. Most of the following information derives from an 1882 census of population and property in Constantinople. A copy of the entire census can be found in the Istanbul University Library and is classified *"evrak"* #89946. Although the period covered by the census occurs about fifteen years after the municipal developments in Galata studied here, the figures and proportions of 1882 are at least approximate for the earlier period. In Galata, the great fire of 1870 greatly inhibited the growth of that district while a few base figures given in the 1882 census reveal little growth for the city as a whole between 1879 and 1882. In addition, in 1857 Nassau Senior also estimated the population of Galata at 200,000. Nassau Senior, *Journal*, London, 1859, p. 73.

6. Ibid., p. 2.

7. Ibid., p. 23.

8. Ibid., p. 2.

9. Ibid., p. 2.

10. Ibid., pp. 88–91.

11. Ibid., p. 88.

12. *Levant Herald* (French Edition), 23 October 1867.

13. *Levant Herald*, 23 October 1867.

14. "Dar as Saadat ve Bilad-i Selese Nufus Sayımı" (cited n. 5), pp. 88–91.

15. Ibid., pp. 49–50.

16. Ibid., p. 57.

17. Ibid., p. 24.

18. Ibid., p. 45.

19. Ibid., pp. 28–30.

20. *Levant Herald* (French Edition), 16 July 1870.

21. Ibid.

22. Ibid.

23. Public Record Office, F.O. 195/732, Gribble to Baron, 11 January 1870.

24. "Dar as Saadat ve Bilad-i Selese Nufus Sayımı" (cited n. 5), p. 51.

25. Mantran (cited n. 1). For the traditional institutions of Istanbul, Mantran's work is the best available. Osman Nuri's (Ergin) *Mecelle-i Umur-i Belediye*, Istanbul, 1914–1922, is the classic work on the municipal history of Turkey. Though sketchy in its account of the period after the nineteenth century its reproduction of many unavailable documents render the work an invaluable primary source. A much shorter account by Nuri, written in modern Turkish, is *Türkiyede Belediye İnkişafı*, Istanbul, 1936. Also in modern Turkish and somewhat dependent on Nuri's work is Siddik Tumerkan, *Türkiye' de Belediyeler*, Istanbul, 1946. In English, H. A. R. Gibb and Harold Bowen,

Islamic Society and the West, 1 vol., 2 parts, London, 1950–1957 provides a general account of Ottoman municipal institutions. The best short treatment of the subject is Bernard Lewis, "Baladiyya," *E.I.*² vol. 2, pp. 972–975. Much of the same material also appears in Lewis, *The Emergence of Modern Turkey,* London, 1961 pp. 393–400.

26.   For the text of the treaty see Charles Issawi, ed., *The Economic History of the Middle East, 1800–1914,* Chicago, 1966, pp. 39–40. For a general treatment see V. S. Puryear, *International Economics and Diplomacy in the Near East,* Stanford, 1935.

27.   Ahmed Refik, *Istanbul Nasıl Eğleniyordu,* Istanbul, 1927, p. 192.

28.   *Journal de Constantinople,* 29 November 1849.

29.   For the problem of the Allies see F.O. 78, 1062/137, Office of Quartermaster to Foreign Office, 23 July 1855.

30.   Regulations of the Prefecture reproduced in Osman Nuri, *Mecelle* (cited n. 25), pp. 1374–1376.

31.   Ibid., p. 51.

32.   For a list of members see *Journal de Constantinople,* 10 April 1856; also Nuri, *Mecelle* (cited n. 25), p. 1386.

33.   On Camondo see M. Franco, *Essai sur l'histoire des Israélites de la Empire ottoman depuis les origines jusqu'à nos jours,* Paris, 1897.

34.   *Journal de Constantinople,* 1856.

35.   Memorandum of High Council of Reform, reproduced in Nuri, *Mecelle* (cited n. 25), p. 1377.

36.   On the projects of the commission see Başbakanlık Arşivi, Hariciye Tasnifi, no. 6429.

37.   Mazbata reproduced in Nuri, *Mecelle* (cited n. 25) p. 1402.

38.   Mazbata of the Meclis-i Tanzimat, 21 Rebiülahir 1274/9 December 1857 reprinted ibid., p. 1416.

39.   *Takvım-ı Vekayi,* 30 Cemaziyül'ahır 1274.

40.   Mazbata of the Meclis-i Tanzimat, 21 Rebiülahir 1274/9 December 1857 reprinted in Nuri, *Mecelle* (cited n. 25) p. 1418.

41.   Ibid., p. 1461.

42.   List of members reprinted ibid., p. 1432.

43.   Organic Regulations of the District 24 Şevval 1274, in F.O. 195/612 undated; *Dustur* Istanbul, 1289/1972, vol. 1, p. 464.

44.   Ibid.

45.   Report of the Study Commission, Nuri, *Mecelle* (cited n. 25), p. 1425.

46.   Başbakanlık Aşivi, Yildiz Tasnifi evrak, no. 553/257. Also *Düstur* (cited n. 43), vol. 1, p. 478.

47.   *Journal de Constantinople,* 20 April 1859.

48.   *Journal de Constantinople,* 13 February 1861; also F.O. 195/73, Aali to Bulwer, 16 June 1863.

49.   F.O. 78, 1429/120, Bulwer to Malmesbury, 16 March 1859.

50.   *Journal de Constantinople,* 21 October 1859.

51.   Başbakanlık Arşivi, no. 27015, 10 Cemaziyelevvel 1276/19 December 1859.

52.   *Journal de Constantinople,* 22 November 1860.

53.   *Journal de Constantinople,* 4 June 1861, 5 June 1861.

54.   Başbakanlık Arşivi, no. 31009, 28 Sevval 1277/10 May 1861.

55.   Başbakanlık Arşivi Belediye Tasnifi, no. 2223, 31 July 1863.

56.   *Journal de Constantinople,* 1 September 1861.

57. *Levant Herald,* 21 November 1861.

58. Ibid.

59. Josiah Brewer, *A Residence in Constantinople in 1827,* New Haven, 1830, p. 60.

60. Julia Pardoe, *The City of the Sultan and Domestic Manners of the Turks,* Philadelphia, 1837, p. 44.

61. Sir Edmund Hornby, *Autobiography,* Boston, 1928, p. 134.

62. On Server Efendi (later Paşa) see Osman Nuri, *İstanbul Şehiremaneti Mecmuası,* no. 40, pp. 195–205. Also Mehmed Süreyya, *Sicill-i Osmanı,* 4 vols. Istanbul, 1308–11/1891–1894, vol. 3, pp. 11–12.

63. Başbakanlık Arşivi Dahiliye Tasnifi no. 34256, 27 Şaban 1279/27 February 1863.

64. Başbakanlık Arşivi, Meclis-i Vala Tasnifi no. 22261, 10 July 1863.

65. *Journal de Constantinople,* 11 February 1864, 20 February 1864, 19 September 1864.

66. *Journal de Constantinople,* 2 December 1864.

67. *Journal de Constantinople,* 10 May 1865. Somewhat later, Murray's *Guide to Constantinople* was able to state that in Galata, "such advances have been made since 1865 that there is good reason to look forward to Constantinople on both sides of the Golden Horn, becoming in the main Europeanized." Murray's *Guide,* p. 76.

68. Budget reproduced in Nuri, *Mecelli* (cited n. 25), p. 1445.

69. *Levant Herald,* 30 August 1865.

18

Non-Muslim Representatives in the First Constitutional Assembly, 1876–1877

ENVER ZIYA KARAL

The religious principles upon which the Ottoman Empire was founded determined the relations between government and society. The peoples of the empire were divided in two, Muslims and non-Muslims. The Muslim peoples were subject to a sort of constitution, the *Sharīʿa,* which included the Quran and supplementary laws compatible with it. The *Sharīʿa* covered, over and above the requirements of religious belief and practice, politics, law, culture, and the principles which regulate society. This is why Islam signifies not only religion, but also a way of life, a civilization.

Since the *Sharīʿa* could not be applied to the non-Muslim peoples, they were allowed to organize themselves as communities to govern themselves, as far as the laws of personal status were concerned, according to their own religious traditions. While the non-Muslims had freedom in the matter of religion and laws of personal status, they were denied the right to perform public service. For all these reasons there came into being two societies, Muslim and non-Muslim, which did not have equal rights. Turks, Arabs, Albanians, and others who constituted the first social group were considered the first class while the Christians and Jews who constituted the second social group were considered the second class.

The *Sharīʿa* which was responsible for this division also affected Ottoman international relations. Because they considered Muslim civilization superior to Christian, they belittled the latter and were suspicious of it. Because of this the Ottomans ignored the system of European international law and persisted in closing their eyes to European material and spiritual progress. The retreat of Ottoman armies in the face of Western attacks led to the questioning of these attitudes—at least with regard to non-Muslim states.[1] In the first half of the eighteenth century Ottomans started to become acquainted with the West. Special envoys to European capitals were instructed to describe their observations in reports—some twenty-one did so during the century.[2] Consequently the

Ottoman Empire attempted to adopt aspects of Western civilization. Military technology and organization, as well as other techniques in administration and organization, were welcomed. Later innovations in government institutions, education, and international diplomacy followed the Western model.[3]

During the first half of the nineteenth century, as the Ottomans were confronted with the prospect of collapse brought on by revolts, notably those in Serbia, Greece, and Egypt, it became clear that the empire must be reformed according to Western principles. The first attempt at initiating such a policy was made in 1830 by Sultan Mahmud II with the following statement:

> I distinguish among my subjects, Muslims in the mosque, Christians in the church, and Jews in the synagogue, but there is no difference among them in any other way. My affection and sense of justice for all of them is strong and they are all indeed my children.[4]

Undoubtedly this statement, an annunciation of egalitarian principles, needed to be embodied in a formal document openly announced to the empire in a public ceremony in order to gain legal value.

After the death of Mahmud II in 1839 and immediately following the coronation of his son Abdülmecid, a decree embodying these principles was proclaimed by Mustafa Reşid Paşa. The text was circulated to the Western ambassadors in the capital. The *Hatt-ı Şerif* of Gülhane, or Noble Rescript of the Rose Chamber, as it came to be called, was based on Western notions of human rights. It proclaimed such principles as security of life, honor and property, regular and orderly recruitment into the armed forces, abolition of tax-farming, and the equality of all, whatever their religion, in the application of its provisions. It also committed the Council of Judicial Ordinances *(Meclis-i Ahkam-i Adliye)* to further these goals.

The Imperial Rescript resembled a constitution. As such it was described by the West and the French press in particular.[5] However, it did not unequivocally set forth freedom of religion and creed nor did it proclaim the political equality of Muslims and non-Muslims. In practice established non-Muslim communities did have freedom of religion. Certain non-Muslims also fulfilled what might be called an auxiliary role in Ottoman institutions. Greeks served as interpreters and special envoys.[6] From the eighteenth century Greeks from the Phanar district of Istanbul controlled the principalities of Moldavia and Wallachia.[7] Particularly during the first half of the nineteenth century Greeks, Armenians, and Jews served as physicians, secretaries, and consultants for sultans and notables, even in the absence of a formal right to perform such services. The *Hatt-ı Hümayun* ("Imperial Rescript") of 1856 made explicit the provisions of the earlier decree: it stated that Ottoman citizens, regardless of religion, may be accepted into government service and are free to enroll in both military and civilian state schools.

Following the Imperial Rescript, Greeks, Armenians, and Jews assumed positions in the administration, judiciary, and educational system of the empire. Within a decade non-Muslims formed the majority of Ottoman diplomats abroad.

Armenians and Greeks were appointed ambassadors in such capitals as London, Paris, Brussels, Berlin, Vienna, and Saint Petersburg.[8]

After the proclamation of this decree for reorganizing the empire, *Tanzimat* as it came to be known, the initiative for reform passed from the grand vezirs to those who had been brought up under the influences of Western education, the Young Ottomans. Rather than a political party they were a literary society which became involved in politics. They felt that the reforms of the *Tanzimat* were inadequate.[9] Unable to pursue their work in Turkey they fled to Europe. There they developed modern political notions which they secretly spread in the empire. Their ideas had three aspects: One, to uncover the imperialist designs of the powers upon the empire, designs advanced by claims of protection for the non-Muslim communities. Two, to show the absolutism and prodigality of the sultan and the decay of the empire, decay embodied in economic crisis to the point of bankruptcy and in lack of public confidence expressed through insurrections in the Christian territories of the Balkans. And three, stemming from this analysis, they proposed that in order to prevent the empire from collapsing the process of reform should continue—constitutional government should replace absolutism; Muslims and non-Muslims should unite to form "the Ottoman Nation" based on the principles of freedom, justice, and patriotism.

The ten-year-long efforts of the Young Ottomans succeeded in changing the opinions of some of the public.[10] The public which was persuaded included some statesmen in Istanbul, a small group of young army officers, and a few teachers and students in the institutions of higher education. Among the statesmen, the firmest proponent of constitutionalism was Midhat Paşa. There were two sources for his beliefs. First, in the course of exchanging French and Turkish lessons with the Hungarian scholar Arminius Vambery, he had acquired familiarity with the political, administrative, and economic systems of the West. Second, his governorship of the Danube, Salonica, Baghdad, and Nis provinces, where he ruled beneficently, brought him into close contact with Muslims and non-Muslims which taught him the benefit of cooperation between the communities.

The events of 1876—revolt in Bulgaria, war with Serbia and Montenegro, student rebellion in the capital, and depositions of Sultan Abdülaziz, and later, for reasons of insanity, of Sultan Murat V—promoted the idea of a constitution. Midhat Paşa was recognized as the master of this subject.

Preparations for the document had begun under Sultan Murat. Upon the sultan's request, a French lawyer in Istanbul had made preliminary studies. His proposals included coeducation of Muslims, Christians, Jews, and even atheists so that from childhood they would be able to look upon each other as brothers, not enemies. Perhaps in the expectation that Sultan Murat, a Freemason, would approve such a notion, this educational reform was included; however, it proved too radical for the times and even Midhat Paşa was not in sympathy with it.[11]

The Grand Vezir, Ruştu Paşa, regarded a constitution as an impossible dream. The Ottoman Empire was composed of too many ignorant peoples with conflicting desires. Namık Paşa, an important Young Ottoman, felt the parliament should be composed solely of Muslims. Kara Halil, a leading *alim* (religious-legal scholar), was against the constitution, but did not make his opposition open. As for Sultan Abdülhamid II, Murat's successor, at first he appeared to support it. Hastening preparation of the document was the hope that its promulgation would ease foreign pressures upon the empire even as it promoted long-considered reforms.

The major objections to the constitution arose from the *Sharīᶜa,* that is the Holy Law of Islam, which was the fundamental law of the empire. By contrast the constitution was a man-made law, designed to eliminate distinctions based upon religion and to promote equality and liberty for all subjects of the empire. The proponents had to make the constitution not conflict with *Sharīᶜa*.

As their proof-text the constitutionalists pointed to the Quranic verse, 42:38, "Discuss among yourselves."[12] They also claimed that the *Sharīᶜa* already enumerated the rights of Muslims and non-Muslims—taken together these equaled a constitutional system. As long as the *Sharīᶜa* was implemented in all its aspects there was no need for either discussion *(meşveret)* or constitution *(meşrutiyet)*. During the reign of an absolute monarch there was no possibility of discussion. In the present situation when the administration of a state is undergoing transition, discussion should be regarded as the guarantee of the *Sharīᶜa*. In addition to the arguments made on religious grounds, constitutionalists claimed that the Ottoman Empire was in fact a European state. European nations, despite the fact that they were composed of different ethnic stocks, were able to coalesce around the concept of nationality. Their efforts on behalf of their fatherlands brought them goodness, peace, affluence, and happiness. A constitution would achieve the same unity for the Ottoman Empire.

As for the opponents of constitutionalism, their arguments ran as follows: God did in fact order discussion, but this applies only to Muslims. If non-Muslims were to join the parliament, this would be contrary to religion. If the constitution, with its promotion of cooperation among all the peoples within the empire, is being adopted solely to please the West, this would also be wrong. It should not be forgotten that the appearance of non-Muslims in the administration of the state would dishonor the state and nation *(devlet ve millet)*, particularly the Muslims. What state in the world today would consider forming a partnership with her subjects? There are millions of Muslims ruled by Russia. Are they provided high government posts such as those we propose to allow to our subjects? Although England has a constitutional government, does she ever admit Indian representatives to her parliament?[13]

There was yet a third party to this debate, those revolutionary intellectuals who put forth the notion that a constitution should not be given by the state, it must be seized by the people. Their argument reflected the fact that the constitution did not arise from a popular revolutionary movement. Midhat Paşa came up with a means of answering this objection—Abdülhamid, the protector of freedom, both desired and ordered a constitution from his people. Quoting the sultan, Midhat explained in Abdülhamid's name, "As the representative of my people *(mil-*

letimdenim) I desire a law *(kanun)* from my state on behalf of my people. And as the head of state and Sultan I order that which I desire on behalf of my people.''[14]

Abdülhamid's peculiar statement suggested a basic weakness in the entire constitutional movement. It lacked a strong popular base. The Quranic instruction—"Discuss among yourselves"—did not stir public debate or prompt demands for representative government among Muslim countries. In fact in the Ottoman Empire it did not even attract attention until the second half of the nineteenth century. Since the exact meaning of the phrase was subject to the varying interpretations of scholars of the Quran, it was very difficult to derive a political injunction from these words. Moreover, the demand that the constitution should be seized by the people had little impact in the empire. European constitutions developed out of popular revolutions in states which already had a degree of national awareness. The Ottoman Empire was not such a state, rather it was a collection of different peoples. Nonetheless there were certain similarities to the European model, for, from the beginning of the nineteenth century, revolts by Muslims and non-Muslims alike forced reform upon the government. Moreover, the Balkan conflicts of 1876, which had the character of an internal revolt, did indeed force the promulgation of the Ottoman constitution.

Because of the conditions in which the empire found itself it was impossible to call a constitutional assembly. Thus in its place, responsible to the sultan and led by Midhat Paşa, a commission was formed. Some twenty different proposals had been submitted to Abdülhamid. The proposals of Said Paşa and Midhat Paşa were accepted as the basis for the commission's deliberations. Said Paşa's draft was a translation of the French constitution, while Midhat Paşa's was based mainly on the constitutions of Belgium and Prussia. A friend and advisor of Midhat Paşa, Krikor Odian Efendi, was of great service in preparing the draft. The final draft of the constitution was the work of a twenty-eight person commission which included three non-Muslims.

The constitution accepted the sultan as ruler of the Ottoman state and defender of the religion of Islam. By considering Muslim and non-Muslim as equal before the law, without regard to religion, a new nation was brought into being. The Ottoman nation was to be ruled by a senate chosen by the sultan and by an assembly whose representatives were to be elected by the people, in other words, a parliament.

Every innovation in the Ottoman Empire was confronted with opposition and reaction. In this instance a group of members of the *ulema* and of *medrese* students stirred the people. They claimed that the constitution would enslave Muslims to non-Muslims, that Midhat Paşa and his associates were infidels, and that they had deceived Abdülhamid. Midhat Paşa banished whatever members of this group he could and embarked on a campaign to enlighten the public about the constitution. He published popular defenses of the document. One of the more interesting was the following dialogue which sought to explain the relation of Muslim and non-Muslim under the new law:

Question: Is the constitution in accord with our traditions and the Holy Law of Islam?

Answer: Yes it is, for wisdom and the Holy Law entitle an individual to seek account of the sum he pays in taxes and the administration he receives in turn.

Question: Will our Christian subjects be admitted into the parliament?

Answer: Undoubtedly they will.

Question: What will be said to those who oppose this?

Answer: No opposition is expected. It is right that Muslims as well as our Christian citizens participate in parliament.

Question: Will the Christian representatives be elected by Christians?

Answer: A division of that sort would bifurcate the Ottoman nation *(millet)* into Muslim and non-Muslim. The people will choose whom they wish without regard to religion.

Question: The *Sharīᶜa* is the Holy Law for Muslims. Might not non-Muslims resist it? Might not parliament raise objections to it?

Answer: The *Sharīᶜa* is indeed the Holy Law for all Muslims. It is also the civil code for non-Muslims in the Ottoman Empire. In any event the question is moot since religious affairs remain outside the purview of parliament.[15]

Not all objections to the constitution came from religious quarters. Certain defenders of the sultanate and certain members of the palace establishment opposed it. The latter owed their social position and political influence not to their own abilities, but to the grace of the sultan. They were suspicious of attempts to restrict the power of the sultan. They disliked public opinion and they were alarmed at the thought of parliamentary interference. Their constant claim was that society was not ready for a constitution. The palace establishment had a peculiar status. From the point of view of Ottoman law they were either slaves *(köle)* of the sultan or descendants of such slaves. The liberty of the constitution meant nothing for them.[16]

Midhat Paşa believed that after the proclamation of the constitution all of these objections would disappear. He expected that like his predecessor, Mustafa Reşid Paşa, who proclaimed the Noble Rescript of 1839, he too would be hailed by the West.

However, the situation had changed in the forty years since the declaration of 1839. The Powers now followed a program of interference in the internal affairs of the Ottoman Empire. After the Treaty of Paris in 1856 each power promoted a reform program to benefit the empire's non-Muslim subjects.

The Constitution did indeed serve non-Muslims' needs. Its provisions even surpassed the reform programs of the Powers. Midhat Paşa scheduled the proclamation of the Constitution to coincide with the meeting of an international conference in Istanbul called to settle a dispute in the Balkans and to establish a reform program on behalf of Ottoman non-Muslims. When the booming of the cannon heralding the proclamation of the Constitution was heard in the conference room, the Ottoman delegation announced the reforms demanded by the

Powers were no longer at issue, since they had been incorporated into their new law; hence there was no further need to continue the conference. The manner in which the Constitution was proclaimed proved to be a serious tactical error. The delegates assumed that the entire event was intended to obstruct their deliberations and they did not take the proclamation of the Constitution seriously. The unfortunate Midhat Paşa, who had been anticipating the kind of support and congratulation which Reşid Paşa had received earlier, was sorely disappointed. Neither the chanceries nor public opinion in Europe supported the new Constitution.[17] Since its goal was a strong and united empire it ran counter to the interests of the Powers who continued to promote their own demands for reform in the status of non-Muslims.

The reaction in Istanbul was different. Muslims and non-Muslims greeted the proclamation of the Constitution with demonstrations of support. One could claim that these were the first gatherings in the Ottoman Empire in which Muslims, Christians, and Jews came together in support of a political cause. Because of the joyous reaction of the people, the day of the Constitution's proclamation was made an official holiday. Another bold new step were the official visits paid by the Grand Vezir to the leaders of the non-Muslim communities. Midhat Paşa paid ceremonial visits to the Greek patriarch, the Armenian patriarch, and the Jewish chief rabbi to thank them individually for their understanding and cooperation in the realization of reform.[18] Such an event had never before occurred in the Ottoman Empire.

Once the Constitution was proclaimed there remained the problem of elections. Since the Senate was to be appointed, electoral arrangements had to be made for the Assembly alone. However, there was no existing electoral law and the creation of such a law would have entailed long delays. Therefore it was decided to choose the first Parliament through an indirect electoral procedure using an existing mechanism. Once chosen, this Parliament would determine the practice to be followed in the future. The mechanism that was in fact used was the Provincial Administrative Council. These bodies had been chosen by direct election and they now acted as electors for Parliament. Furthermore the number of Muslim and non-Muslim representatives from each province should reflect the population of that province. In Istanbul a different system was adopted. The city's twenty departments served as electoral districts. Each chose two electors, one Muslim and one non-Muslim, according to the votes cast by all members of the district regardless of religion. These forty electors then met at the municipality on election day and selected ten representatives, five Muslims and five non-Muslims.[19] The names and professions of the twenty non-Muslim electors of Istanbul illustrate their ethnic and economic backgrounds: Davichon Efendi (former member of the State Supreme Court), Artin Efendi (lumber merchant), Nikolaki Efendi (tradesman), Anastas Efendi (member of the Galata Commercial Court), Ohanes Efendi (minister of commerce), Vasilaki Efendi (businessman), Kostaki Efendi (undersecretary in Ministry of Interior), Behor Efendi (a merchant), Vicin Hulas (a city notable), Paskal Zamin Efendi (a city notable),

Kamanlo Efendi (community leader), Grichen Efendi (president of the Medical Society), Maksutzade Simon Bey (a notable), Bedros Efendi (a member of the Supreme Court), Haci Yorgi Aga (member of the Town Assembly), Istefan Paşa (member of the Military Court), Ezekiel Efendi (member of the Court of Justice), Kostaki Efendi (district mayor of the Sixth District), Haci Tanas Efendi (dealer in desks and caskets), and a second Nikolaki Efendi (a state notable).[20]

Legally, an assembly deputy had to be twenty-five years or older, without convictions for political or nonpolitical offenses, an owner of property within the empire, respected by his fellow citizens, and to know the official language of the state. Deputies were to regard themselves as representing the entire empire, not merely the interests of their particular province.

The results of the election yielded a Parliament composed of 115 deputies, 67 Muslims and 48 non-Muslims. The 9 Balkan provinces sent 22 Muslims and 22 non-Muslims. The 10 provinces of Anatolia sent 21 Muslims and 12 non-Muslims. The 7 provinces of Africa and non-Anatolian Asia sent 17 Muslims and 5 non-Muslims. The Mediterranean province sent 2 Muslims and 4 non-Muslims. Istanbul, as we said earlier, sent 5 Muslims and 5 non-Muslims.[21]

The election of Christian deputies was widespread. However, provinces such as Basra, Hejaz, Yemen, and Tripoli of Libya, which were overwhelmingly Arab Muslim, had no Christian deputies. In Anatolia, Kastamonu's delegation was all Muslim. Neither Egypt nor the district of Mt. Lebanon sent deputies at all, though both were included in the electoral arrangements. Egypt claimed that under the Khedivate it enjoyed an autonomous status, while the district of Mt. Lebanon feared that electing deputies might jeopardize its internationally recognized autonomy. In both instances Ottoman authorities, without success, assured the hold-out areas that their special arrangements would not be prejudiced. Eventually after the drawn-out election procedure was completed and a full complement of deputies was able to reach the capital, Parliament opened on 19 March 1877. The opening ceremony was perhaps more remarkable for who was absent than for who was present. The Young Ottomans, whose decade-long agitation had paved the way for Parliament, were not present. The "father of the Constitution," Midhat Paşa himself, was not present. On 5 February 1877 he had been dismissed from his vezirial position and banished from the country. The inability of the international conference in Istanbul to solve the Balkan crisis in a fashion satisfactory to the Ottomans contributed to Midhat Paşa's fall from favor, but this failure was but one manifestation of Western lack of sympathy for the empire's efforts at reform. More telling was the widespread press criticism throughout Western Europe and particularly in England directed against the Ottoman Constitution.

Nonetheless, despite the hostility of Western Europe and in the absence of its most vigorous proponents, the Ottoman Parliament opened in a gala ceremony marked by a formal speech of the sultan, read by his secretary. This inaugural address commented on the relations between Muslims and non-Muslims.

Abdülhamid's comments on constitutionalism suggest the attitude which characterized his approach to this innovation:

If we have not reached the level of progress of other parts of the civilised world, the cause of this must be traced to the instability of the institutions necessary to the State. . . . This instability proceeded from everything, being in the hands of an absolute government, which disregarded the salutary principle of common deliberation. The progress effected by civilised States, the security and wealth they enjoy, are the fruit of the participation of all in the enactment of laws and in the administration of public affairs. This is why we thought it necessary to seek in that course the means of arriving at progress, and of enacting and enforcing laws adopted by the common consent of the population. For this purpose I have granted and promulgated the Constitution. By the promulgation of the Constitution, I have not simply designed to invite the population to share in the direction of public affairs; I have had the firm resolution of employing the deliberative system as an effective means for the amelioration of the administrative system of the country, to preserve it from maladministration and absolutism. . . . The Constitution guarantees the unity of the governed, and confirms the principle of the welfare and fraternal solidarity of the population; for our illustrious ancestors, having, by God's grace, extended their possessions and aggrandised the Empire, have combined under their rule a large number of peoples. . . . Henceforth all my subjects will be considered children of the same country, and will be placed under the protection of one law. They will be designated by the name borne by the illustrious race of the Founders of the Empire—a name associated with the glorious annals of a history of 600 years. I have a firm conviction that from this moment all my subjects will unite their efforts to make the name Osmanli retain the force and power hitherto surrounding it.[22]

These last lines urged the formation of an Ottoman (Osmanli) nation. What the speech significantly omitted was any mention of *Sharīᶜa*, the Holy Law of Islam.

The day after the ceremonial opening both the Senate and the Assembly began their deliberations in a building near Haghia Sophia which had originally been intended to house a university. The deputies, as mentioned above, had been chosen by local administrative councils. They represented the notables. Prosperous and well-educated for the most part, they knew the problems of their districts well, but they were not strangers to national problems either. They were accustomed to sitting and discussing such issues, whatever their religious community. They were all strict supporters of the Constitution and they shared a belief that theirs was a mission to chart the administration of the empire.

In fact the Parliament was to attempt the greatest democratic experiment in history. This was the first time that representatives from three continents, Asia, Africa, and Europe, from Janina to Basra, and from Van to Tripoli of Libya, and members of different religious communities and different races all came together. One newspaper suggested that they represented "United Ottoman Nations."

The sentiment for unity appeared in the deputies' inaugural oath of office. Until then such an oath might have been a cause for division between Muslims, Christians, and Jews, but this problem was avoided with a secular oath—"I pledge to respect my Sultan, my country, and the laws of the Constitution and to perform no actions which might oppose them."[23]

The disunity of language was also overcome. The assembled deputies spoke some fourteen different languages, but all, as was required by law, knew some Turkish. They spoke something called "rough Turkish," quite different from *Osmanlıca,* the pastiche of Turkish, Arabic, and Persian used by the educated elite of Istanbul. "Rough Turkish," the language of the common people, contained short simple sentences and proved an adequate means of communication in Assembly deliberations.

The sources of division among the representatives, religion, culture, and language, seemed to lose their divisive appeal. Their heritages did, however, inspire them in a different and unifying way. Muslims, Christians, and Jews sought in their respective traditions the sources of the political and legal thought of the eighteenth century. Their goodwill and intentions worked for the survival of an empire based upon constitutional principles.

The Assembly held two sessions, the first from 20 March to 28 June 1877 and the second from 13 December 1877 to 16 February 1878. Their task was to decide upon a number of legislative proposals which had been presented in the sultan's inaugural address. They dealt with internal regulations, an election law, provincial administration, organization of the judiciary, promotion and retirement policies for judges, the duties of bureaucrats, privileges and retirement regulations for civil servants, regulation of the press, proposals concerning the Exchequer and Audit Department, and a law dealing with the budget.[24] In this way the new administrative bodies established by the Constitution were directed by the Ottoman nation composed of Muslims and non-Muslims.

However, before beginning work on these proposals, the Council of Ministers took up the territorial demands of Montenegro. Montenegro had a privileged position within the empire, for it had gained autonomy. It had risen in revolt in order to press its case for additional territory. These claims were rejected by Ottoman authorities on the grounds that they violated the provisions of the Constitution which forbade the separation of territory from the Empire.

International affairs continued to cloud the deliberations of Ottoman authorities. In April 1877 Russia declared war against the Ottoman Empire. One pretext behind this declaration was Russia's claim to be acting in the interest of the empire's non-Muslims. To undermine Russia's claims a number of the non-Muslim deputies declared their loyalty to the empire and their disavowal of Russia's protection.[25]

Manok Efendi (deputy from Aleppo) declared:

> As Armenians and Christians we stated that we have no need of protection. Under no circumstances do we accept this protection. Furthermore we do not need it. Until the very end we will oppose the unjust military attacks, mounted under the pretext of protection.

A group of Bulgarian deputies—Karamihaloğlu Yorgi (Edirne), Dimitri (Salonica), Mişo Todari (Sofia), Zahari (Sofia), Istifanaki (Danube), Dimitraki (Danube)—issued a jointly signed declaration which they presented to the president of the Parliament. In it they declared that the Bulgarian atrocities and the necessity to prevent their recurrence were false reports. "We, Bulgarian subjects of the Ottoman Empire, reject such claims. Our intentions are to work for the Ottoman nation founded under the Constitution."

Sebuh Efendi (Istanbul) declared that he too opposed Russia's claim of protection. Rather than offering a long speech of his own he joined with the sentiments of Manok Efendi. He added that as Christians he and his fellows were prepared to offer whatever was needed, in life and property.

Nufel Efendi (Syria) added his own declaration when he offered a Christian point of view:

> History proved that Christians have always been satisfied by the Government. In some respects they have been even more satisfied than Muslims. Protection is a pretense for Russia. They wish to use us as a pair of tongs to hold against the fire.

Nakkaş Efendi (Syria) echoed the other deputies' opposition to Russian claims to protection and added that Ottoman Christians wanted nothing to do with it.

The rallying of Christian deputies to the defense of the empire did not require extraordinary persuasion. It would be a mistake to dismiss their statements as insincere. Rather this expression of Christian sentiment should be regarded as a testimony to the success that the Ottomans and the hopes for Ottomanism had in creating an alliance between Muslim and Christian notables. Many Christians had prospered under Ottoman rule and therefore had reason to retain its benefits. Furthermore this was a time of great hopefulness. The Constitution formally opened the way for all to participate in deliberating upon the empire's future—of course the way was subsequently blocked, but that is a different matter—as long as the way did remain open, Christian deputies gratefully seized the opportunity to participate.

Christian deputies enthusiastically participated in the deliberations of the Assembly. Perhaps no issue stirred more feeling and indicated more hopeful expectation than did the discussion of the term "Ottoman." This issue arose in the course of the debate on the proposed electoral law. The selection of deputies had taken place in an atmosphere of acute awareness of Greek, Armenian, Jew, and Muslim. On the other hand the Constitution abolished the distinction between Muslim and non-Muslim with its creation of the "Ottoman." As introduced by the government, the proposed electoral law maintained the old distinctions. The majority of deputies preferred the new term of unity. Sayyid Ahmed Efendi (Hejaz) declared, "serving the entire society is the intention of Parliament. When this is the case, there is no need to differentiate by religion." Vasilaki Efendi (Istanbul) announced to applause, "Discrimination is against the Constitution. Let no such discussion occur here. Let us refrain from terms such as 'Muslim' and 'non-Muslim,' 'Greek' and 'Armenian.' Let us not speak such words here again." Manok Efendi (Aleppo) argued, "We are not becoming Ottomans now; we have been Ottomans for six hundred years. Thanks to our Sultan, our Ottomanism has been strengthened." Solidi Efendi warned that expressions such as "believer" and "infidel" were more appropriate to the time of the Spanish Inquisition than they "are to our own day and age." In accordance with such sentiments, the terms "Muslim" and "non-Muslim" were removed from the electoral proposal.[26]

Non-Muslim deputies played an active role in the debate about the press law. Bedros Efendi, acting on behalf of the State Court, introduced the legislation. Ninety-eight speeches on this question were delivered by non-Muslims. Muslims spoke sixty-five times. The debate was not along communal lines. Support, opposition, and amendment to the proposal cut across the different communities. On the whole, though, non-Muslim deputies supported liberalization of the proposal. They sponsored a provision which would decrease the fines to be levied against violators. They opposed the requirement that newspaper publishers should post a bond, arguing that such a practice was not followed in Europe. They also opposed the ban on humor magazines, which the law dismissed as buffoonery. A number of deputies spoke in defense of humor: Solidi Efendi argued that it was essential to have humor magazines, that many antedated the serious journals and that without humor the world would have no means of defeating evil. Manok Efendi added that if the goal of the law was to prevent buffoonery, then *Karagöz,* the Turkish Punch and Judy show, should also be banned. A more serious charge was also raised. It was claimed that an unfettered press might unfairly attack individuals. In the end that argument was countered with the claim that libelous statements should be answered in court, not anticipated in Parliament. The press law was passed.[27]

The budget debate provided another opportunity for certain non-Muslim deputies to express patriotic sentiments. One source of revenue for the Ottoman budget was the *bedel-i askeri,* a tax which non-Muslims paid in lieu of actual military service.[28] In fact this tax corresponded in amount and method of collection to the *cizye,* a Quranically enjoined levy upon the recognized non-Muslim subjects of the Ottoman state. A number of Christian deputies proposed that this tax be excluded from the budget. Vasilaki (Istanbul) asked:

> How can we claim equality under the Constitution and still keep a certain group of our citizens from the honorable task of military service? How can we suggest that they compensate with payment while the rest of the citizenry pays with blood? Shedding blood in the nation's defense is an honorable task for each son of the fatherland. Blood cannot be bought or sold, but it can be freely expended on behalf of the fatherland. Of even more importance, service in the military will instill unity through the comradeship of battle.[29]

Loud applause greeted these remarks.

However inspiring the patriotic words of this Greek deputy from Istanbul, Parliament did not survive the strains of invasion and war. On 16 February 1878 the second session, which had opened on 13 December 1877, was adjourned under unfavorable circumstances. In the face of hostile incursions in the Balkans and in eastern Anatolia, the Ottoman army was forced to withdraw. The populace was shocked, the government helpless, and the deputies fierce with anger. Rumors abounded that the government had sent its spies into the halls of Parliament itself. There were charges of incompetence in the military. An allowance for six hundred thousand soldiers had been authorized by Parliament, but only half that number were actually in battle—or so it was believed at the end of the first session. Although not stating this openly, the deputies believed that Sultan Abdülhamid was responsible for the military failure. Reacting to such charges, the sultan dismissed Parliament and halted this constitutional experiment.

The introduction of a Constitution was part of the process of Westernization which had begun during the first half of the eighteenth century. Although short-lived, the parliamentary intentions of the Constitution reflected practical aims—to save a decaying empire from collapse by creating one Ottoman nation out of many Ottoman subjects. The Parliament acted in a way consistent with this goal. There were no political parties. Neither Muslims nor non-Muslims formed factions in opposition to each other. Indeed these two groups were complementary. Muslims, for the most part, were agriculturalists, government officials, and small tradesmen. Relatively few non-Muslims were engaged in agriculture. Generally speaking they were artisans, merchants, sailors, and financiers. A number of the deputies had received a Western education and knew Western languages. Many had taken advantage of the opportunities the country offered and had become wealthy. Taken together, these different factors contributed to the success which this first parliamentary effort did achieve. The accomplishments of the Ottoman Parliament were greeted with surprise, particularly in those countries which had long lived under constitutional regimes.

Unfortunately this parliamentary effort was not long-lived. A factor in its end was, as we said earlier, Abdülhamid's fear of parliamentary accusations against him arising from failures on the war front. There were other causes as well. Muslim reaction must be included. Another was the panic on the part of a small group of non-Muslim bankers and government contractors who feared a government examination of past financial matters.

Another important cause was foreign influence. The Great Powers, who had for many years insisted on reform of the Ottoman Empire, were taken aback by the success of Parliament and worked against it. Their reaction and behavior suggest that their actual aim was something other than disinterested sponsorship of reform. Rather, they sought to advance their own imperial goals. It is from this perspective that the historian should view the international events of this period—the war between Russia and the Ottoman Empire, the Western response to the conflict, the Treaty of San Stefano which ended it, and the proposed parceling of Ottoman territory at the subsequent Congress of Berlin.

In conclusion it should be noted that although the First Constitutional Period did not achieve its ultimate goal of uniting the Muslim and non-Muslim peoples of the empire, it did represent an impressive historical achievement.

Notes

1. Enver Ziya Karal, "Turkey, from Oriental Empire to Modern National State," *Journal of World History,* 4 (1958) reprinted in Guy S. Métraux and François Crouzet, *The New Asia,* New York, 1969, p. 80.

2. Faik Reşit Unat, *Osmanlı Sefirler ve Sefaretnameleri,* Ankara, 1968.

3. Bernard Lewis, *The Emergence of Modern Turkey,* second edition, London, 1968, pp. 74–128.

4. Reşat Kaynar, *Mustafa Paşa ve Tanzimat,* Ankara, 1954, p. 100.

5. Sabri Esat Siyavuşgil, "Tanzimat'ın Fransız Efkarı Umumiyesinde Uyandırdığı Akisler," *Tanzimat,* Istanbul, 1940, vol. 1, p. 747.

6. Bedrettin Tuncel, "L'Age des Drogmans," *Bulletin de l'Association internationale d'étude du sud-est europeen,* 12 (1974), p. 237.

7. İsmail Hakkı Uzunçarşılı, "18ci Asırda Bugdan'a Voyvuda Tayını," *Tarih Semineri Dergisi,* 1 (1937), p. 32.

8. Based on an examination of Ottoman government yearbooks, *Salnameler,* from 1846 to 1876.

9. Ihsan Sungu, "Tanzimat ve Yeni Osmanlılar" in *Tanzimat* (cited n. 5), p. 795.

10. Ebuzziya Tevfik, *Yeni Osmanlılar Tarihi,* Istanbul, 1973–1974, vol. 3, p. 272.

11. Osman Nuri [Ergin], *Abdulhamit-i Sani ve Devri Saltanatı,* Istanbul, 1327/1909, p. 11.

12. M.K., *Türkiyede Meclis-i Mebusan,* Cairo, 1907, p. 159. The Arberry translation of the Quranic source is "counsel between them"—see Arthur J. Arberry, *The Koran Interpreted,* New York, 1955, vol. 2, p. 196.

13. Ahmed Midhat, *Üss-ü İnkilap,* Istanbul, 1295/1878, vol. 2, p. 320.

14. Ibid., p. 193.

15. Esat Efendi, *Bab-i Ali,* Istanbul, 1293/1876, pp. 3–4.

16. Enver Ziya Karal, *Osmanlı Tarihi,* Ankara, 1962, vol. 7, p. 220.

17. Robert Devereux, *The First Ottoman Constitutional Period,* Baltimore, 1963, pp. 87–90.

18. Roderic Davison, *Reform in the Ottoman Empire, 1856–1876,* Princeton, 1963, p. 383.

19. Provisional Instructions concerning the Election of Representatives in Turkish Historical Society Archives, Serkis Karakoç. Collection, no. 4357.

20. M.K. (cited n. 12), pp. 21–25.

21. *İrade-i Seniye,* 10 Şevval 1293/October 1876, in Karakoç Collection (cited n. 19).

22. Translated and quoted in Ali Haydar Midhat, *Life of Midhat Pasha,* London, 1903, pp. 157–158.

23. *Basiret Gazetesi,* 22 March 1877, no. 2044.

24. Midhat (cited n. 13), p. 396.

25. Hakkı Tarik Us, *Meclis-i Mebusan, 1293:1877 Zabıt Ceridesi,* Istanbul, 1940, vol. 1, pp. 170–175. This work is a reconstruction of parliamentary debates on the basis of contemporary newspaper accounts.

26. Ibid., pp. 250–252.

27. Ibid., pp. 210–217.

28. See H. Bowen, "Badal," *EI,*[2] vol. 1, p. 855.

29. Us (cited n. 25), pp. 322–326.

19

Unionist Relations with the Greek, Armenian, and Jewish Communities of the Ottoman Empire, 1908–1914*

Feroz Ahmad

In July 1908, all the ethnic and religious communities of the Ottoman Empire greeted the restoration of the Constitution with great enthusiasm. Communal leaders fraternized together and joined in the public demonstrations celebrating the opening of a new era. "At Uskub, Monastir, and Salonica," reported The *Times* (London), "Mussulmans and Christians alike are mingling in the popular rejoicing. At Monastir the Greek Metropolitan harangued the crowd, and afterwards joined with the Mussulman Mufti and the Bulgarian priests in mutual embraces. . . ."[1] In Jerusalem, a city held in great reverence by all the religious communities, "a curious mixture of sheikhs, priests, and rabbis delivered speeches denouncing the old régime, and Muslims, Christians, Jews, Samaritans, Turks, and Armenians all fraternized and formed into a procession, preceded by banners with emblems of liberty—the Jews by the Torah covered with gilt embroidery."[2] Beirut, which had been the stage for religious and communal strife only five years previously, staged demonstrations in favor of the Constitution. Muslims and Christians fraternized in the streets and much hope for the future was expressed by all.[3]

The reason for this spontaneous jubilation among the communities is not difficult to discern for it was the principal theme of almost all the public speeches: "For thirty-three years thirty-three million people suffered under the yoke of a cruel sultan and his three hundred lackeys and spies. This cruel régime was overthrown by thirty brave men who raised the flag of liberty. Liberty for everyone; for the Turks and for the Christians. Now we are all brothers; Muslim, Christian, Jew, Turk, Arab, Greek, Bulgarian, we are all citizens of the free Ottoman state."[4]

*The author would like to thank the American Research Institute in Turkey for the summer grant (1977) which facilitated research for this paper.

After the initial outburst of enthusiasm for the constitutional regime, the attitude of the Greek and Armenian leaders was no longer unambiguous; the Jewish community, however, continued to support actively the new regime.

Among the Greeks there were those who hoped to aggrandize the Greek Kingdom at the expense of the Ottoman Empire, and those who hoped to Hellenize it. The former wanted Athens to adopt an aggressive and hostile policy toward the Turks. The latter preferred an alliance between Athens and Istanbul to help preserve the empire which would otherwise be partitioned amongst the Powers and irrevocably lost to Hellenism. To such people "the Young Turk revolution offered a gleam of hope" for if the Young Turks really did try to modernize the multinational empire, the "[Ottoman] Greek élite would come back into its own, it would run the empire and restore to it many of the characteristics of its Byzantine predecessor. . . ."[5] For this reason Dimitrios Rallis, an important Greek politician and statesman was initially enthusiastic about the constitutional regime. After the revolution he visited Salonica and Istanbul "to confer with Greek circles there." But he soon "changed his views: he was all for continuing the Macedonian struggle and even sending bands to Thrace and Asia Minor."[6] Athens's hold over the Ottoman Greeks was overwhelming and they, in turn, identified emotionally and politically with it rather than Istanbul. In their relations with the new regime, their principal concern was to retain the traditional privileges of their community and thus maintain their virtually autonomous existence. The Ottoman Greek community was sufficiently monolithic so that within it nationalism overshadowed class consciousness. In its annual report for 1909–1910, the Socialist Workers' Federation of Salonica noted that after the 1908 revolution "nationalist propaganda amongst the workers suffered a setback within a short time. But this kind of propaganda made gains only amongst the Ottoman Greek workers."[7] Such was the hold of the Orthodox Church and the patriarch over the entire community.

The Armenian community was not as monolithic as the Greek and that was reflected in its attitude toward the constitutional régime. It was divided politically between the patriarchate which spoke for the interests of the merchant community of Istanbul and its own traditional privileges, and the Dashnak—members of the nationalist Armenian Revolutionary Federation *(Hai Heghapokhakan Dashnaksutiun)*—who represented the aspirations of the rising intelligentsia, the artisans and tradesmen of small-town Anatolia, and the agricultural communities. Unlike the Greeks, the Armenians had no existing state they could identify with. But the growing sense of nationalism among the intelligentsia created a strong desire for autonomy and eventual statehood.

The Ottoman Jewish community, except for the community of Iraq, was predominantly Sefardi. Its ancestors had been the Jews expelled from Spain and Portugal in the late fifteenth and sixteenth centuries. and the community had succeeded in retaining much of its traditional language and culture, though somewhat modified by the new environment. It was totally untouched by political Zionism, the Jewish nationalist movement which began to flourish in Eastern Europe in the last quarter of the nineteenth century. Thus when Zionist propagandists sought support for their movement amongst Ottoman Jews, they found their coreligionists unresponsive. Ottoman Jewry seemed too well integrated to seek a separate destiny. This was due to historical factors. In the nineteenth century as the Ottoman Empire was integrated into the European world system and converted into a semicolony, the Jews—unlike the Greeks and Armenians who actually benefited from it—suffered with the Turks the consequences of that process. For this reason the Jews alone identified with the constitutional movement, and particularly with the Committee of Union and Progress (CUP), for they also stood to gain from Ottoman resurgence and the restoration of complete Ottoman sovereignty.

The initial exuberance of the non-Muslim communities at the fall of Abdülhamid's despotism may be explained by the fact that they assumed that any regime would be an improvement on the old one. If the new regime happened to be liberal and committed to administrative decentralization and private initiative, as promised by Prince Sabaheddin, so much the better.[8] Kâmil Paşa's grand vezirate (August 1908) must have suggested that the Liberals, and not the Unionists, were about to come to power. But that was not the case. The CUP emerged as the principal political organization and played the role of guardian of the Constitution. Though it could not assume power directly, its members behaved as though they were the real power behind the throne and they often tried to force the government to implement Unionist policies. Before very long, Greek and Armenian leaders realized that Unionist aspirations were not compatible with their own traditional privileges and long-term interests.

The atmosphere of distrust and confrontation between the two communities and the Unionists arose out of this realization. It must be emphasized, however, that the basis of the antagonism was neither ethnic nor religious; it was rooted in class conflict in so far as the Unionist scheme to transform Ottoman society undermined the position of all privileged classes, regardless of race or religion, and brought the petty bourgeoisie to the helm of affairs. Thus the reactionaries and conservatives, who had been ousted from power, and the upper-class liberal Turks and Muslims, who thought that they ought to inherit it, were as hostile to the Unionists as the Greeks and Armenians. Not surprisingly, all these groups soon reached a tacit understanding against the CUP. But before we discuss the CUP's relations with the three communities, let us briefly examine Unionist aspirations.

The fundamental Unionist aim was to restore full sovereignty to the Ottoman state. Only then would the state be capable of carrying out all its duties and obligations. Without full sovereignty, the empire would remain a semicolony under the hegemony of the Great Powers. They would continue to control its finances through the public debt, maintain the totally dependent character of its economy by regulating its import and export duties, and, generally speaking, uphold the *status quo* buy their insistence on exercising extraterritorial privileges under the capitulations which made a mockery of Ottoman sovereignty. Thus one of the first acts of the Unionists after the revolution was to attack the capitulations, and that brought them into conflict with the Great Powers.

Non-Muslim communities also enjoyed extensive privileges under the *millet* system, and by the late eighteenth century each community was virtually responsible to its own religious leaders, who acted as intermediaries between the community and the state. As the empire declined, the Great Powers began to adopt the *millet*s as clients, exploiting them to further their own interests in the empire. Thus the Treaty of Küçük Kaynarca of 1774 became the pretext for Russia to establish a protectorate over the Greek *millet*. France claimed a similar right to protect the Catholic subjects of the sultan. By the end of the nineteenth century all the non-Muslim *millet*s, save the Jews, had found a *de facto* protector. The powers sometimes intervened in concert in Ottoman internal affairs so as to prevent one of their number from making unilateral gains. Such was the case during the Greek War of Independence and again during the Eastern Crisis of 1875–1878 which culminated in the Congress of Berlin. At Berlin, Armenian leaders sought Great Power support for reform in the eastern provinces of Anatolia which had the largest concentration of Armenians.[9] Article LXI of the Treaty of Berlin granted that support and thereafter the "Armenian question" was internationalized.

Parallel with this process of Great Power protection of minorities and intervention in Ottoman affairs was the process by which non-Muslims began adopting what amounted to foreign citizenship. Thus Ottoman Greeks tended to become Russian or, after 1830, subjects of Greece, or indeed, subjects of any other power willing to grant protection. Other Christians followed their example, and even some Jews became Italian subjects after 1871. This practice was restricted largely to the commerical community which could then benefit from the capitulations and also serve as an intermediary between the Europeans and Ottoman society. Until January 1869, when the Ottoman citizenship law was introduced, there were good reasons why a merchant might require foreign citizenship for legal and commercial purposes.[10] The 1869 law should have put an end to this practice. But it did not, and non-Muslims continued to adopt foreign citizenship for the privileges it conferred rather than from necessity.

As a result of these nineteenth-century trends, the Turks, of whom the majority were peasants, became the most depressed element in the empire. Except for the minute Turkish ruling class composed of military officers, officials, and landowners, some of whom now produced for the export market, the vast majority of the Turkish population suffered the consequences of the old regime. This regime lacked the will and the power to regain its sovereignty and assert itself against the encroachments of an aggressive Europe. Unable to increase its revenues by raising customs duties or commercial taxes, the state simply extorted more from the peasantry. The condition of the peasant, wrote Count Ostrorog,

> is very like that of the peasants in seventeenth-century France. . . . They also, bending under brazen law, painfully earn the wherewithal to pay taxes and maintain just sufficient strength to pay them. If they fail, then Constantinople is hard pressed for money, the tax gatherers dun them mercilessly, and beat them if need be, like tired horses whom pain alone can goad to climb the steep hill. And if, even then, they cannot pay, their poor property is distrained and everything sold save that

which is necessary for the accomplishment of their primary function of tax paying. For they have a secondary function: that of providing fodder for cannon. . . . They are weighed down by the heavy burden of almost perpetual obligatory military service.[11]

The condition of the urban petty bourgeoisie, composed of minor officials, school teachers, artisans, and tradesmen, was only a little better than that of the peasants. This class, being more politically conscious than the peasantry, realized the need for a strong sovereign state to deal with all existing problems. They therefore supported the CUP which, after 1908, began to rectify the situation by attacking the privileges of both the foreigners and their non-Muslim clients. The Unionists were convinced that only the end of privilege would enable Muslims to compete on equal terms with their rivals. In their opinion, the *Tanzimat* reforms and the Constitution had already created *de jure* equality. But foreign protection and traditional communal privilege created *de facto* inequality and that had to be changed by the implementation of the laws.

The question of equality had both psychological and socioeconomic dimensions for the minorities. They had always lived outside the mainstream of Ottoman society, isolated and secure within their own communities. Now they were being asked to be Ottomans, sharing the same rights and obligations as all other citizens. For obvious reasons the minorities resisted this policy; as the British ambassador observed "equal rights for all Ottoman subjects—a basis which inspired the Greeks and other national entities within the Empire with a certain uneasiness, as, by implication, it threatened their old established privileges."[12]

The Unionists and and the Ottoman Greek Community

In 1908 the Ottoman Greek population was about 2,900,000, of whom about 1,800,000 lived in Anatolia (175,000 in Istanbul) and the rest in Thrace and Macedonia.[13] Ostrorog, who drew vivid sketches of various communities, wrote:

> The Greek is almost as much a townsman as a mariner, banker, trader, lawyer, doctor, he competes with and frequently surpasses the Armenian. At Constantinople the only great native bankers are Greek. Finally, owing to their inclination and gift for the retail sale of spirits and colonial [imported] products, well-neigh every grocer (or *bakkal*) in the Ottoman Empire is a Greek.[14]

Sussnitzki, who gave a more detailed account of the ethnic division of labor, observed that almost every aspect of the economy was dominated by the minorities, especially the Greeks and the Armenians. Yet the Turkish role was not as insignificant as one is often led to believe. The Greeks monopolized coastal trade, and if they engaged in agriculture as in western Anatolia it was to raise cash crops for the local and export markets. Trade and commerce were generally controlled by the two Christian communities to the extent that they were able to establish virtual monopolies, "the Greeks in western Asia Minor and the Armenians in the eastern.'' Sussnitzki furnishes various reasons for this state of affairs but as a "final cause" puts forward "the protection they enjoyed from foreign powers, whose subjects they sometimes were, thus becoming, thanks to the former Capitulations, exempt from taxation."[15]

The CUP's attitude towards the Greek community, however, was not based on the latter's economic standing in the empire. Initially the Unionists were Ottoman patriots rather than Turkish nationalists; their main concern was to make Ottomanism viable by including rather than excluding the non-Turkish elements. The success of this principle depended on the positive responses of the communities and Greek cooperation would have been of great significance. But the Greek response was negative, and the reason is not difficult to find.

Despite the citizenship law of 1869 there was no attempt to dissolve the *millet* system and create an Ottoman identity. The Greeks continued to live as in the past "organized in separate legal communities of an autonomous nature, discharged all their communal functions themselves, worshipped freely and supported their churches and schools which had kept alive through centuries the national sentiment. . . . In this way, the Christian population did not assimilate with Moslem society and, more important, kept its national consciousness."[16] Moreover, the Greeks saw themselves as the people from whom the sultans had seized the empire in earlier times, and now as the empire declined they believed they were the rightful successors, the heirs of Byzantium. This tendency had found encouragement following the creation of the Greek state and the developments of the nineteenth century. Ottoman Greeks were loyal either to Athens or a resurgent Byzantium, two sides of the same coin. Ottoman, and later Turkish, revival was seen as the greatest threat to such aspirations and therefore to be prevented at all cost.

The Unionist-Greek relationship was further complicated by Russia's traditional use of the Greek community to pursue her political and economic goals in the empire. This process was legitimized by the Treaty of 1774 but became effective only after the Russo-Turkish war of 1877–1878 which enabled Russia to use the Turkish war indemnity for political and economic ends.[17] By this period a "significant number of residents of the Ottoman Empire held patents conferring Russian citizenship upon them" and some Greek merchants even enjoyed diplomatic status as consular officials. "The [Russian] vice consuls at Bursa and Tekirdağ (Rodosto) were both Greeks. The former had interests in mining and commerce. The latter owned a *çiftlik* (estate) at Lüleburgaz. The consular agents at Aydın and Rethyennon (Crete) were also Greeks. One owned a *çiftlik* and the other was engaged in commerce."[18]

Despite these negative factors, the Unionists were optimistic that representative government would soon remove all elements of disunity and fuse the various communities into a pluralistic Ottoman nation. The Constitution had already bestowed equal rights and obligations. The new Assembly, soon to be elected, was expected to provide unity and cooperation amongst the different ethnic and religious groups. But events soon proved Unionist hopes to be both sanguine and naive.

The Greek patriarch, Yuvakim (Joāchim Efendi, clearly perceived the threat posed by the new regime to the privileges of his community. He attempted to meet this threat by issuing a proclamation urging the Ottoman government to make concessions that would undercut the program of Ottomanism. He urged the Porte to: guarantee the freedom of person and conscience and accept the traditionally acquired rights of the *millets* as fundamental principles; confirm ecclesiastical and educational privileges; restore completely the privileges accorded to the Ecumenical Patriarchate and the Greek community *(millet-i Rûm)* in the past, as well as privileges that had been violated; permit the various communities of the empire to develop on the basis of their religion, beliefs, traditions, and characteristics; implement a system of military recruitment in which units would be formed on the basis of religious affiliation and be used in the district of recruitment; and enlarge and make independent of Istanbul all existing local councils.[19]

If the Unionists were disappointed by the patriarch's proclamation they did not express their disappointment publicly. Instead, they sent Fazlı [Tung] to see Yuvakim Efendi to assure him that the CUP did not intend to curtail in any way the special rights and privileges heretofore enjoyed by the patriarchate.[20] The choice of Fazlı Bey was significant since he was a member of Sabaheddin's decentralist group and not a Unionist, and therefore more likely to seem convincing to the patriarch. Some days later Sebaheddin himself visited Yuvakim Efendi and "reassured him as to the maintenance of the privileges conferred by Mahmoud [sic] the Conqueror on the Greek Patriarchate. . . ."[21]

However, by September 1908 the patriarch was more concerned with the outcome of the general election than with Turkish assurances. The advantage seemed to lie with the non-Muslim communities with their long tradition of communal elections. They were already well organized and could therefore expect to elect candidates far out of proportion to the size of their population merely through the process of mobilization and voter turnout. The Turks and Muslims, on the other hand, were totally divided and lacked any such organization or voting tradition. The Unionists attempted to make up this shortcoming by hurriedly founding chapters throughout the empire and by reaching an understanding with local forces that controlled the votes.

At the polls the patriarch learned that large numbers of his flock were not allowed to vote as they could not establish their Ottoman citizenship. Many were in fact foreign subjects, though the majority had never registered as citizens, or applied for a *tezkere* (identity paper) so as to evade taxation.[22] For the Greeks, these explanations were only a thin disguise for what they denounced as fraud and foul play in the elections, designed to keep down their representation in the Assembly.

There is no doubt that there were irregularities during the elections; it would be surprising had there not been in such an unstable and immature political environment. Initially, only the Greeks felt aggrieved and the patriarch complained to the authorities. Receiving no satisfaction, he decided to complain directly to Grand Vezir Kâmil Paşa. He obtained no satisfaction there either for

Kâmil declared that he saw no evidence of fraud or foul play and that Greek claims must be based on false information. Thereupon Yuvakim Efendi threatened to boycott the elections and to resign unless the Porte took measures to rectify the injustices.[23]

The atmosphere in Istanbul was tense. The Unionists therefore decided to mediate and break the deadlock between the Porte and the patriarch. On 23 October a deputation of two Turks and a Greek visited Yuvakim Efendi and offered him representation in the Assembly proportional to his community's population. The offer was accepted and the Patriarch appointed two representatives to work out the details with the CUP. Responding to public speculation, the Committee denied any connection between its initiative and the deadlock between Kâmil and the patriarch. Its sole purpose in holding these meetings was to bring about union and harmony between the communities and to assure them all fair and proportional representation in the Assembly.[24]

The patriarch began to have second thoughts about negotiating with the CUP. The Committee was, after all, only a political body and by dealing with it he was adding to its prestige while undermining his own. He ought to have been dealing with the Porte on a "government to government" level as he had traditionally done instead of coming down to the level of a political party.

At the beginning of November, when discussions with the CUP ran into difficulties, the patriarch again approached the government. But this time he was received not by the Grand Vezir but the minister of the interior, Ibrahim Hakkı Bey. Yuvakim Efendi repeated his grievances and accused the government of discriminating against his community in the election. To the specific question of the eligibility of the Greek peasants in Epirus, the minister replied that as they were not Ottoman citizens they would not be permitted to vote. However, there would be Greek deputies representing that region. Meanwhile, the government would do its best to correct any injustices that may have taken place.[25]

A few days later, Greek and Armenian leaders agreed to present a common front in the Istanbul election. Their first joint venture was a delegation that went to the Porte to present a list of grievances. The two communities complained that they were not receiving representation appropriate to their numbers, the Greeks claiming forty deputies and the Armenians twenty.[26] Hakkı Bey defended the government and said that thus far elections had been conducted in a manner more honest than those in many other states with longer-established constitutional traditions. He accused the delegation of inflating the claims of the two communities totally out of proportion to their populations, and assured them that the authorities had made every effort to respect the rights of the minorities. He concluded the interview by expressing sorrow at the fact that a sense of Ottomanism had not yet replaced the communal identity.[27]

The elections continued to generate controversy, especially in Istanbul where voters were asked to produce identity papers before they could vote. On 21 November the Greeks of Pera protested against this measure and the next day, led by their notables, they demonstrated outside the Sublime Porte. After hearing their grievances, Kâmil Paşa pointed out that only the Greek community kept complaining of electoral irregularities. If there were in fact complaints, he asked that they be brought before the Assembly, which could then decide whether or not to invalidate particular elections. The Grand Vezir's statement appeared to satisfy the notables. But the large crowd of demonstrators became unruly and had to be dispersed by the cavalry, almost turning the occasion into a riot.[28] Thereafter, the elections were conducted more or less without incident and the new Assembly opened its proceedings on 17 December.

Thus far, the Unionists' relations with the patriarch could hardly be judged a success. They had failed to persuade him to support the election of Greek deputies like Orfanides Efendi, one of the very few Unionist Greeks, who believed in Ottomanism. On the whole, Greek deputies in the Assembly were pan-Hellenists and their contempt for Ottomanism may be illustrated by Boşo (Boussios) Efendi's remark "I am as Ottoman as the Ottoman Bank!"[29] Few were quite as blunt, but almost all shared this sentiment.

The reasons for the Greek attitude are not far to seek. Unlike the Armenian (and Bulgarian) community whose divisions found expression in political parties, the Greek community was politically monolithic, accepting without question the absolute authority of the Orthodox Church and the patriarch. Even the Greek proletariat and its trade unions accepted the Church's political supremacy, refusing to work within the broad Ottoman socialist movement that emerged in 1908. Implicit in the attitude of the Greek community was its total identification with Athens where the twin flames of irredentism and the *Megali Idea* burned strongly and for whom the Ottoman community was composed of "unredeemed Greeks." That remained true until the "Anatolian adventure" of 1919–1922, and ended only with the exchange of populations.

One of the most important factors that helps to explain the relationship between the Unionists and the patriarchate was the latter's informal electoral alliance with the Ottoman Liberals. Initially the Liberals collaborated with the CUP but they soon learned that they would not be able to dominate their partners. Therefore, in September 1908 they formed a political party, the Liberal Union *(Osmanlı Ahrar Fırkası)*, to oppose the CUP. In contrast to "union and progress" the Liberals proposed "administrative decentralization and personal initiative," and in general espoused the ideas of Prince Sabaheddin, their unofficial, spiritual leader. This program appealed to the Greeks and some Armenian groups, as did the proposal for an economic system that would guarantee the *status quo,* and they supported the party enthusiastically.

On 11 November a Liberal delegation visited the patriarch to discuss the possibility of cooperation in the election. Yuvakim Efendi agreed to the proposal in principle. But after consulting his notables, he declared that his position obliged him to remain above politics and he therefore could not agree to open cooperation with a political party. However, he continued, he saw no reason why Greek and Liberal deputies should not support each other in the Assembly.[30] The two sides did support each other's electoral lists though that did not help Liberal candidates, not one of whom was elected in Istanbul. In the Assembly the Liberal Union attracted all the anti-Unionist elements, the Muslim Arabs and Albanians as well as the non-Muslim groups. The Greeks in particular supported the Liberals and that marked the end of any further contacts between the Committee and the patriarchate.

After their abysmal electoral performance against the Unionists, the Liberals, led by Kâmil Paşa, decided to eliminate the Committee's political strength by establishing control over the armed forces where they thought the CUP had its basis of power. In February 1909 Kâmil appointed his nominees as ministers of war and marine. But the Unionists challenged the constitutionality of his appointments in the Assembly and brought about his fall by a vote of no confidence. Kâmil's fall was a severe blow to the Liberals and their supporters and they resolved to destroy the CUP even by the use of extralegal methods.

In the reactionary anti-Unionist campaign which followed in the wake of Kâmil's fall and culminated in the abortive counterrevolution of 13 April 1909, the Greek press of Istanbul played a prominent role. On 25 March, Grand Vezir Hilmi Paşa brought this matter before the Assembly. He appealed for a press law that would not allow divisive and subversive journalism which poisoned relations between the different ethnic and religious groups. He singled out for mention an article in *Neologos* which he claimed was particularly irresponsible. In the debate that followed Hilmi's statement the activities of *Prodos* were also discussed and criticized. The proposed press law failed to pass because of the anti-Unionist opposition in the Chamber.[31] As a result the Liberal and reactionary press continued its activities unrestrained until it came into its own during the counterrevolution.

The true character of the "reactionary movement" was soon revealed by the attitude of the Greek press toward it. An outbreak of "Muslim fanaticism" should have struck terror in the hearts of the non-Muslim minorities. This time, however, they had no cause for alarm for the "fanatics" were carefully seeking out the "godless Unionists," and not harming the more Westernized and therefore "more godless Liberals" let alone "infidel" Christians and Europeans. The Greek press was full of praise for the anti-Unionists and *Neologos,* in particular, congratulated the rebellious soldiers for the role they had played: "The Army has gained the great prize for patriotism, and April 13, 1909 ought to be henceforth marked with no less splendor than July 24, 1908. The Army was inspired yesterday by its love for the country and by no other sentiment."[32]

Until the counterrevolution the Unionists tried to accomplish their goal of Ottomanism by negotiating with the minorities. The bankruptcy of that method led them to try and achieve it through the Assembly. Therefore, in June 1909 they began to introduce legislation whose aim was to curb the political and cultural autonomy of the minorities, and to give control of these activities—for example, education—to the state, which would then set about creating a common Ottoman culture through the schools.

This policy is sometimes described as "Ottomanization," yet that term does not have the same meaning as "Germanization" or "Magyarization" had for the Slavs in the Austro-Hungarian Empire. Ottoman was a dynastic designation and as such lacked national overtones. In a sense the small upper crust amongst the minorities that served the state had already been "Ottomanized." But that was accomplished without violating the religious or ethnic identity of the subject. The Unionists wanted to extend this process on a broader scale so as to embrace all subjects of the empire.

As this policy required the teaching of Ottoman Turkish *(Osmanlıca)*—strictly speaking, the language of the Ottomans and not of the Turks, certainly not the peasants—as well as a common history designed to encourage unity rather than particularism, it is also described by its critics as Turcification. Yet in 1909 it was too early to talk of a general awareness of Turkishness even amongst Unionists; such a tendency would become noticeable only around the time of the Balkan Wars. Hüseyin Cahit Yalçın makes the point that the new regime stifled Turkism in order to promote Ottomanism. "The word 'Ottoman' had never been valued so highly as it was after the Constitution, not even during the period of repression [i.e., under Abdülhamid]. . . . As soon as the Constitution was restored events forced us to forget that we were Turks. The only word we used was 'Ottoman'."[33] Yet even Unionist implementation of Ottomanism was half-hearted. They wanted to introduce the Ottoman-Arabic script in Albania. But confronted with opposition and rebellion they abandoned this scheme and allowed the Latin script to prevail.[34] After the Balkan Wars the Unionists began to compromise even on the principle of centralization.

The language question was never the crux of the problem though it was certainly exploited as such by the minorities. So far as the school-going population of the minorities was concerned, it read and wrote better Ottoman Turkish than the majority of its Muslim counterpart. That was simply because Christian schools, except for the elite state schools and the newly founded Unionist *Terakki* schools, were far superior to the average Turkish school.

Ahmed Şerif, who described the state of Anatolia in this period, was confronted with this fact time and again. For example, in December 1909 he visited two schools in Nallıhan, a small town in Ankara province. The Turkish school consisted of "a tiny, damp, smelly classroom into which twenty pupils belonging to three different levels were crammed together." The teacher was as

> old and decrepit as the school itself. . . . If you had been with me [he laments to his reader] you would have seen how helpless the children were when the *kaymakam* tested them; you would have wept with me. Some pupils did not even have books. . . . Not one understood what he read for he only learned by rote. . . . In contrast to the terrible situation of the schools I have described today, the picture we see from comparing them with Armenian schools should provide a model for action and an encouraging shot-in-the-arm *(darbe)*.
>
> I went to a school belonging to our esteemed Armenian citizens in the company of our *kaymakam*. In a long classroom there were fifty pupils. A kind and polite headmaster received us. He told us about the organization and education in his school. His bearing and manner suggested that he was proud of his living products, namely his pupils. The *kaymakam* asked for four or five young gentlemen and tested them on a variety of subjects like geography, arithmetic, Turkish and Arabic grammar, and the boys gave good answers to all the questions. . . .

> The truth is that the pupils in this school have a much better education and training than the pupils in other [Turkish] schools, and are even more advanced in their knowledge of Turkish grammar as well as reading and writing.[35]

If Ahmed Şerif had any misgivings about such schools, it was that "the children of this country [*Vatan*] do not learn the names of continents and countries in geography, and certain arithmetical terms in Turkish. I do not find that right because these respected citizens of ours know Turkish as well as we do. If they use Turkish in their classes [to teach other subjects] I believe it will be easier and more profitable."[36]

Throughout his reports, Ahmed Şerif constantly repeats the Unionist conviction that the only formula for union and progress was a common education for all Ottomans. The CUP proposed to do that by passing laws making the minister of education responsible for supervising the curricula of all the schools in the empire. Non-Muslim fears concerning their right to provide spiritual guidance to school children were to be met by including in the law "the guarantee of religious instruction *ab antiquo*." When the new law came before the Assembly on 8 June 1909, the non-Muslim deputies—Greeks, Armenians and Slavs, but not Jews—asked that it be amended to read "the systems of education *ab antiquo* shall be maintained."

The debate that followed showed the wide gulf between the ideas of the Unionists and the non-Muslims. Kozmidi Efendi, Greek deputy for Istanbul, pointed out that each communal school taught subjects peculiar to its community and asked whether Greek students would be forbidden to read Aristotle and Plato under the new law. He asked whether the study of national literature—meaning Greek literature!—would be forbidden, for as the law stood the minister had the right to do so. He agreed that education did tend to unite the country but maintained that each community should be allowed its own program of education. He ended by asking if the law would in fact permit the maintenance of Greek and Armenian schools. Kozmidi's line of argument was supported by Yorgi Huneyos (Salonica), Pançedoref (Monastir), Krikor Zohrab (Istanbul), and Boşo Efendi (Serfice), but only the latter raised the question of traditional and time-honored privileges of the *millet*s that were being threatened by the new law.

The question of communal privilege was the fundamental issue in this and other debates, and Cavid Bey (Salonica), who spoke for the CUP, took up the challenge. All the speakers before him, except Boşo Efendi, he said, had not spoken openly and had carefully avoided raising the question of "privileges." He personally failed to understand, now that equality had been established, how people still found it possible to speak of privileges other than those of a purely religious kind. ("It is a matter of national survival," heckled Kozmidi and Zohrab Efendi.) If the inviolability of the educational system were established, how, asked Cavid, would the Ministry of Education be able to make any future observations on the state of affairs contrary to Ottoman unity? In his opinion, the desire to maintain the old system based on communal privileges proved that "Ottoman unity exists only in your words and not in your hearts." He concluded by saying that while primary education would be free in all communities, "we [the state] must have control over the ideas which pervade the schools otherwise it is impossible to have a constitution and Ottoman unity."[37]

Mustafa Rahmi (Unionist deputy for Salonica) responded to the question whether the government intended to prohibit the study of classical Greek literature. He said that that was not the government's intention, and furthermore, classical Greek literature was not the exclusive property of the Greeks but belonged to all humanity.[38] He could have added that the Assembly was privileged to have in its midst Süleyman Bustani (Beirut), the translator of the *Iliad* into Arabic. Finally, Talât Bey (Edirne) said that he failed to understand how, at a time when the Capitulations were about to be abolished, educational privileges could be retained. Soon afterward the minorities' amendment was put to the vote and defeated.

The non-Muslims, especially the Greeks, also raised problems about the implementation of the Military Service Law which provided for the conscription of all Ottoman subjects, regardless of race or religion. They welcomed the law in principle but they neither wanted to serve nor pay the military exemption tax. The patriarch, for example, "insisted on separate companies and barracks for the Christian recruits and safeguards against 'conversion' to Islam."[39] The Unionists, while providing the option to serve in the army, would have preferred the non-Muslims to continue paying the exemption tax for it raised an estimated TL 120,000 *per annum* for the treasury. Moreover, integrating non-Muslims into the armed forces was bound to create problems, especially if the patriarch's demands were met. Thus the law was passed and the constitutional requirements of equality fulfilled. But the *de facto* situation continued to permit non-Muslims (and Muslims) to buy their way out though many non-Muslims did enroll in the Ottoman army during this period. Finally, on 15 February 1915 the Assembly officially restored the tax on exemption of military service, thus restoring the *status quo ante*.[40]

The debate on the Law of Associations was as controversial as the one on education. The government wanted to place all associations under its supervision and to proscribe political ones whose basis was ethnic, national, or religious. The Unionists claimed that such political bodies encouraged separatism and undermined the unity of the empire. The aim of the law was to prevent that, and its intention was not to subvert the cultural pluralism of Ottoman society. The law would therefore be no obstacle to the formation of cultural and literary societies.

Non-Muslim deputies were not satisfied by such explanations. Vartakes Efendi (Armenian depty for Erzurum) claimed that the object of the law was nothing less than an imposed Ottoman union which could only be obtained, he suggested, by a policy of justice. He warned the government that if the law passed, it would provoke great discontent in certain communities and be an incitement to rebellion. Pançedoref defended the right of all communities to develop separately, each contributing to the general progress of Ottoman state and society according to its own genius. The Turks and Bulgarians, he said, were agricultural, the Greeks and Armenians, commercial peoples. The combination of these different elements constituted the strength of the Ottoman nation. Karolidi Efendi (Izmir) also spoke against the law because, he said, its effect would be contrary to that desired by the government. He concluded with the remarks: "I cannot be a good Ottoman without being a good Greek, I cannot love the Muslims without being a good Christian. We have the 'Great Idea' because we are the descendents of a great people."[41] But it was Haristo Dalçef (Serez) who remarked "that union of different elements would not be brought about by the passing of laws, but by community of interests."[42] That was precisely what was lacking amongst the peoples of the Ottoman Empire.

The interests of the communities were in fundamental conflict, and the Greeks and Armenians had much to lose if the Unionists successfully applied what Sir Gerard so aptly described as "the 'levelling' policy of the Turkish Government."[43] That is what would happen if certain communities were deprived of their privileges, thus losing their advantage over the Turkish petty bourgeoisie, the class whose aspirations the Unionists represented.

Moreover, the Unionists deeply resented the division of labor Pançedoref had described in which the vast majority of the Turkish population was made up of a backward and exploited peasantry, while the bulk of the urban population was composed of lower rank officials and soldiers serving a bankrupt state, and tradesmen and artisans who were incapable of competing against the protected minorities and Levantines. They resented the Greco-Armenian economic domination established, they thought, by unfair methods, and the refusal of these communities to participate in Ottoman regeneration. The Unionists were determined to raise the level of their own social class even at the expense of the minorities and the Ottoman ruling class. They would have preferred the collaboration of these groups but counterrevolution had proved that such hopes were a pipe dream.

In late 1909 the Porte began to implement the new laws, particularly the Law for the Prevention of Brigandage and Sedition and the Associations Law. It wanted to disarm the non-Muslim population in Macedonia and close down the political clubs. This brought it into conflict with Greek and Bulgarian bands which soon began to cooperate against the forces of Istanbul. This law and order policy was initiated, not by the CUP, but by Mahmud Şevket Paşa and the generals who assumed power after the counterrevolution. The Unionists understood band warfare too well and knew that such a war was impossible to win.

While they half-heartedly supported repression in Macedonia, the Unionists were more actively engaged in a general boycott of Greek commerce aimed at punishing Athens for supporting the Cretan declaration of *enosis*. But the aim of the boycott was also to raise political and national consciousness amongst the Turks. In time, this factor became more important than the original aim, for the Committee became aware of the need for a "national economy" and a Turkish bourgeoisie.

However, neither the boycott nor anti-Greek militancy proved effective. The boycott did not catch the imagination of the masses as Crete was too far removed from their consciousness. Therefore, by the second half of 1910 the CUP became more moderate and conciliatory. In its proclamation on the second anniversary of the revolution, the Committee confessed that it had shown excessive zeal during the first two years to bring about a speedy union. It now hoped that the communities would themselves work for gradual unity. As for the flagging boycott, the proclamation noted that "Our people's spirit of moderation is a sign of very great affection; from the moment Greece's interference in Crete seemed to be ending they made the boycott less severe."[44]

In Istanbul, the Liberal opposition, supported by the non-Turkish elements, again began to challenge the CUP. It formed, in November 1911, the *Entente Libérale (Hürriyet ve Itilâf Fırkası)*, an anti-Unionist coalition in which Turkish liberals and conservatives, Arabs, Albanians, Greeks and Armenians harnessed their energies in order to defeat the CUP. The party's program appeased the minorities by promising to respect all the privileges that had been granted to them by Imperial *irades, fermans*, and *berats*. But Greek support for the Liberals was half-hearted, suggesting a desire to retain freedom of action. Initially they agreed to disband their political clubs and merge with the Liberal party. But that never materialized, and Greek members were never appointed to the central committee though, writes Dr. Rıza Nur, "they continued to help us in our work."[45]

Just prior to the founding of the *Entente Libérale*, the government made important concessions to the Christian communities. The privileges of the religious heads were officially recognized once again and the situation was restored virtually to what it had been in 1908.[46] The Unionists seemed to be back on square one.

During the course of the Turco-Italian war which broke out in September 1911, Italian forces occupied a number of Aegean islands and encouraged pan-Hellenism amongst the Greek inhabitants. When it became clear that the great powers would not insist on the restoration of these islands to Ottoman sovereignty, Athens put forward her claim to them and carried out propaganda in favor of union with Greece. The support for union was quite general among Ottoman Greeks on the islands, but not all were in favor of it. Describing the situation on Castellorizo, Vice-Consul Biliotti wrote:

> Two parties have arisen in the island. One, consisting of the wealthier inhabitants, who have important interests on the [Anatolian] mainland, do not wish any change in their present situation, the other consisting of the very low class, who have nothing to lose and aspire to annexation to Greece. It is said that a great number of the former, fearing the presence of the insurgents [who wanted union], have fled to the mainland.[47]

Was that the prevailing pattern of political attitudes among Ottoman Greeks?

As the Unionists prepared for an early election in the spring of 1912, they too became more accommodating toward the minorities. Hacı Adıl's mission to Macedonia in February was designed primarily to placate the Greeks, Bulgarians and Albanians. The CUP still hoped to elect an Assembly with which it could work in harmony. Moreover, intercommunal warfare in Macedonia had assumed such proportions that there was fear of Great Power intervention to restore peace, an eventuality the Unionists desperately wanted to avoid. Hacı Adıl's mission was the last attempt to find a peaceful solution. He remained in Macedonia for three and a half months but failed to win over the militant minority organizations.

However, in Istanbul there seems to have been no attempt by the Unionists to reach an electoral agreement with the patriarch. The patriarchate remained politically aloof, seeming not to take the elections seriously this time. The Unionists used violence to win these elections but against the liberal opposition and not the minorities. Without an agreement with the CUP the Greek party did not fare as well as it had in 1908; there were only fifteen Greek deputies in the 1912 Assembly compared to twenty-six in 1908. Relations with the Greek community, though cooling, remained correct, and a Greek continued to serve in the cabinet regardless of its political complexion. This remained true until the end of the First Balkan War, during and after which relations between the two communities deteriorated beyond repair. The policy of appointing Greeks to administrative and diplomatic posts probably also came to an end about that time. We see, for example, Hüseyin Hilmi Pasha replacing Mavroyeni Bey, a member of a prominent Phanariot family, as ambassador to Vienna on 28 October 1912.[48]

The outbreak of the Balkan War on 8 October and the rapid collapse of Turkish armies brought allied troops to the very outskirts of the capital. Greek forces landed at Limni (Lemnos) on 21 October and occupied other offshore islands not held by the Italians. There were grave fears that while the Turks defended Istanbul from the Bulgarians, Greek forces might land on the Aegean coast. Despite that threat, however, no measures were taken against local Greeks, as they would be during the First World War.

The conquest of Ottoman territories by Montenegro, Serbia, Greece, and Bulgaria prompted a migration of Turks and Muslims to Anatolia. The mass migration was caused partly by the ravages of war which simply forced people to abandon their homes in search of security. But the major cause was the policy of terror adopted by each of these states to purge conquered territories of alien peoples. In some regions the character of the population was very mixed and in many cases Turks and Muslims constituted the largest single group if not the majority. In such circumstances, they were expelled, or in the case of the *Pomaks,* Muslims who were Bulgarian by race and language, converted by force to Christianity.[49] Only in this way could the conquering state "nationalize" this newly acquired territory or become the majority community. Such methods are said to have a long history in this region, and may be described rather appropriately as "demographic warfare."[50] They could be justified by nationalism and the prerogatives of the nation state, and the Unionists, latecomers to nationalism, soon adopted these methods though never so explicitly as Greece or Bulgaria for they still retained the illusions of empire.

As their former homelands changed hands and acquired a new national character, hundreds of thousands of Turks and Muslims fled from the Balkans to Anatolia. The Turkish press of this period is full of accounts of inhuman treatment to which Muslims were being subjected. Some of these accounts were undoubtedly exaggerated, though many were verified in the European press and by non-Turkish sources. The Greeks, with their missionary zeal for the *Megali Idea,* were most thorough in Hellenizing the conquered lands. Here is how the "de-Turkification" of Salonica took place following the Greek occupation on 9 November 1912:

> L'entrée des Grecs avait changé considerablement l'aspect de la ville. Dès les premiers jours, pour éviter les services, tous les habitants non musulmans s'étaient empressés des troquer les fez contre les chapeaux. Militaires, fonctionnaires et rentiers turcs, s'étaient embarqués avec leurs familles pour Constantinople et l'Anatolie. . . . La ville s'était déturquisée comme par miracle. Le Turc, langue commune des rues, disparut presque complètement de la circulation. Sur les places, dans les cafés, dans les tramways, encombrés d'officiers et des soldats, on n'entendit plus resonner que le grec châtié des Athéniens. . . .[51]

The resettlement of these refugees posed a serious problem for the government, truly Unionist since the *coup d'état* of 23 January 1913. Initially its primary concern was to obtain the most favorable peace terms so as to retain as much territory as possible in eastern Thrace and regain the Aegean Islands, considered vital for the defense of Istanbul. Consequently, it hardly found time for the refugee question. The CUP was totally preoccupied with regaining Edirne from Bulgaria and that was accomplished in July 1913. But by the end of the year the Unionists began to recover from the trauma of the Balkan disaster and began to deal with the urgent problems confronting them.

The Unionists decided that one way to resolve the refugee problem was to implement a *de facto* exchange of population by forcing Greeks (and Bulgarians) to migrate from Anatolia and Thrace. In their view the Balkan states had begun this process—the Bulgarians after they declared their independence in 1908 and the Greeks in October 1912—it was for the Turks to reciprocate. But it was never official policy, for the Porte feared foreign intervention on behalf of the Christians. In fact the government was embarrassed by the activities of the *Teşkilât-ı Mahsusa,* a Unionist organization that dealt with such matters.[52] It is worth noting that the Unionists had been in power too short a time to establish complete control over state and government, so that initially there were differences over policy between the Committee, the government, and the bureaucracy.

The period of the Balkan Wars also coincided with the growing awareness of Turkish nationalism, a response to the increasing isolation of the Turkish element in the empire. At this point the CUP began to see the commercial boycott as more than an instrument to use against a foreign enemy. The anti-Greek boycott of 1912–13 was used as a weapon against Greek (indeed Christian) economic domination and, at the same time, to promote Muslim enterprise and Muslim entrepreneurs. The boycott went hand in hand with refugee resettlement which was partially accomplished by placing Turks in jobs monopolized by Greeks, as in the case of the railway workers on the French-owned Izmir-Kasaba line.[53]

Throughout 1913 the Porte protested against the Greek persecution of Muslims in Macedonia. In the press there were articles expressing fears that such actions might lead to reprisals against the Greeks of Turkey.[54] Such reprisals began in earnest after January 1914, and Athens and Istanbul protested and made claims and counterclaims. By the summer of 1914 the situation had reached an impasse and the two states seemed prepared to negotiate an agreement on the exchange of populations.[55] But war intervened and the project was postponed until 1923.

Despite the hostile climate after the Balkan Wars, the Ottoman Greek community was too powerful and well organized to be disrupted by Unionist pressures. In the 1914 general election, the Committee was again forced to negotiate with the patriarch and accept his choice of Greek candidates for the Assembly. Far from being demoralized by the general state of affairs, the outcome of the Balkan Wars seemed to strengthen the faith of the Greek leaders in Hellenism and the *Megali Idea*.[56] Their optimism was not totally misplaced for it came very close to fruition in the aborted Treaty of Sevrès.

The Unionists and the Armenian Community

Compared to the Greek community, the Ottoman Armenian community was not as politically homogeneous. For one thing, there was no Armenian state to provide a focus of loyalty or a comparable yearning for union. For another, the community was divided between two repressive empires (Ottoman and Russian) and forced to struggle on two fronts, hardly a guarantee of success. Moreover, the Armenians were split into two factions along essentially socioeconomic lines: the Dashnak—members of the Armenian Revolutionary Federation *(Hai Heghapokhakan Dashnaksutiun)*—who, like the Unionists, spoke for the Armenian petty bourgeoisie of Anatolia and sought autonomy if not ultimate freedom and statehood; and the patriarchate which represented the interests of the "clerico-wealthy" commercial community—the *amira* class—of Istanbul and other commercial centers like Izmir. This group had prospered during the second half of the nineteenth century though it had lost some of its political power as a result of constitutional reform within the community.[57] Its goal after the revolution was to regain its hegemony within the community and protect its traditional privileges from the encroachments of the Porte.

Before the revolution the Porte recognized the patriarch as the official leader of the community; the Dashnak had the status of a proscribed revolutionary party. In July 1908 when the Dashnak became legal, the patriarch tried to establish his authority over this body and bring it under his control. But the Revolutionary Federation, which enjoyed greater support and prestige in the community because of its struggle against the old regime, refused to submit, denouncing the patriarch and his supporters as "money-worshipers and psuedo-patriots."[58] The attitude of the Dashnaks toward the *amira* class resembled the attitude to the Unionists toward the Liberals; both resented the privileged position of their upper classes.

Relations between the Unionists and the Dashnaks were cordial. According to Cemal Paşa, the aim of Unionist policy with regard to minority organizations was "to form the various revolutionary political committees [Bulgarian, Greek and Armenian] in the country into one 'Political Committee of Ottoman Unity.' " None of these groups was willing to dissolve its political organization and merge

There may be something in Babikyan's line of thought though it is not a very satisfactory explanation for the massacres. If it were valid we would expect attacks on the Armenians of Istanbul and the eastern provinces, but there were none. The provocation of foreign intervention seems a more valid motive, especially for the massacres of 25–27 April.

The Liberals, the true architects of the counterrevolution, hoped that the army would acquiesce to the destruction of the CUP and support a Liberal Union government. Their propaganda that the events of 13 April had in no way affected the constitutional regime was designed to achieve that end. The Third Army may have accepted these arguments but it could not allow a military rebellion to go unpunished. Supported by the Unionists in Salonica it marched on the capital. The Liberals tried to use the influence of the British embassy to win over the Third Army but to no avail.[68] Their last resort was to instigate the second phase of the massacres in Adana on the very day Mahmud Şevket Paşa began to occupy Istanbul. Foreign ships had already sailed to Mersin from where they could send marines to Adana. But the Great Powers were too divided to be able to agree on a joint intervention. Unilateral intervention was too dangerous in the diplomatic climate of the time.

The events of April struck a grave blow to the prestige of the CUP and constitutional government. Both had been caught off-guard and neither acted decisively in a critical situation. The massacres destroyed whatever sense of confidence the Committee had managed to create among the Christians. On 6 May the government tried to make amends by providing TL 30,000 for the relief of victims in Adana. But that was too little and too late. Some days later (12 May), the Assembly passed a resolution expressing regret for the events at Adana and proposed that a proclamation be addressed to all Anatolian provinces enjoining concord and fraternity on all communities of the population. The following day, the Grand Vezir announced a special commission to investigate the events at Adana. The Assembly voted to attach two of its own members to the government commission and Şefik Bey (Karesi) and Agop Babikyan (Edirne) were elected for the task.[69] Meanwhile, a martial law tribunal carried out its own investigations and punished—in some cases by hanging—those found guilty of complicity in the massacres. Among those executed there were some local notables who exercised great political influence in the region.[70]

In the Assembly debates on education, military service, and the Associations Law, Armenian deputies joined forces with the Greeks (see above). They also criticized government policy but not quite so vehemently. The Armenian patriarch protested more sharply than the Dashnak against the infringement of his community's privilege. Later, when the Porte required Armenian schools to submit to government inspection, his subordinate, the bishop of Erzurum, refused to comply. The bishop denounced the measure as a violation of the guaranteed privileges of the Armenian patriarchate, and as "a first step towards the realization of the chauvinistic policy of the new régime in educational matters. . . ."[71] Faced with such determined opposition the government made no attempt to enforce the new law, preferring to wait for better circumstances.

Despite the patriarch's opposition to the Unionists, the Dashnak continued to cooperate with them. In September 1909 the two bodies signed an agreement "to work together on behalf of progress, the constitution, and unity." They promised to fight against reactionaries and 'to dispel old faulty ideas sown by the previous despotic régime that the Armenians are striving for independence.'"⁷² *Puzantion* (18 September 1909), the organ of the patriarchate, questioned the sincerity of the agreement. It claimed that this declaration of cooperation was only political expediency on the part of the Dashnak who saw it as a means of survival in the face of the recent Associations Law.⁷³

If that was indeed the case, Dashnak strategy paid off for their organization remained intact and their relations with the CUP correct and without open friction. But any agreement concerning Armenian (and Greek) presence in the cabinet was probably reached well before September 1909 as The *Times* (London) of 23 September had reported. An Armenian and a Greek usually served in cabinets formed after 6 August 1908, occupying such posts as public works, and forests, mines and agriculture. However, Gabriel Efendi Nora-dungian was minister of foreign affairs during the critical months of the First Balkan War. But he was removed by the Unionists who did not trust a non-Muslim in such a sensitive post. Only in the first Unionist cabinet (23 January–11 June 1913) was there no Greek, the latter being replaced by, first, a Kutzo-Vlach (Batzarya Efendi), and then by a Syrian Protestant, Süleyman Bustani.

Unionist-Dashnak cooperation continued into 1912. Prior to the second general election, the two parties agreed on a common platform as well as the numerical representation for the Armenians, which remained the same as in 1908, namely fourteen deputies. They also agreed that if the Committee fulfilled its electoral pledges, they would sign a second agreement providing for cooperation in the Assembly, for the duration of its term.⁷⁴ The life of that Assembly was unduly short because of the military intervention in July 1912. However, when new elections were held in February–March 1914 the CUP and the Armenian Revolutionary Federation again worked together. The patriarch, on the other hand, presented a memorandum to the minister of justice and demanded proportional representation for his community, about twenty deputies for an estimated population of two million. The minister rejected the demand on the grounds that any matter relating to the rights of the Ottoman nation was outside the competence of the patriarch. The matter ended there, though Izmirlian Efendi continued to put his case before the public through the columns of the press.⁷⁵ All that had no effect on the Unionist-Dashnak agreement and the Armenian community again emerged from the elections with fourteen deputies.⁷⁶

Throughout this brief period before 1912, Unionist-Dashnak relations were viable because the Unionists recognized that the Armenians of Anatolia had genuine grievances which needed to be satisfied and which could be achieved with reforms. As for the *amira* class, linked as it was with the world of the capitulations and traditional privileges, the Unionists resented its total lack of Ottoman patriotism. But they also hoped to win it over with a generous dose of economic incentives and by integration into the new bourgeoisie.

Unionist desire to ameliorate the situation in the eastern provinces was not mere altruism. Article LXI of the Treaty of Berlin (1878) which promised reform for these provinces, was theoretically still in effect and could be called upon to justify Great Power intervention while there was no reform. The Porte disliked this article as limiting Ottoman sovereignty but it made no attempt to repudiate it. The Unionists wanted to neutralize it by carrying out the necessary reforms. Their first attempt in February 1909 to send a commission had been foiled by the opposition of local landlords. In February 1912 the Said Paşa government reopened the question and allotted TL 100,000 for the settlement of Armeno-Kurdish land disputes. Armenians who had been dispossessed of their land illegally were to be reinstated, and Kurdish squatters thus removed were to be given financial compensation. Moreover, the powers of the local governments of Bitlis and Erzurum were extended so as to enable them to carry out reform.[77]

A year later, after the disasters of the Tripoli and the Balkan Wars, the Unionists began to compromise on administrative centralization. They recognized that what remained of the empire could only be maintained by a policy of stringent reform and decentralization. Professor Hovannisian suggests that "the Ottoman Government, excluded from the preliminary negotiations [of the Great Powers], attempted to counter the Russian project [for reform in eastern Anatolia] by declaring general reform measures for the entire Empire."[78] But Russian proposals were put forward only in June–July 1913 whereas, according to the British ambassador, a committee had already convened in Istanbul, by January 1913 at the latest, "to consider reforms in the administration of Asiatic Turkey on decentralizing lines."[79] A new law on provincial administration was promulgated on 26 March 1913 and went into effect two days later. It increased local autonomy in administrative and financial matters, increased and defined the powers of the governor, and allowed for general provincial councils to be elected by voters of the second degree, namely by local notables and landlords.[80]

The Unionists were inclined to resolve the "Armenian question" through reform. Did Russian pressure promote this endeavor? Quite the contrary, the CUP became suspicious of Petrograd's motives and intentions, and with good reason. Hovannisian writes that by 1912 Russian policy toward Ottoman Armenians had changed: "There were important reasons in 1912 for satisfying the Armenians. By reviving the Armenian question in Turkey, the Tsar would not only regain the loyalty of his Armenian subjects but also would strike a blow against possible anarchy in Transcaucasia. . . ." In order to protect her sphere of influence in the northern Persian provinces "and to plan for future expansion, Russia needed a loyal Transcaucasia and a peaceful Turkish Armenia. Moreover, St. Petersburg feared German economic penetration" in this region and reasoned that "Russia-supervised reforms" would be sufficient to keep the Germans out. Given these motives, Tsar Nicholas and his advisors "were therefore prepared, after fifteen years of silence, to resurrect the Armenian question."[81]

Armenian leaders, encouraged by Ottoman defeats in the Balkans and the success of Balkan nationalities in achieving their independence, judged the time ripe for achieving their own liberation. As in the past (in 1828–1829 and

1877–1878) they appealed to Russia for active support against the Porte. In Turkish eyes they became the instruments of Russian policy.

Russian reform proposals, submitted to the other Powers, included the main provisions proposed by local Armenian leaders. They soon became a bone of contention between the Triple Entente and the Triple Alliance, supported by the former and obstructed by the latter. The Porte was kept out of the preliminary talks and confronted with a virtual *fait accompli* only after the Powers had reached agreement. However, "Turkish interests" were safeguarded by the German ambassador at Istanbul as Berlin refused to leave the field entirely to Russia. After protracted discussions, the Russians were forced to compromise on the final agreement which, though sanctioned by all six Powers, was signed by only Russia and the Ottoman Empire on 8 February 1914.[82]

For the Unionists, with their experience of Macedonian reform and its consequences, this agreement seemed like a prelude to a Russian protectorate over eastern Anatolia, with eventual Armenian independence. That is precisely how the Russians viewed it.[83] So great was the CUP's fear of Russian occupation that it considered the Şeyh Said Molla Selim rebellion in Bitlis as the pretext for such a move; another Adana massacre but this time on Russia's back door.[84]

Signs of Kurdish unrest in the Bitlis region were visible by March 1914. As a precaution government troops began patrolling the city streets under a 6 PM curfew on 14 March. On the 31st, the Kurds of the region rose in rebellion and Bitlis prepared for an attack. Two days later, the Kurds in the city rioted but government forces crushed the riot and captured most of the leaders. Şeyh Said Molla managed to escape and took refuge in the Russian consulate! The other leaders were tried and eleven were hanged, and their bodies were prominently displayed in the city as a warning to other rebels. Şeyh Said, sentenced to death *in absentia*, remained in the Russian consulate until November when Turkey entered the First World War. With the closing of the consulate he was captured, along with a companion, and both were hanged. According to an official dispatch, his last words were: "The Russians will wreak vengeance on you for me."[85]

Tanin's reaction to the uprising, especially its sense of panic, reflected the Committee's attitude. There was fear that this incident would lead to foreign intervention and the loss of the eastern provinces. That is why the government was urged to act quickly and decisively. "Surely," lamented *Tanin*, "they [the Kurds] must be ignorant of the seriousness of the step they are taking or of the intentions they have, when they attack Bitlis. They naturally can have no idea how serious and how injurious to their own interests and to those of their compatriots is this step of theirs. We cannot believe there are brothers of ours ready to let loose in Anatolia forces such as have just resulted in the loss of Macedonia. . . ."[86]

The Porte acted decisively and one-hundred and fifty people are said to have been killed in putting down the rebellion. Troops were called in from Van and Muş and arms were distributed to the Armenians so that they could defend themselves and fight the rebels. This measure had a good effect on the Armenian community, restoring some badly needed confidence in the government. An

Armenian paper congratulated the government on its policy during the uprising, commenting that "for us Armenians there is another fact still more significant and satisfactory, and that is that the Government has complete confidence in the Armenians. In fact, arms were distributed to the Armenians in Bitlis that they might defend the city against the reactionaries. . . ."[87]

By April 1914 the two foreign inspectors-general (a Dutchman and a Norwegian) had been selected to supervise reform in the eastern provinces. On 13 July the Assembly voted the budget to meet the salaries and expenses of their staffs. It seemed as though all obstacles to reform had been removed and that it was a matter of time before Armenian grievances were removed. But the outbreak of war in Europe opened a new and more tragic chapter in Turkish-Armenian relations.

The Unionists and the Ottoman Jewish Community

Anyone who studies the revolution of 1908 on the basis of British Foreign Office reports, the dispatches of the Istanbul correspondent of *The Times* (London), or the conservative press of the Ottoman capital, is likely to be struck by the outstanding role of the Jews in the CUP movement. All these sources misunderstood the true character of the movement and therefore misrepresented it as a Jewish Freemason conspiracy manipulated by the Jews for their own ends. The British ambassador spoke of the CUP as the "Jew Committee of Union and Progress," and of the "combination of self-seeking spurious freemasons and Jews that represent the Committee of Union and Progress."[88] Philip Graves of *The Times*, who probably received much of his information from British embassy sources, repeated this theme. The indigenous conservative press, in some cases owned by Greeks, also sought the scapegoat for Unionist policies in the Jews and so-called crypto-Jews (the *Dönme*) of Salonica, thereby implying that Unionist policies could not but be harmful to the Islamic community.

Those who saw the Jewish connection in the CUP—though it was never international—were not totally wrong, however. They were mistaken in their explanation, in seeing the CUP as a front for Jewish aims and aspirations as though the Turks were mere dupes of such ambition. Ottoman Jews did play an important part in the Unionist movement before and after 1908, but never as the force capable of manipulating the movement for their own ends. Historical circumstances united the destinies of Jews and Turks and, as a result, the two elements ended up cooperating within the CUP. In fact, such was the unity of interest that the Jewish community's support for the committee was virtually unconditional.

Scholars such as Goitein and Chouraqui claim that the destiny of the Middle Eastern Jewish community was linked intimately with that of the Muslims, virtually from the rise of Islam.[89] Abraham Galanté holds the same views for Ottoman Jewry and his historical periodization for Ottoman Jewish history fits closely the history of the Ottoman Turks. The period from 1453 to 1602 for both was one of greatness and glory. 1602 to 1856 was a long period of decline, and from 1856 to 1908 one of revival. Finally, the years after 1908 were years of reassertion and resurgence.[90]

The centuries of decline for the Jews were centuries of Greek and Armenian revival when the two Christian *millets* began to replace the Jews in many economic and administrative functions. Ottoman Christian communities benefited and developed as European merchant capital penetrated the Ottoman economy, and thrived in the shadow of the Capitulations. By the second half of the eighteenth century, the interests of these communities began to diverge from those of the Turks (and the Jews). Their prosperity and power now depended on the continuing weakness of the Ottoman state whose very revival posed the most deadly threat.

Ottoman Jews are sometimes described in the same terms as the Greeks and Armenians, as members of a comprador bourgeoisie that enjoyed foreign protection, and in some cases foreign citizenship. This may have been true for individuals, but the description did not fit the outlook of the community as a whole. Those Jews who adopted foreign citizenship became Italian subjects, and Italy was a latecomer among the Great Powers, as was Germany, but without the latter's potential. Therefore its political and economic standing in the empire was very limited, and in order to break the monopoly of the dominant powers, England and France, Italy was often willing to renegotiate the Capitulations in return for some advantage over its rivals. The Jews could hardly play a comprador role on behalf of Italy and there is no evidence that they did. On the contrary, they suffered social and economic decline as part of the same process that affected the Turkish community; thus the common interest in the revival of the Ottoman state.

Apart from the economic motive, there was another more potent reason which drew Jews politically to the Turks: the fear as to the future of their community if Ottoman lands were lost to Greece or Bulgaria. This fear applied to the Jews of Macedonia and western Anatolia, and not to those of Iraq. But it united the entire community in its allegiance to the CUP, for Ottoman rule was the best protection against Christian anti-Semitism. Traditionally, Christian communities had persecuted Jews in the empire and the Ottoman state had guaranteed that justice prevailed. Fear of such persecution motivated the steady Jewish migration to territory ruled by the Porte as the Ottoman frontier receded during the nineteenth century. It was particularly true after the Balkan Wars.[91]

After the revolution we do not find any declarations of principle or agreements of cooperation between the CUP and the Jewish community as we do with the other communities. After all, Ottoman Jews had neither political nor national aspirations separate from those of the Committee and therefore no separate political organization to pursue them. While the Zionist movement had an office in Istanbul, it found virtually no support amongst local Jews. In fact, the Zionists were hard put to find a Jewish deputy who would put forward the case for Zionism before the Assembly. Finally, Vlahof Efendi, the Socialist deputy for Salonica, agreed to speak on their behalf.[92]

Amongst the minorities, only the Jewish community identified totally with the

CUP. It alone provided a front line leader, in the person of Emanuel Karasu, for the collective leadership of the party. He was never a member of the Central Committee or a minister, yet he was an important figure in the movement both before and after the revolution. For those who viewed the Committee as a front for a Jewish-Freemason conspiracy, he was the evil genius. He was elected deputy for Salonica in 1908 and served also in the 1912 and 1914 Assemblies along with three other Jewish deputies.[93]

There was a general revival in the fortunes of the Jewish community under the new regime. The merchants, long depressed on account of Greco-Armenian economic domination, benefited from the policy of anti-Greek boycotts which went into effect in 1909 and continued intermittently thereafter. It is important to note that this policy was selective. The first boycott of 1908 was against Austrian goods. In 1909 Greek goods and shops were boycotted because of the Cretan question, and during and after the Balkan Wars the boycott was extended to Christian commerce generally. *The Orient,* a publication of the Bible House in Istanbul, emphasized this fact and noted that "the trouble does not extend to Hebrew shops."[94]

The Unionists also encouraged Turks and Jews to challenge the economic hegemony of the Christians, and these two groups became an important feature of the indigenous bourgeoisie the CUP wanted to create. By 1912 Unionists were discussing the possibility of establishing a "national economy," a concept they derived from the German political economist Friedrich List. Prominent amongst the promoters of this concept was Moise Cohen, a Jew from Salonica who settled in Istanbul in 1912. He also tried to popularize the idea of Jews identifying themselves primarily as Turks, as Turkish Jews, and he himself adopted the Turkish name Tekinalp, under which he wrote and is generally known. Judging by his writings, his contribution to the development of the nationalist ideology, especially in the economic field, is considerable though it has yet to be evaluated.[95]

So far what we have said applies to the Jewish communities of Macedonia and western Anatolia where their principal rivals were the Greeks. The province of Iraq, especially the city of Baghdad, was also a major center of Jewish life. The community witnessed a revival in the second half of the nineteenth century as Baghdad and Basra became important points in the developing trade with Asia. The "Jews gradually acquired an important share in the country's foreign trade, until they displaced Muslims, Christians, and even European merchants, including the British who settled in Iraq. The latter found it difficult to compete with local Jewish merchants, and local Muslims were compelled to take Jewish partners. . . ."[96]

Does Jewish preponderance in Iraq explain Unionist reluctance to permit the takeover of the Hamidiye Steamboat Company by the English Lynch Company? It was undoubtedly an important factor, for the merger would have strengthened England's economic position in Iraq—hence the opposition of deputies from that region, and especially the Unionist writer and deputy for Baghdad, Ismail Hakkı Babanzâde, "who cherished a sincere, if unfounded, belief that the scheme of amalgamation covered an ingenious design on the part of Great Britain to effect the economic conquest of Iraq.''[97]

In Baghdad there were violent demonstrations against the granting of the navigational monopoly on the Tigris and Euphrates to a foreign company. The situation became sufficiently serious for the Porte to consider martial law for both Baghdad and Basra. After long debate in the Assembly, the cabinet was given a vote of confidence and therefore the authority to grant the concession to Lynch. In practice, however, this authority was annulled when the Grand Vezir resigned on 28 December 1909, for his successor claimed that he was no longer bound by the vote.[98]

Until 1914 the coincidence of interest between the CUP and the Jews of Iraq remained strong. But with the outbreak of war, and especially after the British occupation of Basra in November, the Jews rallied to Britain. Many left for Basra to evade military service, and after the war the Iraqi community welcomed the British mandate.[99] The Anatolian Jewish community, on the other hand, remained loyal to the Ottoman ideal throughout the war.

As we would expect, Jewish deputies did not oppose the policy of Ottomanization when various laws were discussed in the Assembly, laws bitterly opposed by Christian deputies. The Jews had no vested interest in the old order and a great deal to gain from the new one.

It is true that there were never any Jewish cabinet ministers. But there was never any question of satisfying the *amour-propre* of the community by making token appointments and the Jews never made an issue of it. Unionist Jews did, however, occupy important positions as undersecretaries and technocrats in key ministries where their role in policymaking was probably more significant than that of the minister. Emanuel Salem prepared the new laws to be introduced in the Assembly; Ezechiel Sasoon (deputy for Baghdad), formerly undersecretary at the Ministry of Agriculture was moved to Commerce; Nissim Russo served as *chef du cabinet privé* at the Ministry of Finance, while Vitali Stroumsa was a member of the Supreme Council for Financial Reform. Samuel Israel occupied the most sensitive post of chief of the political section of the capital's police; he was with Enver Paşa when the latter carried out the coup on 23 January 1913![100]

If Ottoman Jews benefited from the Unionist alliance, they also suffered the consequences. In October 1908 reactionaries demonstrating against the new regime attacked Jews in Baghdad for supporting the CUP.[101] During and after the Balkan Wars Jews in Macedonia and Thrace suffered persecution along with the Muslims and also migrated to Anatolia.[102] So great was the concern of Ottoman Jews for the future of the empire during these wars, that those residing in southern Africa joined local Indian Muslims to raise money for the Ottoman army.[103] In the spring of 1913, when there was a threat of a Greek landing in Anatolia, the Unionist government armed not only the peasantry but also the Jews of the region, demonstrating its total confidence in the community.[104] This mutual sense of trust guided the relations between Turks and Jews until the end of the empire and into the republic.

Notes

1. The *Times* (London), 27 July 1908 (hereafter cited as *The Times*); Leon Sciaky, *Farewell to Salonica,* New York, 1946, pp. 185–187; P. Risal, *La ville convoitée Salonique,* Paris, 1914, p. 308.

2. *The Times,* 11 August 1908.

3. Ibid., 14 August 1908; and Lowther to Grey, no. 544 confidential, Therapia 5 September 1908, F.O. 371/546/31555.

4. "Abraam Benaroya'nın Anıları" in George Haupt and Paul Dumont (eds.), *Osmanlı İmparatorluğunda Sosyalist Hareketler,* Istanbul, 1977, p. 283. Though Benaroya and others speak of Ottoman brotherhood, that was not one of the promises of the 1908 Revolution. The Unionist slogan was "Liberty (*hürriyet*), Equality (*müsavat*), and Justice (*adalet*)," and not "Liberty, Equality, Fraternity"!

5. Douglas Dakin, *The Unification of Greece 1770–1923,* London, 1972, pp. 176–177. The Unionists were aware that amongst Ottoman Greeks there were two factions: those who wanted the empire to break up so that parts could be annexed by Greece, and those who hope to restore Byzantium, albeit in a new form. They described these factions as *Yunancı* and *Bizanscı.* See Celâl Bayar, *Ben de Yazdım,* Istanbul, 1967, vol. 5, p. 1589 where he quotes from the unpublished memoirs of Eşref Kuşçubaşı.

6. Dakin (cited n. 5), p. 177.

7. See Document 6 in Haupt and Dumont (cited n. 4), pp. 78, 88; and Risal (cited n. 2), pp. 321–322.

8. On Prince Sabaheddin's pre-1908 ideas concerning decentralization and personal initiative see E.E. Ramsaur, *The Young Turks,* Princeton, 1957, passim; and Bernard Lewis, *The Emergence of Modern Turkey,* second edition, London, 1968, pp. 202–204. After he returned to Turkey in September 1908, Sabaheddin revised some of his ideas. The "Prince gave some conferences in which he explained that by decentralization he meant not autonomy of particular geographical areas—e.g., Armenia—but the conferring on the provincial authorities of the existing vilayets of the Empire of wider administrative powers on the lines laid down in Midhat Pasha's Constitution". See Lowther to Grey, no. 621 confidential, Therapia, 28 Sept 1908, F.O. 371/559/34308.

9. On the Armenian population, whose details need not concern us here, see S.J. Shaw and E.K. Shaw, *History of the Ottoman Empire and Modern Turkey,* Cambridge, England, 1977, vol. 2, pp. 200–205. The authors conclude that in none of the provinces claimed by Armenian nationalists did they have a majority. Richard Hovannisian, *Armenia on the Road to Independence 1918,* Los Angeles, 1967, pp. 34–37, gives higher figures but agrees with the Shaws' conclusion.

10. The law is published in George Young, *Corps de droit Ottoman,* Oxford, 1905, vol. 2, pp. 238–240. In fact a *mahmi* (a protected person or protégé) did not actually become a citizen of the protecting power. But the Ottoman authorities had to treat him as though he were. I owe this observation to Professor Sina Akşin of Ankara University.

11. Count Leon Ostrorog, *The Turkish Problem,* London, 1919, pp. 95–96. That the state exacted more from the peasant during this period is shown by Shaw and Shaw (cited n. 9), p. 233. Tithes increased from 425.7 million kuruş (1877–1878) to 690.5 million kuruş (1908–1909) while grain exports went up from 465 million kuruş (1877–1878) to 753.9 million (1907–1908).

12. Lowther to Grey (cited n. 8).

13. Dimitri Pentzopoulos, *The Balkan Exchange of Minorities and its Impact upon Greece,* Thessaloniki, 1962, pp. 29–31; Shaw and Shaw (cited n. 9), pp. 241–242.

14. Ostrorog (cited n. 11), pp. 12–14. See the occupational makeup of Istanbul's population in 1886 in Shaw and Shaw (cited n. 9), p. 244.

15. For A.J. Sussnitzki's article published in 1917 see Charles Issawi (ed.), *The Economic History of the Middle East 1800–1914,* Chicago, 1966, pp. 120–121.

16. Pentzopoulos (cited n. 13), p. 33; see also Roderic Davison, *Reform in the Ottoman Empire 1856–1876*, Princeton, 1963, pp. 114–135.

17. Michael Milgrim, "The War Indemnity and Russian Commercial Investment Policy in the Ottoman Empire: 1878–1914" in Osman Okyar (ed.), *Türkiye İktisat Tarihi Semineri*, Ankara, 1975, p. 298.

18. Ibid., p. 356, and *passim*.

19. *Tanin*, 27 and 28 August 1908. *The Times* (28 August 1908) observed that the third demand implied the suppression of the Bulgarian Exarchate as well as Rumanian religious communities which had been Orthodox in the past.

20. *Tanin*, 29 and 30 August 1908; see also Lowther to Grey, no. 535 confidential, Therapia 1 Sept. 1908, F.O. 371/546/30971.

21. Lowther to Grey (cited n. 8).

22. İkdam, 4, 5, and 6 November 1908; D. Dakin, *The Greek Struggle in Macedonia 1897–1913*, Salonica, 1966, p. 391, n. 47. Abraham Galanté, *Turcs et Juifs*, Istanbul, 1932, p. 116, writes concerning the activities of an Ottoman official: "Lors des fonctions à Salonique, Joseph Krieger fit rentrer à la sujétion ottomane onze mille Grecs et à Rhôdes . . . plus de mille Grecs, qui se reclamaient de sujétion hellène."

23. *Stamboul*, 23 and 24 October 1908.

24. *Tanin*, 24–26 October 1908.

25. *Tanin*, 4 November 1908.

26. *Stamboul*, 11 November 1908. In fact the Greeks had twenty-six and the Armenians fourteen deputies in the 1908 Assembly. See F. Ahmad and D.A. Rustow, "İkinci Meşrutiyet Döneminde Meclisler 1908–1918" in *Güney–Doğu Avrupa Araştırmaları Dergisi*, 4–5 (1976), p. 247.

27. *Stamboul*, 11 November 1908.

28. Ibid., 22–24 November 1908; Hüseyin Cahit Yalçın, *Siyasal Anılar*, Ankara, 1976, p. 52.

29. The remark may be apocryphal but it catches the spirit of the time; and it is widely quoted. See H.C. Yalçın, "On Yılın Hikayesi," *Yedi Gun*, vol. 7, no. 176 (July 1936), p. 22.

30. *Stamboul*, 12–14 November 1908.

31. *Tanin*, 26 March 1909; enclose of Hilimi Paşa's memorandum in Lowther to Grey, no. 223 confidential, Pera 30 March 1909, F.O. 371/761 12788. On the hostility of the Istanbul Greek press towards *Tanin*, and therefore toward the CUP, see Yalçın (cited n. 28), pp. 52–53.

32. Quoted in Feroz Ahmad, *The Young Turks*, Oxford, 1969, p. 43; the text of the *Neologos* article republished in *İkdam*, 15 April 1909, is given in Ismail Hami Danişmend, *31 Mart Vakası*, Istanbul, 1961, pp. 210–211. The most detailed account of the counterrevolution is Sina Akşin, *31 Mart Olayı*, Istanbul, 1970.

33. Yalçın (cited n. 28), p. 39.

34. Stavro Skendi, *The Albanian National Awakening 1878–1912*, Princeton, 1967, 389–390 and *passim*.

35. Ahmed Şerif, *Anadolu'da Tanin*, Istanbul 1325/1909, pp. 137–139; pp. 120–122 in new modern Turkish edition, edited by Çetin Börekçi, Ankara, 1977, hereafter cited as Şerif, 1977. In the Assembly on 3 July 1909, Hasbi Efendi's remarks that Greek schools were superior to Turkish ones drew protests from the ranks of clerical deputies.

36. Şerif (cited n. 35) p. 140; Şerif, 1977 (cited n. 35), p. 111.

37. The account of the debate is from the Istanbul press, 9 June 1909; see also Yalçın (cited n. 28), p. 145 where he quotes an article he wrote in *Tanin*, 13 June 1909. A brief account of these discussions may be read in Lowther to Grey, no. 624, Therapia, 4 August 1909, F.O. 371/761/29787.

38. Istanbul press, 9 June 1909.

39. Dakin (cited n. 22), p. 414, n. 24; Assembly discussions may be followed in the Istanbul press, 10, 16, 21, and 26 June, and 1, 3, and 5 July 1909. The law was finally passed in August. See *Takvim-i Vekayi* 11 August 1909. For the implementation of the law see Annual Report 1910 in Lowther to Grey, no. 103 confidential, Constantinople 14 February 1911, F.O. 371/1245/6167.

40. *The Orient,* vol. 6, no. 9, 3 March 1915, p. 62.

41. Istanbul press, 20 and 21 July 1909. Karolidi Efendi had been professor of history at Athens University and was the author of the article "Turkey" in the 11th edition of *Encyclopaedia Britannica.* After his election, his Ottoman citizenship was questioned in the Assembly.

42. Ahmad (cited n. 32), p. 62.

43. Lowther to Grey, no. 611 confidential, Therapia 29 August 1910, F.O. 371/998/32221.

44. *Tanin,* 27 July 1910; see also Dakin (cited n. 5), p. 178.

45. Rıza Nur, 'Hürriyet ve Itilâf Nasıl Doğdu, Nasıl Öldü', in *Cumhuriyet* 23 October 1946; and Tarık Z. Tunaya, *Türkiyede Siyasî Partiler 1859–1952,* Istanbul, 1952, pp. 315–344, who gives the founding members.

46. Y. H. Bayur, *Türk İnkılâbı Tarihi,* Istanbul, 1943, vol. 2, part 1, pp. 245–247, where the author quotes from cabinet minutes. No doubt war with Italy forced the Porte to be conciliatory toward the minorities.

47. Vice-Counsul Sir A. Biliotti to Consul-General Barnham, Rhodes, 17 March 1913, in Bilâl N. Şimşir, *Ege Sorunu,* Istanbul, 1976, vol. 1, pp. 566–567.

48. M. K. İnal, *Osmanlı Devrinde Son Sadriazamlar,* Istanbul, 1940–1953, pp. 1674–1675. Ahmed Şerif writes that in Haçın, today's Saimbeyli, a Greek was traditionally appointed *kaymakam,* and Yorgi Efendi, he heard, opposed and discouraged public collections for the navy fund and was openly hostile to the CUP. With Greek officials, their loyalty to the Ottoman state had become suspect. See Şerif, 1977 (cited n. 35), pp. 269–270.

49. Carnegie Endowment for International Peace, *Report of the International Commission to Inquire into the Causes and Conduct of the Balkan Wars,* Paris, 1914, pp. 71–78, 148–151, 155–157, 186, 201–202. The Bulgarian Holy Synod conceived of a novel way to convert the Pomaks *en masse.* They were lined up in the fields and a priest went down the line making them take a bite from a pork sausage!

50. The term is taken from Mark Pinson's unpublished Ph.D. thesis, Harvard 1970, entitled "Demographic Warfare."

51. Risal (cited n. 1), pp. 338–339; Aram Andonyan, *Balkan Harbı Tarihi,* 1975, pp. 400–404. This book was originally published in Armenian (Istanbul, 1912–1913).

52. Bayar (cited n. 5), pp. 1568–1600.

53. Ibid., pp. 1554–1558.

54. See in particular H. C. Yalcın's article published in *Revue Politique International* (n.d.) quoted in *The Orient,* vol. 5, no. 6 (11 February 1914), p. 54.

55. Dakin (cited n. 5), p. 202.

56. According to Pallis, after 1913 "the national idea is no more the creation of a purely Hellenic Greece but the establishment of a large Hellenic state in which many foreign elements would coexist with the Hellenic one, keeping naturally their particular national consciousness under the sovereignty of the Hellenic element and [using] as their connecting link the Greek language—the official language of the state." A. A. Pallis, "Racial Migration in the Balkans during the years 1912–1924," *The Geographical Journal,* vol. 66, no. 4 (October 1925), p. 330, quoted in Pentzopoulos (cited n. 13), p. 28.

57. Louise Nalbandian, *The Armenian Revolutionary Movement,* Berkeley, 1963, and Davison (cited n. 16), pp. 114–135.

58. Sarkis Atamian, *The Armenian Community: The Historical Development of a Social and Ideological Conflict,* New York, 1955, pp. 159–165, where he quotes from *Puzantion,* 9 October

1909 (the patriarch's paper) and *Azadamard,* 13 and 14 October 1909 (the organ of the Dashnak). Atamian also discusses the Hinchaks, the socialist revolutionaries, but they were not significant in Ottoman politics.

59.   Djemal Pasha, *Memories of a Turkish Statesman 1913–1919,* London, 1922, pp. 252–253. The Hinchak, he wrote, "absolutely refused to negotiate with us". These may be the same negotiations as the ones reported by *The Times* 14 September 1908 and which took place in Van "the most important [Armenian] revolutionary centre in Turkey," according to the British consul. See Dickson to Sir Nicholas O'Conor, Van, 2 March 1908, F.O. 371/533.

60.   E. J. Dillon, "The Reforming Turk," *Quarterly Review,* 210 (1909), p. 247.

61.   Fitzmaurice to Lowther, 54 D, 30 November 1908, F.O. 195/228.

62.   Heck to Secretary of State, Constantinople, 17 January 1919, 867.00/846. Adam Block, a longtime resident of Istanbul, had served as first dragoman at the British embassy, as British representative on, and president of the Ottoman Public Debt Administration, and in 1919 he was also financial adviser to the British high commissioner at Istanbul. Lewis Heck was US commissioner at Istanbul.

63.   Djemal (cited n. 59), pp. 254–255.

64.   Ibid., pp. 255–262; Esat Uras, *Tarihte Ermeniler ve Ermeni Meselesi,* Istanbul, 1976, pp. 551–570; Mehmed Hocaoğlu, *Tarihte Ermeni Mezâlimi ve Ermeniler,* n.p. 1976, pp. 572–573; Abdullah Yaman, *Ermeni Meselesi ve Türkiye,* Istanbul, 1973, p. 122; this book is a reissue of the 1916 government publication.

65.   Djemal (cited n. 59), pp. 254–255.

66.   Babikyan's report was first published in Istanbul in 1919 though it was presented to the Assembly a decade earlier. It is quoted by Uras (cited n. 64), p. 559; Djemal (cited n. 59), p. 259 writes that he had heard a rumor that members of the Muhammadan Union, responsible for the reactionary movement in Istanbul, had been active in the Adana region warning the Muslims of an impending Armenian uprising. Şerif (cited n. 35), *passim,* also heard that outside elements had been very active in the region before and during the massacres.

67.   Babikyan quoted by Uras (cited n. 64), pp. 559–560.

68.   Ahmad (cited n. 32), pp. 43–45.

69.   "Report of Proceedings of the Ottoman Parliament from April 26 to May 20, 1909" in Lowther to Grey, no. 377 confidential, Pera, 20 May 1909, F.O. 371/761/20292; Akşin (cited n. 32), p. 193. Later, when Cemal Paşha went as governor of Adana, he says TL 200,000 were put at his disposal to compensate victims of the massacres. See Djemal (cited n. 59), p. 261.

70.   Djemal (cited n. 59), p. 262. The Armenian community, however, found the sentences inadequate and thought that the culprits had gotten off too lightly. There was also much anger at the fact that Armenians were punished by the tribunal and the patriarch resigned in protest, though he probably retracted his resignation. See Lowther to Grey, no. 843 confidential, Therapia, 12 October 1909, F.O. 371/774/38364.

71.   Consul McGregor to Mr. Marling, Erzerum, 6 December 1910 in Marling to Grey, no. 908 confidential, Constantinople, 18 December 1910, F.O. 371/1017/46557.

72.   Atamian (cited n. 58), pp. 160–161, quoting *Azadamard,* 19 September 1909. The text of the declaration was published in *Tanin,* 16 September 1909 and is given in Uras (cited n. 64), pp. 576–577. *The Times,* 23 September 1909 also reported an agreement to the effect that the Unionists agreed that there would always be an Armenian in the cabinet.

73.   Atamian (cited n. 58), p. 163.

74.   The *Times,* 1 March 1912.

75.   *Tanin,* 19 November 1913 and *Stamboul,* 31 October, 15 and 19 November, and 9, 12, 13, and 15 December 1913.

76.   Ahmad and Rustow (cited n. 26), p. 247.

77. The *Times,* 14 February 1912.

78. Hovannisian (cited n. 9), pp. 33–34.

79. Lowther to Grey, no. 104 confidential, Constantinople, 7 February 1913, F.O. 371/788/7281. *The Times,* 22 April 1913, wrote that the Porte had turned toward decentralization since the beginning of 1912.

80. Rommily to Secretary of State, Constantinople, 29 April 1913, no. 480, 867.00/53; Shaw and Shaw (cited n. 9), p. 306.

81. Hovannisian (cited n. 9), p. 31.

82. Ibid., pp. 32–34 and Djemal (cited n. 59), pp. 272–274. The Unionists would have preferred an agreement with Britain to reform the eastern provinces and Cemal Paşa said so to Sir Henry Wilson, who was in Istanbul in October 1913. See Sir Charles Calwell, *Field-Marshal Sir Henry Wilson,* New York, 1927, vol. 1, p. 128ff. Ostrorog (cited n. 11), p. xi, confirms this, but thwarting Russia did not suit Britain's interests in Europe and the world. See Feroz Ahmad, "Great Britain's Relations with the Young Turks 1908–1914," *Middle Eastern Studies,* 2 (1966).

83. Djemal (cited n. 59), pp. 274–275, quoting from Russian documents. The growing importance that Russia attached to eastern Anatolia may be seen in its decision to establish consulates at Diyarbakır, Sivas, Harput, and Mosul. See *The Orient,* vol. 5, no. 28 (15 July 1914), p. 279.

84. Bayur (cited n. 46), vol. 2, part 3, pp. 188–189.

85. The account is based on reports in *The Orient,* vol. 5, nos. 14, 15, 16 (8, 15, and 22 April 1914 respectively), and vol. 5, no. 51 (23 December 1914), p. 463.

86. *Tanin,* n.d., quoted in *ibid.,* vol. 5, no. 14 (8 April 1914), p. 131.

87. *The Orient,* vol. 5, no. 4 (8 April 1914), p. 131.

88. Elie Kedourie, "Young Turks, Freemasons and Jews," *Middle Eastern Studies* 7 (1971); B. Lewis (cited n. 8), p. 211, n. 41. See also a dispatch on Freemasonry from Lowther to Grey (1910) in F.O. 371/1010/20761 and a dispatch on Zionism (internal, i.e. in the Ottoman Empire) written in February 1911 and given in F.O. 371/1244. Such views were not unique to the British but were held by conservative circles throughout Europe. Father Herman Gruber, a clerical adviser to Archduke Ferdinand of Austria-Hungary, wrote a treatise in three volumes on "the role of Freemasons in contemporary revolutionary movements since 1776." He "claimed that the revolution in Brazil in 1889, the uprising in Cuba in 1899, the revolution of the Young Turks in 1908, and the revolution in Portugal in 1910 were all organized by Freemasonry." See Vladmir Dedijer, *The Road to Sarajevo,* New York, 1966, p. 113 and *passim.*

89. André Chouraqui, *Letter to an Arab Friend,* Amherst, 1972, and S. D. Goitein, *Jews and Arabs,* New York, 1955.

90. Abraham Galanté, *Rôle économique des Juifs d'Istanbul,* Istanbul, 1942, p. 4ff.

91. *Idem., Histoire des Juifs d'Anatolie,* Istanbul, 1937, vol. 1, p. 161ff.

92. "Vlahof Efendi'nin Anıları" in Haupt and Dumont (cited, n. 4), pp. 257–262. In Palestine there were not enough Ottoman Jews to elect a representative to the Assembly; see Walter Laqueur, *A History of Zionism,* New York, 1976, p. 222, though Iraq sent a Jewish deputy to Istanbul. S. Landshut, *Jewish Communities in the Muslim Countries of the Middle East,* London, 1950, p. 45, wrote: "there never has been any feeling of solidarity with the political aspirations of Zionism." The same was true of Salonica, see Ben Gurion, *Ben Gurion Looks Back,* New York, 1970, pp. 43–46; and even Egypt, see Jacob Landau, *Jews in Nineteenth Century Egypt,* 1969, p. 275.

93. Ahmad and Rustow (cited n. 26), p. 267. Karasu was a lawyer by profession. Before the revolution, as grand master of the 'Macedonia Risorta' Lodge, he provided a cover for Unionist clandestine activities, and acted as a courier. After 1908, he belonged to the 'Jacobin' wing of the CUP and was close to Talât. During the war he was appointed a food controller and is said to have amassed a fortune. In 1919 he migrated to Italy and this suggests that he may have been an Italian subject.

94. *The Orient,* vol. 5, no. 11 (18 March 1914), p. 105.

95.   Moise Cohen was born in Salonica (date unknown) and settled in Istanbul in 1912 after Salonica was lost to Greece. He then adopted the name Tekinalp and wrote in *Yeni Mecmua* and *İktisadiyat Mecmuası,* which he also edited during 1915–1917. Through his writing he helped to popularize the idea of a national economy and the need for a Turkish bourgeoisie. In 1915 his *Türkismus und Pantürkismus* was published in Weimar and it explained Turkish nationalism to the CUP's German allies. After the war, Tekinalp supported the nationalists, and in 1935 wrote *Kemalizm* (*Le Kemalisme,* Paris, 1937), an important contribution to the articulation of the nationalist ideology. In the multiparty period after 1945, he supported the Demokrat Parti, especially its promotion of a *laissez-faire* economy. See Galanté (cited n. 22) p. 127, and idem. (cited n. 90), pp. 58–64. Despite Tekinalp's significance, he is not given a place in Hilmi Ziya Ülken, *Türkiyede Çağdaş, Düsünce Tarihi,* Konya, 1966.

96.   Hayyim Cohen, *The Jews of the Middle East 1860–1972,* New York, 1973, p. 90, where he seems to follow Phebe Marr, ''Yasin al-Hashimi: The Rise and Fall of a Nationalist,'' unpublished Ph.D. dissertation Harvard University 1966, p. 30; and Landshut (cited n. 92), p. 42.

97.   *The Times,* 11 December 1909. Sasoon Efendi, Jewish deputy for Baghdad, had been director of the Ottoman Steamer Company (Hamidiye) and was said to be opposed to the merger. See Lowther to Grey, no. 510 confidential, Therapia 1 July 1909. F.O. 371/778/25436.

98.   Ahmad (cited n. 32), p. 67.

99.   Landshut (cited n. 92), p. 43.

100.   Galanté (cited n. 90), pp. 51–52; *idem.* (cited n. 22), pp. 116–117, 123–124; Tunaya (cited n. 45), p. 412.

101.   Yusuf Ghanima, *Nuzhat al-mushtāq fī tarīkh yahud al-ʿIrāq,* Baghdad, 1924, p. 180, cited in Cohen (cited n. 96), p. 24. Note the striking contrasts to the reactionaries' attitude toward non-Muslims who were not Unionists.

102.   Galanté (cited n. 22), pp. 41–47; idem. (Avram Galanti), *Türkler ve Yahudiler,* Istanbul, 1947, pp. 25, 42–46.

103.   Ibid., p. 64 and 67–68 respectively.

104.   Acting Vice-Consul Harris to Sir G. Lowther, Dardanelles, 26 March 1913, and Lowther to Grey, Constantinople, 9 April 1913 with reports from the Dardanelles and Izmir, in Şimşir (cited n. 47), pp. 574–575 and 591–594.

V

SOURCES

20

Ottoman Archival Materials on *Millets*

HALIL INALCIK

Kadi Court Records

The *kadı* court records, *sicillāt,* constitute an extensive collection,[1] scattered across the former area of the empire, and perhaps the most important source for the social life and actual legal conditions of the non-Muslims under Ottoman rule. This happened not only because the non-Muslims, as the *ahl al-dhimma,* were under the jurisdiction of *kadis* is so many areas of the law, but also because the *dhimmīs* often preferred to seek a *kadi's* decision or certificate. The use of Muslim courts provided greater assurance, or the means to escape the more rigid stipulations of their own religious law in such matters as marriage, divorce, and parenthood rights, which were supposed to be under the exclusive jurisdiction of the Christian or Jewish authorities. In the eighteenth century the Greek Patriarchate had to take serious measures to prevent the latter practice, as a result of which the infiltration of Islamic and customary law was being seen in such areas as marriage and dowry practices.[2] At any rate the *kadi sicillāt* abound with court decisions, as well as contracts, transactions, certificates and other kinds of documents, drawn up not only between Muslims and non-Muslims but also between non-Muslim parties.

Since the *sicillāt* were deposited in the *kadi* courts of the cities and towns throughout the empire, their rediscovery has given existence from the 1930s on to many local archives in the lands once under Ottoman rule—Yugoslavia, Bulgaria, Albania, Greece, Syria, Turkey, Israel, Jordan, and Egypt. One of the most extensive, and for obvious reasons the most important collections, is that in Istanbul, under the office of the *Muftı.* About ten thousand well-preserved volumes of the *kadi* records of Istanbul, Galata, Eyüp, and adjacent districts, collected under Abdülhamid II, have been barely touched for study. The Bursa collection, comprising the oldest *kadi* registers dating back to the 1460s, is the best known to the students of Ottoman history, and has been exploited since the 1930s.[3] Also, a number of publications have been made from the collections in such centers as Monastir, Sarajevo, Vidin, Sofia, Salonica, Cyprus, Damascus,

Jerusalem, and Cairo.[4] Documents from the *sicillāt* of Vidin and Sofia concerning the Church and ecclesiastical matters have been collected and studied by
Joseph Kabrda.[5]

Monastery Archives

Ottoman documents preserved in monastery archives bear a special interest not
only for the history of particular monasteries and the administration of monastic
properties under Ottoman rule, but also for Ottoman history in general, since
some monasteries preserved documents from the earliest Ottoman times, even
the fourteenth century. Monastic documents have been published by Paul Wittek
and Paul Lemerle, Elizabeth Zachariadou-Oikonomides (Greece), D. Ihčiev
(Bulgaria), P. Džansazov and J. Jastrebov (Yugoslavia), Eutimo Castellani
(Jerusalem), Klaus Schwarz (Sinai) and Zdenka Veselá-Prenosilová (Sinai).[6] It
should be added that the Ottoman survey registers of the fifteenth and sixteenth
centuries preserved in the central archives in Istanbul contain complete lists of
the monasteries in Ottoman territories and often copies of their *ferman*s and
statutes.

Collections in the Central Archives (Başvekâlet Arşivi, Istanbul)

The collection of *Mühimme* registers in the Ottoman archives, containing
copies of the decrees decided upon in the Imperial Council, and covering the
period from 1553 to 1905, is definitely one of the most important sources for
affairs concerning the non-Muslims and their organizations in the Ottoman
Empire. Among the collections of documents on this subject selected from this
source, those published by Ahmed Refik Altınay and Uriel Heyd are particularly
worthy of mention.[7] Ahmed Refik, in his selection, included principally documents concerning the non-Muslim communities in Istanbul and their organization. Uriel Heyd selected those on the Jews in Palestine. A brief examination of
these publications will suffice to show that the *Mühimme* collection documents
deal with all aspects of the relations of non-Muslims individually or collectively
with the Ottoman government. They also show the government's concern for
matters affecting its *dhimmī* subjects, especially in relation to taxation, security
and peace among them. A great number of the decrees are concerned with the
enforcement of the restrictions that Islamic law imposed upon non-Muslims as,
for example: the bans upon selling wine in public, upon dressing as Muslims,
riding horses, possessing slaves, having houses too close to Muslim places of
worship, upon any construction of churches or synagogues beyond the maintenance of those Mehmet the Conqueror had permitted to remain in use. A need to
reinforce restrictions of this sort was apparently felt in times of war against
Christian powers and in times of public distress, when the sultan made a show to
the Muslim public of the fact that he was scrupulously applying the prescriptions
of the *Sharīᶜa*.

On the other hand, since the *dhimmī*s were involved in every aspect of public life in the Ottoman Empire, the papers and registers dealing with public affairs, especially with public finances, are important, such as the *māliye aḥkām*, the *mukataᶜa* registers, the *ᶜavāriz-i dīvāniyye* registers, and the registers of petitions and complaints, *şikāyāt* and *aḥkām*. Of special interest is a register called *Avrupa [tüccārı]* containing decrees and diplomas issued to non-Muslim merchants of the empire who were engaged in trade with European countries and who were given special privileges and tax exemptions to enable them to compete on an even footing with those enjoying capitulary privileges.[8] It is important to emphasize that these documents show that the Ottoman government dealt with non-Muslims directly as its *dhimmī* subjects.

The *taḥrīr*, or *tapu, defterleri*, the population and tax survey books of the Ottoman state,[9] are of basic importance for statistical data on the non-Muslims in the areas of demography, economic conditions, and taxation. Frequently the contents of important fermans, or of diplomas granting exemptions or appointments, as well as laws and regulations, *kānūnnāme*s, are entered in these registers along with the persons or groups to whom they apply. These are the best known registers in the Ottoman archives and a number of publications have already been made based on them with full reproductions or summaries.[10] Mention should be made here of the surveys of imperial *evḳāf*, comprising valuable statistical data on the non-Muslims who paid their taxes to *evḳāf*. The best example is the sultanic *evḳāf* of the *Fatih* mosque (Tapu registers n. 240, dated 952 cumadelûlâ I/1545 July, and no. 210),[11] which is a mine of information on the Greek, Armenian, Jewish, and European *(Efrenciyān)* communities of Istanbul. From this register we learn, for example, not only the population of each district and the taxes paid, but also individual and group places of origin. These records attest to a large immigration of Armenians and Greeks from Anatolian towns into Istanbul before 1545. As for the nineteenth century, starting from 1831 several detailed population surveys have been the subject of research and publication by E. Z. Karal, K. Karpat, and J. McCarthy.[12]

As for the principal registers concerning only the non-Muslim communities in the Ottoman Empire, they are:

1. the *cizye* registers, registers of the Islamic poll tax, which go back to the fifteenth century. The important *cizye* register of the year 1489 has been studied and published by N. Todorov and Ö. L. Barkan.[13]

2. the *peskopos mukātaᶜası* registers, on which we will focus our attention below.

3. the *cemāᶜat-i gayr-i Muslima* registers, altogether eighteen registers containing copies of papers on all matters of affairs concerning the non-Muslim communities from the year 1837 on.

4. the *kilise defterleri*, which start in 1837, and contain permissions for construction and repair of churches, schools and other buildings, as well as cemeteries, run by the non-Muslim communities or foreigners.

From 1916 on imperial orders, *irāde*s, were classified in dossiers according to individual subject. Among the *irāde dosyaları*, dossier no. 62 is devoted to the non-Muslim communities and includes such important documents as petitions from the Greek Patriarchate for the appointment of a new patriarch, the reaffirmation of the regulations governing the Armenian Patriarchate, and the resignation of the Haham-başı, Hayim Nahum.

In the nineteenth century important events involving the non-Muslim communities prompted special investigations by the government and resulted in such special *defter*s as that on the *Rum fesādı*, the Greek insurrection, a survey of all Greek merchants in Istanbul *hān*s, one on Serbian affairs, and other registers on the Bulgarian uprising in Vidin, the question of the Bulgarian Exarchate, the disorders in Lebanon, and the question of Crete.[14]

Briefly speaking, all of these documents show that the Ottoman government treated the non-Muslims simply as its *dhimmī* subjects, and that their religious leaders were given full independence of action only in matters concerning the church hierarchy and property. It was only in 1764 that for the first time the sultan gave the Greek and Armenian patriarchs direct authorization to punish troublemakers in their community without having to bring the case to the attention of the Porte; at the same time *ḳadı* courts were ordered to refuse cases involving dubious marriages.[15]

A Study of the Peskopos Muḳāta‘ası Registers, Başvekâlet Archives, Istanbul, Kâmil Kepeci Tasnîfi nos. 2539-2542

In this series the introduction to register no. 2540-2 reads: "This is a register of the diplomas and decrees *(berevāt ve ahkām)* concerning the Office of the Public Revenues from the Appointments of Bishops *(Ḳalem-i Muḳata‘a-ı Peskopos)*, during the time of his Excellency ‘Abdullāh Nā’ilī Efendi, *Defterdār-i Şikk-i Evvel*, and ‘Alī Efendi, secretary to the grand vezir's *kethudā* and chief secretary of the said office. First of Muharrem 1167/Oct. 29, 1753)."

The introduction makes clear the following points:

1. There is a special office at the department of imperial finances responsible for the collection of the revenues connected with appointment of the religious heads of the Christian communites in the empire.
2. The head of this office is a *hoca*, head-secretary, under the finance minister, but at the same time he is a secretary to the grand vezir's deputy, thus under the direct control of the grand vezir's office.

The register contains diplomas and decrees on appointments, changes and other matters concerning the title and jurisdiction of the metropolitans *(medrepolid)* and bishops *(peskopos)* in the empire. In other words the registers kept at this office are essential for the study of church organization throughout the empire and its relations with the Ottoman government. The records concern the Orthodox Greek Patriarchate of Istanbul and the Patriarchates of Jerusalem, Alexandria, and Antioch, Ohrid (Ohri) and peč (İpek) as well as the Armenian Patriarchate of Istanbul. It also includes decrees concerning monasteries. The first register in this series contains documents from the period 1051–1061/ 1641–1651, but it also has notes on circumstances dating back to the sixteenth century as well as marginal records of the years 1061–1082/1651–1671. The office was then under the *Defterdār* of the *şikk-i sānī*. There are four registers in this series, covering the period between 1051–1253/1641–1837. The office of *Peskopos Halīfeliği Muḳataᶜası* was abolished in 1837; after that, diplomas and decrees concerning the non-Muslim communities were copied in the registers of the *Cemāᶜat-i Gayr-i Muslima* in the *Dīvān-i Hümāyūn* under the direct control of the grand vezir or prime minister.[16]

The following list of the Metropolitan and Episcopal sees under the Patriarchate of the Orthodox Greeks *(Rumiyan)* with the amount of *pīş-keş* is based upon the *Peskopos Muḳataᶜası* register no. 2539 covering the period 1641–1651.

	Pīş-keş
Patriarchate of Istanbul, over the Christians in Istanbul and its dependencies. 105 *oḳḳa* meat per day for the Imperial gardeners *(bostancı)*	20,000 *kuruş*
Metropolitanate of the Christians in the *nāḥiyes* (counties) of Terkoz and Hâslar (area between Bosphorus, Marmara Sea and Black Sea) and the city of Galata	4 gold pieces
Bishopric of the town of Çatalca with the villages of Hamillu(?) and Haridin(?) and Büyük-Çekmece and its dependencies	800 akça
Metropolitanate of the Christians of Bigados and its dependencies	1440 akça
Metropolitanate of the Christians of the district *(vilāyet)* of Ereglü (Heraclea) and its dependencies	20 gold pieces
Metropolitanate of the *nāḥiye* (county) of Istanimaka and its dependencies	20 gold pieces
Metropolitanate of the district *(vilāyet)* of Siroz (Serrès) and its dependencies	65 gold pieces
Metropolitanate of the district of Zihne and its dependencies	9 gold pieces
Bishopric of the Christians of the village of Potemkali(?) and its dependencies in the *ḳazā* of Argirikasrı	2000 akça
Gumenot-i Manastır-i Prokri or Panaya along with the Christians of Kızıl-Kaya	5 gold pieces
Metropolitanate of the Christians of Salonica with the Bishopric of Liti and Andelissa(?) in Sidre-Kapsi (Siderokavsja)	150 gold pieces
Metropolitanate of Arhi, and its dependencies in the *ḳazā* of Sidre-Kapsi	30 gold pieces
Metropolitanate of Kara-Ferye (Pherrai) and its dependencies	25 gold pieces
Kethudalık of the Christians of the *ḳazā* of Sidre-Kapsi	10 gold pieces
Kethudalık of the salt-works in the area of Salonica	730 akça
Metropolitanate of the Christians of the district of Varna and its dependencies	10 gold pieces

Metropolitanate of the Christians of the district of Kortos (Corinth) and its dependencies	130 gold pieces (100 for metropolitan and 30 for bishop)
Metropolitanate of the Christians of the church of Koron with Kalamata	15 gold pieces
Metropolitanate of the Christians of Narda with the church of Inebahtı and its dependencies	30 gold pieces
Fixed sum paid annually by the monks in the Aynaroz (Athos) monasteries	200,000 akça
For *zarar-ı kassābān* and *kirbas-bahā* for the *bostancı*s as ordered in the year 1063/1652	200,000 akça
Metropolitanate containing the bishopric of the district of Moton (Modon)	8 gold pieces
Bishopric of the Christians of Yeni-Kale in the provinces of Morea with the districts of Moton, Koron and Arkadya, comprising fifty villages	7 gold pieces
Metropolitanate of the Christians of the Island of Sakız (Chios) and its dependencies	35 gold pieces
Tercumanlık (office of dragoman) at Sakız	500 akça
Metropolitanate of the Christians of the islands of Rhodes and Limnos and their dependencies	24 gold pieces
Bishopric of the Christians of the islands in the Marmara Sea	20 gold pieces
Bishopric of the Latin Christians *(efrenciyye)* in the *kazā* of Bar and its dependencies	1800 akça
Metropolitanate of the Christians in the villages of Ganos and Khora and its dependencies in the *kazā*s of Gallipoli and Magalkara	8 gold pieces
Metropolitanate in the district of Bursa and its dependencies	15 gold pieces
Metropolitanate of the Christians in Mudanya, Sigi (Sige), Pulad, Gusi and Subashi in the *kazā* of Kite	25 gold pieces
Bishopric of the Christians in the villages of Kurşunlu (Megas Agros), Mir-Ali and Yeni-Köy	6 gold pieces
Kethudalık of Mir-Ali and its dependencies	30 gold pieces
Metropolitanate of the Christians in the district *(vilāyet)* of Amasya with the *kazā*s of Sinop, Samsun, Bafra, Aydinat and their dependencies	40 gold pieces
Metropolitanate of the province *(livā-sancak)* of Canik with the church of Panaya	10 gold pieces
Metropolitanate of the Christians of Trabzon, Torul (Ardasa) with the districts *(nāhiye)* of Gümüş (Argyropolis), Bayburt (Paipert) and their dependencies	50 gold pieces
Metropolitanate of the Christians of the district of Rize (Rizaion)	20 gold pieces
Metropolitanate of Konya and its dependencies	9 gold pieces
Metropolitanate of the Christians of the district of Niğde and its dependencies	12 gold pieces
Metropolitanate of the Christians of the district of Antalya	20 gold pieces
Metropolitanate of the Christians of the district of Aydıncık (near Cyzicus)	20 gold pieces

Metropolitanate of the Christians of the district of Kefe (Caffa) and its dependencies	50 gold pieces
Metropolitanate of the Christians of the district of Mangup	20 gold pieces
Metropolitanate of the Christians of Tat-Ili (in the Crimea) and its dependencies	15 gold pieces
Metropolitanate of the Christians of the district of Kayseriye and its dependencies	12 gold pieces
Metropolitanate of the Christians of the district of Ankara and its dependencies	10 gold pieces
Metropolitanate of the Christians of the district of Filibe (Philippopoli) with the *ḳazā*s of Hasköy and Tatar-Pazarı and their dependencies	50 gold pieces
Metropolitanate of the Christians of the district of Sofya (Sofia), and its dependencies	112 gold pieces
Metropolitanate of the Christians of the district of Ayaslug (Ephesus) and its dependencies	20 gold pieces
Metropolitanate of the Christians of the district of Izmir (Smyrna)	10 gold pieces

Under the Patriarch of the
Christians of the island of Cyprus

	Pīş-keş
Patriarchate of the Christians of the province of Cyprus and its dependencies	73,500 akça
Dragoman at the Court of Cyprus	1,600 akça
Bishopric of the Christians of the *ḳazā* of Baf and its dependencies	5,400 akça
Bishopric of the Christians of the *ḳazā* of Kirine and its dependencies	1,400 akça
Bishopric of the Christians of the *ḳazā* of Gilani and its dependencies	2,400 akça
Bishopric of the Christians of the *ḳazā* of Limasson and its dependencies	2,400 akça
Bishopric of the Christians of the *ḳazā* of Lefkoşa and its dependencies	3,600 akça
Bishopric of the Christians of the *ḳazā* of Hirishora and its dependencies	2,800 akça

Under the Patriarch of Ohri (Ohrid)

Patriarchate of the Christians of the province of Ohri and its dependencies and the fixed lump sum to be delivered to the imperial treasury annually	1,000 gold pieces 60,000 akça
Bishopric of the Latin Christians *(Efrenciyān)* on the island of Andrea and its dependencies	8 gold pieces

Under the Patriarch of İpek (Peč)

Patriarch of the Serbian Christians of the province of İpek with the provinces of Budin (Buda), Temešvar, Bosnia[17], Gyula, Egre, Kanija, İskenderiyye, Prizrin and their dependencies as found on July 1, 1615. Besides the *pīş-keş* he agreed to pay each year to the imperial treasury	100,000 akça

a lump sum in the amount of 100,000 akça, as fixed down.

Metropolitanate of the Christians of the districts of Iştip (štip), Maleşeva, Kratova, İslavişte and their dependencies; later on with an addition of 6200 akça	45 gold pieces
Metropolitanate of the Christians of the province of İpek later on with addition that was fixed down as 3000 akça	22 gold pieces

Since the aforesaid metropolitanate lies at İpek, the Patriarch himself holds it, and paying the *pīş-keş* he possesses it independently; this was decided on March 27, 1584.

Bishopric of the Christians of the church belonging to the Latin clergy *(ruhbānān-i Latin)* in the province of Bosnia, Kilis, Hersek and their dependencies. Bishop is nominated by the Patriarch of İpek	40 gold pieces
Metropolitanate of the Christians of the city of Budin (Buda) and its dependencies. Its holder is nominated by the Patriarch of İpek	10 gold pieces
Metropolitanate of the Christians of the districts of Sigetvar with Peçuy. Its holder is nominated by the Patriarch of İpek.	10 gold pieces

The following is a list of all the Metropolitan and Episcopal sees in their hierarchical order as found in the *berāt* renewed for Kyrillos, patriarch of the Greek Orthodox Church, on the occasion of Osman III's accession to the throne in 1753 (Register no. 2540/2, p. 39). For the titles Metropolitanate (M), Archbishopric (AB), Bishopric (B) we followed the list in T. Papadopoullos, *Studies and Documents Relating to the History of the Greek Church and People under Turkish Domination*, Brussels, *1952*, p. 82–122.

1. Istanbul and its dependencies (M)
2. Kayseriye (Kayseri) (M)
3. Lititisa (AB)
4. Kuş-Adası (Ephesus) (M)
5. Ereğli (Hrakleia) (M)
6. Radoscuk (Rodosto) (B)
7. Gelibolu (Kallioupoli, Gallipoli) (B)
8. Mirtofona (Miriofiton, Mürefte) (B)
9. Çatalca (Metrai) (AB)
10. Çorlu (Tsuralon) (AB)
11. Ankara (Ancyra) (M)
12. Kapıdagı (Cyzicus) (M)
13. İznikmid (Izmit) (Nicomedia) (M)
14. İznik (Nicaea) (M)
15. Kadıköyü (Chalcedon) (M)
16. Selanik (Salonica) (M)
17. Çitroz (Kitros) (B)
18. Kapaniya (Kampania) (B)
19. Balatomina (Platamuno) (B)

20. Serfice (Serfion) (B)
21. Toyran (Tolvan) (B)
22. Petros (Petras) (B)
23. Ardamiri (Ardamerion) (B)
24. Aynaroz (Mount Athos)
25. Silstre (Dristra) (B)
26. Tırnovi (M)
27. Çirmen (Tsernevon) (B)
28. Lofca (Lovec) (B)
29. Şumnu (formerly Preslav) (B)
30. Edirne (M)
31. Ahtabolu (Agathopoli) (B)
32. Amasya (Amasea) (M)
33. Bursa (M)
34. Niksar (Neokaisaria) (M)
35. Konya (Iconion) (M)
36. Kara-Ferye (Pherrai) (M)
37. Antalya (formerly Pisidia) (M)
38. Talantova (Talantion) (formerly Athens) (M)
39. Girit (Crete) (M)
40. Trabzon (Trebizond) (M)
41. Yenişehir (Larissa) (M)
42. Tırhala (Trikkala) (B)
43. Narda (B)
44. İnebahtı (Lepanto, Naupakhton) (M)
45. Filibe (Philippopoli) (M)
46. Rodos (Rhodes) (M)
47. Siroz (Serez, Serrai) (M)
48. Dırama (Philippi) (M)
49. Zihne (Zichna)
50. Midillü (Mytilene) (M)
51. Yanya (Ioannina) (M)
52. Dimetoka (Didymoteichon) (M)
53. Alaşehir (Philadelphia) (M)
54. Menlik (Melenikon) (M)
55. Badracık (Neo-Patras) (M)
56. İstifa (Tsivon) (M)
57. Inoz (Enez, Ainos) (M)
58. Melo (Melos island) (AB)
59. Nakşa (Naxos)
60. Misivri (Mesambria) (M)
61. Vidin (M)
62. Ağriboz (Euboea) (M)
63. Sofya (M)
64. Vize (Byzon) (M)
65. Ahyolu (Anchialus) (M)
66. Varna (M)
67. Ibrail (Braila) (M)
68. Gömülcine (Komotene) (M)

69. Silivri (Silivria) (M)
70. Süzebolu (Sozopoli) (M)
71. İskete (Xanthi) (M)
72. Golos (Volo) (M)
73. Kefe (Caffa) (M)
74. Gözleve (Kozlov, Jevpatorya)
75. Sakız (Chios) (AB)
76. Limni (Lemnos) (M)
77. Imroz (Imbros) (M)
78. Hâslar (Villages between Istanbul and Bosphorus formerly Derkos or Terkos) (M)
79. Kördos (Kortos, Corinthos) (M)
80. Benefşe (Monemvasia) (M)
81. Ravendos (Reontos) (B)
82. Balya-Badra (Palaia Patra) (M)
83. Moston (Mothonis?) (B)
84. Mezistre (Misithra, Mistra) (M)
85. Arkadya (Christianoupolis) (M)
86. Anabolu (Nauplion) (M)
87. Marmara (Marmora island)
88. Ilıca
89. Santorin (Santorin island) (AB)
90. Mesta
91. Alosonya (Elassonia) (AB)
92. Sisam (Samos) (AB)
93. İstanköy (Karpathos) (AB)
94. Fenar (Phanarion) (AB)
95. Gümüşhane (Argyropolis)
96. Mezid Adası
97. Kesendire (Kassandra) (AB)
98. Değirmen Adası
99. Sifnos (Sifnos) (AB)
100. Andre (Andros) (AB)
101. Egin (Aigina) (AB)
102. Bogonyani (Pogonianis) (AB)
103. Kirine
104. Ayamavra (Levkas) (AB)
105. Ala-Kilisa (Phersalon?) (AB)
106. Kefalya (Kephallenia) (AB)
107. Istendin (Tinos) (AB)
108. Kördos (Corinthos) (B)
109. Eflak (Wallachia) (M)
110. Bogdan (Moldavia) (M)
111. Venice (M); in 1782 the patriarchate notified the Ottoman Porte that since 1557 the Orthodox Greeks resident in Venice had been electing a metropolitan for themselves with the approval of the patriarch.[18]

The list of the metropolitan sees under Ottoman rule as established by T. Papadopoullos on the basis of seven *Notitiae Episcopatum* and the Synodal

Acta can be checked against the above lists drawn up on the basis of Ottoman documents. The amount of the *pīş-keş* to be paid by each metropolitan or bishop can be an indication of the importance of the see and the size of the Orthodox population in the area under its jurisdiction. Among the *Notitiae* the one drawn up by the Patriarch Serapheim in 1759 is chronologically the closest to our document. The next *Notitiae* known is dated 1855, while the *Peskopos Mukātaᶜ a* registers contain lists of the same character for the whole period after 1641. The hierarchical structure of the Greek church during the Ottoman period, T. Papadopoullos said, exhibited essentially the same structure as it had in Byzantine times. Under the immediate jurisdiction of the Ecumenical Patriarch we find metropolitans at the head of dioceses, which constitute the essential subdivisions of the hierarchy. Under the immediate jurisdiction of a metropolitan is placed a bishop, *peskopos*. Those metropolitans under the direct jurisdiction of the Ecumenical Patriarchate who have no bishops under their own dominion, are considered higher in rank than a bishop but lower than an independent metropolitan. Otherwise, the metropolitans are all of equal importance, distinguished only according to an established order of precedence. As our document makes clear, the respective boundaries of metropolitan dioceses and espiscopal sees are determined by Ottoman administrative divisions. T. Papadopoullos stressed the fact that a metropolitan diocese or an episcopal see owes its historical continuity to the continuing existence of the Orthodox population in that particular area. They flourish, decline and disappear as the Orthodox population increases, decreases and disappears. Thus the actual geographic distribution of the Orthodox population is reflected in the *Notitiae Episcopatum*. The Ottoman *cizye* registers on the other hand furnish us with complete lists of the Orthodox population subject to the poll tax in Istanbul and the provinces; these lists can be used as reliable sources for actual population estimates.[19]

Peşkeş or Pīş-keş

Peşkeş or originally *pīş-keş* meaning gift, present in general usage, was actually "an offering made by an inferior as a mark of respect and dependence" (Redhouse). In the Ottoman Empire, *pīş-keş* was given at the moment of a governor's acceptance of his diploma of appointment. The rate for each rank was fixed by regulation in the sixteenth century. For example, the governor of Rumeli gave to the *mīr-ᶜalem* at the Porte, ten thousand *akça*. Originally, the exchange of presents was a symbolic act, used to establish a bond of dependency between lord and retainer in the Turco-Mongol world. The exchange of presents was, from the beginning of Ottoman history, a persistent custom practiced by the Ottomans (as an early example see Sultan Orhan's *temlīknāme* in *Arşiv Klavuzu*, Istanbul, 1938, document no. 1). Officials of lesser grades paid a fixed amount of money called *resm-i berāt* accompanied by some costly presents from the sultan, such as a caftan, a horse with gilded saddle, or a sword. These presents symbolizing the authority delegated by the ruler in Islamic states were generally called *al-ᶜalāmāt-i mulūkiyya*, (see *al-ᶜUmarī, Al-taᶜrīf*, Cairo 1312/1894, pp.

209–211). It should be noted that *pīş-keş* cannot be interpreted as bribery from the Ottoman viewpoint. The money paid by high clergy at the moment of receiving their *berāt* from the Porte was also called *berāt pīşkeşi*, *pīş-keş* paid for *berāt*.[20]

According to a tradition perpetuated in the circles of the patriarchate, Gennadios, at the time of his appointment as the first patriarch under the Ottomans, was granted one thousand gold pieces for his maintenance.[21] The contemporary historian Kritovoulos confirms that "the sultan loaded him with noble and costly gifts."[22] It is known from documentary evidence that before the Conqueror's time metropolitans and bishops were assigned regular income from the Ottoman treasury in the form of *timar*.[23] Hence, these metropolitans, as well as Gennadios, must have given customary *pīş-keş* to the sultan. What was, perhaps, striking for the contemporaries was the extravagant increase of the amount of *pīş-keş*, first to 2,000 gold pieces, and then to 2,500 by the rival metropolitans to obtain the patriarchate.[24] As a result of the competition for the patriarchal throne in the Greek church[25] and the growing tendency of the Ottomans to farm out public offices to the highest bidders, *pīş-keş* was over time substantially increased and considered a source of revenue for the state.

Notes

1. For a bibliography of the *sicillāt* in Turkey, see Osman Ersoy, "Şer'iyye Sicillerinin Toplu Kataloğuna Doğru," *Ankara Üniversitesi, Dil ve Tarih-Cografya Fakültesi Mecmuası*, 21 (1963), pp. 35–65 and Mücetba İlgürel, "Şer'iyye Sicillerinin Toplu Kataloğuna Doğru," *Istanbul Üniversitesi Edebiyat Fakültesi, Tarih Dergisi*, 28–29 (1975), pp. 123–166.

2. N. J. Pantazapoulos, *Church and Law in the Balkan Peninsula During Ottoman Rule*, Salonica, 1967, pp. 91–112.

3. See H. Inalcik, "Bursa şer'iye sicillerinde Fatih Sultan Mehmed'in fermanları," *Belleten*, 11 (1944), p. 693. *Sicillāt* were extensively exploited for local history in the publications made by *Halkevleri* in Turkey.

4. For the publications made in these places see J. Reychman and A. Zajaczkowski, *Handbook of Ottoman-Turkish Diplomatics*, revised ed. A. S. Ehrenkreutz and T. Halasi-Kun, The Hague and Paris 1968, index.

5. In his book, *Le système fiscal de l'Eglise orthodoxe dans l'Empire Ottoman*, Brno, 1969, and his articles, cited in the book's bibliography, p. 163.

6. See for a bibliography, Klaus Schwarz, *Osmanische Staatsurkunden des Sinai-Klosters in türkischer Sprache*, Freiburg im Breisgau, 1970, pp. 197–205.

7. Ahmed Refik (Altınay), *Istanbul Hayatı*, 3 vols., Istanbul, 1930–1935; U. Heyd, *Ottoman Documents on Palestine*, Oxford, 1960; also see Bernard Lewis, *Notes and Documents from the Turkish Archives*, Jerusalem, 1952.

8. For all these *defters* see Midhat Sertoğlu, *Muhteva bakımından Başvekâlet Arşivi*, Ankara, 1955; and B. Lewis (cited n. 7), p. 2–4.

9. See Ö. L. Barkan, "Türkiye'de imparatorluk devirlerinin büyük nüfus ve arazi tahrirleri ve hakana mahsus istatistik defterleri," *Istanbul Üniversitesi Iktisat Fakültesi Mecmuası*,2 (1941), pp. 20–59; 2 (1941), pp. 214–47; B. Lewis (cited n. 7) pp. 4–5.

10. For a bibliography see Reychman and Zajaczkowski (cited n. 4), pp. 24–103.

11. See H. Inalcik, "Istanbul," *EI²*, vol. 3, pp. 244–45.

12. See H. Inalcik, "Impact of the *Annales* School on Ottoman Studies and New Findings," *Review*, 1 (1978), p. 76; K. Karpat, "Ottoman Population Records and Census of 1881–1893," *I JMES*, 9 (1978), pp. 237–74; mention should also be made of the important data in the *Sālnāme*s or Yearbooks of the Ottoman Provinces, for a bibliography of these see H. R. Ertug, "Osmanlı devrinde salnameler," *Hayat Tarih Mecmuası*, 9 (1973).

13. N. Todorov, "La situation démographique de la péninsule balkanique au cours des XVᵉ et XVIᵉ siècles," *Annuaire de l'universite de Sofia, Faculté de Philosophie et d'histoire*, 53 (1959); Ö. L. Barkan, "894 (1488/1489) yılı cizye muhasebesine âit muhasebe bilançoları," *Belgeler*, 1 (1964), pp. 1–117.

14. See M. Sertoğlu (cited n. 8).

15. See A. Refik, *Istanbul Hayatı, 1000–1100*, Istanbul, 1931, p. 206; for marriages see orders in Kabrda (cited n. 5), no. xxvi, xxviii, xxxiv and Pantazapoulos (cited n. 2), pp. 98–103.

16. See M. Sertoğlu (cited n. 3), pp. 27–29.

17. In a register of *mukātaᶜa* dated 1479 (Başvekâlet Archives, Maliyeden Müdevver no. 176) the metropolitan of Bosnia *(Medrepolid-i vilāyet-i Bosna)* was to pay fifty gold pieces each year. The high rate of *pīş-keş* can be interpreted as an indication of the importance of the Greek Orthodox church in Bosnia at that time; cf. John Fine, *The Bosnian Church, A New Interpretation*, New York and London 1975, p. 375–78.

18. See the document published by A. Refik (cited n. 15), pp. 227–29.

19. See note 13.

20. See Kabrda (cited n. 5), p. 59.

21. Pantazapoulos (cited n. 2), p. 25.

22. *History of Mehmed the Conqueror*, trans. C. T. Riggs, Princeton, 1954, p. 94.

23. See *Sûret-i defter-i sancak-i Arvanid*, ed. H. Inalcik, Ankara, 1954, nos. 100, 122, 148, 162, 186, 200, 270, 299.

24. See M. Crusius, *Turcograecia libri octo*, Basel, 1584 cited by S. Runciman, *The Great Church in Captivity*, Cambridge, 1968, pp. 193–94; Pantazapoulos (cited n. 2), p. 25.

25. See for the situation in later times T. Papadopoullos, *Studies and Documents Relating to the History of the Greek Church and People under Turkish Domination*, Brussels, 1952, pp. 132–35; O. Kersten, *Das Patriarchat von Konstantinopel im ausgehenden 16. Jahrhundert*, Wien, 1970, pp. 82–83.